STUDY GUIDE to accompany *Macroeconomics*
ISBN 0-07-549705-0

Answers to the even-numbered problems at the end of each text chapter can be found in the supplementary *Study Guide*, a specially-designed learning aid for students of macroeconomics. Available now in your campus bookstore!

Macroeconomics

Third Canadian Edition

Macroeconomics

Third Canadian Edition

Rudiger Dornbusch
Massachusetts Institute of Technology

Stanley Fischer
Massachusetts Institute of Technology

Gordon R. Sparks
Queen's University

McGraw-Hill Ryerson Limited

Toronto Montreal New York Auckland Bogotá Caracas Hamburg
Lisbon London Madrid Mexico Milan New Delhi
Paris San Juan São Paulo Singapore Sydney Tokyo

Macroeconomics, Third Canadian Edition

Copyright © McGraw-Hill Ryerson Limited, 1989, 1985, 1982. Copyright © 1987, 1981, 1978 by McGraw-Hill Inc. All rights reserved. No part of this publication may be reproduced, stored in a data base or retrieval system, or transmitted, in any form or by any means, electronic, mechanical, photocopying, recording, or otherwise, without prior written permission of McGraw-Hill Ryerson Limited.

ISBN 0-07-549703-4

1 2 3 4 5 6 7 8 9 0   JD   8 7 6 5 4 3 2 1 0 9

Printed and bound in Canada

Care has been taken to trace ownership of copyright material contained in this text. The publishers will gladly take any information that will enable them to rectify any reference or credit in subsequent editions.

Technical illustrations by Dianna Little
Design by Christopher Griffin

Canadian Cataloguing in Publication Data

Dornbusch, Rudiger
   Macroeconomics

3rd Canadian ed.
Includes index.
ISBN 0-07-549703-4

1. Macroeconomics.   I. Fischer, Stanley.
II. Sparks, Gordon R.   III. Title.

HB172.5.D618 1989   339   C88-094386-6

To
Sandra, Leslie, and Ian

SUMMARY OF CONTENTS

CONTENTS

PREFACE

This third edition of *Macroeconomics* remains faithful to our basic approach—presenting the relevant theory and at the same time showing both its empirical relevance and policy applications. We have stayed with our general eclectic outlook on macroeconomics but there have been changes in details of the presentation and the weight given various topics in light of the changing emphasis of macroeconomics issues and theory over the last few years. In particular, we have added material on the microfoundations of macroeconomics, and substantially increased the space devoted to the rational expectations–equilibrium approach.

There are two major organizational changes in this edition:

- We have moved "Aggregate Supply and Demand: An Introduction" to Chapter 7, so that instructors can present a complete aggregate supply-demand model earlier in the course. Students can now discuss inflation using a simple model well before the midterm. Those instructors who prefer the arrangement of the first two editions, in which the detailed material developing the aggregate demand side of the economy (contained now in Chapters 8 to 13) precedes aggregate supply, may choose to defer Chapter 7 for later.

- We have added a new Chapter, 17, "Money, Deficits, and Inflation," that both presents new material and brings together material on these topics previously spread through the book. Our experience has shown that students are fascinated by the topics treated in this chapter.

By popular request we have restored to this edition the dynamic model of aggregate supply and demand (originally Chapter 13), whose removal from the second edition caused far more dismay than we had anticipated. That now appears in Chapter 15, and is used also in Chapter 17. The simplest aggregate supply-demand model (now Chapter 7) has also been revised after suggestions by users (including ourselves) and reviewers.

The publication of the report and supporting research studies of the Royal Commission on the Economic Union and Development Prospects for Canada provides a large volume of material for supplementary reading. References to specific research studies are provided at several points in the text in special boxes.

An *Instructor's Manual*, prepared by Patricia Pando and Gordon Sparks, is available to accompany this edition. It is an updated and improved version of the manual that accompanied the previous edition.

Although there are major changes from earlier editions, the book remains recognizably the same in that it develops, and teaches students to use, a broad-based, critical, and useful macroeconomics. Our overriding objective is to explain how modern macroeconomics is used in understanding important economic issues, and to help the reader analyze macroeconomic issues for herself or himself. The book provides full coverage of all major topics in macroeconomics. No important topic has been omitted because it is too difficult, but we have taken great pains to make nothing more difficult than it need be.

ACKNOWLEDGEMENTS

We are indebted to many users of our book who have given us the benefit of their teaching experience and offered comments and suggestions. In particular we would like to thank Stephan Kaliski, Manfred Keil, Isidore Masse, Kanta Marwah, Duncan McDougall, and Connie Smith. We have also benefited from detailed reviews of the manuscript provided by Stuart Landon (University of Alberta), Angela Redish (University of British Columbia), and Peter Sephton (University of New Brunswick).

We would also like to thank Charlotte David and Leslie Sparks who assisted in the preparation of the manuscript for the present edition.

PART 1

Determination of
National Income

CHAPTER

Introduction

Macroeconomics is concerned with the behaviour of the economy as a whole —booms and recessions, the economy's total output of goods and services and the growth of output, the rates of inflation and unemployment, the balance of payments, and exchange rates. To study the overall performance of the economy, macroeconomics focusses on the economic policies and policy variables that affect that performance such as monetary and fiscal policies, the money stock and interest rates, the public debt, and the federal government budget. In brief, macroeconomics deals with many of the major economic issues and problems of the day.

Macroeconomics is interesting because it deals with important issues, but it is fascinating and challenging too, because it reduces complicated details of the economy to manageable essentials. *Those essentials lie in the interactions among the goods, labour, and assets markets of the economy.*

In dealing with the essentials, we have to disregard details of the behaviour of individual economic units, such as households and firms, or the determination of prices in particular markets, or the effects of monopoly on individual markets. These are the subject matter of microeconomics. In macroeconomics we deal with the market for goods as a whole, treating all the markets for different goods, such as the markets for agricultural products and for medical services, as a single market, and treating all these different goods as a single good. Similarly, we deal with the labour market as a whole, abstracting from differences between the markets for, say, migrant labour and doctors. We deal with the assets markets as a whole, abstracting from the differences between the markets for provincial bonds and Rembrandt paintings. The cost of the abstraction is that omitted details sometimes matter. The benefit of the abstraction is increased understanding of the vital interactions among the goods, labour, and assets markets.

Despite the contrast between macroeconomics and microeconomics, there is no basic conflict between them. After all, the economy in the aggregate is nothing but the sum of its submarkets. The difference between microeconomics and macroeconomics is therefore primarily one of emphasis and exposition. In studying price determination in a single industry, it is convenient for microeconomists to assume that prices in other industries are given. In macroeconomics, where we study the price level, it is for the most part sensible to ignore changes in relative prices of goods among different industries. In microeconomics, it is convenient to assume the total income of all consumers is given and to ask how consumers divide their spending out of that income among different goods. In macroeconomics, by contrast, the aggregate level of income or spending is among the key variables to be studied.

The great macroeconomists, including Keynes, and modern American leaders in the field—the older Nobel Prize-winning generation such as Milton Friedman of the University of Chicago and the Hoover Institution, Franco Modigliani of the Massachusetts Institute of Technology, and James Tobin of Yale University, and the younger generation such as Martin Feldstein of Harvard University, Robert Lucas of the University of Chicago, and Thomas Sargent of the University of Minnesota — have all had a keen interest in the applications of macrotheory to problems of policy making. Indeed, developments in macrotheory are closely related to the economic problems of the day. Keynesian economics developed during the great depression of the 1930s and showed the way out of such depressions. Monetarism developed during the 1960s, promising a way of solving the inflation problem. *Supply-side economics* became a fad in the United States in the early 1980s, promising an easy way out of the economic mess of low growth and high inflation by cutting taxes. However, supply-side economics promised far too much and there was no easy way out.

Because macroeconomics is closely related to the economic problems of the day, it does not yield its greatest rewards to those whose primary interest is theoretical. The need for compromise between the comprehensiveness of the theory and its manageability inevitably makes macroeconomic theory a little untidy at the edges. The emphasis in macroeconomics is on the manageability of the theory and on its applications, and to demonstrate that emphasis, this book uses the theories we present to illuminate economic events from the great depression to the 1980s. We also refer continually to real world events to elucidate the meaning and the relevance of the theoretical material.

Schools of Thought

There have for long been two intellectual traditions in macroeconomics. One school of thought believes that markets work best if left to themselves; another believes that government intervention can significantly improve the operation of the economy. In the 1960s the debate on these questions involved *monetarists*, led by Milton Friedman, on one side and *Keynesians*, including Franco

Modigliani and James Tobin, on the other side. In the 1970s the debate on much the same issues brought to the fore a new group — the *new classical macroeconomists* — including among the leaders Robert Lucas and Thomas Sargent. That group remains influential in the macroeconomics of the 1980s.

The new classical macroeconomics shares many policy views with Friedman. It sees the world as one where individuals act rationally in their self-interest in markets that adjust rapidly to changing conditions. The government, it is claimed, is likely only to make things worse by intervening. That model is a challenge to traditional macroeconomics, which sees a role for useful government action in an economy which is viewed as adjusting sluggishly, with rigidities, poor information, and social customs impeding the rapid clearing of markets.

Macroeconomics if often presented as the battleground between implacably opposed schools of thought. There is no denying that there are conflicts of opinion and even theory between different camps. Because macroeconomics is about the real world, the differences that exist are sure to be highlighted in political and media discussions of economic policy. Nevertheless, there are significant areas of agreement and the different groups, through discussion and research, continually evolve new areas of consensus and a sharper idea of where precisely the differences lie. In this book we do not emphasize the debate, preferring to discuss the substantive matters while indicating alternative views of an issue whenever relevant.

We shall now, in Section 1-1, present an overview of the key concepts with which macroeconomics deals. Section 1-2 examines relationships among the main macroeconomic variables, while Section 1-3 discusses stabilization policy. Section 1-4 presents a diagrammatic introduction to aggregate demand and supply and their interaction; it gives a very general perspective on the fundamentals of macroeconomics and the organization of this book. In Section 1-5 we outline the approach of the book to the study of macroeconomics and macropolicy making, and present a preview of the order in which topics are taken up. Section 1-6 contains brief remarks on how to use the book.

1-1   KEY CONCEPTS

Gross Domestic Product

Gross domestic product (GDP) is the value of all goods and services produced in the economy during a given time period. GDP is the basic measure of economic activity prepared by Statistics Canada.[1]

---

[1] An alternative measure of output, gross national product (GNP), is sometimes used. The difference between GDP and GNP is explained in Chapter 2.

Figure 1-1 shows two measures of GDP—*nominal*, or *current dollar*, GDP and *real*, or *constant dollar*, GDP.[2] Nominal GDP measures the value of output at the prices prevailing in the period the output is produced, while real GDP measures the output at the prices of some base year. At present, 1981 serves as the base year for real output measurement. GDP statistics become available quarterly.

Note: Real GDP is calculated using 1981 prices.
The scale is logarithmic. The logarithmic scale is explained in footnote 2.

FIGURE 1-1   REAL AND NOMINAL GDP, 1966–1987

(*Source*: Adapted from Statistics Canada, 13-201, 11-003)

---

[2] Notice that the scale for GDP in Chart 1-1 is not linear. For example, the distance from 60 to 65 is bigger than the distance from 145 to 150. The scale is logarithmic, which means that equal ratios are represented by equal distances. For instance, the distance from 60 to 120 is the same as the distance from 75 to 150, since GDP doubles in both cases. On a logarithmic scale, a variable growing at a constant rate (e.g., 4 percent per annum) is represented by a straight line.

Figure 1-1 shows that nominal GDP was equal to $509.9 billion in 1986 and $356.0 billion in 1981. Thus nominal GDP grew at an average rate of 7.5 percent during that period. On the other hand, real GDP was $406.9 billion in 1986 and $356.0 billion in 1981,[3] implying an average annual growth rate of real GDP of only 2.7 percent over the period.

Inflation and Nominal GDP

Figure 1-1 shows that nominal GDP has risen much more rapidly than real GDP. The difference between the growth rates of real and nominal GDP occurs because the prices of goods have been rising, or there has been *inflation*. The inflation rate is the percentage rate of increase of the level of prices during a given period.

Real GDP grew at an average rate of 3.1 percent over the 10 years from 1976 to 1986, while nominal GDP grew at an average annual rate of 9.9 percent. Because real GDP is calculated holding the prices of goods constant, the difference is entirely due to inflation, or rising prices. Over the 10-year period, prices were on average rising at 6.8 percent per year. In other words, the average rate of inflation over that period was 6.8 percent per year.

With 1981 as the base year for the prices at which output is valued, we observe in Figure 1-1 two implications of the distinction between nominal and real GDP. First, in 1981 the two are equal because, in the base year, current and constant dollars are the same dollars. Second, with inflation, nominal GDP rises faster than real GDP and therefore, after 1981, nominal GDP exceeds real GDP. The opposite is true of course before 1981.

Growth and Real GDP

We turn next to the reasons for the growth of real GDP. The growth rate of the economy is the rate at which real GDP is increasing. Anytime we refer to growth or the growth rate without any qualifying word, we mean the growth rate of GDP. On average, most economies grow by a few percent per year over long periods. For instance, Canadian real GDP grew at an average rate of 4.0 percent per year from 1966 to 1986.

What causes GDP to grow? The first reason real GDP changes is that the available amount of resources in the economy changes. The resources are conveniently split into capital and labour. The labour force, consisting of people either working or looking for work, grows over time and thus provides one source of increased production. The capital stock, including buildings and machines, likewise has been rising over time, thereby making increased output

---

[3] Why are real and nominal GDP the same in 1981? This is because we use 1981 prices to calculate real GDP.

possible. Increases in the availability of factors of production—the labour and capital used in the production of goods and services—thus account for part of the increase in real GDP.

The second source of real GDP growth is *productivity increase*. Over time, the same factors of production can produce more output. These increases in the efficiency of production result from changes in knowledge, including learning by doing, as people learn through experience to perform familiar tasks better.

Employment and Unemployment

The third source of change in GDP is a change in the employment of the given resources available for production. Not all the capital and labour available to the economy are actually used at all times.

The *unemployment rate* is the fraction of the labour force that cannot find jobs. For example, in 1982, a reduction in the employment of labour, or a rise in unemployment, shows up in Figure 1-1 as a fall in real GDP. Indeed, in that year unemployment rose to 12.8 percent, the highest unemployment rate in the post-World War II period. More than one person out of every eight who wanted to work could not find a job. Such unemployment levels had not been experienced since the great depression of the 1930s.

Inflation, Growth, and Unemployment: The Record

Macroeconomic performance is judged by the three broad measures we have introduced: the *inflation* rate, the *growth* rate of output, and the rate of *unemployment*. Because they affect our daily lives, news of these three variables makes the headlines.

When the inflation rate is high, the prices of goods people buy are rising. Partly for this reason, inflation is unpopular, even if people's incomes rise along with the prices. Inflation is also unpopular because it is often associated with other disturbances to the economy, such as the oil price increases of the 1970s, that would make people worse off even if there were no inflation.

When the growth rate is high, the production of goods and services is rising, making possible an increased standard of living. Along with the high growth rate typically goes lower unemployment, and more jobs. High growth is a target and hope of most societies.

For the long run, the growth rate of real GDP per person is the most important of all the macroeconomic performance indicators. Per capita GDP doubles every 35 years if it grows at 2 percent a year. In that case, each generation could look forward to a material standard of living double that of its parents. If per capita GDP grows at 1 percent per annum, it takes 70 years to double. Over long periods, small differences in growth rates mount up to big differences in the material standard of living.

High unemployment rates are a major social problem. Jobs are difficult to find. The unemployed suffer a loss in their standard of living, personal distress, and sometimes a lifetime deterioration in their career opportunities. When unemployment exceeds 10 percent—and even well short of that—it becomes the number one social and political issue.

Table 1-1 shows that economic performance in Canada deteriorated sharply from the decade of the sixties to the seventies. Inflation and unemployment increased and growth fell. In the early eighties the inflation rate came down, but this was accompanied by a large increase in unemployment.

TABLE 1-1   MACROECONOMIC PERFORMANCE, 1952-1987

PERIOD	INFLATION % PER ANN.	GROWTH % PER ANN.	UNEMPLOYMENT %
1952-1962	1.2	4.3	5.5
1962-1972	3.3	5.5	4.4
1972-1982	9.6	2.5	6.6
1983-1984	7.0	2.1	11.4
1984-1987	4.2	3.8	9.7

Source: Dept. of Finance, *Economic Review* and Bank of Canada *Review*. Note: Inflation and growth rates are year over year changes. Unemployment rate is average of years shown.

As we develop macroeconomics in this book, we are looking for answers to the questions that recent macroeconomic performance raises. Why did the inflation rate rise from the fifties to the seventies and then fall? Will the growth rate return to levels of the sixties? Can the unemployment rate be brought down, and what economic policies, if any, can produce low inflation, low unemployment and high growth?

The Business Cycle and the Output Gap

Inflation, growth, and unemployment are related through the *business cycle*. The business cycle is the more or less regular pattern of expansion (recovery) and contraction (recession) in economic activity around the path of trend growth. At a cyclical *peak*, economic activity is high relative to trend, and at a cyclical *trough*, the low point in economic activity is reached. Inflation, growth, and unemployment all have clear cyclical patterns as we will show below. For the moment we concentrate on measuring the behaviour of output or real GDP relative to trend over the business cycle.

Figure 1-2 shows as the straight line the trend path of real GDP and the fluctuations around this trend over the business cycle. During an *expansion* (or *recovery*) the *employment* of factors of production increases, and that is a source of increased production. Output can rise above trend because people work

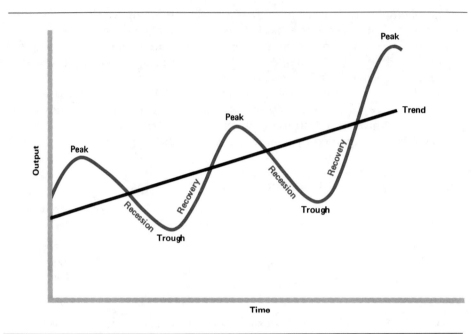

FIGURE 1-2   THE BUSINESS CYCLE. Output or GDP does not grow smoothly at its trend rate. Rather, it fluctuates irregularly around trend, showing business cycle patterns from trough, through recovery, to peak, and then from peak, through recession, back to the trough. Business cycle output movements are not regular in timing or in size.

overtime, and machinery is used for several shifts. Conversely, during a *recession* unemployment develops and less output is produced than can in fact be produced with the existing resources and technology. The wavy line in Figure 1-2 shows these cyclical departures of output from trend. Deviations of output from trend are referred to as the *output gap*. The output gap measures the gap between actual output and the output the economy could produce at full employment given the existing resources. Full-employment output is also called *potential output*.

$$\text{Output gap} \equiv \text{potential output} - \text{actual output} \qquad (1)$$

The output gap allows us to measure the cyclical deviations of output from potential output or trend output (we use there terms interchangeably). Figure 1-3 shows actual and potential output for Canada.

The figure shows the output gap growing during a recession, such as in 1982. More resources become unemployed, and actual output falls below potential. Conversely, during an expansion, most strikingly in the long expansion of the

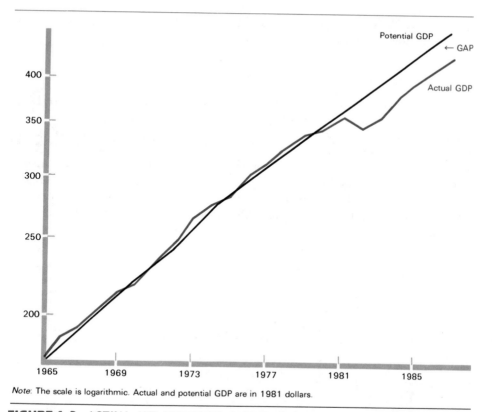

Note: The scale is logarithmic. Actual and potential GDP are in 1981 dollars.

FIGURE 1-3   ACTUAL AND POTENTIAL OUTPUT, 1965–1987. Potential output is the full employment level of output. It grows like trend output in Figure 1-2. Actual GDP fluctuates around potential, falling below during recession, and rising back toward the potential level during recoveries.

(*Source:* Adapted from Statistics Canada, 13-201)

1960s, the gap declines and ultimately even becomes negative. A negative gap means that there is overemployment, overtime of workers, and more than the usual rate of utilization of machinery.

Establishing the level of potential output is a difficult problem. In the 1960s it was believed that full employment corresponds to a measured rate of unemployment of 4 to 4.5 percent of the labour force. Changes in the composition of the labour force toward younger workers, and female workers who change jobs more frequently, raised the estimate of the full employment rate of unemployment to a range above 6 percent in the 1970s. This is a benchmark for calculating what potential output or full employment output is, but it is only a benchmark, not a rigid, undebatable rule. Even so, the output gap provides an important indicator of how the economy is performing and in which direction policies should try to move the level of activity.

Seasonal Variation

Figure 1-4 shows the actual monthly unemployment rate from October 1982 to December 1983 together with the *seasonally adjusted* rate, as calculated by Statistics Canada. The seasonally adjusted series is corrected for the typical seasonal pattern observed in the past and is a measure of the underlying cyclical movement. For example, from October 1982 to March 1983, the unadjusted rate rose from 11.7 to 14 percent but this was somewhat below the increase typically experienced in the winter months. Thus, when seasonal factors are removed, the seasonally adjusted rate shows a decline from 12.8 to 12.5 percent.

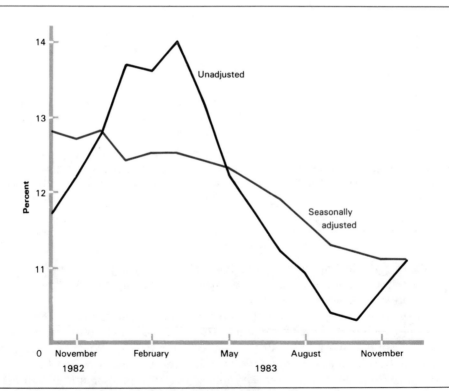

FIGURE 1-4   ACTUAL AND SEASONALLY ADJUSTED UNEMPLOYMENT RATE

(*Source*: Adapted from Statistics Canada, 11-003)

Balance of Payments

The balance of payments is the record of transactions of the economy with the rest of the world. It includes borrowing and lending and exchange of assets between countries as well as imports and exports of goods and services. Trade in goods is recorded in the merchandise trade balance. Figure 1-5 shows Canada's trade balance for 1966 through 1986. There have been wide swings, but exports exceeded imports in every year except 1975.

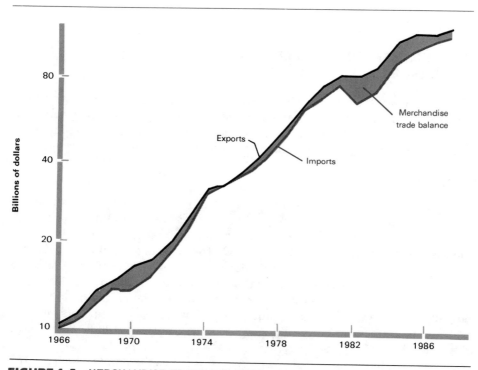

FIGURE 1-5 MERCHANDISE TRADE BALANCE, 1966–1987

(*Source:* Adapted from *Bank of Canada Review*)

Exchange Rates

An exchange rate is the relative value of the currencies of two countries. For example, at the beginning of 1988 the Canadian dollar traded for about 78 U.S. cents or equivalently one U.S. dollar cost $1.28 in Canadian funds. The British pound was worth $2.40 and the German mark was worth $0.81.

Under a fixed exchange rate, the external value of the country's currency is pegged within narrow bounds around a preannounced value. This system was followed by Canada from 1962 to 1970 when the Canadian dollar was fixed at 92.5 U.S. cents. If a country allows the value of its currency to be determined by market forces, it is said to have a flexible or floating exchange rate. This practice was followed by Canada in the 1950s and from 1970 to the present the value of our dollar has fluctuated between a high of about 105 U.S. cents and recent lows near 70 cents. In 1988 it returned to above 80 cents for the first time since 1984.

1-2   RELATIONSHIPS AMONG MACROECONOMIC VARIABLES

The preliminary look at the data presented above, and our discussion of the business cycle, correctly suggests that we should expect to find simple relationships among the major macroeconomic variables: growth, unemployment, and inflation. There are indeed such relationships, as we now document.

Growth and Unemployment

We have already noted that changes in the employment of factors of production provide one of the sources of growth in real GDP. We would then expect high GDP growth to be accompanied by declining unemployment. That is indeed the case, as we observe from Figure 1-6. On the vertical axis, Figure 1-6 shows the growth rate of output in a particular year and on the horizontal axis the change in the unemployment rate in that year. For example, in both 1964 and 1965, the growth rate of output was 6.7 percent and the reduction in the unemployment rate was 0.8 percentage points. Thus we plot the points labelled 64-65 in the upper left-hand region. That region corresponds to a period of expansion and falling unemployment rates.

By contrast, in the lower right-hand region, such as the points labelled 1975 and 1982, are periods of recession — low growth and rising unemployment rates. Note that even when there is some growth, such as in 1981, unemployment rates may be rising. It takes growth rates above about 3 percent to cause unemployment rates to come down.

Okun's Law

A relationship between real growth and changes in the unemployment rate is known as *Okun's law*, named after is discoverer, the late Arthur Okun of the Brookings Institution, former chairperson of the U.S. Council of Economic Advisers. Okun's law says that for every 2½ percentage points of growth in real GDP above the trend rate that is sustained for a year, the unemployment rate declines by 1 percentage point. This 2½-to-1 relationship, the status of which is somewhat exaggerated by calling it a law rather than an empirical

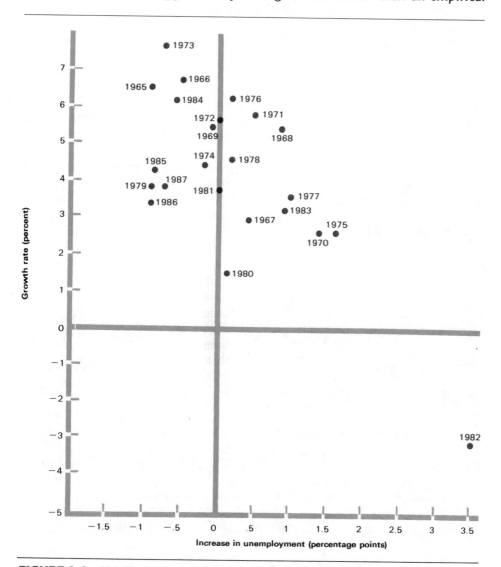

FIGURE 1-6 GROWTH AND THE CHANGE IN THE UNEMPLOYMENT RATE, 1965–1987. High rates of growth cause the unemployment rate to fall, and low or negative rates of growth are accompanied by increases in the unemployment rate. The relationship shown by the scatter of the points in this figure is summarized by *Okun's law*, linking the growth rate to the change in the unemployment rate.

(*Source*: Department of Finance, *Economic Review*)

regularity, provides a rule of thumb for assessing the implications of real growth for unemployment.[4] While the rule is only approximate and will not work very precisely from year to year, it still gives a sensible translation from growth to unemployment.

The relation is a useful guide to policy because it allows us to ask how a particular growth target will affect the unemployment rate over time. Suppose we were in a deep recession with 9 percent unemployment. How many years would it take us to return to, say, 6 percent unemployment? The answer depends, of course, on how fast the economy grows in the recovery. Assume the growth rate of potential output is 3 percent per year. One possible path to return to 6 percent unemployment is for output to grow at 5½ percent per year for 3 years. On this path, each year we are growing 2½ percent above trend, and thus each year we take 1 percentage point off the unemployment rate. An alternative recovery strategy is front-loaded: growth is high at the beginning and then slows down. Such a path might be one of growth rates in successive years equal to 6½, 5½, and 4½ percent, also allowing a return to 6 percent unemployment in 3 years.

Inflation and the Cycle

Inflation is the rate of increase of prices. An expansion of aggregate demand tends to produce inflation, unless it occurs when the economy is at high levels of unemployment. Protracted periods of low aggregate demand tend to reduce the inflation rate. Figure 1-7 shows one measure of inflation for the Canadian economy for the period since 1960. The inflation measure in the figure is the rate of change of the *consumer price index*, the cost of a given basket of goods, representing the purchases of a typical urban consumer.[5]

The rate of inflation shown in Figure 1-7 fluctuates considerably. Just as we could tell much about the recent history of the economy from looking at Figure 1-3's picture of the course of actual and potential GDP, we can likewise see much of recent economic history in Figure 1-7. In particular, there is the long period of steady inflation from 1957 through 1964 when the inflation rate hovered around the 2 percent level. Then there is a slow climb in the inflation rate from 1965 to 1969, followed by a brief pause in 1970. Subsequently there are the inflationary bursts from 1971 through 1974 and 1977 to 1980, when the

---

[4] The analysis of Canada's medium-term prospects shown in the Economic Council of Canada's *Sixteenth Annual Review* (1979) suggests a ratio of about 2 to 1.

[5] By contrast, the measure of inflation obtained in Figure 1-1 by comparing nominal and real GDP is the rate of change of the GDP *deflator*. The consumer price index (CPI) is most frequently used to measure inflation, and the GDP deflator is next most popular. Chapter 2 presents more details on the different price indexes.

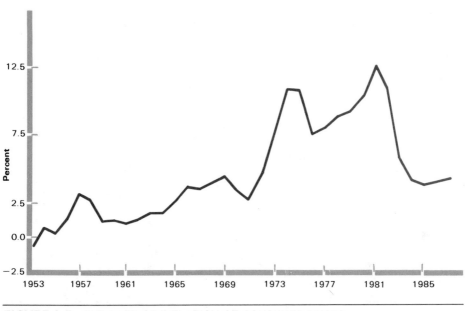

FIGURE 1-7   THE RATE OF INFLATION OF CONSUMER PRICES

(*Source*: Department of Finance, *Economic Review*)

inflation rate rose to 12 percent and above. Finally, in 1982–83, inflation came down to the 4-5 percent range under the impact of a deep recession.

Figure 1-7 shows the rate of increase of prices. We can also look at the level of prices. All the inflation of the 1970s and 1980s adds up to a large increase in the price level. From 1972 to 1986, the price level tripled so that a product that cost $1 in 1972 cost $3 in 1986.

Inflation-Unemployment Tradeoffs

The *Phillips curve* describes a relationship between inflation and unemployment: the higher the rate of unemployment, the lower the rate of inflation. The Phillips curve is an empirical relationship that relates the behaviour of wage and price inflation to the rate of unemployment. It was made famous in the 1950s in Great Britain and has since become a cornerstone of macroeconomic discussion. Figure 1-8 presents a typical downward-sloping Phillips curve showing that high rates of unemployment are accompanied by low rates of inflation and vice versa. The curve suggests that less unemployment can always be attained by incurring more inflation and that the inflation rate can always be

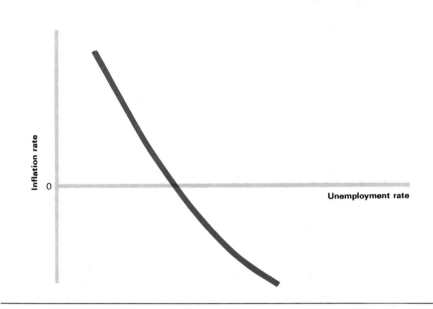

FIGURE 1-8 A PHILLIPS CURVE. The Phillips curve suggests a tradeoff between inflation and unemployment: less unemployment can always be obtained by incurring more inflation — or inflation can be reduced by allowing more unemployment. Recent events, particularly the combination of high inflation *and* high unemployment in years such as 1981 and 1982, have led to skepticism about the Phillips curve. It nonetheless remains useful, as we shall show later.

reduced by incurring the costs of more unemployment. In other words, the curve suggests there is a tradeoff between inflation and unemployment.

Figure 1-9 shows that the Phillips curve broadly describes Canadian experience in the period 1956–1966. However, we can see also that economic events of the last 20 years, particularly the combination of high inflation *and* high unemployment, are not consistent with the curve traced out in the earlier years.

Nonetheless, there remains a tradeoff between inflation and unemployment which is more sophisticated than a glance at Figure 1-8 would suggest, and which will enable us to make sense of Figure 1-9. In the short run of, say, 2 years, there is a relation between inflation and unemployment of the type shown in Figure 1-8. The *short-run Phillips curve*, however, does not remain stable. It shifts as expectations of inflation change. In the long run, there is no tradeoff worth speaking about between inflation and unemployment. In the long run, the unemployment rate is basically independent of the long-run inflation rate.

The short- and long-run tradeoffs between inflation and unemployment are obviously a major concern of policy making and are the basic determinants of the potential success of stabilization policies.

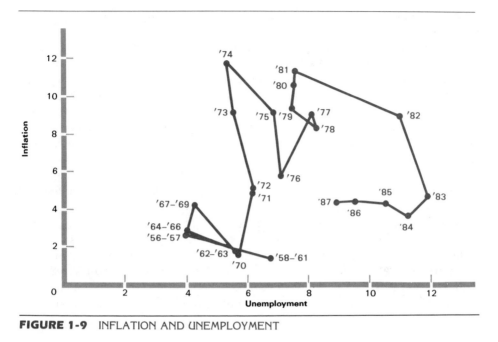

FIGURE 1-9   INFLATION AND UNEMPLOYMENT

(*Source:* Adapted from *Bank of Canada Review*)

1-3   MACROECONOMIC POLICY

Policy makers have at their command two broad classes of policies with which to affect the economy. *Monetary policy* is controlled by the Bank of Canada. The instruments of monetary policy are changes in the stock of money, changes in the interest rate—the bank rate—at which the Bank of Canada lends money to banks, and some controls over the banking system. *Fiscal policy* is under the control of Parliament, and usually is initiated by the government of the day. The instruments of fiscal policy are tax rates and government spending.

One of the central facts of policy is that the effects of monetary and fiscal policy on the economy are not fully predictable, neither in their *timing* nor in the *extent* to which they affect demand or supply. These two uncertainties are at the heart of the problem of stabilization policy. *Stabilization policies* are monetary and fiscal policies designed to moderate the fluctuations of the economy; in particular, fluctuations in the rates of growth, inflation, and unemployment. Stabilization policy is also known as *countercyclical policy*, that is, policy to moderate the trade cycle or business cycle.

Figure 1-9, which showed the recent fluctuations of the rates of inflation and unemployment, suggests strongly that stabilization policy has not been fully successful in keeping them within narrow bounds. The failures of stabilization policy are due mostly to uncertainty about the way it works.

However, questions of political economy are also involved in the way stabilization policy has been operated. The speed at which to proceed in trying to eliminate unemployment, at the risk of increasing inflation, is a matter of judgment about both the economy and the costs of mistakes. Those who regard the costs of unemployment as high, relative to the costs of inflation, will run greater risks of inflation to reduce unemployment than will those who regard the costs of inflation as high and unemployment as a relatively minor misfortune.

Political economy affects stabilization policy in more ways than through the costs which policy makers of different political persuasions attach to inflation and unemployment, and the risks they are willing to undertake in trying to improve the economic situation. There may be a *political business cycle* if election results are affected by economic conditions. When the economic situation is improving and the unemployment rate is falling, there is an environment favourable to the government. There is thus the incentive to policy makers running for reelection, or who wish to affect the election results, to use stabilization policy to produce booming economic conditions before elections.

Monetarists and Activists

We noted above that there is some controversy over the existence of the tradeoff between inflation and unemployment. That controversy arose around 1967–1968 in the context of the debate in macroeconomics between monetarists and nonmonetarists, or fiscalists. We have already identified some of the major participants in the debate as Milton Friedman on the monetarist side and Franco Modigliani and James Tobin on the nonmonetarist side. Among Canadian economists, prominent exponents of monetarism include Tom Courchene and David Laidler (University of Western Ontario) and their views have been vigorously challenged by Clarence Barber (University of Manitoba). However, macroeconomists cannot be neatly classified into one camp or the other. Instead, there is a spectrum of views. There are monetarists who make Friedman look like a fiscalist or Keynesian, and Keynesians who make Modigliani look like a monetarist. Not only that; there is no compelling unity in the views that are identified with monetarism, and the balanced economist is likely to accept some monetarist arguments and reject others. Nor is the debate one in which there is no progress. For example, both theory and empirical evidence have been brought to bear on the issue of the inflation-unemployment tradeoff, and it is no longer central to the monetarist-fiscalist debate.

Another major point of contention is the relation between *money* and *inflation. Monetarists* tend to argue that the quantity of money is the prime determinant of the level of prices and economic activity, and that excessive monetary growth is responsible for inflation and unstable monetary growth for economic fluctuations. Since they contend that variability in the growth rate of money accounts for variability of real growth, they are naturally led to argue for a monetary policy of low and constant growth in the money supply—a monetary growth rule. *Activists*, by contrast, point out that there is no close relationship between monetary growth and inflation in the short run and that monetary growth is only one of the factors affecting aggregate demand. Activists maintain that policy makers are, or at least can be, sufficiently careful and skillful to be able to use monetary and fiscal policy to control the economy effectively.

The skill and care of the policy makers are important because monetarists raise the issue of whether aggregate demand policies might not worsen the performance of the economy. Monetarists point to episodes, such as the over-expansionary policies followed by the Bank of Canada in 1971, to argue that policy makers cannot and do not exercise sufficient caution to justify using activist policy. On this issue the activists are optimists, suggesting that we can learn from our past mistakes.

A further issue that divides the two camps concerns the proper role of government in the economy. This is not really an issue that can be analysed using macroeconomic theory, but it is difficult to follow some of the debate without being aware that the issue exists.

Monetarists tend to be conservatives who favour small government and abhor budget deficits and a large public debt. They favour tax cuts during recessions and cuts in public spending during booms, with the net effect of winding up with a smaller share of government in the economy. Activists, by contrast, tend to favour an active role for government and are therefore quite willing to use increased government spending and transfers as tools of stabilization policy. Differences between monetarists and activists must, therefore, be seen in a much broader perspective than their particular disagreements about the exact role of money in the short run.

Expectations, the New Classical Macroeconomics, and Activism

The monetarist challenge to Keynesian activism warmed up in the sixties and still continues today. But its importance has been superseded by the more fundamental and theoretically innovative *rational expectations equilibrium approach* to macroeconomics, or the *new classical macroeconomics*. The approach and challenge, associated with Robert Lucas and Thomas Sargent, has been developed by many other well-known economists, including Neil Wallace of the University of Minnesota and Robert Barro of the University of Rochester.

The essence of the rational expectations equilibrium approach is the assumption that markets are continuously in equilibrium. In particular, new classical macroeconomists regard as incomplete or unsatisfactory any theory that leaves open the possibility that private individuals could make themselves better off by trading among themselves.

This may not sound radical, but consider for instance unemployment. There is unemployment when people who want jobs cannot find them. It is quite easy to explain unemployment if wages do not adjust and are too high for firms who want to employ everyone who wants to work at that wage. New classical macroeconomists insist that such an assumption is too easy and unsatisfactory. After all, they say, if the unemployed are willing to work for less than existing workers, firms would increase their profits by hiring them and firing any of their existing workers who are not willing to work at the lower wage. Thus, if wages are indeed slow to adjust, economists have to explain why it is not in someone's interest to adjust them more rapidly. The new classical macroeconomics has developed a sophisticated alternative explanation of unemployment that we discuss later.

The new classical macroeconomists also assume that expectations are *rational*; that is, that they are based on all economically relevant information. This is consistent with the assumption that individuals do not act arbitrarily or without thought in their economic life in forming expectations, as in other economic decisions.

New classical macroeconomists, like monetarists, tend to be conservatives, who see only a relatively small role for active government policy in the economy. This follows from the view that markets are mostly in equilibrium; people look after their own interests, leaving little for the government to do to improve the situation. They argue also that activist policy is difficult to carry out successfully because reactions of thinking firms and consumers to government actions depend on what the private sector thinks the government is trying to achieve, and may be difficult to predict.

Although they share many policy views, new classical macroeconomists are not necessarily monetarists. We discuss the equilibrium approach, rational expectations, and the new classical macroeconomics throughout the book, and in detail in Chapter 18.

1-4   AGGREGATE DEMAND AND SUPPLY

We have sketched the major issues and variables we shall be discussing and using in the book.

The key overall concepts in analysing output, inflation and growth, and the role of policy are *aggregate demand* and *aggregate supply*. In this section we provide a brief preview of those concepts and of their interaction, with the aims of showing where we are heading and of keeping the material of Chapter 3 through 6 in perspective.

The level of output and the price level are determined by the interaction of aggregate demand and aggregate supply. Under some conditions, employment depends only on total spending, or aggregate demand. At other times, supply limitations are an important part of the policy problem and have to receive major attention. From the 1930s to the late 1960s, macroeconomics was very much oriented towards the influence of aggregate demand on employment.

However, in recent years the emphasis has shifted, and aggregate supply and *supply-side economics* have gained in importance. This shift of emphasis and interest was no doubt fostered by the slow growth and high inflation experienced by the industrialized countries in the 1970s.

Figure 1-10 shows aggregate demand and supply curves. The vertical axis P is the price level, and the horizontal axis Y is the level of real output or income. Although the curves look like the ordinary supply and demand curves of microeconomics, a full understanding of them will not be reached until Chapter 7.

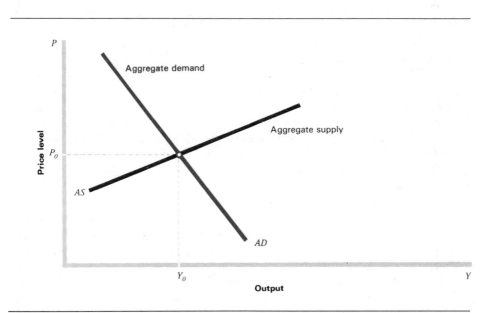

FIGURE 1-10   AGGREGATE DEMAND AND SUPPLY. The basic tools for analyzing output, inflation, and growth are the aggregate supply and demand curves. Shifts in either aggregate supply or demand will cause the level of output to change — thus affecting growth — and will also change the price level — thus affecting inflation. Through *Okun's law*, changes in output are linked to changes in the unemployment rate. For the first 6 chapters, we concentrate on aggregate demand. Then in the later chapters we introduce the aggregate supply curve, thereby completing the analysis.

Aggregate demand is the total demand for goods and services in the economy. It depends on the aggregate price level, as shown in Figure 1-10. It can be shifted through monetary and fiscal policy. The aggregate supply curve shows the price level associated with each level of output. It can, to some extent, be shifted by fiscal policy.

Aggregate supply and demand interact to determine the price level and output level. In Figure 1-10, P_0 is the equilibrium price level and Y_0 the equilibrium level of output. If the AD curve in the figure shifts up to the right, then the extent to which output and prices, respectively, are changed depends on the steepness of the aggregate supply curve.[6] If the AS curve is very steep, then a given increase in aggregate demand mainly causes prices to rise and has very little effect on the level of output. If the AS curve is flat, a given change in aggregate demand will be translated mainly into an increase in output and very little into an increase in the price level.

One of the crucial points about macroeconomic adjustment is that the aggregate supply curve is not a straight line. Figure 1-11 shows that at low levels of output, below potential output Y^*, the aggregate supply curve is quite flat. When output is below potential, there is very little tendency for prices of goods and factors (wages) to fall. Conversely, for output above potential, the aggregate supply curve is steep and prices tend to rise continuously. The effects of changes in aggregate demand on output and prices therefore depend on the level of output relative to potential.

All these observations are by way of a very important warning. In Chapters 3 through 6 we focus on aggregate demand as the determinant of the level of output. We shall assume that prices are given and constant, and that output is determined by the level of demand — that there are no supply limitations. We are thus talking about the very flat part of the aggregate supply curve, at levels of output below potential.

The suggestion that output rises to meet the level of demand without a rise in prices leads to a very activist conception of policy. Under these circumstances, without any obvious tradeoffs, policy makers would favour very expansionary policies to raise demand and thereby cause the economy to move to a high level of employment and output. There are circumstances where such a policy view is altogether correct. The early 1960s are a case in point. Figure 1-3 shows that in those years output was substantially below potential. There were unused resources, and the problem was a deficiency of demand. By contrast, in the late 1960s and the early 1970s the economy was operating at full employment. There was no significant output gap. An attempt to expand output further would run into supply limitations and force up prices rather than the production

---

[6] Experiment with graphs like Figure 1-10 to be sure you understand this fact.

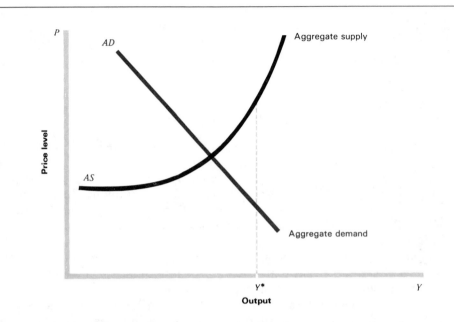

FIGURE 1-11 AGGREGATE DEMAND AND NONLINEAR AGGREGATE SUPPLY. A key fact about the aggregate supply curve is that it is not linear. At low levels of output, prices do not change much on the aggregate supply schedule, implying that more output will be supplied without much increase in prices. However, as the economy gets close to full employment or potential output, further increases in output will be accompanied by increased prices.

of goods. In these circumstances, a model that assumes that output is demand-determined and that increased demand raises output and *not* prices is simply inappropriate.

Should we think that the model with fixed prices and demand-determined output is very restricted and perhaps artificial? The answer is no. There are two reasons for this. First, the circumstances under which the model is appropriate — those of high unemployment — are neither unknown nor unimportant. Unemployment and downward price rigidity are continuing features of the Canadian economy. Second, even when we come to study the interactions of aggregate supply and demand in Chapter 7 and later, we need to know how given policy actions *shift* the aggregate demand curve at a given level of prices. Thus all the material of Chapters 3 through 6 on aggregate demand plays a vital part in the understanding of the effects of monetary and fiscal policy on the price level as well as output in circumstances where the aggregate supply curve is upward-sloping.

What, then, is the warning of this section? It is simply that the very activist spirit of macroeconomic policy under conditions of unemployment must not cause us to overlook the existence of supply limitations and price adjustment when the economy is near full employment.

1-5 OUTLINE AND PREVIEW OF THE TEXT

We have sketched the major issues we shall discuss in the book. We can now outline our approach to macroeconomics and the order in which the material will be presented. The key overall concepts, as already noted, are aggregate demand and aggregate supply. Aggregate demand is influenced by monetary policy, primarily via interest rates and expectations, and by fiscal policy. Aggregate supply is affected by fiscal policy and also by disturbances such as changes in the supply of oil.

Figure 1-12 presents a schematic view of the approach of the book to macroeconomics. Being schematic, the diagram is not comprehensive, but it does show the most important relationships we shall examine.

The coverage by chapters starts in Chapter 2 with national income accounting, emphasizing data and relationships that are used repeatedly later in the book. Chapters 3 and 4 are concerned with aggregate demand in a closed economy without external economic relationships, and Chapters 5 and 6 extend the analysis to an open economy with trade and international capital flows. Chapter 7 introduces aggregate supply and shows how aggregate supply and demand interact to determine both output and the price level.

Chapters 8–13 presents material which clarifies and deepens understanding of aggregate demand and of the ways in which monetary and fiscal policies affect the economy. Chapters 14–20 perform a similar service for aggregate supply and the interactions of aggregate supply and demand.

1-6 PREREQUISITES AND RECIPES

A few words on how to use this book are helpful in concluding this introductory chapter. First, we note that there is no mathematical prerequisite beyond high school algebra. We do use equations whenever they appear helpful, but they are not an indispensable part of the exposition. Nevertheless, they can and should be mastered by any serious student of macroeconomics.

The technically harder chapters or sections are marked by an asterisk (*). They can be skipped or dipped into. Either we present them as supplementary material, or we provide sufficient nontechnical coverage to help the reader get on without them later in the book. The reason we do present more advanced

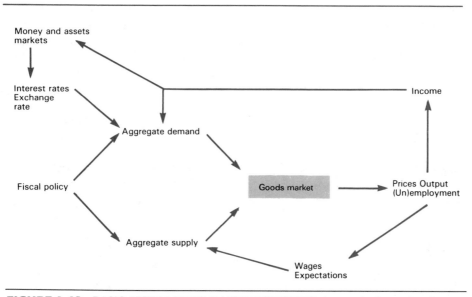

FIGURE 1-12   BASIC APPROACH TO MACROECONOMICS. Aggregate demand and aggregate supply are the key elements in determining prices and output. Aggregate supply is affected by fiscal policy and by wage behaviour and expectations. Aggregate demand is affected by fiscal policy and by monetary policy. There are also feedbacks through the money market — a high level of income increases the demand for money, which raises interest rates and reduces aggregate demand. This figure is a road map for the rest of the book. It will be helpful to return to it later, to see where the material being covered in later chapters fits in to the overall approach to the economy outlined here.

material or treatment is to afford a complete and up-to-date coverage of the main ideas and techniques in macroeconomics. Even though you may not be able to grasp every point of a section marked by an asterisk on first reading — and should not even try to — these sections should certainly be read to get the main message and an intuitive appreciation of the issues that are raised.

The main problem you will encounter comes from the interaction of several markets and many variables. As Figure 1-12 already suggests, the direct and feedback effects in the economy constitute a quite formidable system. How can you be certain to progress efficiently and with some ease? The most important thing is to ask questions. Ask yourself, as you follow the argument: Why is it that this or that variable should affect, say, aggregate demand? What would happen if it did not? What is the critical link?

There is no substitute for an active form of learning. Reading sticks at best for 7 weeks. Are there simple rules for active study? The best way to study is to use pencil and paper and work the argument by drawing diagrams, experimenting with flowcharts, writing out the logic of an argument, working out the problems at the end of each chapter, and underlining key ideas. The *Study Guide*, by Gordon Sparks and Richard Startz, contains much useful material and problems that will help in your studies. Another valuable exercise is to take issue with an argument or position, or to spell out the defence for a particular view on policy questions. Beyond that, if you get stuck, read on for half a page. If you are still stuck, go back five pages.

You should also learn to use the Index. Several concepts are discussed at different levels in different chapters. If you come across an unfamiliar term or concept, check the Index to see whether and where it was defined and discussed earlier in the book.

As a final word, this chapter is designed for reference purposes. You should return to it whenever you want to check where a particular problem fits or where a particular subject matter is relevant. The best way to see the forest is from Chapter 1.

KEY TERMS

Monetarists   *Recovery or expansion*
Keynesians   *Recession*
New classical macroeconomists   *Output gap*
GDP, nominal and real   *Okun's law*
Inflation   *Phillips curve*
Growth   *Monetary policy*
Unemployment   *Fiscal policy*
Business cycle   *Stabilization policies*
Trend or potential output   *Activists*
Peak   *Aggregate demand and supply*
Trough

CHAPTER

National Income Accounting

Macroeconomics is ultimately concerned with the determination of the economy's total output, the price level, the level of employment, interest rates, exchange rates, and other variables discussed in Chapter 1. A necessary step in understanding how these variables are determined is *national income accounting*.

The national income accounts give us regular estimates of GDP, the basic measure of the performance of the economy in producing goods and services. The first part of the chapter discusses the measurement and meaning of GDP, and the second part describes the relationships between three key macroeconomic variables: output, income, and spending. These relationships are summarized in the circular flow diagram, Figure 2-1.

Figure 2-1 illustrates the interactions of firms and households in the economy. Output is produced by firms. The value of the output produced is the gross domestic product. GDP includes the value of goods produced, such as automobiles and eggs, along with the value of services, such as haircuts and medical services.

Firms produce the output by employing factors of production—land, labour, and capital—and paying for their use. The payments made by the firms are the *incomes* earned in the economy. The flow of income is shown in the lower bottom loop of the circular flow diagram. Thus the value of output is equal to the value of incomes received in the economy.

The goods produced by the firms are sold to households (and to other firms) or are added to inventories. Total *spending* on goods including accumulation of inventories is thus equal to the value of output. The flow of spending is also shown in Figure 2-1.

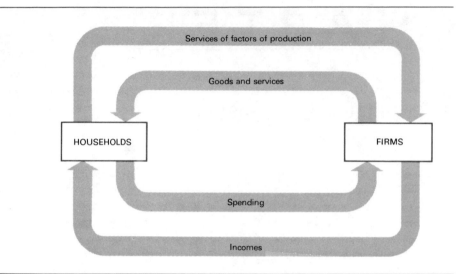

FIGURE 2-1 THE CIRCULAR FLOW OF INCOME AND SPENDING. Production is carried out by firms whose total output is equal to GDP. The output is produced using the services of factors of production, mostly labour, owned by households and paid for by the firms. The payments for the use of factors of production generate the households' income. Household spending out of those incomes, in turn, generates the demand for the goods produced by the firms. Spending on goods is, in the simple case shown here where there is no government and no foreign trade, equal to GDP, and also equal to the income of households. The diagram shows the key relation: output is equal to income is equal to spending.

Looking at the relationships summarized in Figure 2-1, we see that *the value of total output is equal to total income earned in the economy, and is also equal to total spending.* That is the main lesson of this chapter, and the single most important point to remember about national income accounting. There is, however, considerable complexity in the actual national income accounts in relating GDP to incomes and spending. Those complexities arise in large part from the role of the government and from the presence of foreign trade, and we shall have to explain some of them.

We start in Section 2-1 by examining GDP and its measurement, and then move, in Sections 2-2 and 2-3, to the relationships among output, income and spending summarized in the circular flow diagram. Section 2-4 returns to the distinction between real and nominal GDP, and Section 2-5 compares alternative measures of the price level.

Section 2-6 paves the way for the economic analysis of the determination of the level of output, that begins in Chapter 3, by systematically setting out the national income relationships studied in this chapter.

2-1   CALCULATING GROSS DOMESTIC PRODUCT

GDP is the value of all final goods and services produced in Canada within a given period. It includes the value of such goods produced as houses and whiskey, and the value of services, such as brokers' services and economists' lectures. The output of each of these is valued at its market price, and the values are added together to give GDP.

Table 2-1 shows the calculation of GDP in a simple economy that produces only bananas and oranges. Twenty bananas and sixty oranges are produced. The bananas are valued at $0.30 each and oranges at ¢0.25 each. GDP is equal to $21, the total value of output.

TABLE 2-1   CALCULATING GDP IN A SIMPLE ECONOMY

	Output	Price per unit	Value of output	GDP
Bananas	20	$0.30	$ 6.00	
Oranges	60	$0.25	$15.00	
				$21.00

GDP in Canada in 1986 was $509.9 billion. Dividing by population, equal to 25.6 million in 1986, we obtain GDP per person or per capita of just under $20 000. We can also calculate output per person employed. In 1986 there were on average 11.634 million people employed. Thus GDP per person employed or output per person employed was $43 828.

Final Goods and Value Added

GDP is the value of *final* goods and services produced. The insistence on final goods and services is simply to make sure that we do not double-count. For example, we would not want to include the full price of an automobile in GDP and then also include the value of the tires that were sold to the automobile producer as part of the GDP. The components of the car, sold to the manufacturers, are called *intermediate* goods, and their value is not included in GDP. Similarly, the wheat that goes into bread is an intermediate good, and we do not count the value of the wheat sold to the miller and the value of the flour sold to the baker, as well as the value of the bread, as part of GDP.

In practice, double counting is avoided by working with *value added*. At each stage of the manufacture of a good, only the value added to the good at that stage of manufacture is counted as part of GDP. The value of the wheat produced by the farmer is counted as part of GDP. Then the value of the flour sold by the miller minus the cost of the wheat is the miller's value added. If we follow this process along, we will see that the sum of value added at each stage of processing will be equal to the final value of the bread sold.[1]

Current Output

GDP consists of the value of output *currently produced*. It thus excludes transactions in existing commodities such as old masters or existing houses. We count the construction of new houses as part of GDP, but we do not add trade in existing houses. We do, however, count the value of realtor's fees in the sale of existing houses as part of GDP. The realtor provides a current service in bringing buyer and seller together, and that is appropriately part of current output.

Market Prices

GDP values goods at *market prices*. The market price of many goods includes indirect taxes such as the sales tax and excise taxes, and thus the market price of goods is not the same as the price the seller of the good receives. The price net of indirect taxes is the *factor cost*, which is the amount received by the factors of production that manufactured the good. GDP is valued at market prices and not at factor cost. This point becomes important when we relate GDP to the incomes received by the factors of production.

Valuation at market prices is a principle that is not uniformly applied, because there are some components of GDP that are difficult to value. There is no very good way of valuing the services of housepersons, or a self-administered haircut, or, for that matter, the services of the police force or the government bureaucracy. Some of these activities are simply omitted from currently measured GDP, as, for instance, housepersons' services. Government services are valued at cost, so that the wages of government employees are taken to represent their contribution to GDP. There is no unifying principle in the treatment of these awkward cases, but rather a host of conventions is used.

Domestic Product Versus National Product

Statistics Canada provides an alternative measure of output called *gross national product*, or *GNP*. GNP is the value of current output *produced by domestically owned factors of production*, while GDP measures *production within*

---

[1] How about the flour that is directly purchased by households for baking in the home? It is counted as a contribution toward GDP since it represents a *final* sale.

Canada using both Canadian and nonresident factors of production. Interest and dividends paid by Canadian companies to nonresidents are part of Canadian GDP but not GNP. Since income paid to nonresidents typically exceeds income earned by Canadians from foreign sources, GDP exceeds GNP. As shown in Table 2-2, the difference in 1986 was $16.9 billion.[2]

TABLE 2-2 GROSS DOMESTIC PRODUCT AND NATIONAL PRODUCT, 1986
(billions of dollars)

Gross domestic product (GDP)		$509.9
Plus: Investment income received from nonresidents	$7.2	
Less: Investment income paid to nonresidents	24.1	
Gross national product (GNP)		493.0
Less: Capital consumption allowances	57.6	
Net national product		435.4

Source: Statistics Canada, 11-010.

Net national product (NNP), as distinct from GNP, deducts from GNP the depreciation of the existing capital stock over the course of the period. Production causes wear and tear; for example, machines wear out as they are used. If resources were not used to maintain or replace the existing capital, GNP could not be kept at the current level. Accordingly, we can use NNP as a measure of the rate of economic activity that could be maintained over long periods, given the existing capital stock and labour force.

Depreciation, or capital consumption allowances, is a measure of the part of GNP that has to be set aside to maintain or replace worn out capital. As shown in Table 2-2, in 1986 capital consumption allowances amounted to $57.6 billion.

2-2 GDP AND INCOME

We now consider the relation between the value of output or GDP and the incomes that are generated in the production process. In this section we show that income is equal to the value of output because the receipts from the sale of

---

[2] Prior to 1986, Canada's national accounts were presented on a national product rather than a domestic product basis. For a brief discussion of the revisions, see Department of Finance, Quarterly Economic Review, Sept., 1986.

output must accrue to someone as income. The purchaser of bread is indirectly paying the farmer, the miller, the baker, and the supermarket operator for the labour and capital used in production.

GDP and Domestic Income

Our statement above, equating the value of output and income, is correct with three qualifications:

1. The first correction arises from depreciation. As already noted, part of GDP has to be set aside to maintain the productive capacity of the economy. Depreciation should not be counted as part of income, since it is a cost of production.
2. The second adjustment arises from indirect taxes, in particular, sales and excise taxes, that introduce a discrepancy between market price and prices received by producers. GDP is valued at market price, but the income accruing to producers does not include the sales and excise taxes that are part of the market price.
3. Finally there is a statistical discrepancy that represents errors in measurement of the value of output and total incomes.

With these three deductions we can derive *net domestic income* from GDP as shown in Table 2-3. This gives us the value of output at *factor cost* rather than market prices.

TABLE 2-3 GROSS DOMESTIC PRODUCT AND DOMESTIC INCOME, 1986
(billions of dollars)

Gross domestic product (GDP		$509.9
Less: Indirect taxes less subsidies	$53.9	
Capital consumption allowances	57.6	
Statistical discrepancy	1.8	
Net domestic income at factor cost		396.5

Source: Statistics Canada, 11-010.

Factor Shares in Net Domestic Income

Table 2-4 shows how domestic income is split among different types of income. The most striking fact is that wages and salaries make up nearly 70 percent of the total. The inventory valuation adjustment is made in order to exclude capital gains or losses on inventories that appear as part of profits measured under business accounting procedures but are not related to current production. Rental income includes not only rents received by landlords but also *imputed* income of owner-occupied housing.[3]

TABLE 2-4   NET DOMESTIC INCOME AND ITS DISTRIBUTION, 1986
(billions of dollars)

Net domestic income		$396.5	100.0%
Wages, salaries and other labour income		274.0	69.1
Corporation profits	45.4		
Less inventory valuation adjustment	1.1	44.3	11.2
Interest and misc. investment income		40.8	10.3
Net income of unincorporated business			
Farm	5.1		
Nonfarm, including rent	32.3	37.4	9.4

Source: Statistics Canada, 11-010

Net Domestic Income and Personal Income

A considerably more important question from the macroeconomic viewpoint is how much the personal sector—households and unincorporated business—actually receives as income including transfers. This is measured by *personal income. Transfers* are those payments that do *not* arise out of current productive activity. Thus, welfare payments and unemployment benefits are examples of transfer payments. The level of personal income is important because it is a prime determinant of household consumption and saving behaviour.

To go from net domestic income to personal income, we have to remove the part of net domestic income that accrues to the corporate sector and add back dividends. As shown in Table 2-5, we also add transfers from government and interest on government debt. These interest payments are part of personal income, but are excluded from GDP because much of the debt has been incurred to finance past government expenditure which does not contribute to current production of goods and services.

Although we have derived personal income in Table 2-5 by starting with net domestic income and making adjustments, we could also obtain it by adding up the components in a way similar to that shown in Table 2-4. In particular, personal income consists of wages and salaries, plus net income of unincorporated business, plus interest and dividends, plus transfers.

---

[3] GDP includes an estimate of the services homeowners receive by living in their homes. This is estimated by calculating the rent on an equivalent house. Thus the homeowner is treated as if she pays herself rent for living in her house.

TABLE 2-5   NET DOMESTIC INCOME AND PERSONAL INCOME, 1986
(billions of dollars)

Net domestic income		$396.5
Less: Corporation profits	45.4	
Other adjustments	-1.4	
Plus: Dividends and interest on govt. debt	16.3	
Transfers from government	62.3	
Other transfers	1.4	
Personal income		432.5

Source: Statistics Canada, 11-010.

Personal Disposable Income and Its Allocation

Not all personal income is available for spending by households. The amount available for spending, *personal disposable income*, deducts from personal income the personal tax payments and other transfers to government made by the household sector. The other transfers include such items as licence fees and traffic tickets.

Personal disposable income is then available for personal consumption expenditure, other transfers, and saving. By far the largest outlay is for personal consumption, as shown in Table 2-6.

TABLE 2-6   DISPOSITIONS OF PERSONAL INCOME, 1986
(billions of dollars)

Personal income		$432.5
Less: Personal taxes	$85.1	
Other transfers to government	3.9	
Personal disposable income		343.5
Less: Personal consumption expenditure	298.7	
Other transfers	5.2	
Personal saving		39.6

Source: Statistics Canada, 11-010.

In summary, this section has shown the relation between GDP, which is a measure of productive activity in the economy, and income receipts that accrue to the household sector. The main steps in the long chain we have followed arise from taxes, transfers between sectors, depreciation, and corporation profits.

These intermediate steps remind us that there is an important difference between GDP as the value of output at market prices and the spendable receipts of the household sector. We could have a positive personal disposable income even if GDP were zero, provided there was someone to make the necessary transfer payments. Likewise, GDP could be large and disposable income small if the government sector took in a lot of taxes. The larger taxes are relative to government transfers, the smaller is disposable income relative to GDP.

Summary

We summarize here in a few identities (and in Figure 2-2 which appears on page 38) the relationships reviewed in Tables 2-3 through 2-6:

$$
\begin{aligned}
\text{GDP} \quad &- \text{ indirect taxes} \\
&- \text{ capital consumption allowances} \\
&= \text{ net domestic income (Table 2-3)} \qquad (1)
\end{aligned}
$$

$$
\begin{aligned}
\text{Net domestic income} \\
&= \text{ wages and salaries} \\
&+ \text{ corporation profits} \\
&+ \text{ interest} \\
&+ \text{ net income of unincorporated} \\
&\quad\ \text{business (Table 2-4)} \qquad (2)
\end{aligned}
$$

$$
\begin{aligned}
\text{Net domestic income} \\
&- \text{ corporation profits} \\
&+ \text{ dividends and interest on govt. debt.} \\
&+ \text{ transfers} \\
&= \text{ personal income (Table 2-5)} \qquad (3)
\end{aligned}
$$

$$
\begin{aligned}
\text{Personal income} \\
&- \text{ personal taxes and other transfers to govt.} \\
&= \text{ personal disposable income (Table 2-6)} \qquad (4)
\end{aligned}
$$

$$
\begin{aligned}
\text{Personal disposable income} \\
&= \text{ personal consumption expenditure} \\
&+ \text{ other transfers} \\
&+ \text{ personal saving (Table 2-6)} \qquad (4a)
\end{aligned}
$$

2-3   EXPENDITURE COMPONENTS OF GDP

In the previous section, we started with GDP and asked how much of the value of goods and services produced is actually obtained by households. In this section we present a different perspective on GDP by asking who buys the output, rather than who receives the income. More technically, we look at the demand for output and speak of the components of the aggregate demand for goods and services.

Total demand for domestic output is made up of four components: (1) consumption spending by households; (2) investment spending by businesses;

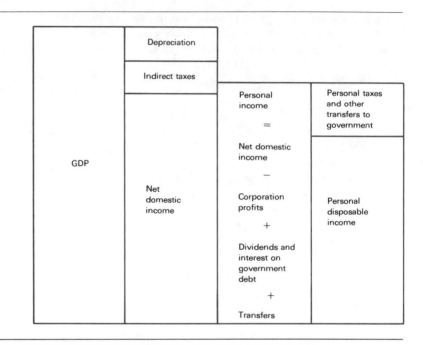

FIGURE 2-2   THE RELATION BETWEEN GDP AND PERSONAL DISPOSABLE INCOME

(3) government (federal, provincial and municipal) expenditure on goods and services; and (4) net foreign demand. We shall now look more closely at each of these components.

Consumption

Table 2-7 presents a breakdown of GDP in 1986 by components of demand. The table illustrates that the chief component of demand is consumption spending by the personal sector. This includes anything from food to golf lessons but involves also, as we shall see in discussing investment, consumer spending on durable goods such as automobiles — spending which might be regarded as investment rather than consumption.

Government

Next in importance we have government expenditure on goods and services. Here we have such items as national defence expenditures, road paving by provincial and municipal governments, and salaries of government employees. It is important to note here that the government component of GDP is expenditure on *goods and services* and excludes transfer payments. For all levels of

TABLE 2-7   GROSS DOMESTIC PRODUCT, EXPENDITURE BASED, 1986
(billions of dollars)

Personal consumption expenditure		$298.7	58.6%
Gross business investment		93.0	18.2
Government exp. on goods and services		113.9	22.3
Net exports of goods and services			
Exports	138.2		
Less imports	132.1	6.1	1.2
Statistical discrepancy		−1.8	−0.3
Gross domestic product		$509.9	100.0%

Source: Statistics Canada, 11-010.

government in 1986 the transfer component of spending amounted to about $62 billion, so that total budgetary spending was about $176 billion.

Investment

Gross business investment is an item that requires some definitions. First, throughout this book, we will mean by investment, additions to the physical stock of capital. As we use the term, investment does *not* include buying a bond or purchasing stock in General Motors. In practice, investment includes expenditure on machinery and equipment, nonresidential construction, residential construction, and additions to business inventories of goods. The classification of spending as consumption or investment remains to a significant extent a matter of convention. From the economic point of view, there is little difference between a household building up an inventory of peanut butter and a grocery store doing the same. Nevertheless, in the national income accounts, the individual's purchase is treated as a personal consumption expenditure, whereas the store's purchase is treated as investment in the form of inventory investment. Although these borderline cases clearly exist, we can retain as a simple rule of thumb that investment is associated with the business sector's adding to the physical stock of capital, including inventories.

Similar issues arise in the treatment of household sector expenditures. For instance, how should we treat purchases of automobiles by households? Since automobiles usually last for several years, it would seem sensible to classify household purchases of automobiles as investment. We would then treat the *use* of automobiles as providing consumption services. (We could think of imputing a rental income to owner-occupied automobiles.) However, the convention is to treat all household expenditures as consumption spending. This is not quite so bad as it might seem, since the accounts do separate our households' purchases of durable goods like cars and refrigerators from their other purchases. There is thus information in the accounts on those parts of household spending that, with considerable justification, could be categorized as investment spending. When consumer spending decisions are studied in detail, expenditures on consumer durables are usually treated separately.

The convention that is adopted with respect to the household sector's purchases of houses also deserves comment. The accounts treat the building of a house as investment by the business sector. When the house is sold to a private individual, the transaction is treated as the transfer of an asset, and not then an act of investment. Even if a house is custom-built by the owner, the accounts treat the builder who is employed by the owner as undertaking the act of investment in building the house. The investment is thus attributed to the business sector.

In passing, we note that in Table 2-7, investment is defined as "gross." It is gross in the sense that depreciation is not deducted. Net investment is gross investment minus depreciation.

Net Exports

The item net exports appears in Table 2-7 to show the effects of foreign trade on the demand for domestic output. Exports are added in as they represent spending by foreigners on our goods. Imports are subtracted out since they represent the part of domestic spending that is not for domestically produced goods. The practice in the national accounts is to include under consumption, investment and government expenditure all spending by Canadian residents both on domestically produced and foreign goods. To obtain total spending on domestically produced goods (GDP), imports are subtracted out.

The point can be illustrated with an example. Assume that instead of having spent $299 billion, the personal sector had spent $2 billion more. What would GDP have been? If we assume that government and investment spending had been the same as in Table 2-7, we might be tempted to say that GDP would have been $2 billion higher. That is correct if all the additional spending had fallen on our goods. The other extreme, however, is the case where all the additional spending falls on imports. In that event, consumption would be up $2 billion *and* net exports would be down $2 billion, with no net effect on GDP.

Final Demand

Sometimes it is important to distinguish total spending by domestic residents from the level of output produced. The two can differ because spending can exceed output when imports exceed exports. Domestic demand is thus defined by:

$$\text{Domestic demand} = \text{GDP} + \text{imports} - \text{exports}$$

It is also useful to have a concept of spending that nets out changes in inventories. This is *final domestic demand* and is defined as:

Final domestic demand = domestic demand
– inventory change

In 1986, final domestic demand was $501.9 billion as compared with a GDP of $509.9 billion. The difference reflects the positive value of net exports and positive inventory accumulation.

2-4 REAL AND NOMINAL GDP

Nominal GDP measures the value of output in a given period in the prices of that period or, as it is sometimes put, in *current dollars*. Thus 1985 nominal GDP measures the value of the goods produced in 1985 at the market prices that prevailed in 1985, and 1976 GDP measures the value of goods produced in 1976, at the market prices that prevailed in 1976. Nominal GDP changes from year to year for two reasons. The first is that the physical output of goods changes. The second is that market prices change. As an extreme and unrealistic example, one could imagine the economy producing exactly the same output in two years, between which all prices have doubled. Nominal GDP in the second year would be double nominal GDP in the first year, even though the physical output of the economy has not changed at all.

Real GDP measures changes in *physical* output in the economy between different time periods by valuing all goods produced in the two periods *at the same prices*, or in *constant dollars*. Real GDP is now measured in the national income accounts in the prices of 1981. That means that, in calculating real GDP, today's physical output is multiplied by the prices that prevailed in 1981 to obtain a measure of what today's output would have been worth had it been sold at the prices of 1981.

We return to the simple example of Table 2-1 to illustrate the calculation of real GDP. The hypothetical outputs and prices of bananas and oranges in 1981 and 1989 are shown in the first two columns of Table 2-8. Nominal GDP in

TABLE 2-8 REAL AND NOMINAL GDP: AN ILLUSTRATION

1981 nominal GDP		1989 nominal GDP		1989 real GDP*	
15 bananas at $0.10	$1.50	20 bananas at $0.30	$6.00	20 bananas at $0.10	$ 2.00
50 oranges at $0.15	$7.50	60 oranges at $0.25	$15.00	60 oranges at $0.15	$ 9.00
	$9.00		$21.00		$11.00

*Measured in 1981 prices

1981 was $9, and nominal GDP in 1989 was $21, or an increase in nominal GDP of 133 percent. However, much of the increase in nominal GDP is purely a result of the increase in prices between the two years and does not reflect an increase in physical output. When we calculate real GDP in 1989 by valuing 1989 output in the prices of 1981, we find real GDP equal to $11, which is an increase of 22 percent rather than 133 percent. The 22 percent increase is a better measure of the increase in physical output of the economy than the 133 percent increase.

We see from the table that the output of bananas rose by 33 percent, while the output of oranges increased by 20 percent from 1981 to 1989. We should thus expect our measure of the increase in real output to be somewhere between 20 and 33 percent, as it is.[4]

Figure 2-3 shows the behaviour of real and nominal GDP over the past few years. It is particularly noteworthy that nominal GDP rose continuously during the period, even while real GDP fell as it did, for example, during 1982. It would clearly be a mistake to regard the increases in nominal GDP as indicating that the performance of the economy was improving during 1982 despite the fall in physical output. Real GDP is the better measure of the performance of the economy in producing goods and services, and it is the measure we use in comparing output in different years.

Price Indexes

The calculation of real GDP gives us a useful measure of inflation known as the *GDP deflator*. Returning to the hypothetical example of Table 2-8, we can get a measure of inflation between 1981 and 1989 by comparing the value of 1989 GDP in 1989 prices and 1981 prices. The ratio of nominal to real GDP in 1989 is 1.91 (= 21 ÷ 11). In other words, output is 91 percent higher in 1989 when it is valued using the higher prices of 1989 than valued in the lower prices of 1981. We ascribe the 91 percent increase to price changes or inflation, over the period 1981–1989.

The GDP deflator is the ratio of nominal GDP in a given year to real GDP, and it is a measure of inflation from the period from which the base prices for

---

[4] The increase in real GDP that is calculated depends on the prices that are used in the calculation. If you have a calculator, you might want to compare the increase in real GDP between 1981 and 1989 if the prices of 1989 are used to make the comparison. (Using 1989 prices, real GDP rises 23.5 percent from 1981 to 1989, compared with 22.2 percent using 1981 prices.) The ambiguities that arise in comparisons using different prices to calculate real GDP are an inevitable result of the attempt to use a single number to capture the increase in output of both bananas and oranges when those two components did not increase in the same proportion. However, the ambiguity is not a major concern when there is inflation at any substantial rate, and that is precisely when we most want to use real (rather than nominal) GDP to study the performance of the economy.

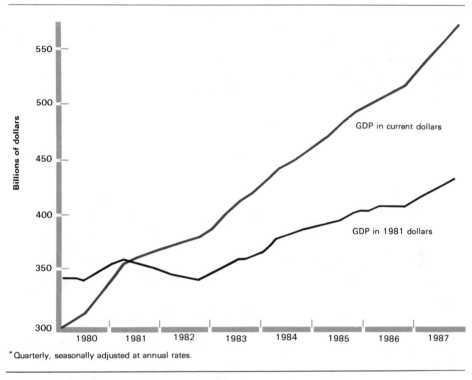

FIGURE 2-3   REAL AND NOMINAL GDP*

(*Source*: Adapted from Statistics Canada, 11-003, 11-206)

calculating real GDP are taken, to the current period. Since the GDP deflator is based on a calculation involving all the goods produced in the economy, it is a very widely based price index that is frequently used to measure inflation.

The Consumer Price Index

The *consumer price index (CPI)* measures the cost of buying a fixed bundle of goods, representative of the purchases of consumers. The GDP deflator differs in three main ways from the CPI. First, it measures the prices of a much wider group of goods than the CPI, which is based on the market basket of goods purchased by an average consumer. Second, the CPI measures the cost of a given basket of goods, which is the same from year to year. The basket of goods included in the GDP deflator, however, differs from year to year, depending on what is produced in the economy in each year. The goods valued in the deflator in a given year are the goods that are produced in the economy in that year. When wheat production is high, wheat receives a relatively large weight in the computation of the GDP deflator. By contrast, the CPI measures the cost of a fixed bundle of goods that does not vary over time.[5] Third, the CPI directly includes prices of imports, whereas the deflator includes only prices of goods *produced* in Canada. The behaviours of the two main indexes used to compute inflation, the GDP deflator and the CPI, accordingly differ from time to time. For example, at times when the price of imported oil rises rapidly, the CPI is likely to rise faster than the deflator.

BOX 2-1　PRICE INDEX FORMULAS

The CPI is a price index which compares the current and base year cost of a basket of goods of *fixed* composition. If we denote the base year quantities of the various goods by q_0^i and their base year prices by p_0^i, the cost of the basket in the base year is $\Sigma p_0^i q_0^i$, where the summation (Σ) is over all the goods in the basket. The cost of a basket of the *same* quantities but at today's prices is $\Sigma p_t^i q_0^i$, where p_t^i is today's price. The CPI is the ratio of today's cost to the base year cost, or

$$\text{Consumer price index} = \frac{\Sigma p_t^i q_0^i}{\Sigma p_0^i q_0^i} \times 100$$

This is a so-called *Laspeyres*, or *base-weighted*, price index.

The GDP deflator by contrast uses the weights of the *current* period to calculate the price index. Let q_t^i be the quantities of the different goods produced in the current year.

$$\text{GDP deflator} = \frac{\text{GDP measured in current prices}}{\text{GDP measured in base year prices}}$$
$$= \frac{\Sigma p_t^i q_t^i}{\Sigma p_0^i q_t^i} \times 100$$

This is known as a *Paasche*, or *current-weighted*, price index.

Comparing the two formulas we see that they differ only in that q_0^i, or the base year quantities, appears in both numerator and denominator of the CPI formula, whereas q_t^i appears in the formula for the deflator. In practice, the CPI and GDP deflator indexes differ also because they involve different collections of goods.

---

[5] Price indexes are, however, occasionally revised to change weights to reflect current expenditure patterns.

Industry Selling Price Index

A third important price index is the industry selling price index. Like the CPI, this is a measure of the cost of a given basket of goods. If differs from the CPI partly in its coverage, which includes, for example, semifinished goods. It differs, too, in that it is designed to measure prices at an early stage of the distribution system. Whereas the CPI measures prices where households actually do their spending, that is at the retail level, the industry selling price index is constructed from prices at the level of the first significant commercial transaction. This difference is important because it makes the latter a relatively flexible price index and one that signals changes in the general price level, or the CPI, some time before they actually materialize.

Table 2-9 shows the CPI, the industry selling price index, and the GDP deflator for the last 15 years. We note from the table that all three indexes have been increasing throughout the period. This is a reflection of the fact that the average price of goods has been rising, whatever basket we look at. We note, too, that the cumulative increase (price 1986/price 1971) differs across indexes. This difference occurs because the indexes represent the prices of different commodity baskets.[6]

TABLE 2-9   THREE PRICE INDEXES (1981 = 100)

	Consumer Price Index	Industry Selling Price Index	GDP Deflator
1971	42.2	36.7	41.9
1976	62.9	59.3	65.8
1981	100.0	100.0	100.0
1986	132.4	119.6	124.2
percent increase			
1971-1986	214%	226%	196%

Source: Statistics Canada, 11-003, 11-505.

2-5   PROBLEMS OF GDP MEASUREMENT

GDP data are, in practice, used not only as a measure of how much is being produced, but also as a measure of the welfare of the residents of a country.

---

[6] The mechanics of price indexes are briefly described in the appendix to this chapter. Detailed discussion of the consumer price index can be found in Statistics Canada, 62-010.

Economists and politicians talk as if an increase in real GDP means that people are better off, but GDP data are far from perfect measures of either economic output or welfare.

Badly Measured Outputs

Most of the difficulties of measuring GDP arise because some outputs do not go through the market. We already noted that government production is valued at cost. That is because much of government output is not sold in the market, nor is anything comparable available that would make it possible to estimate the value of government output. How would we measure the value of output of safety from criminals that police expenditures are supposed to produce?

There is also a conceptual problem with much of government output. We include in GDP the value of wages paid for the police and the defence forces. Suppose there was an improvement in public safety and police were taken out of the police force and put to work making candy — at their previous wage. GDP would not change, but the economy's output of useful goods and services certainly would seem to rise.

The problem in this case is that we generally do not deduct negative outputs, or *bads*, from GDP. We do not attempt to value the decline in public safety that requires increased police forces. Nor do we deduct from GDP the value of pollution produced by factories and cars. These are bads, but they do not show up in the GDP accounts. If we were somehow able to value the amount of public safety provided by society, then a shift of labour out of the police force resulting from an increase in public safety would indeed show up as an increase in GDP. Similarly, the improvement in the quality of the environment in the 1970s would show up as having raised output over that decade.

Other nonmarket activities, including do-it-yourself work and volunteer activities, are also excluded from GDP. The most important category here is the value of work done in the home by housepersons. Measured GDP would increase if someone stopped cleaning the house by himself and instead hired a cleaning service to do the same thing, but the output of the economy would not really have risen.

Thus real GDP suffers from weaknesses even as a measure of goods and services produced in the economy.

Real GDP as a Measure of Well-being

The second use of GDP is as a *measure of economic welfare* or well-being of the residents of a country. When GDP rises, it is assumed that people are better off. Of course, it is necessary first to divide real GDP by the number of people to use GDP in this sense: it is per capita (per person) GDP that is used as a welfare measure.

The difficulties of measuring nonmarket outputs already suggest that real GDP per capita is an imperfect measure of economic well-being. In addition, real GDP has to be adjusted to include the value of leisure. If the value of output falls because people have decided they would like to work less, that is not necessarily a sign that they are worse off. Much economic progress over the last century is reflected in a falling workweek. One hundred years ago the average workweek was well above 60 hours and in manufacturing it was higher still. Now it is under 40 hours. Real GDP should be adjusted to include the value of the increased leisure people have as a result of the declining workweek, if GDP is to be used as a measure of economic welfare.

An ideal measure of welfare is not available, and thus we continue to use real GDP as the chief measure of the economy's output and, although we know its shortcomings, as a measure of how the economy is performing in providing material well-being. The justification for doing so, in addition to the lack of choice, is that, in the short run, changes in real GDP are probably in the same direction as changes in welfare.

2-6   SOME IMPORTANT IDENTITIES

In this section we formalize the discussion of the preceding sections by writing down a set of relationships which we use extensively in Chapter 3. We introduce here some notation and conventions that we follow throughout the book.

For analytical work in the following chapters, we simplify our analysis by omitting the distinction between GDP and net domestic income. For the most part we disregard depreciation and thus the difference between gross and net investment. We refer simply to investment spending. We also disregard indirect taxes and non government transfer payments. With these conventions in mind *we refer to net domestic income and GDP interchangeably as income or output.* These simplifications have no serious consequence and are made only for expositional convenience. Finally, and only for a brief while, we omit both the government and foreign sector. Thus the assumptions we are making conform to those of the circular flow diagram, Figure 2-1.

A Simple Economy

We denote the value of output in our simple economy, which has neither a government nor foreign trade, by Y. Consumption is denoted by C and investment spending by I. The first key identity we want to establish is that between output produced and spending. Output produced is Y, which can be written in terms of the components of demand as the sum of consumption and investment spending. (Remember, we have assumed away the government and foreign sectors.) Accordingly, we can write the identity of output sold and output pro-duced as[7]

$$Y \equiv C + I \tag{5}$$

Now, is Equation (5) really an identity? Is it inevitably true that all output produced is either consumed or invested? After all, do not firms sometimes make goods that they are unable to sell? The answer to each of the questions is yes. Firms do sometimes make output that they cannot sell, and that accu-mulates on their shelves. *However, we count the accumulation of inventories as part of investment* (as if the firms sold the goods to themselves to add to their inventories), and therefore, all output is either consumed or invested. Note that we are talking here about *actual* investment, which includes investment in inventories that firms might be very unhappy to make. Because of the way investment is defined, output produced is identically equal to output sold.

Identity (5) formalizes the basis of Table 2-7 (we are still assuming away the government and external sectors). The next step is to draw up a corresponding identity for Table 2-6 and identity (4), which examined the disposition of per-sonal income. For that purpose, it is convenient to ignore the existence of corporations and consolidate or add together the entire private sector. Using this convention, we know that private sector income is Y, since the private sector receives as income the value of goods and services produced. Why? Because who else would get it? There is no government or external sector yet. Now the private sector receives, as disposable personal income, the whole of income Y. How will that income be allocated? Part will be spent on consump-tion, and part will be saved. Thus we can write

$$Y \equiv S + C \tag{6}$$

where S denotes private sector saving. Identity (6) tells us that the whole of income is allocated to either consumption or saving.

Next, identities (5) and (6) can be combined to read:

$$C + I \equiv Y \equiv C + S \tag{7}$$

The left-hand side of Equation (7) shows the components of demand, and the right-hand side shows the allocation of income. The identity emphasizes that

---

[7] Throughout the book we distinguish identities from equations. Identities are state-ments that are *always* true because they are directly implied by definitions of variables or accounting relationships. They do not reflect any causality based on economic behav-iour but are extremely useful in organizing our thinking. Identities, or definitions, are shown with the sign $\equiv$, and equations with the usual equality sign $=$.

output produced is equal to output sold. The value of output produced is equal to income received, and income received, in turn, is spent on goods or saved.

The identity in Equation (7) can be slightly reformulated to look at the relation between saving and investment. Subtracting consumption from each part of Equation (7), we have

$$I \equiv Y - C \equiv S \tag{8}$$

Identity (8) is an important result. It shows first that in this simple economy, saving is identically equal to income less consumption. This result is not new, since we have already seen it in Equation (6). The new part concerns the identity of the left and right sides: *investment is identically equal to saving.*

One can think of what lies behind this relationship in a variety of ways. In a very simple economy, the only way the individual can save is by undertaking an act of physical investment — by storing grain or building an irrigation channel. In a slightly more sophisticated economy, one could think of investors financing their investing by borrowing from individuals who save.

However, it is important to recognize that Equation (8) expresses the identity between investment and saving, and that some of the investment might well be undesired inventory investment, occurring as a result of mistakes by producers who expected to sell more than they actually did. The identity is really only a reflection of our definitions — output less consumption is investment, output is income, and income less consumption is saving. Even so, we shall find that identity (8) plays a key role in Chapter 3.

Reintroducing the Government and Foreign Trade

We can now reintroduce the government sector and the external sector. First, for the government we denote purchases of goods and services by G and all taxes by TA. Transfers to the private sector (including interest) are denoted by TR. Net exports (exports minus imports) are denoted by NX.

We return to the identity between output produced and sold, taking account now of the additional components of demand G and NX. Accordingly, we restate the content of Table 2-7 by writing

$$Y \equiv C + I + G + NX \tag{9}$$

Once more we emphasize that in Equation (9) we use actual investment in the identity and thus do not rule out the possibility that firms might not all be content with the level of investment. Still, as an accounting identity, Equation (9) must hold.

Next we turn to the derivation of the very important relation between output and disposable income. Now we have to recognize that part of income is spent on taxes, and that the private sector receives net transfers TR in addition to factor income. Disposable income is thus equal to income plus transfers less taxes:

$$YD \equiv Y + TR - TA \tag{10}$$

We have written YD to denote disposable income. Disposable income, in turn, is allocated to consumption and saving, so that we can write

$$YD \equiv C + S \tag{11}$$

Combining identities (10) and (11) allows us to write consumption as the difference between income, plus transfers minus taxes, and saving:

$$C + S \equiv YD \equiv Y + TR - TA \tag{12}$$
$$\text{or} \quad C \equiv YD - S \equiv Y + TR - TA - S \tag{12a}$$

Identity (12a) states that consumption is disposable income less savings, or alternatively, that consumption is equal to income plus transfers less taxes and saving. Now we use the right-hand side of Equation (12a) to substitute for C an identity (9). With some rearrangement we obtain

$$S - I \equiv (G + TR - TA) + NX \tag{13}$$

Saving, Investment, the Government Budget, and Trade

Identity (13) cannot be overemphasized. Its importance arises from the fact that the first set of terms on the right-hand side $(G + TR - TA)$ is the *government budget deficit*. $(G + TR)$ is equal to government[8] expenditures on goods and services (G) plus government transfer payments (TR), which is total government spending. TA is the amount of taxes received by the government. The difference $(G + TR - TA)$ is the excess of government spending over its receipts, or its budget deficit. The second term on the right-hand side is the excess of exports over imports, or the *trade surplus*.

Thus identity (13) states that the excess of savings over investment $(S - I)$ of the private sector is equal to the government budget deficit plus the trade surplus. The identity correctly suggests that there are important relations among the accounts of the private sector, $S - I$, the government budget, $G + TR - TA$, and the external sector. For instance, if, for the private sector, savings is equal to investment, then the government's budget deficit (surplus) is reflected in an equal external deficit (surplus).

---

[8] *Government* throughout this chapter means the federal government plus provincial and municipal governments. A breakdown by level of government can be found in Statistics Canada publications.

Table 2-10 shows the significance of Equation (13). To fix ideas, suppose that private sector saving S is equal to $30 (billion). In the first two rows we assume that exports are equal to imports, so that the trade surplus is zero. In row 1, we assume the government budget is balanced. Investment accordingly has to equal $30 billion. In the next row we assume the government budget deficit is $10 billion. *Given the level of saving* of $30 billion and a zero trade balance, it has to be true that investment is now lower by $10 billion. Rows 3 and 4 show how these relationships are affected when there is a trade surplus.

TABLE 2-10   THE BUDGET DEFICIT, TRADE, SAVING, AND INVESTMENT

S	I	BD (budget deficit)	NX (trade surplus)
30	30	0	0
30	20	10	0
30	25	0	5
30	15	10	5

To interpret these relationships, realize that any sector that spends more than it receives in income has to borrow to pay for the excess spending. The private sector has three ways of disposing of its saving. It can make loans to the government, which thereby pays for the excess of its spending over the income it receives from taxes, or it can lend to foreigners, who are buying more from us than we are buying from them. They therefore are earning less from us than they need to pay for the goods they buy from us, and we have to lend to cover the difference. Finally, the private sector can lend to business firms which use the funds for investment.

In Table 2-10 we take saving as fixed at $30 billion. When the budget and trade are balanced, the private sector has to lend the $30 billion to firms, which invest that amount. But suppose the government runs a budget deficit of $10 billion. Then the private sector has to lend $10 billion to government to cover its excess of spending over revenue. Only $20 billion is left to lend to firms for investment. Similarly, if we export more than we import, foreigners need to borrow from us to pay for the excess of what they buy from us over what they sell to us. In rows 3 and 4 we are using $5 billion of our saving to lend to foreigners. Then only $25 billion is left to lend either to firms or to the government.

2-7   SUMMARY

1. As the circular flow diagram shows, output is equal to income and spending.

2. Gross domestic product (GDP) is the value at market prices of all final goods and services produced within a country.

3. Gross national product is the value of output produced by domestically owned factors of production. GDP differs from gross national product since it includes net payments to nonresident factors of production.

4. Net domestic income is equal to GDP minus depreciation and indirect taxes and represents the value of output at factor cost.

5. Gross domestic product is conveniently divided into consumption, investment, government expenditure on goods and services, and net exports. The division between consumption and investment in the national income accounts is somewhat arbitrary at the edges.

6. Real GDP is the value of the economy's output measured in the prices of some base year. Real GDP comparisons, based on the same set of prices for valuing output, provide a better measure of the change in the economy's physical output than nominal GDP comparisons, which also reflect inflation.

7. The GDP deflator is the ratio of nominal to real GDP. It reflects the general rise in prices from the base date by which real GDP is valued. Other frequently used price indexes are the consumer and producer price indexes.

8. The excess of the private sector's saving over investment is equal to the sum of the budget deficit and the foreign trade surplus.

9. For the remainder of the book we use a simplified model for expositional convenience. We assume away depreciation, indirect taxes, business transfer payments, and the difference between households and corporations. For this simplified model, Figure 2-4 and Equation (14) review the *basic macroeconomic identity.*

KEY TERMS

Gross domestic product (GDP)	*Personal disposable income*
Final goods	*Consumption*
Value added	*Government expenditure on goods and*
Market prices	*services*
Factor cost	*Investment*
Gross national product	*Net exports*
Depreciation	*Consumer durables*
Net domestic income	*Real GDP*
Factor shares	*GDP deflator*
Personal income	*Consumer price index*
Transfers	*Government budget deficit*

FIGURE 2-4   THE BASIC MACROECONOMIC IDENTITY.

$$C + G + I + NX \equiv Y \equiv YD + (TA - TR) \equiv C + S + (TA - TR) \quad (14)$$

The left-hand side is the demand for output by components which is identically equal to output supplied. Output supplied is equal to income. Disposable income is equal to income plus transfers less taxes. Disposable income is allocated to saving and consumption.

PROBLEMS

1. Show from national income accounting that:
    (a) An increase in taxes (while transfers remain constant) must imply a change in the trade balance, government purchases or the saving-investment balance.
    (b) An increase in disposable income must imply an increase in consumption or an increase in saving.
    (c) An increase in both consumption and saving must imply an increase in disposable income.

2. The following is information from the national income accounts for a hypothetical country:

GDP	240
Gross investment	40
Net Investment	15
Consumption	150
Government expenditure on goods and services	48
Net domestic income	190
Wages and salaries	146
Net income of unincorporated business	16
Dividends	5
Interest income	13
Government budget surplus	− 15
Interest on government debt	7
Government transfer payments	25

   What are:
   (a) Net exports?
   (b) Indirect taxes?
   (c) Corporate profits?
   (d) Personal income?
   (e) Personal disposable income?
   (f) Personal saving?

3. What would happen to GDP if the government hired unemployed workers,
who had been receiving amount TR in unemployment benefits, as government employees to do nothing, and now paid them TR? Explain.

4. What is the difference in the national income accounts between:
   (a) A firm's buying an auto for an executive and the firm's paying the exec-
       utive additional income to buy himself a car?
   (b) Your hiring your spouse (who takes care of the house) rather than just
       having him or her do the work without pay?
   (c) Your deciding to buy a Canadian-made car rather than a German car?

5. Explain the following terms:
   (a) Value added
   (b) Factor cost
   (c) Inventory investment
   (d) GDP deflator

6. This question deals with price index numbers. Consider a simple economy
where only three items are in the CPI: food, housing, and entertainment
(fun). Assume in the base period, say, 1981, the household consumed the
following quantities at the then prevailing prices:

	Quantities	Prices per unit, $	Expenditure, $
Food	5	14	70
Housing	3	10	30
Fun	4	5	20
Total			120

(a) Define the consumer price index.

(b) Assume that the basket of goods that defines the CPI is as given in the table. Calculate the CPI for 1990 if the prices prevailing in 1990 are: food, $30 per unit; housing, $20 per unit; and fun, $6 per unit.

(c) Show that the change in the CPI relative to the base year is a weighted average of the individual price changes, where the weights are given by the base year expenditure shares of the various goods.

7. Refer to Table 2-4 to answer the following.

(a) How would a shift by corporations from equity to debt finance affect the distribution of national income?

(b) How would the incorporation of a business affect the table?

(c) What difference would it make if some existing houses were owned by corporations instead of individuals?

8. Assume that GDP is $120, personal disposable income is $100, and the government budget deficit is $7. Consumption is $85 and the trade surplus is $2.

(a) How large is saving S?

(b) What is the size of investment I?

(c) How large is government spending?

*9. Calculate both Laspeyres and Paasche price indexes for the information in Table 2-8.

---

* An asterisk denotes a more difficult problem.

CHAPTER

Aggregate Demand and
Equilibrium Income and Output

In Chapter 2 we studied the measurement of national income and output. With these fundamental concepts, we are now able to begin our study of the factors that determine the level of national income and product. Ultimately, we want to know why real GDP sometimes falls (and the rate of unemployment rises), as it did in 1982, and why at other times income rises very rapidly (and unemployment falls), as it did in 1972–1973.

We also want to know what determines the rate of inflation. Why was it so high in 1975 and 1981? Why did it rise from 1978 to 1981? We want to know whether public policies, such as changes in government spending and tax rates, or changes in the growth rate of the money supply, or changes in interest rates, can affect the level of income and the rates of inflation and unemployment. If they can, we want to know how.

The study of those questions occupies the rest of the book but to make progress we proceed slowly. We begin in this chapter with a simplified model of the economy that isolates the crucial concept of *aggregate demand*, while still omitting both some factors that affect aggregate demand and considerations of aggregate supply. In later chapters we gradually introduce those other factors. By the time we have completed Chapter 7, we shall be able to understand the behaviour of the key macroeconomic variables — the rates of unemployment and inflation and the level of GDP.

We start from the macroeconomic identities in equation (14) of Chapter 2 and in Figure 2-4. First, GDP is equal to total spending on goods and services, consisting of consumption C, investment I, government purchases of goods and services G, and net exports NX. Second, GDP is also equal to income received in the economy.[1] Income, in turn, increased by transfers TR and reduced by taxes TA, is allocated to consumption C and saving S. Thus

$$C + I + G + NX \equiv Y \equiv C + (TA - TR) + S$$

In this chapter we go beyond that *accounting identity* to begin our study of the factors that determine the level of national product or output. In particular, we focus on the interactions between the level of output and aggregate demand. The main point of the chapter is to show that *there is a single level of equilibrium output at which the aggregate (total) demand for goods and services is equal to the level of output.*

To begin with, we simplify our task by discussing a hypothetical world without a government ($G \equiv TA \equiv TR \equiv 0$) and without foreign trade ($NX \equiv 0$). In such a world, the accounting identity simplifies to

$$C + I \equiv Y \equiv C + S \tag{1}$$

where Y denotes the *real* value of output and income. Throughout this chapter a change in a macroeconomic aggregate is a change in its *real* value. For instance, when we speak of a change in consumption spending, we mean a change in real consumption spending.

The key concept of *equilibrium output* is introduced immediately, in Section 3-1. To keep the analysis as simple as possible, we assume to begin with that the demand for goods is *autonomous* — that is, independent of the level of income.[2] In fact, though, increases in income increase the demand for consumption goods. Accordingly, in Section 3-2 we extend the basic analysis by introducing the *consumption function*, which relates the demand for consumption goods to the level of income. In Sections 3-2 and 3-3 we derive explicit formulas for the equilibrium level of income.

The government sector is reintroduced in Section 3-4, which includes the first discussion of fiscal policy. The government budget is examined in Section 3-5 and foreign trade is introduced in Section 3-6.

---

[1] Because output is equal to income received in the economy, economists tend to use the terms *income* and *output* interchangeably when discussing the level of economic activity.

[2] The terms *autonomous* and *induced* are traditionally used to indicate spending that is independent of the level of income and dependent on the level of income, respectively. More generally, autonomous spending is spending that is independent of the other variables explained in a given theory.

3-1   EQUILIBRIUM OUTPUT

In this chapter and the next we assume a world where all prices are given and constant.[3] In terms of Figure 1-10, the aggregate supply curve is horizontal.

What would determine the level of output actually produced if firms could supply any amount of output at the prevailing level of prices? *Demand* must enter the picture. Firms would produce at a level just sufficient to meet demand.

To develop this point, we define the concepts of *aggregate demand* and *equilibrium output*.

Aggregate Demand

Aggregate demand is the total amount of goods demanded in the economy. In general, the quantity of goods demanded, or aggregate demand, depends on the level of income in the economy and — as we shall see later — on interest rates. But for now we shall assume that the amount of goods demanded is constant, independent of the level of income.

Aggregate demand is shown in Figure 3-1 by the horizontal line *AD*. In the diagram, aggregate demand is equal to 300 (billion dollars). This means that the total amount of goods demanded in the economy is $300 billion, no matter what the level of income.

But if the quantity of goods demanded is constant, independent of the level of income, what determines the actual level of income? We have to turn to the concept of equilibrium output.

Equilibrium Output

Output is at its *equilibrium* level when the quantity of output produced is equal to the quantity demanded. An equilibrium situation is one which no forces are causing to change. We now explain why output is at its equilibrium level when it is equal to aggregate demand.

In Figure 3-1 we show the level of output on the horizontal axis. This 45° line serves as a reference line that translates any horizontal distance into an equal vertical distance. For any given level of output *Y* on the horizontal axis, the 45° line gives the level of aggregate demand that is equal to that level of output. For instance, at point *E*, both output and aggregate demand are equal to 300.

---

[3] The assumption that prices are constant is made to simplify the exposition of Chapters 3 and 4. In later chapters, starting with Chapter 7, we use the theory of aggregate demand developed here to study the factors that determine the price level and cause it to change over time.

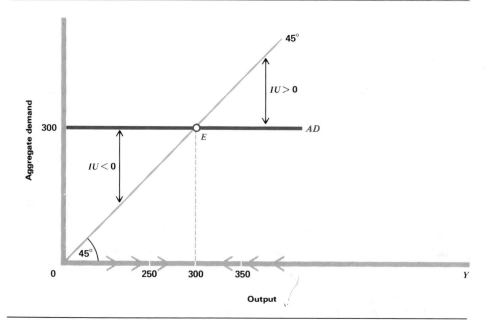

FIGURE 3-1   EQUILIBRIUM WITH CONSTANT AGGREGATE DEMAND. Aggregate demand is shown by the *AD* line, and is equal to 300. Output is at its equilibrium level when it is equal to aggregate demand, equal to 300. Thus the equilibrium is shown at point *E*. At any other output level, inventories are changing in a way that causes firms to change their production in a direction that moves output toward the equilibrium level.

Point *E* is the point of equilibrium output, at which the quantity of output produced is equal to the quantity demanded. To understand why this should be the equilibrium level of output, suppose that firms were producing some other amount, say, 350 units. Then output would exceed demand. Firms would be unable to sell all they produce and would find their warehouses filling with inventories of unsold goods. They would then cut their output. This is shown by the horizontal arrow pointing left at the output level of 350 on the horizontal axis.

Similarly, if output were less than 300, say, at 250, firms would either run out of goods or be running down their inventories. They would therefore increase output, as shown by the horizontal arrow pointing to the right from the output level of 250.

Thus at point *E*, the equilibrium level of output, firms are selling as much as they produce, people are buying the amount they want to purchase, and there is no tendency for the level of output to change. At any other level of output, the pressure from increasing or declining inventories causes firms to change the level of output.

Equilibrium Output and the National Income Identity

We have defined equilibrium output as that level of output at which aggregate demand for goods is equal to output. To clarify that definition, we have to dispose of an unsettling issue that arises from the accounting identity in equation (1), derived from our study of national income accounting. The identity in equation (1) states that demand, $C + I$, is *identically* equal to supply Y, *whatever* the level of output. That seems to mean that demand equals supply at *any* level of output, so that any level of output could be the equilibrium level.

The issue is resolved by recalling that aggregate demand is the amount of goods people *want to buy*, whereas in the national income accounts investment and consumption are the amounts of the goods *actually* bought for investment or consumption, whether or not people wanted to or planned to buy them. In particular, the investment measured in equation (1) includes *involuntary*, or *unintended* (or *undesired*), inventory changes, which occur when firms find themselves selling more or less goods than they had planned to sell. Similarly, if households cannot buy all the goods they want, the consumption measured in equation (1) will be different from planned consumption.

We have to make a distinction between the actual aggregate demand that is measured in an accounting context and the relevant economic concept of planned (desired, intended) aggregate demand.

Actual aggregate demand $(C + I)$ is, by the accounting identity in equation (1), equal to the level of output (Y). The output level is determined by firms. In deciding how much to produce, firms calculate how much investment, including inventory investment, they want to undertake. They also produce to meet the demand for consumption they forecast will be forthcoming from households. *Planned aggregate demand* consists of the amount of consumption that households plan to carry out plus the amount of investment planned by firms.[4]

If firms miscalculate households' consumption demands, planned aggregate demand does not equal actual aggregate demand. Suppose first that firms overestimate consumption demand. In terms of Table 3-1, suppose that firms decide to produce 350 units of output, expecting to be able to sell that amount. However, aggregate demand is only 300. The firms thus sell 300 units of output.

---

[4] From now on we shall assume that actual consumption is equal to planned consumption, so that all differences between actual and planned aggregate demand are reflected in unintended inventory changes. In practical terms, this means we are not considering situations where firms put "Sold Out" signs in their windows and customers cannot buy what they want.

TABLE 3-1   EQUILIBRIUM OUTPUT AND INVOLUNTARY INVENTORY CHANGE.

Output	Aggregate demand	Involuntary inventory changes
200	300	− 100
250	300	− 50
300	300	0
350	300	+ 50
400	300	+ 100

But they are left with 50, which they have to add to their inventories. It is as if they buy those extra 50 units of output themselves. In the national income accounts, additions to inventories count as investment. Of course, this is not *planned* or *desired* investment, but it does count as part of investment. Looking at the national income accounts for such an economy, we would see output equal to 350 and consumption plus investment equal to 350. However, the equality of output and $(C + I)$ does not mean that 350 is the equilibrium level of output, because 50 units of investment were undesired additions to inventories.

When aggregate demand, the amount people *want* to buy, is not equal to output, there is unplanned inventory investment. We summarize this as where *IU* is unplanned additions to inventory.

In terms of Figure 3-1, unplanned inventory investment is shown by the vertical arrows. When output exceeds 300, there is unplanned inventory investment. When output is less than 300, there are unplanned reductions in inventories. In Table 3-1, unplanned inventory investment is shown in the last column.

An alternative way of seeing the link between the national income accounting relations and the economic concepts is in equation (2a). Here we state that actual output is equal to planned spending or aggregate demand, plus involuntary inventory adjustment.

$$\text{Output} = \text{planned spending} + \text{involuntary inventory adjustment} \quad (2a)$$

The *equilibrium* level of income is the level of income (or output) at which planned spending is equal to actual output, so that there is no involuntary inventory accumulation or decumulation.

Equilibrium Output and Demand

We can now define equilibrium output more formally, using equation (2). Output is at its equilibrium level when it is equal to aggregate demand, or when unplanned inventory accumulation is zero. That is, output is at its equilibrium level when

$$Y = AD \tag{3}$$

There are three essential notions from this section:

1. Aggregate demand determines the equilibrium level of output.
2. At equilibrium, unintended changes in inventories are zero, and households consume the amount they want to consume.
3. An adjustment process for output based on unintended inventory changes will actually move output to its equilibrium level.[5]

Note, too, that the definition of equilibrium implies that actual spending on consumption and investment equals planned spending. In equilibrium, aggregate demand, which is planned spending, equals output. Since output identically equals income, we see also that *in equilibrium, planned spending equals income*.

3-2   THE CONSUMPTION FUNCTION AND AGGREGATE DEMAND

The preceding section studied the equilibrium level of output (and income) on the assumption that aggregate demand was simply a constant. Now we move to a more realistic specification of aggregate demand and begin to examine the economic variables that determine it.

In the simplified model we are working with, which excludes both the government and foreign trade, aggregate demand consists of the demands for consumption and investment. The demand for consumption goods is not in practice autonomous as we have so far assumed, but rather increases with income—families with higher income consume more than families with lower income, and countries where income is higher typically have higher levels of

---

[5] You may have noticed that the adjustment process we describe raises the possibility that output will temporarily exceed its new equilibrium level during the adjustment to an increase in aggregate demand. This is the *inventory cycle*. Suppose firms desire to keep on hand inventories which are proportional to the level of demand. When demand unexpectedly rises, inventories are depleted. In subsequent periods, the firms have to produce not only to meet the new higher level of aggregate demand, but also to restore their depleted inventories and to raise them to a higher level. While they are rebuilding their inventories and also producing to meet the higher level of demand, their total production will exceed the new higher level of aggregate demand.

total consumption. The relationship between consumption and income is described by the *consumption function.*

The Consumption Function

We assume that consumption demand increases along with the level of income[6]:

$$C = \overline{C} + cY$$

where $\quad\quad\overline{C} > 0 \quad$ and $\quad 0 < c < 1$ $\hfill$ (4)

This consumption function is shown in Figure 3-2a on page 64. The consumption function in equation (4) implies that at low levels of income consumption exceeds income, whereas at high levels of income consumption is less than income. The *intercept of the consumption function is* $\overline{C}$ and the *slope is* c. Along the consumption function the level of consumption rises with income.

The coefficient c is sufficiently important to have a special name, the *marginal propensity to consume.* (The marginal propensity to consume is the increase in consumption per unit increase in income.) In our case, the marginal propensity to consume is less than 1, which implies that out of a dollar increase in income, only a fraction, c, is spent on consumption. For example, if c is 0.8, then when income rises by $1, consumption increases by $0.80

Consumption and Saving

What happens to the rest, the fraction $(1 - c)$ that is not spent on consumption? If it is not spent, it must be saved. Income is either spent or saved; there are no other uses to which income can be put.

More formally, look at equation (1) which says that income that is not spent on consumption is saved, or

$$S \equiv Y - C$$ $\hfill$ (5)

Equation (5) tells us that by definition, *saving is equal to income minus consumption.* This means that we cannot postulate, in addition to the consumption function, an independent saving function and still expect consumption and saving to add up to income.

---

[6] Equation (4) is special because consumption is assumed to be a *linear* function of income. That means that in terms of Fig. 3-2, we can show the consumption function as a straight line. You might want to experiment with nonlinear consumption functions. Note also that because income is equal to output, we use the same symbol, Y, for both income and output.

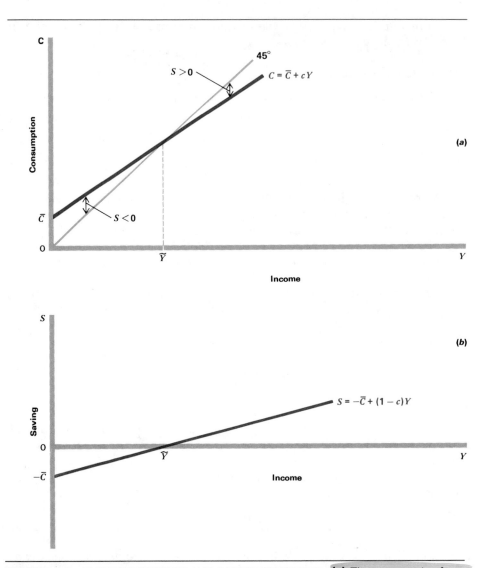

FIGURE 3-2   THE CONSUMPTION AND SAVING FUNCTIONS. **(a)** The consumption function shows consumption increasing with income. Its intercept is $\bar{C}$, and its slope, the marginal propensity to consume, is c. At low levels of income, consumption is above the level of income, implying that people spend more than they earn. At higher levels of income, consumption is below the level of income, implying that people save part of their income. **(b)** The saving function in Figure 3-2b is consistent with the consumption function above it, at low income levels, saving is negative, and it is positive at higher income levels. At income level $\widetilde{Y}$, saving is exactly zero.

The consumption function in equation (4), together with equation (5), which we call the *budget constraint*, implies a saving function. The saving function is the function that related the level of saving to the level of income. Substituting the consumption function in equation (4) into the budget constraint in equation (5) yields the saving function

$$S \equiv Y - C$$
$$= Y - (\overline{C} + cY) \qquad\qquad (6)$$
$$= -\overline{C} + (1 - c)Y$$

From equation (6), saving is an increasing function of the level of income because the *marginal propensity to save*, $s = 1 - c$, is positive. For instance, suppose the marginal propensity to consume, c, is 0.8, meaning that 80 cents out of each extra dollar of income is consumed. Then the marginal propensity to save, s, is 0.2, meaning that the remaining 20 cents of each extra dollar of income is saved.

The interrelationship between the consumption and savings functions examined in equation (6) can also be seen in Figure 3-2, where the vertical distance between the consumption function and the 45° line at each level of income measures saving. At low levels of income, saving is negative, reflecting the fact that consumption exceeds income. An individual can have negative saving by using up his or her assets — bank account or stocks — to pay for purchases in excess of income. Conversely, at sufficiently high levels of income, saving becomes positive, reflecting the fact that not all income is spent on consumption.

The saving function is the mirror image of the consumption function. Figure 3-2*b* shows the saving function that is derived from the consumption function in Figure 3-2*a* by plotting the vertical distance between income and consumption spending at each level of income. Of course, Figure 3-2*b* is merely a representation of equation (6). Note that the slope of the saving function in Figure 3-2*b* is the marginal propensity to save, $s = 1 - c$, as defined above.

Planned Investment and Aggregate Demand

We have now specified one component of aggregate demand, consumption demand. We must also consider the determinants of investment spending, or an *investment function*. We cut short the discussion for the present by simply assuming that planned investment spending is at a constant level $\overline{I}$.[7]

---

[7] In Chapters 4 and 9, investment spending will become a function of the rate of interest and will gain an important place in the transmission of monetary policy.

Aggregate demand is the sum of consumption and investment demands:

$$AD = C + \bar{I}$$
$$= \bar{C} + cY + \bar{I} \qquad (7)$$
$$= \bar{A} + cY$$

The aggregate demand function (7) is shown in Figure 3-3. Part of aggregate demand, $\bar{A}$ ($= (\bar{C} + \bar{I})$), is independent of the level of income, or autonomous. But aggregate demand also depends on the level of income. It increases with the level of income, because consumption demand increases with income.

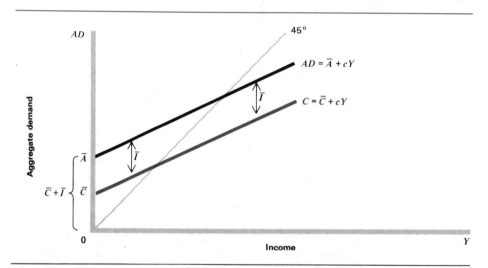

FIGURE 3-3   AGGREGATE DEMAND. Aggregate demand is the sum of the demands for consumption and investment goods. The consumption function is upward-sloping. Investment demand $\bar{I}$ is assumed constant and is added to consumption demand to obtain the level of aggregate demand at each level of income. The line AD shows how aggregate demand increases with income. Its slope is c, the marginal propensity to consume.

Equilibrium Income and Output

The next step is to use the aggregate demand function AD in Figure 3-3 and equation (7) to determine the equilibrium level of output and income. We plot the AD schedule again in Figure 3-4.

Recall the basic point of this chapter: the equilibrium level of income is such that aggregate demand equals output (which in turn equals income). The 45° line in Figure 3-4 shows points at which output and aggregate demand are equal. The aggregate demand schedule in Figure 3-4 cuts the 45° line at E,

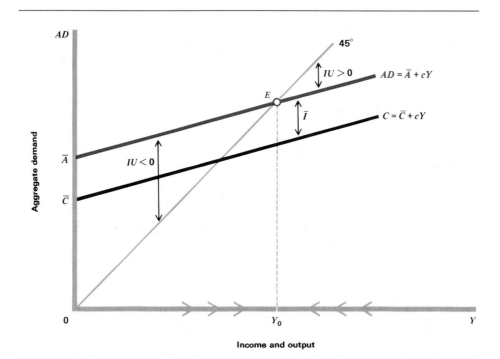

FIGURE 3-4 DETERMINATION OF EQUILIBRIUM INCOME AND OUTPUT. Output is at its equilibrium level when aggregate demand is equal to output. This occurs at point E, corresponding to the output (and income) level Y_0. At any higher level of output, aggregate demand is below the level of output, firms are unable to sell all they produce and there is undesired accumulation of inventories. Firms therefore reduce output, as shown by the arrows. Similarly, at any level of output below Y_0, aggregate demand exceeds output, firms run short of goods to sell, and they therefore increase output. Only at the equilibrium output level Y_0 are firms producing the amount that is demanded, and there is no tendency for the level of output to change.

and it is accordingly at E that aggregate demand is equal to output (equals income). Only at E, and at the corresponding equilibrium level of income and output, Y_0, does aggregate demand exactly equal output.[8] At that level of output and income, planned spending precisely matches production.

The arrows in Figure 3-4 indicate once again how we reach equilibrium. If firms expand production whenever they face unintended decreases in their inventory holdings, then they increase output at any level below Y_0, because below Y_0, aggregate demand exceeds output and inventories are declining. Conversely, for output levels above Y_0, firms find inventories piling up and

---

[8] We frequently use the subscript $_0$ to denote the equilibrium level of a variable.

therefore cut production. This process leads to the output level Y_0, where current production exactly matches planned aggregate spending, and unintended inventory changes are therefore equal to zero. Again, the arrows in Figure 3-4 represent the dynamic process by which the economy moves to the equilibrium level of output Y_0.[9]

The Formula for Equilibrium Output

The determination of equilibrium output in Figure 3-4 can also be described using equation (7) and the equilibrium condition in the goods market that output is equal to aggregate demand:

$$Y = AD \qquad (8)$$

The level of aggregate demand AD is specified in equation (7). Substituting for AD in equation (8), we have the equilibrium condition as

$$Y = \overline{A} + cY \qquad (9)$$

Since we have Y on both sides of the equilibrium condition in equation (9), we can collect the terms and solve for the equilibrium level of income and output, denoted by Y_0:

$$Y - cY = \overline{A}$$

or

$$Y(1 - c) = \overline{A}$$

Thus the equilibrium level of income, at which aggregate demand equals output, is

$$Y_0 = \frac{1}{1-c}\overline{A} \qquad (10)$$

Figure 3-4 sheds light on equation (10). The position of the aggregate demand schedule is characterized by its slope c and intercept $\overline{A}$. The intercept $\overline{A}$ is the level of autonomous spending, that is, spending that is independent of the level of income. The other determinant of the equilibrium level of income is the marginal propensity to consume, c, which is the slope of the aggregate demand schedule.

Given the intercept, a steeper aggregate demand function — as would be implied by a higher marginal propensity to consume — implies a higher level of equilibrium income. Similarly, for a given marginal propensity to consume,

---

[9] Do you see that there is once more the possibility of an inventory cycle? Refer to footnote 5.

a higher level of autonomous spending — in terms of Figure 3-4 a larger inter-cept — implies a higher equilibrium level of income. These results, suggested by Figure 3-4, are easily verified from equation (10), which gives the formula for the equilibrium level of income.

Thus, the equilibrium level of output is higher, the larger the marginal pro-pensity to consume, c, and the larger the level of autonomous spending $\bar{A}$.

Saving and Investment

There is an alternative, useful formulation of the equilibrium condition that aggregate demand is equal to output. *In equilibrium, planned investment equals saving.* This condition applies only to an economy in which there is no govern-ment and no foreign trade.

To understand this relationship, return to Figure 3-4. The vertical distance between the aggregate demand and consumption schedules in that figure is equal to planned investment spending $\bar{I}$. Recall in addition (from Figure 3-2) that the vertical distance between the consumption schedule and the 45° line measures saving at each level of income.

We thus have two vertical distances: between the AD and C schedules in Figure 3-4 and between the 45° line and the C schedule in Figure 3-2a. The equilibrium level of income is one where AD crosses the 45° line, at E. Accord-ingly, at the equilibrium level of income — and only at that level — the two vertical distances are equal. Thus at the equilibrium level of income, saving equals (planned) investment. By contrast, above the equilibrium level of income Y_0, saving (the distance between the 45° line and the consumption schedule) exceeds investment, while below Y_0, investment exceeds saving.

Now, is the equality between saving and investment at equilibrium an essen-tial characteristic of the equilibrium level of income, or is it a mere curiosity? It is an essential characteristic of equilibrium. We can see that by starting with the basic equilibrium condition, equation (8), which states that in equilibrium, $Y = AD$. If we subtract consumption from both Y and AD, we realize that $Y - C$ is saving and $AD - C$ is planned investment. In symbols,

$$
\begin{aligned}
Y &= AD \\
Y - C &= AD - C \\
S &= \bar{I}
\end{aligned}
\tag{11}
$$

Thus, the condition $S = \bar{I}$ is merely another way of stating the basic equilibrium condition.[10]

---

[10] In problem 3 at the end of this chapter, we ask you to derive equation (10) for Y_0 by starting from $S = \bar{I}$ and substituting for S from equation (6).

There is also a diagrammatic derivation of the equilibrium level of income in terms of equation (11)'s balance between saving and investment. In Figure 3-5, we show the saving function that was derived in Figure 3-2. We have drawn, too, planned investment spending, indicated by the horizontal line with intercept $\bar{I}$. Equilibrium income is shown at the level Y_0.

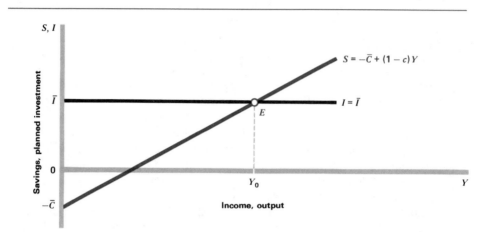

FIGURE 3-5 SAVING AND INVESTMENT. An alternative definition of the equilibrium level of output is that it occurs where saving is equal to (planned) investment. This is shown at point E, with corresponding output level Y_0. At higher levels of output, consumers want to save more than $\bar{I}$. They do not buy all of output, inventories accumulate, and actual investment is made equal to saving because firms undertake undesired inventory investment. They therefore cut output, and the economy moves to output level Y_0.

3-3 THE MULTIPLIER

In this section we develop an answer to the following question: By how much does a $1 increase in autonomous spending raise the equilibrium level of income?[11] There appears to be a simple answer. Since, in equilibrium, income equals aggregate demand, it would seem that a $1 increase in (autonomous) demand or spending should raise equilibrium income by $1. That answer is wrong. Let us now see why.

Suppose first that output increased by $1 to match the increased level of autonomous spending. This increase in output and income would in turn give

[11] Recall that autonomous spending $\bar{A}$ is spending that is independent of the level of income. Note also that the answer to this question is contained in equation (10). Can you deduce the answer directly from equation (10)? This section provides an explanation of that answer.

rise to further *induced* spending as consumption rises because the level of income has risen. How much of the initial $1 increase in income would be spent on consumption? Out of an additional dollar of income, a fraction c is consumed. Assume then that production increases further to meet this induced expenditure, that is, that output and so income increase by $1 + c$. That will still leave us with an excess demand, because the very fact of an expansion in production and income by $1 + c$ will give rise to further induced spending. This story could clearly take a long time to tell. We seem to have arrived at an impasse where an expansion in output to meet excess demand leads to a further expansion in demand without an obvious end to the process.

It helps to lay out the various steps in this chain more carefully. We do this in Table 3-2. We start off in the first round with an increase in autonomous spending $\Delta\bar{A}$. Next we allow an expansion in production to meet exactly that increase in demand. Production accordingly expands by $\Delta\bar{A}$. This increase in production gives rise to an equal increase in income and, therefore, via the consumption function, $C = \bar{C} + cY$, gives rise in the second round to induced expenditures of size $c(\Delta\bar{A})$. Assume again that production expands to meet the increase in spending. The production adjustment this time is $c(\Delta\bar{A})$, and so is the increase in income. This gives rise to a third round of induced spending

TABLE 3-2   THE MULTIPLIER

Round	Increase in demand this round	Increase in production this round	Total increase in income
1	$\Delta\bar{A}$	$\Delta\bar{A}$	$\Delta\bar{A}$
2	$c\Delta\bar{A}$	$c\Delta\bar{A}$	$(1+c)\Delta\bar{A}$
3	$c^2\Delta\bar{A}$	$c^2\Delta\bar{A}$	$(1+c+c^2)\Delta\bar{A}$
4	$c^3\Delta\bar{A}$	$c^3\Delta\bar{A}$	$(1+c+c^2+c^3)\Delta\bar{A}$
.	.	.	.
.	.	.	.
.	.	.	$\frac{1}{1-c}\Delta\bar{A}$
1	1.0	1.0	1.0
2	0.6	0.6	1.6
3	0.36	0.36	1.96
4	0.216	0.216	2.176
5	0.1296	0.1296	2.3056
.	.	.	.
.	.	.	.
.	.	.	2.5

equal to the marginal propensity to consume, times the increase in income $c(c\,\Delta\overline{A}) = c^2\,\Delta\overline{A}$. Careful inspection of the last term shows that induced expenditures in the third round are smaller than those in the second round. Since the marginal propensity to consume, c, is less than 1, the term c^2 is less than c. This can be seen also in the lower part of the table, where we assume $c = 0.6$ and show the steps corresponding to those in the upper part of the table.

If we write out the successive rounds of increased spending, starting with the initial increase in autonomous demand, we obtain

$$\Delta AD = \Delta\overline{A} + c\,\Delta\overline{A} + c^2\,\Delta\overline{A} + c^3\,\Delta\overline{A}) + \ldots$$

$$= \Delta\overline{A}\,(1 + c + c^2 + c^3 + \ldots) \qquad (12)$$

For the value of $c < 1$, the successive terms in the series become progressively smaller. In fact, we are dealing with a geometric series, the sum of which is calculated as

$$\Delta AD = \frac{1}{1 - c}\Delta\overline{A} = \Delta Y_0 \qquad (13)$$

From equation (13) therefore, the cumulative change in aggregate spending is equal to a multiple of the increase in autonomous spending. This could also have been deduced from equation (10).[12] The multiple $1/(1 - c)$ is called the *multiplier*. The multiplier is the amount by which equilibrium output changes when autonomous aggregate demand increases by one unit. Because the multiplier exceeds unity, we know that a \$1 change in autonomous spending increases equilibrium income and output by more than \$1.[13] The concept of the multiplier is sufficiently important to create a new notation. Defining the multiplier as α, we have

$$\alpha \equiv \frac{1}{1 - c} \qquad (14)$$

---

[12] If you are familiar with the calculus, you will realize that the multiplier is nothing other than the derivative of the equilibrium level of income, Y_0, in equation (10) with respect to autonomous spending. Use the calculus on equation (10) and later on equation (22) to check the statements of the text.

[13] *Two warnings:* (1) The multiplier is necessarily greater than 1 in this very simplified model of the determination of income, but as we shall see in the discussion of "crowding out" in Chapter 4, there may be circumstances in which it is less than 1. (2) The term *multiplier* is used more generally in economics to mean the effect on some endogenous variable (a variable whose level is explained by the theory being studied) of a unit change in an exogenous variable (a variable whose level is not determined within the theory being examined). For instance, one can talk of the multiplier of a change in the income tax rate on the level of unemployment. However, the classic use of the term is as we are using it here—the effects of a change in autonomous spending on equilibrium output.

Inspection of the multiplier in equation (14) shows that the larger the marginal propensity to consume, the larger the multiplier. With a marginal propensity to consume of 0.6 as in Table 3-2, the multiplier is 2.5; for a marginal propensity to consume of 0.8, the multiplier is 5. The reason is simply that a high marginal propensity to consume implies that a large fraction of an additional dollar income will be consumed. Accordingly, expenditures induced by an increase in autonomous spending are high and, therefore, so is the expansion in output and income that is needed to restore balance between income and demand (or spending).

Note that the relationship between the marginal propensity to consume, c, and the marginal propensity to save, s, allows us to write equation (14) in a somewhat different form. Remembering from the budget constraint that saving plus consumption adds up to income, we realize that the fraction of an additional dollar of income consumed plus the fraction saved must add up to a dollar, or $1 \equiv s + c$. Substituting $s \equiv 1 - c$ in equation (14), we obtain an equivalent formula for the multiplier in terms of the marginal propensity to save: $\alpha \equiv 1/s$.

The Multiplier in Pictures

Figure 3-6 provides a graphic interpretation of the effects of an increase in autonomous spending on the equilibrium level of income. The initial equilibrium is at point E with an income level Y_0. Now autonomous spending increases from $\overline{A}$ to $\overline{A}'$. This is represented by a parallel upward shift of the aggregate demand schedule to AD'. The upward shift means that now, at each level of income, aggregate demand is higher by an amount $\Delta \overline{A} \equiv \overline{A}' - \overline{A}$.

At the initial level of income, Y_0, aggregate demand now exceeds income or output. Consequently, unintended inventory decumulation is taking place at a rate equal to the increase in autonomous spending, equal to the vertical distance $\Delta \overline{A}$. Firms will respond to the excess demand by expanding production, say, to income level Y'. This expansion in production gives rise to induced expenditure, increasing aggregate demand to the level $\overline{A}'$. At the same time, it reduces the gap between aggregate demand and output to the vertical distance FG. The gap between demand and output is reduced because the marginal propensity to consume is less than 1.

Thus, a marginal propensity to consume that is positive but less than unity implies that a sufficient expansion in output will restore the balance between aggregate demand and output. In Figure 3-6 the new equilibrium is indicated by point E', and the corresponding level of income is Y'_0. The change in income required is therefore $\Delta Y_0 = Y'_0 - Y_0 (= EP = PE')$ with the change in autonomous spending that is equal to the vertical distance between the new and old aggregate demand schedule (QE'). It is clear from Figure 3-6 that the change in income PE' exceeds the change in autonomous spending QE'.

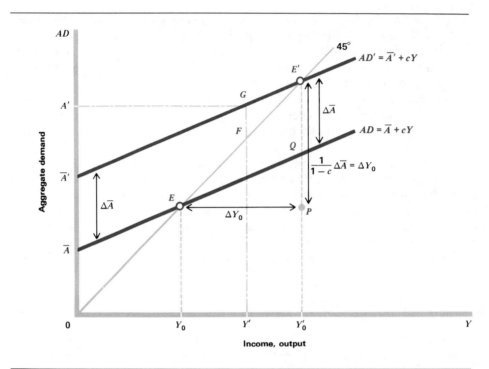

FIGURE 3-6 GRAPHICAL DERIVATION OF THE MULTIPLIER. When there is an increase in autonomous aggregate demand, the aggregate demand schedule shifts up to AD'. The equilibrium moves from E to E'. The increase in equilibrium output ($Y_0' - Y_0$), equal to distance PE, equal to PE', exceeds the increase in autonomous demand $E'Q$. From the diagram we see that is a result of the AD curve having a positive slope rather than being horizontal. In other words, the multiplier exceeds 1 because consumption demand increases with output — any increase in output produces further increases in demand.

Another Derivation

Finally, there is yet another way of deriving the multiplier. Remember that in equilibrium, aggregate demand equals income or output. From one equilibrium to another, it must therefore be true that the change in income ΔY_0 is equal to the change in aggregate demand ΔAD:

$$\Delta Y_0 = \Delta AD \tag{15}$$

Next we split the change in aggregate demand into the change in autonomous spending $\Delta \overline{A}$ and the change in expenditure induced by the consequent change in income—that is, $c\,\Delta Y_0$.

$$\Delta AD = \Delta \overline{A} + c\,\Delta Y_0 \qquad (16)$$

Combining equations (15) and (16), the change in income is

$$\Delta Y_0 = \Delta \overline{A} + c\,\Delta Y_0 \qquad (17)$$

or, collecting terms,

$$\Delta Y_0 = \frac{1}{1-c}\Delta \overline{A} = \alpha\,\Delta \overline{A} \qquad (18)$$

Summary

There are three points to remember from this discussion.

1. An increase in autonomous spending raises the equilibrium level of income.
2. The increase in income is a multiple of the increase in autonomous spending.
3. The larger the marginal propensity to consume, the larger the multiplier, arising from the relation between consumption and income.

As a check on your understanding of the material of this section, you should develop the same analysis, and the same answers, in terms of Figure 3-5.

3-4 THE GOVERNMENT SECTOR

So far we have ignored the role of the government sector in the determination of equilibrium income. The government affects the level of equilibrium income in two separate ways. First, government expenditures on goods and services, G, is a component of aggregate demand. Second, taxes and transfers affect the relation between output and income, Y, and the *disposable income* — income that is available for consumption or saving—that accrues to the private sector, YD. In this section, we are concerned with the way in which government expenditures, taxes, and transfers affect the equilibrium level of income.

We start again from the basic national income accounting identities. The introduction of the government restores government expenditures (G) on the expenditure side of equation (1) of this chapter, and taxes (TA) less transfers (TR) on the allocation of income side. We can accordingly rewrite the identity in equation (1) as

$$C + I + G \equiv S + (TA - TR) + C \qquad (1a)$$

The definition of aggregate demand has to be augmented to include government expenditures on goods and services — the purchases of military equipment and services of bureaucrats, for instance. Thus we have

$$AD \equiv C + \bar{I} + G \tag{7a}$$

Consumption will no longer depend on income, but rather on *disposable income YD*. Disposable income *YD* is the net income available for spending by households after paying taxes to, and receiving transfers from, the government. It thus consists of income less taxes plus transfers, $Y + TR - TA$. The consumption function is now

$$C = \bar{C} + cYD = \bar{C} + c(Y + TR - TA) \tag{4a}$$

A final step is a specification of *fiscal policy*. Fiscal policy is the policy of the government with regard to the level of government expenditures, the level of transfers, and the tax structure. We assume that the government purchases a constant amount $\bar{G}$, that it makes a constant amount of transfers, $\overline{TR}$, and that it collects a fraction t of income in the form of taxes. For example, if t equals 0.2, there is an income tax equal to 20 percent of income.

$$G = \bar{G} \qquad TR = \overline{TR} \qquad TA = tY \tag{19}$$

With this specification of fiscal policy, we can rewrite the consumption function, after substitution from equation (19) for TR and TA in equation (4a), as

$$\begin{aligned} C &= \bar{C} + c(Y + \overline{TR} - tY) \\ &= (\bar{C} + c\overline{TR}) + c(1 - t)Y \end{aligned} \tag{20}$$

Note from equation (20) that the presence of transfers raises autonomous consumption spending by the marginal propensity to consume out of disposable income c times the amount of transfers.[14] The presence of income taxes, by contrast, lowers consumption spending at each level of income. That reduction arises because households' consumption is related to *disposable* income rather than income itself, and income taxes reduce disposable income relative to the level of income.

---

[14] We are assuming no taxes are paid on transfers from the government. As a matter of fact, taxes are paid on some transfers, such as interest payments on the government debt, and not paid on other transfers, such as welfare and unemployment benefits.

While the marginal propensity to consume out of disposable income remains c, now the marginal propensity to consume out of income is $c(1-t)$, where $1-t$ is the fraction of income left after taxes. If the marginal propensity to consume, c, is 0.8 and the tax rate is 0.25, then the marginal propensity to consume out of income, $c(1-t)$, is 0.6 [$= 0.8 \times(1-0.25)$].

Combining (7a), (19), and (20), we have now

$$AD = (\overline{C} + c\overline{TR} + \overline{I} + \overline{G}) + c(1-t)Y \qquad (21)$$
$$= \overline{A} + c(1-t)Y$$

The effects of the introduction of government on the aggregate demand schedule are shown in Figure 3-7. The new aggregate demand schedule, denoted AD' in the figure, starts out higher than the original schedule AD, but has a flatter slope. The intercept is larger because it now includes both government spending $\overline{G}$ and the part of consumption resulting from transfer payments by the government, $c\overline{TR}$. The slope is flatter because households now have to pay part of every dollar of income in taxes, and are left with only $(1-t)$ of that dollar. Thus, as (21) shows, the marginal propensity to consume out of income is now $c(1-t)$ instead of c.

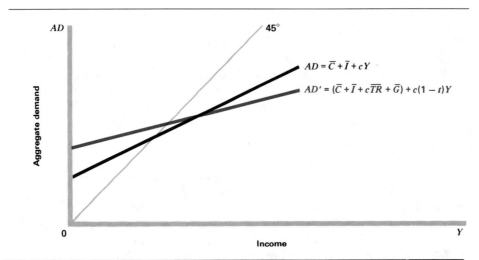

FIGURE 3-7 GOVERNMENT AND AGGREGATE DEMAND. Government affects aggregate demand through its own expenditures assumed here to be fixed at the autonomous level $\overline{G}$, through transfers $\overline{TR}$, and through taxes. Taxes are assumed to be a constant proportion, t, of income. Under these assumptions, the introduction of government shifts the intercept of the aggregate demand curve up and flattens the curve.

Equilibrium Income

We are now set to study income determination when the government is included. We return to the equilibrium condition for the goods market, $Y = AD$, and using (21), write the equilibrium condition as

$$Y = \overline{A} + c(1 - t)Y$$

We can solve this equation for Y_0, the equilibrium level of income, by collecting terms in Y:

$$Y[1 - c(1 - t)] = \overline{A} \tag{22}$$

$$Y_0 = \frac{1}{1 - c(1 - t)}\overline{A}$$

In comparing equation (22) with equation (10), we see that the government sector makes a substantial difference. It raises autonomous spending by the amount of government expenditures, $\overline{G}$, and by the amount of induced spending out of net transfers, $c\overline{TR}$.

Income Taxes and the Multiplier

At the same time *income taxes lower the multiplier*. As can be seen from equation (22), if the marginal propensity to consume is 0.8 and taxes are zero, the multiplier is 5; with the same marginal propensity to consume and a tax rate of 0.25, the multiplier is cut in half to $1/[1 - 0.8(0.75)] = 2.5$. Income taxes reduce the multiplier because they reduce the induced increase of consumption out of changes in income. This can be seen in Figure 3-7, where the inclusion of taxes flattens the aggregate demand curve—recall from Figure 3-6 that the larger the multiplier, the steeper the aggregate demand schedule.

Effects of a Change in Government Expenditures

We now consider the effects of changes in fiscal policy on the equilibrium level of income. We distinguish three possible changes in fiscal variables: changes in government expenditures, changes in transfers, and income tax changes. The simplest illustration is that of a change in government expenditures. This case is shown in Figure 3-8, where the initial level of income is Y_0.

An increase in government purchases is a change in autonomous spending and therefore shifts the aggregate demand schedule upward by an amount equal to the increase in government expenditures. At the initial level of output and income, the demand for goods exceeds output, and accordingly, firms expand production until the new equilibrium at point E' is reached. By how much does income expand? Recall that the change in equilibrium income will equal the change in aggregate demand, or

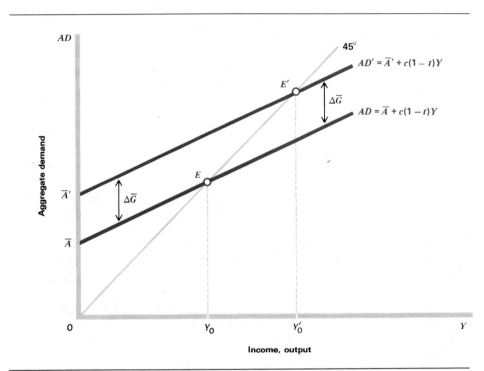

FIGURE 3-8 THE EFFECTS OF AN INCREASE IN GOVERNMENT EXPENDITURES. An increase in government spending shifts the aggregate demand schedule up from AD to AD'. Output rises from Y_0 to Y_0'. The multiplier is smaller now than it was in Figure 3-6.

$$\Delta Y_0 = \Delta \overline{G} + c(1 - t)\,\Delta Y_0$$

where the remaining terms ($\overline{C}$, $\overline{TR}$, and I-) are constant by assumption. Thus, the change in equilibrium income is

$$\Delta Y_0 = \frac{1}{1 - c(1 - t)}\Delta \overline{G} = \overline{\alpha}\Delta \overline{G} \qquad (23)$$

where we have introduced the notation $\overline{\alpha}$ to denote the multiplier in the presence of income taxes:

$$\overline{\alpha} \equiv \frac{1}{1 - c}(1 - t) \qquad (24)$$

From equation (23) it is apparent that a $1 increase in government expenditures will lead to an increase in income in excess of a dollar. Thus, as we have already seen, with a marginal propensity to consume of $c = 0.8$ and an income tax rate of $t = 0.25$, we would have a multiplier of 2.5: a $1 increase in government spending raises equilibrium income by $2.50.

Income Taxes as Automatic Stabilizers

We have just seen that a proportional income tax reduces the multiplier. This means that if any component of autonomous demand changes, output will change by less if there is a proportional income tax than in the absence of such taxes. The proportional income tax is one example of the important concept of *automatic stabilizers*. An automatic stabilizer is any mechanism in the economy that reduces the amount by which output changes in response to a charge in autonomous demand.

We shall see later that one explanation of the business cycle, the more or less regular movements of real GDP around trend, is that it is caused by shifts in investment demand. Sometimes, it is argued, investors are optimistic and investment is high — and so, therefore, is output. But sometimes they are pessimistic, and both investment and output are low.

Swings in investment demand will have a smaller effect on output when automatic stabilizers are in place. This means that in the presence of automatic stabilizers we should expect output to fluctuate less than it would without them. Higher income tax rates in the post–World War II period are one possible reason why the business cycle has been less pronounced since 1945 than it was earlier.

The proportional income tax is not the only automatic stabilizer. Unemployment benefits enable the unemployed to continue consuming even if they do not have a job. This means that demand falls less when someone becomes unemployed than it would if there were no benefits. This too makes the multiplier smaller and output more stable. Unemployment benefits and a proportional income tax are two automatic stabilizers that keep the multiplier small, thereby protecting the economy from responding strongly to every small movement in autonomous demand and stabilizing the economy.

Effects of Increased Transfer Payments

An increase in transfer payments increases autonomous demand, as can be seen from equation (21), where autonomous demand includes a term $c\overline{TR}$. A $1 increase in transfers therefore increases autonomous demand by an amount c. For instance, if the marginal propensity to consume, c, is 0.8, a $1 increase in transfers increases autonomous demand by $0.80. The increase is less than the full $1 increase in transfers because part of the transfer — $0.20 in this case — is saved.

Given that a $1 increase in transfers increases autonomous demand by the amount c, it is clear that the multiplier for an increase in transfers is c times the multiplier for an increase in government spending. For instance, with c equal to 0.8, and a tax rate of 0.25, the government spending multiplier is 2.5. The multiplier for transfers is 0.8 times 2.5, or 2.0.

Effects of an Income Tax Change

The final fiscal policy question is the effects of a reduction in the income tax rate. This is illustrated in Figure 3-9 by an increase in the slope of the aggregate demand function, because that slope is equal to the marginal propensity to spend out of income, $c(1 - t)$. At the initial level of income, the aggregate demand for goods now exceeds output because the tax reduction causes increased consumption. The new higher equilibrium level of income is Y'_0.

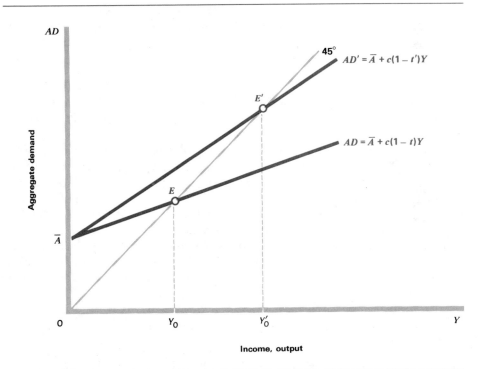

FIGURE 3-9 THE EFFECTS OF A DECREASE IN THE TAX RATE. A reduction in the income tax rate leaves the consumer with a larger proportion of every dollar of income earned. Accordingly, a larger proportion of every extra dollar of income is consumed. The aggregate demand curve swings upward, from AD to AD'. It becomes steeper because the income tax cut, in effect, acts like an increase in the propensity to consume. The equilibrium level of income rises from Y_0 to Y'_0.

To calculate the change in equilibrium income, we equate the change in income to the change in aggregate demand. The change in aggregate demand has two components. The first is the change in spending at the initial level of income that arises from the tax cut. This part is equal to the marginal propensity to consume out of disposable income times the change in disposable income due to the tax cut, $cY_0 \Delta t$, where the term $Y_0 \Delta t$ is the initial level of income times the change in the tax rate. The second component of the change in aggregate demand is the induced spending due to higher income. This is now evaluated at the new tax rate t' and has the value $c(1 - t')\Delta Y_0$. We can therefore write[15]

$$\Delta Y_0 = -cY_0 \Delta t + c(1 - t') \Delta Y_0 \qquad (25)$$

or

$$\Delta Y_0 = -\frac{1}{1 - c(1 - t')}cY_0 \Delta t \qquad (26)$$

Example

An example clarifies the effects of an income tax cut. Initially the level of income is $Y_0 = 100$, the marginal propensity to consume is $c = 0.8$, and the tax rate $t = 0.2$. Assume now a tax cut that reduces the income tax rate to only 10 percent, or $t' = 0.1$.

At the initial level of income, disposable income rises by $Y_0\Delta t = 100(t - t') = \$10$. Out of the increase in disposable income of $10, a fraction $c = 0.8$ is spent on consumption, so that aggregate demand, at the initial level of income, increases by $8. This corresponds to the first term on the right-hand side of equation (25). The increase in aggregate demand causes an expansion in output and income. Per dollar increase in income, disposable income rises by a fraction $(1 - t')$ of the increase in income. Furthermore, of the increase in disposable income, only a fraction, c, is spent. Accordingly, induced consumption spending is equal to $c(1 - t')\Delta Y_0$, which is the second term in equation (25).

How much does the income tax cut achieve in terms of output expansion? Substituting our numbers in equation (26), we have

$$Y_0 = \frac{1}{1 - 0.8(1 - 0.1)} (0.8)(100)(0.2 - 0.1) = (3.57)(8) \qquad (26a)$$
$$= 28.56$$

---

[15] You should check equation (26) by using equation (22) to write out Y_0 corresponding to a tax rate of t, and Y'_0 corresponding to t' Then subtract Y_0 from Y'_0 to obtain ΔY_0 as given in equation (26).

In our example, a cut in the tax rate, such that taxes fall by $10 at the initial level of income, raises equilibrium income by $28.56.

Note, however, that although taxes are initially cut by $10, the government's total taxes received fall by less than $10. Why? The reason is that the government receives 10 percent of the induced increase in income, or $2.856, as taxes. Thus the final reduction in tax receipts by the government is not the initial $10, but rather $7.144.[16]

Active Fiscal Policy

Changes in government spending and taxes affect the level of income. This immediately raises the possibility that fiscal policy can be used to stabilize the economy. When the economy is in a recession, perhaps taxes should be cut or spending increased to get output to rise. When the economy is booming, perhaps taxes should be increased or government spending cut to get back down to full employment.

Fiscal policy is in practice actively used to try to stabilize the economy, as we shall see in the next section when we examine the behaviour of the budget. It is also true that there is dispute over whether such fiscal policy actions really work. The disputes center on two issues: first, whether they work fast enough to help; and second, and more complicated, whether government policy actions don't merely result in private individuals taking offsetting actions. For instance, when government spending rises, private spending might fall.

We cannot at this stage evaluate the arguments against the active use of fiscal policy. Starting in Chapter 4, and continuing in Chapters 12 and 13, we resume the discussion.

Summary

1. Government expenditures and transfer payments act like increases in autonomous spending in their effects on equilibrium income.
2. A proportional income tax reduces the proportion of each extra dollar of output that is received as disposable income by consumers, and thus has the same effects on equilibrium income as a reduction in the propensity to consume.[17]

---

[16] We leave it to you to calculate the multiplier relating the change in equilibrium income to the total change in taxes received by the government.

[17] It might be helpful to note that all the results we have derived can be obtained in a straightforward manner by taking the change in aggregate demand at the initial level of income times the multiplier. (Check this proposition for each of the fiscal policy changes we have considered.) You should consider, too, the effect on equilibrium income of an increase in government expenditures combined with an equal reduction in transfer payments, $\Delta \overline{G} = - \Delta \overline{TR}$. (See problem 9 at the end of this chapter.)

3-5   THE BUDGET

The budget — and especially the budget deficit — became a major preoccupation of economic policy in the first half of the 1980s. By 1985 the federal government budget deficit exceeded $30 billion, or 6 percent of GDP, meaning that the federal government was spending $30 billion more per year than it was receiving in taxes. It had to borrow that $30 billion. The prospect of equally large deficits threatened for the rest of the decade unless taxes were raised or government spending cut. The fear was so strong that the economy could not prosper with the threat of large deficits hanging over it.

Why the concern? The fear was that the government's borrowing would make it difficult for private firms to borrow and invest, and thus slow the economy's growth. Full understanding has to wait to Chapter 9, but we start now, dealing with the government budget, its effects on output, and the effects of output on the budget. The first important concept is the *budget surplus*, denoted by *BS*. The budget surplus is the excess of the government's revenues, consisting of taxes, over its total expenditures, consisting of purchases of goods and services, and transfer payments.

$$BS \equiv TA - G - TR \tag{27}$$

A negative budget surplus, an excess of expenditure over taxes, is a *budget deficit*, denoted *BD*:

$$BD \equiv -BS = G + TR - TA$$

Of course, at the present time, government deficits are the norm, and surpluses are nowhere a prospect, but it was not always so. For example, there were surpluses in the years 1947–1953 and 1964–1974.

In Box 3-1 on page 86, we describe the concepts of government budget surplus and deficit that appear in the national income accounts. For that purpose, the federal government and provincial and municipal governments are added together. Thus the government sector in the national income accounts, and in the theory we are developing here, is not just the federal government; it is all government.

However, the budget deficit on which the media and politicians focus is the federal budget deficit. Later in this section we look at the behaviour of the federal budget. For now we study the behaviour of the budget surplus in relation to income, in the simple theory of this chapter.

Substituting in Equation (27) the assumption of a proportional income tax that yields a tax revenue $TA = tY$ gives us

$$BS = tY - G - TR \tag{27a}$$

In Figure 3-10 we plot the budget surplus as a function of the level of income for given $G = \overline{G}$, $TR = \overline{TR}$, and income tax rate t. At low levels of income, the budget is in deficit (the surplus is negative) because payments $\overline{G} + \overline{TR}$ exceed income tax collection. For high levels of income, by contrast, the budget shows a surplus, since income tax collection outweighs expenditures in the form of government expenditures and transfers.

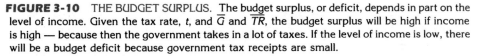

FIGURE 3-10   THE BUDGET SURPLUS.   The budget surplus, or deficit, depends in part on the level of income. Given the tax rate, t, and $\overline{G}$ and $\overline{TR}$, the budget surplus will be high if income is high — because then the government takes in a lot of taxes. If the level of income is low, there will be a budget deficit because government tax receipts are small.

Figure 3-10 demonstrates a significant point about budget surpluses and deficits. The point is that the budget deficit depends not only on the government's policy choices, reflected in the tax rate t, in expenditures $\overline{G}$, and in transfers $\overline{TR}$, but also on anything else that shifts the level of income. For instance, suppose there is an increase in investment demand that increases the level of output. Then the budget deficit will fall, or the surplus will increase because tax revenues have risen even though the government has done nothing that changed the deficit.

We should accordingly not be surprised to see budget deficits in recessions. Those are periods when the government's tax receipts are low. In practice, transfer payments, through unemployment benefits, also increase in recessions, even though in our model we are taking $\overline{TR}$ as autonomous.

The Effects of Government Expenditures and Tax Changes on the Budget Surplus

Next we show how changes in fiscal policy affect the budget. In particular, we want to find out whether an increase in government expenditures must reduce

BOX 3-1   GOVERNMENT IN THE NATIONAL INCOME ACCOUNTS

We distinguish three aspects of fiscal policy in the text. G is government expenditures on goods and services, TR is government transfers, and TA is taxes or government receipts. We now give the data for these variables in 1987, when GDP was $549.7 billion. We also show the breakdown of the variables among federal, provincial and municipal governments.

GOVERNMENT EXPENDITURE (billions of dollars)[a]

	Goods and Services	Transfer Payments	
		Interest on Public Debt	Other
Federal	$ 26.6	$27.7	$45.5
Provincial	39.2	13.8	28.0
Municipal[b]	53.3	3.7	1.7
Total	$119.1	$45.2	$75.2
Percent of GDP	21.7%	8.2%	13.7%

Federal and provincial transfer payments are considerably larger than expenditures on goods and services, and interest payments on the public debt are a substantial portion of transfer payments.

GOVERNMENT REVENUE (billions of dollars)[a]

	Income Taxes	Pension Contributions	Sales, Excise, and Property Taxes	Other
Federal	$ 65.6	$5.4[c]	$23.3	$ 8.8
Provincial	38.5	1.7[d]	29.4	18.7
Municipal[b]			17.9	1.7
Total	$104.1	$7.1	$70.6	$29.2
Percent of GDP	18.9%	1.3%	12.8%	5.3%

[a] *Source:* Statistics Canada, 13-001.
[b] Includes hospitals
[c] Canada Pension Plan
[d] Quebec Pension Plan

SURPLUS OR DEFICIT (–)[a]

	$ billions	Percent of GDP
Federal	– 21.9	– 4.0
Provincial	– 3.2	– 0.6
Municipal[b]	– 5.9	– 1.1
Total	– 19.2	– 3.5

In 1987, the total deficit of the government sector was $19.2 billion or 3.5 percent of GDP. Most of this deficit was incurred at the federal level. It should be noted that transfers between levels of government are netted out of these figures. In 1987, the federal government transferred $22.7 billion to provinces and municipalities.

[a] *Source:* Statistics Canada, 13-001.
[b] Includes hospitals
[c] Canada Pension Plan
[d] Quebec Pension Plan

the budget surplus. At first sight, this appears obvious, because increased government expenditures, from equation (27), are reflected in a reduced surplus, or increased deficit. At further thought, however, the increased government expenditures will cause an increase (multiplied) in income and, therefore, increased income tax collection. This raises the interesting possibility that tax collection might increase by more than government expenditures.

A brief calculation shows that the first guess is right—increased government expenditures reduce the budget surplus. From equation (23) the change in income due to increased government expenditures is equal to $\Delta Y_0 \equiv \bar{\alpha} \Delta \bar{G}$. A fraction of that increase in income is collected in the form of taxes, so that tax revenue increases by $t \bar{\alpha} \Delta \bar{G}$. The change in the budget surplus, using equation (24) to substitute for $\bar{\alpha}$, is therefore

$$
\begin{aligned}
\Delta BS &= \Delta TA - \Delta \bar{G} \\
&= t \bar{\alpha} \Delta \bar{G} - \Delta \bar{G} \\
&= \left[\frac{t}{1 - c(1 - t)} - 1 \right] \Delta \bar{G} \\
&= - \frac{(1 - c)(1 - t)}{1 - c(1 - t)} \Delta \bar{G}
\end{aligned}
$$

which is unambiguously negative.

We have, therefore, shown that an increase in government expenditures will reduce the budget surplus, although by considerably less than the increase in spending. For instance, for $c = 0.8$ and $t = 0.25$, a $1 increase in government purchases will create a $0.375 reduction in the surplus.[18]

In the same way, we can consider the effects of an increase in the tax rate on the budget surplus. We know that the increase in the tax rate will reduce the level of income. It might thus appear that an increase in the tax rate, keeping the level of government spending constant, could reduce the budget surplus. In fact, an increase in the tax rate increases the budget surplus, despite the reduction in income that it causes, as you are asked to show in problem 7 at the end of this chapter.[19]

A Simultaneous Change in Taxes and Expenditures

Finally, we can investigate the budgetary effects of simultaneous changes in taxes and government expenditures. We do this by working out an example, in Table 3-3. We assume a fiscal policy change that reduces the tax rate and government expenditures. The reduction is such that at the initial equilibrium level of income, of 100, the cut in taxes is exactly equal to the cut in government expenditures.

What effect would we expect such a fiscal policy to have? A first reaction would be that since taxes are being cut the same amount as spending, there will be no effect. But the table shows that is not right. The combined effect of the two actions is actually to lower income.

Why? The reason is that part of the cut in taxes is saved, so that not all the tax cut goes to increase aggregate demand, but the entire cut in government spending reduces aggregate demand. Therefore this fiscal policy actually reduces aggregate demand, and therefore income.

Notice also from the table that the budget deficit in the end increases slightly — as a result of the fall in income — even though at the initial level of income the cuts in taxes and spending are equal.

Balanced Budget Multiplier

In the previous example, the combined tax cut and reduction of government purchases raised the budget deficit. What would happen to the level of income if government expenditures and taxes changed by exactly the same amount, so that the budget surplus remained unchanged between the initial and final level of income? The answer to this question is contained in the famous *bal-*

---

[18] In this case, $\bar{\alpha} = 1/[1 - 0.8(0.75)] = 2.5$. So $\Delta BS = -2.5(0.2)(0.75) = -0.375$.

[19] The theory that tax rate cuts would increase government revenue (or tax rate increases reduce government revenue) is associated with Arthur Laffer of Pepperdine University. Laffer's argument, however, did not depend on the aggregate demand effects of tax cuts, but rather on the possibility that a tax cut would lead people to work more. This was a strand in supply-side economics, which we examine in Chapter 18.

TABLE 3-3 EFFECTS OF COMBINED TAX CUT AND GOVERNMENT SPENDING DECREASE

Parameters: Initial tax rate, $= 0.2$

New tax rate, $t' = 0.1$

Initial level of income, $Y_0 = \$100$

Marginal propensity to consumer, $c = 0.8$

Change in government spending, $\Delta \overline{G} = -10$

Multiplier: $\overline{\alpha} = \dfrac{1}{1 - c(1 - t')} = \dfrac{1}{1 - 0.72} = 3.57$

Effects of Tax cut: [See equation (26)]

Change in income: $\overline{\alpha} c Y_0 \Delta t = -(3.57)(0.8)(100)(-0.1) = 28.56$

Effects of cut in government spending: [See equation (23)]

Change in income: $\overline{\alpha} \Delta \overline{G} = -35.70$

Total effect on income: $\Delta Y_0 = -35.70 + 28.56$

$= -7.14$

Therefore: $Y_0' = 100 - 7.14 = 92.86$

Effect on tax receipts: Initial taxes $= 20$

Taxes in new situation $= 0.1 \times 92.86 = 9.29$

Therefore: Change in taxes, $\Delta TA = -10.71$

Effects on budget surplus: $\Delta BS = \Delta TA - \Delta \overline{G}$

$= -10.71 + 10.00$

$= -0.71$

---

anced budget multiplier result. The result is that the balanced budget multiplier is exactly 1. That is, an increase in government spending, accompanied by an equal increase in taxes, increases the level of income by exactly the amount of the increase in spending.[20] This interesting result is derived in the appendix at the end of this chapter.

The major points of the preceding discussion are that a balanced budget cut in government expenditures lowers equilibrium income and that a dollar increase in government spending has a stronger impact on equilibrium income than a dollar cut in taxes. A dollar cut in taxes leads only to a fraction of a dollar's increase in consumption spending, the rest saved, while government spending is reflected dollar for dollar in a change in aggregate demand.[21]

---

[20] Note that the balanced budget multiplier may well be less than 1 in the more sophisticated models of Chapter 4, in which investment spending depends on the interest rate.

[21] Rather than go through the analysis of changes in transfer payments, we leave it to you to work through an example of the effects on the budget of a change in transfer payments in problem 10 at the end of the chapter.

The Full-Employment Budget Surplus

A final topic to be treated here is the concept of the full-employment budget surplus.[22] Recall that increases in taxes add to the surplus and that increases in government expenditures reduce the surplus. Increases in taxes have been shown to reduce the level of income, and increases in government spending and transfers to increase the level of income. It thus seems that the budget surplus is a convenient, simple measure of the overall effects of fiscal policy on the economy. For instance, when the budget is in deficit, we would say that fiscal policy is expansionary, tending to increase GDP.

However, the budget surplus by itself suffers from a serious defect as a measure of the direction of fiscal policy. The defect is that the surplus can change passively because of changes in autonomous private spending, as we have seen. Thus, if the economy moves into a recession, tax revenue automatically declines and the budget moves into a deficit (or reduced surplus). Conversely, an increase in economic activity causes the budget to move into a surplus (or reduced deficit). These changes in the budget take place automatically for a given tax structure. This implies that we cannot simply look at the budget deficit as a measure of whether government fiscal policy is expansionary or deflationary. A given fiscal policy may imply a deficit if private spending is low and a surplus if private spending is high. Accordingly, an increase in the budget deficit does not necessarily mean that the government has changed its policy in an attempt to increase the level of income.

Since we frequently want to measure the way in which fiscal policy is being actively, rather than passively, used to affect the level of income, we require some measure of policy that is independent of the particular position of the business cycle — boom or recession — in which we may find ourselves. Such a measure is provided by the *full-employment budget surplus*, which we denote by BS^*. The full-employment (high-employment) budget surplus measures the budget, not at the actual level of income, but rather at the full-employment level of income or at potential output. Thus, a given fiscal policy summarized by G, $\overline{TR}$, and t is assessed by the level of the surplus, or deficit, that is generated at full employment. Using Y^* to denote the full-employment level of income, we can write

$$BS^* = tY^* - \overline{G} - \overline{TR} \tag{29}$$

Alternative names for the full-employment surplus have been proliferating. Included are the *cyclically adjusted surplus* (or deficit), the *high-employment surplus*, the *standardized employment surplus*, and the *structural surplus* or deficit. All these names refer to the same concept. The new names are intended

---

[22] The concept of the full-employment surplus was first used by E. Cary Brown, "Fiscal Policy in the Thirties: A Reappraisal," *American Economic Review*, December 1956.

to divert attention from the notion that there is a unique level of full employ-ment output that the economy has not yet reached. They suggest instead that the concept is merely a convenient measuring rod that fixes a given level of employment as the reference point. Given the difficulty of knowing exactly what is the full-employment level of output, the new names have some justification.

In Figure 3-11 we show the budget surplus schedule from Figure 3-10 but add the full-employment level of income Y^*. The full-employment budget sur-plus is indicated by the corresponding point on the budget surplus schedule.

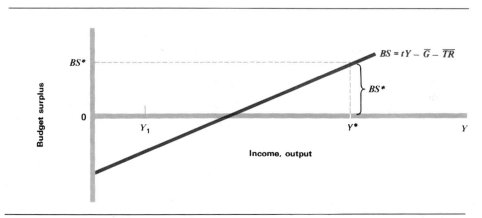

FIGURE 3-11 THE ACTUAL AND FULL-EMPLOYMENT BUDGET SURPLUSES. Y^* is the full-employment level of output. The full-employment budget surplus BS^* is the budget surplus that would exist if the economy were at full employment. If output is below the full-employment level, at a level such as Y_1, the budget surplus would be smaller than BS^*. Indeed, at income level Y_1 the actual budget is in deficit even though there is a full-employment surplus.

To see the difference between the actual and the full-employment budgets, we subtract the actual budget in equation (27a) from equation (29) to obtain

$$BS^* - BS = t(Y^* - Y) \qquad\qquad (30)$$

The only difference arises from income tax collection.[23] Specifically, if output is below full employment, the full-employment surplus exceeds the actual sur-plus. Conversely, if actual output exceeds full-employment (or potential) out-put, the full-employment surplus is less than the actual surplus.

---

[23] In practice, transfer payments, such as welfare and unemployment benefits, are also affected by the state of the economy, so that TR also depends on the level of income. However, the major cause of differences between the actual surplus and the full-employ-ment surplus is taxes.

Budget Trends

Figure 3-12 shows the actual and cyclically adjusted surplus as a fraction of GDP for the years 1961 to 1986. In periods of rapid growth and relatively low unemployment, such as 1964–1969, the actual surplus rises above the adjusted one, while in recession years such as 1961, 1970, 1975 and 1982, the growth of tax revenues slows down and the actual surplus falls below the adjusted one. The emergence of large cyclically adjusted deficits in the period 1975–1978 reflects the expansionary fiscal policy adopted during that period in response to rising unemployment rates. Conversely, the very large actual deficits in 1982–1985 reflect the emergence of very high unemployment rates.

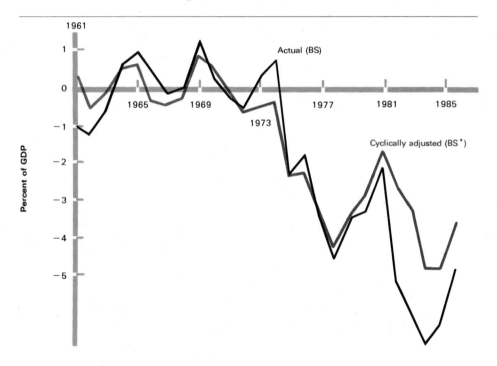

FIGURE 3-12 THE ACTUAL AND CYCLICALLY ADJUSTED BUDGET SURPLUS AS A PERCENT OF GDP

(*Source*: Department of Finance, *Economic Review*; The Fiscal Plan, Feb., 1986)

One final word of warning: The high-employment surplus is a better measure of the direction of active fiscal policy than the actual budget surplus, but it is not a perfect measure of the thrust of fiscal policy. The reason is that balanced budget increases in government purchases are themselves expansionary, so that an increase in government purchases matched by a tax increase that keeps the surplus constant leads to an increase in the level of income. Because fiscal policy involves the setting of a number of variables — the tax rate, transfers, and government purchases—it is difficult to describe the thrust of fiscal policy perfectly in a single number. The high-employment surplus is nevertheless a useful guide to the direction of fiscal policy.

3-6 THE FOREIGN SECTOR

For a country like Canada, which exports about one-quarter of its total output and spends a similar fraction of its income on imports, foreign trade plays an important role in the determination of equilibrium income. When foreign trade is taken into account, we return to the general case represented by the basic accounting identity given at the beginning of the chapter. Aggregate demand becomes

$$AD = C + I + G + NX$$

Denoting exports by X and imports by Q, we have

$$NX = X - Q$$

As in the case of planned investment and government spending, we assume that exports are fixed at a given level (denoted by $\overline{X}$). On the other hand, since imports represent part of domestic demand, they are assumed to depend on income. Using a linear relationship we have

$$Q = \overline{Q} + mY \tag{31}$$

where the slope m is called the *marginal propensity to import.*
   To determine the equilibrium level of income, we use the equilibrium condition, $Y = AD$ together with the consumption function (20) and the import function (31)

$$
\begin{aligned}
Y &= (\overline{C} + c\overline{TR}) + c(1 - t)Y + \overline{I} + \overline{G} + \overline{X} - \overline{Q} - mY \\
&= (\overline{C} + c\overline{TR} + \overline{I} + \overline{G} + \overline{X} - \overline{Q}) + [c(- t) - m]Y \\
&= \overline{A} + [c(1 - t) - m]Y
\end{aligned}
$$

Solving for the equilibrium level of income Y_0, we obtain

$$Y_0 = \frac{1}{1 - c(1 - t) + m} \overline{A} \tag{32}$$

Comparing Equation (32) with Equation (22), we see that exports add to and imports subtract from autonomous spending. In addition, imports are similar to taxes in that they reduce the increases in demand for domestic output induced by increases in income, and thereby lower the multiplier. The higher the marginal propensity to import, the lower the multiplier.

Interdependence and Repercussion Effects

When we include the foreign sector in our analysis and consider the interaction among countries, we find that income determination in the individual countries of the world economy is interdependent. An increase in income in one country (country A), by increasing country A's imports, affects demand for output abroad and leads, in turn, to a foreign expansion in imports from country A. There is thus a *repercussion effect* that we have so far ignored by assuming that export demand is autonomous.

Estimated Repercussion Effects

Table 3-4 provides estimates of the size of repercussion effects and the importance of international linkages. The table, derived from an econometric model of the OECD, shows income multipliers associated with an expansion in one country on that country itself and on other countries.[24] Consider first the case

TABLE 3-4   THE INTERNATIONAL TRANSMISSION OF AGGREGATE DEMAND DISTURBANCES

INITIATING COUNTRY OR GROUP (1 PERCENT INCREASE IN AUTONOMOUS SPENDING)	AFFECTED COUNTRY OR GROUP (PERCENTAGE CHANGE IN INCOME)				
	United States	Germany	Japan	Canada	OECD
United States	1.47	0.23	0.25	0.68	0.74
Germany	0.05	1.25	0.60	0.60	0.23
Japan	0.04	0.05	1.26	0.06	0.21
Canada	0.06	0.03	0.03	1.27	0.10
OECD	1.81	2.38	1.84	2.32	2.04

Source: OECD Occasional Paper, "The OECD International Linkage Model" January 1979.

[24] The OECD (Organization for Economic Cooperation and Development) is a grouping of 24 industrialized countries, based in Paris, which serves as a framework for international policy discussion. Among the members are the few listed in Table 18-4, plus Italy, the United Kingdom, France, and seventeen others.

of the United States. An increase of 1 percentage point in U.S. autonomous spending would raise U.S. income by 1.47 percent.

What is the impact on selected other countries? Looking at the top row, we find that German income rises by about 0.25 percent, and the same is true for Japan. Thus, U.S. expansion does affect these countries, although the size of the effect is not overwhelming. The comparison with Canada is of interest here. A U.S. expansion by 1.47 percent raises Canadian income by nearly 0.7 percent. Thus Canada appears considerably affected by U.S. expenditure disturbances. The last entry in the top row of Table 3-4 shows the impact of a U.S. expansion on industrialized countries as a group. The impact here is to increase the group's combined income by three-quarters of a percentage point.

Consider for comparison a Canadian expansion. The multiplier for Canadian income of a 1 percent increase in Canadian autonomous spending is 1.27, about the same as the 1.47 multiplier for the United States. The impact on the rest of the world is quite minor, though. The most substantial impact is on the United States (0.06 percent induced income increase) and only 0.03 percent increased income for Germany or Japan.

What determines the size of the multipliers and spillover effects? Three chief factors should be taken into account in interpreting the multiplier patterns revealed in Table 3-4. First, the size of the country is important. A Canadian expansion, for example, induces only a small percentage increase in U.S. income because a given dollar change in Canadian income and imports will be only a small fraction of U.S. income. By contrast, however, a given increase in U.S. income and imports will be a relatively large fraction of Canadian income.

The second important determinant of multiplier patterns is openness to trade. The spillover effects of an expansion in any one country on the rest of the world will be more substantial the more open the expanding economy.

The third point to note is the extent to which trade patterns are reflected in the multipliers. The United States, for example, benefits relatively more from a Canadian expansion than does Germany. This reflects the fact that Canada has a high marginal propensity to import from the United States in comparison with its propensity to import from Germany.

Table 3-4 allows us to study not only the effects of an individual country's expansion and the induced spillovers but also the effect of a simultaneous joint expansion in all industrialized countries. The last row of the table provides the multipliers for this experiment. Clearly, if all countries expand together—each raising autonomous expenditure by 1 percent—the multiplier effects are much more substantial. Each country benefits not only from its own expansion and its repercussion effects through induced expansion abroad, but also from the autonomous foreign expansion. Accordingly, the multipliers are around 2 in this case, while being in the range of 1.2 to 1.5 for the case of an isolated expansion.

3-7 SUMMARY

1. Output is at its equilibrium level when the aggregate demand for goods is equal to the level of output.

2. Aggregate demand consists of planned spending by households on consumption, by firms on investment goods, and by government on goods and services. When foreign trade is taken into account, net exports are added.

3. When output is at its equilibrium level, there are no unintended changes in inventories and all economic units are making precisely the purchases they had planned to. An adjustment process for the level of output based on the accumulation or decumulation of inventories leads the economy to the equilibrium output level.

4. The level of aggregate demand is itself affected by the level of output (equal to the level of income) because consumption demand depends on the level of income.

5. The consumption function relates consumption spending to income. Income that is not consumed is saved, so that the saving function can be derived from the consumption function.

6. The multiplier is the amount by which a one-dollar change in autonomous spending changes the equilibrium level of output. The greater the propensity to consume, the higher the multiplier.

7. Government expenditures on goods and services and government transfer payments act like increases in autonomous spending in their effects on the equilibrium level of income. An increase in the rate of a proportional income tax has the same effects on the equilibrium level of income as a reduction in the propensity to consume. A proportional income tax thus reduces the multiplier.

8. The budget surplus is the excess of government receipts over its expenditure. When the government is spending more than it receives, the budget is in deficit. The size of the budget surplus (deficit) is affected by the government's fiscal policy variables — government purchases, transfer payments, and tax rates.

9. The budget surplus is also affected by changes in tax revenue and transfers resulting from changes in the level of income occurring as a result of changes in private autonomous spending. The *cyclically adjusted* or *full-employment* (high-employment) budget surplus is accordingly frequently used as a measure of the active use of fiscal policy. The full-employment surplus measures the budget surplus that would exist if output were at its potential (full-employment) level.

10. When foreign trade is taken into account, exports add to and imports subtract from autonomous spending. The dependence of imports on income affects the size of the multiplier: the higher the marginal propensity to import, the lower the multiplier.

11. There are *repercussion effects* by which an increase in foreign income eventually induces an increase in the demand for foreigners' goods through exports. The size of these interdependence and repercussion effects depends on the relative size and openness of the economy. A small economy may be very dependent on a larger one, but a larger economy's level of income does not depend much on the income level in small foreign economies.

KEY TERMS

Aggregate demand
Equilibrium output
Unintended (undesired) inventory
    accumulation
Planned aggregate demand
Consumption function
Marginal propensity to consume
Marginal propensity to save
Multiplier

Automatic stabilizer
Budget surplus
Budget deficit
Balanced budget multiplier
Full-employment (high-employment)
    surplus
Marginal propensity to import
Repercussion effect

PROBLEMS

1. Here we investigate a particular example of the model studied in Sections 3-2 and 3-3 with no government. Suppose the consumption function is given by $C = 100 + 0.8Y$, while investment is given by $I = 50$.
   (a) What is the equilibrium level of income in this case?
   (b) What is the level of saving in equilibrium?
   (c) If, for some reason, output was at the level of 800, what would the level of involuntary inventory accumulation be?
   (d) If $\bar{I}$ were to rise to 100 (we discuss what determines $\bar{I}$ in later chapters), what would the effect be on equilibrium income?
   (e) What is the multiplier α here?
   (f) Draw a diagram indicating the equilibriums in both 1a and 1d.

2. Suppose consumption behaviour were to change in problem 1 so that $C = 100 + 0.9Y$, while $\bar{I}$ remained at 50.

    (a) Would you expect the equilibrium level of income to be higher or lower than in 1a? Calculate the new Y' to verify this.

    (b) Now suppose investment increases to $\bar{I} = 100$ just as in 1d. What is the new equilibrium income?

    (c) Does this change in investment spending have more or less of an effect on Y than in problem 1? Why?

    (d) Draw a diagram indicating the change in equilibrium income in this case.

3. We showed in the text that the equilibrium condition $Y = AD$ is equivalent to the $S = \bar{I}$, or saving = investment, condition. Starting from $S = \bar{I}$ and the saving function, derive the equilibrium level of income, as in equation (10).

4. This problem relates to the so-called *paradox of thrift*. Suppose that $I = \bar{I}$ and that $C = \bar{C} + cY$.

    (a) What is the saving function, that is, the function that shows how saving is related to income?

    (b) Suppose individuals want to save more at every level of income. Show, using a figure like Figure 3-5, how the saving function is shifted.

    (c) What effect does the increased desire to save have on the new equilibrium level of saving? Explain the paradox.

5. Now let us look at a model which is an example of the ones presented in Sections 3-4 and 3-5; that is, it includes government expenditure, taxes, and transfers. It has the same features as the one in problems 1 and 2, except that it also has a government. Thus, suppose consumption is given by $C = 100 + 0.8YD$ and $\bar{I} = 50$, while fiscal policy is summarized by $G = 200$, $\overline{TR} = 62.5$, and $t = 0.25$.

    (a) What is the equilibrium level of income in this more complete model?

    (b) What is the new multiplier $\bar{\alpha}$? Why is this less than the multiplier in problem 1e?

6. Using the same model as in problem 5, determine the following:

    (a) What is the value of the budget surplus BS when $\bar{I} = 50$?

    (b) What is BS when $\bar{I}$ increases to 100?

    (c) What accounts for the change in BS from 6a to 6b?

    (d) Assuming that the full-employment level of income $\bar{Y}$ is 1 200, what is the full-employment budget surplus BS^* when $\bar{I} = 50$? 100? (Be careful.)

    (e) What is BS^* if $\bar{I} = 50$ and $\bar{G} = 250$, with $\bar{Y}$ still equal to 1 200?

    (f) Explain why we use BS^* rather than simply BS to measure the direction of fiscal policy.

7. Suppose we expand our model to take account of the fact that transfer payments TR do depend on the level of income Y. When income is high,

transfer payments such as unemployment benefits will fall. Conversely, when income is low, unemployment is high and so are unemployment benefits. We can incorporate this into our model by writing transfers as $TR = \overline{TR} - bY, b > 0$. Remember that equilibrium income is derived as the solution to $Y_0 = C + \overline{I} + \overline{G} = \overline{C} + cYD + \overline{I} + \overline{G}$, where $YD = Y + TR - G$, where $YD = Y + TR - TA$ is disposable income.

(a) Derive the expression for Y_0 in this case, just as equation (22) was derived in the text.

(b) What is the new multiplier now?

(c) Why is the new multiplier less than the standard one, $\overline{\alpha}$?

(d) How does the change in the multiplier relate to the concept of automatic stabilizers?

8. Now we look at the role taxes play in determining equilibrium income. Suppose we have an economy of the type in Sections 3-4 and 3-5, described by the following functions:

$$
\begin{aligned}
C &= 50 + 0.8\,YD \\
\overline{I} &= 70 \\
\overline{G} &= 200 \\
\overline{TR} &= 100 \\
t &= 0.20
\end{aligned}
$$

(a) Calculate the equilibrium level of income and the multiplier in this model.

(b) Calculate also the budget surplus BS.

(c) Suppose that t increases to 0.25. What is the new equilibrium income? The new multiplier?

(d) Calculate the change in the budget surplus. Would you expect the change in the surplus to be more or less if $c = 0.9$ rather than 0.8?

(e) Can you explain why the multiplier is 1 when $t = 1$?

9. Suppose the economy is operating at equilibrium with $Y_0 = 1\,000$. If the government undertakes a fiscal change so that the tax rate t increases by 0.05 and government spending increases by 50, will the budget surplus go up or down? Why?

10. Suppose the government decides to reduce transfer payments (such as welfare), but to increase government expenditure on goods and services by an equal amount. That is, it undertakes a change in fiscal policy such that $\Delta \overline{G} = -\Delta \overline{TR}$.

(a) Would you expect equilibrium income to rise or fall as a result of this change? Why? Check out your answer with the following example: Suppose initially, $c = 0.8$, $t = 0.25$, and $Y_0 = 600$. Now let $\Delta \overline{G} = 10$ and $\Delta \overline{TR} = -10$.

(b) Find the change in equilibrium income ΔY_0.

(c) What is the change in the budget surplus ΔBS? Why has BS changed?

*11. We have seen in problem 10 that an increase in G accompanied by an equal decrease in TR does not leave the budget unchanged. What would the effect on equilibrium income be if TR and G change to leave the budget surplus BS fixed? [Hint: Notice that $BS = TA - TR - G$. We want $\Delta BS = \Delta TA - \Delta TR - \Delta G = 0(*)$ so that $\Delta TR = \Delta TA - \Delta G$. Since t is constant, $\Delta TA = t\Delta Y_0(**)$. We also know that $Y_0 = \bar{\alpha}\,(\bar{C} + \bar{I} + \bar{G} + c\bar{R})$ and $\Delta Y_0 = \bar{\alpha}(\Delta\bar{G} + c\Delta\overline{TR})$.]

[Substituting (*) and (**) into this last equation, derive an expression for ΔY in terms of ΔG. Simplify that expression, using the fact that $\bar{\alpha} = \{1/[1 - c(1 - t)]\}$, to obtain the balanced budget result in the case of changes in transfers and government spending. If you have trouble with this problem, check the appendix to this chapter.]

*12. In the preceding problem and in the appendix we derived the balanced budget multiplier result. It states that if $\Delta G = \Delta TA$ from the initial to final equilibrium, then $\Delta Y = \Delta G$. Let us look at an example of this balanced budget multiplier in action.

Consider the economy described by the following functions:

$$C = 85 + 0.75YD$$
$$\bar{I} = 50$$
$$\bar{G} = 150$$
$$\overline{TR} = 100$$
$$t = 0.20$$

(a) Derive the multiplier $\bar{\alpha}$ and the level of autonomous spending $\bar{A}$.

(b) From 12a calculate the equilibrium level of income and the budget surplus.

(c) Now suppose G rises to 250 while t increases to 0.28. Repeat step 12a for the new fiscal policy.

(d) What are ΔTA, ΔG, ΔY, and ΔBS?

(e) In view of this result and that of problem 10, what do you think the effect on income would be if we had a balanced budget change where $\Delta TR = \Delta TA$?

*13. Suppose the aggregate demand function is as in the figure on page 101. Notice that at Y_0 the slope of the aggregate demand curve is greater than 1. (This would happen if $c > 1$.) Complete this picture as is done in Figure 3-1 to include the arrows indicating adjustments when $Y \neq Y_0$ and show what IU is for $Y < Y_0$ and $Y > Y_0$. What is happening in this example, and how does it differ fundamentally from Figure 3-1?

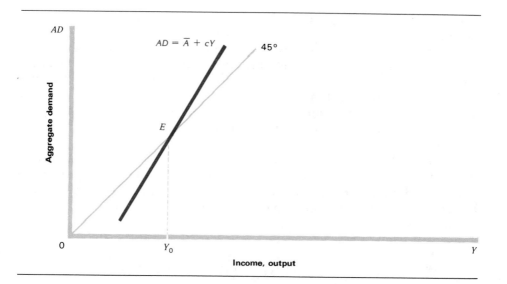

14. Let us look at the effect of foreign sector by adding the following equations to the model in problem 8:

$$\overline{X} = 150$$
$$Q = 10 + 0.14\,Y$$

(a) Calculate the equilibrium level of income and the multiplier in this model.

(b) Why is the multiplier less than the one obtained in problem 8?

*(c) Derive an expression for the trade balance, NX, as a function of income and plot it in a diagram with Y on the horizontal axis.

*(d) Show the effect of a change in income on the trade balance, using your diagram. Show also the effect on the trade balance of a change in exports, given income.

*(e) Calculate the effect on equilibrium income and the trade balance of an increase in exports.

APPENDIX: THE BALANCED BUDGET MULTIPLIER

This appendix considers the balanced budget multiplier result mentioned earlier. The balanced budget multiplier refers to the effects of an increase in government expenditures accompanied by an increase in taxes such that, in the new equilibrium, the budget surplus is exactly the same as in the original equilibrium. The result is that the multiplier of such a policy change, the balanced budget multiplier, is 1.

A multiplier of unity implies that output expands by precisely the amount of the increased government expenditures with no induced consumption spending. It is apparent that what must be at work is the effect of higher taxes that exactly offset the effect of the income expansion, thus maintaining disposable income, and hence consumption, constant. With no induced consumption spending, output expands simply to match the increased government purchases.

We can derive this result formally by noting that the change in aggregate demand ΔAD is equal to the change in government expenditures plus the change in consumption spending. The latter is equal to the marginal propensity to consume out of disposable income, c, times the change in disposable income, ΔYD; that is, $\Delta YD = \Delta Y_0 - \Delta TA$, where ΔY_0 is the change in output. Thus,

$$\Delta AD = \Delta \overline{G} + c(\Delta Y_0 - \Delta TA) \tag{A1}$$

Since from one equilibrium to another the change in aggregate demand has to equal the change in output, we have

$$\Delta Y_0 = \Delta \overline{G} + c(\Delta Y_0 - \Delta TA)$$

or

$$\Delta Y_0 = \frac{1}{1 - c}(\Delta \overline{G} - c\Delta TA) \tag{A2}$$

Next we note that by assumption the change in government purchases between the new equilibrium and the old one is exactly matched by a change in tax collection so that $\Delta \overline{G} = \Delta TA$. It follows from this last equality, after substitution in equation (A2), that with this particular restriction on fiscal policy we have

$$\Delta Y_0 = \frac{1}{1 - c}(\Delta \overline{G} - c\Delta \overline{G}) = \Delta \overline{G} = \Delta TA \tag{A3}$$

so that the multiplier is precisely unity.

Another way of deriving the balanced budget multiplier result is by considering the successive rounds of spending changes caused by the government policy changes. Suppose each of government expenditures and taxes increased by \$1. Let $c(1 - t)$, the induced increase in aggregate demand caused by a \$1 increase in income in the presence of taxes, be denoted by $\overline{c}$.

Table A3-1 shows the spending induced by the two policy changes. The first column shows the changes in spending resulting from the change in govern-

TABLE A3-1 THE BALANCED BUDGET MULTIPLIER CHANGE IN SPENDING RESULTING FROM:

Spending round	$\Delta \bar{G} = 1$	$\Delta TA = 1$	Net this round	Total
1	1	$-\bar{c}$	$1 - \bar{c}$	$1 - \bar{c}$
2	$\bar{c}$	$-\bar{c}^2$	$\bar{c} - \bar{c}^2$	$1 - \bar{c}^2$
3	$\bar{c}^2$	$-\bar{c}^3$	$\bar{c}^2 - \bar{c}^3$	$1 - \bar{c}^3$
4	$\bar{c}^3$	$-\bar{c}^4$	$-\bar{c}^3 - \bar{c}^4$	$1 - \bar{c}^4$
$\vdots$				
n	$\bar{c}^{n-1}$	$-\bar{c}^n$	$\bar{c}^{n-1} - \bar{c}_n$	$1 - \bar{c}^n$

ment expenditures and its later repercussions. The second column similarly gives the spending effects in successive rounds of the tax increase. The third column sums the two effects for each spending round, while the final column adds all the changes in spending induced so far. Since $\bar{c}$ *is less than 1*, $(\bar{c})^n$ becomes very small as the number of spending rounds, n, increases, and the final change in aggregate spending caused by the balanced budget increase in government spending is just equal to $1.

Finally, the balanced budget multiplier can also be thought of from a somewhat different perspective. Consider the goods market equilibrium condition in terms of saving, taxes, investment, transfers, and government expenditures:

$$S + TA - TR = \bar{I} + G \tag{A4}$$

Now, using the definition of the budget surplus, $BS \equiv TA - TR - G$,

$$BS = \bar{I} - S \tag{A5}$$

If there is no change in the budget deficit, nor a change in investment, the equilibrium change in saving is zero. For saving not to change, disposable income must remain unchanged. This says that $\Delta YD = \Delta Y - \Delta TA = 0$, and hence shows once more that the change in income equals the change in taxes. This in turn equals the change in government expenditures.

Hence, the balanced budget multiplier, or more precisely, the multiplier associated with an unchanging budget surplus or deficit, is equal to unity. This perspective on the income determination process is very useful because it emphasizes the fact that a change in the surplus or deficit of one sector is matched by a corresponding change in the deficit or surplus of the remaining sectors. If the government surplus is constrained by fiscal policy to be unchanged, so too must be the private sector's surplus, $S - \bar{I}$.

CHAPTER

Money, Interest, and Income

The stock of money, interest rates, and the Bank of Canada seemingly had no place in the model of income determination developed in Chapter 3. Clearly, though, we know that money has an important role to play in the determination of income and employment. Interest rates are frequently mentioned as an important determinant of aggregate spending, and the Bank of Canada and monetary policy receive at least as much public attention as fiscal policy. For instance, the blame for the deep 1980–1982 recession and its extraordinary high interest rates is often placed on the tight money policy pursued in the U.S. and Canada. This chapter introduces money and monetary policy, and builds an explicit framework of analysis in which the interaction of goods and assets markets can be studied.

This new framework leads to an understanding of the determination of interest rates and of their role in the business cycle. Figure 4-1 shows the interest rate on Treasury bills. The interest rate on Treasury bills represents the payment, per dollar per year, that someone receives who lends to the Government of Canada. Thus an interest rate of 10 percent means that someone who lends $100 to the government for 1 year will receive 10 percent, or $10, in interest. Figure 4-1 immediately suggests some questions: What factors cause the interest rate to increase, as occurred, for example, in 1980–1981, and what factors cause rates to decline as they did in 1982 and 1985? Furthermore, when interest rates increase, what are the effects on output and employment?

The model we introduce in this chapter, the *IS-LM model*, is the core of modern macroeconomics. It maintains the spirit and, indeed, many details of the previous chapter. The model is broadened, though, by introducing the interest rate as an additional determinant of aggregate demand. In Chapter 3, autonomous spending and fiscal policy were the chief determinants of aggregate spending. Now we add the interest rate and argue that a reduction in the rate

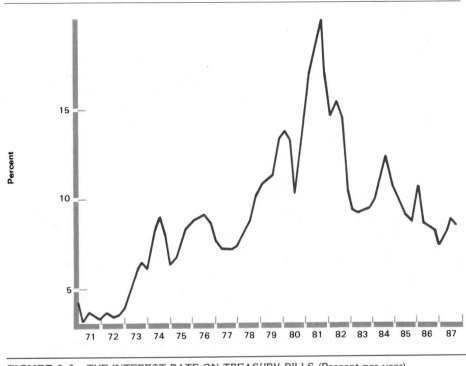

FIGURE 4-1   THE INTEREST RATE ON TREASURY BILLS (Percent per year)

(*Source*: Adapted from *Bank of Canada Review*)

of interest raises aggregate demand. This seems a minor extension, which can readily be handled in the context of Chapter 3. This is not entirely correct, because we have to ask what determines the rate of interest. That question extends our model to include the markets for financial assets and forces us to study the interaction of goods and assets markets. Interest rates and income are jointly determined by equilibrium in goods and assets markets.

What is the payoff for that complication? The introduction of assets markets and interest rates serves three important purposes:

1. The extension shows how monetary policy works.
2. The analysis qualifies the conclusions of Chapter 3. Consider Figure 4-2, which lays out the logical structure of the model. So far we looked at the submodel of autonomous spending and fiscal policy as determinants of aggregate demand and equilibrium income. Now the inclusion of assets markets—money demand and supply, as we shall see—introduces an additional channel. An expansionary fiscal policy, for example, would in the first

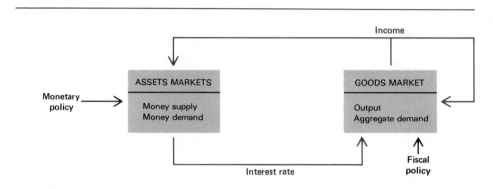

FIGURE 4-2   THE STRUCTURE OF THE *IS-LM* MODEL. The *IS-LM* model emphasizes the interaction between goods and assets markets. The model of Chapter 3 looks at income determination by arguing that income affects spending, which in turn determines output and income. Now we add the effects of interest rates on spending and thus income, and the dependence of assets markets on income. Higher income raises money demand and thus interest rates. Higher interest rates lower spending and thus income. Spending, interest rates, and income are determined jointly by equilibrium in goods *and* assets markets.

place raise spending and income. That increase in income, though, would affect the assets markets by raising money demand and thereby raising interest rates. The higher interest rates in turn reduce aggregate spending and thus, as we shall show, dampen the expansionary impact of fiscal policy. Indeed, under certain conditions, the increase in interest rates may be sufficiently important to offset *fully* the expansionary effects of fiscal policy. Clearly, such an extreme possibility is an important qualification to our study of fiscal policy in Chapter 3.

3. Even if the interest rate changes just mentioned only dampen (rather than offset fully) the expansionary effects of fiscal policy, they nevertheless have an important side effect. The *composition* of aggregate demand between investment and consumption spending will depend on the rate of interest. Higher interest rates dampen aggregate demand mainly by reducing investment. Thus, an expansionary fiscal policy would tend to raise consumption through the multiplier, but it would tend to reduce investment through the induced increase in interest rates. The side effects of fiscal expansion on interest rates and investment continue to be a sensitive and important issue in policy making. Because fiscal expansion tends to reduce investment, an influential view is that fiscal policy should not be used as a tool for demand management.

These three reasons justify the more complicated model we study in this chapter. There is the further advantage that the extended model helps us to understand the functioning of financial markets.

Outline of the Chapter

We use Figure 4-2 once more to lay out the structure of this chapter. We start in Section 4-1 with a discussion of the link between interest rates and aggregate demand. Here we use the model of Chapter 3 directly, augmented to include an interest rate as a determinant of aggregate demand. We derive a key relationship — the *IS* curve — that shows combinations of interest rates and levels of income for which the goods markets clear. In this chapter, we restrict the analysis to the case of a closed economy with no foreign trade or capital flows. The open economy case is taken up in Chapters 5 and 6.

In section 4-2, we turn to assets markets and, in particular, to the money market. We show that the demand for money depends on interest rates and income and that there is a combination of interest rates and income levels, the *LM* curve, for which the money market clears.[1] In Section 4-3, we combine the two schedules to study the joint determination of interest rates and income. Section 4-4 lays out the adjustment process toward equilibrium. Monetary policy is discussed in Section 4-5. Fiscal policy and the important issue of the monetary-fiscal policy mix are considered in sections 4-6 and 4-7.

4-1   THE GOODS MARKET AND THE *IS* CURVE

In this section we derive a *goods market equilibrium schedule*. The goods market equilibrium schedule, or *IS* schedule, shows combinations of interest rates and levels of output such that planned spending equals income. The goods market equilibrium schedule is an extension of income determination with a 45° line diagram. What is new here is that investment is no longer fully exogenous but is also determined by the interest rate. To appreciate the extension of Chapter 3 we briefly review what we found there.

In Chapter 3 we derived an expression for equilibrium income:

$$Y_0 = \frac{\overline{A}}{1 - \overline{c}} \qquad \overline{c} = c(1 - t) \tag{1}$$

Equilibrium income in this simple Keynesian model has two determinants: autonomous spending, $\overline{A}$, and the propensity to consume out of income, $\overline{c}$.

---

[1] The terms *IS* and *LM* are shorthand representations, respectively, of investment equals saving (goods market equilibrium) and money demand (*L*) equals money supply (*M*), or money market equilibrium. The classic article that introduced this model is J. R. Hicks, "Mr. Keynes and the Classics: A Suggested Interpretation," *Econometrica*, 1937, pp. 147–159.

Autonomous spending includes government spending, investment spending, and autonomous consumption spending. The propensity to consume out of income, as seen from (1), depends on the propensity to consume out of disposable income, c, and on the fraction of a dollar of income retained after taxes, $(1 - t)$. The higher the level of autonomous spending and the higher the propensity to consume, the higher the equilibrium level of income.

Investment and the Interest Rate

So far, investment spending $\bar{I}$ has been treated as *entirely* exogenous — some number like $70 billion determined altogether outside the model of income determination. Now, as we make our macromodel more complete by introducing interest rates as part of the model, investment spending, too, becomes endogenous. The desired or planned rate of investment is lower the higher the interest rate.

A simple argument shows why. Investment is spending on additions to the capital stock (machinery, structures, inventories). Such investment is undertaken with the aim of making profits in the future by operating machines and factories. Suppose firms borrow to buy the capital (machines and factories) that they use. Then the higher the interest rate, the more firms have to pay out in interest each year from the earnings they receive from their investment. Thus, the higher the interest rate the less the profits to the firm after paying interest, and the less it will want to invest. Conversely, a low rate of interest makes investment spending profitable and is, therefore, reflected in a high level of planned investment.

The Investment Demand Schedule

We specify an interest spending function of the form[2]

$$I = \bar{I} - bi \quad b > 0 \tag{2}$$

where i is the rate of interest and b measures the interest response of investment. $\bar{I}$ now denotes autonomous investment spending, that is, investment spending that is independent of both income and the rate of interest.[3] Equation

---

[2] Here and in other places in the book, we specify linear (straight-line) versions of behavioural functions. We use the linear specifications to simplify both the algebra and the diagrams. The linearity assumption does not lead to any great difficulties so long as we confine ourselves to talking about small changes in the economy. You should often draw nonlinear versions of our diagrams to be sure you can work with them.

[3] In Chapter 3, investment spending was defined as autonomous with respect to income. Now that the interest rate appears in the model, we have to extend the definition of

(2) states that <u>the lower the interest rate, the higher is planned investment</u>, with the <u>coefficient b measuring the responsiveness of investment spending to the interest rate.</u>

Figure 4-3 shows the investment schedule of equation (2). The schedule shows for each level of the rate of interest the rate at which firms plan to spend on investment. The <u>schedule is negatively sloped</u> to reflect the assumption that <u>a reduction in the rate of interest increases the profitability of additions to the capital stock and therefore to a larger rate of planned investment spending.</u>

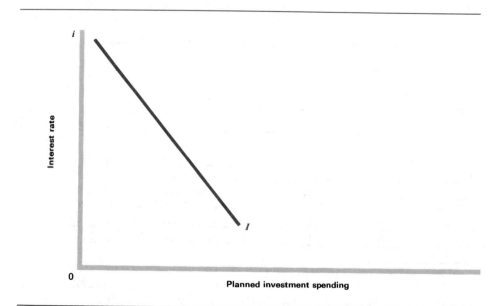

FIGURE 4-3   THE INVESTMENT SCHEDULE. The investment schedule shows the planned level of investment spending at each rate of interest. Because higher interest rates reduce the profitability of additions to the capital stock, higher interest rates imply lower planned rates of investment spending. Changes in autonomous investment shift the investment schedule.

The <u>position of the investment schedule is determined</u> by the slope — the <u>term b</u> in equation (2) — and by the level of autonomous investment spending <u>I</u>. If investment is highly responsive to the interest rate, a small decline in interest rates will lead to a large increase in investment, so that the schedule is almost flat. Conversely, if investment responds little to interest rates, the

autonomous to mean independent of *both* the interest rate and income. To conserve notation, we continue to use I to denote autonomous investment, but recognize that the definition is broadened.

schedule is more nearly vertical. Changes in autonomous investment spending I shift the investment schedule. An increase in $\bar{I}$ means that at each level of the interest rate firms plan to invest at a higher rate. This would be shown by a rightward shift of the investment schedule.

The Interest Rate and Aggregate Demand: The *IS* Curve

We now modify the aggregate demand function of Chapter 3 to reflect the new planned investment spending schedule. Aggregate demand still consists of the demand for consumption, investment, and government spending on goods and services. Only now investment spending depends on the interest rate. We have

$$
\begin{aligned}
AD &\equiv C + I + G \\
&= \bar{C} + c\overline{TR} + c(1 - t)Y + \bar{I} - bi + \bar{G} \\
&= \bar{A} + \bar{c}Y - bi
\end{aligned}
\tag{3}
$$

where
$$
\bar{A} \equiv \bar{C} + c\overline{TR} + \bar{I} + \bar{G}
\tag{4}
$$

From equation (3) we observe that an increase in the interest rate reduces aggregate demand at a given level of income because an interest rate increase reduces investment spending. Note that the term $\bar{A}$, which is the part of aggregate demand unaffected by either the level of income or the interest rate, does include part of investment spending, namely, $\bar{I}$. As noted earlier, $\bar{I}$ is the *autonomous* component of investment spending, which is independent of the interest rate (and income).

At any given level of the interest rate, we can still proceed as in Chapter 3 to determine the equilibrium level of income and output. As the interest rate changes, however, the equilibrium level of income changes. Figure 4-4 is used to derive the *IS* curve.

For a given level of the interest rate, say, i_1, the last term of equation (3) is a constant (bi_1), and we can in Figure 4-4a draw the aggregate demand function of Chapter 3, this time with an intercept $\bar{A} - bi_1$. The equilibrium level of income obtained in the usual manner is Y_1 at point E_1. Since the equilibrium level of income was derived for a given level of the interest rate i_1, we plot that pair (i_1, Y_1) in the bottom panel as point E_1. We now have one point, E_1, on the *IS* curve.

Consider next a lower interest rate, i_2. At a lower interest rate, aggregate demand would be higher at each level of income because investment spending is higher. In terms of Figure 4-4a, that implies an upward shift of the aggregate demand schedule. The curve shifts upward because the intercept $\bar{A} - bi$ has been increased. Given the increase in aggregate demand, the equilibrium level of income rises to point E_2, with an associated income level Y_2. At point E_2, in

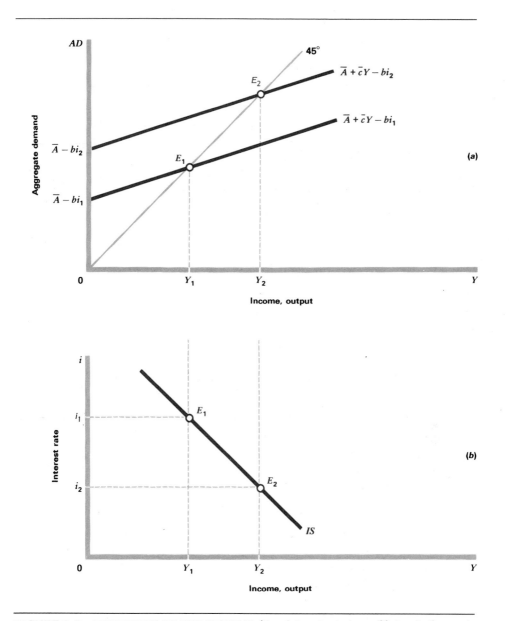

FIGURE 4-4 DERIVATION OF THE *IS* CURVE. At an interest rate i_1, equilibrium in the goods market obtains at point E_1 in the upper panel with an income level Y_1. In the lower panel this is recorded as point E_1. A fall in the interest rate to i_2 raises aggregate demand, increasing the level of spending at each income level. The new equilibrium income level is Y_2. In the lower panel, point E_2 records the new equilibrium in the goods market corresponding to an interest rate i_2.

the bottom panel, we record the fact that an interest rate i_2 implies an equilibrium level of income, Y_2—equilibrium in the sense that the goods market is in equilibrium (or that the goods market *clears*). Point E_2 is another point on the *IS* curve.

We can apply the same procedure to all conceivable levels of the interest rate and thereby generate all the points which make up the *IS* curve. They have in common the property that they are combinations of interest rates and income (output) such that the goods market clears. That is why the *IS* curve is called the *goods market equilibrium schedule*.

Figure 4-4 shows that the *IS* curve is negatively sloped, reflecting the increase in aggregate demand associated with a reduction in the interest rate. We can also derive the *IS* curve by using the goods market equilibrium condition, income equals planned spending, or

$$Y = AD$$
$$= \overline{A} + \overline{c}Y - bi \qquad (5)$$

which can be simplified to

$$Y = \overline{\alpha}(\overline{A} - bi) \qquad \overline{\alpha} = \frac{1}{1 - \overline{c}} \qquad (6)$$

where $\overline{\alpha}$ is the multiplier of Chapter 3. Equation (6) should now be compared with (1) at the beginning of this chapter. Note from equation (6) that a higher interest rate implies a lower level of equilibrium income for a given $\overline{A}$, as Figure 4-4 shows.

The construction of the *IS* curve is quite straightforward and may even be deceptively simple. We can gain further understanding of the economics of the *IS* curve by asking and answering the following questions:

- What determines the slope of the *IS* curve?

- What determines the position of the *IS* curve, given its slope, and what causes the curve to shift?

- What happens when the interest rate and income are at levels such that we are not on the *IS* curve?

The Slope of the *IS* Curve

We have already noted that the *IS* curve is negatively sloped because a higher level of the interest rate reduces investment spending, therefore reducing aggregate demand and thus the equilibrium level of income. The steepness of the curve depends on how sensitive investment spending is to change in the interest rate, and also on the multiplier $\bar{\alpha}$ in equation (6).

Suppose that investment spending is very sensitive to the interest rate, so that b in equation (6) is large. Then, in terms of Figure 4-4, a given change in the interest rate produces a large change in aggregate demand, and thus shifts the aggregate demand curve in Figure 4-4a by a large distance. A large shift in the aggregate demand schedule produces a correspondingly large change in the equilibrium level of income. If a given change in the interest rate produces a large change in income, the IS curve is very flat. This is the case if investment is very sensitive to the interest rate, that is, if b is large. Correspondingly, with b small and investment spending not very sensitive to the interest rate, the IS curve is relatively steep.

The Role of the Multiplier

Consider next the effects of the multiplier $\bar{\alpha}$ on the steepness of the IS curve. Figure 4-5 shows aggregate demand curves corresponding to different multipliers. The coefficient $\bar{c}$ on the darker aggregate demand curves is smaller than the corresponding coefficient $\bar{c}'$ on the lighter aggregate demand curves. The multiplier is accordingly larger on the lighter aggregate demand curves. The initial levels of income, Y_1 and Y'_1, correspond to the interest rate i_1 on the lower of each of the darker and lighter aggregate demand curves, respectively.

A given reduction in the interest rate, to i_2, raises the intercept of the aggregate demand curves by the same vertical distance, as shown in the top panel. However, the implied change in income is very different. For the lighter curve, income rises to Y'_2, while it rises only to Y_2 on the darker line. The change in equilibrium income corresponding to a given change in the interest rate is accordingly larger as the aggregate demand curve is steeper; that is, the larger the multiplier, the greater the rise in income. As we see from the lower figure, the larger the multiplier, the flatter the IS curve. Equivalently, the larger the multiplier, the larger the change in income produced by a given change in the interest rate.

We have thus seen that the smaller the sensitivity of investment spending to the interest rate and the smaller the multiplier, the steeper the IS curve. This conclusion is confirmed using equation (6). We can turn equation (6) around to express the interest rate as a function of the level of income:

$$i = \frac{\bar{A}}{b} - \frac{Y}{\bar{\alpha} b} \tag{6a}$$

Thus, for a given change in Y, the associated change in i will be larger in size as b is smaller and $\bar{\alpha}$ is smaller.

Given that the slope of the IS curve depends on the multiplier, fiscal policy can affect that slope. The multiplier $\bar{\alpha}$ is affected by the tax rate: an increase in

FIGURE 4-5 EFFECTS OF THE MULTIPLIER ON THE STEEPNESS OF THE *IS* CURVE. The diagram shows that corresponding to a higher marginal propensity to spend, and hence a steeper aggregate demand schedule, there is a flatter *IS* schedule.

the tax rate reduces the multiplier. Accordingly, the higher the tax rate, the steeper the *IS* curve.[4]

The Position of the IS Curve

Figure 4-6 shows two different *IS* curves, the lighter one of which lies to the right and above the darker *IS* curve. What might cause the *IS* curve to be at *IS'* rather than at *IS*? The answer is an increase in the level of autonomous spending.

In Figure 4-6a we show an initial aggregate demand curve drawn for a level of autonomous spending $\overline{A}$ and for an interest rate i_1. Corresponding to the initial aggregate demand curve is the point E_1 on the *IS* curve in Figure 4-6b. Now, at the same interest rate, let the level of autonomous spending increase to $\overline{A}'$. The increase in autonomous spending increases the equilibrium level of income at the interest rate i_1. The point E_2 in Figure 4-6b is thus a point on the new goods market equilibrium schedule *IS'*. Since E_1 was an arbitrary point on the initial *IS* curve, we can perform the exercise for all levels of the interest rate and thereby generate the new curve *IS'*. Thus, an increase in autonomous spending shifts the curve out to the right.

By how much does the curve shift? The change in income, as a result of the change in autonomous spending, can be seen from the top panel to be just the multiplier times the change in autonomous spending. That means that the *IS* curve is shifted horizontally by a distance equal to the multiplier times the change in autonomous spending as in the lower panel.

The level of autonomous spending is, from equation (4):

$$\overline{A} \equiv \overline{C} + c\overline{TR} + \overline{I} + \overline{G}$$

Accordingly, an increase in government purchases or transfer payments will shift the *IS* curve out to the right, the extent of the shift depending on the size of the multiplier. A reduction in transfer payments or in government purchases shifts the *IS* curve to the left.

Positions off the IS Curve

We gain understanding of the meaning of the *IS* curve by considering points off the curve. Figure 4-7 reproduces Figure 4-4, along with two additional points — the *disequilibrium points* E_3 and E_4. Consider first the question of what is true for points off the schedule, points such as E_3 and E_4. In Figure 4-7b at point

[4] In problem 3 we ask you to relate this fact to the discussion of automatic stabilizers in Chapter 3.

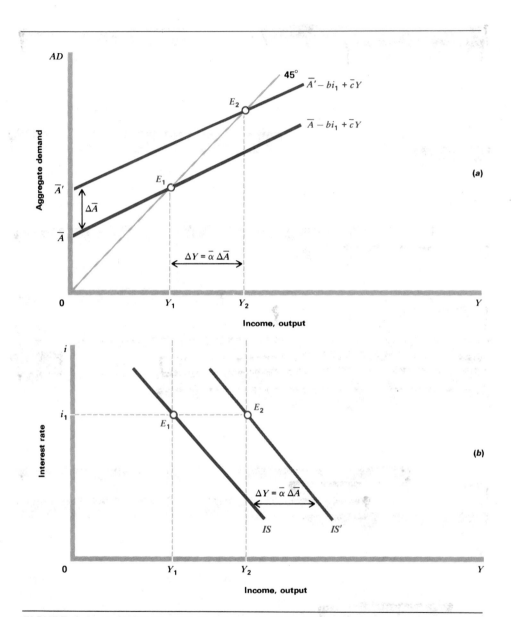

FIGURE 4-6   A SHIFT IN THE *IS* CURVE CAUSED BY A CHANGE IN AUTONOMOUS SPENDING. An increase in aggregate demand due to higher autonomous spending shifts the aggregate demand curve in **(a)** up, raising the equilibrium level of output at interest rate i_1. The *IS* schedule shifts. At each level of the interest rate, equilibrium income is now higher. The horizontal shift of the *IS* schedule is equal to the multiplier times the increase in autonomous spending.

E_3 we have the same interest rate i_2 as at point E_2, but the level of income is lower than at E_2. Since the interest rate i_2 at E_3 is the same as at E_2, we must have the same aggregate demand function corresponding to the two points. Accordingly, looking now at Figure 4-7a, we find both points are on the same aggregate demand schedule. At E_3 on that schedule, aggregate demand exceeds the level of output. Point E_3 is therefore a point of *excess demand for goods*; the interest rate is too low or output is too low for the goods market to be in equilibrium. Demand for goods exceeds output.

Next, consider point E_4 in Figure 4-7b. Here we have the same rate of interest i_1 as at E_1, but the level of income is higher. Given the interest rate i_1, the corresponding point in Figure 4-7a is at E_4, where we have an *excess supply of goods* since output is larger than aggregate demand — that is, aggregate demand, given the interest rate i_1 and the income level Y_2.

The preceding discussion shows that points above and to the right of the *IS* curve — points like E_4 — are points of excess supply of goods. This is indicated by *ESG* (excess supply of goods) in Figure 4-7b. Points below and to the left of the *IS* curve are points of excess demand for goods *(EDG)*. At a point like E_3, the interest rate is too low and aggregate demand is therefore too high, relative to output. *EDG* shows the region of excess demand in Figure 4-7.

Summary

The major points about the *IS* curve are:

1. The *IS* curve is the schedule of combinations of the interest rate and level of income such that the goods market is in equilibrium.
2. The *IS* curve is negatively sloped because an increase in the interest rate reduces planned investment spending and therefore reduces aggregate demand, thus reducing the equilibrium level of income.
3. The smaller the multiplier and the less sensitive investment spending is to changes in the interest rate, the steeper the curve.
4. The *IS* curve is shifted by changes in autonomous spending. An increase in autonomous spending, including an increase in government purchases, shifts the *IS* curve out to the right.
5. At points to the left of the curve, there is excess supply in the goods market, and at points to the left of the curve, there is excess demand for goods.

We turn now to examine behaviour in the assets markets.

4-2   THE ASSETS MARKETS AND THE *LM* CURVE

In the preceding section, we discussed aggregate demand and the goods market. In the present section, we turn to the assets markets. The assets markets

FIGURE 4-7   EXCESS SUPPLY (*ESG*) AND DEMAND (*EDG*) IN THE GOODS MARKET. Points above and to the right of the *IS* schedule correspond to an excess supply of goods, and points below and to the left to an excess demand for goods. At a point such as E_4, interest rates are higher than at E_2 on the *IS* curve. At the higher interest rates, investment spending is too low, and thus output exceeds planned spending and there is an excess supply of goods.

are the markets in which money, bonds, stocks, houses, and other forms of wealth are traded. Up to this point in the book, we have ignored the role of those markets in affecting the level of income, and it is now time to remedy the omission.

There is a large variety of assets, and a tremendous volume of trading occurs every day in the assets markets. But we shall simplify matters by grouping all available financial assets into two groups, *money* and *interest-bearing assets*.[5] By analogy with out treatment of the goods market, we proceed in the assets markets as if there are only two assets, money and all others. It will be useful to think of the other assets as marketable claims to future income such as *bonds*.

A bond is a promise to pay to its holder certain agreed-upon amounts of money at specified dates in the future. For example, a borrower sells a bond in exchange for a given amount of money today, say, $100, and promises to pay a fixed amount, say, $6, each year to the person who owns the bond, and to repay the full $100 (the principal) after some fixed period of time, such as 3 years, or perhaps longer. In this example, the interest rate is 6 percent, for that is the percentage of the amount borrowed that the borrower pays each year.

BOX 4-1   ASSETS AND ASSET RETURNS

There are four kinds of assets in the economy: money, interest-bearing assets, equities or stocks, and real assets.

MONEY
The money stock consists of assets that can be immediately used for making payments. It includes currency (notes and coins) and deposits on which cheques can be written. There is no interest paid on currency and most chequable deposits. However, in recent years, interest-bearing chequing accounts have become more common, thus blurring the distinction between money and nonmonetary financial assets. The definition of the stock of money is discussed in more detail in Chapter 10.

---

[5] We assume in this section that certain assets, such as the capital that firms use in production, are not traded. That too is a simplification. A more complete treatment of the assets markets would allow for the trading of capital and would introduce a relative price for the capital operated by firms. This treatment is usually reserved for advanced graduate courses. For such a treatment of the assets markets, see James Tobin, "A General Equilibrium Approach to Monetary Theory." *Journal of Money, Credit and Banking*, February 1969, pp. 15–29, and by the same author, "Money, Capital, and Other Stores of Value," *American Economic Review*, May 1961, pp. 26–37.

INTEREST-BEARING ASSETS

These include savings accounts in banks and other financial institutions, mortgages and bonds. A bond is a promise by a borrower to pay the lender a certain amount (the principal) at a specified date (the maturity of the bond) and in the meantime to pay a given amount of interest per year. Thus we might have a bond, issued by the Government of Canada, that pays $10 000 on June 1, 1985, and until that time pays 8 percent interest per year, or $800 each year. Bonds are issued by many types of borrower — the government, municipalities, corporations. The interest rates on bonds issued by different borrowers reflect the differing risk of default. Default occurs when a borrower is unable to meet the commitment to pay interest or principal. Corporations sometimes default, and during the great depression of the 1930s, so did some cities. In the early 1980s there was fear that many foreign governments would do so.

EQUITIES OR STOCKS

Equities or stocks are claims to a share of the profits in an enterprise. For example, a share in Alberta Energy entitles the owner to a share of the profits of that corporation. The shareholder or stockholder receives the return on equity in two forms. Most firms pay regular *dividends*, which means that stockholders receive a certain amount of dollars for each share they own. Firms may also decide not to distribute profits to the stockholders, but rather retain them and reinvest these profits by adding to their stock of machines and structures. When this occurs, the shares become more valuable since they now represent claims on the profits from a larger capital stock. Therefore, the price of the stock in the market will rise, and stockholders make *capital gains*. A capital gain is an increase, per period of time, in the price of an asset. Of course, when the outlook for a corporation turns sour, stock prices can fall and stockholders make capital losses.

Thus the return on stocks or the yield to a holder of a stock is equal to the dividend (as a percent of price) plus the capital gain.

Suppose we look at 1988 and 1989 and consider the yield on a stock in an imaginary company, BioMiracles, Inc. In 1988 the stock trades for $15. In 1989 the stock pays a dividend of $0.75 and the stock price increases to $16.50. What is the yield on the stock? The yield per year is equal to 15.0 percent, which is the dividend as a percent of initial price [5 percent = (0.75/15) × 100] plus 10.0 percent, which is the $1.50 capital gain as a percent of initial price.

REAL ASSETS

Real assets, or tangible assets, are the machines, land, and structures owned by corporations, and the consumer durables (washing machines, stereos, etc.) and houses owned by households. These assets carry a return that differs from one asset to another. Owner-occupied houses provide a return to owners who enjoy living in them and not paying monthly rent; the machines a firm owns contribute to producing output and thus making profits. The assets are called *real* to distinguish them from *financial* assets (money, stocks, bonds).

The value of equities and bonds held by individuals cannot be added to tangible wealth to get the total wealth of individuals. The reason is that the equities and bonds they hold are claims on part of the tangible wealth, that part held by corporations. The equity share gives an individual a part ownership in the factory and machinery.

In macroeconomics, to make things manageable, we lump assets into two categories. On one side we have money, with the specific characteristic that it is the only asset that serves as a means of payment. On the other side we have all other assets. Because money offers the convenience of being a means of payment, it carries a lower return than other assets, but that differential depends on the relative supplies of assets. As we see in this chapter, when the Bank of Canada reduces the money stock and increases the supply of other assets (we say "bonds"), the yield on other assets increases.

The Appendix to Chapter 9 develops the relationship between interest rates and asset prices or present values. The Appendix can be read independently of Chapter 9, and the interested student can study that material now.

The Wealth Constraint

An any given time, an individual has to decide how to allocate his or her financial wealth between alternative assets. The more bonds held, the more interest received on total financial wealth. The more money held, the less likely the individual is not to have money available when he or she wants to make a purchase. The person who has $1 000 in financial wealth has to decide whether to hold, say, $900 in bonds and $100 in money, or rather, $500 in each type of asset, or even $1 000 in money and none in bonds. Decisions on the form in which to hold assets are *portfolio decisions*.

The example makes it clear that the portfolio decision on how much money to hold and the decision on how many bonds to hold are really the same decision. Given the level of financial wealth, the individual who has decided how many bonds to hold has implicitly also decided how much money to hold. There is thus a *wealth budget constraint* which states that the sum of the individual's demand for money and demand for bonds has to add up to that person's total financial wealth.

Real and Nominal Money Demand

At this stage we have to reinforce the crucial distinction between *real* and *nominal* variables. The nominal demand for money is the individual's demand for a given number of dollars, and similarly, the nominal demand for bonds is the demand for a given number of dollars' worth of bonds. The real demand for money is the demand for money expressed in terms of the number of units of goods that money will buy: it is equal to the nominal demand for money divided by the price level. If the nominal demand for money is $100 and the price level is $2 per good—meaning that the representative basket of goods costs $2— then the real demand for money is 50 goods. If the price level later doubles to $4 per good and the demand for nominal money likewise doubles to $200, the real demand for money is unchanged at 50 goods.

Real money balances—*real balances* for short—are the quantity of nominal money divided by the price level, and the real demand for money is called the demand for real balances. Similarly, real bond holdings are the nominal quantity of bonds divided by the price level.

The wealth budget constraint in the assets markets states that the demand for real balances, which we denote L, plus the demand for real bond holdings, which we denote DB, must add up to the real financial wealth of the individual. Real financial wealth is, of course, simply nominal wealth WN divided by the price level P:

$$L + DB \equiv \frac{WN}{P} \qquad (7)$$

Note, again, that the wealth budget constraint implies, given an individual's real wealth, that a decision to hold more real balances is also a decision to hold less real wealth in the form of bonds. This implication turns out to be both important and convenient. It will allow us to discuss assets markets entirely in terms of the money market. Why? Because, given real wealth, when the money market is in equilibrium, the bond market will turn out also to be in equilibrium. We now show why that should be.

The total amount of real financial wealth in the economy consists of real money balances and real bonds in existence. Thus, total real financial wealth is equal to

$$\frac{WN}{P} \equiv \frac{M}{P} + SB \qquad (8)$$

where M is the stock of nominal money balances and SB is the real value of the supply of bonds. Total real financial wealth consists of real balances and real bonds. The distinction between equations (7) and (8) is that equation (7) is a constraint on the amount of assets individuals wish to hold, whereas equation (8) is merely an accounting relationship which tells us how much financial wealth there is in the economy. There is no implication in the accounting relationship in equation (8) that individuals are necessarily happy to hold the amounts of money and bonds that actually exist in the economy.

Now substitute equation (7) into equation (8) and rearrange terms to obtain

$$\left(L - \frac{M}{P}\right) + (DB - SB) \equiv 0 \tag{9}$$

Let us see what equation (9) implies. Suppose that the demand for real balances L is equal to the existing stock of real balances. M/P. Then the first term in parentheses in equation (9) is equal to zero, and therefore the second term in parentheses must also be zero. Thus, if the demand for real money balances is equal to the real money supply, the demand for real bonds DB must be equal to the supply of real bonds SB.

Stating the same proposition in terms of "markets," we can say the following: *The wealth budget constraint* implies that when the money market is in equilibrium ($L = M/P$), the bond market, too, is in equilibrium ($DB = SB$). Similarly, when there is excess demand in the money market, so that $L > M/P$, there is an excess supply of bonds: $DB < SB$. We can therefore fully discuss the assets markets by concentrating our attention on the money market.

The Demand for Money

We now turn to the money market and initially concentrate on the demand for real balances.[6] The demand for money is a demand for *real* balances because the public holds money for what it will buy. The higher the price level, the more nominal balances a person has to hold to be able to purchase a given quantity of goods. If the price level doubles, then an individual has to hold twice as large a nominal balance in order to be able to buy the same amount of goods.

The demand for real balances depends on the level of real income and the interest rate. It depends on the level of real income because individuals hold money to finance their expenditures, which, in turn, depend on income. The demand for money depends also on the cost of holding money. The cost of holding money is the interest that is foregone by holding money rather than other assets. The higher the interest rate, the more costly it is to hold money, rather than other assets and, accordingly, the less cash will be held at each level of income.[7] Individuals can economize on their holdings of cash, when the interest rate rises, by being more careful in managing their money, or by making transfers from money to bonds whenever their money holdings reach any appreciable magnitude. If the interest rate is 1 percent, then there is very little benefit from holding bonds rather than money. However, when the interest rate

---

[6] The demand for money is studied in depth in Chapter 10; here we only briefly present the arguments underlying the demand for money.

[7] In recent years, it has become more common to pay interest on some forms of money holdings. Nevertheless there do remain sizable parts of money holding, including currency, on which no interest is paid, so that overall, money earns less interest than other assets and the analysis of this chapter is still applicable.

is 10 percent, one would probably go to some effort not to hold more money than needed to finance day-to-day transactions.

On these simple grounds, then, the demand for real balances increases with the level of real income and decreases with the interest rate. The demand for real balances is accordingly written[8]

$$L = kY - hi \qquad k > 0 \qquad h > 0 \tag{10}$$

The parameters k and h reflect the sensitivity of the demand for real balances to the level of income and the interest rate, respectively. A \$5 increase in real income raises money demand by $5k$ real dollars. An increase in the interest rate by 1 percentage point reduces real money demand by h real dollars.

The demand function for real balances, equation (10), implies that for a given level of income, the quantity demanded is a decreasing function of the rate of interest. Such a demand curve is shown in Figure 4-8 for a level of income Y_1.

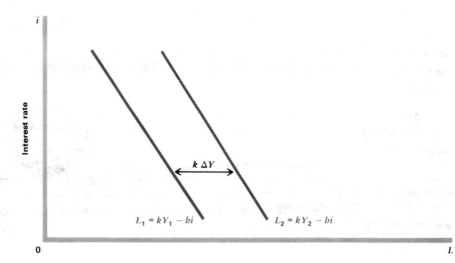

Demand for money

FIGURE 4-8 THE DEMAND FOR REAL BALANCES AS A FUNCTION OF THE INTEREST RATE AND REAL INCOME. The demand for real balances is drawn as a function of the rate of interest. The higher the rate of interest, the lower the quantity of real balances demanded, given the level of income. An increase in income raises the demand for money. This is shown by a rightward shift of the money demand schedule.

[8] Once again, we use a linear equation to describe a relationship. You should experiment with an alternative form, for example, $L = kY + h'/i$, where k and h' are positive. How would the equivalent of Figure 4-8 look for this demand function?

The higher the level of income, the larger the demand for real balances, and therefore the further to the right the demand curve. The demand curve for a higher level of real income Y_2 is also shown in Figure 4-8.

The Supply of Money, Money Market Equilibrium, and the *LM* Curve

Now we study equilibrium in the money market. For that purpose we have to say how the supply of money is determined. The nominal quantity of money M is controlled by the Bank of Canada, and we take it as given at the level $\overline{M}$. We assume the price level is constant at the level $\overline{P}$, so that the real money supply is at the level $\overline{M}/\overline{P}$.[9]

In Figure 4-9, we show combinations of interest rate and income levels such that the demand for real balances exactly matches the available supply. Starting with the level of income Y_1, the corresponding demand curve for real balances L_1, is shown in Figure 4-9b. It is drawn, as in Figure 4-8, as a decreasing function of the interest rate. The existing supply of real balances $\overline{M}/\overline{P}$ is shown by the vertical line, since it is given and therefore is independent of the interest rate. The interest rate i_1 has the property that it clears the money market. At that interest rate, the demand for real balances equals the supply. Therefore, point

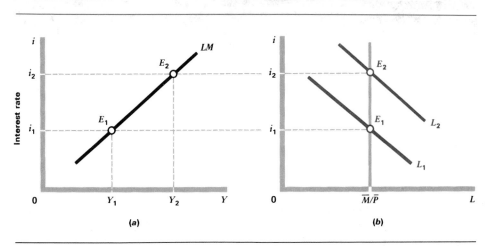

(a)   (b)

FIGURE 4-9   DERIVATION OF THE *LM* CURVE. The right-hand panel shows the money market. The supply of real balances is the vertical line $\overline{M}/\overline{P}$. The nominal money supply $\overline{M}$ is fixed by the central bank, and the price level $\overline{P}$ is assumed given. Demand for money curves L_1 and L_2 corresponds to different levels of income. When the income level is Y_1, L_1 applies, and the equilibrium interest rate is i_1. This gives point E_1 on the *LM* schedule in **(a)**. At income level Y_2, greater than Y_1, the equilibrium interest rate is i_2, yielding point E_2 on the *LM* curve.

[9] Since for the present we are holding constant the money supply and price level, we refer to them as exogenous and denote that fact by a bar.

E_1 is an equilibrium point in the money market. That point is recorded in Figure 4-9a as a point on the *money market equilibrium schedule*, or the *LM curve*.

Consider next the effect of an increase in income to Y_2. In Figure 4-9b the higher level of income causes the demand for real balances to be higher at each level of the interest rate, and so the demand curve for real balances shifts up and to the right, to L_2. The interest rate increases to i_2 to maintain equilibrium in the money market at that higher level of income. Accordingly, the new equilibrium point is E_2. In Figure 4-9a we record point E_2 as a point of equilibrium in the money market. Performing the same exercise for all income levels, we generate a series of points that can be linked to give us the *LM* schedule.

The *LM* schedule, or money market equilibrium schedule, shows all combinations of interest rates and levels of income such that the demand for real balances is equal to the supply. Along the *LM* schedule, the money market is in equilibrium.

The *LM* curve is positively sloped. An increase in the interest rate reduces the demand for real balances. To maintain the demand for real balances equal to the fixed supply, the level of income has, therefore, to rise. Accordingly, money market equilibrium implies that an increase in the interest rate is accompanied by an increase in the level of income.

The *LM* curve can be obtained directly by combining the demand curve for real balances, equation (10), and the fixed supply of real balances. For the money market to be in equilibrium, demand has to equal supply, or

$$\frac{\overline{M}}{\overline{P}} = kY - hi \tag{11}$$

Solving for the interest rate:

$$i = \frac{1}{h}\left(kY - \frac{\overline{M}}{\overline{P}}\right) \tag{11a}$$

The relationship (11a) is the *LM* curve.

Next we ask the same questions about the properties of the *LM* schedule that we asked about the *IS* curve.

The Slope of the LM Curve

The larger the responsiveness of the demand for money to income, as measured by k, and the lower the responsiveness of the demand for money to the interest rate h, the steeper the *LM* curve will be. This point can be established by experimenting with Figure 4-9. It can also be confirmed by examining equation (11a), where a given change in income ΔY has a larger effect on the interest rate i, the larger is k and the smaller is h. If the demand for money is relatively insensitive to the interest rate, so that h is close to zero, the LM curve is nearly vertical. If the demand for money is very sensitive to the interest rate, so that h is large, then the LM curve is close to horizontal. In that case, a small change in the interest rate is accompanied by a large change in the level of income to maintain money market equilibrium.

The Position of the LM Curve

The real money supply is held constant along the LM curve. It follows that a change in the real money supply will shift the LM curve. In Figure 4-10, we show the effect of an increase in the real money supply. In Figure 4-10b, we draw the demand for real money balances for a level of income Y_1. With the initial real money supply $\overline{M}/\overline{P}$, the equilibrium is at point E_1, with an interest rate i_1. The corresponding point on the LM schedule is E_1.

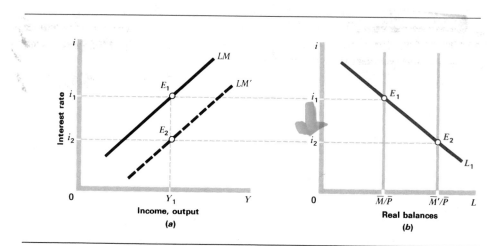

FIGURE 4-10 A SHIFT IN THE LM CURVE CAUSED BY AN INCREASE IN THE SUPPLY OF MONEY. An increase in the stock of real balances shifts the supply schedule in the right panel from $\overline{M}/\overline{P}$ to $\overline{M}'/\overline{P}$. At the initial income level Y_1, the equilibrium interest rate in the money market falls to i_2. In the left panel we show point E_2 as one point on the new LM schedule, corresponding to the higher money stock. Thus an increase in the real money stock shifts the LM schedule down and to the right.

Consider the effect of an increase in the real money supply to $\overline{M}'/\overline{P}$, which is represented by a rightward shift of the money supply schedule. At the initial level of income and, hence, on the demand schedule L_1, there is now an excess supply of real balances. To restore money market equilibrium at the income level Y_1, the interest rate has to decline to i_2. The new equilibrium is, therefore, at point E_2. This implies that in Figure 4-10a, the LM schedule shifts to the right and down to LM'. At each level of income the equilibrium interest rate has to be lower to induce people to hold the larger real quantity of money. Alternatively, at each level of the interest rate the level of income has to be higher so as to raise the transactions demand for money and thereby absorb the higher real money supply. These points can be noted, too, from inspection of the money market equilibrium condition in equation (11).

Positions off the *LM* Curve

Next we consider points off the *LM* schedule, to characterize them as points of excess demand or supply of money. For that purpose, look at Figure 4-11, which reproduces Figure 4-9 but adds the disequilibrium points E_3 and E_4. Look first at point E_1, where the money market is in equilibrium. Next assume an increase in the level of income to Y_2. This will raise the demand for real balances and shift the demand curve to L_2. At the initial interest rate, the demand for real balances would be indicated by point E_4 in Figure 4-11b, and we would have an excess demand for money — an excess of demand over supply — equal to the distance E_1E_4. Accordingly, point E_4 in Figure 4-11a is a point of excess demand for money: the interest rate is too low and/or the level of income too high for the money market to clear. Consider, next, point E_3 in Figure 4-11b. Here we have the initial level of income Y_1, but an interest rate that is too high

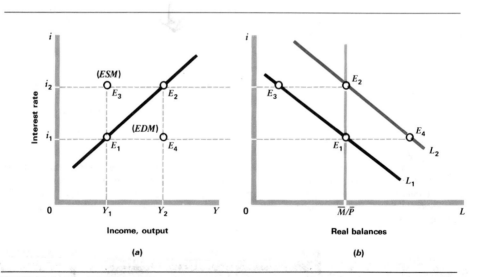

FIGURE 4-11   EXCESS DEMAND (*EDM*) AND SUPPLY (*ESM*) OF MONEY. Points above and to the left of the *LM* schedule correspond to an excess supply of real balances; points below and to the right to an excess demand for real balances. Starting at point E_1 in the left panel, an increase in income takes us to E_4. At E_4 in the right panel, there is an excess demand for money — and thus at E_4 in the left panel there is an excess demand for money. By a similar argument, we can start at E_2 and move to E_3, at which the level of income is lower. This creates an excess supply of money.

to yield money market equilibrium. Accordingly, we have an excess supply of money equal to the distance E_3E_2. Point E_3 in Figure 4-11a therefore corresponds to an excess supply of money.

More generally, any point to the right and below the *LM* schedule is a point of excess demand for money, and any point to the left and above the *LM* curve is a point of excess supply. This is shown by the *EDM* and *ESM* notations in Figure 4-11a.

Summary

The following are the major points about the *LM* curve.

1. The *LM* curve is the schedule of combinations of the interest rate and level of income such that the money market is in equilibrium.
2. When the money market is in equilibrium, so is the bond market in equilibrium. The *LM* curve is, therefore, also the schedule of combinations of the level of income and the interest rate such that the bond market is in equilibrium.
3. The *LM* curve is positively sloped. Given the fixed money supply, an increase in the level of income, which increases the quantity of money demanded, has to be accompanied by the increase in the interest rate. This reduces the quantity of money demanded and thereby maintains money market equilibrium.
4. The *LM* curve is shifted by changes in the money supply. An increase in the money supply shifts the *LM* curve to the right.
5. At points to the right of the *LM* curve, there is an excess demand for money, and at points to its left, there is an excess supply of money.

We are now ready to discuss the joint equilibrium of the goods and assets markets.

4-3   EQUILIBRIUM IN THE GOODS AND ASSETS MARKETS

The conditions that have to be satisfied for the goods and money markets, respectively, to be in equilibrium are summarized by the *IS* and *LM* schedules. The task now is to determine how these markets are brought into *simultaneous* equilibrium. For simultaneous equilibrium, interest rates and income have to be such that *both* the goods market *and* the money market are in equilibrium. That condition is satisfied at point *E* in Figure 4-12. The equilibrium interest rate is therefore i_0, and the equilibrium level of income is Y_0, given the exogenous variables, in particular, the real money supply and fiscal policy.[10] At point *E*, both the goods market and the assets markets are in equilibrium.

---

[10] Recall that exogenous variables are those whose values are not determined within the system being studied.

FIGURE 4-12   GOODS AND ASSETS MARKET EQUILIBRIUM. Goods and assets markets clear at point E. Interest rates and income are such that the public holds the existing stock of money and planned spending equals output.

Figure 4-12 summarizes our analysis: the interest rate and the level of output are determined by the interaction of the assets (LM) and goods (IS) markets.

It is worth stepping back now to review our assumptions and the meaning of the equilibrium at E. The major assumption is that the price level is constant and that firms are willing to supply whatever amount of output is demanded at that price level. Thus, we assume the level of output Y_0 in Figure 4-12 will be willingly supplied by firms at the price level P. We repeat that this assumption is one that is temporarily needed for the development of the analysis; it will be dropped in Chapter 7 when we begin to study the determinants of the price level.

At the point E, in Figure 4-12, the economy is in equilibrium, given the price level, because both the goods and money markets are in equilibrium. The demand for goods is equal to the level of output on the IS curve. And on the LM curve, the demand for money is equal to the supply of money. That also means the supply of bonds is equal to the demand for bonds. as the discussion of the wealth budget constraint showed. Accordingly, at point E, firms are producing the amount of output they plan to (there is no unintended inventory accumulation or decumulation), and individuals have the portfolio compositions they desire.

Changes in the Equilibrium Levels of Income and the Interest Rate

The equilibrium levels of income and the interest rate change when either the *IS* or the *LM* curve shifts. Figure 4-13, for example, shows the effects of an increase in the rate of autonomous consumption $\overline{C}$ on the equilibrium levels of income and the interest rate. Such an increase raises autonomous spending $\overline{A}$ and therefore shifts the *IS* curve to the right. That results in a rise in the level of income and an increase in the interest rate at point E'.

Recall that an increase in autonomous spending $\Delta\overline{C}$ shifts the *IS* curve to the right by the amount $\overline{\alpha}\Delta\overline{C}$, as we show in Figure 4-13. In Chapter 3, where we dealt only with the goods market, we would have argued that $\overline{\alpha}\Delta\overline{C}$ would be the change in the level of income resulting from the change of $\Delta\overline{C}$ in autonomous spending. It can be seen in Figure 4-13 that the change in income here is only ΔY_0, which is clearly less than the shift in the *IS* curve $\overline{\alpha}\Delta\overline{C}$.

What explains the fact that the increase in income is smaller than the increase in autonomous spending $\Delta\overline{C}$ times the simple multiplier $\overline{\alpha}$? Diagrammatically, it is clear that it is the slope of the *LM* curve. If the *LM* curve were horizontal,

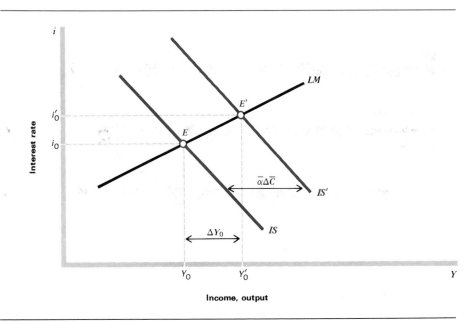

FIGURE 4-13 EFFECTS OF AN INCREASE IN AUTONOMOUS SPENDING ON INCOME AND THE INTEREST RATE. An increase in autonomous spending shifts the *IS* schedule out and to the right. Income increases, and the equilibrium income level rises. The increase in income is less than is given by the simple multiplier $\overline{\alpha}$. This is because interest rates increase and dampen investment spending.

there would be no difference between the extent of the horizontal shift of the *IS* curve and the change in income. If the *LM* curve were horizontal, then the interest rate would not change when the *IS* curve shifts.

What is the economics of what is happening? The increase in autonomous spending does tend to increase the level of income. But an increase in income increases the demand for money. With the supply of money fixed, the interest rate has to rise to ensure that the demand for money stays equal to the fixed supply. When the interest rate rises, investment spending is reduced because investment is negatively related to the interest rate. Accordingly, the equilibrium change in income is less than the horizontal shift of the *IS* curve $\overline{\alpha}\Delta\overline{C}$.

We have now provided an example of the use of the *IS-LM* apparatus. That apparatus is most useful for studying the effects of monetary and fiscal policy on income and the interest rate, and we so use it in Sections 4-5 and 4-6. Before we do, however, we discuss how the economy moves from one equilibrium, such as *E*, to another, such as *E'*.

4-4   ADJUSTMENT TOWARD EQUILIBRIUM

Suppose the economy were initially at a point like *E* in Figure 4-13, and that one of the curves then shifted, so that the new equilibrium was at a point like *E'*. How would that new equilibrium actually be reached? The adjustment will involve changes in both the interest rate and the level of income. To study how they move over time, we make two assumptions.

1. Output increases whenever there is an excess demand for goods and contracts whenever there is an excess supply of goods. This assumption reflects the adjustment of firms to undesired decumulation and accumulation of inventories.
2. The interest rate rises whenever there is an excess demand for money and falls whenever there is an excess supply of money. This adjustment occurs because an excess demand for money implies an excess supply of other assets (bonds). In attempting to acquire more money, people sell off bonds and thereby cause their prices to fall or their yields (interest rate) to rise.

A detailed discussion of the relationship between the price of a bond and its yield is presented in the appendix to Chapter 9. Here we give only a brief explanation. For simplicity, consider a bond which promises to pay the holder of the bond $5 per year forever. The $5 is known as the bond *coupon*, and a bond which promises to pay a given amount to the holder of the bond forever is known as a *perpetuity*. If the yield available on other assets is 5 percent, the perpetuity will sell for $100 because at that price it too yields 5 percent (= $5/$100). Now suppose that the yield on other assets rises to 10 percent. Then the price of the perpetuity will drop to $50, because only at that price does the perpetuity yield 10 percent; that is, the $5 per year interest on a bond costing $50 gives its owners a 10 percent yield on their $50. This example makes it clear that the price of a bond and its yield are inversely related, given the coupon.

In point 2 above we assumed that an excess demand for money causes asset holders to attempt to sell off their bonds, thereby causing their prices to fall and their yields to rise. Conversely, when there is an excess supply of money, people attempt to use their money to buy up other assets, raising their prices and lowering their yields.

In Figure 4-14 we apply the analysis to study the adjustment of the economy. Four regions are represented, and they are characterized in Table 4-1. We know from Figure 4-11 that there is an excess supply of money above the LM curve, and hence we show ESM in regions I and II in Table 4-1. Similarly, we know from Figure 4-7 that there is an excess demand for goods below the IS curve. Hence, we show EDG for regions II and III in Table 4-1. You should be able to explain the remaining entries of Table 4-1.

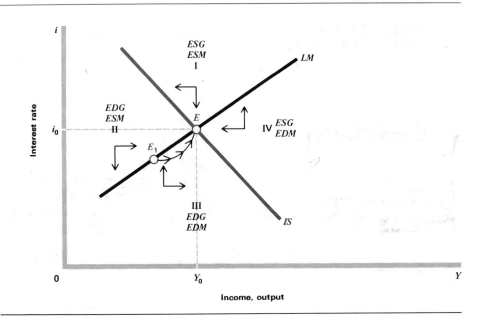

FIGURE 4-14 DISEQUILIBRIUM AND DYNAMICS IN THE GOODS AND MONEY MARKETS. Income and interest rates adjust to the disequilibrium in goods markets and assets markets. Specifically, interest rates fall when there is an excess supply of money and rise when there is an excess demand. Income rises when aggregate demand for goods exceeds output and falls when aggregate demand is less than output. The system converges over time to the equilibrium at E.

TABLE 4-1 DISEQUILIBRIUM AND ADJUSTMENT

Region	GOODS MARKET Disequilibrium	Adjustment: output	MONEY MARKET Disequilibrium	Adjustment: interest rate
I	ESG	Falls	ESM	Falls
II	EDG	Rises	ESM	Falls
III	EDG	Rises	EDM	Rises
IV	EDG	Falls	EDM	Rises

The adjustment directions specified in assumptions 1 and 2 above are represented by arrows. Thus, for example, in region IV we have an excess demand for money that causes interest rates to rise as other assets are sold off for money and their prices decline. The rising interest rates are represented by the upward-pointing arrow. There is, too, an excess supply of goods in region IV, and, accordingly, involuntary inventory accumulation to which firms respond by reducing output. Declining output is indicated by the leftward-pointing arrow. The adjustments shown by the arrows will lead ultimately, perhaps in a cyclical manner, to the equilibrium point E. For example, starting at E_1 we show the economy moving to E, with income and the interest rate increasing along the *adjustment path* indicated.

Rapid Asset Market Adjustment

For many purposes it is useful to restrict the dynamics by the reasonable assumption that the money market adjusts very quickly and the goods market adjusts relatively slowly. Since the money market can adjust merely through the buying and selling of bonds, the interest rate adjusts rapidly and the money market effectively is always in equilibrium. Such an assumption implies that we are always on the LM curve: any departure from the equilibrium in the money market is almost instantaneously eliminated by an appropriate change in the interest rate. In disequilibrium, we therefore move along the LM curve, as is shown in Figure 4-15.

The goods market adjusts relatively slowly because firms have to change their production schedules, which takes time. For points below the IS curve, we move up along the LM schedule with rising income and interest rates, and for points above the IS schedule, we move down along the LM schedule with falling output and interest rates until point E is reached. The adjustment process is *stable* in that the economy does move to the equilibrium position at E.

The adjustment process shown in Figure 4-15 is very similar to that of Chapter 3. To the right of the IS curve, there is an excess supply of goods, and firms are therefore accumulating inventories. They cut production in response to their

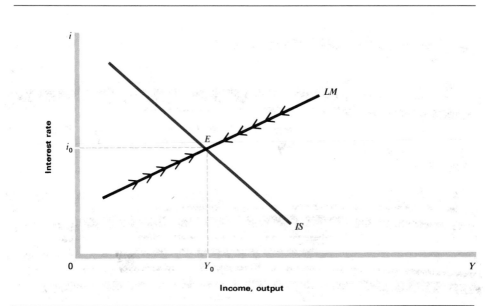

FIGURE 4-15 ADJUSTMENT TO EQUILIBRIUM WHEN THE MONEY MARKET ADJUSTS QUICKLY. If the money market adjusts very rapidly, then the economy is always in monetary equilibrium. In the diagram this corresponds to always being on the *LM* schedule. When there is excess demand for goods, output and interest rates are rising, and when there is excess supply of goods, output and interest rates are falling.

inventory buildup, and the economy moves down the *LM* curve. The difference between the adjustment process here and in Chapter 3 is the following: here, as the economy moves toward the equilibrium level of income, with a falling interest rate, desired investment spending is actually rising.[11]

Now that we have established that the economy does adjust toward its equilibrium position, we turn to examine the effects of monetary and fiscal policy on the equilibrium interest rate and level of income.

4-5 MONETARY POLICY

In this section we are concerned with the effect of an increase in the real quantity of money on the interest rate and level of income. We break up that inquiry into two separate questions. First, what is the ultimate effect of the increase in

[11] In a more detailed analysis, one would want to allow for the possibility that desired investment would be cut back in response to excess inventories. This again rises the possibility of the inventory cycle, referred to in Chapter 3.

the money supply when the new equilibrium is reached? Second, how is that new equilibrium reached, or what is the transmission mechanism?

Through monetary policy the Bank of Canada affects the quantity of money and thereby the interest rate and income. The chief instrument, studied in more detail in Chapter 11, is *open market operations*. In an open market operation the Bank of Canada purchases bonds in exchange for money, thus increasing the stock of money, or it sells bonds in exchange for money paid by the purchasers of the bonds, thus reducing the money stock.

We take here the case of an open market purchase of bonds. The purchase is made by the Bank of Canada, which pays for its purchases with money that it can create. One can usefully think of the Bank printing money with which to buy bonds, even though that is not strictly accurate, as we shall see in Chapter 11. The purpose of an open market operation is to change the available *relative* supplies of money and bonds and thereby change the interest rate or yield at which the public is willing to hold this modified composition of assets. When the Bank buys bonds, it reduces the supply of bonds available in the market and thereby tends to increase their price, or lower their yield. Only at a lower interest rate will the public be prepared to hold a larger fraction of their given wealth in the form of money, and a lower fraction in the form of bonds.

In Figure 4-16 we show graphically how the open market purchase works. The initial equilibrium at point E is on the initial LM schedule that corresponds to a real money supply, $\overline{M/P}$. Consider next an open market operation that increases the nominal quantity of money, and given the price level, the real quantity of money. We showed before that, as a consequence, the LM schedule will shift to LM'. Therefore, the new equilibrium will be at point E' with a lower interest rate and a higher level of income. The equilibrium level of income rises because the open market purchase reduces the interest rate and thereby increases investment spending.

By experimenting with Figure 4-16, you will be able to show that the steeper the LM schedule, the larger the change in income. If money demand is very sensitive to the interest rate, then a given change in the money stock can be absorbed in the assets markets with only a small change in the interest rate. The effects of an open market purchase on investment spending would then be small. By contrast, if the demand for money is not very sensitive to the interest rate, a given change in the money supply will cause a large change in the interest rate and have a big effect on investment demand.[12] Similarly, if the demand for money is very sensitive to income, a given increase in the money stock can be absorbed with a relatively small change in income.

---

[12] In problem 3 we ask you to provide a similar explanation of the role of the slope of the *IS* curve, which is determined by the multiplier and the interest sensitivity of investment demand, in determining the effect of monetary policy on income.

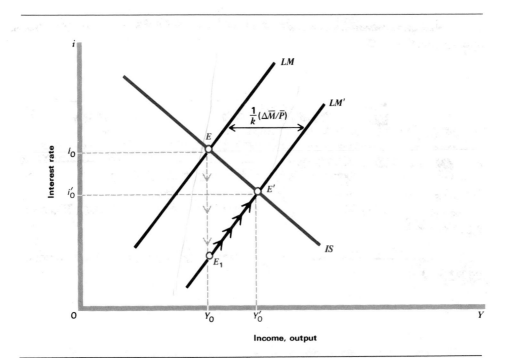

FIGURE 4-16 THE ADJUSTMENT PATH OF THE ECONOMY FOLLOWING AN INCREASE IN THE MONEY STOCK. An increase in the real money stock shifts the *LM* schedule down and to the right. Interest rates immediately decline from E to E_1 and then, through their effect on investment, cause spending and income to rise until a new equilibrium is reached at E'. Once all adjustments have taken place, a rise in the real money stock raises equilibrium income and lowers equilibrium interest rates.

Consider next the adjustment process to the monetary expansion. At the initial equilibrium point E, the increase in the monetary supply creates an excess supply of money to which the public adjusts by attempting to reduce its money holdings by buying other assets. In the process, asset prices increase and yields decline. By our assumption that the assets markets adjust rapidly, we move immediately to point E_1, where the money market clears, and where the public is willing to hold the larger real quantity of money because the interest rate has declined sufficiently. At point E_1, there is an excess demand for goods. The decline in the interest rate, given the initial income level Y_0, has raised aggregate demand and is causing inventories to run down. In response, output expands and we start moving up the *LM'* schedule. Why does the interest rate rise in the adjustment process? Because the increase in output raises the demand for money and that increase has to be checked by higher interest rates.

Thus the increase in the money stock first causes interest rates to fall as the public adjusts its portfolio and then — through lower interest rates — increase aggregate demand.

The Transmission Mechanism

Two steps in the *transmission mechanism* — the process by which changes in monetary policy affect aggregate demand — are essential. The first is that an increase in real balances generates a *portfolio disequilibrium* — at the prevailing interest rate and level of income, people are holding more money than they want. This causes portfolio holders to attempt to reduce their money holdings by buying other assets, thereby changing asset prices and yields. In other words, the change in the money supply changes interest rates. The second stage of the transmission process occurs when the change in interest rates affects aggregate demand.

These two stages of the transmission process are essential in that they appear in almost every analysis of the effects of changes in the money supply on the economy. The details of the analysis will often differ — some analyses will have more than two assets and more than one interest rate; some will include an influence of interest rates on other categories of demand, such as consumption.[13]

Table 4-2 provides a summary of the stages in the transmission mechanism. There are two critical links between the change in real balances and the ultimate effect on income. First, the change in real balances, by bringing about portfolio disequilibrium, must lead to a change in interest rates. Second, that change in interest rates must change aggregate demand. Through those two linkages, changes in the real money stock affect the level of output in the economy. This immediately implies the following: if portfolio imbalances do not lead to significant changes in interest rates — for whatever reason — or if spending does not respond to changes in interest rates, the link between money and output does not exist.[14] We now study these linkages in more detail.

---

[13] Some analyses also include a mechanism by which changes in real balances have a direct effect on aggregate demand through the real balance effect. The argument is that wealth affects consumption demand (as we shall see in Chapter 8) and that an increase in real balances increases wealth and therefore consumption demand. This effect would not apply in the case of an open market purchase, which merely exchanges one asset for another (bonds for money) without changing wealth. The real balance effect is not very important empirically because the relevant real balances are only a small part of wealth.

[14] We refer to the responsiveness of aggregate demand, rather than investment demand, to the interest rate because consumption demand may also respond to the interest rate. Higher interest rates may lead to more saving and less consumption at a given level of income. Empirically, it has been difficult to isolate such an interest rate effect on consumption.

TABLE 4-2 THE TRANSMISSION MECHANISM

(1)	(2)	(3)	(4)
Change in real money supply	Portfolio adjustments lead to a change in asset prices and interest rates	Spending adjusts to the change in interest rates	Output adjusts to the change in aggregate demand

Monetary Policy and the Liquidity Trap

In discussing the effects of monetary policy on the economy, two extreme cases have received much attention. The first is the *liquidity trap*, a situation in which the public is prepared, at a given interest rate, to hold whatever amount of money is supplied. This implies that the *LM* curve is horizontal and that changes in the quantity of money do not shift it. In that case, monetary policy carried out through open market operations[15] has no effect on either the interest rate or level of income. In the liquidity trap, monetary policy is powerless to affect the interest rate.

There is a liquidity trap at a zero interest rate. At a zero interest rate, the public would not want to hold any bonds, since money, which also pays zero interest, has the advantage over bonds of being usable in transactions. Accordingly, if the interest rate ever, for some reason, was zero, increases in the quantity of money could not induce anyone to shift into bonds and thereby reduce the interest rate on bonds even below zero. An increase in the money supply in that case would have no effect on the interest rate and income, and the economy would be in a liquidity trap.

The belief that there was a liquidity trap at low positive (rather than zero) interest rates was quite prevalent during the forties and fifties. It was a notion associated with the Keynesian followers and developers of the theories of the great English economist John Maynard Keynes—although Keynes himself did state that he was not aware of there ever having been such a situation.[16] The importance of the liquidity trap stems from its presenting a circumstance under which monetary policy has no effect on the interest rate and thus on the level

---

[15] We say "through open market operations" because an increase in the quantity of money carried out simply by giving the money away increases individuals' wealth and, through the real balance effect, has some effect on aggregate demand. An open market purchase, however, increases the quantity of money and reduces the quantity of bonds by the same amount, leaving wealth unchanged.

[16] J. M. Keynes, *The General Theory of Employment, Interest and Money* (New York: Macmillan, 1936), p. 207.

of real income. Belief in the trap, or at least the strong sensitivity of the demand for money to the interest rate, was the basis of the Keynesian belief that monetary policy has no effects on the economy. There is no strong evidence that there ever was a liquidity trap, and there certainly is not one now.

The Classical Case

The polar opposite of the horizontal *LM* curve — which implies that monetary policy cannot affect the level of income — is the vertical *LM* curve. The *LM* curve is vertical when the demand for money is entirely unresponsive to the interest rate. Under those circumstances, any shift in the *LM* curve has a maximal effect on the level of income. Check this by moving a vertical *LM* curve to the right and comparing the resultant change in income with the change produced by a similar horizontal shift of a nonvertical *LM* curve.

The vertical *LM* curve is called the *classical case*. It implies that the demand for money depends only on the level of income and not at all on the interest rate. The classical case is associated with the classical *quantity theory of money*, which argues that the level of nominal income is determined solely by the quantity of money. As we shall see, a vertical *LM* curve implies not only that monetary policy has a maximal effect on the level of income, but also that fiscal policy has no effect on income. The vertical *LM* curve, implying the comparative effectiveness of monetary policy over fiscal policy, is sometimes associated with the view that "only money matters" for the determination of output. Since the *LM* curve is vertical only when the demand for money does not depend on the interest rate, the interest sensitivity of the demand for money turns out to be an important issue in determining the effectiveness of alternative policies.

These two extreme cases, the liquidity trap and the classical case, suggest that the slope of the *LM* curve is a key determinant of the effectiveness of monetary policy in affecting output. The slope of the *LM* curve in turn depends on the interest sensitivity of money demand. The more sensitive to the interest rate is the quantity of money demanded, the flatter the *LM* curve.

4-6 FISCAL POLICY AND CROWDING OUT

Whenever governments run budget deficits, borrowing to pay for the excess of their spending over the tax revenue they receive, the talk turns to *crowding out*. Crowding out occurs when expansionary fiscal policy causes interest rates to rise, thereby reducing private spending, particularly investment.

When we introduced fiscal policy in Chapter 3, we had not yet included the assets markets in the analysis. Thus we could not discuss the effects of changes in fiscal policy on interest rates. In this section we consider how fiscal policy works when the interdependence of goods and assets markets is taken into account in the *IS-LM* model.

Our aim is to see how explicit consideration of the role of interest rates affects the conclusions we reached in Chapter 3 about fiscal policy. Is it still the case that an increase in government spending raises output and employment? Do tax cuts still increase output, or is it possible that the effects of fiscal policy on interest rates are so important that our previous conclusions about the effects of fiscal policy on the economy are reversed?

Fiscal Policy in the *IS-LM* Model

Figure 4-17 shows how fiscal policy fits into the *IS-LM* model. Fiscal policy affects aggregate demand directly. For instance, an increase in government spending increases aggregate demand, tending to raise output. However, the higher output level raises the interest rate by increasing money demand, and thereby dampens the effects of the fiscal policy on output. The higher interest rates reduce the level of investment spending, or crowd out investment. Thus a fiscal policy that increases output may actually reduce the rate of investment.

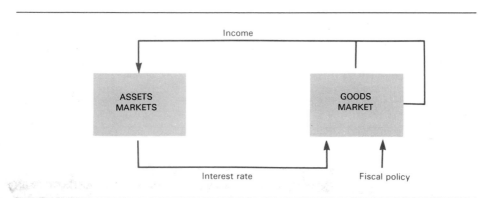

FIGURE 4-17   FISCAL POLICY IN THE *IS-LM* MODEL. Fiscal policy affects aggregate demand and thus has an impact on output and income. But changes in income affect the demand for money and thereby equilibrium interest rates in assets markets. These interest rate changes feed back to the goods market and dampen the impact of fiscal policy.

Figure 4-18 illustrates the effect of an increase in government spending. At unchanged interest rates, a higher level of government spending will increase aggregate demand and output will rise. At each level of the interest rate, equilibrium income rises by the multiplier times the increase in government spending. For example, if government spending rises by 100 and the multiplier is 2, then equilibrium income must increase at each level of the interest rate by 200. Thus the *IS* schedule shifts to the right by 200.

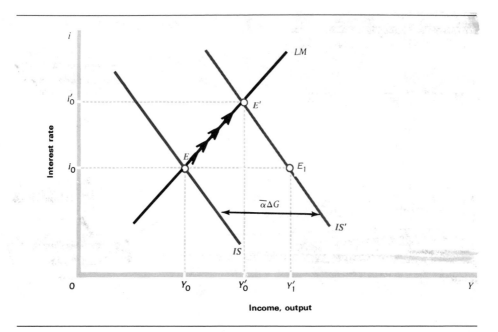

FIGURE 4-18 EFFECTS OF AN INCREASE IN GOVERNMENT SPENDING. An increase in government spending raises aggregate demand at each level of the interest rate and thus shifts the *IS* schedule out and to the right to *IS'*. At point *E* there is now an excess demand for goods. Output rises, and with it the interest rate, because the income expansion raises money demand. The new equilibrium is at point *E'*. The increase in income ($Y_0' - Y_0$) is less than the amount indicated by the simple multiplier ($Y_1 - Y_0$) because higher interest rates crowd out some investment spending.

If the economy is initially in equilibrium at point *E* and now government spending rises by 100, we would move to point E_1 *if the interest rate stayed constant*. At E_1 the goods market is in equilibrium in that planned spending equals output, but the assets market is no longer in equilibrium. Income has increased, and therefore the quantity of money demanded is higher. At interest rate i_0, the demand for real balances now exceeds the given real money supply. Because there is an excess demand for real balances, the interest rate rises, but as interest rates rise, private spending is cut back. Firms' planned investment spending declines at higher interest rates, and thus aggregate demand falls off.

What is the complete adjustment, taking into account the expansionary effect of higher government spending and the dampening effects of higher interest rates on private spending? Figure 4-18 shows that only at point *E'* do *both* the goods and assets markets clear. Only at point *E'* is planned spending equal to income and, at the same time, the quantity of real balances demanded equal to the given real money stock. Point *E'* is therefore the new equilibrium point.

The Dynamics of Adjustment

We continue to assume that the money market clears fast and continuously, while output adjusts only slowly. This implies that as government spending increases, we stay initially at point E, since there is no disturbance in the money market. The excess demand for goods, however, leads firms to increase output, and that increase in output and income raises the demand for money. The resulting excess demand for money, in turn, causes interest rates to be bid up, and we proceed up along the LM curve with rising output and rising interest rates, until the new equilibrium is reached at point E'

The Extent of Crowding Out

Comparing E' to the initial equilibrium at E, we have seen that increased government spending raises both income and the interest rate. Another important comparison is between points E' and E_1, the equilibrium in the goods market at unchanged interest rates. Point E_1 corresponds to the equilibrium we studied in Chapter 3 where we neglected the impact of interest rates on the economy. In comparing E_1 and E' it becomes clear that the adjustment of interest rates and their impact on aggregate demand dampen the expansionary effect of increased government spending. Income, instead of increasing to the level Y_1, rises only to Y'_0. This leads us to the following question: What factors determine the extent to which interest rate adjustments dampen the output expansion induced by increased government spending?

The extent to which a fiscal expansion raises income and the interest rate depends on the slopes of the IS and LM schedules and on the size of the multiplier. By drawing for yourself different IS and LM schedules you will be able to show the following:

1. Income increases more, and interest rates increase less, the flatter the LM schedule.
2. Income increases less, and interest rates increase less, the flatter the IS schedule.
3. Income and interest rates increase more the larger the multiplier $\bar{\alpha}$ and thus the larger the horizontal shift of the IS schedule.

To illustrate these conclusions, we turn to the two extreme cases we discussed in connection with monetary policy, the liquidity trap and the classical case.

The Liquidity Trap

If the economy is in the liquidity trap so that the LM curve is horizontal, then an increase in government spending has its full multiplier effect on the equilibrium level of income. There is no change in the interest rate associated with the change in government spending, and thus no investment spending is cut off. There is therefore no dampening of the effects of increased government spending on income.

You should draw your own *IS-LM* diagrams to confirm that if the *LM* curve is horizontal, monetary policy has no impact on the equilibrium of the economy and fiscal policy has a maximal effect on the economy. Less dramatically, if the demand for money is very sensitive to the interest rate, so that the *LM* curve is almost horizontal, fiscal policy changes have a relatively large effect on output, while monetary policy changes have little effect on the equilibrium level of output.

So far, we have taken the money supply to be constant at the level $\overline{M}$. It is possible that the central bank might instead manipulate the money supply so as to keep the interest rate constant. In that case the money supply is responsive to the interest rate: the central bank increases the money supply whenever there are signs of an increase in the interest rate, and reduces the money supply whenever the interest rate seems about to fall. The more responsive the money supply with respect to the interest rate, the flatter will be the *LM* curve, and fiscal policy will again have large impacts on the level of output.

The Classical Case and Crowding Out

If the *LM* curve is vertical, then an increase in government spending has *no* effect on the equilibrium level of income. It only increases the interest rate. This case is shown in Figure 4-19a, where an increase in government spending shifts the *IS* curve to *IS'* but has no effect on income. If the demand for money is not related to the interest rate, as a vertical *LM* curve implies, then there is a unique level of income at which the money market is in equilibrium.

Thus, with a vertical curve, an increase in government spending cannot change the equilibrium level of income, but only raises the equilibrium interest rate. However, if government spending is higher and output is unchanged, there must be an offsetting reduction in private spending. The increase in interest rates *crowds out* private investment spending. Crowding out, as defined earlier, is the reduction in private spending (and particularly investment) associated with the increase in interest rates caused by fiscal expansion. There will be full crowding out if the *LM* curve is vertical.[17]

In Figure 4-19 we show the crowding out in panel (*b*), where the investment schedule of Figure 4-3 is drawn. The fiscal expansion raises the equilibrium interest rate from i_0 to i'_0 in panel (a). In panel (b), as a consequence, investment spending declines from the level I_0 to I'_0. Now it is easy to verify that if the *LM* schedule were positively sloped rather than vertical, interest rates would rise less with a fiscal expansion and as a result investment spending would decline less. The extent of crowding out thus depends on the slope of the *LM* curve and

---

[17] Note again that, in principle, consumption spending could be reduced by increases in the interest rate, and then both investment and consumption would be crowded out.

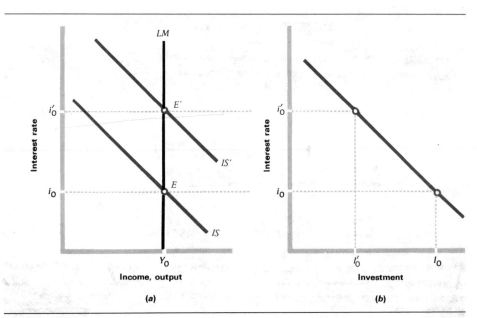

FIGURE 4-19   FULL CROWDING OUT. With a vertical *LM* schedule, a fiscal expansion, shifting out the *IS* schedule, raises interest rates, not income. Government spending displaces, or crowds out, private spending, one-for-one.

therefore on the interest responsiveness of money demand. The less interest-responsive is money demand, the more a fiscal expansion crowds out investment rather than raising output.

The view that increased government spending crowds out private spending, largely or even completely, is held by most monetarists.[18] They believe money determines income or, as we saw above, that money demand does not depend on the interest rate, implying a vertical *LM* schedule. However, there is also another case where crowding out can be complete, as we shall see in Chapter 7. If the economy is at full employment so that output cannot expand, then, of course, increased expenditure on goods by the government must mean that some other sector uses less goods and services. Interest rates increase to crowd out private spending by an amount exactly equal to the higher level of government spending.

Is Crowding Out Likely?

How seriously must we take the possibility of crowding out? Here three points must be made. First, in an economy with unemployed resources there will *not* be full crowding out because the *LM* schedule is not, in fact, vertical. A fiscal

---

[18] We discuss monetarism in Chapter 18.

expansion will raise interest rates, but income will also rise. Crowding out thus, rather than being full, is a matter of degree. The increase in aggregate demand raises income, and with the rise in income, it raises the level of saving. This expansion in saving, in turn, makes it possible to finance a larger budget deficit without *completely* displacing private borrowing or investment.

We can look at this proposition with the help of Equation (12), which states the equilibrium condition in the goods market already studied in Chapter 3[19]:

$$S \equiv I + (G + TR - TA) \tag{12}$$

Here the term $G + TR - TA$ is the budget deficit. Now from (12) it is clear that an increase in the deficit, given saving, must lower investment. In simple terms, when the deficit rises, the government has to borrow to pay for its excess spending. That borrowing "uses up" part of saving, leaving less available for firms to borrow to further their investment plans. But it is equally apparent that if saving rises with a government spending increase, because income rises, then there need not be a one-for-one decline in investment. In an economy with unemployment, crowding out is incomplete because increased demand for goods raises real income and output; savings rise and interest rates do not rise enough (because of interest-responsive money demand) to choke off investment.

The second point is that, with unemployment and thus a possibility for output to expand, interest rates need not rise at all when government spending rises, and there need not be any crowding out. This is because the monetary author- ities can *accommodate* the fiscal expansion by an increase in the money supply. Monetary policy is *accommodating* when, in the course of a fiscal expansion, the money supply is increased so as to prevent interest rates from increasing. Monetary accommodation is also referred to as *monetizing budget deficits*, meaning that the Bank of Canada prints money to buy the bonds with which the government pays for its deficit.[20] When the Bank accommodates a fiscal expansion, both the *IS* and the *LM* schedule shift to the right as in Figure 4-20. Output will clearly increase, but interest rates need not rise. Accordingly, there need not be any adverse effects on investment.

The third comment on crowding out is an important warning. So far we are assuming an economy with given prices and less than full employment. When we talk about fully employed economies in Chapter 15, crowding out becomes

---

[19] We have simply rearranged Eq. (1a) in Chapter 3, cancelling consumption on both sides.

[20] The term *accommodation* is used more generally. For instance, when oil prices increased in the 1970s, there was much discussion of whether central banks should accommodate the higher prices by raising the money stock. This issue, and the meaning of *accommodation* in that context, are discussed in Chapter 15.

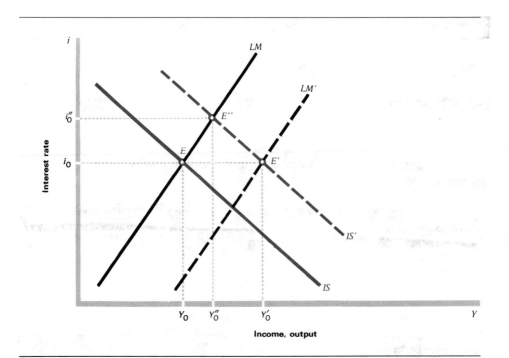

FIGURE 4-20 MONETARY ACCOMMODATION OF FISCAL EXPANSION. A fiscal expansion shifts the IS curve to IS', and moves the equilibrium of the economy from E to E''. Because the higher level of income has increased the quantity of money demanded, the interest rate rises from i_0 to i_0'', thereby crowding out investment spending. However, the central bank can accommodate the fiscal expansion, creating more money and shifting the LM curve to LM', and the equilibrium of the economy to E'. The interest rate remains at level i_0, and the level of output rises to Y_0'.

a much more realistic possibility, and accommodating monetary policy may turn into an engine of inflation.

4-7 THE COMPOSITION OF OUTPUT

We have now seen that both monetary and fiscal policy can be used to expand aggregate demand and thus raise the equilibrium level of output. Since the liquidity trap and the classical case represent, at best, extremes useful for expositional purposes, it is apparent that policy makers can use either monetary or fiscal policy to affect the level of income.

Table 4-3 summarizes the effects of expansionary monetary and fiscal policy on output and the interest rate. These are the effects shown in Figures 4-16 and 4-18.

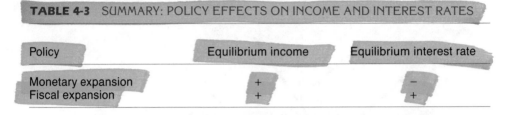

TABLE 4-3   SUMMARY: POLICY EFFECTS ON INCOME AND INTEREST RATES

Policy	Equilibrium income	Equilibrium interest rate
Monetary expansion	+	−
Fiscal expansion	+	+

We now examine the policy choices of an economy that is in equilibrium with an output level Y_0, below the full-employment level Y^*. What can be done to raise output? From the preceding analysis and Table 4-3, it is obvious that we could use an expansionary monetary policy. By increasing the money supply, we could shift the *LM* curve down and to the right, lower interest rates, and raise aggregate demand. Alternatively, we can use an expansionary fiscal policy to shift the *IS* curve up and to the right. Finally, we can use a combination of monetary and fiscal policy. What package should we choose?

The choice of monetary and fiscal policy as tools of stabilization policy is an important and controversial topic. In Chapter 12 we address some technical issues that deal with the flexibility and speed with which these policies can be implemented and can take effect. Here we do not discuss speed and flexibility, but rather look at what these policies do to the composition of aggregate demand.

In that respect, there is a sharp difference between monetary and fiscal policy. Monetary policy operates by stimulating interest-responsive components of aggregate demand, primarily investment spending and, in particular, residential construction. There is strong evidence that the earliest and strongest effect of monetary policy is on residential construction.

Fiscal policy, by contrast, operates in a manner that depends on precisely what goods the government buys or what taxes and transfers it changes. Here we might be talking of government expenditures on goods and services such as defence spending, or a reduction in the corporate profits tax, or in sales taxes, or social insurance contributions. Each policy affects the level of aggregate demand and causes an expansion in output, except that the type of output and the beneficiaries of the fiscal measures differ. An investment subsidy, discussed below, increases investment spending. An income tax cut has a direct effect on consumption spending. Given the quantity of money, all expansionary fiscal policies have in common is that they will raise the interest rate.

An Investment Subsidy

Table 4-4 shows examples of the impact of different fiscal policies on key variables. One interesting case is an *investment subsidy*, shown in Figure 4-21. When the government subsidizes investment, it essentially pays part of the cost of each firm's investment. A subsidy to investment shifts the investment sched-

TABLE 4-4 ALTERNATIVE FISCAL POLICIES

	Interest rate	Consumption	Investment	Income
Income tax cut	+	+	−	+
Government spending	+	+	−	+
Investment subsidy	+	+	+	+

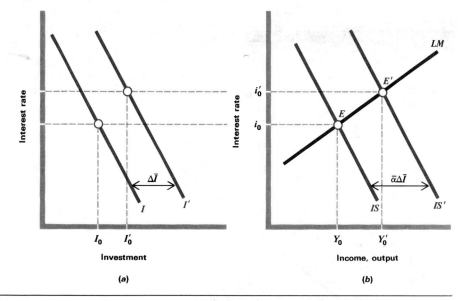

(a)   (b)

FIGURE 4-21 AN INVESTMENT SUBSIDY. An investment subsidy shifts the investment schedule in panel **(a)** at each interest rate out and to the right. The increase in planned investment shows in panel **(b)** as a shift of the IS curve. Equilibrium income rises to Y_0', and the interest rate increases to i_0'. At the higher interest rate, investment is still higher, I_0', than it was initially. Thus an investment subsidy raises interest rates, income, and investment.

ule in panel (a). At each interest rate, firms now plan to invest more. With investment spending higher, aggregate demand increases.

In panel (b), the IS schedule shifts by the multiplier times the increase in autonomous investment brought about by the subsidy. The new equilibrium is at point E', where goods and money markets are again in balance. But note now that although interest rates have risen, we see in panel (a) that investment is higher. Investment is at the level I'_0 up from I_0. The interest rate increase thus has only dampened but not reversed the impact of the investment subsidy. Here is an example where both consumption, induced by higher income, and investment rise as a consequence of fiscal policy.

The Policy Mix

In Figure 4-22 we show the policy problem of reaching full-employment output Y^* for an economy that is initially at point E with unemployment. Should we choose a fiscal expansion, moving to point E_1 with higher income and higher interest rates, or should we choose a monetary expansion, leading to full employment with lower interest rates at point E_2? Or should we pick a policy mix of fiscal expansion and accommodating monetary policy, leading to an intermediate position?

Once we recognize that all the policies raise output but differ significantly in their impact on different sectors of the economy, we open up a problem of political economy. Given the decision to expand aggregate demand, who should get the primary benefit? Should the expansion take place through a decline in interest rates and increased investment spending, should it take place through a cut in taxes and increased personal spending, or should it take the form of an increase in the size of government?

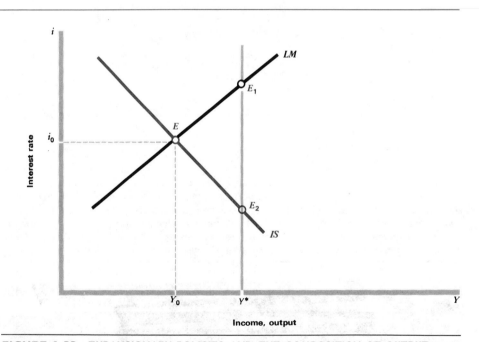

FIGURE 4-22   EXPANSIONARY POLICIES AND THE COMPOSITION OF OUTPUT. In an economy with output Y_0 below the full-employment level Y^*, there is a choice of using monetary or fiscal expansion to move to full employment. Monetary expansion would move the LM curve to the right, putting the equilibrium at E_2. Fiscal expansion shifts the IS curve, putting the new equilibrium at E_1. The expansionary monetary policy reduces the interest rate, while the expansionary fiscal policy raises it. The lower interest rate in the case of monetary policy means that investment is higher at E_2 than it is at E_1.

Questions of speed and predictability of policies apart, the issues raised above have been settled by political preferences. Conservatives will argue for a tax cut anytime. They will favour stabilization policies that in a recession cut taxes and in a boom cut government spending. Over time, given enough cycles, the government becomes very small, just as a conservative would want it to be. The counterpart view belongs to those who feel that there is much scope for government spending on education, environment, job training and rehabilitation, and the like, and who, accordingly, favour expansionary policies in the form of increased government spending. Growth-minded people and the construction industry finally argue for expansionary policies that operate through low interest rates.

The recognition that monetary and fiscal policy changes have different effects on the composition of output is important. It suggests that policy makers can choose a *policy mix* that will both get the economy to full employment and also make a contribution to solving some other policy problem. We anticipate here several subsequent discussions in which we point out two other targets of policy which have been taken into account in setting monetary and fiscal policy —growth and balance of payments equilibrium.

*4-8 A FORMAL TREATMENT OF THE *IS-LM* MODEL

Our exposition so far has been verbal and graphic. We now round off the analysis with a more formal treatment that uses the equations of the *IS* and *LM* schedules to derive and discuss fiscal and monetary policy multipliers.

Equilibrium Income and the Interest Rate

The intersection of the *IS* and *LM* schedules determines equilibrium income and the equilibrium interest rate. We can derive expressions for these equilibrium values by using the equations of the *IS* and *LM* schedules. From Section 4-1 we remember the equation of the *IS* schedule or goods market equilibrium schedule as

IS schedule: $Y = \overline{\alpha}\,(\overline{A} - bi)$ (13)

and the equation describing money market equilibrium as[21]

LM schedule: $i = \dfrac{1}{h}\left(kY - \dfrac{\overline{M}}{\overline{P}}\right)$ (14)

---

[21] To deal with the case where liquidity preference is not only high but at some rate, say i', *perfectly* elastic, we could rewrite the LM equation as $\overline{M}/\overline{P} = kY - h(i - i')$, so that real money demand depends on the excess of the interest rate above some floor level i'. With this information, (14) becomes $i = i' + (1/h)[kY - \overline{M}/\overline{P}]$. If h is extremely high, the interest rate is $i = i'$ or the LM schedule is horizontal at the level i'.

The intersection of the *IS* and *LM* schedules in the diagrams corresponds to a situation where both the *IS* and *LM* equations hold — the *same* interest rate and income levels assure equilibrium in *both* the goods and money market. In terms of the equations, that means we can substitute the interest rate from the *LM* Equation (14) into the *IS* Equation (13):

$$Y = \overline{\alpha}\left[\overline{A} - \frac{b}{h}\left(kY - \frac{\overline{M}}{\overline{P}}\right)\right] \tag{15}$$

Collecting terms and solving for the equilibrium level of income, we obtain

$$Y_0 = \frac{h\overline{\alpha}}{h + kb\overline{\alpha}}\overline{A} + \frac{b\overline{\alpha}}{h + kb\overline{\alpha}}\frac{\overline{M}}{\overline{P}} \tag{15a}$$

Equation (15a) shows the equilibrium level of income depending on two exogenous variables: autonomous spending $\overline{A}$, including fiscal policy parameters $(\overline{C}, \overline{I}, \overline{G}, t, \overline{TR})$ and the real money stock $\overline{M}/\overline{P}$. Equilibrium income is higher the higher the level of autonomous spending $\overline{A}$ and the higher the stock of real balances.

The equilibrium rate of interest, i_0, is obtained by substituting the equilibrium income level Y_0 from (15a) into the equation of the *LM* schedule, (14):

$$i_0 = \frac{k\overline{\alpha}}{h + kb\overline{\alpha}}\overline{A} - \frac{1}{h + kb\overline{\alpha}}\frac{\overline{M}}{\overline{P}} \tag{16}$$

Equation (16) shows that the equilibrium interest rate depends on the parameters of fiscal policy captured in the multiplier and the term $\overline{A}$, and on the real money stock. A higher real money stock implies a lower equilibrium interest rate.

For policy questions we are interested in the precise relation between changes in fiscal policy or changes in the real money stock and the resulting changes in equilibrium income. The *monetary* and *fiscal policy multipliers* provide the relevant information.

The Fiscal Policy Multiplier

The fiscal policy multiplier tells us how much an increase in government spending changes the equilibrium level of income, holding the real money supply constant. Examine Equation (15a) and consider the effect of an increase in government spending on income. The increase in government spending $\Delta\overline{G}$ is a change in autonomous spending, so that $\Delta\overline{A} = \Delta\overline{G}$. The effect of the change in $\overline{G}$ is given by

$$\frac{\Delta Y_0}{\Delta \overline{G}} = \frac{h\overline{\alpha}}{h + bk\overline{\alpha}} \qquad (17)$$

We note that the expression in Equation (17) is zero if h is very small and will be equal to $\overline{\alpha}$ if h approaches infinity. This corresponds, respectively, to vertical and horizontal LM schedules. Similarly, a large value of either b or k serves to reduce the effect on income of government spending. Why? A high value of k implies a large increase in money demand as income rises and hence a large increase in interest rates in order to maintain money market equilibrium. In combination with a high b, this implies a large reduction in private aggregate demand. Equation (17) thus presents the algebraic analysis that corresponds to the graphical analysis of Figures 4-18 and 4-19.

The Monetary Policy Multiplier

The monetary policy multiplier tells us by how much an increase in the real money supply increases the equilibrium level of income, keeping fiscal policy unchanged. Using Equation (15a) to examine the effects of an increase in the real money supply on income, we have

$$\frac{\Delta Y_0}{\Delta(\overline{M}/P)} = \frac{b\overline{\alpha}}{h + bk\overline{\alpha}} \qquad (18)$$

The smaller h and k and the larger b and $\overline{\alpha}$, the more expansionary the effect of an increase in real balances on the equilibrium level of income. Large b and $\overline{\alpha}$ correspond to a very flat IS schedule. Equation (18) thus corresponds to the graphical analysis presented in Figure 4-16.

The Classical Case and the Liquidity Trap

We now turn to two special cases that demonstrate the role of the demand function for real balances in the effectiveness of monetary and fiscal policies. Consider first the possibility that money demand does not depend at all on interest rates and is simply proportional to real income. This happens if the parameter h is zero, so that real money demand is simply

$$L = kY \qquad (19)$$

In this case monetary equilibrium, equating the demand and supply of money, leads to[22]

---

[22] The demand for real balances is $L = kY$ and the supply $\overline{M}/P$. Thus with demand equal to supply, $\overline{M}/P = kY$ or $Y = (1/k)\overline{M}/P$.

$$Y = (1/k)\ \frac{\overline{M}}{\overline{P}} \tag{20}$$

This case is called the *classical case* because classical (that is, nineteenth century) economists did not give much emphasis to the interest response of money demand. The case is important because it has the following implication: If money demand does not depend on the interest rate and only on the level of income, as in (19), the money supply alone determines income.

In this classical case the level of nominal income, $\overline{P}Y$, is proportional to the nominal money stock. Changes in the nominal money stock lead to changes in income in the same proportion. Furthermore, while income does respond to money, it is *totally* unresponsive to fiscal policy. We also can see the point from (15a) by setting $h = 0$.

Interest Rates and Fiscal Policy

How is it possible that fiscal policy should have no effect at all on income? After all, if the government were to spend more, how is it possible that the increased spending should *not* raise income? The reasoning is as follows. An increase in government spending does lead to an incipient rise in aggregate demand and income, but that immediately raises the demand for money. With the money supply unchanged, interest rates will shoot up to clear the money market. But the rise in interest rate does nothing to reduce the quantity of money demanded. It does, however, have an impact on private investment spending. As interest rates rise because of the excess demand for money, investment spending declines. The fall in investment spending compensates exactly for the higher government spending, and the level of income is unchanged.

We can see this by looking at the investment equation (21), obtained by substituting in the equilibrium interest rate from (16):

$$I = \bar{I} - bi_0 = \bar{I} - \frac{bk\overline{\alpha}}{h + bk\overline{\alpha}}\overline{A} + \frac{b}{h + bk\overline{\alpha}}\frac{\overline{M}}{\overline{P}} \tag{21}$$

In the case where $h = 0$, the coefficient multiplying $\overline{A}$ in (21) is 1. This means that a \$1 increase in $\overline{A}$, given the real money stock, leads to an equal reduction of investment. That is what we call *full* crowding out. In general, with h not equal to zero, the coefficient of $\overline{A}$ is a fraction, as shown in (21). The larger h, the smaller the fraction of an extra dollar of government spending that is offset by reduced investment spending.

Liquidity Trap

The other extreme for monetary and fiscal policy is represented by a world where h is infinite. Then money and other assets are effectively perfect substitutes. In such a world, Equation (15a) reduces to

$$Y = \bar{\alpha}\,\overline{A} \qquad\qquad (22)$$

This is the "multiplier world" of Chapter 3, where autonomous spending entirely determines the level of real income. It occurs if the economy is in a liquidity trap.

In the liquidity trap, money does not matter for income determination because money demand is *so* responsive to interest rates. The smallest change in interest rates is sufficient to eliminate imbalances in the money market that might arise from changes in money supply or in income. And because these corrective changes in interest rates are so small, they do not even affect aggregate demand. The interest rate effect can be verified from (11). With *h* extremely high, investment spending is not influenced by either monetary or fiscal policy.

4-9   SUMMARY

1. The *IS-LM* model presented in this chapter incorporates the assets markets as well as the goods market. It lays particular stress on the channels through which monetary and fiscal policy affect the economy.

2. The *IS* curve shows combinations of the interest rate and level of income such that the goods market is in equilibrium. Increases in the interest rate reduce aggregate demand by reducing the demand for investment goods. Thus, at higher interest rates, the level of income at which the goods market is in equilibrium is lower: the *IS* curve slopes downward.

3. The demand for money is a demand for *real* balances. The demand for real balances increases with income and decreases with the interest rate, the cost of holding money rather than other assets. With an exogenously fixed supply of real balances, the *LM* curve, representing money market equilibrium, is upward-sloping. Because of the wealth constraint, equilibrium of the money market implies equilibrium of the remaining assets markets, summarized here under the catch-all "bond market."

4. The interest rate and level of output are jointly determined by simultaneous equilibrium of the goods and money markets. This occurs at the intersection point of the *IS* and *LM* curves.

5. Assuming that output is increased when there is an excess demand for goods, and that the interest rate rises when there is an excess demand for money, the economy does move toward the new equilibrium when one of the curves shifts. Typically we think of the assets markets as clearing rapidly, so that in response to a disturbance, the economy tends to move along the *LM* curve to the new equilibrium.

6. Monetary policy affects the economy in the first instance by affecting the interest rate, and then by affecting aggregate demand. An increase in the

money supply reduces the interest rate, increases investment demand and aggregate demand, and thus increases equilibrium output.

7. There are two extreme cases in the operation of monetary policy. In the classical case the demand for real balances is independent of the rate of interest. In this case monetary policy is highly effective. The other extreme is the liquidity trap, where the public is willing to hold *any* amount of real balances at the going interest rate. In that case changes in the supply of real balances have no impact on interest rates and therefore do not affect aggregate demand and output.

8. Taking into account the effects of fiscal policy on the interest rate modifies the multiplier results of Chapter 3. Fiscal expansion, except in extreme circumstances, still leads to an income expansion. However, the rise in interest rates that comes about through the increase in money demand caused by higher income dampens the expansion.

9. Fiscal policy is more effective the smaller are the induced changes in interest rates and the smaller is the response of investment to these interest rate changes.

10. In the liquidity trap, the interest rate is constant because money demand is completely elastic with respect to the interest rate. Monetary policy has no effect on the economy, whereas fiscal policy has its full multiplier effect on output, and no effect on interest rates.

11. In the classical case, the demand for money is independent of the interest rate. In that case, changes in the money stock change income, but fiscal policy has no effect on income — it affects only the interest rate. In this case there is complete crowding out of private spending by government spending.

12. Neither the liquidity trap nor the classical case applies in practice. But they are useful cases to study in order to show what determines the magnitude of monetary and fiscal policy multipliers.

13. A fiscal expansion, because it leads to higher interest rates, displaces or crowds out some private investment. The extent of crowding out is an important issue in assessing the usefulness and desirability of fiscal policy as a tool of stabilization policy.

14. In an economy that is less than fully employed, crowding out need not occur. The monetary authorities can provide an accommodating monetary policy that avoids the rise in interest rates associated with the output expansion.

15. The question of the monetary-fiscal policy mix arises because expansionary monetary policy reduces the interest rate while expansionary fiscal

policy increases the interest rate. Accordingly, expansionary fiscal policy increases output while reducing the level of investment; expansionary monetary policy increases output and the level of investment.

16. Governments have to choose the mix in accordance with their objectives for economic growth, or increasing consumption, or from the viewpoint of their beliefs about the desirable size of the government.

KEY TERMS

IS Curve

LM Curve

Bond

Money

Portfolio decisions

Real balances (real money balances)

Wealth budget constraint

Open market operation

Transmission mechanism

Liquidity trap

Classical case

Crowding out

Monetary-fiscal policy mix

Investment subsidy

PROBLEMS

1. The following equations describe an economy. (Think of C, I, G, etc., as being measured in billions and i as percent; a 5 percent interest rate implies $i = 5$.)

$$C = 0.8 (1 - t)Y \qquad 1$$
$$t = 0.25 \qquad 2$$
$$I = 900 - 50i \qquad 3$$
$$\overline{G} = 800 \qquad 4$$
$$L = 0.25Y - 62.5i \qquad 5$$
$$\frac{\overline{M}}{P} = 500 \qquad 6$$

(a) What is the equation that describes the IS curve?

(b) What is the general definition of the IS curve?

(c) What is the equation that describes the LM curve?

(d) What is the general definition of the LM curve?

(e) What are the equilibrium levels of income and the interest rate?

(f) Describe in words the conditions that are satisfied at the intersection of the IS and LM curves, and why this is an equilibrium.

2. Continue with the same equations.
    (a) What is the value of $\bar{\alpha}$, which corresponds to the simple multiplier (with taxes) of Chapter 3?
    (b) By how much does an increase in government spending of $\Delta \bar{G}$ increase the level of income in this model, which includes the assets markets?
    (c) By how much does a change in government spending of $\Delta \bar{G}$ affect the equilibrium interest rate?
    (d) Explain the difference between your answers to 2a and b.

3. (a) Explain in words how and why the multiplier $\bar{\alpha}$ and the interest sensitivity of aggregate demand affect the slope of the IS curve.
    (b) Explain why the slope of the IS curve is a factor in determining the working of monetary policy.

4. Explain in words how and why the income and interest sensitivities of the demand for real balances affect the slope of the LM curve.

5. (a) Why does a horizontal LM curve imply that fiscal policy has the same effects on the economy as we derived in Chapter 3?
    (b) What is happening in this case in terms of Figure 4-2?
    (c) Under what circumstances might the LM curve be horizontal?

6. We mentioned in the text the possibility that the interest rate might affect consumption spending. An increase in the interest rate could, in principle lead to increases in saving and therefore a reduction in consumption, given the level of income. Suppose that consumption were in fact reduced by an increase in the interest rate. How would the IS curve be affected?

7. Suppose that the money supply, instead of being constant, increased (slightly) with the interest rate. How would this change affect the construction of the LM curve?

8. (a) How does an increase in the tax rate affect the IS curve?
    (b) How does it affect the equilibrium level of income?
    (c) How does it affect the equilibrium interest rate?

9. Draw a graph of how i and Y respond over time (that is, use time as the horizontal axis) to an increase in the money supply. You may assume that the money market adjusts much more rapidly than the goods market.

10. (a) Show that a given change in the money stock has a larger effect on output the less interest sensitive the demand for money.
    (b) How does the response of the interest rate to a change in the money stock depend on the interest sensitivity of money demand?

11. The economy is at full employment. Now the government wants to change the composition of demand toward investment and away from consumption without, however, allowing aggregate demand to go beyond full

employment. What is the required policy mix? Use the *IS-LM* diagram to show your policy proposal.

12. Discuss the role of the parameters $\bar{\alpha}$, h, b, and k in the transmission mechanism linking an increase in government spending to the resulting change in equilibrium income. In developing the analysis use the following table:

(1)	(2)	(3)
Increase in G raises aggregate demand and output	The increase in income raises money demand and hence interest rates	The increase in interest rates reduces investment spending and hence dampens the output expansion

13. Consider an economy where the government considers two alternative programs for contraction. One is the removal of an investment subsidy; the other is a rise in income tax rates. Use the *IS-LM* schedule and the investment schedule, as shown in Figure 4-21, to discuss the impact of these alternative policies on income, interest rates, and investment.

*14. Suppose the parameters k and $\bar{\alpha}$ are 0.5 and 2, respectively. Assume there is an increase of $1 billion in government spending. By how much must the real money stock be increased to hold interest rates constant?

CHAPTER

International Trade and Capital Flows with Fixed Exchange Rates

This is the first of two chapters analysing international macroeconomic linkages. Canada is linked to the rest of the world through two broad channels: *trade* and *finance*. This trade linkage arises from the fact that some of our output is exported to foreign countries, while some purchases are on goods that are produced elsewhere and imported. In 1986, exports amounted to 27 percent of GDP, while imports were 26 percent of GDP.

The international linkages in the area of finance arise from the fact that Canadian residents, whether households, banks or corporations, can hold assets in foreign countries, and foreigners can choose to hold Canadian assets. Although households are likely to hold mainly domestic assets, portfolio managers for banks and corporations also consider the relative attractiveness of lending and borrowing in the U.S., Europe or Japan as well as in Canada.

International investors provide a link between asset markets in Canada and abroad, and their actions have fundamental effects on the determination of income, exchange rates, and the ability of monetary policy to affect interest rates. We show in this chapter how the *IS-LM* analysis has to be modified to take international trade and finance linkages into account. A first step is to discuss exchange rates and the balance of payments.

5-1 THE BALANCE OF PAYMENTS AND EXCHANGE RATES

The balance of payments is the record of transactions of the residents of a country with the rest of the world. There are two main accounts in the balance of payments: the current account and the capital account.

The current account records trade in goods and services, as well as transfer payments. Services include freight, royalty payments, and interest payments, while transfer payments consist of remittances, gifts, and grants. The current account balance is equal to exports, less imports and net transfers to foreigners. Net exports of goods alone is referred to as the *merchandise trade balance*.

The capital account records borrowing and lending as well as purchases and sales of assets such as stocks, bonds and land. There is a capital account surplus, or a net capital inflow, when our receipts from borrowing and the sale of assets exceeds our payments for lending and the purchase of assets.

Surpluses and Deficits

The simple rule for balance of payments accounting is that any private transaction that gives rise to disbursement of foreign currency is recorded as a payment. Thus, imports of goods, foreign travel, purchase of foreign stocks and lending to foreigners are all payment items. Conversely, any transactions, such as exports and borrowing from foreigners, that give rise to the acquisition of foreign exchange, are recorded as receipts.

The overall balance of payments is the sum of the current and capital account balances. An overall deficit in the balance of payments means that Canadian residents make more payments to foreigners than they receive from foreigners. Any such gap must be matched by *net official financing*. This item records foreign currency transactions carried out by the Bank of Canada on behalf of the government of Canada. The foreign exchange held for this purpose is referred to as *official international reserves*.

Table 5-1 shows the details of Canada's balance of payments in 1987 and Figure 5-1 shows the movements in the major categories since 1966. With the

TABLE 5-1   CANADIAN BALANCE OF INTERNATIONAL PAYMENTS, 1987
(billions of dollars)

	RECEIPTS (+)	PAYMENTS (−)	BALANCE
Current account			
Merchandise trade	$125.8	$115.4	
Travel	6.3	8.8	
Investment income	7.0	23.6	
Freight and shipping	4.9	4.3	
Other services and transfers	12.3	13.8	
Balance on current account			$−9.6
Capital account			
Net private capital movements*			15.0
Net official financing			−5.4

*Includes statistical discrepancy

Source: *Bank of Canada Review*

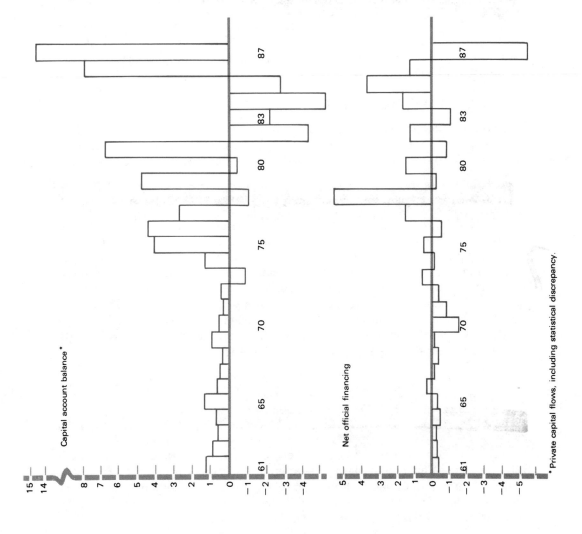

FIGURE 5-1   CANADA'S BALANCE OF INTERNATIONAL PAYMENTS, BILLIONS OF DOLLARS

(Source: Bank of Canada Review)

exception of 1982–1984, the typical pattern has been a surplus on merchandise trade more than offset by a deficit on services and transfers, leaving a substantial current account deficit. Much of this deficit is attributable to a large outflow of dividend and interest payments associated with accumulated foreign indebtedness and foreign ownership of Canadian businesses.

In 1987 there was a large surplus on capital account. This reflected the fact that receipts arising from borrowing from foreigners and sales of Canadian assets to foreigners exceeded payments arising from lending to foreigners and purchases of foreign assets by Canadians.

Fixed Versus Flexible Exchange Rates

We now examine in more detail the way in which central banks, through their official transactions, finance, or provide the means of paying for, balance of payments surpluses and deficits. At this point we distinguish between fixed and floating rate systems.

Under a flexible (or floating) exchange rate, the central bank allows the exchange rate to be determined by the foreign exchange market. In Figure 5-2 we illustrate the supply and demand for Canadian dollars in the exchange market. The exchange rate is measured on the vertical axis as the domestic currency price of foreign exchange (for example $1.25 Canadian dollars per U.S. dollars). The supply of Canadian dollars offered in exchange for foreign currency equals imports and capital outflows. It is upward sloping since an increase in the price reduces the cost of imports and shifts demand from domestic to imported goods. The demand curve represents exports and capital inflows and is downward sloping since an increase in the price raises the cost of exports in foreign markets. The equilibrium exchange rate is e_1, determined by the intersection.

Fixed Exchange Rates

In a fixed rate system, central banks stand ready to buy and sell their currencies at a fixed price in terms of dollars. For example, from May 1962 to June 1970 the Bank of Canada would buy or sell any amount of foreign currency at 92.5 U.S. cents per Canadian dollar.[1] The fact that the Bank was prepared to buy or sell *any* amount of Canadian dollars at this fixed price or exchange rate meant that the market price would indeed be equal to 92.5 U.S. cents. Why? Clearly, nobody who wanted to buy Canadian dollars with U.S. dollars would pay more than 92.5 U.S. cents if they could be gotten at that price from the Bank of

---

[1] The Bank of Canada was not committed to maintaining exactly this rate. Under the rules of the Internationall Monetary Fund in effect at that time, countries on fixed exchange rates maintained the value of their currencies within one percent of the stated fixed rate.

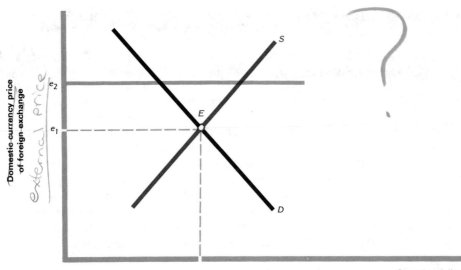

FIGURE 5-2 THE FOREIGN EXCHANGE MARKET. The exchange rate is measured on the vertical axis as the domestic currency price of foreign exchange. The supply of Canadian dollars equals imports and capital outflows and is upward sloping since an increase in the price reduces the cost of imports. The demand curve represents exports and capital inflows and is downward sloping since an increase in the price raises the price of exports. To fix the exchange rate at e_2 above the equilibrium rate e_1, the central bank has to exchange the excess supply of Canadian dollars for foreign currency.

Canada. Conversely, nobody would part with Canadian dollars for less than 92.5 U.S. cents if the Bank of Canada was prepared to buy them at that price.

In a fixed rate system, the central banks have to finance any balance of payments surplus or deficit that arises at the official exchange rate. They do that simply by buying or selling all the foreign currency that is not supplied in private transactions.

Figure 5-2 illustrates the fact that fixed exchange rates operate like any other price support scheme, such as in agricultural markets. If the price is fixed above the equilibrium level, say at e_2, the central bank has to take up the excess supply of Canadian dollars by exchanging Canadian dollars for foreign currency. In order to be able to ensure that the price (exchange rate) stays fixed, it is obviously necessary to hold an inventory of foreign exchange that can be sold in exchange for domestic currency. Thus, the Bank of Canada holds *reserves* of U.S. dollars, and gold that can be sold for U.S. dollars, for the purpose of exchange market intervention.

Intervention

Intervention is buying or selling of foreign exchange by the central bank. What determines the amount of intervention that a central bank has to do in a fixed exchange rate system? We already have the answer to that question. The balance of payments measures the amount of foreign exchange intervention needed from the central banks. So long as the central bank has the necessary reserves, it can continue to intervene in the foreign exchange markets to keep the exchange rate constant. However, if a country persistently runs deficits in the balance of payments, the central bank eventually will run out of reserves of foreign exchange and will be unable to continue its intervention.

Before that point is reached, the central bank is likely to decide that it can no longer maintain the exchange rate, and will devalue the currency. In 1967, for instance, the British devalued the pound from $2.80 per pound to $2.40 per pound. That meant it became cheaper for foreigners to buy British pounds, and the devaluation thus affected the balance of payments. We shall study the way in which devaluation affects the balance of payments in Section 5-3.

Floating, Clean and Dirty

In a system of *clean floating*, central banks stand aside completely and allow exchange rates to be freely determined in the foreign exchange markets. The central banks do not intervene in the foreign exchange markets in a system of clean floating, and official reserve transactions would, accordingly, be zero in such a situation. That means the balance of payments would be zero in a system of clean floating. The exchange rate would adjust to make the current and capital accounts sum to zero.

In practice, the flexible rate system has not been one of clean floating. Instead, the system has been one of *managed*, or *dirty*, *floating*. Under managed floating, central banks intervene to buy and sell foreign currencies, in attempts to influence exchange rates. Official reserve transactions are, accordingly, not equal to zero. The reasons for this central bank intervention under floating rates are discussed in Chapter 6.

Terminology

The use of language with respect to exchange rates can be very confusing. In particular, the terms *depreciation* and *appreciation* and *devaluation* and *revaluation* will recur throughout this chapter and the next.

A *devaluation* takes place when the price of foreign currencies under a fixed rate regime is increased by official action. A devaluation thus means that foreigners pay less for the devalued currency or that residents of the devaluing country pay more for foreign currencies. The opposite of a devaluation is a *revaluation*.

Changes in the price of foreign exchange under flexible exchange rates are referred to as *currency depreciation* or *appreciation*. A currency depreciates when, under floating rates, it becomes less expensive in terms of foreign currencies. For instance, if the exchange rate of the Canadian dollar moves from 90 U.S. cents to 84 U.S. cents, we talk of a depreciation of the Canadian dollar. Conversely, an appreciation means that the value of our currency rises in terms of foreign exchange.

Summary

1. The balance of payments accounts are a record of the transactions of the economy with other economies. The capital account describes transactions in assets, while the current account covers transactions in goods and services and transfers.

2. Transactions that give rise to the disbursement of foreign exchange are recorded as payments, while those that give rise to the acquisition of foreign exchange are recorded as receipts. The balance of payments deficit (or surplus) is the sum of the deficits (or surpluses) on current and capital accounts.

3. Under fixed exchange rates, central banks stand ready to meet all demands for foreign currencies arising from balance of payments deficits or surpluses at a fixed price in terms of the domestic currency. They have to *finance* the excess demands for, or supplies of, foreign currency (that is, the balance of payments deficits or surpluses, respectively), at the pegged (fixed) exchange rate by running down, or adding to, their reserves of foreign currency.

4. Under flexible exchange rates, the demands for, and supplies of, foreign currency can be made equal through movements in exchange rates. Under clean floating, there is no central bank intervention and the balance of payments is zero. Central banks sometimes intervene in a floating rate system, engaging in so-called dirty floating.

5-2 TRADE IN GOODS, MARKET EQUILIBRIUM, AND THE BALANCE OF TRADE

We now study the effects of trade in goods on the level of income, and the effects of various disturbances on both income and the trade balance—which, from now on, we use as shorthand for the current account. We also examine policy problems which arise when the balance of trade and the level of income require different corrective actions. We do not at this stage include the capital account, so that for the present the current account and the balance of payments are the same.

In this section we fit foreign trade into the *IS-LM* framework. As in Chapters 3 and 4, we assume that the price level is given, and that output that is demanded will be supplied. A word of warning is in order before you start working through the following sections. The exposition assumes you are thoroughly at home with the *IS-LM* analysis and therefore proceeds quite rapidly. However, the material is not more difficult than that of the previous chapters and should be accessible with careful reading.

Domestic Spending and Spending on Domestic Goods

In this subsection we want to establish how foreign trade fits into the *IS* schedule. In an open economy, part of domestic output is sold to foreigners (exports), and part of spending by domestic residents falls on foreign goods (imports). We accordingly have to modify our analysis of aggregate demand developed in Chapter 4.

The most important change is that it is no longer true that domestic spending determines domestic output. What is true now is that *spending on domestic goods* determines domestic output. Spending by domestic residents falls in part on domestic goods but also in part on imports. On the other hand, demand for domestic goods includes exports.

The way in which external transactions affect the demand for domestic output was examined in Section 3-6. Aggregate demand for domestically produced goods is

$$AD \equiv C + I + G + NX \tag{1}$$

where *NX* is the trade balance (net exports). Assuming that exports are fixed and that imports depend on income, we have

$$NX \equiv X - Q \equiv \overline{X} - \overline{Q} - mY \tag{2}$$

The relationship expressed in Equation (2) is illustrated in Figure 5-2. Imports are small at low levels of income, so that given the fixed level of exports, there is a trade surplus, $NX > 0$. As income rises, import spending increases until we reach income level $\overline{Y}$, where imports match exports, so that trade is balanced. A further increase in income gives rise to a trade deficit.

Goods Market Equilibrium

With these modifications, the equation for the *IS* curve becomes

$$Y = \overline{\alpha}(\overline{A} - bi) \tag{3}$$

where autonomous spending now includes exports minus the autonomous component of imports and is thus given by

$$\overline{A} = C + c\overline{TR} + \overline{I} + \overline{G} + \overline{X} - Q \tag{4}$$

and the open economy multiplier is

$$\overline{\alpha} = 1/[1 - c(1 - t) + m] \tag{5}$$

Figure 5-3 illustrates the goods market equilibrium condition (3). We still refer to it as a goods market equilibrium, or *IS* curve, although it is important to recognize that now the trade surplus appears as a component of demand for output. The schedule is downward-sloping because an increase in output causes an excess supply of goods: the increase in income is only partly spent on domestic goods, the rest being either saved or spent on imports. To compensate for the excess supply, interest rates have to decline to induce an increase in aggregate demand, and the *IS* curve therefore slopes down. The *IS* schedule is drawn for the given level of foreign demand $\overline{X}$.

We have also shown, in Figure 5-3, the trade balance equilibrium schedule *NX*. Given exports, we see from Figure 5-2 and Equation (3) that there is some level of income, $\overline{Y}$, at which import spending exactly matches export revenue, so that trade is balanced. Points to the left of the *NX* schedule are points of trade surplus. Here income and hence import spending are low relative to exports. Exports accordingly exceed imports. Points to the right of the *NX* schedule, by contrast, are deficit points. Here income and hence import spending are too high relative to exports for trade to be balanced. Finally, we have drawn, too, the *LM* schedule, which is precisely the same as in our study of the closed economy.

Equilibrium Income and the Balance of Trade

The next question to address, using Figure 5-3, is where the short-run equilibrium of the economy will be. It will be at point *E*, the intersection of the *IS* and *LM* curves. At point *E*, demand for domestic goods equals supply, and money demand equals money supply. Therefore, both the goods and money markets are in equilibrium.

The trade balance need not be in equilibrium since a deficit can be financed by running down foreign exchange reserves, and a surplus can be financed by building up reserves. The assumption is that the central bank finances the trade deficit by selling foreign exchange and thus maintains the exchange rate at its pegged level in the face of a trade and balance of payments deficit, or that the bank purchases foreign exchange if there is a surplus.[2] We assume the goods

---

[2] We are abstracting here from a complication discussed in Section 5-5. Foreign exchange transactions will have an effect on the domestic money supply unless offsetting action is taken by the central bank. At this point we are assuming that there is no link between the balance of payments and the money supply.

and money markets clear sufficiently quickly so that equilibrium is determined at point E in Figure 5-3. As we have drawn the equilibrium, the trade balance is in surplus.

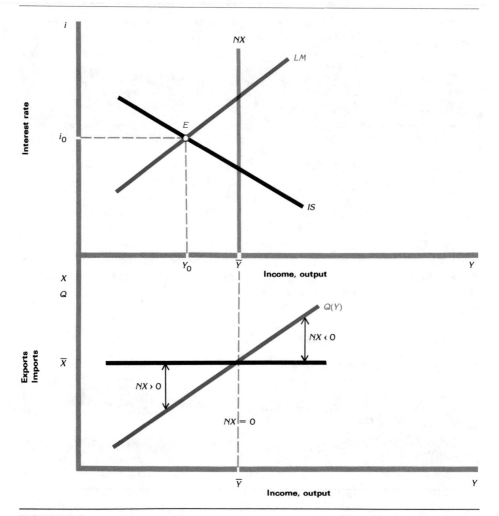

FIGURE 5-3 GOODS AND MONEY MARKET EQUILIBRIUM. The *LM* schedule is familiar from the closed economy. The *IS* schedule represents goods market equilibrium but now includes net exports as a component of demand. As shown in the lower panel, imports depend on the level of income so that, given exports there is a level of income $\overline{Y}$ at which trade is balanced. This is shown by the vertical *NX* schedule in the upper panel. Equilibrium obtains at point E, where goods and money markets clear. At E there is a trade surplus.

Disturbances

How do internal and external disturbances—shifts in the level or composition of spending, or changes in exports—affect equilibrium income and the balance of trade? To answer that question, it is important to remember that both the *IS* and the trade balance schedules are drawn for a given level of exports, $\overline{X}$.

We can think of three types of disturbances, the effects of which we will briefly analyse in turn: (1) an increase in autonomous domestic spending that falls on our own goods, (2) an increase in exports, and (3) a shift in demand from domestic goods to imports.

Before going through the exercises, we indicate the results we expect to find. First, any autonomous increase (decrease) in spending on our goods should result in an increase (decrease) in equilibrium output and income. But we would expect the trade balance to worsen if domestic income expands because the higher income leads to increased import spending. Second, it is not so clear how an increase in exports affects the trade balance. Say exports increase, and as a consequence domestic income rises. This income increase, in turn, raises import spending, and we are not certain whether the net effect on the trade balance is an improvement or a worsening. In fact we can show that the net effect is actually an improvement—induced import spending dampens but does not offset the trade balance improvement resulting from an increase in exports. Table 5-2 summarizes those results.

TABLE 5-2   THE EFFECT OF DISTURBANCES ON INCOME AND ON THE TRADE BALANCE

	Autonomous increase in spending on domestic goods	Autonomous increase in exports	Shift in demand from imports to domestic goods
Income	+	+	+
Trade Balance	−	+	+

The Effects of an Increase in Autonomous Spending

We now proceed to our analysis. First, consider an autonomous increase in our spending on domestic goods, perhaps because of expansionary fiscal policy. In Figure 5-4, we show the effect to be a shift in the *IS* curve. At the initial equilibrium *E* there is an excess demand for goods, and accordingly, the equilibrium income level increases. The new equilibrium is at point *E'*, where output and interest rates have risen and where we have a reduction in the trade surplus.

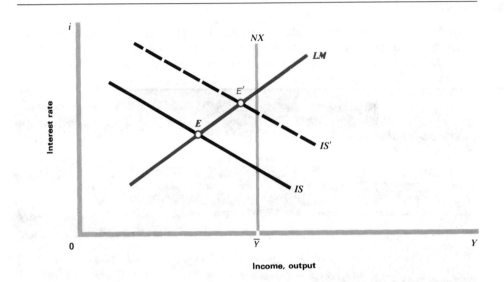

FIGURE 5-4   THE EFFECTS OF AN INCREASE IN DOMESTIC SPENDING. Starting from equilibrium at E, there is an increase in our spending that falls on domestic goods. Accordingly, the IS schedule shifts to the right to IS', and the new equilibrium is at point E', where goods and assets markets clear. The increase in demand raises income. It also worsens the trade balance because of increased import spending.

The expansion in output increases import spending, and thus at E' the trade surplus is less than at E. The first lesson is, therefore, that expansionary domestic policies or autonomous increases in spending raise income but cause a worsening of the trade balance.

A second point worth making concerns the size of the income expansion induced by an expansionary policy, that is, the size of the multiplier. By comparison with a closed economy, we have less of an expansion in an open economy. Multipliers are smaller because induced spending on domestic goods is less. Part of an increase in income is now spent on imports rather than domestic goods. Imports are a *leakage* from the domestic multiplier process. Indeed, the larger the fraction of an increase in income that is spent on imports, the smaller the multiplier, because there is relatively little induced spending on domestic goods.

The Effects of an Increase in Exports

The next disturbance we consider is an increase in exports. An increase in exports raises the demand for domestic goods and thus shifts the IS curve to the right (to IS'), as shown in Figure 5-5. At the same time, the increase in

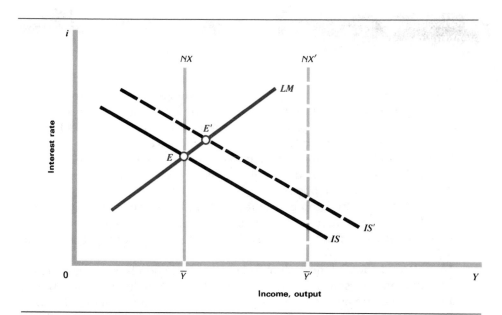

FIGURE 5-5   THE EFFECT OF AN INCREASE IN EXPORTS. Starting from an equilibrium at E, there is an increase in exports. The trade balance improves at each income level. It now takes a higher level of income to induce enough import spending to match the higher level of exports. Accordingly, the trade balance equilibrium schedule shifts to the right to NX'. Higher exports means increased demand for domestic goods. Therefore the IS schedule also shifts to the right. But it shifts by less than the trade balance schedule. The new equilibrium is at point E'. Interest rates and income rise. At the same time, the trade balance improves.

exports implies that at each level of income the trade balance is improved. Given the higher exports, trade will now be balanced at a higher level of income. Thus, the trade balance schedule shifts to NX'.

Starting from a position of balanced trade at point E, we find that the increase in exports raises equilibrium income and improves the balance of trade at point E'. The first part is quite intuitive. Higher demand for our goods leads to an increase in equilibrium output. The trade balance improvement, though, is less intuitive. The increase in exports by itself improves the trade balance, but the increase in income leads to increased import spending, which, it seems, could perhaps offset the direct improvement from the export increase. This is, in fact, not the case, and we leave the demonstration of that result to Problem 1 at the end of this chapter.

A Shift in the Composition of Demand

The last disturbance we consider is a shift in demand from imports to domestic goods. You will recognize that this has the same effects as an increase in exports. It means increased demand for domestic goods and also an improvement in the trade balance.

Summary

1. The introduction of trade in goods means that spending by domestic residents is no longer equal to the demand for domestically produced goods. Some of our demand for goods goes for imports, and some of the demand for our goods comes from foreigners, to whom we export.
2. There is equilibrium in the goods market when the demand for our goods, consisting of spending by domestic residents, plus net exports, is equal to the output of domestic goods.
3. In equilibrium, there is no guarantee that trade balances. In our simplest model, there is a unique level of income at which trade balances, and this is not necessarily the income level at which the economy comes into equilibrium.
4. An increase in autonomous demand for domestic goods increases domestic output and worsens the trade balance. An increase in exports increases domestic income and reduces the trade deficit. A shift in demand toward domestically produced goods increases the level of income and reduces the trade deficit, or increases the trade surplus.

5-3   INTERNAL AND EXTERNAL BALANCE

We have now constructed and used, in Figure 5-3 through 5-5, our basic diagrammatic apparatus for embodying trade in the *IS-LM* model. We draw on the analysis of income and trade balance determination to ask about economic policy making. From a policy perspective we would want to be able to achieve both *internal* and *external balance*. Internal balance means that output is at the full-employment level. External balance occurs when the trade balance is zero.

It is clear enough why internal balance should be an aim of policy, but why is external balance desirable? In a fixed exchange rate world, a balance of payments deficits cannot be maintained indefinitely, as the financing of the deficits requires the country to use its reserves of foreign currency. Such reserves will run out in the face of continual deficits. Hence, a country on a fixed exchange rate cannot aim to run a balance of payments deficit indefinitely. On the other hand, a country on fixed rates wants to avoid running a permanent surplus, because that causes it to acquire foreign currencies to add to its reserves indefinitely. Since the foreign exchange could be used to buy and consume foreign goods, the country is permanently forgoing some consumption it could otherwise have had, when it chooses to run permanent balance of payments surpluses.

The policy problem is illustrated in Figure 5-6. The problem is that for a given level of exports we may not be able to achieve *both* internal and external balance. In Figure 5-6, we have drawn the trade balance schedule, *NX*, for the given level of exports. We have drawn, too, the full-employment level of output *Y*,* and the two lines do not coincide.

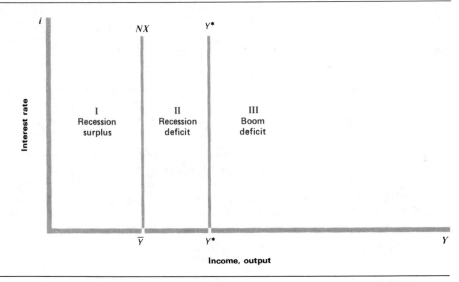

FIGURE 5-6   INTERNAL AND EXTERNAL BALANCE AND THE POLICY DILEMMA

We can break up Figure 5-6 into three regions. To the left of the trade balance schedule, we have a trade surplus, and to the right we have a deficit. To the left of the *Y** schedule, we have unemployment, and to the right we have overemployment, or a boom.

From a policy viewpoint, regions I and III present no problem. In region I we want to pursue an expansionary policy so as to raise employment *and* reduce the trade surplus. Until we get to trade balance equilibrium, there is no issue, since both the internal and external targets call for expansionary policies. Similarly, in region III we want to pursue restrictive policies to reduce overemployment and the trade deficit. Until we get to full employment, there is no issue.

Policy Dilemmas

The dilemma area is region II. Here we have to choose whether we want to use tight policies to achieve trade balance equilibrium or expansionary policies to achieve full employment. Not only are we unable to reach both targets simultaneously by manipulating aggregate demand, but any attempt to reach one target gets us further away from the other. Such a situation is called a *policy dilemma*, and it can always arise when there are more targets of policy than instruments with which to move the economy toward its targets. In our case we have only one policy instrument — aggregate demand policies — but we have two independent targets — external and internal balance.

The policy dilemma can be solved by finding another policy instrument to cope with the multiple targets. What is needed is some policy that shifts the trade balance schedule to the right until it overlaps with the full-employment level of output line, Y^*. An obvious policy would be to cut down on imports at each level of income. Such a policy would reduce import spending at each level of income and thus shift the trade balance schedule to the right.

How can we cut import spending? We can use any of a number of tools, among them tariffs and exchange rate changes. Tariffs are taxes on imported goods. A tariff raises the cost of imports to domestic residents and thereby diverts demand away from imports to domestic goods. A 10 percent tariff on imported shoes, for instance, makes imported shoes more expensive relative to domestically made shoes. However, tariffs cannot be freely used to adjust the balance of trade, partly because there are international organizations and agreements such as GATT (General Agreement on Tariffs and Trade) and the IMF (International Monetary Fund) that outlaw, or at least frown on, the use of tariffs. Tariffs have generally fallen in the post-World War II period as the industrialized world has moved to freer trade between countries.

Devaluation

An alternative to tariffs for reconciling internal and external balance is a *devaluation* that achieves the same effect by increasing the domestic currency price of foreign exchange.

Devaluation and Relative Prices

Assuming that nominal prices in the home currency in each country are fixed, a devaluation increases the relative price of imported goods in the devaluing country and reduces the relative price of exports from the devaluing country. These effects are illustrated in Table 5-3. We assume that Canada produces and exports rye whiskey and Britain produces the exports Scotch whiskey. Scotch is priced at £6.00 and rye at $10.00. These prices, in terms of the respective producer's currencies, are assumed to remain constant. Now, at an exchange rate of $2.00 per pound, the relative price of Scotch in terms of rye is $12.00/$10.00 = 6/5, meaning that Scotch costs 20 percent more than rye. Next, consider a devaluation of the Canadian dollar by 25 percent. The table shows that the Canadian dollar price of Scotch rises and that the sterling price of rye declines. Both in Canada and Britain, rye becomes *relatively* cheaper, or Scotch becomes relatively more expensive. The Canadian dollar devaluation lowers

TABLE 5-3   THE EFFECT OF EXCHANGE RATE CHANGES
ON RELATIVE PRICES

	Scotch Whiskey	Rye Whiskey
Canadian dollar price		
(a) $2.00/pound	$12.00	$10.00
(b) $2.50/pound	$15.00	$10.00
Sterling price		
(a) $2.00/pound	£6.00	£5.00
(b) $2.50/pound	£6.00	£4.00

the sterling price of Canadian goods and raises the dollar price of British goods. The exchange ratio for Scotch and rye now becomes $15.00/ $10.00 = 3/2, so that Scotch now costs 50 percent more than rye. Clearly, the decrease in the relative price of Canadian goods will affect the pattern of demand, increasing both Canadian and British demands for rye at the expense of the demand for Scotch.

Effect of a Devaluation

The analysis of a devaluation is complicated by the fact that policies that shift spending from imports to domestic goods generally also affect aggregate demand in the goods market. Accordingly, policies to shift the NX line generally have to be accompanied by policies that adjust aggregate demand.

Figure 5-7 shows a situation in which the level of output in the economy is at Y^*, but the balance of payments is in deficit, since the NX line is to the left of Y^*. As we saw earlier in this chapter, aggregate demand policies cannot, in this case, both keep us at full employment and reduce the trade deficit. Consider using a devaluation which shifts demand from imports to domestic goods and shifts the trade balance line to the right until it coincides with the full-employment line.

However, the devaluation will also affect the demand for domestic goods. The spending which at a given level of income no longer goes to imports goes to domestic goods instead. We are simply *switching* expenditures from imports to domestic goods. Accordingly, the IS curve shifts out to the right to *IS'*. We therefore have to use a further policy to offset the expansionary effect of the devaluation in the domestic goods market. We could use either monetary or fiscal policy to shift the economy's equilibrium back to the full-employment level Y^*.

The important point is: In general it is necessary to combine both *expenditure switching policies*, which shift demand between domestic and imported goods, and *expenditure reducing* (or *expenditure increasing*) *policies*, to cope with the

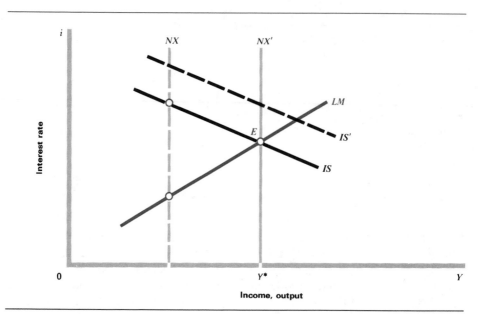

FIGURE 5-7 THE POLICY DILEMMA WITH A TRADE DEFICIT. An initial equilibrium at E involves a trade deficit. To correct the external balance there is a devaluation, and this policy move shifts demand from imports to domestic goods. The trade balance equilibrium schedule shifts to $NX' = 0$ because imports are reduced at each income level. The IS schedule shifts right to IS' because of increased demand for domestic goods. A further policy change is now required to avoid the overemployment equilibrium at the intersection of IS' and LM. A reduction in money, shifting the LM schedule up and to the left, could restore full-employment equilibrium.

targets of internal and external balance. This point is of general importance and continues to apply when we take account of capital flows and other phenomena omitted in this section.

Targets and Instruments of Policy

In general we cannot secure both external and internal balance following a disturbance by using just one instrument of policy. A general rule of policy making is that we need to use as many policy instruments as we have policy targets. Thus, if a disturbance occurs that causes a trade deficit, it will, in general, not be enough just to have a devaluation.

To make that point we look at a reduction in saving or an autonomous increase in spending at home. The increased spending, by assumption, falls entirely on imports. Interest rates and income at home are unchanged because demand for domestic goods is unchanged, but there is now a trade deficit.

Since we are no longer in external balance, corrective action requires some measure to improve the trade balance. Suppose a devaluation is used and successfully shifts demand from imports to domestic goods. External balance now is secured, but we have done so by shifting demand to domestic goods. If initially there was full employment, the higher level of demand now means overemployment. Accordingly, we need a further policy, in addition to the devaluation, that ensures maintenance of full employment. A restrictive monetary or fiscal policy would do the job. Thus, external balance adjustment involves an adjustment of the entire economy.

We should not fool ourselves into believing that just because full employment can be maintained, current account adjustment with a devaluation is costless. Current account adjustment involves not only a cut in spending to the level of income, but also, in many instances, a worsening of the *terms of trade* — the price of exports relative to imports. Foreign goods become more expensive, thus reducing the purchasing power of the goods we produce. Therefore our standard of living falls.

Finally, a comment on the role of the exchange rate in a fixed rate system: In the fixed rate system, the exchange rate is an *instrument of policy*. The central bank can change the exchange rate for policy purposes, devaluing when the current account looks as though it will be in for a prolonged deficit. In a system of clean floating, by contrast, the exchange rate moves freely to equilibrate the balance of payments. In a system of dirty floating, the central bank attempts to manipulate the exchange rate while not committing itself to any given rate. The dirty floating system is thus intermediate between a fixed rate system and a clean floating system.

5-4 CAPITAL MOBILITY

In this section we consider the role of the capital account in determining the balance of payments and equilibrium income. It plays an important role because of the high degree of international integration of capital markets. For example, yields on Canadian assets are closely linked to yields on comparable assets in the United States. If Canadian interest rates fall relative to U.S. rates, there will be a capital outflow from Canada as lenders move their funds out of Canada and borrowers attempt to raise funds in the domestic market rather than abroad.

The recognition that interest rates affect capital flows and the balance of payments has important implications for stabilization policy. First, because monetary and fiscal policy affect interest rates, they have an effect on the balance of payments through the capital account as well as through the trade account as discussed above. Second, the effect of interest rates on the balance of payments makes it possible to use a monetary-fiscal policy mix to achieve internal and external balance.

The Balance of Payments and Capital Flows

In introducing capital flows, we assume that the foreign rate of interest (i^*) is given and that capital flows into the home country at a rate that is higher, the higher the home country's rate of interest. In Figure 5-8 we show the rate of capital inflow CF, or the capital account surplus, as an increasing function of the rate of interest. When the domestic interest rate equals the foreign rate, the capital flow is zero. If the domestic interest rate is higher, there will be an inflow, and conversely, if the domestic rate is lower, there will be an outflow.

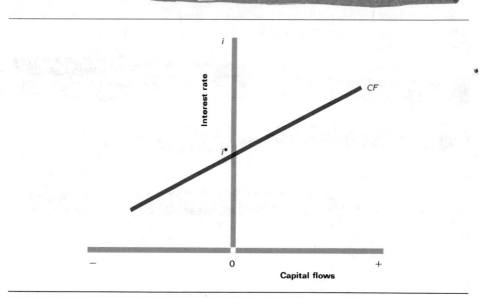

FIGURE 5-8   INTEREST-RESPONSIVE CAPITAL FLOWS

Under the assumptions given above, the capital account surplus is given by a relationship of the form:

$$CF = a(i - i^*) \tag{6}$$

Combining this with Equation (2) from Section 5.2 above we obtain the overall balance of payments surplus BP as:

$$BP = \overline{X} - \overline{Q} - mY + a(i - i^*) \tag{7}$$

Equation (7) shows that an increase in income worsens the trade balance and reduces the overall surplus, while an increase in the interest rate increases the capital inflow and increases the overall surplus.

If we set the overall balance of payments surplus equal to zero, we obtain from Equation (7) the combinations of income and the interest rate for which we have balance of payments equilibrium. This relationship is illustrated in Figure 5-9 as the positively sloped *BP* curve. It is drawn for given exports and a given foreign interest rate. To derive the slope, start with an income expansion that raises imports and worsens the balance of payments. To restore balance of payments equilibrium, interest rates must be raised to attract capital inflows and offset the trade deficit. Thus a higher level of income must be matched by higher interest rates to maintain a zero balance of payments surplus.

As shown in Figure 5-9, at points above the *BP* curve we have a balance of payments surplus and at points below the curve we have a deficit. To see why this is so, consider what happens if we hold income constant and vary the domestic interest rate. At the interest rate for which we are on the curve, we have a zero balance. At a higher rate the trade balance will be the same but

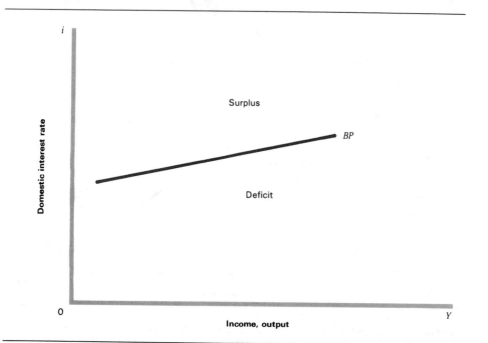

FIGURE 5-9 THE BALANCE OF PAYMENTS EQUILIBRIUM SCHEDULE. Along the *BP* curve the balance of payments is in equilibrium. A rise in income worsens the trade balance, and therefore higher interest rates are required to attract capital inflows that offset the trade deficit. Points above and to the left of the *BP* schedule correspond to surpluses and points below and to the right to deficits in the balance of payments. The higher the degree of capital mobility, the flatter the *BP* schedule, since then a small increase in our interest rates creates large capital inflows.

there will be a higher net capital inflow (or smaller net outflow) and therefore an overall surplus. Conversely, a lower interest rate will reduce the capital account surplus (or increase the deficit) and lead to an overall deficit.

Equilibrium Income and the Balance of Payments

Figure 5-10 illustrates the equilibrium of an economy with both trade and capital flows. As was the case in Section 5-2 above, the intersection of the *IS* and *LM* curves determines the equilibrium income and interest rate. Since the balance of payments need not be in equilibrium, the *BP* curve serves to determine whether there will be a balance of payments surplus or deficit. The case illustrated in Figure 5-10 involves a surplus at equilibrium.

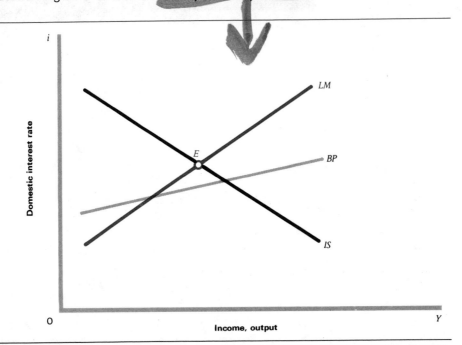

FIGURE 5-10 GOODS AND MONEY MARKET EQUILIBRIUM WITH CAPITAL FLOWS. Equilibrium income and the interest rate are determined by the intersection of the *IS* and *LM* schedules. The position of the *BP* schedule determines whether there is a surplus or deficit in the balance of payments. At the point *E* there is a surplus.

The Slope of the BP Curve

The slope of the *BP* curve depends on the marginal propensity to import and the degree of capital mobility as measured by the effect on capital flows of a change in the domestic interest rate. The higher the degree of capital mobility, the flatter is the schedule. If capital flows are highly responsive to interest rates, then a small increase in the interest rate will bring about very large flows and thus allow a large increase in the trade deficit. The larger the marginal propensity to import, the steeper is the schedule. An increase in income worsens the trade balance by the increase in income times the marginal propensity to import. Thus a high propensity means that a given increase in income produces a large deficit, and requires a large increase in interest rates to bring about a matching increase in capital inflow.

Since the BP and LM curves are both positively sloped, the assumption made as to which is steeper may have an important effect on the conclusions of our analysis. In Figure 5-10, we have made the BP curve relatively flat under the assumption that there is a high degree of capital mobility. This is likely to be appropriate for a country like Canada whose financial markets are closely integrated with those in the United States. This assumption is maintained throughout this section and is discussed further in Section 5-5 below.[3]

Monetary and Fiscal Policy

The effect of an expansionary fiscal policy on income and the balance of payments is illustrated in Figure 5-11. For simplicity we assume that we begin with IS and LM curves that intersect at the point E which is on the BP curve; that is, we assume that we begin at an equilibrium at which we have a zero balance of payments surplus. The IS curve shifts to the right and the new equilibrium is at E' where income and the interest rate are higher.

What will be the effect of expansionary fiscal policy on the balance of payments? The answer to this question is complicated by the fact that both the trade account and the capital account are affected. As in Section 5-2 above, the trade balance worsens because the higher income increases import spending. On the other hand, the higher interest rate increases the net capital inflow and improves the balance of payments. Since the point E' in Figure 5-11 is above the BP curve, the net effect is an *improvement* in the overall balance of payments. The capital account effect dominates the trade account effect because of our assumption that capital is highly mobile.

Monetary Policy

Turning to monetary policy, Figure 5-12 shows the effect of an increase in the money supply. The LM curve shifts to the right and the equilibrium income rises and interest rate falls as we move from E to E'. The new equilibrium point

[3] In problem 7 at the end of this chapter you are asked to consider the opposite case in which the BP curve is steeper than the LM curve.

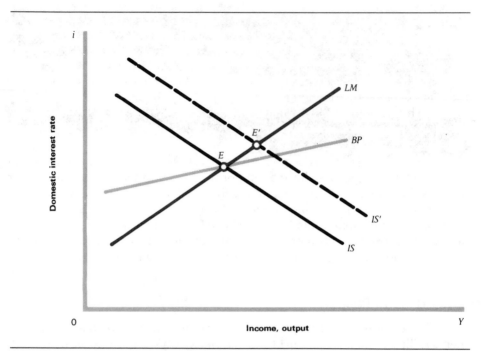

FIGURE 5-11   FISCAL POLICY AND THE BALANCE OF PAYMENTS. Expansionary fiscal policy shifts the *IS* curve up and to the right and the economy moves from *E* to *E'* where both income and the interest rate are higher. The trade account worsens since higher income increases imports, while the capital account improves since higher interest rates attract capital inflows. The net effect is an improvement since *E'* is above the *BP* schedule. This reflects the assumption that capital is highly mobile.

is below the *BP* curve so that an expansionary monetary policy leads to a balance of payments deficit. In this case, the trade account and capital account effects work in the same direction. The higher level of income causes a worsening of the trade account and the lower interest rate causes a worsening of the capital account.

Internal and External Balance

Figure 5-13 illustrates internal and external balance in an economy with capital flows. The full-employment output is shown as *Y** so that at the point *E*, we have both full employment and balance of payments equilibrium. The four quadrants represent the four possible policy problems. For example if we are at point E_1, we have deficient demand and a balance of payments deficit. The appropriate policy to produce internal and external balance requires a higher level of employment for internal balance and higher interest rates and/or a lower level of income for external balance.

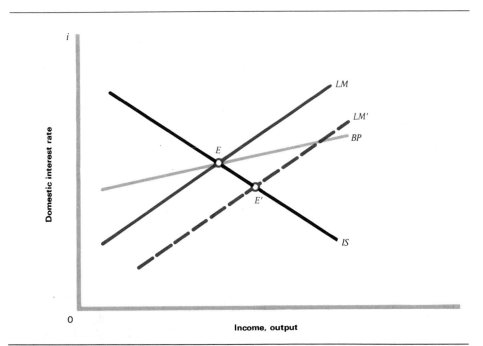

FIGURE 5-12   MONETARY POLICY AND THE BALANCE OF PAYMENTS. An increase in the money supply shifts the *LM* curve down and to the right so that income rises and the interest rate falls. The balance of payments worsens since the higher income increases imports and the lower interest rate reduces the net capital inflow.

In terms of the earlier analysis there is a policy dilemma at E_1 because employment considerations suggest income should be raised and balance of payments considerations suggest it should be reduced. However, now there is a way out of the dilemma. Suppose we reduce the money supply and thus raise interest rates. To offset the effects of the higher interest rates on income, we could use expansionary fiscal policy. Clearly, we would keep income constant and reach balance of payments equilibrium by getting interest rates high enough. However, we can do better. We can use fiscal policy to get us all the way to full employment and use tight money, in the form of higher interest rates, to achieve balance of payments equilibrium. Thus we can get to point E with both internal and external balance.[4]

[4] The idea of the policy mix for internal and external balance was suggested by Robert Mundell in his important paper. "The Appropriate Use of Monetary and Fiscal Policy under Fixed Exchange Rates," *I.M.F. Staff Papers*, March 1962. Mundell's work on international macroeconomics has been extraordinarily important, and the adventurous student should certainly consult his two books: *International Economics* (New York: Macmillan, 1967) and *Monetary Theory* (Pacific Palisades, Calif.: Goodyear, 1971).

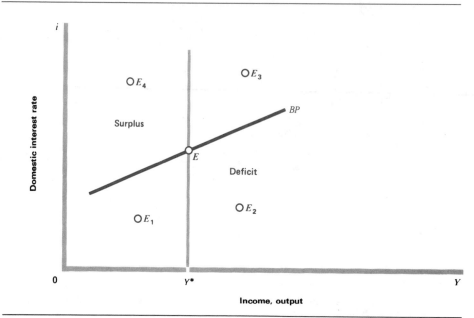

FIGURE 5-13   INTERNAL AND EXTERNAL BALANCE. The internal balance schedule is a vertical line at the full employment level of income. Along the *BP* schedule, the overall balance of payments is zero. The four quadrants represent the four possible policy problems. An appropriate combination of monetary and fiscal policy can be used to move the economy to the point *E*.

The lesson we have just derived is that under fixed exchange rates, we should expand income through fiscal policy whenever there is unemployment and use tight money whenever there is a balance of payments deficit. The combination of policies moves us to both internal and external balance. With a situation like point E_4, we want to use the same principle, but the economic conditions are different. Here we have a surplus and unemployment. Accordingly, we need expansionary fiscal policy to achieve full employment and expansionary monetary policy to reduce interest rates. Actually there is no dilemma at point E_4, since any form of expansionary policy moves us in the right direction with respect to both targets.

We leave it to you to work through the remaining cases and note here merely the principle: Under fixed exchange rates and with capital mobility, we use monetary policy to achieve external balance and fiscal policy to achieve full employment. What is the experience with such a rule? There is little doubt that tight money, for balance of payments reasons, is the oldest remedy in the policy maker's medicine chest. Since monetary policy is a flexible tool, attainment of external balance in the short run through tight money is relatively easy.

Limitations of the Policy Mix

The argument for a fiscal-monetary policy mix to handle both internal and external balance problems is persuasive, but it overlooks two important limitations. The first problem is that a country will typically not be indifferent to the level of domestic interest rates. Even if fiscal policy were sufficiently flexible to implement the policy mix, it would still be true that the composition of domestic output would depend on the mix. Thus, a country that attempts an expansion in aggregate demand, together with tight money, effectively restricts the construction sector and investment spending in general. The notion of a policy mix with monetary policy devoted to the balance of payments therefore overlooks the fact that the interest rate determines the composition as well as the level of aggregate spending.

The second consideration concerns the composition of the balance of payments. Countries are not indifferent about the makeup of their balance of payments between the current account deficit and the capital account surplus. Even if the overall balance is in equilibrium so that one target is satisfied, there is still the problem that a capital account surplus or capital inflow means net external borrowing: our country's debts to foreigners are increasing. Those debts will eventually have to be repaid.

Under a system of fixed exchange rates, there are circumstances under which a country, much like an individual, will find it useful to borrow in order to finance, say, a transitory shortfall of export earnings. But continued large-scale borrowing from abroad is not consistent with a fixed exchange rate over long periods. Large-scale borrowing eventually places the country in a position where the interest payments to foreigners become a major burden. Faced with the prospect of continued foreign borrowing on a large scale in order to maintain its fixed exchange rate, a country would be well advised to implement adjustment policies that improve the current account balance. Such policies would typically be a devaluation accompanied by restrictive monetary and/or fiscal policy to reduce domestic demand.

*5-5   BALANCE OF PAYMENTS AND MONEY SUPPLY

The analysis in the preceding sections has been based on the assumption that there is no link between the domestic money supply, and the foreign exchange market intervention that is required to maintain a fixed exchange rate when the balance of payments is not in equilibrium. However, such a link does exist since intervention involves buying and selling foreign currency in exchange for domestic currency.

Consider, for example, the foreign exchange transactions required when there is a balance of payments deficit. The central bank offsets the excess demand for foreign currency by selling foreign currency out of its reserves. It receives domestic currency in payment and thus withdraws money from circulation.[5] In general, a balance of payments deficit leads to a decline in the domestic money supply and a surplus leads to an increase in the money supply.

Sterilization

It is possible, of course, for the central bank to offset the effects of foreign exchange transactions and insulate the domestic money supply from the balance of payments. The process by which offsetting open market operations are used for this purpose is called *sterilization*.[6] For example, if the Bank of Canada sells U.S. dollars in exchange for Canadian dollars, it can prevent a reduction in the money supply by simultaneously purchasing an equal Canadian dollar amount of bonds. Thus, we can say that in the preceding sections we have assumed that the central bank breaks the link between the balance of payments and the money supply through sterilization.

The Adjustment Process without Sterilization

Suppose we assume that the central bank does not carry out sterilization operations and permits the money supply to be determined by the balance of payments surplus or deficit. How will this affect the analysis of monetary and fiscal policy carried out in Section 5-4?

Monetary Policy

We consider first the effect of an increase in the money supply as illustrated in Figure 5-12 of the previous section. The *LM* curve shifts to the right and the economy moves from E to E' where there is a balance of payments deficit. In the absence of sterilization, the money supply will fall and the *LM* curve will shift back until balance of payments equilibrium is restored at the starting point E. Thus, we conclude that in the absence of sterilization, monetary policy has no effect since the money supply is automatically determined by the balance of payments and cannot be controlled by the central bank.

Fiscal Policy

The effect of an expansionary fiscal policy is illustrated in Figure 5-14. As in Figure 5-11, the *IS* curve shifts to the right and the economy moves to E' where

---

[5] Strictly speaking, it is the *monetary base* rather than the total money supply that is affected. The change in the money supply is then determined by the multiplier process discussed in Chapter 10.

[6] *Open market operations* are purchases and sales of bonds by the central bank. The process by which these transactions affect the money supply is described in detail in Chapter 11.

there is a balance of payments surplus. In the absence of sterilization, the money supply will rise, the *LM* curve will shift to the right, and the economy will move along the adjustment path shown to the new equilibrium at *E"*. In this case the effect of fiscal policy is reinforced by the automatic adjustment of the money supply so that we get a larger increase in income than occurs with sterilization.

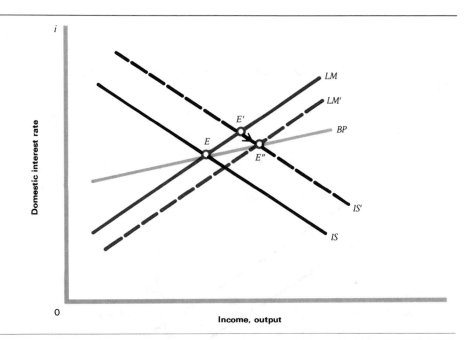

FIGURE 5-14 ADJUSTMENT TO AN EXPANSIONARY FISCAL POLICY WITHOUT STERILIZATION. An expansionary fiscal policy moves the economy to the point *E'* where there is a balance of payments surplus. As a result the money supply increases until a new equilibrium is reached at *E"*.

In general, if no sterilization operations are undertaken by the central bank, the equilibrium point is determined by the intersection of the *IS* and *BP* curves. The *LM* curve shifts automatically as the money supply changes in response to balance of payment surpluses or deficits.

Perfect Capital Mobility

We conclude this chapter with a discussion of the special case in which international capital is *perfectly mobile.* This means that there will be very large capital flows whenever the domestic interest rate deviates from the foreign rate, so that we can have balance of payments equilibrium only when the domestic rate is equal to the foreign rate. For many purposes this is a useful approximation to the Canadian case.

The assumption of perfect capital mobility leads to a considerable simplification of our model of the balance of payments. Since the domestic interest rate is constrained to be equal to the foreign rate, Equation (8), which describes the BP schedule is replaced by:

$$i = i^* \tag{8a}$$

As illustrated in Figure 5-15 the BP curve will be a horizontal line at the interest rate $i = i^*$.

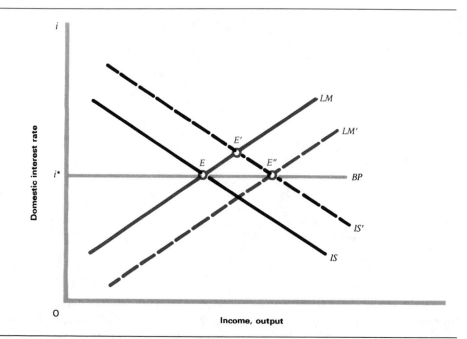

FIGURE 5-15   THE EFFECT OF FISCAL POLICY WITH PERFECT CAPITAL MOBILITY. With perfect capital mobility, the BP schedule is horizontal at the foreign interest rate. An expansionary fiscal policy moves the economy from E to E'' and has a full multiplier effect. The money supply must expand to maintain the domestic interest rate equal to the foreign rate and prevent a massive capital inflow.

The implications of this assumption are very strong. To begin with, under fixed exchange rates and perfect capital mobility, sterilization is not possible and the central bank has no control over the domestic money supply. This follows from the fact that at any point off the *BP* curve, there will be a very large capital account surplus or deficit. The central bank is forced to allow the money supply to adjust so as to maintain the domestic interest rate equal to the foreign rate, and the equilibrium must be at a point like *E* in Figure 5-15 where all three curves intersect at the same point. This will be assured by the automatic adjustment of the money supply and the *LM* curve.

Fiscal Policy with Perfect Capital Mobility

The effect of an expansionary fiscal policy is illustrated in Figure 5-15. The *IS* curve shifts to the right and intersects the *LM* curve at *E'*. However, at *E'* the economy cannot be in equilibrium since the domestic interest rate is above the foreign rate. To prevent a massive capital inflow, the money supply must expand, shifting the *LM* curve to the right until it intersects the *IS* curve at *E"*. At this point, income has increased, but the interest rate is unchanged from the initial equilibrium level.

Thus, we find that under fixed exchange rates and perfect capital mobility, there is no crowding out and fiscal policy changes have a full multiplier effect on income. The effect of an increase in government spending as shown in Figure 5-15 is exactly the same as we obtained in Figure 4-20 of the previous chapter. There we assumed, in the context of a closed economy, that the fiscal expansion was *accommodated* by a discretionary money supply increase so as to maintain a constant interest rate. In the present case, the monetary accommodation is forced on the central bank for balance of payments reasons.

5-6 SUMMARY

1. The balance of payments accounts are a record of the international transactions of the economy. The current account records trade in goods and services, as well as transfer payments. The capital account records borrowing and lending and purchases and sales of assets.

2. The overall balance of payments is the sum of the current and capital accounts. If the overall balance is in deficit, we have to make more payments to foreigners than they make to us. The foreign currency for making these payments is supplied by central banks.

3. Under fixed exchange rates, the central bank maintains constant the price of foreign currencies in terms of the domestic currency. It does this by buying and selling foreign exchange at that fixed exchange rate. For that purpose, it has to keep reserves of foreign currency.

4. Under floating or flexible exchange rates, the exchange rate may change from moment to moment. In a system of clean floating, the exchange rate is determined by supply and demand without central bank intervention to affect the rate. Under dirty floating, the central bank intervenes by buying and selling foreign exchange in an attempt to influence the exchange rate.

    The remainder of the chapter studies the role of trade in goods and capital flows under fixed exchange rates:

5. The introduction of trade in goods means that some of the demand for our output comes from abroad and that some spending by our residents is on foreign goods. There is equilibrium in the goods market when the demand for domestically produced goods is equal to the output of those goods.

6. In equilibrium, the trade account may be in deficit. If there are no capital flows, there may be a policy dilemma in that trade balance and full employment cannot be attained using monetary and fiscal policy. An expenditure switching policy, such as devaluation, is needed to change the allocation of spending between imports and domestic goods.

7. When capital flows are introduced with a high degree of capital mobility, an expansionary fiscal policy leads to an improvement in the balance of payments as a result of the effect of a higher interest rate on capital inflows. An expansionary monetary policy causes a worsening of both the trade account and the capital account.

8. Policy dilemmas can be handled by combining restrictive monetary policy, that improves the capital account through higher interest rates, with expansionary fiscal policy that increases domestic employment. However, if the balance of payments problem is not temporary then ultimately the imbalance must be dealt with by an alternative policy such as devaluation.

9. The domestic money supply can be insulated from foreign exchange transactions by sterilization operations. If there is no sterilization, then the money supply is automatically determined by the balance of payments and cannot be controlled by the central bank.

10. With perfect capital mobility, sterilization is not possible. The money supply must be allowed to adjust so as to maintain the domestic interest rate equal to the foreign rate. In this case there is no crowding out effect from changes in fiscal policy.

KEY TERMS

Fixed exchange rates	Revaluation
Flexible exchange rates	Currency depreciation
Balance of payments	Currency appreciation
Current account	Internal and external balance
Capital account	Targets and instruments of policy
Trade balance	Capital mobility
Intervention	Policy mix
Clean floating	Sterilization
Dirty (managed) floating	Perfect capital mobility
Devaluation	

PROBLEMS

1. This problem formalizes some aspects of income and trade balance deter-
    mination in the open economy. We assume, as a simplification, that the
    interest rate is given ($i = i_0$). In terms of Figures 5-3 and 5-4, the central
    bank holds the interest rate constant at i_0 so that the LM curve is effectively
    horizontal at this level. We assume aggregate demand is

    $$AD = \overline{A} + cY - hi + X - Q$$

    Import spending is given by

    $$Q = \overline{Q} + mY$$

    where $\overline{Q}$ is autonomous import spending. Exports are given and equal to

    $$X = \overline{X}$$

    (a) What is the balance of trade?
    (b) What is the equilibrium level of income?
    (c) What is the balance of trade at that equilibrium level of income?
    (d) What is the effect of an increase in exports on the equilibrium level of
        income? What is the multiplier?
    (e) What is the effect of increased exports on the trade balance?

2. Suppose that, in problem 1,

    $$\overline{A} = 400 \qquad c = 0.8 \qquad h = 30 \qquad i_0 = 5 \text{ (percent)} \qquad \overline{Q} = 0$$
    $$m = 0.2 \qquad \overline{X} = 250$$

(a) Calculate the equilibrium level of income.
(b) Calculate the balance of trade.
(c) Calculate the open economy multiplier, that is, the effect of an increase in $\overline{A}$ on equilibrium output.
(d) Assume there is a reduction in export demand of $\Delta\overline{X} = 1$ (billion). By how much does income change? By how much does the trade balance worsen?
(e) How much does a 1 percentage point increase in the interest rate (from 5 to 6 percent) improve the trade balance? Explain why the trade balance improves when the interest rate rises.
(f) What policies can the country pursue to offset the impact of reduced exports on domestic income and employment as well as on the trade balance?

3. Consider a country that is in a position of full employment and balanced trade. Which of the following types of disturbances can be remedied with standard aggregate demand tools of stabilization? Indicate in each case the impact on external and internal balance as well as the appropriate policy response.
(a) A loss of export markets
(b) A reduction in saving and corresponding increase in demand for domestic goods
(c) An increase in government spending
(d) A shift in demand from imports to domestic goods
(e) A reduction in imports with a corresponding increase in saving

4. (a) Use the formula for the foreign trade multiplier to discuss the impact on the trade balance of an increase in autonomous domestic spending.
(b) Comment on the proposition that the more open the economy, the smaller the domestic income expansion.

5. Consider an economy with capital flows that is initially in internal and external balance. (Draw the *IS*, *LM*, and *BP* schedules.) Assume there is an increase in the foreign interest rate.
(a) Show the effect on the *BP* schedule.
(b) What policy response would immediately restore internal and external balance?
(c) If the central bank did not undertake sterilization operations, what would be the adjustment process?

6. Given the existence of capital flows, what mix of monetary and fiscal policy should be pursued to offset the following disturbances?
(a) A temporary gain in exports
(b) A permanent gain in exports
(c) A decline in autonomous spending

      (d) An increased rate of capital outflow (at each level of the domestic inter-
          est rate)

  7. Suppose we have a limited degree of capital mobility so that the *BP* curve
      is steeper than the *LM* curve. What would be the effects on the following
      of an increase in government spending?
      (a) Income and the domestic interest rate
      (b) Trade balance
      (c) Capital account balance
      (d) Overall balance of payments

 *8. Reinterpret the conditions of Problem 1 as a case with perfect capital mobil-
      ity rather than a discretionary monetary policy to maintain a constant inter-
      est rate. Illustrate graphically the effect on income of an increase in exports.
      What would be the effect on the trade account and the capital account?

CHAPTER

Trade and Capital Flows Under Flexible Exchange Rates

6

The Canadian economy has operated at various times under both fixed and flexible exchange rate regimes. Figure 6-1 shows the fluctuations in the value of the Canadian dollar since 1926. Between 1926 and 1929, Canada and most other countries fixed their rates by maintaining convertibility into gold at a fixed price. A floating rate was in effect during the 1930s until the outbreak of World War II when a fixed rate of 90.5 U.S. cents was established. The Canadian dollar was revalued to 100 U.S. cents in 1946 and this rate was abandoned in 1950 in favour of a floating rate. Under the influence of market forces, our dollar soon rose above 100 U.S. cents and remained there until 1961.

After a rapid downward movement of the Canadian dollar in 1961 and early 1962, the government decided to return to a fixed rate and a value of 92.5 U.S. cents was established in May 1962. In 1970, the Canadian dollar came under strong upward pressure and a floating rate was adopted again. By 1972, the rate had risen above 100 U.S. cents and was close to 104 cents in 1974. Subsequently the value of the Canadian dollar drifted down and in early 1984 it dropped below 80 U.S. cents for the first time. After reaching a low below 70 cents, it recovered and by early 1988 it was back above 80 cents.

This chapter is concerned with macroeconomic adjustment under flexible exchange rates. We begin with the development of a model that simultaneously determines income, the interest rate and the exchange rate.[1] In the light of this theory, we then review the experience of the Canadian economy under a flexible exchange rate in the 1950s. The chapter concludes with a discussion of the role of exchange rate expectations.

---

[1] The model used here is generally known as the Mundell-Fleming model. See Robert A. Mundell "Capital Mobility and Stabilization Policy under Fixed and Flexible Exchange Rates," *Canadian Journal of Economics*, November 1963, and Marcus Fleming "Domestic Financial Policies under Fixed and under Floating Exchange Rates," International Monetary Fund *Staff Papers*, vol. 9, 1962, pp. 369–379. An up-to-date discussion can be found in Jacob Frenkel and Michael Mussa, "Asset Markets, Exchange Rates and the Balance of Payments," in R. W. Jones and P. Kenen (eds.), *Handbook of International Economics*, vol. 2 (Amsterdam, North-Holland, 1985).

FIGURE 6-1   THE CANADIAN DOLLAR, 1926–1987

(*Source*: Adapted from *Bank of Canada Review, Federal Reserve Bulletin*)

6-1   EXCHANGE RATES AND EQUILIBRIUM INCOME

Under a flexible exchange rate regime, the external value of the country's currency is determined by market forces and thus becomes a variable that is simultaneously determined along with income and interest rates. In this section we consider how the analysis of the previous chapter can be extended to the flexible rate case.

The Exchange Rate and Goods Market Equilibrium

As we indicated in our discussion of devaluation in Section 5-3, the exchange rate affects the trade balance and aggregate demand through its effect on the relative price of foreign and domestic goods. Assuming that nominal prices in the home currency are given in each country, a depreciation increases the relative price of imported goods in the home market and lowers the relative price of exports in the foreign market.

This relationship can be summarized in terms of the international competitiveness of the domestic economy. An exchange rate depreciation leads to a gain in home country competitiveness, and an appreciation leads to a loss in home country competitiveness. Thus a depreciation will cause an increase in net exports and an appreciation will cause a decrease in net exports.

As we have seen, aggregate demand for domestic goods consists of total spending by residents (including spending on imports) plus net exports. Thus the level of aggregate demand and the position of the *IS* curve depend on the exchange rate. We show in Figure 6-2 the *IS* schedule that represents goods market equilibrium, given the level of the exchange rate. What happens to the schedule if there is a depreciation?

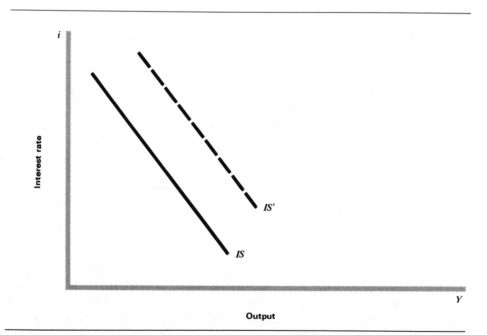

FIGURE 6-2   EFFECT OF CURRENCY DEPRECIATION ON THE *IS* CURVE. Each *IS* curve is drawn for a given exchange rate. A depreciation which makes us more competitive and thus increases aggregate demand shifts the *IS* curve to the right. The shift is larger the larger the response of the trade balance to a change in competitiveness and the larger the multiplier.

Exchange rate depreciation will improve competitiveness and increase the net export component of aggregate demand. Thus, for a given interest rate and income level, there will be excess demand for domestic goods. To restore equilibrium, output must rise or the interest rate must rise. Accordingly, in Figure

6-2 we show that a depreciation shifts the *IS* schedule up and to the right. An appreciation would, of course, lead to an excess supply of domestic goods and a shift of the schedule down and to the left.

Monetary Equilibrium and Payments Balance

The condition for money market equilibrium is the familiar *LM* schedule as shown in Figure 6-3. For the present, we draw the balance of payments equilibrium schedule under the simplifying assumption of *perfect capital mobility*. This means that there will be very large capital flows whenever the domestic interest rate deviates from the foreign rate so that we can have balance of payments equilibrium only when the domestic rate is equal to the foreign rate. This implies that the *BP* curve will be a horizontal line at the foreign interest rate.

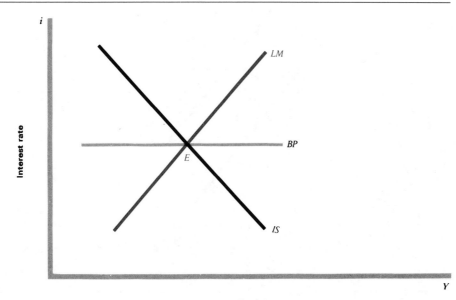

FIGURE 6-3   EQUILIBRIUM OF THE GOODS AND MONEY MARKETS AND THE BALANCE OF PAYMENTS. The *LM* schedule is familiar from the closed economy. The *IS* schedule is drawn for a given exchange rate. The schedule *BP* shows equilibrium in the balance of payments with capital flows matching trade imbalances. The schedule is horizontal in the case of perfect capital mobility where any divergence of home interest rates from those abroad leads to unlimited capital flows. Only at an interest rate $i = i^*$ can the balance of payments then be in equilibrium.

The Effect of an Increase in Exports

We have now completed the specification of our model as represented by Figure 6-3, and can ask how the economy will adjust to disturbances. The first change we look at is an exogenous increase in foreign demand for our goods, or an increase in exports.

Starting from an initial equilibrium at point E in Figure 6-4, we see that the increase in foreign demand implies an excess demand for our goods. At the initial interest rate, exchange rate, and output level, demand for our goods now exceeds the available supply. For goods market equilibrium, at the initial interest rate and exchange rate, we require a higher level of output. Accordingly, the IS schedule shifts out and to the right.

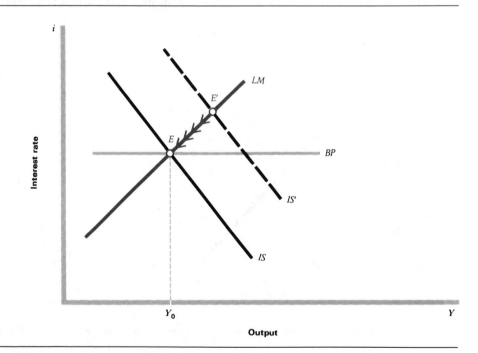

FIGURE 6-4 EFFECTS OF AN INCREASE IN THE DEMAND FOR EXPORTS. A rise in foreign demand for our goods, at the initial exchange rate and interest rate at point E, creates an excess demand for goods. The IS schedule shifts out to IS', and the new goods and money market equilibrium is at point E' where our interest rate exceeds that abroad. Capital will tend to flow into our country in response to the increased interest rate, and the resulting balance of payments surplus leads to currency appreciation. The appreciation means that we become less competitive. The IS schedule starts shifting back as a result of the appreciation, and the process continues until the initial equilibrium at E is reached again. In the end, increased exports (or a fiscal expansion) do not change output. They simply lead to currency appreciation and thereby to an offsetting change in net exports.

Now consider for a moment point E', where the goods and money markets clear. Here output has increased to meet the increased demand. The rise in income has increased money demand and thus raised equilibrium interest rates. Is point E' an equilibrium? It is not, because the balance of payments is not in equilibrium. In fact, we would not reach point E' at all. The tendency for the economy to move in that direction, as we show now, will bring about an appreciation that will take us all the way back to the initial equilibrium at E.

The Adjustment Process

Suppose, then, that the increase in foreign demand takes place and that, in response, there is a tendency for output and income to increase. The induced increase in money demand will raise interest rates and thus will bring us out of line with interest rates internationally. The resulting capital inflows immediately put pressure on the exchange rate. The capital inflow causes our currency to appreciate.

The appreciation means, of course, that import prices fall and that domestic goods become relatively more expensive. Demand shifts away from domestic goods, and net exports decline. In terms of Figure 6-4, the appreciation implies that the IS schedule shifts back from IS' to the left. Next, we have to ask how far the appreciation will go and to what extent it will therefore dampen the expansionary effect of increased net exports.

The currency will keep appreciating as long as our interest rate exceeds the world level. This implies that the appreciation must continue until the IS schedule has shifted back all the way to its initial position. Thus adjustment is shown by the arrows along the LM schedule. Only when we return to point E will output and income have reached a level consistent with monetary equilibrium at the world rate of interest.

We have now shown that under conditions of perfect capital mobility, an expansion in exports has no lasting effect on equilibrium output. With perfect capital mobility the tendency for interest rates to rise, as a result of the increase in export demand, leads to currency appreciation and thus to a complete offset of the increase in exports. Once we return to point E, net exports are back to their initial level. Imports will increase as a consequence of the appreciation, and the initial expansion in exports is in part offset by the appreciation of our currency.

Fiscal Policy

We can extend the usefulness of this analysis by recognizing that it is valid not only for an increase in exports. The same analysis applies to a fiscal expansion. A tax cut or an increase in government spending would lead to an expansion in demand in just the same way as increased exports do. Again, the tendency for interest rates to rise leads to appreciation and therefore to a fall in exports and increased imports. There is, accordingly, complete crowding out here. The crowding out takes place not as in Chapter 4 because higher interest rates reduce investment, but because the appreciation reduces competitiveness and causes a decline in net exports.

BOX 6-1 FISCAL POLICY AND EXCHANGE RATES IN THE 1980s

In the early 1980s the U.S. dollar appreciated massively in world markets. A ready explanation is given by the fiscal policies in the United States and other countries. As can be seen in Table 1 below, the U.S. budget surplus declined while the opposite occurred in Germany and Japan. The model used in this chapter implies that as a result the U.S. dollar should have appreciated causing the U.S. current account to worsen. This is of course exactly what happened.

TABLE 1 CHANGE IN BUDGET AND CURRENT ACCOUNT SURPLUSES (% of GNP or GDP), 1980–85

	Budget Surplus	Current Account
United States	−2.1	−3.0
Germany	1.8	4.0
Japan	3.2	4.7
Canada	−4.2	
Other than U.S.		−4.2
U.S.		4.3

The budget surplus in Canada declined even more, relative to GDP, than in the U.S. and there was an appreciation of the Canadian dollar against the major currencies other than the U.S. dollar. However, since the U.S. deficit was much

TABLE 2 RATES OF APPRECIATION, 1980–85

| Against: | Appreciation of: | |
	U.S. Dollar	Canadian Dollar
Canada	16.8%	
Other Group of 10 countries	49.6%	20.7%

Source: Dept. of Finance, *Quarterly Economic Review*, Annual Reference Tables.

larger in dollar terms, there was an appreciation of the U.S. dollar against the Canadian dollar. There was little change in our total current account, but there was an increase in our surplus with the U.S. and an increase in our deficit with our other trading partners.

In mid-1985 the value of the U.S. dollar reached a peak and a substantial depreciation followed. This episode illustrated an important limitation of our analysis. An equilibrium with a large current account deficit financed by capital inflow can be sustained only as long as foreigners are willing to accumulate claims against the deficit country. This borrowing from, and sale of assets to, foreigners worsens the current account deficit since it increases the outflow of dividends and interest. As investors lost confidence in the ability to the U.S. to deal with its balance of payments problem, they became unwilling to expose themselves to the risk of holding U.S. dollars and suffering losses in the event of a depreciation. As a result the demand for U.S. assets fell and a depreciation occurred.

The important lesson here is that disturbances to the goods market do not affect equilibrium income under flexible rates with perfect capital mobility. This is in contrast to the effect of a fiscal expansion under fixed rates. In section 5-5, we showed that with fixed exchange rate and perfect capital mobility, there is no crowding out and fiscal policy changes have a full multiplier effect on income. With a flexible rate, fiscal policy has no effect on income. Instead, it merely causes an offsetting loss of competitiveness and a shift in the composition of spending towards domestic goods and away from net exports.

Adjustment to a Monetary Disturbance

We now show that under flexible exchange rates, an increase in the money stock leads to an increase in income and a depreciation of the currency. The analysis uses Figure 6-5. We start from an initial position at point E and consider an increase in the nominal quantity of money, M. Since prices are given, we have an increase in the real money stock, M/P. At E there will be an excess supply of real balances. To restore equilibrium, interest rates would have to be lower or income would have to be larger. Accordingly, the LM schedule shifts down and to the right to LM'.

We ask once again whether point E' is the new equilibrium. At E', goods and money markets are in equilibrium (at the initial exchange rate), but it is clear that interest rates have fallen below the foreign level. Capital outflows will therefore put pressure on the exchange rate. The depreciation caused by the low level of interest rates implies that import prices increase, domestic goods become more competitive and, as a result, demand for our output expands.

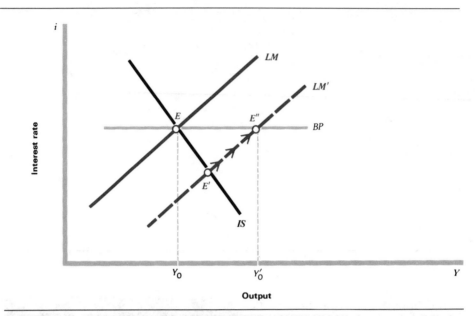

FIGURE 6-5 EFFECTS OF AN INCREASE IN THE MONEY STOCK. A monetary expansion shifts the *LM* schedule to *LM'*. At point *E'* the goods and money markets clear, but our interest rate is below the world level. Therefore capital will tend to flow out, the balance of payments goes into deficit, and the currency depreciates. The depreciation means that we become more competitive. Net exports rise, and therefore the *IS* curve shifts out and to the right. The process continues until we reach point *E''*. Interest rates are again at the foreign level, and the depreciation has led to a higher level of income. Monetary policy thus works by increasing net exports.

The depreciation therefore shifts the *IS* curve out and to the right. As the arrows indicate, depreciation continues until the relative price of domestic goods has fallen enough to raise demand and output to the level indicated by point *E''*. Only at *E''* do we have goods and money market equilibrium compatible with the foreign rate of interest. Consequently, there is no further tendency for exchange rates and relative prices, and hence demand, to change.[2]

We have now shown that a monetary expansion leads to an increase in output and a depreciation of the currency under flexible rates. The depreciation raises net exports, and that increase in net exports, in turn, sustains the higher level of output and employment. One interesting implication of our analysis, then, is the proposition that monetary expansion improves the current account through the induced depreciation.

[2] In Problem 8 at the end of this chapter, we ask you to show that the current account improves between *E* and *E''*, even though the increased level of income increases imports.

How do our results compare with those of the fixed exchange rate case? We argued in Section 5-5 that under fixed rates and perfect capital mobility, the central bank cannot control the money supply. An attempt to expand the money supply will merely lead to a reserve loss as the central bank attempts to prevent a depreciation on the currency in response to declining interest rates. Under flexible rates, by contrast, there is no intervention and the money supply increase is not reversed through foreign exchange transactions.

The fact that the central bank *can* control the money stock under flexible exchange rates is one of the most important aspects of the flexible rate system. As we shall see, it has important implications for the ability of the Bank of Canada to carry out an independent monetary policy. Under a fixed exchange rate the money supply in Canada is largely determined by monetary policy in other countries, particularly the United States.

Beggar-Thy-Neighbour Policy and Competitive Depreciation

It is useful to extend our analysis to a brief discussion of the international implications of currency depreciation and changes in net exports. We showed that a monetary expansion in the home country leads to depreciation, an increase in net exports, and therefore an increase in output and employment. However, our increased net exports correspond to a deterioration in the trade balance abroad. The domestic depreciation shifts demand from foreign goods toward domestic goods. Abroad, output and employment therefore decline. It is for this reason that the depreciation-induced change in the trade balance has been called a *beggar-thy-neighbour policy* — it is a way of exporting unemployment or of creating domestic employment at the expense of the rest of the world.

The recognition that exchange depreciation is mainly a way of shifting demand from one country to another, rather than changing the level of world demand, is important. It implies that exchange rate adjustment can be a useful policy when countries find themselves in different stages of a business cycle — for example, one in a boom (with overemployment) and the other in a recession. In that event, a depreciation by the country experiencing a recession would shift world demand in that direction and thus work to reduce divergences from full employment in each country.

By contrast, when countries' business cycles are highly synchronized, such as in the 1930s or in the aftermath of the oil shock in 1973, exchange rate movements will not contribute much toward world full employment. The problem is then one of the level of total world spending being deficient or excessive while exchange rate movements affect only the allocation of a *given* world demand between countries. Nevertheless, from the point of view of an individual country, currency depreciation works to attract world demand and raise domestic output. If every country tried to depreciate to attract world demand, we would have *competitive depreciation* and a shifting around of world demand.

rather than an increase in the world level of spending. Coordinated monetary and/or fiscal policies are needed to increase demand and output in each country.

* Imperfect Capital Mobility

In Chapter 5, we considered the effects of monetary and fiscal policy under fixed exchange rates in the more general model in which capital is not perfectly mobile. In this case, the rate of capital flow increases as the interest differential increases, but at a finite rate, so that there can be equilibrium with the domestic rate different from the foreign rate.

How would policy work with flexible exchange rates and imperfect capital mobility? We leave as an exercise at the end of the chapter the demonstration of the following results: First, a fiscal expansion at home raises our interest rate and increases our income. With the higher interest rate, there will be an increased inflow of capital. This implies a deterioration in the current account, since the sum of the current and capital accounts is zero. However, the current account deteriorates by less than the fiscal expansion. There is less than full crowding out, and hence, income rises.

In the case of a monetary expansion, our interest rate falls, income rises, and the current account must improve. We know that the current account must improve since the lower interest rate implies increased capital outflows which, for payments to balance, must be offset by an improvement in the current account.

The case of imperfect capital mobility clearly qualifies our earlier results. Now both monetary and fiscal policies are effective and the extent to which fiscal policy can affect income depends on the extent to which changes in interest differentials affect capital flows.

Summary

An examination of goods market and monetary disturbances under flexible exchange rates, and perfect capital mobility gave us the following results, summarized in Table 6-1.

1. A fiscal expansion leaves output unchanged. The fiscal expansion tends to increase income and raise interest rates. The tendency for interest rates to rise leads to appreciation of the exchange rate as capital is attracted from abroad. The appreciation, by lowering import prices, shifts demand away from our goods and thus offsets the expansionary effect of fiscal policy.

2. This result is the opposite of that derived under fixed exchange rates. The difference results from the fact that under flexible rates, the money stock is exogenous and is kept fixed when fiscal policy changes, while under

TABLE 6-1   THE EFFECTS OF MONETARY AND FISCAL POLICY UNDER PERFECT CAPITAL MOBILITY

	FIXED RATES	FLEXIBLE RATES
MONETARY EXPANSION	No output change; reserve losses equal to money increase	Output expansion; trade balance improves; currency depreciation
FISCAL EXPANSION	Output expansion; trade balance worsens	No output change; reduced net exports; currency appreciation

fixed rates, exchange rate stabilization makes money endogenous and thus accommodates the fiscal expansion.

3.   For a monetary expansion, conclusions were also opposite to those for fixed rates. A monetary expansion leads to an increase in income and to exchange depreciation. The tendency for interest rates to fall as a consequence of monetary expansion leads to a capital outflow that causes the exchange rate to depreciate and thereby to raise demand for domestic output.

4.   In the case of a fiscal expansion, the induced appreciation of the exchange rate leads to a reduction in net exports, offsetting the increased domestic spending. With a monetary expansion, the depreciation that ensues leads to an improvement in net exports. The trade balance effects of the two policies are thus quite different.

5.   With imperfect capital mobility, interest rates can differ internationally, and both monetary and fiscal policies can affect the level of output.

6-2   CANADIAN EXPERIENCE WITH FLEXIBLE EXCHANGE RATES IN THE 1950s

Since World War II, Canada has operated under both fixed and flexible exchange rate regimes. A flexible rate was in effect from 1950 to mid-1962 and from mid-1970 to the present. In this section we examine the performance of the Canadian economy in the earlier period. A discussion of the more recent experience is postponed to Chapter 18 after we have introduced inflation into our analysis.

Figure 6-6 shows the performance of the Canadian economy over the period 1953–1961. There was a sharp but brief recession in 1954 followed by an investment boom in 1955 and 1956, which resulted in rapid growth in GNP and a decline in the unemployment rate below 4 percent. In 1957 the growth rate slowed and the unemployment rate rose sharply. The entire period from 1957 to 1961 was characterized by slow growth and relatively high unemployment.

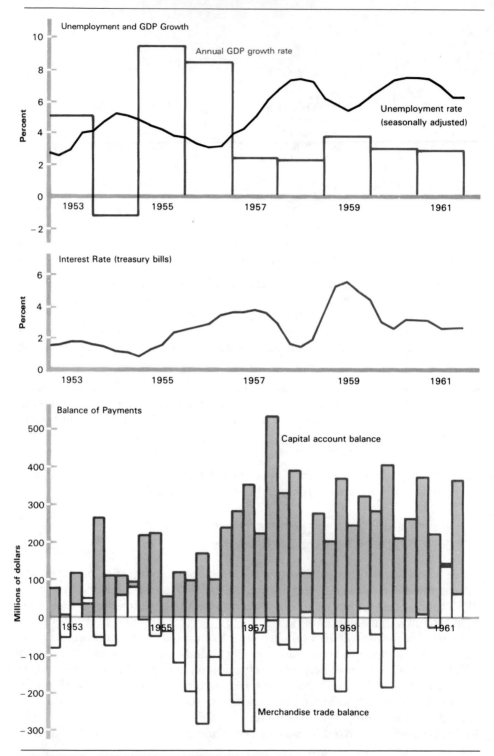

FIGURE 6-6   THE CANADIAN ECONOMY, 1953–1961

(*Source*: Adapted from Department of Finance, *Economic Review*; Statistics Canada, 11-206)

The Natural Resource Boom of the Mid-1950s

During the mid-1950s Canada experienced boom conditions fueled by high world demand for natural resources. Further, the attractive investment opportunities that existed in Canada attracted large capital inflows. As can be seen in Figure 6-1, the effect of the capital account surplus was to push up the value of the Canadian dollar which remained above 100 U.S. cents and at times rose as high as 105 U.S. cents. This in turn had the effect of reducing exports and increasing imports so that there were deficits in merchandise trade.

This appreciation of the Canadian dollar acted as a stabilizer and had a desirable dampening effect on aggregate demand. The economy was subject to expansionary disturbances as represented by the outward shift in the IS schedule shown in Figure 6-4. At the point E' we have a balance of payments surplus which causes an appreciation and a movement of the IS back to E.

The question that remains is why did the Canadian economy go through a prolonged period of slow growth and high unemployment during the years 1957 to 1961? We now turn to a detailed examination of that period.

The Slow Growth Period, 1957–1961

During 1957 the Canadian economy weakened and the unemployment rate rose, subsequently reaching a peak of 7.9 percent in mid-1958. There was an effort to stimulate the economy in 1958 and 1959 through expansionary fiscal policy and the cyclically adjusted federal budget balance moved into a deficit position. However, as we have seen, we would not expect fiscal policy to have a lasting effect on income under a flexible exchange rate. An increase in the government deficit leads to a crowding out of private demand in the form of net exports. Clearly, it is necessary for a country with a flexible exchange rate to use monetary policy for stabilization purposes.

How was monetary policy used in this period? During 1958, the money supply was expanded at a rapid rate, but this policy was reversed in 1959 and 1960. During these two years there was virtually no growth in the money supply and as a result interest rates rose sharply in 1959 and remained relatively high until mid-1961. Thus, the period 1959 to 1961 was characterized by a very restrictive monetary policy in spite of a clear need for economic stimulus.

A review of statements by the Bank of Canada during this period suggests that the restrictive monetary policy being followed was based on two major concerns. First, rising inflation was seen as an important threat to the Canadian economy even after 1957 when it was clear that a recession had taken hold. Second, the Governor placed great emphasis on what he regarded as the unsatisfactory state of Canada's balance of payments. In his *Annual Report* for 1959 (pp. 7–8) he stated:

> For some years, as I see it, the Canadian economy has been under the influence of excessive overall spending, which even in periods of relatively high unemployment resulted in a net inflow of imports from other countries. . . . The

attempt to accomplish too much too fast has given rise to huge deficits in our international balance of payments on current account, . . . to a large and growing volume of foreign debt, . . . and has gone hand-in-hand with a growing degree of foreign predominance in Canadian business.

Continuing this theme in his *Annual Report* for 1960 (p. 22), he concluded that:

> . . . to engage in further large over-all monetary expansion in an attempt to drive down interest rates generally, with or without the motive of thereby reducing the inflow of capital from abroad, is an unsound and dangerous approach. . . .

It appears that the Bank of Canada's prescription for these supposed ills was to maintain high interest rates so as to reduce imports by curtailing overall aggregate demand, and to reduce the capital inflows by encouraging domestic saving. In retrospect, it is clear that this policy was at odds with the theory of an open economy under a flexible exchange rate.

Consider Figure 6-7 in which the point *E* is assumed to represent equilibrium at the full-employment level of output. The adoption of restrictive monetary policy means the *LM* schedule shifts up and to the left to *LM'*. At *E'*, output is below the initial (full-employment) level and the domestic interest rate is above the foreign rate. The higher interest rate induces a capital account surplus and

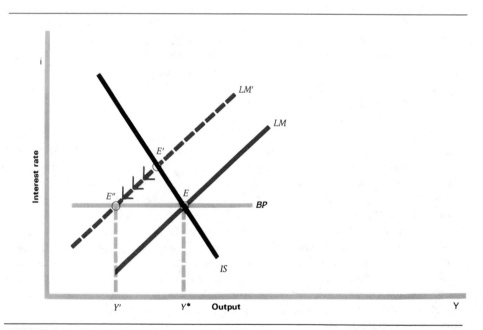

FIGURE 6-7   EFFECTS OF A RESTRICTIVE MONETARY POLICY. The adjustment process is the same as that shown in Figure 6-5 except that in this case we have a decrease in the money supply.

an appreciation of the Canadian dollar. As a result, the trade account moves toward a deficit position so that the IS curve shifts in and to the left and the economy moves toward E''. This adjustment process is quite consistent with the observed behaviour of the Canadian economy over the period 1959 to 1961.

Thus we conclude that mistakes in monetary policy were a major cause of the stagnation of the Canadian economy in the late fifties and early sixties. There was indeed considerable controversy at the time, and in 1960, a group of academic economists called upon the Minister of Finance to dismiss the Governor of the Bank of Canada. Subsequently, there was an acrimonious confrontation between the Minister and the Governor, and the latter finally resigned in July of 1961.[3]

*6-3 EXCHANGE RATE EXPECTATIONS AND THE INTEREST PARITY CONDITION

A cornerstone of our theoretical model of exchange rate determination in Section 6-1 was international capital mobility. In particular, we assumed that capital markets were highly integrated so that interest rates would be equalized across the countries. How does this assumption stand up to the facts?

In Figure 6-8, we show Canadian and U.S. interest rates on 90-day paper. These rates follow a similar pattern over time but they are by no means equalized. Exchange rate expectations provide the key to squaring this fact with our theory.

Exchange Rate Expectations

The theory that implies international equalization of interest rates is incomplete in a world where exchange rates frequently do and are expected to change. For example, consider a situation where the German mark is expected to appreciate by 5 percent over the next year relative to the Canadian dollar. Suppose the interest rate in Germany is 6 percent. Then anyone buying German bonds will earn a return in marks of 6 percent. Suppose now that the Canadian interest rate is 10 percent. A German investing in Canada for a year will, at the beginning of the year, exchange his marks for dollars, and then earn 10 percent on his dollars. At the end of the year, he will want to change his dollars back into marks to spend in Germany. However, he expects that by the end of the year, each dollar will be worth 5 percent less in terms of marks, as a result of the expected depreciation. Therefore, in terms of marks, he will expect to earn only

---

[3] See H. Scott Gordon, *The Economists Versus the Bank of Canada* (Toronto: The Ryerson Press, 1961).

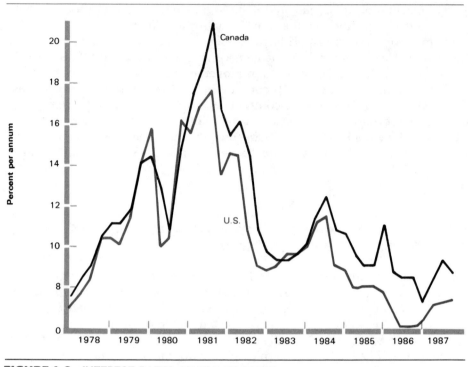

FIGURE 6-8 INTEREST RATES ON 90-DAY PAPER

(*Source:* Adapted from *Bank of Canada Review*)

5 percent (10 percent minus 5 percent) by investing in Canadian bonds, whereas he earns 6 percent by investing in German bonds. He will naturally prefer to invest in German bonds.[4]

It is clear, therefore, that we must extend our discussion of interest rate equalization to incorporate expectations of exchange rate changes. Table 6-2 gives some combinations of the domestic interest rate, the foreign interest rate, and exchange rate changes. Suppose we want to know the return, in terms of domestic currency, of investments here compared with those abroad. For domestic investments we just look at our interest rate. For foreign investments, we look at the foreign rate, *and* at the exchange depreciation. Suppose foreign interest rates were 5 percent and exchange rates did not change. In Table 6-2 this is the

---

[4] You should confirm that a Canadian who expects the dollar to depreciate by 5 percent would, given the 6 percent and 10 percent interest rates, also prefer to buy German bonds.

TABLE 6-2   INTEREST RATES AND CURRENCY DEPRECIATION
(in percentages)

	Domestic interest rate (1)	Foreign interest rate (2)	Depreciation (3)	Adjusted interest differential (1) − (2) − (3)
1.	10	5	0	5
2.	10	15	−5	0
3.	10	15	−2	−3
4.	10	15	−10	5

case of row 1, and the *adjusted* interest differential is 5 percent in favour of the home country. Row 2 considers the case where interest rates abroad are high (15 percent), but where our currency appreciates at the rate of 5 percent or the foreign currency depreciates by that amount. Here the depreciation exactly offsets the higher foreign interest rates and the adjusted differential is zero — what would be gained in interest is lost through the foreign depreciation. Cases 3 and 4 show circumstances where the foreign depreciation falls short of, and exceeds, the interest differential, respectively. Clearly, in cases 1 and 4, we would want to invest in the home country; in case 2 we are indifferent; and case 3 favours the foreign country.

The trouble, of course, is that we do not know ahead of time how the exchange rate will move. We know the interest rates on, say, three-month treasury bills in Canada and the United Kingdom, so that we can compute the interest differential, but we do not know whether the pound will appreciate or depreciate over the next three months. Even if we somehow knew the direction, we would certainly not know the precise amount.

Investors then have to form *expectations* about the behaviour of the exchange rate; that is, in deciding whether to invest a home or abroad, they have to make forecasts of the future behaviour of the exchange rate. Given these forecasts, we would expect that in a world of high capital mobility, the interest differentials, adjusted for expected depreciation, should be negligible. That means that a country that is certain to depreciate will have interest rates above the world level, and conversely, a country that is expected to appreciate will have interest rates below the world level.

The Interest Parity Condition

The introduction of exchange rate expectations modifies our condition for balance of payments equilibrium. We maintain the assumption of perfect capital mobility, but replace the condition that the domestic rate i is equal to the foreign rate i^* with

$$i = i^* + x \tag{1}$$

where x is the expected rate of depreciation of the domestic currency. This condition is called the *interest parity condition*.

Using this equation to describe the balance of payments equilibrium implies that the *BP* schedule will still be horizontal but its position will depend on exchange rate expectations. This implies that speculative capital flows related to expectations of changes in exchange rates will have macroeconomic consequences. In Figure 6-9, the *BP* schedule is drawn for a given foreign interest rate and a given expected rate of depreciation, say, zero. Suppose that we start in full equilibrium at point E and that the market develops the expectation that the home currency will appreciate. This implies that even with a lower home

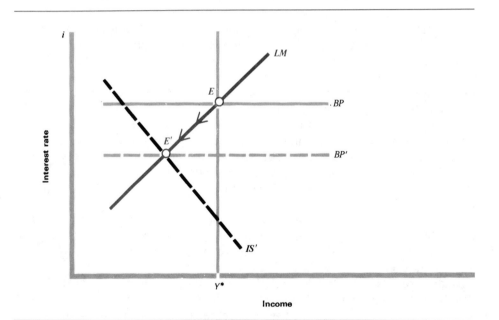

FIGURE 6-9   RESPONSE TO AN EXPECTED APPRECIATION OF THE CURRENCY. The initial equilibrium at E is disturbed by the expectation that the home currency will appreciate. The *BP* schedule shifts down to *BP'*, reflecting the fact that people are willing to hold domestic assets at a reduced interest rate since they are compensated for the differential by anticipated appreciation. At E' there is now a capital inflow that leads to currency appreciation. The *IS* schedule (not drawn) shifts to *IS'*, and the economy moves into a recession. The capital inflow has brought about a loss of trade competitiveness and thus unemployment at point E'.

interest rate, domestic assets are attractive, and so the BP schedule shifts down by the amount of expected appreciation.

Point E is no longer an equilibrium, given the shift of the BP schedule to BP', but rather a position of surplus with large-scale capital inflows motivated by the anticipation of appreciation. (This might well describe the case of the United Kingdom after awareness of British oil discoveries spread in the market.) The surplus causes the exchange rate to start appreciating, and we move in a southwesterly direction, as indicated by the arrow. The speculative attack causes appreciation, a loss in competitiveness, and, consequently, falling output and employment.

This analysis confirms that exchange rate expectations, through their impact on capital flows and thus on actual exchange rates, are a potential source of disturbance to macroeconomic equilibrium.

Exchange Rate Overshooting

The interest parity condition also has important implications for the adjustment process in response to monetary changes. Consider the adjustment path shown in Figure 6-5. It is drawn under our usual assumption that the money market adjusts instantaneously so that the adjustment path is along the LM curve from E' to E''. Along this path, the currency is depreciating while the domestic interest rate is below the foreign rate. However, to the extent that this depreciation is anticipated, the interest parity condition is violated since we have $x > 0$ and $i - i^* < 0$.

Figures 6-10 and 6-11 illustrate an adjustment process that is consistent with the interest parity condition. Figure 6-11 shows the time paths of the money supply, the exchange rate and income. Note that the exchange rate is measured by the domestic currency price of foreign exchange so that a depreciation is shown as an increase.

When the money supply is increased at time T_0, there is an immediate depreciation and a fall in the domestic interest rate. As shown in Figure 6-11 this depreciation *overshoots* the final equilibrium value. Thereafter, the domestic currency *appreciates* towards its new equilibrium. Meanwhile in Figure 6-10, the economy moves initially to E'. At this point, the interest parity condition holds since we have $i - i^* < 0$ and $x < 0$ (i.e., investors anticipate an appreciation). As we move towards the new equilibrium, income increases in response to the initial improvement in competitiveness, the currency appreciates, and the interest rate rises back to the level of the foreign rate.

At the new equilibrium, income is higher, the domestic interest rate is unchanged, and the currency has depreciated. However, the exchange rate overshoots the new equilibrium level since, in response to the disturbance, it initially moves beyond the equilibrium it ultimately will reach and then gradually returns to the new equilibrium. Overshooting means that changes in monetary policy produce large changes in exchange rates.

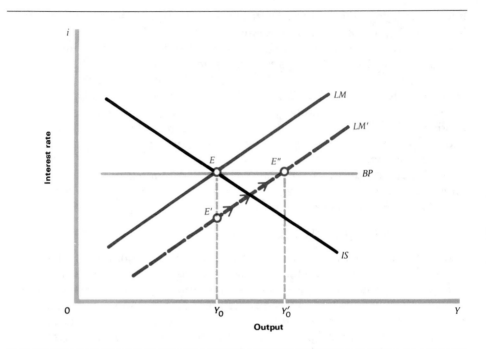

FIGURE 6-10   INTEREST PARITY AND THE ADJUSTMENT TO AN INCREASE IN MONEY. When the money supply is increased, the economy initially moves to E' where $i < i^*$ and investors anticipate an appreciation of the currency. As we move to E'', income increases, the currency appreciates, and i rises back to the level of i^*.

6-4   SUMMARY

1.   Under flexible exchange rates, without government intervention, the exchange rate adjusts to ensure equilibrium in the overall balance of payments. The sum of the current and capital account deficits is zero with floating rates and no intervention.

2.   The demand for our goods depends on the exchange rate which, given foreign and domestic prices, affects the relative price of imports versus exports. An increase in the exchange rate—a depreciation—increases the demand for domestically produced goods by reducing imports and increasing exports.

3.   When capital is perfectly mobile, so that the interest rate essentially cannot differ from the foreign rate, fiscal policy becomes totally ineffective in changing the level of income. An increase in government spending merely

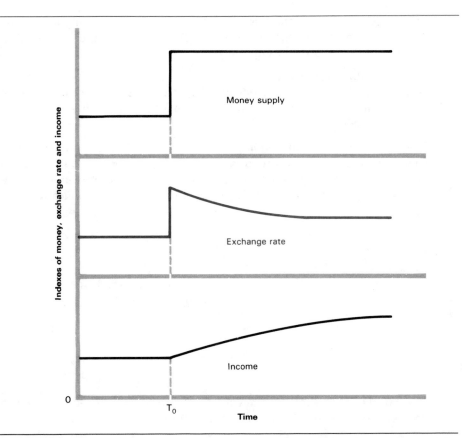

FIGURE 6-11 EXCHANGE RATE OVERSHOOTING. The diagram shows indexes of the money supply, exchange rate and income to illustrate the time paths corresponding to the adjustment process shown in Figure 6-10. An increase in the money stock at time T_0 causes an immediate depreciation. The gain in competitiveness leads to an increase in income over time while the currency appreciates, partially reversing the initial overshooting.

reduces net exports, with the trade deficit being matched by a capital inflow.

4. Monetary policy retains its effectiveness when capital is very mobile. An increase in the money stock leads to a depreciation of the exchange rate and an improved trade balance, which increases demand for domestic output.

5. If an economy finds itself with unemployment, the central bank can intervene to depreciate the exchange rate and increase net exports and thus

aggregate demand. Such policies are known as beggar-thy-neighbour policies, because the increase in demand for domestic output comes at the expense of demand for foreign output.

6. When exchange rate expectations are taken into account, balance of payments equilibrium is described by the interest parity condition which equates the domestic interest rate with the foreign rate plus the expected rate of depreciation.

7. The interest parity condition implies that there will be exchange rate overshooting in response to a change in the money supply. An increase in money causes a depreciation beyond the final equilibrium value followed by an appreciation along an adjustment path to the new equilibrium.

KEY TERMS

Competitiveness
Perfect capital mobility
Beggar-thy-neighbour policy

Interest parity condition
Exchange rate overshooting

PROBLEMS

1. Explain why the belief that a devaluation is imminent makes a devaluation more likely in a fixed exchange rate system.

2. Explain why an expansionary fiscal policy "beggars our neighbours" less than direct intervention by the central bank in the foreign exchange markets to depreciate the currency.

3. Assume that capital is perfectly mobile, the price level is fixed, and the exchange rate is flexible. Now let the government increase expenditure. Explain first why the equilibrium levels of output and the interest rate are unaffected. Then show whether the current account improves or worsens as a result of the increased government expenditure on goods and services.

4. Assume that there is perfect mobility of capital. How does the imposition of a tariff affect the exchange rate, output, and the current account? (*Hint:* Given the exchange rate, the tariff reduces our demand for imports.)

5. Explain how and why monetary policy retains its effectiveness when there is perfect mobility of capital.

6. Consult *The Globe and Mail* or some other newspaper which has foreign exchange rates listed in its financial pages. For some countries, such as Britain and the United States, you should find future prices listed. This is the price to be paid today to receive one unit of the foreign currency in the future. A 30-day future price for the pound sterling, say, is the price paid today to receive £1 30 days from now. Explain why the future prices are not generally equal to the spot prices—the price paid today to receive the foreign currency today.

7. Assume you expect the pound to depreciate by 6 percent over the next year. Assume that the Canadian interest rate is 8 percent. What interest rate would be needed on pound securities, such as government bonds, for you to be willing to buy those securities with your dollars today, and then sell them in a year in exchange for dollars? Can you relate your answer to this question to your answer to problem 6?

8. This problem deals with the current account effect of an expansion in the money stock, given prices, perfect capital mobility, and flexible exchange rates.
    (a) Given the interest rate i^*, the real money stock M/P, and the money market equilibrium condition

    $$\frac{M}{P} = kY - hi$$

    solve for the equilibrium level of income Y_0 that is compatible with monetary equilibrium.
    (b) Consider next the goods market equilibrium condition:

    $$Y = A(Y,i) + NX$$

    Let $A = \overline{A} + cY - bi$. Substitute for $i = i^*$ and the equilibrium level of income from (a). What is the equilibrium value of the trade balance NX?

9. Assume capital is imperfectly mobile, so that the higher the interest rate at home, the higher the rate of capital inflow, but that the flows remain finite. Then we can write the balance of payments as

    $$BP = NX(e, Y) + CF(i - i^*)$$

    where CF denotes the net rate of capital inflow, i^* is the given foreign interest rate, and e is the exchange rate.

(a) Suppose the exchange rate adjusts to maintain payments equilibrium. Then $BP = 0$, and the current account surplus equals the capital account deficit:

$$NX(e, Y) = -CF(i - i^*)$$

Suppose the goods market is *also* in equilibrium, so that

$$Y = A(i, Y) + NX(Y, e)$$

Substituting for the current account in the goods market equilibrium condition yields

$$Y = A(i, Y) - CF(i - i^*)$$

Show this equation graphically in i, Y space and interpret it.
(b) Also draw an LM schedule in the same space and interpret the intersection point.
(c) Show now the effect of a fiscal expansion in the home country on interest rates, income, and the current account.
(d) Show the effect of a monetary expansion on income, interest rates, and the current account.

10. This problem draws on the discussion of stabilization policy and beggar-thy-neighbour policy in Section 6-1. Suppose we have two countries with full-employment output levels $\bar{Y}$ and $\bar{Y}^*$ at home and abroad, respectively.
(a) Draw a diagram with actual output levels, Y and Y^*, on the axes. Draw also lines corresponding to potential output levels. Label the resulting four quandrants, I, II, III, and IV.
(b) Identify for each of the quadrants the state of demand in each country as boom or recession.
(c) Which policies can be pursued when output exceeds potential in each country? When output exceeds potential in one but falls short of potential in another?
(d) In which quadrants are beggar-thy-neighbour policies particularly dangerous? Where is coordination of policies essential?

CHAPTER 7

Aggregate Supply and Demand:
An Introduction

So far our analysis has assumed that the price level is fixed. We studied the impacts of changes in the money supply, or of taxes, or of government spending, assuming that whatever amount of goods was demanded would be supplied *at the existing price* level.

To put the same point in different words, we have not yet analyzed *inflation*, but of course inflation is one of the major concerns of citizens, policy makers, and macroeconomists. The time therefore has come to bring the price level and inflation rate — the rate of change of the price level — into our analysis of the economy. We have to study the determination of both the level of output — on which we have concentrated so far — and the price level. In this chapter, we confine our discussion to an economy without international trade or capital flows. The open economy case is taken up again in Chapter 19.

Figure 7-1 shows the model of *aggregate demand and supply* that we shall use to study the joint determination of the price level and the level of output. The aggregate demand curve *AD*, which is downward-sloping, is based entirely on the material of the earlier chapters, in particular Chapter 4. We define the aggregate demand curve in this chapter, and show why it slopes downward and what causes it to shift. The aggregate supply curve will be introduced in this chapter and developed further in Chapter 14. The intersection of the *AD* and *AS* schedules at *E* determines the equilibrium level of output, Y_0, and the equilibrium price level, P_0. Shifts in either schedule cause the price level and the level of output to change.

The aggregate demand-supply model is the basic macroeconomic model for studying output and price level determination — just as in microeconomics, demand and supply curves are the essential tools for studying output and price

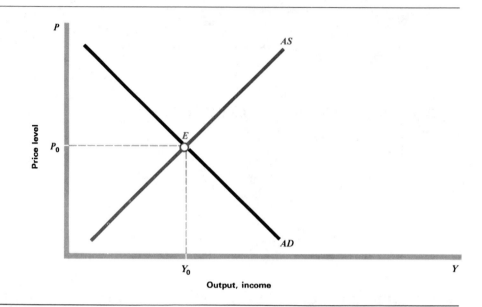

FIGURE 7-1 AGGREGATE SUPPLY AND DEMAND. The diagram shows the complete model of aggregate demand and supply that is used to explain the joint determination of the levels of output and prices. The aggregate demand curve, *AD*, is based on the *IS-LM* model studied in earlier chapters. The aggregate supply curve *AS* is developed in this chapter and Chapter 14. Their intersection at point *E* determines the level of output Y_0 and the price level P_0.

determination in a single market. However, the aggregate demand and supply curves are not as simple as the microeconomic demand and supply curves. There is more going on in the background of the aggregate curves than there is in that of the microeconomic curves.[1]

7-1 INTRODUCING AGGREGATE DEMAND AND SUPPLY

Before we go deeply into the factors underlying the aggregate demand and supply curves, we show how the curves will be used. Suppose that the money

[1] The aggregate demand curve is sometimes referred to as the *macroeconomic demand curve*, both to emphasize that it is different from a regular demand curve in microeconomics and to distinguish it from the aggregate demand schedule in Chapter 3. We stay with the same name, *AD*, here after warning that the present *AD* schedule represents a considerable extension of that in Chapter 3 since it makes interest rates endogenous along the curve.

supply is increased. What effects will that have on the price level and output? In particular, does an increase in the money supply cause the price level to rise, thus producing inflation? Or does the level of output rise, as it did in the analysis of earlier chapters? Or do both output and the price level rise?

Figure 7-2 shows that an increase in the money supply shifts the aggregate demand curve AD to the right, to AD'. We see later in this chapter why that should be so. The shift of the aggregate demand curve moves the equilibrium of the economy from E to E'. The price level rises from P_0 to P_0', and the level of output from Y_0 to Y_0'. Thus an increase in the money stock causes both the level of output and the price level to rise.

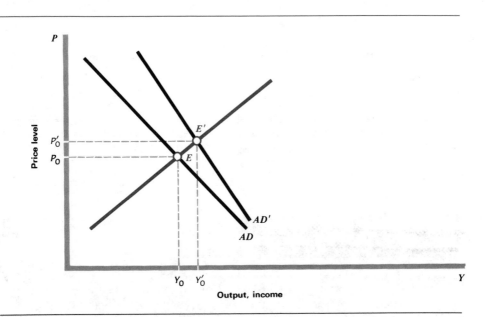

FIGURE 7-2 THE EFFECTS OF AN INCREASE IN THE NOMINAL MONEY STOCK. An increase in the money stock shifts the aggregate demand curve from AD to AD'. The equilibrium moves from E to E', resulting in higher levels of both prices and output. Thus an increase in the money stock in part results in higher prices and not entirely in higher output.

The Slope of the Aggregate Supply Curve

What determines how much the price level rises and how much output increases? Looking at Figure 7-3a we see that if the aggregate supply curve is relatively flat, a shift in the AD curve raises output a lot and prices very little. By contrast, in Figure 7-3b we see that when the aggregate supply curve is

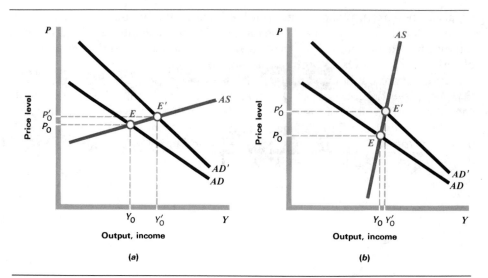

FIGURE 7-3 THE INTERACTION OF AGGREGATE SUPPLY AND DEMAND. The effects of a shift in the aggregate demand curve from AD to AD' depend on the slope of the aggregate supply curve. If the AS curve is relatively flat, as in panel **(a)**, the shift in the aggregate demand curve results mainly in an increase in output. By contrast, in panel **(b)**, the shift in the aggregate demand curve results almost entirely in an increase in the price level and very little in an increase in output.

nearly vertical, an increase in the money supply mainly causes prices to rise and hardly increases output at all.

If the aggregate supply curve is vertical, or nearly so as in Figure 7-3b, then the analysis of the earlier chapters that showed an increase in the money stock raising output could be very misleading. For example, if the aggregate supply curve is vertical, an increase in the money stock will lead only to higher prices, not to more output. Thus one of the key questions we shall concentrate on is what determines the shape of the aggregate supply curve. When is it vertical, or nearly so as in Figure 7-3b? When is the aggregate supply curve more nearly horizontal as in Figure 7-3a?

We start the analysis here by defining aggregate demand and supply.

Aggregate Demand and Supply Defined

The *aggregate demand curve* shows the combinations of the price level and level of output at which the goods and assets markets are simultaneously in equilibrium. At any point on the aggregate demand curve, for instance point B in Figure 7-4, we see that for the given price level, P_B in this case, the level of output at which the goods and assets markets are in equilibrium is Y_B.

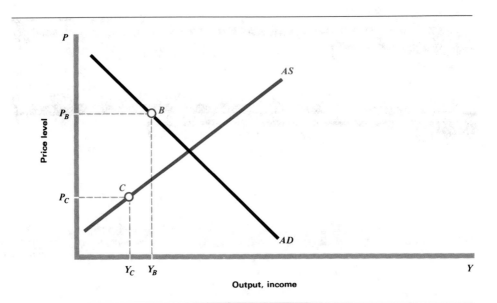

FIGURE 7-4   AGGREGATE DEMAND AND SUPPLY CURVES DEFINED. At any point on the aggregate demand curve, such as point B, both the goods and assets markets are in equilibrium. This is the equilibrium described by the intersection of IS and LM curves in Chapter 4. For instance, with price level P_B, the level of output at which both goods and assets markets are in equilibrium is Y_B. The aggregate supply curve AS describes the relation between the price level and the amount of output firms wish to supply. For instance, at price level P_C, firms want to supply output Y_C.

We can already give a preliminary explanation of why the aggregate demand curve slopes downward, based on the discussion of monetary policy in Chapter 4. Suppose that the goods and assets markets are in equilibrium at a level of output like Y_B, with a given price level P_B. Now suppose the price level falls. With a given nominal stock of money, a fall in the price level creates an increase in the quantity of *real balances*. Recall from Chapter 4 that an increase in the quantity of real balances reduces interest rates, increases investment demand, and therefore increases aggregate spending. Accordingly, when the price level falls, the equilibrium level of spending rises; therefore the AD curve slopes down. We go into the details in Section 7-3.

We can also see, from the definition of the aggregate demand curve, why the analysis of the previous chapters is not at all wasted. The aggregate demand curve describes the joint equilibrium of the goods and assets markets. That is precisely what the IS-LM analysis describes. Thus the material we studied in earlier chapters is an essential part of the aggregate demand and supply model we shall use to analyze the simultaneous determination of the levels of output and prices.

The *aggregate supply curve* describes the combinations of output and the price level such that firms are willing, at the given price level, to supply the given quantity of output. For instance, at point C in Figure 7-4, with price level P_C, firms are willing to supply output equal to Y_C. The amount of output firms are willing to supply depends on the prices they receive for their goods and the amounts they have to pay for labour and other factors of production. *Accordingly, the aggregate supply curve reflects conditions in the factor markets — especially the labour market — as well as the goods markets.*

7-2 AGGREGATE SUPPLY: TWO SPECIAL CASES

In this chapter we concentrate on two special cases in discussing aggregate supply. The first, the *Keynesian case*, shown in Figure 7-5a, is a horizontal

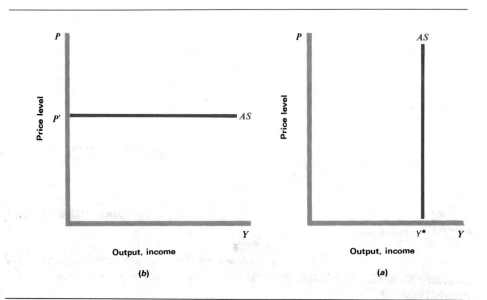

FIGURE 7-5 KEYNESIAN AND CLASSICAL SUPPLY FUNCTIONS. The Keynesian aggregate supply curve is horizontal, implying that any amount of output will be supplied at the existing price level. This is shown in panel **(a)**, where the AS curve is horizontal at price level P'. The classical supply function is based on the assumption that there is always full employment of labour, and thus that output is always at the level of output corresponding to full employment of labour, Y^*, and *independent of the price level*. This is shown by the vertical aggregate supply curve in panel **(b)**.

aggregate supply curve. The *Keynesian aggregate supply curve* is horizontal, indicating that firms will supply at the existing price level whatever amount of goods is demanded.

The idea underlying the Keynesian aggregate supply curve is that because there is unemployment, firms can obtain as much labour as they want at the current wage. Their average costs of production therefore are assumed not to change as their output levels change. They are accordingly willing to supply as much as is demanded at the existing price level.

The Classical Supply Curve

Figure 7-5*b* shows the opposite extreme, of a vertical supply curve. In the *classical case*, the *aggregate supply curve* is vertical, indicating that the same amount of goods will be supplied whatever the price level.

The classical supply curve is based on the assumption that the labour market is always in equilibrium with full employment of the labour force. If the entire labour force is being employed, then output cannot be raised above its current level even if the price level rises. There is no more labour available to produce any extra output. Thus the aggregate supply curve will be vertical at a level of output corresponding to full employment of the labour force, Y^* in Figure 7-5*b*.

Underlying the vertical schedule is the assumption that the labour market is always in equilibrium because the wages adjust rapidly to maintain equilibrium. For example, suppose that the economy is in equilibrium and the aggregate demand curve shifts to the right, as in Figure 7-2. At the existing price level, the quantity of goods demanded increases.

Now firms try to obtain more labour. Each firm attempts to hire more labour, offering to pay higher wages if necessary. But there is no more labour available in the economy, and so firms are unable to obtain more workers. Instead, in competing against each other for workers, they merely bid up wages. Because wages are higher, the prices the firms charge for their output will also be higher, but output will be unchanged.

The difference between the classical and Keynesian aggregate supply curves is that the classical supply curve is based on the belief that the labour market works smoothly, always maintaining full employment of the labour force. Movements in the wage are the mechanism through which full employment is maintained. The Keynesian aggregate supply curve is instead based on the assumption that the wage does not change much or at all when there is unemployment, and thus that unemployment can continue for some time.

These two cases—the classical, representing continuing labour market equilibrium, and the Keynesian, assuming wages do not adjust — are the two extremes. In Chapter 14 we develop the theory of aggregate supply and show why the aggregate supply curve is in practice positively sloped — in between the Keynesian and classical cases.

7-3   THE AGGREGATE DEMAND SCHEDULE

The aggregate demand curve, or schedule, shows, for each price level, the level of output at which the goods and assets markets are simultaneously in equilibrium. At any given price level, we use the *IS-LM* model to determine the level of output at which the goods and assets markets are in equilibrium.

In Figure 7-6 we show the *IS-LM* model. The position of the *IS* curve depends on fiscal policy. The *LM* schedule is drawn for a given nominal money stock M and a given price level P_0 and thus for a given real money stock M/P_0. The equilibrium interest rate is i_0, and the equilibrium level of income and spending is shown as Y_0.

A Change in the Price Level

Consider the effect of a fall in the price level from P_0 to P_0'. This reduction in the price level increases the real money stock from M/P_0 to M/P_0'. To clear the money market with an increased real money stock, either interest rates must fall, inducing the public to hold more cash balances, or output must rise, thus increasing the transactions demand for money.

Accordingly, the *LM* curve shifts downward and to the right, to *LM'*. The new equilibrium is shown at point E', where once again both the money market clears — because we are on the *LM* curve — and the goods market clears — because we are on the *IS* curve. The new equilibrium level of output is Y_0', corresponding to the lower price level P_0'. Thus a reduction in the price level, *given the nominal quantity of money*, results in an increase in equilibrium income and spending. The derivation of the *AD* schedule can be seen in Figure 7-6. The economy is initially in equilibrium at points E in both the upper and lower panels. The equilibrium interest rate is i_0, the level of output is Y_0, and the corresponding price level is P_0. Now the price level drops to P_0'. In the upper panel, the equilibrium moves to E', as a result of the shift of the *LM* curve to *LM'*. Corresponding to point E' in the upper panel is point E' in the lower panel, at price level P_0' and the level of income and output Y_0'.

Thus E and E' in the lower panel are both points on the *AD* schedule. We could now consider all possible price levels and the corresponding levels of real balances. For each level of real balances there is a different *LM* curve in the upper panel. Corresponding to each *LM* curve is an equilibrium level of income, which would be recorded in the lower panel at the price level that results in the *LM* curve in the upper panel. Connecting all these points gives us a downward-sloping aggregate demand curve *AD*, as shown in Figure 7-6.

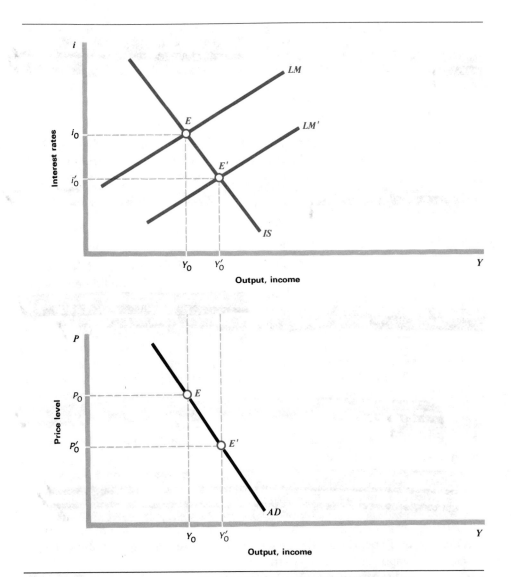

FIGURE 7-6 DERIVATION OF THE AGGREGATE DEMAND SCHEDULE. The upper panel shows the *IS* schedule and the initial *LM* schedule drawn for the real money stock M/P_0. Equilibrium is at point *E*. In the lower panel we record that at a price level P_0 the equilibrium level of income and spending is Y_0. This is shown by point *E*. At a lower level of prices, say, P_0', the real money stock is M/P_0', and therefore the *LM* schedule shifts to *LM'*. Equilibrium income now is Y_0'. Again in the lower panel we show at point *E'* the combination of the price level P_0' and the corresponding equilibrium level of income and spending Y_0'. Considering different levels of prices and connecting the resulting points such as *E* and *E'*, we derive the aggregate demand schedule *AD*. The schedule shows the equilibrium level of spending at each level of prices, given the nominal money stock and fiscal policy.

The *AD* curve is downward-sloped because there is a definite relation between equilibrium spending and the price level: The higher the price level, the lower are real balances, and hence the lower the equilibrium level of spending and output.

Properties of the *AD* Schedule

The *AD* schedule shows how the level of real spending changes with the level of prices, given fiscal policy, the quantity of money, and autonomous private spending. What are the precise properties of the *AD* schedule? We start with the slope, which tells us how much real spending changes in response to a change in the level of prices.

The Slope of the *AD* Schedule

In Figure 7-6 we derived the *AD* schedule by considering the effect of changes in the price level, and hence in real balances, on the *LM* schedule and hence on equilibrium income and spending. The slope of the *AD* curve therefore reflects the extent to which a change in real balances changes the equilibrium level of spending, taking both assets and goods markets into account.

However, we have already examined the effects of a change in the stock of real balances on the level of output that equilibrates the goods and assets markets. In Chapter 4 we showed the effect of an increase in the nominal stock of money on equilibrium spending and output, with the price level given. Now we ask what is the effect of a change in real balances due to lower prices, given nominal money.

In discussing monetary policy in Chapter 4 we showed the following results using the *IS-LM* schedules:

> An increase in real balances leads to a larger increase in equilibrium income and spending, the smaller the interest response of money demand and the higher the interest response of investment demand.
> An increase in real balances leads to a larger increase in equilibrium income and spending, the larger the multiplier and the smaller the income response of money demand.

Because the slope of the AD curve is determined by the effect of a change in real balances on equilibrium spending and output, the same factors that determine the effects of a change in the stock of money on equilibrium output and spending also determine the slope of the AD curve. If a given change in real balances has a large impact on equilibrium spending, then the *AD* curve will be very flat — because a small change in the price level creates a large change in equilibrium spending. But if a given change in real balances has a small effect on equilibrium spending and output, then the *AD* curve will be steep: in that case it takes a large change in the price level to create a small change in spending and output.

Accordingly, we see that:

1. The *AD* curve is flatter (*a*) the smaller the interest responsiveness of the demand for money, and (*b*) the larger the interest responsiveness of investment demand.
2. The *AD* curve is flatter (*a*) the larger the multiplier, and (*b*) the smaller the income responsiveness of the demand for money.

To fix ideas further, it is useful to think for a moment about the *AD* schedule in terms of the extreme classical and liquidity trap cases that we learned about in Chapter 4. In the classical case, where money demand is entirely unresponsive to interest rates and the *LM* curve is vertical, changes in real balances have a big effect on income and spending. As illustrated in Figure 7-7 that corresponds to a very flat *AD* schedule, such as *AD'*, as we should expect based on point 1*a* above. Conversely, in the liquidity trap case, where the public is willing to hold any amount of real balances at unchanged interest rates, a fall in prices and a rise in the real money stock have very little effect on income and

FIGURE 7-7   THE SLOPE OF THE *AD* SCHEDULE. The diagram shows two possible *AD* schedules. Along *AD"* a change in prices from P_0 to P_0' has a smaller effect on spending than along *AD'*. The former corresponds to the case where changes in real balances have little impact on equilibrium income and spending: the latter to the case where real balance changes exert significant effects.

spending.[2] In Figure 7-7 that would correspond to an almost vertical AD curve, as suggested again by point 1a above. A vertical AD curve means that the planned level of spending is unresponsive to the price level.

You should now experiment with alternative IS and LM schedules to see how the effects of a change in the price level depend on the slopes of the IS and LM curves and the factors underlying those slopes. In doing so you will confirm the points summarized above. In problem 4 at the end of the chapter, we ask you to demonstrate these links.

Next we consider the factors that determine the position of the AD curve.

The Effect of a Fiscal Expansion

We noted above that the same factors that determine the positions of the IS and LM schedules also determine the position of the AD curve. We now show how changes in fiscal and monetary policy shift the AD curve, starting with a fiscal expansion.

In Figure 7-8 the initial LM and IS schedules correspond to a given nominal quantity of money and the price level P_0. Equilibrium obtains at point E, and there is a corresponding point on the AD schedule in the lower panel.

Now the government increases the level of spending. As a consequence, the IS schedule shifts outward and to the right. At the initial price level there is a new equilibrium at point E' with higher interest rates and a higher level of income and spending. Thus at the initial level of prices, P_0, equilibrium income and spending now are higher. We show this by plotting point E' in the lower panel. Point E' is a point on the new schedule AD' reflecting the effect of higher government spending.

Of course, we could have started with any other point on the original AD curve, and we would then have shown how in the lower panel the rise in government spending leads to a higher equilibrium level of output at each price level. In that way we trace out the entire AD' schedule, which lies to the right of AD.

In fact, we can say more: At each level of prices, and hence of real balances, the AD schedule shifts to the right by an amount indicated by the fiscal policy multiplier developed in Chapter 4. As we saw there, a fiscal expansion leads to a higher level of income and spending, the larger the interest response of money demand, the smaller the interest response of aggregate demand, and the larger the marginal propensity to consume.

---

[2] The reason a reduction in prices increases output in this case is the *real balance effect*: with lower prices, the value of real balances held by the public is higher, their wealth is accordingly higher, and therefore their consumption spending and output are higher. The real balance effect is central to monetary theory as developed in the classical treatise by Don Patinkin, *Money, Interest, and Prices* (New York: Harper & Row, 1965).

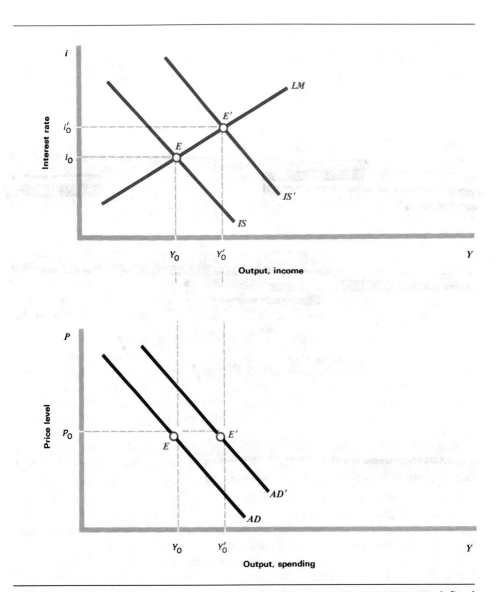

FIGURE 7-8 THE EFFECT OF A FISCAL EXPANSION ON THE *AD* SCHEDULE. A fiscal expansion, such as an increase in government spending, shifts the *IS* curve in the upper panel to *IS'*. At any given price level, such as P_0, the equilibrium in the upper panel shifts to E', with higher level of output Y_0' and higher interest rate i_0'. Point E' in the lower panel is a point on the new aggregate demand schedule *AD'* corresponding to price level P_0. We could similarly trace the effect of increased government spending on the equilibrium level of output and spending in the lower panel for every price level, and thus show that the *AD* curve shifts out to *AD'* when fiscal policy is expansionary.

Thus if the fiscal policy multiplier derived in Chapter 4 was, for example, 1.5, then a $1 (billion) dollar increase in government spending would increase equilibrium income and spending by $1.5 billion, at the given price level. In response to any change in government spending, the *AD* schedule would shift to the right by 1.5 times the increase in *G*.[3]

The Effect of a Monetary Expansion on the *AD* Schedule

An increase in the nominal money stock implies, at each level of prices, a higher real money stock. In the assets markets interest rates decline to induce the public to hold higher real balances. That decline in interest rates, in turn, stimulates aggregate demand and thus raises the equilibrium level of income and spending. In Figure 7-9 we show that an increase in the nominal money stock shifts the *AD* schedule up and to the right.

The extent to which an increase in nominal money shifts the *AD* schedule to the right depends on the monetary policy multiplier. If the monetary policy multiplier is large, say, because money demand is not very interest elastic and goods demand is, the *AD* schedule will shift a lot. Conversely, if the *LM* schedule is nearly flat, in which case monetary policy is ineffective, the *AD* schedule will shift very little.

We can also ask about the *upward* shift of the schedule. Here an interesting and important point emerges. Recall that what matters for equilibrium income and spending is the *real* money supply *M/P*. If an increase in nominal money is matched by an equiproportionate increase in prices, *M/P* is unchanged, and hence interest rates, aggregate demand, and equilibrium income and spending will remain unchanged. This gives us the clue to the vertical shift of the *AD* schedule.

An increase in the nominal money stock shifts the AD *schedule up exactly in proportion to the increase in nominal money.* Thus if, starting at point *E* in the lower panel of Figure 7-9, we have a 10 percent increase in *M*, real spending will be unchanged only if prices also rise by 10 percent, thus leaving real balances unchanged. Therefore the *AD* schedule shifts upward by 10 percent. At point *K* in Figure 7-9, *real* balances are the same as at *E*, and therefore interest rates and equilibrium income and spending are the same as at *E*.

We now have completed the derivation of the aggregate demand schedule. The important points to recall are that the *AD* schedule is shifted to the right both by increases in the money stock and by expansionary fiscal policy. In the remainder of this chapter we show how to use this tool to discuss the effects of

---

[3] In Chapter 4 we showed that the fiscal policy multiplier is given by the expression $h\bar{\alpha}/(h + kb\bar{\alpha})$, where *h* is the interest responsiveness of money demand, $\bar{\alpha}$ the simple Keynesian multiplier, *k* the income response of money demand, and *b* the interest response of investment demand.

monetary and fiscal policy *on both the level of output and the price level* under alternative assumptions about the supply side.

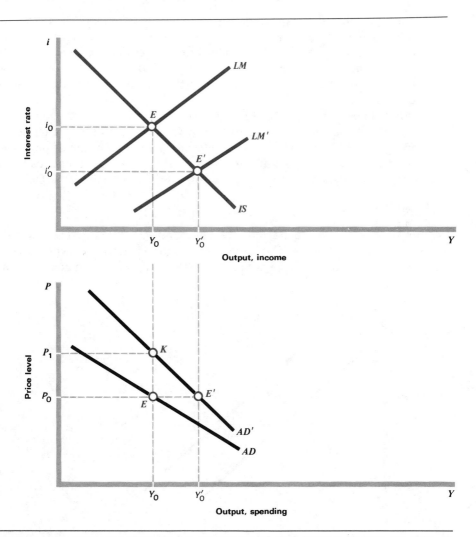

FIGURE 7-9   THE EFFECTS OF AN INCREASE IN THE MONEY STOCK ON THE *AD* SCHEDULE. An increase in the money stock shifts the *LM* curve to *LM'* in the upper panel. The equilibrium level of income rises from Y_0 to Y_0' at the initial price level P_0. Correspondingly, the *AD* curve moves out to the right, to *AD'*, with point *E'* in the lower panel corresponding to *E'* in the upper panel. The *AD* curve shifts up in exactly the same proportion as the money stock increases. For instance, at point *K* the price level P_1 is higher than P_0 in the same proportion that the money supply has risen. Real balances at *K* on *AD'* are therefore the same as at *E* on *AD*.

7-4 MONETARY AND FISCAL POLICY UNDER ALTERNATIVE SUPPLY ASSUMPTIONS

In Figure 7-2 we showed how the aggregate supply and demand curves together determine the equilibrium level of income and prices in the economy. Now that we have shown how the aggregate demand curve is derived, and how it is shifted by policy changes, we use the aggregate demand and supply model to study the effects of monetary and fiscal policy in the two extreme supply cases — Keynesian and classical.

We should expect that the conclusions we reach in the Keynesian supply case are precisely the same as those reached in Chapter 4. In those chapters, in developing the *IS-LM* model, we assumed that whatever amount of goods was demanded would be supplied at the existing price level. Of course, as Figure 7-5a shows, the Keynesian supply curve implies that this will be the case.

The Keynesian Case

In Figure 7-10 we combine the aggregate demand schedule with the Keynesian aggregate supply schedule. The initial equilibrium is at point *E*, where *AS* and *AD* intersect. At that point the goods and assets markets are in equilibrium.

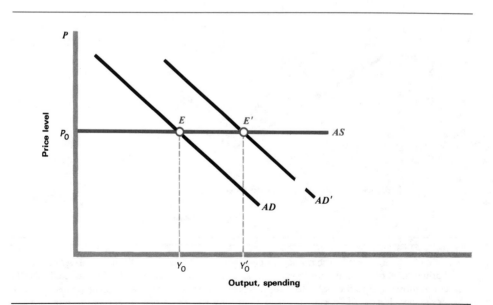

FIGURE 7-10 A FISCAL EXPANSION: THE KEYNESIAN CASE. In the Keynesian case, with output in perfectly elastic supply at a given price level, a fiscal expansion increases equilibrium income from Y_0 to Y_0'. This is exactly the result already derived with *IS* and *LM* schedules.

Consider now a fiscal expansion. As we have already seen, increased government spending, or a cut in tax rates, shifts the *AD* schedule out and to the right from *AD* to *AD'*. The new equilibrium is at point *E'*, where output has increased. Because firms are willing to supply *any* amount of output at the level of prices P_0, there is no effect on prices. The only effect of higher government spending in Figure 7-10 is to increase output and employment. In addition, as we know from the *IS-LM* model that lies behind the *AD* schedule, the fiscal expansion will raise equilibrium interest rates. Because interest rates do increase, the fiscal expansion raises output less than suggested by the simple multiplier of Chapter 3.

We leave it to you to show that in the Keynesian case an increase in the nominal quantity of money likewise leads to an expansion in equilibrium output. With a horizontal *AS* schedule there is again no impact on prices. The magnitude of the output expansion then depends, in this Keynesian case, only on the monetary policy multiplier that determines the extent of the horizontal shift of the *AD* schedule.

Thus, as we expected, all our conclusions about the effects of policy changes in the Keynesian supply case are those of the simple *IS-LM* model.

The Classical Case: Fiscal Policy

In the classical case the aggregate supply schedule is vertical at the full-employment level of output. Firms will supply the level of output *Y** whatever the price level. Under this supply assumption we obtain results very different from those reached using the Keynesian model. Now the price level is not given, but rather depends on the interaction of supply and demand.

In Figure 7-11 we study the effect of a fiscal expansion under classical supply assumptions. The aggregate supply schedule is *AS*, with equilibrium initially at point *E*. Note that at point *E* there is full employment because, by assumption, firms supply the full-employment level of output at any level of prices.

The fiscal expansion shifts the aggregate demand schedule from *AD* to *AD'*. At the initial level of prices, P_0, spending in the economy rises to point *E'*. At price level P_0 the demand for goods has risen, but firms cannot obtain the labour to produce more output, and output supply cannot respond to the increased demand. As firms try to hire more workers, they only bid up wages and their costs of production, and therefore they charge higher prices for their output. The increase in the demand for goods therefore leads only to higher prices, and not to higher output.

The increase in prices reduces the real money stock and leads to an increase in interest rates and a reduction in spending. The economy moves up the *AD'* schedule until prices have risen enough, and real balances have fallen enough, to raise interest rates and reduce spending to a level consistent with full-employment output. That is the case at a price level P_0'. At point *E''* aggregate

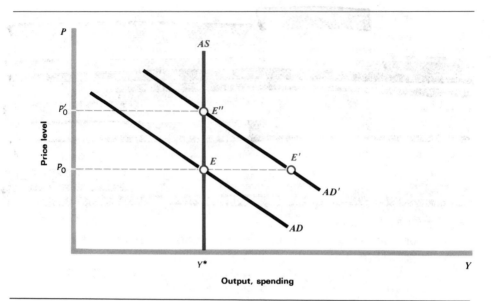

FIGURE 7-11 A FISCAL EXPANSION: THE CLASSICAL CASE. The supply of output is perfectly inelastic at the full-employment level of output, Y^*. A fiscal expansion raises equilibrium spending, at the initial price level P_0, from E to E', but now there is an excess demand because firms are unwilling to supply that much output. Prices increase, and that reduces real balances until we reach point E''. At E'' government spending is higher, but the higher price level means lower real balances, higher interest rates, and hence reduced private spending. At E'' increased government spending has crowded out an equal amount of private spending.

demand, at the higher level of government spending, is once again equal to aggregate supply.

Crowding Out Again

Note what has happened in Figure 7-11: output is unchanged at the full-employment level Y^*, but government spending is higher. That must imply less spending by the private sector. There is thus *full*, or complete, *crowding out*. Recall that crowding out occurs when an increase in government spending results in less spending by the private sector. Typically, as we showed in Chapter 4, government spending crowds out investment. In the case shown in Figure 7-11, with a classical supply curve, every dollar increase in real government spending is offset by a dollar reduction in private spending, so that crowding out is complete.

We thus reach the following important result: *In the classical case increased real government spending leads to full crowding out.* We now explain the mechanism through which crowding out occurs.

Figure 7-12 shows the *IS-LM* diagram, augmented with the line Y^* at the full-employment level of output. The initial equilibrium is at point E, where the money market clears and planned spending equals output. The fiscal expansion shifts the *IS* schedule to *IS'*. At an unchanged price level, and assuming firms were to meet the increase in demand by expanding production, we would move to point E'. However, this is not possible under classical supply assumptions. Faced with an excess demand for goods, firms end up raising prices rather than output. The price increase, in turn, reduces real balances and therefore shifts the *LM* schedule up. Prices will increase until the excess demand has been eliminated. That means the *LM* schedule shifts up and to the left until we reach a new equilibrium at point E''.

At E'' the goods market clears at the full-employment level of output. Interest rates have increased compared with the initial equilibrium at E, and that increase in interest rates has reduced private spending to make room for increased government purchases. Note that the money market is also in equilibrium. Output and income are the same as at point E. The higher interest rate

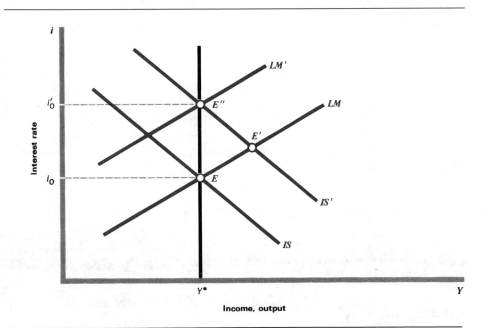

FIGURE 7-12 CROWDING OUT IN THE CLASSICAL CASE. A fiscal expansion in the classical case leads to full crowding out. The fiscal expansion shifts the *IS* schedule to *IS'*. At the initial price level the economy would move to point E', but there is excess demand since firms supply only Y^*. Prices increase, shifting the *LM* schedule up and to the left until *LM'* is reached. The new equilibrium is at point E'', where interest rates have risen enough to displace an amount of private spending equal to the increase in government demand.

reduces the demand for real balances, matching the decline in the real money stock.

Note that we have now seen two mechanisms that produce full crowding out. In Chapter 4, crowding out is complete if the *LM* curve is vertical. In that case, crowding out occurs because money demand is interest inelastic. In this chapter, full crowding out occurs because aggregate supply limits total output. In brief, in Chapter 4 crowding out is a demand phenomenon; here it is a supply phenomenon.

In Table 7-1 we summarize the effects of a fiscal expansion in the cases of classical and Keynesian supply conditions. In each case we show what happens to output, interest rates, and the price level.

TABLE 7-1   THE EFFECTS OF A FISCAL EXPANSION

Aggregate supply	Output	Interest rate	Prices
Keynesian	+	+	0
Classical	0	+	+

The table reinforces our understanding of the two models; in one case only prices adjust; in the other case only output. These models are clearly extremes, and we would expect that often adjustment occurs in both output and prices. That is the adjustment process we study in Chapter 14. We shall see there that the Keynesian case comes close to describing the short-run effects of a fiscal expansion, while the classical case more accurately predicts what happens in the long run after all adjustments have taken place.

Monetary Expansion under Classical Conditions

We have already seen the impact of monetary policy under Keynesian supply conditions: With prices given, a rise in the nominal money stock is a rise in the real money stock. Equilibrium interest rates decline as a consequence, and output rises. Consider now the adjustments that occur in response to a monetary expansion when the aggregate supply curve is vertical and the price level is no longer fixed.

In Figure 7-13 we study an expansion in the nominal money stock under classical supply conditions. The initial full-employment equilibrium is at point *E*, where the *AD* and *AS* schedules intersect. Now the nominal money stock is increased, and accordingly, the aggregate demand schedule shifts up and to the right to *AD'*. If prices were fixed, the economy would move to *E'*, the Keynesian equilibrium, but now output is in fixed supply. The increase in aggregate demand leads to an excess demand for goods. Firms that attempt to expand,

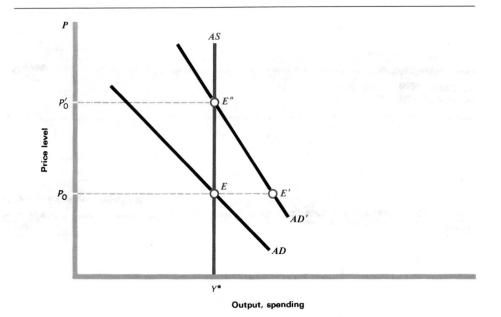

FIGURE 7-13   THE EFFECT OF A MONETARY EXPANSION UNDER CLASSICAL SUPPLY ASSUMPTIONS. Starting from the full-employment equilibrium at point E, an increase in the nominal money stock shifts the aggregate demand schedule to AD'. At the initial price level there is now an excess demand for goods. Prices increase, and thus the real money stock declines toward its initial level. Price increases continue until the economy reaches point E''. Here the *real* money stock has returned to its initial level, and with output unchanged, interest rates are again at their initial level. Thus a monetary expansion affects only prices, not output or interest rates.

hiring more workers, bid up wages and costs. Prices increase in response to the excess demand, and that means real balances fall back toward their initial level. In fact prices keep rising until the excess demand for goods disappears. Thus they must increase until the economy reaches point E'', where AS intersects the new aggregate demand schedule AD'. Only when aggregate demand is again equal to full-employment supply does the goods market clear and the pressure for prices to rise disappear.

Consider now the adjustment that takes place in moving from E to E''. There is no change in output, only a change in the price level. Note, moreover, that prices rise in exactly the same proportion as the nominal quantity of money.[4]

---

[4] In problem 7 we ask you to use the IS and LM curves to show how the change in the money supply works. To answer the problem you have to use Fig. 7-9 along with the fact that the LM schedule shifts as the price level changes.

This we know because we saw earlier that in response to an increase in nominal money the *AD* schedule shifts upward in the same proportion as the increase in money. Thus at point *E″* the real money stock *M/P* is back to its initial level. At *E″* both nominal money and the price level have changed in the same proportion, leaving real money, and hence interest rates and aggregate demand, unchanged. We thus have an important implication of the classical model: *Under classical supply conditions an increase in nominal money raises the price level in the same proportion, but leaves interest rates and real output unchanged.*

In Table 7-2 we summarize the effects of an increase in the nominal money stock under Keynesian and classical supply conditions. Once again we look at the effects on output, prices, and interest rates. In addition we show the effect on real balances *M/P*. The table brings out the fact that under classical supply conditions, none of the *real* variables, such as output, interest rates, or real balances, are affected by a change in the nominal money stock. Only the price level changes.

TABLE 7-2 THE EFFECTS OF AN INCREASE IN THE NOMINAL MONEY STOCK

Aggregate supply	Output	Interest rate	Prices	Real balances
Keynesian	+	−	0	+
Classical	0	0	+	0

7-5 THE QUANTITY THEORY AND THE NEUTRALITY OF MONEY

The classical model of supply, in combination with the *IS-LM* model describing the demand side of the economy, has extremely strong implications. Because, by assumption, output is maintained at the full-employment level by full wage and price flexibility, monetary and fiscal policy do not affect output. Fiscal policy affects interest rates and the *composition* of spending between the government and the private sector and between consumption and investment. Monetary policy only affects the price level.

These implications about the effects of monetary policy on output are consistent with the *quantity theory of money* The quantity theory of money in its strongest form asserts that the price level is proportional to the stock of money. For instance, in the case of the classical supply curve, an increase in the quantity of money produces, in equilibrium, a proportional increase in the price level. In this case, money is *neutral*.

The Neutrality of Money

Money is *neutral* when changes in the money stock lead only to changes in the price level, with no real variables (output, employment, and interest rates) changing. For instance, money is neutral in the second row of Table 7-2, where in response to a change in the money stock, only the price level changes, with output, interest rates, and real balances remaining unchanged.

We saw above that the classical supply curve has the powerful and important implication that fiscal policy cannot affect output. The neutrality of money likewise has strong policy implications. For instance, if money were neutral, there would be an easy way to reduce the inflation rate if we ever wanted to do that. All we would have to do would be to reduce the rate at which the money stock is growing.

In practice, it is very difficult to change the inflation rate without producing a recession, as for instance in the period 1979–1983. When a lower growth rate of money leads first to unemployment, and only later to lower inflation, as it did in the recession in 1982, then we know that money is not neutral. Changes in the quantity of money then have real effects — monetary policy affects the level of output. This means that the aggregate supply curve cannot be vertical in the short run. In Chapter 14 we develop the aggregate supply curve, showing why in the short run it is quite flat, whereas over longer periods it is more nearly vertical.

The Modern Quantity Theory: Monetarism

The strict quantity theory asserts that the price level is proportional to the quantity of money. Although the quantity theory is centuries, and perhaps millennia, old, few have believed in the strict quantity theory. That is, few have believed that the price level is strictly proportional to the money stock, or that money is the *only* factor affecting the price level. Rather, quantity theorists argued and argue that the money stock is, in practice, the single most important factor producing inflation.

Box 7-1 presents quotations from Irving Fisher (1867–1947), widely thought to be the greatest American economist of his time, and from Milton Friedman, the leading exponent of the quantity theory and the importance of money in the modern era. The two differ in emphasis: Fisher comes close to asserting that *only* changes in the quantity of money affect the price level; Friedman is more clear in arguing that other factors can affect the price level, but that these other factors are of secondary importance.

Friedman is the recognized intellectual leader of an influential group of economists, called *monetarists*, who emphasize the role of money and monetary policy in affecting the behaviour of output and prices. Leading monetarists include Professor Karl Brunner and Robert Barro of the University of Rochester, Allen Meltzer of Carnegie Mellon University, William Poole of Brown University, and Anna Schwartz of the National Bureau of Economic Research and Hunter College, David Laidler and Michael Parkin of the University of Western Ontario, and other scholars, both in North America and elsewhere.

Modern quantity theorists differ also from the strict quantity theory in not believing that the supply curve is vertical in the short run. Monetarists such as Friedman argue that a reduction in the money stock does in practice *first* reduce the level of output, and only later has an effect on prices.

Thus Friedman and other monetarists make an important distinction between the short- and long-run effects of changes in money. They argue that in the long run money is more or less neutral. Changes in the money stock, after they have worked their way through the economy, have no real effects and only change prices: the quantity theory and the neutrality of money are, from this long-run perspective, not just theoretical possibilities, but instead a reasonable description of the way the world works. But in the short run, they argue, monetary policy and changes in the money stock can and do have important real effects.

There is more to monetarism than the argument that money is the most important determinant of macroeconomic performance, but we leave the evidence on this and the other tenets of monetarism for further discussion in Chapters 12 and 18.

BOX 7-1 THE QUANTITY THEORY OF MONEY

Irving Fisher (1867–1947) and Milton Friedman (born 1912) are two of the foremost monetary economists in the United States in this century. Both strongly advocated the quantity theory of money as the right model of price level determination.

Fisher stated:*

> In recent popular discussions a great variety of reasons have been assigned for the "high cost of living," *e.g.*, "profiteering"; speculation; hoarding; the middleman; . . . the tariff; cold storage; longer hauls on railroads; marketing by telephone; the free delivery system; the individual package; the enforcement of sanitary laws; the tuberculin testing of cattle; the destruction of tainted meat; sanitary milk; the elimination of renovated butter and of "rots" and "spots" in eggs; food adulteration; advertising; unscientific management; extravagance; higher standards of living; the increasing cost of government; the increasing cost of old-age pensions, and of better pauper institutions, hospitals, insane asylums, reformatories, jails and other public institutions; . . .

* Irving Fisher, *Stabilizing the Dollar* (New York: Macmillan, 1920), pp. 10–11 and 29.

I shall not discuss in detail this list of alleged explanations. While some of them are important factors in raising particular prices, none of them . . . has been important in raising the *general* scale of prices. . . .

The ups and downs of prices roughly correspond with the ups and downs of the money supply. Throughout all history this has been so. For this general broad fact the evidence is sufficient even where we lack the index numbers by which to make accurate measurements. Whenever there have been rapid out-pourings from mines, following discoveries of the precious metals used for money, prices have risen with corresponding rapidity. This was observed in the sixteenth century, after great quantities of the precious metals had been brought to Europe from the New World, and again in the nineteenth century, after the Californian and Australian gold mining of the fifties; and, still again, in the same century after the South African, Alaskan, and Cripple Creek mining of the nineties. Likewise when other causes than mining, such as paper money issues, produce violent changes in the quantity or quality of money, violent changes in the price level usually follow.

Friedman wrote:†

Since men first began to write systematically about economic matters they have devoted special attention to the wide movements in the general level of prices that have intermittently occurred. Two alternative explanations have usually been offered. One has attributed the changes in prices to changes in the quantity of money. The other has attributed the changes in prices to war or to profiteers or to rises in wages or to some other special circumstance of the particular time and place and has regarded any accompanying change in the quantity of money as a common consequence of the same special circumstance. The first explanation has generally been referred to as the quantity theory of money, although that designation conceals the variety of forms the explanation has taken, the different levels of sophistication to which it has been developed, and the wide range of the claims that have been made for its applicability.

In its most rigid and unqualified form the quantity theory asserts strict pro-portionality between the quantity of what is regarded as money and the level of prices. Hardly anyone has held the theory in that form, although statements capable of being so interpreted have often been made in the heat of argument or for expository simplicity. Virtually every quantity theorist has recognized that changes in the quantity of money that correspond to changes in the volume of trade or of output have no tendency to produce changes in prices. Nearly as many have recognized also that changes in the willingness of the community to hold money can occur for a variety of reasons and can introduce disparities between changes in the quantity of money per unit of trade or of output and changes in prices. What quantity theorists have held in common is the belief that these qualifications are of secondary importance for substantial changes in either prices or the quantity of money, so that the one will not in fact occur without the other.

---

† Milton Friedman, "Money: The Quantity Theory," in *The International Encyclopedia of the Social Sciences*, vol. X, 1968, pp. 432–447.

7-6 AGGREGATE SUPPLY: THE QUESTIONS AHEAD

The theory of aggregate supply is among the most controversial and the least settled of any in macroeconomics. Here is the difficulty. From the viewpoint of logic and simplicity, the classical theory of supply — that the labour market clears all the time and that output is always at the full employment level — is compelling. After all, if output is below the full employment level, there are some workers who want to work but cannot find a job. Surely they could find a job by offering to work at lower real wage. Much of microeconomics suggests that markets are mostly in equilibrium (demand is equal to supply) and, if not, are at least moving that way, so economists have a professional bias in favour of equilibrium.

However, the facts do not support the classical theory of supply.

- Output is not always at the full employment level. The unemployment rate varies, and is sometimes very high; there are many people wanting work who cannot find it, and therefore the quantity of labour supplied exceeds the quantity demanded.
- Further, if output is always at the full employment level, then changes in the money stock affect only prices and not output: Money is neutral. However, changes in monetary policy in fact frequently appear not to be neutral. Sharp reductions in money growth, for instance when governments try to reduce inflation, almost always cause recessions, and increases in money growth often appear to cause rapid growth of real output.

Indeed, the broad facts come closer to supporting the Keynesian aggregate supply curve than the classical view. Increases in aggregate demand, caused, for instance, by expansionary fiscal or monetary policy, raise real output much more than prices in the short run.

However, the assumption that prices are completely fixed, which underlies the Keynesian supply function, is bothersome. When prices are fixed and markets do not clear, people can benefit from changing prices. The unemployed would be willing to work at a wage below that earned by the currently employed. Employers should be happy to employ labour at a lower wage. Why do not employers and the unemployed get together, agree on a lower wage, and get rid of the unemployment? In other words, why does the labour market not move quickly to equilibrium?

In a nutshell, the difficulty facing the theory of aggregate supply is that logic and simple microeconomic theory lead us to believe we should be in a classical world, but the real world does not appear to be classical. The challenge for macroeconomics is to explain the real world.

There are three leading approaches to explaining the short-run stickiness of wages and prices, the short-run nonneutrality of money, and varying and often persistently high rates of unemployment that exist in the real world. We give the flavour of the arguments here, and take them up more systematically in Chapters 14, 15, and 18.

Modern Keynesian Approaches

The original Keynesian approach was to assume that the wage is fixed.[5] Modern Keynesian theories argue that the wage and price levels are very slow to change rather than fixed. The aggregate supply curve is viewed as being close to flat in the short run and close to vertical in the long run. Attention focusses mainly on wages and on the adjustment process to explain why adjustment is not immediate or at least very fast.

Contracts

Wages are slow to change because they are fixed in long-term contracts. These contracts may be explicit, as with union contracts, or they may be implicit, an unwritten agreement between firm and employee that the wage will remain fixed for a period of a year and will not be cut.

If wages (and prices) are adjusted at different times for different firms and industries, then the economy-wide average wage and the aggregate price level adjust only slowly to policy changes or other changes. This is so because they are made up of many wages or many prices and only a small part of them will be adjusted at any one time.

Coordination

The nonneutrality of money can be accounted for by the difficulty of coordinating wage and price changes when wages and prices are not all adjusted simultaneously. When the quantity of money is changed, the extent to which any individual should change his or her own price or wage depends on how much others change their prices. If everyone else changes prices in proportion to the change in the money supply, then the last remaining firm would do the same. However, if no one else or only a few firms do, then the firm raising its price in proportion to an increase in the money stock will lose customers because its price is out of line with the others. Because all the firms in an economy cannot get together to coordinate, they will raise prices slowly as the effects of the change in money are felt through increased demand for their goods at the existing prices.

---

[5] In the *General Theory of Employment, Interest and Money* (London: Macmillan, 1936) Keynes assumed for most of the book that the nominal wage was fixed. However, he also argued that flexible wages would not succeed in stabilizing output and employment and that the active use of monetary policy was a preferable means of maintaining full employment.

Efficiency Wages

Another strand of modern Keynesian supply theory, efficiency wage theory, focusses on the wage as a means of motivating labour. The amount of effort workers make on the job is related to how well the job pays relative to alternatives. Firms may want to pay employees wages above the market clearing wage to ensure that they work hard in order not to lose their "good" jobs. By the same token firms are reluctant to cut wages because that affects worker morale and output. This theory does not explain why the average wage is slow to change, but it does help explain the existence of unemployment.

These are not the only recent models that seek to explain aggregate supply along broadly Keynesian lines in which markets may not always clear. Aggregate supply is an area of intensive research. There is not as yet a dominant, completely persuasive microeconomic explanation of the positively sloped aggregate supply curve, but there are many suggestive theories. We will examine the main explanations of upward sloping, but not vertical, supply curves in Chapter 14.

The Imperfect Information-Market Clearing Approach

An alternative explanation for the effects of changes in the money supply on real output is associated with the *rational expectations equilibrium* approach to macroeconomics. This approach, which we review further in later chapters, assumes that markets are in equilibrium even in the short run, but that people typically have imperfect information about the economy.[6]

A frequent assumption made in this approach is that people do not know the aggregate price level but do know the absolute (dollar) price at which they can buy and sell. For instance, at a given moment of time, a worker knows that the going wage rate is $12 per hour but does not know all prices in the economy and hence the aggregate price level, and thus does not know the real wage (the nominal wage divided by the price level, equal to the amount of goods the wage will buy). Since it is the real wage, not the absolute wage, that determines whether and how many working hours are wanted, the worker has somehow to estimate the aggregate price level.

With these assumptions it is possible to explain why changes in the stock of money affect real output. Suppose the stock of money increases *unexpectedly*, and begins to affect the demand for goods and labour, raising the price level and wages. Each firm and worker knows the price at which it can sell goods or labour. However, workers and firms do not know as a fact that the aggregate

---

[6] Robert E. Lucas of the University of Chicago is the intellectual founder of this approach. See his famous article "Some International Evidence on Output-Inflation Tradeoffs," *American Economic Review* June 1973 for an example of the approach.

price level has risen. Each believes that the increase in the absolute price at which it can sell is at least in part an increase in the relative price at which it sells. Workers think their real wage has risen, and want to work more. Because the labour market is always in equilibrium, they can work more. Thus there is an increase in the amount of work and output, because workers think their real wage has risen.

Of course, the workers were wrong. Their real wage had not in fact risen. If they had known the facts, they would not have worked more, prices would have risen in proportion to the money stock, and money would have been neutral. But they had imperfect information, and as a result the increase in the money stock was not neutral.

The imperfect information — market clearing approach does not assert that people make *stupid* mistakes in deciding how much to work and produce. Rather people do their best to understand the situation in which they find themselves but lack the full information to make the correct decision.

Search

The imperfect information — market clearing approach can also be used to explain unemployment. Suppose that workers who become unemployed search for a new job, staying employed until they find a suitable job at the right real wage. Suppose further that they do not know the aggregate price level exactly. Now suppose that the money supply increases, that the aggregate price level goes up (though less than proportionately), and that firms raise the wages they are willing to pay.

Workers are unaware that the price level is up. They find higher wages when they look for a job, think that the real wage is higher, and take the job. The unemployment rate falls as a result of the increase in the money stock. What might look like a Keynesian effect of an increase in the money stock on unemployment is instead explained by imperfect information: The real wage is lower than the worker thought it was when taking the job.

Real Business Cycles and the Role of Money

A third approach, real business cycle theory, starts from the market-clearing view, assuming that markets are always in equilibrium. Its distinctive feature is the argument that changes in the money stock play no serious role in the business cycle.[7] Real business cycle theorists recognize that output fluctuates

---

[7] Carl Walsh "New View of the Business Cycle: Has the Past Emphasis on Money Been Misplaced?", *Business Review*, Federal Reserve Bank of Philadelphia, Jan./Feb. 1986, provides an excellent introduction to the topic.

over time, but argue that the fluctuations are a result of *real* shocks to the economy.

Real shocks are taken as coming mainly from the supply side of the economy. Changes in the weather, or the price of oil, or new methods of production affect the level of output. On the demand side, changes in government spending can also affect the level of output; but real business cycle theory by definition does not give a causal role to changes in the money stock in affecting output.

Rather the argument is that the quantity of money adjusts itself to the level of output. Thus real business cycle theorists argue that changes in output cause changes in the quantity of money rather than the other way around. The explanation is that when the level of output rises, people demand more real balances, and that the banks can generally create more money.

A Look Ahead

We will not evaluate the different approaches here, but we keep returning to them in subsequent chapters, especially Chapter 18 where we discuss current issues in macroeconomics.

In Chapter 14 we develop a theory of aggregate supply which produces a positively sloped aggregate supply curve that is relatively flat in the short run while vertical in the long run. We base the theory largely on the modern Keynesian approach, but combine that with the emphasis on expectations that comes from the rational expectations approach to macroeconomics.

7-7   SUMMARY

1. The aggregate supply and demand model is used to show the determination of the equilibrium levels of *both* output and prices.

2. The aggregate supply schedule *AS* shows at each level of prices the quantity of real output firms are willing to supply.

3. The Keynesian supply schedule is horizontal, implying that firms supply as much goods as demanded at the existing price level. The classical supply schedule is vertical. It would apply in an economy that has full price and wage flexibility. In such a frictionless economy, employment and output are always at the full-employment level.

4. The aggregate demand schedule *AD* shows at each price level the level of output at which the goods and assets markets are in equilibrium. This is the quantity of output demanded at each price level. Along the *AD* schedule fiscal policy is given, as is the nominal quantity of money. The *AD* schedule is derived using the *IS-LM* model.

5. Moving down and along the *AD* schedule, lower prices raise the real value of the money stock. Equilibrium interest rates fall, and that increases aggregate demand and equilibrium spending.

6. A fiscal expansion or an increase in the nominal quantity of money shifts the *AD* schedule outward and to the right.

7. Under Keynesian supply conditions, with prices fixed, both monetary and fiscal expansion raise equilibrium output. A monetary expansion lowers interest rates, while a fiscal expansion raises them.

8. Under classical supply conditions a fiscal expansion has no effect on output, but a fiscal expansion raises prices, lowers real balances, and increases equilibrium interest rates. That is, under classical supply conditions there is full crowding out. Private spending declines by exactly the increase in government demand.

9. A monetary expansion, under classical supply conditions, raises prices in the same proportion as the rise in nominal money. All real variables, specifically output and interest rates, remain unchanged. When changes in the money stock have no real effects, money is said to be *neutral*.

10. The strict quantity theory of money states that prices move in proportion to the nominal money stock. Modern quantity theorists or monetarists accept that there is no exact link between money and prices, but argue that changes in the money stock are, in practice, the most important single determinant of changes in the price level.

KEY TERMS

Aggregate supply curve	Full crowding out
Aggregate demand curve	Quantity theory of money
Keynesian aggregate supply curve	Neutrality of money
Classical aggregate supply curve	Monetarism
Efficiency wage theory	Rational expectations equilibrium approach

PROBLEMS

1. Define the aggregate demand and supply curves.

2. Explain why the classical supply curve is vertical and explain the mechanisms that ensure continued full employment of labour in the classical case.

3. Discuss, using the *IS-LM* model, what happens to interest rates as prices change along a given *AD* schedule.

4. Show graphically that the *AD* curve is steeper (a) the larger the interest responsiveness of the demand for money and (b) the smaller the multiplier.

5. Suppose full-employment output increases from Y^* to $Y^{*'}$. What does the quantity theory predict will happen to the price level?

6. In goods market equilibrium in a closed economy, $S + T = I + G$. Use this equation to explain why, in the classical case, a fiscal expansion must lead to full crowding out.

7. Show, using *IS* and *LM* curves, why money is neutral in the classical supply case. (Refer to footnote 4 for hints.)

8. Suppose the government reduces the personal income tax rate from t to t'.
   (a) What is the effect on the *AD* schedule?
   (b) What is the effect on the equilibrium interest rate?
   (c) What happens to investment?

9. Suppose there is a decline in the demand for money. At each output level and interest rate the public now wants to hold lower real balances.
   (a) In the Keynesian case, what happens to equilibrium output and to prices?
   (b) In the classical case, what is the effect on output and on prices?

10. In question 9, use the quantity theory of money to explain the effect of the money demand shift on prices.

11. Suppose the government undertakes a balanced budget increase in spending. Government spending rises from G to G', and there is an accompanying increase in tax rates so that at the initial level of output the budget remains balanced.
    (a) Show the effect on the *AD* schedule.
    (b) Discuss the effect of the balanced budget policy on output and interest rates in the Keynesian case.
    (c) Discuss the effect in the classical case.

12. (a) Define the strict quantity theory.
    (b) Define monetarism.
    (c) What types of statistical evidence would you need to collect, to support, or refute the major argument of monetarism presented in this chapter?

13. Explain the basic difficulty facing the theory of aggregate supply.

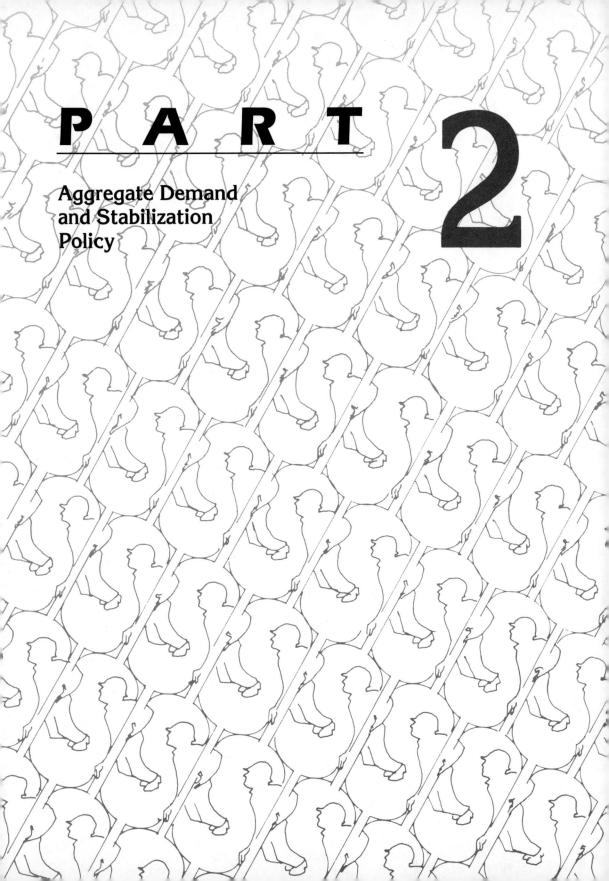

PART

2

Aggregate Demand
and Stabilization
Policy

CHAPTER

Consumption and Saving

The *IS-LM* model provides a comprehensive framework for understanding the interactions of the main macroeconomic variables that determine aggregate demand. Now we retrace our steps to present a more detailed and sophisticated treatment of the key relationships in the *IS-LM* model. The present chapter deals with the consumption function and with saving—since consumption purchases account for about 60 percent of aggregate demand, this is the natural place to begin. The following three chapters flesh out the behaviour of investment, money demand, and money supply, and thus move us to a more realistic and reliable understanding of the working of the economy.

Our starting point in examining consumption behaviour is the consumption function we have been using in previous chapters. Thus far we have assumed that consumption is a linear function of disposable income:

$$C = \overline{C} + cYD \qquad \overline{C} > 0 \qquad 1 > c > 0 \qquad (1)$$

What does the empirical evidence show? Do the data for the postwar period bear out the hypothesis of a consumption function such as Equation (1)? We plot consumption and disposable income (both in 1981 dollars) for each of the years from 1966 through 1987 in Figure 8-1. The diagram clearly reveals a close positive relationship between consumption and disposable income. To find numerical estimates of the intercept (C) and the marginal propensity to consume (c), we "fit" a regression line to the observations. The regression line is fitted to the data using the method of least squares, which produces the linear equation that best characterizes the relation between consumption and disposable income contained in the data.[1]

The estimated regression line is shown in Figure 8-1 as the solid line and is reported in Equation (2). The estimate of the intercept is 1.22 and the estimate of the marginal propensity to consume is 0.86.

$$C = 1.22 + 0.86YD \text{ (annual data 1966–87)} \tag{2}$$

Two characteristics of a consumption function such as Equation (1) are borne out by the empirical Equation (2). There is a positive intercept and the marginal propensity to consume is positive and less than unity.

If we divide through by YD in Equation (2), we obtain an equation that gives the average propensity to consume (C/YD) as a function of disposable income:

$$\frac{C}{YD} = \frac{1.22}{YD} + 0.86 \tag{3}$$

Equation (3) indicates that the average propensity to consume declines as disposable income rises.[2] However, although the intercept, 1.22, is positive, it is very small relative to disposable income, which is $264 billion 1981 dollars, in 1987.[3] If the intercept were actually zero, then we see from Equations (1) and (3) that consumption would be proportional to disposable income, with $C/YD = c$. The marginal and average propensities to consume would be equal. The relationship shown by Figure 8-1 and Equation (2) is essentially one of

---

[1] It is frequently useful to summarize a relationship, such as that of Fig. 8-1, between consumption expenditures and disposable income by writing an equation such as equation (2), which has specific numerical values in it, rather than the more general form of equation (1), which does not specify numerical values of the coefficients $\overline{C}$ and c. The line drawn in Fig. 8-1 is the line represented by equation (2). That line is calculated by minimizing the sum of the squares of the vertical distances of the points in Fig. 8-1 from the line, and it provides a good description of the general relationship between the two variables. For further details on the fitting of such lines, called least-squares regression lines, see Robert S. Pindyck and Daniel L. Rubinfeld, *Econometric Models and Economic Forecasts*, 2d ed. (New York: McGraw-Hill, 1980).

[2] You should check the *Canadian Statistical Review* to see how well Equation (2) predicts consumption for 1988. Disposable income in 1981 dollars can be obtained by dividing the current dollar figure by the implicit price index (deflator) for personal consumption expenditure.

[3] Technically, the intercept is statistically not significantly different from zero. See Pindyck and Rubinfeld, op. cit., for the meaning of tests of significance.

FIGURE 8-1   THE CONSUMPTION-INCOME RELATION, 1966-1987

proportionality, with the average and marginal propensities to consume out of disposable income equal to each other, at about 0.9.

Inspection of the regression line in Figure 8-1 suggests that the estimated equation fits well. There are no points far off the fitted line. As a first approximation then, Equation (2) provides a reasonable summary of consumption behaviour. However, Figure 8-2 gives a different perspective. It shows the annual *changes* in consumption compared with the changes calculated from Equation (2). The errors are quite large, particularly in the last 7 years of the period. In addition, the predicted change remains above the actual change from

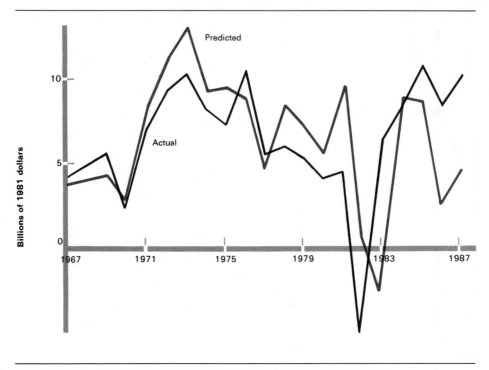

FIGURE 8-2 ACTUAL AND PREDICTED CHANGES IN CONSUMPTION

1970 to 1975 and below the actual change from 1978 to 1982. It appears that the simple consumption function in Equation (2) can be improved upon.

We develop the two basic modern theories of consumption in the remainder of this chapter. They are the *life-cycle* theory, associated primarily with Franco Modigliani[4] of MIT, 1985 Nobel Prize winner in economic science, and the *permanent income* theory, associated primarily with Milton Friedman of the University of Chicago, the 1976 winner of the Nobel Prize in economics. These theories are quite similar. Like much of good macroeconomics, they have in common a careful attention to microeconomic foundations. The life-cycle theory in particular starts from an individual's lifetime consumption planning, and develops from there a macroeconomic theory of consumption and saving.

---

[4] Modigliani developed the life cycle theory together with Richard Brumberg, who died tragically young, and Albert Ando of the University of Pennsylvania. His Nobel Prize lecture, "Life Cycle, Individual Thrift, and the Wealth of Nations," appears in the June 1986 *American Economic Review*.

Box 8-1 describes an empirical puzzle about the simple consumption function that was historically important in leading to the new theories of the consumption function.[5]

BOX 8-1   A CONSUMPTION FUNCTION PUZZLE

The puzzle consists of two types of evidence that made their appearance in the late 1940s and that were apparently in conflict. The first type of evidence came from estimates of the standard consumption function, equation (1), using annual data for the U.S. for the 1929–1941 period. (No earlier data were available then.) The estimated equation (in 1972 dollars) is

$$C = 47.6 + 0.73YD \qquad \text{(annual data, 1929–1941)} \qquad \text{(B1)}$$

Using Canadian data for the period 1926–1940, the estimated equation in 1971 dollars) is

$$C = 3.0 + 0.69Y_D \qquad \text{(annual data, Canada, 1926–1940)} \qquad \text{(B2)}$$

These equations imply that the average propensity to consume falls as the level of income rises. They also have low marginal propensities to consume. If we used Equation (4a) to predict today's average propensity to consume in Canada, the estimate would be around .72, which of course is far off the actual ratio of about .85.

The second piece of evidence was the finding by Nobel Prize winner, Simon Kuznets (1901–1985), using averages of U.S. data over long periods — 10 and 30 years — that there was near proportionality between consumption and

---

[5] The theories of the consumption function developed hereafter are also useful for explaining another empirical puzzle that we shall not go into in detail. In *cross-sectional* studies of the relationship between consumption and income — studies in which the consumption of a sample of families is related to their income—the marginal propensity to consume out of disposable income also appears to be lower than the average propensity to consume, with the average propensity to consume falling as the level of income rises. If you are interested in the reconciliation of this evidence with the long-run evidence of Kuznets, you should look at the ingenious explanation advanced by Milton Friedman through the permanent-income hypothesis. Follow up the reference given in footnote 10.

income.* This is consistent with the intercept term in equation (1) being zero. The average propensity to consume that he found for three overlapping 30-year periods is shown in Table 1. The Kuznets results suggest, using long-term averages, that there is little variation in the ratio of consumption to income and, in particular, that there is no tendency for the average propensity to decline as disposable income rises.

TABLE 1   THE KUZNETS FINDING

	1869–1898	1884–1913	1904–1933
Average propensity	0.867	0.867	0.879

Source: Simon Kuznets, *National Income, A Summary of Findings* (New York: National Bureau of Economic Research, 1946), table 16.

There is clearly a conflict between the implications of the consumption function in equation (B1) and Kuznets' findings. The Kuznets results suggest that the average propensity to consume is constant over long periods, whereas equation (B1) suggests its falls as income rises. It is also clear that the consumption function estimated above on the basis of the prewar data is inconsistent with the same function estimated on the basis of postwar data, that is, equation (2).

The puzzle of the discrepancy was well known by the time the alternative theories we outline below were developed. In resolving the puzzle, both theories draw on the notion that consumption is related to a broader income measure than just current income. The broader measures go under the names of *lifetime income and permanent income*. These concepts have in common the recognition that consumption spending is maintained relatively constant in the face of fluctuations of current income. Consumption spending is not geared to what we earn today, but to what we earn on average. The important question obviously is what "average" means in this context. This is analyzed in the theories developed in the following sections.

---

* Simon Kuznets, *National Product Since 1869* and *National Income, A Summary of Findings* (New York: National Bureau of Economic Research, 1946).

8-1   THE LIFE-CYCLE THEORY OF CONSUMPTION AND SAVING

The consumption function (1) is based on the simple notion that individuals' consumption behaviour in a given period is related to their income in that period. The *life-cycle hypothesis* views individuals, instead, as planning their consumption and saving behaviour over long periods with the intention of allocating their consumption in the best possible way over their entire lifetimes.

The life-cycle hypothesis views savings as resulting mainly from individual's desire to provide for consumption in old age. As we shall see, the theory points to a number of unexpected factors affecting the saving rate of the economy, for instance, the age structure of the population is, in principle, an important determinant of consumption and saving behaviour.

To anticipate the main results of this section, we can already state here that we will derive a consumption function of the form

$$C = aWR + cYL \tag{4}$$

where *WR* is real wealth, *a* is the marginal propensity to consume out of wealth, *YL* is *labour income*, and *c* is the marginal propensity to consume out of labour income. Labour income is the income that is earned by labour, as opposed to the income earned by other factors of production, such as the rent earned by land or the profits earned by capital.

In developing the life-cycle hypothesis of saving and consumption, we show what determines the marginal propensities *a* and *c* in equation (4), why wealth should affect consumption, and how the life-cycle hypothesis helps explain the Kuznets puzzle described in Box 8-1.

Consider a person who expects to live for *NL* years, work and earn income for *WL* years, and be in retirement for $(NL - WL)$ years. The individual's year 1 is the first year of work. We shall, in what follows, ignore any uncertainty about either life expectancy or the length of working life. We shall assume, too, that no interest is earned on savings, so that current saving translates dollar for dollar into future consumption possibilities. With these assumptions, we can approach the saving or consumption decision with two questions. First, what are the individual's lifetime consumption possibilities? Second, how will the individual choose to distribute his or her consumption over a lifetime?

Consider now the consumption possibilities. For the moment we ignore property income (income from assets) and focus attention on labour income *YL*. Income, *YL*, and consumption, *C*, are measured in real terms. Given *WL* years of working, *lifetime income* (from labour) is $(YL \times WL)$, income per working year times the number of working years. Consumption over someone's lifetime cannot exceed this lifetime income unless that person is born with wealth, which we initially assume is not the case. Accordingly, we have determined the first part of the consumer's problem in finding the limit of lifetime consumption.

We assume the individual will want to distribute consumption over a lifetime so that he or she has a flat or even flow of consumption. Rather than consume a lot in one period and very little in another, the preferred profile is to consume exactly equal amounts in each period.[6] Clearly, this assumption implies that consumption is not geared to *current* income (which is zero during retirement), but rather to *lifetime income.*

Lifetime consumption equals lifetime income. This means that the planned level of consumption C, which is the same in every period, times the number of years in life NL equals lifetime income:

$$C \times NL = YL \times WL \tag{5}$$

where WL is working life. Lifetime income is equal to $(YL \times WL)$. Dividing through by NL, we have planned consumption per year, C, which is proportional to labour income:

$$C = \frac{WL}{NL} \times YL \tag{6}$$

The factor of proportionality in equation (6) is WL/NL, the fraction of lifetime spent working. Accordingly, equation (6) states that in each year of working life a fraction of labour income is consumed, where that fraction is equal to the proportion of working life in total life.

Numerical Example

Suppose a person starts working at age 20, plans to work till 65, and will die at 80. The working life WL is thus 45 years (= 65 − 20) and the number of years of life, NL, is 60 years (= 80 − 20). Annual labour income YL is $20 000. Then

$$\begin{aligned} \text{Lifetime income} &= YL \times WL \\ &= \$20\,000 \times 45 \\ &= \$900\,000 \end{aligned}$$

---

[6] Why? The basic reason is the notion of diminishing marginal utility of consumption. Consider two alternative consumption plans. One involves an equal amount of consumption in each of two periods; the other involves consuming all in one period and none in the other. The principle of diminishing marginal utility of income implies that in the latter case, we would be better off by transferring some consumption from the period of plenty toward that of starvation. The loss in utility in the period of plenty is *more* than compensated by the gain in utility in the period of scarcity. And there is a gain to be made by transferring consumption so long as there is any difference in consumption between the two periods. The principle of diminishing marginal utility of consumption conforms well with the observation that most people choose stable life styles — not, in general, saving furiously in one period to have a spending spree in the next, but rather, consuming at about the same level every period.

This person will receive a total of $900 000 over a working lifetime.

The lifetime income, $900 000, has to be spread over the 60 years of life. The consumer wants to spread it evenly, and so

$$C = \frac{\$900\ 000}{60} = \$15\ 000 = \frac{WL}{NL} \times YL$$

$$= \frac{45}{60} \times 20\ 000$$

$$= 0.75 \times 20\ 000$$

In this example, 0.75 of labour income is consumed each year the person works. Why is the propensity to consume out of labour income in this example equal to 0.75? It is simply the fraction of lifetime that the person works.

Saving and Dissaving

The counterpart of equation (6) is the saving function. Remembering that saving is equal to income less consumption, we have

$$S \equiv YL - C = YL \frac{NL - WL}{NL} \tag{7}$$

Equation (7) states that saving during the period in which the individual works is equal to a fraction of labour income, with that fraction being equal to the proportion of life spent in retirement.

Figure 8-3 shows the lifetime pattern of consumption, saving, and *dissaving*.[7] Over the whole lifetime, there is an even flow of consumption at the rate of C, amounting in total to C × NL. That consumption spending is financed during working life out of current income. During retirement the consumption is financed by drawing down the savings that have been accumulated during working life. Therefore the shaded areas (YL − C) × WL and C × (NL − WL) are equal, or equivalently, saving during working years finances, dissaving during retirement.

The important idea of lifetime consumption theory is apparent from Figure 8-3. It is that consumption plans are made so as to achieve a smooth or even level of consumption by saving during periods of high income and dissaving during periods of low income. This is, therefore, an important departure from consumption based on current income. It is an important difference because,

---

[7] Figure 8-3 was developed by Franco Modigliani in "The Life Cycle Hypothesis of Saving, the Demand for Wealth and the Supply of Capital," *Social Research*, vol. 33, no. 2, 1966.

in addition to current income, the whole future profile of income enters into the calculation of lifetime consumption. Before developing that aspect further, however, we return to Figure 8-3 to consider the role of assets.

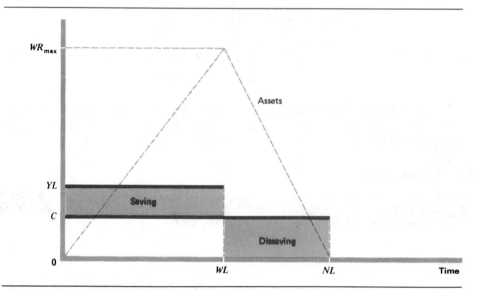

FIGURE 8-3 LIFETIME INCOME, CONSUMPTION, SAVINGS, AND WEALTH IN THE LIFE-CYCLE MODEL. During the working life, lasting WL years, the individual saves, building up assets. At the end of the working life, the individual begins to live off these assets, dissaving for the next $(NL - WL)$ years, till the end of life. Consumption is constant at level C throughout the lifetime. All assets have been used up at the end of life.

Assets

During the working years, the individual saves to finance consumption during retirement. The saving builds up assets, and we accordingly show in Figure 8-3 how the individual's wealth or assets increase over working life and reach a maximum at retirement age. From that time on, assets decline because the individual sells assets to pay for current consumption.

What is the maximum level that assets reach? Remember that assets are built up to finance consumption during retirement. Total consumption during retirement is equal to $C \times (NL - WL)$. All that consumption is financed out of the assets accumulated by the date of retirement, which is when assets are at their peak.

Denote the maximum level of assets by WR_{max}. Then,

$$WR_{max} = C \times (NL - WL)$$

For instance, in the numerical example above, where C was $15 000 and $(NL - WL)$ was equal to 15, the individual would have $15 000 $\times$ 15 = $225 000 saved at the date of retirement. Equivalently, the person has worked for 45 years, saving $5000 each year, meaning an accumulation of $225 000 at age 65.

This simple case gives the spirit of the life-cycle hypothesis of consumption and saving. People do not want to consume over their lifetimes at precisely the same times and amounts they earn income. Thus they save and dissave so as to consume their lifetime incomes in the pattern they want. Typically, the theory argues, they will save while working, and then use the savings to finance spending in their retirement years.

Saving

The life-cycle theory of consumption is also of course a theory of life-cycle saving. In its simplest version, as in Figure 8-3, the theory implies that individuals save for their retirement while working. But there is a more general theory of saving implied by the life-cycle theory. Namely, individuals aim to have smooth patterns of consumption over their lifetimes. Their income patterns may not be so smooth: they may go to school at one stage, or retire at another, or take a year off to find themselves at the age of forty. *The life-cycle theory of saving predicts that people save a lot when their income is high relative to lifetime average income, and dissave when their income is low relative to the lifetime average.*

Introducing Wealth

The next step is to extend this model and allow for initial assets, assuming the individual is born to wealth.[8] We can draw on the previous insight that the consumer will spread any existing resources to achieve an even lifetime consumption profile. The individual who has assets in addition to labour income will plan to use these assets to add to lifetime consumption. A person who is at some point T in life, with a stock of wealth WR and labour income accruing for another $(WL - T)$ years at the rate of YL, and with a life expectancy of $(NL - T)$ years to go, will behave as follows. The person's lifetime consumption possibilities are

$$C(NL - T) = WR + (WL - T)YL \qquad (8)$$

---

[8] The individual may receive wealth early in life through gifts or bequests. In the fully developed life-cycle model, the individual, in calculating lifetime consumption, has also to take account of any bequests he or she may want to leave. We discuss the role of bequests in Box 8-2.

where we have included wealth WR along with lifetime labour income as a source of finance for lifetime consumption. From equation (8), consumption in each period is equal to

$$C = aWR + cYL \qquad a \equiv \frac{1}{NL - T} \qquad c \equiv \frac{WL - T}{NL - T} \qquad WL > T \qquad (9)$$

where the coefficients a and c are, respectively, the marginal propensities to consume out of wealth and out of labour income.

In the numerical example above we considered a person starting work at age 20, who will retire at 65 and die at 80. Thus, $WL = 65 - 20 = 45$; and $NL = 80 - 20 = 60$. We also assumed $YL = 20\,000$.

Now suppose the person is 40 years old. Accordingly, $T = 20$, meaning that the person is in the twentieth year of working life. We can calculate the propensity to consume out of wealth a and the propensity to consume out of income c from equation (9). For this person, at age 40 (i.e., for $T = 20$):

$$a = \frac{1}{NL - T} = \frac{1}{60 - 20} = 0.025$$

$$c = \frac{WL - T}{NL - T} = \frac{45 - 20}{60 - 20} = 0.625$$

Suppose now that the individual's wealth is $200\,000. Then from the consumption function, equation (9), we find:

$$
\begin{aligned}
C &= (0.025 \times 200\,000) + (0.625 \times 20\,000) \\
&= 5000 + 12\,500 \\
&= 17\,500
\end{aligned}
$$

Note that the consumption level here is higher than in the previous example. That is because this individual has more wealth at age 40 than he or she would have if all this wealth came from saving out of labour income. (That amount, at age 40, would from the previous example be $100\,000—since the individual in the previous example saved $5000 per year and at T = 20 has been working 20 years.) We can conclude that we are dealing here with someone who inherited wealth and started out working life with some wealth.

Thus, in our model of individual lifetime consumption, we have derived a consumption function like equation (4), where both wealth and labour income affect the individual's consumption decisions. It is important to recognize from equation (9) that the marginal propensities are related to the individual's position in the life cycle. The closer a person is to the end of lifetime, the higher the marginal propensity to consume out of wealth. Thus, someone with 2 more years of life will consume half his or her remaining wealth in each of the remaining 2 years. The marginal propensity to consume out of labour income is related both to the remaining number of years during which income will be earned, $WL - T$, and to the number of years over which these earnings are spread, $NL - T$. It is quite clear from equation (9) that an increase in either wealth or labour income will raise consumption expenditures. It is apparent, too, that lengthening working life relative to retirement will raise consumption because it increases lifetime income and reduces the length of the period of dissaving. The most basic point, however, is that equation (9) shows both (lifetime) income and wealth as determinants of consumption spending.

To summarize where we have come so far, we note that in this form of the life-cycle model:

1. Consumption is constant over the consumer's lifetime.
2. Consumption spending is financed by lifetime income plus initial wealth.
3. During each year a fraction $1/(NL - T)$ of wealth will be consumed.
4. Current consumption spending depends on current wealth and lifetime income.

Extensions

The model outlined makes very strong simplifying assumptions. It can be extended to remove most of the strong assumptions without affecting the underlying result of equation (9), that consumption is related to both labour income and wealth.

First, it is necessary to take account of the possibility that saving earns interest, so that a dollar not consumed today will provide more than a dollar's consumption tomorrow. Second, the analysis has to be extended to allow for the fact that individuals are uncertain of the length of their lifetimes, and also that they sometimes want to leave bequests to their heirs. In this latter case, they would not plan to consume all their resources over their own lifetimes. Similarly, the model has to be extended to take account of the composition of the family over time, so that some consumption is provided for children before they begin to work. However, to repeat, these extensions do not change the basic results contained in equation (9).

A final extension is very important. In practice, one never knows exactly what one's lifetime labour income will be, and lifetime consumption plans have to be made on the basis of predictions of future labour income. This, of course, raises the issue of how income is to be predicted. We do not pursue this important issue here, but leave it to the next section on permanent income, which is an estimate of lifetime income. However, *expected* lifetime labour income would be related to *current* disposable labour income, leading to a form of the consumption function like equation (4), perhaps with other variables also included.

BOX 8-2   THE LIFE-CYCLE HYPOTHESIS, CONSUMPTION OF THE ELDERLY, AND BEQUESTS

Although the life-cycle hypothesis remains the leading microeconomic theory of consumption behaviour, recent empirical evidence raises questions about the particular form of the theory developed in this chapter. In the form of the theory developed by Modigliani, the assumption is that people save mainly for retirement, and draw down their savings during retirement.

Two recent papers question the assumed motive for saving and the implication that people draw down their savings when old. Laurence Kotlikoff and Lawrence Summers* have made calculations suggesting that most saving is done to provide bequests rather than to provide for consumption when old. Of course, the savings are there for the old to use in retirement, but, they argue, the amount of wealth in the economy is far too large for people to have been saving only for their retirement. Rather, they conclude, people are saving mainly to pass wealth on to their descendants.

A detailed examination of the consumption propensities of the elderly by Sheldon Danziger, Jacques van der Gaag, Eugene Smolensky, and Michael Taussig† contains the remarkable conclusion that the elderly save a higher proportion of their incomes than the young. This fact is inconsistent with the simple form of the life-cycle hypothesis set out in the chapter.

How might this evidence be reconciled with existing theories? First, the facts are not yet definitive. Franco Modigliani is his Nobel Prize lecture (*American Economic Review*, June 1986) takes strong issue with the detailed calculations that underlie the Kotlikoff-Summers claim. In Japan, where similar results have been found,‡ the elderly typically move in and pool their wealth with their children. They thus probably are drawing down wealth during their retirement, but their wealth cannot be distinguished from that of the children who are saving.

If the basic evidence that the elderly who remain on their own accumulate wealth holds up, an explanation will have to take into account their increasing fears of being left alone without financial help from family, and with possibly large medical expenses, as they get older. The need for wealth may increase

* "The Role of Intergenerational Transfers in Aggregate Capital Accumulation," *Journal of Political Economy*, August 1981.

† In their research paper from the University of Wisconsin, "The Life Cycle Hypothesis and the Consumption Behavior of the Elderly," 1982.

‡ See Albert Ando and Arthur Kennickell, "How Much (or Little) Life Cycle Saving Is There in Micro Data?" in Rudiger Dornbusch, and Stanley Fischer (eds.), *Macroeconomics and Finance: Essays in Honor of Franco Modigliani* (Boston: MIT Press, 1986).

with age if complete insurance against medical expenses is not available — as it is not in the United States.

Whether people save for their own lifetimes, or also save to pass wealth on to their children, does not affect the fact that wealth belongs in the consumption function, as in equation (3). But as we shall see below, it has potentially important implications for the effects of fiscal policy on the economy.

Indeed, it is useful to think of the life-cycle and permanent-income theories as being fundamentally the same, with the life-cycle theory developing most carefully the implications of the model for the role of wealth and other variables in the consumption function,[9] and the permanent-income theory concentrating on the best way to predict lifetime income.

Aggregate Consumption and Saving

The theory as so far outlined is strictly a microeconomic theory about consumption and saving by individuals over the course of their lifetimes. How does it relate to aggregate consumption, which is, after all, the focus of macroeconomic interest in consumption? Imagine an economy in which population and income were constant through time. Each individual in that economy would go through the life cycle of saving and dissaving outlined in Figure 8-3. The economy as a whole, though, would not be saving. At any one time, the saving of working people would be exactly matched by the dissaving of retired people. However, if the population were growing, there would be more young people than old, thus more saving in total than dissaving, and there would be net saving in the economy. Thus, aggregate consumption depends in part on the age composition of the population. It also depends on such characteristics of the economy as the average age of retirement and the presence or absence of government pensions. These surprising implications of the theory indicate the richness of the approach.

Implications

We want to return to equation (4) to emphasize again the role of wealth. Note from equation (4) that if there were an increase in wealth, the ratio of consumption to disposable income would rise. This has a bearing on the puzzle described in Box 8-1, where the average propensity to consume seems, on the basis of equation (3), to decline with income and, on the basis of Kuznets' findings, to remain constant on average over long periods.

---

[9] The other variables indicated here will be discussed in the next paragraph.

If we divide through in equation (4) by YD, we obtain

$$\frac{C}{YD} = a\frac{WR}{YD} + c\frac{YL}{YD} \tag{10}$$

Now, if the ratio of wealth to disposable income and the ratio of disposable labour income to total disposable income are constant, then equation (10) shows that the ratio of consumption to disposable income will be constant. However, if the ratio of wealth to disposable income is changing, the average propensity to consume will also be changing.

This suggests, as an explanation of the Kuznets puzzle, the possibility that the ratio of wealth to disposable income is roughly constant over long periods, and that it varies considerably in the short run. This also helps explain the fluctuations in the average propensity to consume shown in Figure 8-2 as resulting from short-run changes in the wealth-income ratio.

One further interesting implication of the life-cycle hypothesis is that it provides a route for the stock market to affect consumption behaviour. The value of stocks held by the public is part of wealth and is included in WR in equation (4). When the value of stocks is high — when the stock market is booming — WR is high and tends to increase consumption, and the reverse occurs when the stock market is depressed.

We continue now to the permanent-income theory of consumption, bearing in mind that we have not yet discussed the determinants of expected lifetime labour income in equation (9) in any detail, and recalling that the two theories should be thought of as complementary rather than competing.

8-2 PERMANENT-INCOME THEORY OF CONSUMPTION

In the long run, the consumption-income ratio is very stable, but in the short run, it fluctuates. The life-cycle approach explains this by pointing out that people want to maintain a smooth profile of consumption even if their lifetime income profile is uneven, and thus emphasizes the role of wealth in the consumption function. Another explanation, which differs in details but entirely shares the spirit of the life-cycle approach, is the permanent-income theory of consumption.

The theory, which is the work of Milton Friedman,[10] argues that people gear their consumption behaviour to their permanent or long-term consumption opportunities, not to their current level of income. A suggestive example provided by Friedman involves someone who is paid or receives income only once

---

[10] Milton Friedman, *A Theory of the Consumption Function* (Princeton, N.J.: Princetown University Press, 1957).

a week, on Fridays. We do not expect that individual to concentrate his or her entire consumption on the one day on which income is received, with zero consumption on every other day. Again we are persuaded by the argument that individuals prefer a smooth consumption flow, rather than plenty today and scarcity tomorrow or yesterday. On that argument, consumption on any one day of the week would be unrelated to income on that particular day but would rather be geared to average daily income — that is, income per week divided by the number of days per week. It is clear that in this extreme example, income for a period longer than a day is relevant to the consumption decision. Similarly, Friedman argues, there is nothing special about a period of the length of one quarter or one year that requires the individual to plan consumption within the period solely on the basis of income within the period; rather, consumption is planned in relation to income over a longer period.

The idea of consumption spending that is geared to long-term or average or permanent income is appealing and essentially is the same as the life-cycle theory. It leaves two further questions. The first concerns the precise relationship between current consumption and permanent income. The second question is how to make the concept of permanent income operational, that is, how to measure it.

In its simplest form the permanent-income hypothesis of consumption behaviour argues that consumption is proportional to permanent income:

$$C = cYP \qquad (11)$$

where YP is permanent (disposable) income. From equation (11), consumption varies in the same proportion as permanent income. A 5 percent increase in permanent income raises consumption by 5 percent. Since permanent income should be related to long-run average income, this feature of the consumption function is clearly in line with the observed long-run constancy of the consumption-income ratio.

Estimating Permanent Income

The next problem is how to think of and measure permanent income. We define permanent income as follows:[11] Permanent income is the steady rate of consumption a person could maintain for the rest of his or her life, given the present level of wealth and income earned now and in the future.

---

[11] There is no standard definition of permanent income in Friedman's exposition of his theory. The definition given above is similar to average lifetime income, but it is not quite the same, because it effectively converts wealth into income in defining permanent income. Someone with no labour income, and only wealth, is defined as having permanent income equal to the amount he or she could consume each year by using up wealth at a steady rate over the remainder of his or her life.

To think about the measurement of permanent income, imagine someone trying to figure out what his or her permanent income is. The person has a current level of income, and has formed some idea of the level of consumption he or she can maintain for the rest of life. Now income goes up. The person has to decide whether that income increase represents a permanent increase, or merely, a *transitory* change, one that will not persist. In any particular case, the individual may know whether the increase is permanent or transitory. A government official who is promoted one grade will know that the increase in income is likely to be maintained, or the worker who has exceptionally high overtime in a given year will likely regard that year's increased income as transitory. In general, though, a person is not so certain about what part of any change in income is likely to be maintained, and is therefore permanent, and what part is not likely to be maintained, and is therefore transitory. Transitory income is assumed not to have any substantial effect on consumption.

The question of how to infer what part of an increase in income is permanent is typically resolved in a pragmatic way by assuming that permanent income is related to the behaviour of current and past incomes. To give a simple example, we might estimate permanent income as being equal to last year's income plus some fraction of the change in income from last year to this year:

$$YP = Y_{-1} + \theta(Y - Y_{-1}) \qquad 0 < \theta < 1$$
$$= \theta Y + (1 - \theta)Y_{-1}$$

(12)

where θ is a fraction and Y_{-1} is last year's income. The second line in equation (12) shows permanent income as a *weighted average* of current and past income. The second formulation is, of course, equivalent to that in the first line. To understand equation (12), assume we had a value of $\theta = 0.6$ and that this year's income was $Y = \$25\ 000$ and last year's income was $Y_{-1} = \$24\ 000$. The value of permanent income would be $YP = \$24\ 600\ (= 0.6 \times \$25\ 000 + 0.4 \times \$24\ 000)$. Thus, permanent income is an average of the two income levels. Whether it is closer to this year's or last year's income depends on the weight θ given to current income. Clearly, in the extreme with $\theta = 1$, permanent income is equal to current income.

Some special features of equation (12) deserve comment. First, if $Y = Y_{-1}$, that is, if this year's income is equal to last year's, then permanent income is equal to the income earned this year and last year. This guarantees that an individual who had always earned the same income would expect to earn that income in the future. Second, note that if income rises this year compared with last year, then permanent income rises by *less* than current income. The reason is that the individual does not know whether the rise in income this year is permanent. Not knowing whether the increase in income will be maintained or not, the individual does not immediately increase the expected or permanent income measure by the full amount of the actual or current increase in income.

Rational Expectations and Permanent Income

An estimate of permanent income that uses only current and last year's income is likely to be an oversimplification. Friedman forms the estimate by looking at incomes in many earlier periods, as well as current income, but with weights that are larger for the more recent, as compared with the more distant, incomes.[12]

The rational expectations approach, discussed in the following section, emphasizes that there is no simple theory that would tell us how expectations are or should be formed without looking at how income changes in practice. If, in practice, changes in income are typically permanent or long-run changes, then a consumer who sees a given change in his income will believe that it is mostly permanent. Such a consumer would have a high θ as in equation (12). If the consumer's income is usually very variable, then he or she will not pay much attention to current changes in income in forming an estimate of permanent income. Such a consumer will have a low value of θ.[13]

At the same time, any sensible theory of expectations, including rational expectations, would emphasize that a formula like (12), based on the behaviour of income in the past, cannot include all the factors that influence a person's beliefs about future income. The discovery of a vast amount of oil in a country, for instance, would raise the permanent incomes of the inhabitants of the country as soon as it was announced, even though a (mechanical) formula like equation (12) based on past levels of income would not reflect such a change.

Permanent Income and the Dynamics of Consumption

Using equations (11) and (12), we can now rewrite the consumption function:

$$C = cYP = c\theta Y + c(1 - \theta)Y_{-1} \qquad (13)$$

The marginal propensity to consume out of *current* income is then just $c\theta$, which is clearly less than the long-run average propensity to consume, c. Hence, the permanent-income hypothesis implies that there is a difference between the short-run marginal propensity to consume and the long-run marginal (equal to the average) propensity to consume.

---

[12] Friedman also adjusted permanent income by taking into account the growth of income over time.

[13] Recall that although we restricted our measure of permanent income to a 2-year average, there is no reason why the average should not be taken over longer periods. If current income is unstable, an appropriate measure of permanent income may well be an average over 5 or more years.

We shall see shortly that this implication is supported by the data, but first we explore it in more detail. The reason for the lower short-run marginal propensity to consume is that when current income rises, the individual is not sure that the increase in income will be maintained over the longer period on which consumption plans are based. Accordingly, the person does not fully adjust consumption spending to the higher level that would be appropriate if the increase in income were permanent. However, if the increase turns out to be permanent, that is, if next period's income is the same as this period's, then the person will (next year) fully adjust consumption spending to the higher level of income. Note, though, that the adjustment here is completed in 2 years only because we have assumed, in equation (12), that permanent income is an average of 2 years' income. Depending on how expectations of permanent income are formed, the adjustment could be much slower.

The argument is illustrated in Figure 8-4. Here we show the long-run consumption function as a straight line through the origin with slope c, which is

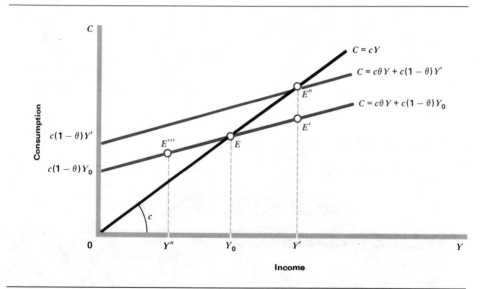

FIGURE 8-4 THE EFFECTS ON CONSUMPTION OF A SUSTAINED INCREASE IN INCOME. The short-run consumption functions, shown in colour, have marginal propensity to consume of $c\theta$. The position of the short-run consumption function depends on the level of income in the previous period. The long-run consumption function is shown by the black line and has average and marginal propensity to consume equal to c. When the level of income rises from Y_0 to Y', consumption rises only to E' in the short run, because consumers are not sure the change in income is permanent. With income remaining at Y', the short-run consumption function shifts up and consumption rises to point E'', as consumers realize their permanent income has changed.

the constant average and marginal propensity to consume out of permanent income. The lower flat consumption function is a short-run consumption function drawn for a given history of income which is reflected in the intercept $c(1 - \theta)Y_0$. Assume that we start out in long-run equilibrium with actual and permanent income equal to Y_0 and consumption therefore equal to cY_0, as is shown at the intersection of long-run and short-run consumption functions at point E. Assume next that income increases to the level Y'. In the short run, which means during the current period, we revise our estimate of permanent income upward by θ times the increase in income and consume a fraction c of that increase in permanent income. Accordingly, consumption moves up along the short-run consumption function to point E'.

Note immediately that in the short run the ratio of consumption to income declines as we move from point E to E'. Going one period ahead and assuming that the increase in income persists so that income remains at Y', we get a shift in the short-run consumption function. The consumption function shifts upward because, as of the given higher level of income, the estimate of permanent income is now revised upward to Y'. Accordingly, consumers want to spend a fraction of c of their new estimate of permanent income Y'. The new consumption point is E'', where the ratio of consumption to income is back to the long-run level. The example makes clear that in the short run, an increase in income causes a decline in the average propensity to consume because people do not anticipate that the increase in income will persist or be permanent. Once they do observe that the increase in income does persist, however, they fully adjust consumption to match their higher permanent income.

Like the life-cycle hypothesis, the permanent-income hypothesis has some unexpected and interesting implications. For instance, we noted above that an individual whose income is very unstable would have a low value of θ, whereas one whose income is more stable would have a higher value of θ. Looking at equation (13), this means that the short-run marginal propensity to consume of someone whose income is very variable will be relatively low—because the short-run marginal propensity to consume is $c\theta$. Friedman shows that this implication is borne out by the facts. Farmers, for instance, have very variable incomes and a low marginal propensity to consume out of current income.

The Life-Cycle and Permanent-Income Hypotheses

To conclude this section, it is worth considering again the relationship between the life-cycle and permanent-income hypotheses briefly. The two hypotheses are not mutually exclusive. The life-cycle hypothesis pays more attention to the motives for saving than the permanent-income hypothesis does, and provides convincing reasons to include wealth as well as income in the consumption function. The permanent-income hypothesis, on the other hand, pays more careful attention to the way in which individuals form their expectations about their future incomes than the original life-cycle hypothesis does. Recall that current labour income entered the life-cycle consumption function to reflect expectations of future income. The more detailed analysis of the determinants of expected future income that is provided by the permanent-income hypothesis can be, and has been, included in the life-cycle consumption function.

Indeed, modern theories of the consumption function combine the expectations formation emphasized by the permanent-income approach with the emphasis on wealth and demographic variables suggested by the life-cycle approach. A simplified version of a modern consumption function would be

$$C = aWR + b\theta YD + b(1 - \theta)YD_{-1} \tag{14}$$

where YD in equation (14) would be disposable labour income. Equation (14) combines the main features that are emphasized by modern consumption theory.[14] It also shows the role of wealth, which is an important influence on consumption spending.

We end this section by repeating a warning that is important enough for us to risk overstating. An equation like (14) performs quite well on average in predicting consumption, but it is always important to remember the underlying theory when using it. Equation (14) embodies the estimate of permanent income implied by equation (12). If we have knowledge about some particular change in income—for example, that it is transitory—then we should use that knowledge in predicting consumption. For instance, as we shall see, a temporary 1-year tax increase that reduced current disposable income would reduce current consumption by much less than a tax increase of the same size that was known to be permanent, even though equation (14) does not show that.

8-3   RATIONAL EXPECTATIONS, EXCESS SENSITIVITY, AND LIQUIDITY CONSTRAINTS

One of the most fascinating areas of research in modern consumption theory concerns the question of whether consumption responds excessively to changes in current income. Modern research in this area, originating with work by Robert Hall of Stanford University and Marjorie Flavin of the University of

---

[14] To fix ideas, you should draw a graph of equation (14) with consumption on the vertical axis and current disposable labour income on the horizontal axis. What is the intercept? How does the diagram differ from Fig. 8-4? Show the effects of (1) a transitory increase in income, (2) a sustained increase in income, and (3) an increase in wealth.

Virginia, focusses on the combined implications of rational expectations and the life-cycle–permanent-income theory of consumption.[15]

In the previous section we noted that if expectations are rational, consumers' estimates of their permanent incomes should be consistent with the way income actually changes in the real world. When current income increases, it is usually impossible to be certain whether this increase represents a transitory or a permanent rise in income, but the consumer can use experience to determine what is the expected relationship between changes in current and changes in permanent income. For example, historically a $1 increase in current income might typically have represented a 25 cent increase in permanent income, with the remaining 75 cents being transitory. Let θ be the fraction of a dollar increase in current income that represents the permanent increase. Then the consumption function in (11) together with this extra information about the current–permanent income relation will yield a propensity to consume out of current equal to $c\theta$. Thus if $c = 0.9$ and $\theta = 0.25$ the marginal propensity to consume out of current income should be 0.225.

The researcher determines the value of θ, the proportion of a current change in income that is permanent, by examining the past behaviour of income.[16] The next step is to see whether consumption reacts to the change in income by the right amount, $c\theta$, implied by the combined rational-expectations–permanent-income theory. The striking finding, for instance in Flavin's 1981 paper referred to above, is that consumption *systematically* responds too much to current income, or is excessively sensitive. When income rises, consumption goes up by more than $c\theta$, and when income falls, consumption goes down by more than $c\theta$.

Still accepting the permanent-income hypothesis as a correct framework of consumption behaviour, there are two possible explanations for this overreaction. The first is that households do not correctly understand how changes in income are divided between permanent and transitory changes. This shortcoming is called a failure of the rational expectations hypothesis (RE) because it implies households have not done their homework and are not forecasting in the best possible way and using all available information about how income

---

[15] See Robert E. Hall, "Stochastic Implications of the Life Cycle-Permanent Income Hypothesis: Theory and Evidence," *Journal of Political Economy*, vol. 86, December 1978, and Marjorie Flavin, "The Adjustment of Consumption to Changing Expectations about Future Income," *Journal of Political Economy*, vol. 89, October 1981.

[16] Income changes over time in a more complicated way than is implied by equation (12), but that does not affect the principle that the test figures out how *estimated* permanent income should change with current income, and then sees whether changes in consumption are in accord with that estimate.

behaves. The alternative hypothesis is that, while households in fact understand
how income changes are divided between permanent and transitory, they fail
to adjust to these changes properly because of liquidity constraints.

Excess Sensitivity and Liquidity Constraints

A liquidity constraint exists when a consumer cannot borrow to sustain current
consumption in the expectation of higher future income. Students in particular
should appreciate the possibility that liquidity constraints exist. Most students
can look forward to much higher income in future than they receive as students.
The life-cycle says they should be consuming on the basis of their lifetime
incomes, which means they should be spending much more than they earn. To
do that, they have to borrow. They can borrow to some extent, through student
loans, but it is entirely possible they cannot borrow enough to support consumption at its permanent level.

Such students are liquidity-constrained. When they leave university and take
jobs, their incomes will rise, and their consumption will rise too. According to
the life-cycle theory, consumption should not rise much when income rises, so
long as the increase was expected. In fact, because of the liquidity constraint,
consumption will rise a lot when income rises. Thus consumption will be more
closely related to *current* income than is implied by the theory.

Alternatively, consider a household that suffers a decline in current income
and believes the decline is transitory because in the past, on average, falls in
income have been mostly transitory. The household would therefore maintain
consumption substantially unchanged, dissaving today. If there are no assets
to run down to finance the excess of consumption over income, the household
would borrow today, repaying the loan when income rises again as expected.
Here imperfect capital markets come in. If the household cannot borrow
because nobody wants to lend against uncertain (though likely) future income, then it faces liquidity constraints and for that reason is forced to consume according to current rather than permanent income. Consumption will
then fall substantially along with current income—an overreaction in terms of
the permanent income theory which occurs because of the impossibility of
borrowing.

How serious are these liquidity constraints in fact? There is substantial evidence that liquidity constraints account for the excess sensitivity of consumption to income, and separate evidence that low income households are indeed
liquidity-constrained.[17] When liquidity constraints are present, consumption

[17] For instance Marjorie Flavin, "Excess Sensitivity of Consumption to Current Income:
Liquidity Constraints or Myopia?" *Canadian Journal of Economics*, vol. 18, February
1985, and Fumio Hayashi, "The Effect of Liquidity Constraints on Consumption:
A Cross-Sectional Analysis," *Quarterly Journal of Economics*, vol. 100, February 1985.

behaves more like the simple Keynesian consumption function equation (2) than life-cycle theory implies.

The strength of liquidity constraints will depend on economic conditions. Suppose the government initiates a tax cut. If we are in a period of deep recession where many households have already run down their assets, the tax cut will translate into a large increase in spending: Liquidity-constrained household members, by definition, are spending less than they would like and hence will spend every extra penny they can lay their hands on. By contrast a tax cut that occurs in a period of prosperity will have much less impact because few households are in a liquidity-constrained position where they spend, at the margin, all of an extra dollar of income.

8-4   FURTHER ASPECTS OF CONSUMPTION BEHAVIOUR

In this section we briefly review three topics in consumption, starting with international comparisons of saving behaviour.

International Differences in Saving Rates

Consumers in Canada and the United States save a lower proportion of their disposable income than consumers in many other countries, as Table 8-1 shows. The first row shows that North American households save about half as much of their disposable income as Japanese households. The second row shows *national* saving rates, which include saving by corporations and governments. Corporations save when they retain profits and use them for investing rather than paying them out as dividends. Similarly, governments that run budget surpluses are saving and contributing to national saving. This adjustment reduces the differences among countries somewhat but Japan remains a relatively large saver.

TABLE 8-1   INTERNATIONAL COMPARISONS OF SAVING RATES, 1970–1980

	U.S.	Japan	France	U.K.	Italy	Canada
Gross household saving	12.6	25.0	16.7	10.9	25.1	13.8
Gross national saving	18.6	35.0	24.1	19.0	22.3	22.1

Source: "Alternative of Measures Saving," *OECD Economic Outlook, Occasional Studies,* June 1983. Household saving rates are a percentage of disposable income; national saving rates are essentially percentages of GDP.

BOX 8-3 SAVING RATES IN CANADA AND THE U.S.

As shown in Table 2 below, in recent years the private savings rates in Canada have been substantially larger than those in the United States. The analysis of Carroll and Summers* suggests that differences in tax structures between the two countries were an important factor in explaining this divergence. The Canadian personal income tax provided greater incentives for saving through deductibility of contributions to Registered Pension Plans and Registered Retirement Savings Plans. In contrast, the U.S. personal income tax provided disincentives to save through the deductibility of interest paid on loans incurred to purchase durable goods and housing.

TABLE 2 SAVING IN CANADA AND THE U.S., 1983–1985
(percent of gross national product)

	Corporate	Personal	Government	Total
Canada	3.5	8.9	−5.3	7.1
U.S.	2.3	3.9	−3.3	2.9

* Chris Carrol and Lawrence H. Summers, "Why Have Private Saving Rates in the United States and Canada Diverged?", National Bureau of Economic Research, Working Paper No. 2319, 1987.

Consumption, Saving and Interest Rates

Since anyone who saves receives a return in the forms of interest, or dividends and capital gains, we might expect that saving would increase if the rate of return available to savers were increased. Think of someone saving and receiving an interest rate of 5 percent each year on accumulated savings. Surely an increase in the rate to, say, 10 percent would make that person save more.

Although it is true that when the interest rate rises, saving is made more attractive, it also makes it less necessary. Consider someone who has decided to save an amount that will ensure $10 000 per year is available for retirement. Suppose the interest rate is now 5 percent, and the person is saving $1000 per year. Now let the interest rate rise to 10 percent. With such a high interest rate, the individual needs to save less now to provide the given $10 000 per year during retirement. It may be possible to provide the same retirement income by saving only about $650 a year. Thus an increase in the interest rate might reduce saving.

What do the facts show? Does saving rise when the interest rate increases, because every dollar of saving generates a higher return? Or does saving fall because there is less need to save to provide a given level of future income? The answers from the data are ambiguous. Many researchers have examined this question, but few have found strong positive effects of interest rate increases on saving. Typically, research suggests the effects are small and certainly hard to find.[18]

Tax Cuts, the Barro-Ricardo Hypothesis and Saving

An argument that tax cuts will increase saving and have little effect on consumption has been put forward by Robert Barro of the University of Rochester.[19] The proposition was originally noted and rejected by David Ricardo in the nineteenth century. Suppose the budget is balanced initially, and the government cuts taxes. There will be a budget deficit, financed by borrowing. The debt that is issued today must be retired next year or in some future year, along with the interest that it carries. To repay the debt the government will have to raise taxes in the future. Thus a tax cut today means a tax increase in the future. Hence changes in taxes should have no effect on consumption because *permanent* income is really unaffected by this intertemporal jiggling of tax rates.

However, if permanent income is unaffected by the tax cut, then consumption should be unaffected. When taxes are cut today, households save the tax cut so they can pay the higher taxes tomorrow. Of course households may not in fact behave exactly in the way prescribed by the Barro-Ricardo hypothesis. They may see themselves as recipients of present cuts, but (perhaps rationally) they do not see themselves but rather future generations (in whose well-being they are not especially interested) as paying the future taxes.[20]

---

[18] The best known study finding positive interest rate effects is that of Michael Boskin, "Taxation, Saving, and the Rate of Interest," *Journal of Political Economy*, pt. 2, April 1978. For more typical results, see Gerald A. Carlino, "Interest Rate Effects and Intertemporal Consumption," *Journal of Monetary Economics*, March 1982.

[19] "Are Government Bonds Net Wealth?" *Journal of Political Economy*, vol. 82, November/December 1974. Recent empirical research on this hypothesis is reported in David A. Aschauer, "Fiscal Policy and Aggregate Demand," *American Economic Review*, March 1985.

[20] We noted above that whether individuals save for their children affects fiscal policy. If parents are concerned enough about their children, they will regard future taxes to be paid by their children as equivalent to taxes on themselves.

8-5   CONSUMPTION AND THE *IS-LM* FRAMEWORK

In this section we discuss briefly how the more sophisticated theories of consumption we have developed in this chapter affect the *IS-LM* analysis of Chapter 4. We focus on two implications. The first is that consumption is a function of wealth, and not only income as we assumed previously. The second is that the response of consumption to various changes—for instance, in autonomous spending — may take time, as individuals gradually adjust their estimates of permanent income.

Wealth in the Consumption Function

The life-cycle hypothesis, and estimated consumption functions of a form like equation (14), show that the rate of consumption depends on the level of wealth, as well as disposable income. This means that the position of the *IS* curve, representing equilibrium in the goods market, depends on the level of wealth.

Figure 8-5 shows how an increase in the level of wealth affects equilibrium output and the interest rate. The economy is initially in equilibrium at point *E*. There is then an increase in wealth: perhaps the stock market has gone up,

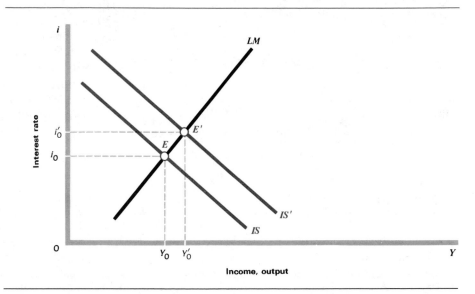

FIGURE 8-5   THE EFFECTS OF A SHIFT IN WEALTH. An increase in wealth shifts the consumption function, raising consumption demand at any level of income. Accordingly, the *IS* curve shifts to *IS'*, the level of output rises from Y_0 to Y_0', and the interest rate rises from i_0 to i_0'.

because everyone is optimistic that the economy is recovering from a recession. The higher wealth raises consumption spending, and the *IS* curve thus shifts up to *IS'*. The new equilibrium is at *E'*.

At *E'*, the interest rate and level of output are higher than at *E*. Thus an increase in wealth raises equilibrium output. Since the increase in wealth was assumed to result from expectations that the economy was recovering from a recession, we see that the expectations are partly self-fulfilling. A self-fulfilling prophecy is one which, purely as a result of being made, produces the prophesied result.

The Dynamics of Adjustment

In Section 8-3 and Figure 8-4, we examined the dynamic response of consumption spending to a shift in disposable income. Now we want to embody that dynamic adjustment in a full *IS-LM* model. The slow adjustment of consumption to a given change in disposable income will mean that income itself adjusts slowly to any given shift in autonomous spending that is not at first recognized as permanent, as we now show.

We assume here that people do not know whether the shift in autonomous demand is permanent or transitory. Rather, the only way they can figure that out is by seeing whether the change in demand persists or goes away. Figure 8-6 illustrates the effects of a permanent shift in autonomous demand, the nature of which (permanent or transitory) is not known to consumers.

Suppose that the economy is initially in equilibrium at point *E*. Now there is a shift in autonomous investment demand. In the long run, such a shift will move the *IS* curve to *IS'*. The extent of the shift is determined by the *long-run* multiplier $[1/(1 - c)]$, where c is the long-run propensity to consume. When expectations of income have fully adjusted, the economy will be at position *E'*, with output level Y_0' and interest rate i_0'.

However, in the short run the marginal propensity to consume is not c, but only $c\theta$. Thus the short-run multiplier is only $[l/(1 - c\theta)]$. In the short run, the *IS* curve shifts only to *IS"*. Thus the immediate effect of the shift in investment demand is to raise income to Y_0'' and the interest rate to i_0''.

Next period, the *IS* curve shifts again. It does not shift all the way to *IS'* though. Consumers have adjusted their estimate of permanent income up, but they have not yet adjusted it all the way to Y_0', because income last period was only Y_0'' and not Y_0'. (To keep the diagram simple, we do not show the *IS* curve for the second or later periods.) Income and the interest rate will rise above Y_0'' and i_0'', but still fall short of Y_0' and i_0'.

This process continues, with the consumption function gradually shifting up over time, as people come to realize that their permanent incomes have risen. A single shock to autonomous demand therefore produces a slow, or *distributed*

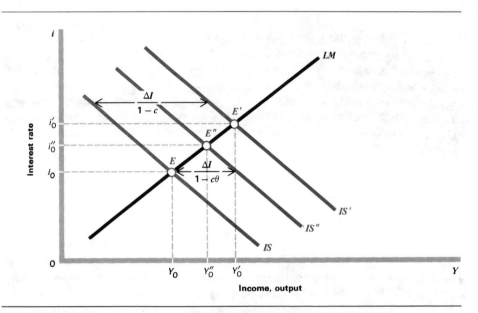

FIGURE 8-6   THE DYNAMICS OF ADJUSTMENT TO A SHIFT IN INVESTMENT DEMAND. Autonomous investment demand rises by amount ΔI, but it is not known whether the shift is permanent or transitory. It is in fact permanent, so that the *IS* curve will eventually be at *IS'*, shifted to the right by an amount $[\Delta I/(1-c)]$, where $[1/(1-c)]$ is the long-run multiplier. But in the first period, the *IS* curve shifts only to *IS"*, by amount $[\Delta I/(1-c\theta)]$, determined by the short-run consumption function and multiplier. Over time, the economy moves gradually from E'' to E', as individuals come to recognize that the shift in investment demand is permanent.

lag, effect on output. Figure 8-7 shows how income adjusts gradually to its new equilibrium level. The time pattern of changes in income caused by the increase in investment demand is called the *dynamic multiplier* of income with respect to autonomous investment.

Policy Implications

Suppose we have a permanent decline in investment expenditure. As we have seen, the decline in spending would lead to a fall in output and employment, occurring over a period of time.

Suppose the government wants to offset the reduction in aggregate demand by using tax cuts to keep income at the full-employment level. Since consumption adjusts only gradually to the changes in income resulting from both the initial fall in investment and tax cuts, the policy maker who wants to stabilize output *over time* will have to know about the adjustment pattern of consumption

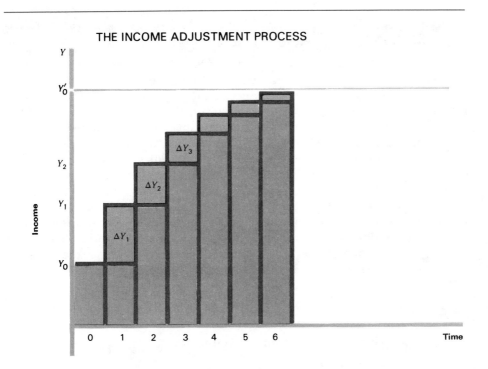

FIGURE 8-7 THE INCOME ADJUSTMENT PROCESS. The figure shows the *dynamic multiplier* of investment spending on income. This is how a given change in autonomous investment spending affects the level of output over time. Income rises in the first period from Y_0 to Y_1. Then in subsequent periods it continues to rise toward its long-run equilibrium level Y_0'.

so as not to overreact. The problems may be further complicated, as we discuss in Chapter 12, by the fact that frequently the policy maker too reacts only with a lag to changed circumstances.

In the short run, consumption does not respond fully to changes in income. Therefore it takes a relatively large tax cut to obtain a given change in consumption with which to offset the decline in investment. Over time, though, consumption adjusts to the change in disposable income, and the tax cut that was initially just sufficient to offset reduced investment now turns out to be too generous. The compensating policy must therefore be one of a tax cut that is *front-loaded* and gradually phased down to the long-run level. The difference between the short-run and the long-run tax cuts is determined by the relative size of the short-run and long-run tax multipliers.

Indeed, the observant reader will recall that we assumed consumers had no special knowledge about the nature of the changes in income they experienced as a result both of the initial change in investment and of subsequent tax adjustments. Remarkably enough, if consumers know that the investment shift was permanent, and if they could be persuaded that the change in government policy was permanent, a one-time reduction in taxes, calculated using the long-run multiplier implied by the consumption function, would precisely stabilize income. In that case, the response to the fall in investment would recognize the permanent nature of the change, implying the long-run multiplier is relevant, and the response to the tax change would also recognize the permanent nature of the change. Consumption would adjust immediately, rather than gradually over the course of time.

The conclusion of this section is that policy making, and understanding of the behaviour of the economy cannot be successful unless careful attention is paid to expectations formation — bearing in mind that expectations depend in part on how the policy makers are perceived to be acting. This is the message of rational expectations, to which we return in Chapters 15 and 18.

8-6   SUMMARY

1. The simple Keynesian consumption function

    $$C = 1.22 + 0.86YD \qquad (2)$$

    accounts well for observed consumption behaviour. The equation suggests that out of an additional dollar of disposable income, 86 cents is spent on consumption. The consumption function implies, too, that the ratio of consumption to income, C/YD, declines somewhat with the level of income.

2. Early empirical work on consumption showed that the average propensity to consume declined with the level of income. Postwar studies, by contrast, find a relatively constant average propensity to consume of about 0.9.

3. The evidence is reconciled by a reconsideration of consumption theory. Individuals want to maintain relatively smooth consumption profiles over their lifetime. Their consumption behaviour is geared to their long-term consumption opportunities — permanent income or lifetime income plus wealth. With such a view, current income is only one of the determinants of consumption spending. Wealth and expected income play a role, too. A consumption function that represents this idea is

    $$C = aWR + b\theta YD + b(1 - \theta)YD_{-1} \qquad (14)$$

which allows for the role of real wealth WR, current disposable income YD, and lagged disposable income YD_{-1}.

4. The life-cycle hypothesis suggests that the propensities of an individual to consume out of disposable income and out of wealth depend on the person's age. It implies that saving is high (low) when income is high (low) relative to lifetime average income. It also suggests that aggregate saving depends on the growth rate of the economy and on such variables as the age distribution of the population.

5. The permanent-income hypothesis emphasizes the formation of expectations of future income. It implies that the propensity to consume out of permanent income is higher than the propensity to consume out of transitory income.

6. Both theories do well, in combination, in explaining aggregate consumption behaviour, but there are still some consumption puzzles, including the excess sensitivity of consumption to current income and the fact that the aged do not appear to draw down their savings as they age.

7. The excess sensitivity of consumption to current income may be caused by liquidity constraints that prevent individuals from borrowing enough to maintain smooth consumption patterns.

8. The rate of consumption, and thus of saving, could in principle be affected by the interest rate, but the evidence for the most part shows little effect of interest rates on saving.

9. The Barro-Ricardo hypothesis implies that cuts in tax rates that produce deficits will not affect consumption.

10. Lagged adjustment of consumption to income results in a gradual adjustment of the level of income in the economy to changes in autonomous spending and other economic changes. An increase in autonomous spending raises income, but the adjustment process is spread out over time because the rising level of income raises consumption only gradually. This adjustment process is described by dynamic multipliers that show by how much income changes in each period following a change in autonomous spending (or other exogenous variables).

KEY TERMS

Life-cycle hypothesis
Dissaving
Permanent income
Rational expectations

Liquidity constraints
Dynamic multiplier
Excess sensitivity
Barro-Ricardo hypothesis

PROBLEMS

1. What is the significance of the ratio of consumption to GDP in terms of the level of economic activity? Would you expect it to be higher or lower than normal during a recession (or depression)? Do you think the ratio would be higher in developed or underdeveloped countries? Why?

The Life-Cycle Hypothesis

2. The text implies that the ratio of consumption to accumulated savings declines over time until retirement.
    (a) Why? What assumption about consumption behaviour leads to this result?
    (b) What happens to this ratio after retirement?

3. (a) Suppose you earn as much as your neighbour but are in much better health and expect to live longer. Would you consume more or less than your neighbour? Why? Derive your answer from Equation (6).
    (b) According to the life-cycle hypothesis, what would the effect of the Canada Pension Plan system be on your average propensity to consume out of (disposable) income?
    (c) How would Equation (9) be modified for an individual who expects to receive $X per year of retirement benefits? Verify your result in 3(b).

4. Give an intuitive interpretation of the marginal propensity to consume out of wealth and income at time T in the individual's lifetime in Equation (9).

5. In equation (6), consumption in each year of working life is given by

$$C = \frac{WL}{NL} \times YL \qquad (6)$$

In equation (9), consumption is given as

$$C = aWR + cYL \qquad a \equiv \frac{1}{NL - T} \qquad c \equiv \frac{WL - T}{NL - T} \qquad (9)$$

Show that equations (6) and (9) are consistent for an individual who started life with zero wealth and has been saving for T years. [*Hint:* First calculate the individual's wealth after T years of saving at rate $YL - C$. Then calculate the level of consumption implied by equation (9) when wealth is at the level you have computed.]

Permanent-Income Hypothesis

6. In terms of permanent-income hypothesis, would you consume more of your Christmas bonus if (a) you knew there was a bonus every year; (b) this was the only year such bonuses were given out?

7. Suppose that permanent income is calculated as the average of income over the past 5 years; that is,

$$YP = \tfrac{1}{5}(Y + Y_{-1} + Y_{-2} + Y_{-3} + Y_{-4})$$

   Suppose, further, that consumption is given by $C = 0.9YP$.
   (a) If you have earned $10 000 per year for the past 10 years, what is your permanent income?
   (b) Suppose next year (period $t + 1$) you earn $15 000. What is your new YP?
   (c) What is your consumption this year and next year?
   (d) What is your short-run marginal propensity to consume (MPC)? Long-run MPC?
   (e) Assuming you continue to earn $15 000 starting in period $t + 1$, graph the value of your permanent income in each period using the equation above.

8. Explain why good gamblers (and thieves) might be expected to live very well even in years when they don't do well at all.

9. The graph (below) shows the lifetime earnings profile of a person who lives for four periods and earns income of $30, $60, and $90 in the first

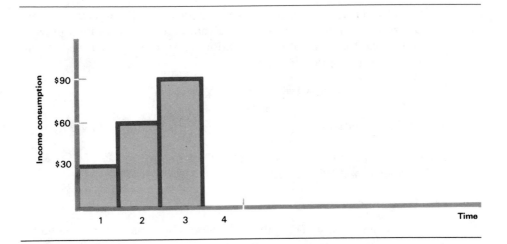

three periods of the life cycle. There are no earnings during retirement. Assume that the interest rate is 0.

(a) You are asked to determine the level of consumption, compatible with the budget constraint, for someone who wants an even consumption profile throughout the life cycle. Indicate in which periods the person saves and dissaves and in what amounts.

(b) Assume now that, contrary to 9a, there is no possibility for borrowing. The credit markets are closed to the individual. Under this assumption, what is the flow of consumption the individual will pick over the life cycle? In providing an answer, continue to assume that if possible, an even flow of consumption is preferred (*Note:* You are assuming here that there are liquidity constraints.)

(c) Assume next that the person described in 9(b) receives an increase in wealth or nonlabour income. The increase in wealth is equal to $13. How will that wealth be allocated over the life cycle with and without access to the credit market? How would your answer differ if the increase in wealth were $23?

(d) Relate your answer to the problem of excess sensitivity of consumption to current income.

10.   Consider the consumption function in equation (14). Assume autonomous investment spending is constant, as is government spending. The economy is close to full employment and the government wishes to maintain aggregate demand precisely constant. In these circumstances, assume there is an increase in real wealth of $10 billion. What change in income taxes will maintain constant the equilibrium level of income in the present period? What change is required to maintain income constant in the long run?

11.   Equation (14) shows consumption as a function of wealth and current and lagged disposable income. To reconcile that consumption function with permanent-income expectations formation, you are asked to use equation (12) and the consumption function

$$C = 0.045WR + 0.55YD + 0.17YD_{-1}$$

to determine the magnitude of θ and $(1 - \theta)$ that is implied by equation (14).

12.   (a) Explain why the interest rate might affect saving.
      (b) Why does it matter?

Adjustment and Dynamics

13.   Here is a challenge to your ability to develop diagrams. You are asked to show short-run and long-run income determination in the 45° diagram

of Chapter 3. Assume that investment demand is totally autonomous and does not respond to the interest rate. Thus you do not need to use the full *IS-LM* model.

(a) Draw the short-run consumption functions and the aggregate demand schedule with $I = \bar{I}$.

(b) Show the initial full equilibrium.

(c) Show the short-run and long-run effects of increased investment on equilibrium income.

CHAPTER

Investment Spending

Consumption spending in Canada is on average about 60 percent of real GDP, and thus accounts for much of aggregate demand. Investment spending is typically about 20 percent of real GDP, but it fluctuates more than consumption. Table 9-1 shows how the components of aggregate demand changed in the most recent recession and recovery. From the peak in the third quarter of 1981 to the trough in the fourth quarter of 1982, real GDP fell sharply mainly because of the large decline in investment spending.[1] In the subsequent recovery investment turned around dramatically.

TABLE 9-1   REAL GDP AND ITS COMPONENTS IN RECESSION AND RECOVERY
(billions of 1981 dollars)

| | CHANGE OVER SIX QUARTERS ENDING | | |
	1982 IV	1984 II	1985 IV
Consumption	−5.1	12.8	15.3
Investment	−30.4	15.5	5.7
Government	3.6	1.1	2.9
Net exports	14.3	2.1	−0.2
GDP	−18.7	32.7	23.0

Source: Statistics Canada, 11-003.

[1] The increase in net exports reflects the depreciation of the Canadian dollar and the greater severity of the recession in Canada as compared with the United States.

The cyclical importance of investment spending, shown in Table 9-1, goes back a long way. For instance, in the Great Depression, gross investment fell to less than 4 percent of output in 1933. Understanding investment, then, is of prime importance in understanding the business cycle.

In this chapter we continue our in-depth analysis of the components of aggregate demand. We provide both a foundation for the essential component of the simple investment function of Chapter 4—that investment demand is reduced by increases in the interest rate—and go further than that investment function, by discussing the roles of output and taxes in determining investment. While much of the reason for studying investment spending is that its fluctuations help account for the business cycle, another reason is that investment spending can be significantly affected by policy. High interest rates, caused by restrictive monetary policy and expansive fiscal policy, reduce investment spending; policies that reduce interest rates and provide tax incentives for investment can increase investment spending.

One simple relationship is vital to the understanding of investment. Investment is spending devoted to increasing or maintaining the stock of capital. The stock of capital consists of the factories, machines, offices, and other durable products used in the process of production. The capital stock also includes residential housing as well as inventories. Investment is spending that adds to these components of capital stock. Recall the distinction drawn in Chapter 2 between *gross* and *net investment.* Gross investment represents total additions to the capital stock. Net investment subtracts depreciation—the reduction in the capital stock that occurs each period through wear and tear and the simple ravages of time—from gross investment. Net investment thus measures the increase in the capital stock in a given period of time.

In this chapter, we disaggregate investment spending into three categories. The first consists of spending by business firms on productive capital in the form of *machinery and equipment* and *nonresidential construction.* The second is *residential construction,* which consists of spending on houses and apartment buildings. These two categories comprise *fixed investment* as opposed to the third one, *inventory investment,* some aspects of which were discussed in Chapter 3.

Table 9-2 shows investment spending in these categories for 1986, and Figure 9-1 shows the components of investment since 1966. Although inventory investment is a small fraction of GDP it shows wide fluctuations. Note that the large negative inventory investment in the recession year 1982 is unusual, since in most years it is positive.

In the remainder of this chapter, we develop theories and discuss evidence about the determinants of the rate of investment in each of the three major categories shown in Table 9-2 and Figure 9-1. We will develop what look like different models to explain each of the categories of investment spending. However, the theories are essentially similar, sharing a common view of the

TABLE 9-2   GROSS BUSINESS INVESTMENT, 1986
(billions of 1981 dollars)

Machinery and equipment	30.3
Nonresidential construction	22.1
Residential construction	25.2
Total fixed investment	77.6
Change in inventories	3.4
Gross business investment	$81.0

Source: Statistics Canada, 11-010.

interaction between a desired capital stock and the rate at which the economy adjusts toward that desired stock.

9-1   INVENTORY INVESTMENT

Inventories consist of raw materials, goods in the process of production, and completed goods held by firms in anticipation of their sale. The ratio of inventories to monthly shipments in Canadian manufacturing has been in the range of 1.5 to 2.5 over the past 30 years.

The inventories of interest to us are those held to meet future demands for goods. Firms hold such inventories because goods cannot be instantly manufactured or obtained from the manufacturer to meet demand. Some inventories are held as an unavoidable part of the production process; there is an inventory of meat and sawdust inside the sausage machine during the manufacture of sausage, for example. Inventories are also held because it is less costly for a firm to order goods less frequently in large quantities than to order small quantities frequently—just as the average householder finds it useful to keep several days' supplies on hand in the house so as not to have to visit the supermarket daily.

Firms have a desired ratio of inventories to final sales that depends on economic variables. The smaller the cost of ordering new goods and the greater the speed with which such goods arrive, the smaller the inventory-sales ratio. The more uncertainty about the demand for the firm's goods, given the expected level of sales, the higher the inventory-sales ratio. The inventory-sales ratio may also depend on the level of sales, with the ratio falling with sales because there is relatively less uncertainty about sales as sales increase. Finally, there is the interest rate. Since firms carry inventories over time, they must tie up money to buy and hold them. There is an interest cost involved in such

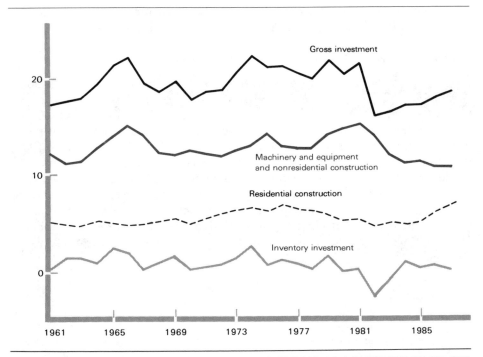

FIGURE 9-1   COMPONENTS OF INVESTMENT SPENDING AS A PERCENTAGE OF GDP

(*Source*: Department of Finance, *Economic Review*)

inventory holding, and the desired inventory-sales ratio should be expected to fall with increases in the interest rate.

Anticipated versus Unanticipated Inventory Investment

The most interesting aspect of inventory investment lies in the distinction between anticipated (desired) and unanticipated (undesired) investment. Inventory investment could be high in two circumstances. First, if sales are unexpectedly low, firms would find unsold inventories accumulating on their shelves; this constitutes unanticipated inventory investment. This is the type of inventory investment discussed in Chapter 3. Second, inventory investment could be high because firms plan to restore depleted inventories. The two circumstances obviously have very different implications for the behaviour of aggregate demand. Unanticipated inventory investment is a result of unexpectedly low aggregate demand. On the other hand, planned inventory investment can be a response to recent, unexpectedly high aggregate demand. That is, rapid accumulation of inventories could be associated with either rapidly declining aggregate demand or rapidly increasing aggregate demand.

Inventories in the Business Cycle

Inventory investment fluctuates substantially in the business cycle — proportionately more than any other component of aggregate demand. This is well illustrated in the 1981–1982 recession. In Figure 9-2, we show sales by Canadian manufacturing industries as measured by shipments and the ratio of inventories to shipments. As we move into the recession in the last quarter of 1981, sales begin to decline. Initially, however, there is relatively little adjustment in production, so there is an *unintended* build up of inventories and the inventory-sales ratio increases. As the recession proceeds, production is cut back and the inventory-sales ratio stops rising. As demand picks up again at the beginning of 1983, increases in production lag behind, allowing inventories to decline. Thus the inventory-sales ratio decreases as the economy moves out of the recession.

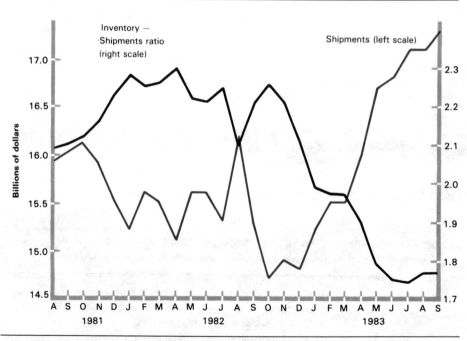

FIGURE 9-2   MANUFACTURING SHIPMENTS AND INVENTORY — SHIPMENTS RATIO

(*Source*: Adapted from Statistics Canada 11-003, 11-206)

Note that this behaviour of inventories reflects the adjustment mechanism for output that we discussed in Chapter 3. When there is a fall in aggregate demand, firms unanticipatedly accumulate inventories. They cut back production in order to get output back in line with demand. As we noted in the footnotes in Chapter 3, though, in the process of reducing production to cut back inventories, firms may cause a larger reduction in GDP for a while than would have happened had inventories not been unintentionally accumulated. This is known as the *inventory cycle*.

To understand the inventory cycle, consider the case of hypothetical automobile dealer who sells, say, thirty cars per month, and holds an average of 1 month's sales, namely thirty cars, in inventory. As long as sales stay steady at thirty cars per month, the dealer will be ordering thirty cars per month from the factory. Now suppose sales drop to twenty-five cars per month, and it takes the dealer 2 months to respond to the change. During those 2 months his or her inventory will have climbed to forty cars. In the future he or she will want an inventory of only twenty-five cars on hand. Thus when the dealer does respond to the fall in demand orders from the factory are cut from thirty to ten in the third month, to get the inventory back to 1 month's sales. After the desired inventory-sales ratio has been restored, the dealer will then order twenty-five cars per month from the factory. We see in this extreme case how the drop in demand of five cars, instead of leading to a simple drop in car output of five cars per month, causes a drop of output of twenty cars in 1 month, followed by the longer-run drop in output of five cars per month.

9-2   BUSINESS FIXED INVESTMENT: THE NEOCLASSICAL APPROACH

The machinery, equipment, and structures used in the production of goods and services constitute the *stock* of business fixed capital. Our analysis of business fixed investment in this section proceeds in two stages. First, we ask how much capital firms would like to use, given the costs and returns of using capital and the level of output they expect to produce. That is, we ask what determines the *desired capital stock*. The desired capital stock is the capital stock that firms would like to have in the long run, abstracting from the delays they face in adjusting their use of capital. However, because it takes time to order new machines, build factories, and install the machines, firms cannot instantly adjust the stock of capital used in production. Second, therefore, we discuss the rate at which firms adjust from their existing capital stock toward the desired level over the course of time. The rate of adjustment determines how much firms spend on adding to the capital stock in each period; that is, it determines the rate of investment.

The Desired Capital Stock: Overview

Firms use capital, along with labour, to produce goods and services for sale. The firms' goal is, of course, to maximize their profits. In deciding how much capital to use in production, they have to balance the contribution that more capital makes to their revenues against the cost of using more capital. The *marginal product of capital* is the increase in output produced by using one more unit of capital production. The *rental (user) cost of capital* is the cost of using one more unit of capital in production.

To derive the rental cost of capital, we think of the firms as financing the purchase of the capital (whether the firm produces the capital itself or buys it from some other firm) by borrowing, at an interest cost *i*. In order to obtain the services of an extra unit of capital, in each period the firm must pay the interest cost *i* for each dollar of capital that it buys. Thus the basic measure of the rental cost of capital is the interest rate.[2] Later we shall go into more detail about the rental cost of capital, but for the meantime we shall think of the interest rate as determining the rental cost.

In deciding how much capital they would like to use in production, firms compare the value of the marginal product of capital with the user or rental cost of capital. The value of the marginal product of capital is the increase in the *value* of output obtained by using one more unit of capital. For a competitive firm, it is equal to the price of output times the marginal product of capital. So long as the value of the marginal product of capital is above the rental cost, it pays the firm to add to its capital stock. Thus the firm will keep investing until the value of the output produced by adding one more unit of capital is equal to the cost of using that capital — the rental cost of capital. In equilibrium, we must have

Value of marginal product of capital = rental cost of capital   (1)

To give content to this relationship, we have to specify what determines the productivity of capital and what determines the user (rental) cost of capital. The marginal product of capital is examined next, and then we turn to the rental cost of the capital.

The Marginal Productivity of Capital

In understanding the marginal productivity of capital, it is important to note that firms can substitute capital for labour in the production of output. Different

---

[2] Even if the firm finances the investment out of profits it has made in the past—retained earnings—it should still think of the interest rate as the cost of using the new capital, since it could otherwise have lent out those funds and earned interest on them, or paid them out as dividends to shareholders.

combinations of capital and labour can be used to produce a given level of output. If labour is relatively cheap, the firm will want to use relatively more labour, and if capital is relatively cheap, the firm will want to use relatively more capital.

The general relationship among the desired capital stock (K^*), the rental cost of capital (rc), and the level of output is given by

$$K^* = g(rc, Y) \qquad (2)$$

Equation (2) indicates that the desired capital stock depends on the rental cost of capital and the level of output. The lower the rental cost of capital, the larger the desired capital stock. And the greater the level of output, the larger the desired capital stock.[3]

The relationship shown in equation (2) makes complete sense. It says that firms want to have more capital on hand if they have to produce more output, and that they want to have more capital the cheaper it is to use capital. We now explain in more detail the factors underlying equation (2).

As the firm combines progressively more capital with relatively less labour in the production of a *given* amount of output, the marginal product of capital declines. This relation is shown in the downward-sloping schedules in Figure 9-3. These schedules show how the marginal product of capital falls as more capital is used in producing a given level of output. The schedule YY_1 is drawn for a level of output Y_1. The schedule YY_2 is drawn for the higher output level Y_2. The marginal product of capital, given the capital stock, say, K_0, is higher on the schedule YY_2 than on YY_1. That is because more labour is being used in combination with the given amount of capital K_0 to produce the level of output Y_2 than to produce Y_1.

Figure 9-3 shows the marginal product of capital in relation to the level of output and the amount of capital being used to produce that output. Figure 9-4 is a similar diagram which shows the desired capital stock as related to the rental cost of capital and the level of output. Given the level of output, say, Y_1, the firm will want to use more capital the lower the rental cost of capital — because at low rental costs of capital, it can afford to use capital even when its marginal productivity is quite low. If the rental cost of capital is high, the firm will be willing to use capital only if its marginal productivity is high — which means that the firm will not want to use very much capital and will instead substitute labour for capital. In producing a higher level of output, say, Y_2, the firm will use both more capital and more labour, given the rental cost of capital. Therefore, at higher levels of output, the desired capital stock is higher.

[3] Throughout this discussion, we have implicitly been assuming that the real wage paid to labour is given and does not change as the rental cost of capital changes.

FIGURE 9-3   THE MARGINAL PRODUCT OF CAPITAL IN RELATION TO THE LEVEL OF
OUTPUT AND THE CAPITAL STOCK. The marginal product of capital decreases as relatively
more capital is used in producing any given level of output. Thus the schedules YY_1 and YY_2 are
downward sloping. The higher the level of output, for any given capital input, the higher the
marginal product of capital. Thus schedule YY_2, with output level Y_2 greater than Y_1, is above
schedule YY_1.

The Cobb-Douglas Production Function

While equation (2) provides the general relationship determining the desired
capital stock, a particular form of the equation, based on the Cobb-Douglas
production function,[4] is frequently used in studies of investment behaviour. The
particular equation that is used is[5]

$$K^* = \frac{\gamma Y}{rc} \tag{3}$$

[4] The Cobb-Douglas production function is written in the form

$$Y = N^{1-\gamma}K^\gamma \qquad 1 > \gamma > 0$$

where N is the amount of labour used. This production function is particularly popular
because it is easy to handle, and also because it appears to fit the facts of economic
experience quite well. The coefficient γ appearing in Eq. (3) is the same as the γ of the
production function. The reader trained in calculus will want to show that γ is the share
of capital in total income.

[5] We draw attention here to a very subtle point: Equation (3) gives the marginal product
of capital (*MPK*) when the *input of labour* is held fixed, while in Figs. 9-3 and 9-4 we work

FIGURE 9-4   THE DESIRED CAPITAL STOCK IN RELATION TO THE LEVEL OF OUTPUT AND THE RENTAL COST OF CAPITAL. Firms' desired capital stock is chosen at the point at which the value of the marginal product of capital is equal to the rental cost of capital. At rental cost rc and output level Y_1, the firm's desired capital stock is K_1^*. An increase in the level of output to Y_2 raises the desired capital stock to K_2^*. An increase in the rental cost of capital (not shown) would reduce the desired capital stock at each level of output.

where γ is a constant. In this case, the desired capital stock varies in proportion to output. Given output, the desired capital stock varies with the rental cost of capital.

Expected Output

In determining the desired stock, we have to specify the relevant time period for which the decision on the capital stock applies. In this section we are discussing the capital stock that the firm desires to hold at some future time.

with the *MPK* when labour is being adjusted so that *output* is kept fixed. The desired capital stock that corresponds to Figs. 9-3 and 9-4 is

$$K^* = \left[\frac{\gamma w}{(1-\gamma)rc}\right]^{1-\gamma} Y \tag{3a}$$

where w is the real wage.

Equation (3a), like Eq. (3), implies that desired capital is proportional to Y and varies inversely with the rental cost of capital. We use Eq. (3) rather than Eq. (3a) in the text because it is the form that has been used in empirical studies.

Accordingly, the level of output in equations (2) and (3) should be the level of output which firms expect to be producing at that time. For some investments the future time at which the output will be produced is a matter of months or only weeks. For other investments — such as power stations — the future time at which the output will be produced is years away.

This suggests that the notion of permanent income (in this case, permanent output) introduced in Chapter 8 is relevant to investment as well as consumption. For longer-lived investments, the firm's capital demand is governed primarily by its views on the level of output it will be producing on average in the future. The firm's long-run demand for business fixed capital, depending on the normal or permanent level of output, is thus relatively independent of the current level of output, and depends on *expectations* of future output levels. However, it is affected by current output to the extent that current output affects expectations of permanent output.[6]

Summary on the Desired Capital Stock

It is worthwhile stepping back for a moment to summarize the main results so far:

1. The firm's demand for capital — the desired capital stock K^* — depends on the rental cost of capital, rc, and the expected level of output.

2. Firms balance the costs and benefits of using capital. The lower the rental cost of capital, the larger the optimal level of capital relative to output. This relation reflects the lower marginal productivity of capital when it is used relatively intensively. The intensive use of capital will be profitable only if the rental cost of capital is low.

3. The higher the level of output, the larger the desired capital stock.

4. The firm plans its capital stock in relation to expected future or permanent output.

5. Current output affects capital demand to the extent that it affects expectations about future output.

The Rental Cost of Capital Again

We have already introduced the notion of the rental or user cost of capital in determining the firm's desired capital stock. As a first approximation, we iden-

---

[6] The role of permanent income in investment has been emphasized by Robert Eisner. Much of his work is summarized in his book *Factors in Business Investment* (Cambridge, Mass.: Ballinger, 1978).

tified the rental cost of capital with the interest rate, on the argument that firms would have to borrow to finance their use of capital. Now we go into more detail on the cost per period of using capital.

To use capital for a single period, say, a year, the firm can be thought of as buying the capital with borrowed funds and paying the interest on the borrowing. At the end of the year, the firm will have some of the capital left, but the capital is likely to have depreciated over the course of the year. We shall assume that the firm intends to continue using the remaining capital in production in future years and that its depreciation simply represents the using up of the capital in the process of production—physical wear and tear. We now examine the rental cost, taking into account interest costs and depreciation. Later we will show that taxes also affect the rental cost of capital.

Leaving aside taxes, the rental cost of using capital consists of interest and depreciation costs.[7] We assume that the rate of depreciation is a constant, equal to d, implying that a fixed proportion d of the capital is used up per period. The rental cost, or user cost, of capital per dollar's worth of capital, which we denote by rc, is therefore

$$rc = \text{interest rate} + d \qquad (4)$$

where d is the depreciation rate.

The Real Rate of Interest

We have now to take a careful look at the interest rate term in equation (4). The distinction between the *real* and *nominal* interest rates is essential here. The real interest rate is the nominal (stated) rate of investment minus the rate of inflation.

The *notion of the real rate of interest is extremely important.* Suppose that the nominal interest rate, the rate stated in the loan agreement, is 10 percent. Then suppose also that prices are rising at 10 percent. Someone borrowing $100 at the beginning of the year pays back $110 at the end of the year. But those dollars in which repayment is made buy less goods than the dollars lent at the beginning of the year when the loan was made. If the inflation rate is 10 percent, then the $110 paid at the end of the year buys the same amount of goods that could have been bought with the original $100 at the beginning of the year. In *real* terms, in terms of the goods which the money can buy, the lender has no more at the end than at the beginning of the year. Thus the *real* interest rate

---

[7] Why is depreciation considered as a cost? The firm continues using the capital and therefore has to devote expenditures to maintaining the productive efficiency of capital and thus offsetting wear and tear. We are assuming that, per dollar of capital, d dollars per period are required to maintain productive efficiency.

actually received was zero, even though the *nominal* interest rate was 10 percent. Given the nominal interest rate, the real interest rate is lower the higher the rate of inflation becomes. In practice, nominal interest rates tend to be higher when inflation is higher.

It is the *expected real* rate of interest that should enter the calculation of the rental cost of capital. Why? The firm is borrowing in order to produce goods for sale. On average, across all firms, it is reasonable to believe that the prices of the goods the firms sell will be rising along with the general price level. Thus the value of what the firm will be producing in the future will be rising with the price level, but the nominal amount of interest it has to pay back on account of its borrowings does not rise with the price level. The real value of the debt it has incurred by borrowing will be falling over time, as a result of inflation, and it should take that reduction in the real value of its outstanding debts into account in deciding how much capital to employ.

Accordingly, we can be more precise in the way we write equation (4) for the rental cost of capital. We write the rental cost of capital, taking account of expected inflation at the rate π^e, as

$$rc \equiv r + d \equiv i - \pi^e + d \tag{5}$$

where r is the real interest rate, i the nominal interest rate, and

$$r \equiv i - \pi^e \tag{6}$$

Equation (6) states that the real rate of interest is the nominal interest rate minus the expected rate of inflation. Implicitly, equation (6) refers to the expected real rate of interest.[8] At the end of the period, when the rate of inflation is known, we can also state what the *actual* or realized real rate of interest for the period was — namely, the nominal interest rate i minus the actual rate of inflation.

To reiterate, it is important to note that the interest rate relevant to the firm's demand for capital is the *real* rate, and not the nominal rate. This makes it clear that the nominal rate of interest is not a good guide to the rental cost of capital. If the rate of inflation is zero and is expected to be zero and the nominal interest rate is 5 percent, then the real interest rate is 5 percent. By contrast, if the nominal interest rate is 10 percent and inflation is at the rate of 10 percent, the real interest rate is zero. Other things equal, the desired capital stock in this example would tend to be higher with the nominal interest rate of 10 percent

---

[8] Some loans to firms carry *variable* interest rates, so that the amount of interest the firm has to pay changes over time as the general level of interest rates changes. In these cases the rate i in Equation (6) would be the expected interest rate over the life of the loan.

than with the nominal rate of 5 percent — because those rates correspond to real rates of zero and 5 percent, respectively. As you have no doubt deduced, and as we shall show, investment spending tends to be higher when the rental cost of capital is lower. However, because of the distinction between real and nominal interest rates, that is *not* the same as saying that investment tends to be higher when the nominal rate of interest is lower.

Taxes and the Rental Cost of Capital

The rental cost of capital is affected by tax variables as well as by the interest rate and depreciation. The two main tax variables to consider are the corporate income tax and the investment tax credit. The corporate income tax is an essentially proportional tax on profits, whereby the firm pays a proportion, say, t, of its profits in taxes. The investment tax credit allows firms to deduct from their taxes a certain function, say, τ, of their investment expenditures in each year. Thus a firm spending $1 million for investment purposes in a given year could deduct 10 percent of the $1 million, or $100\,000$, from the taxes it would otherwise have to pay the federal government.

We want to know what effects the corporate income tax and the investment tax credit have on the rental cost of capital. The easier case is the investment tax credit. The investment tax credit reduces the price of a capital good to the firm by the ratio τ, since the government returns to the firm a proportion τ of the cost of each capital good. The investment tax credit therefore reduces the rental cost of capital.

To a first approximation, the corporate income tax, surprisingly, has no effect on the desired stock of capital. In the presence of the corporate income tax, the firm will want to equate the *after-tax* value of the marginal product of capital with the *after-tax* rental cost of capital in order to ensure that the marginal contribution of the capital to profits is equal to the marginal cost of using it.

Let us focus on the interest component of the rental cost. The basic point is that interest cost is treated as a deduction from revenues in the calculation of the corporation's taxes. Suppose there were no corporate income tax, no inflation, no depreciation, and an interest rate of 10 percent. The desired capital stock would be that level of the capital stock, say, K_0^*, such that the marginal product of capital was 10 percent. Now suppose that the corporate income tax rises to 35 percent and the interest rate remains constant. At the capital stock K_0^*, the after-tax marginal product of capital is now 6.5 percent (since 35 percent of the profits are paid in taxes). If the interest rate stays at 10 percent and the firm gets to deduct 35 percent of its interest payments from taxes, the after-tax cost of capital will be 6.5 percent too. In this case, the desired capital stock is unaffected by the rate of corporate taxation.

However, there are complexities in the tax laws, which we do not go into here, which make the total effect of the corporate income tax on the desired capital stock ambiguous. The ambiguities arise when the special tax treatment of depreciation,[9] of inflation, and of investment financing other than through borrowing is taken into account.[10]

We conclude by noting the two main points. The investment tax credit reduces the rental cost of capital and increases the desired stock of capital. The corporate income tax has ambiguous effects on the desired stock of capital.

The Stock Market and the Cost of Capital

We have so far assumed that the firm finances its investment by borrowing. But a firm can also finance investment by selling shares or equity. That way it raises the capital it needs to pay for the investment. The people buying the shares expect to earn a return from dividends and/or, if the firm is successful, from the increase in the market value of their shares, that is *capital gains*.

When the stock market is high, a company can raise a lot of money by selling relatively few shares. When stock prices are low, the firm has to sell more shares to raise a given amount of money. The owners of the firm, existing shareholders, will be more willing for the firm to sell shares to raise new money if they have to sell few shares to do so. If they have to sell many shares in the company, they will own a smaller share of the company in the future. Thus we expect corporations to be more willing to sell equity to finance investment when the stock market is high than when it is low.

In estimating the rental cost of capital, economists sometimes assume that the investment project will be financed by a mixture of borrowing and equity. The cost of equity capital is frequently measured by the ratio of the firm's dividends to the price of its stock.[11] Then obviously the higher the price of the

---

[9] For tax purposes depreciation is counted as a business expense, but these allowances follow complicated rules and are not generally equal to the depreciation that the capital stock actually undergoes.

[10] Some investment is financed through the sale of equities. Part of the return to equity holders typically takes the form of dividend payments. However, dividends are not treated as a deduction from profits in the calculation of corporate income taxes. Thus the basic argument presented in the case of interest payments, that the corporate income tax does not affect the desired capital stock, would not apply for equity-financed investment.

[11] An alternative measure is the ratio of the firm's *earnings* (some of which are not paid out to shareholders) to the price of its stock. However neither measure is really correct, for the cost of equity capital is the amount the investment is expected to yield *in the future* to the people who buy it now.

stock, the lower the cost of equity capital, and the lower the overall cost of capital.[12] That is why a booming stock market is good for investment.

Summary and Effects of Fiscal and Monetary Policy on the Desired Capital Stock

We summarize, using equation (2), which gives the desired capital stock as a function of the rental cost of capital and the expected level of output, and the preceding discussion of the rental cost of capital. From equation (2) we note that the desired capital stock increases when the expected level of output rises and when the rental cost of capital falls.

The rental cost of capital falls when the real interest rate and the rate of depreciation fall. It likewise falls when the investment tax credit rises. Changes in the rate of corporate taxation have ambiguous effects on the desired capital stock.

The major significance of these results is their implication that monetary and fiscal policy affect the desired capital stock. Fiscal policy exerts an effect through both the corporate tax rate t and the investment tax credit τ. Both these instruments are used to affect capital demand and thus investment spending.

Fiscal policy affects capital demand by its overall effects on the position of the IS curve, as discussed in Chapter 4. A high tax—low government-spending policy keeps the real interest rate low and encourages the demand for capital. (At this point you want to refer to Figure 4.22.) A high government-spending —low-tax policy that produces large deficits raises the real interest rate and discourages the demand for capital.

Monetary policy affects capital demand by affecting the market interest rate.[13] A lowering of the nominal interest rate by the Bank of Canada (given the expected inflation rate), as reflected in a downward shift in the LM curve, will induce firms to desire more capital. This expansion in capital demand, in turn, will affect investment spending, as we shall now see.

---

[12] An alternative approach to the firm's investment decision, Tobin's q theory of investment focusses on the stock market as the primary source of funds. The basic approach is outlined in James Tobin, "A General Equilibrium Approach to Monetary Theory," *Journal of Money, Credit and Banking*, February 1969. For an empirical implementation, see Lawrence H. Summers, "Taxation and Corporate Investment: A q-Theory Approach." *Brookings Papers on Economic Activity*, 1981.

[13] We should note that the Bank of Canada is able to affect *nominal* interest rates directly by its sales and purchases of bonds. Its ability to control *real* interest rates is more limited.

From Desired Capital Stock to Investment

We have now put more content into the general form of equation (2) for the desired capital stock by discussing the rental cost of capital in detail. The actual capital stock will often differ from the capital stock firms would like to have. At what speed do firms change their capital stocks in order to move toward the desired capital stock? In particular, is there any reason why firms do not attempt to move to their desired capital stocks immediately?

Since it takes time to plan and complete an investment project, and because attempts to invest quickly are likely to be more expensive than gradual adjustment of the capital stock, it is unlikely that firms would attempt to adjust their capital stocks to the long-run desired level instantaneously. Very rapid adjustment of the capital stock would require crash programs by the firm which would distract management from its routine tasks and interfere with ongoing production. Thus, firms generally plan to adjust their capital stocks gradually over a period of time rather than immediately.

Capital Stock Adjustment

There are a number of hypotheses about the speed with which firms plan to adjust their capital stock over time; we single out the *gradual adjustment hypothesis* here.[14] The basic notion behind the gradual adjustment hypothesis is that the larger the gap between the existing capital stock and the desired capital stock, the more rapid a firm's rate of investment. The hypothesis is that firms plan to close a fraction λ of the gap between the desired and actual capital stocks each period. Denote the capital stock at the end of the last period by K_{-1}. The gap between the desired and actual capital stocks is $(K^* - K_{-1})$. The firm plans to add to last period's capital stock K_{-1}, a fraction λ of the gap $K^* - K_{-1}$ so that the capital stock at the end of current period, K, will be

$$K = K_{-1} + \lambda(K^* - K_{-1}) \tag{7}$$

Equation (7) states that the firm plans to have the capital stock at the end of the period (K) be such that a fraction λ of the gap (between the desired capital stock K^* and the capital stock K_{-1} that existed at the end of last period) is closed. To increase the capital stock from K_{-1} to the level of K indicated by equation (7), the firm has to achieve an amount of net investment, $I \equiv K - K_{-1}$, indicated by equation (7). We can therefore write net investment as

$$I = \lambda(K^* - K_{-1}) \tag{8}$$

---

[14] The gradual adjustment hypothesis is a generalized form of the older *accelerator* model of investment, in which investment is proportional to the change in the level of output. The accelerator model is examined in Sec. 9-3.

which is the gradual adjustment formulation of net investment. Notice that equation (8) implies that investment is larger, the larger the gap between actual and desired capital stocks.[15] With a zero gap net investment is zero.

In Figure 9-5 we show the adjustment process of capital in a circumstance where the initial capital stock is K_1 and the given desired capital stock is K^*.

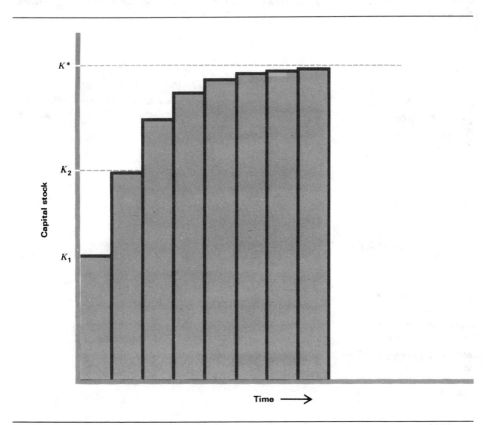

FIGURE 9-5 THE GRADUAL ADJUSTMENT OF THE CAPITAL STOCK. The desired capital stock is K^*, and the current capital stock is K_1. The firms plans to close half the gap between the actual and the desired capital stock each period ($\lambda = 0.5$). Thus, in period one it moves to K_2, with (net) investment equal to $(K_2 - K_1)$, which in turn is equal to one half of $(K^* - K_1)$. In each subsequent period it closes half the gap between the capital stock at the beginning of the period and the desired capital stock, K^*.

[15] Gross investment, as opposed to net investment described in equation (8), includes, in addition, depreciation. Thus, gross investment is $I + dK_{-1}$, where d is again the rate of depreciation.

The assumed speed of adjustment is $\lambda = 0.5$. Starting from K_1, one-half the discrepancy between target capital and current actual capital is made up in every period. First-period net investment is therefore $0.5(K^* - K_1)$. In the second period, investment will be less because the previous period's investment reduces the gap. Investment continues until the actual capital stock reaches the level of target capital. The speed with which this process allows actual capital to reach target capital is determined by λ. The larger λ is, the faster the gap is reduced.

In equation (8), we have reached our goal of deriving an investment function that shows current investment spending determined by the desired stock of capital K^* and the actual stock of capital K_{-1}. According to the flexible accelerator hypothesis, any factor that increases the desired stock increases the rate of investment. Therefore an increase in expected output, or a reduction in the real interest rate, or an increase in the investment tax credit will each increase the rate of investment. We thus have derived a quite complete theory of business fixed investment that includes many of the factors we should expect to affect the rate of investment. Further, the theory of investment embodied in equation (8) also contains aspects of *dynamic behaviour*—that is, of behaviour that depends on values of economic variables in periods other than the current period.

There are two sources of dynamic behaviour in equation (8). The first arises from expectations. The K^* term depends on the firm's estimate of future or permanent output. To the extent that the firm forms its estimates of permanent output as a weighted average of past output levels, there will be lags in the adjustment of the level of permanent output to the actual level of output. In turn, investment will therefore also adjust slowly to a change in the level of output. The second source of dynamic behaviour arises from adjustment lags. Firms plan to close only a proportion of the gap between the actual and desired capital stocks each period, as shown in Figure 9-5. The adjustment lags produce a lagged response of investment to changes in the variables that affect the desired capital stock.

The Timing of Investment and the Investment Tax Credit

The flexible accelerator model provides a useful summary of the dynamics of investment, but it does not sufficiently emphasize the *timing* of investment. Because investment is undertaken for the long run and often requires several years to complete, there is flexibility in the dates on which the actual investment is undertaken. For example, suppose a firm wanted to have some machinery in place within 3 years. Suppose that it knew the investment tax credit would be raised substantially a year from now. Then the firm might be wise to delay the investment for a year and to make or acquire the machinery at a faster rate during the next 2 years, receiving the higher investment tax credit as the reward for waiting the extra year. Similarly, if a firm anticipated that the cost of borrowing next year would be much lower than this year, it might wait a year to undertake its investment project.

The flexibility in the timing of investment leads to an interesting contrast between the effects of the investment tax credit and the income tax on investment and consumption, respectively. We saw in Chapter 8 that a *permanent* change in the income tax has a much larger effect on consumption than a *transitory* change. However, the rate of investment *during the period* that a *temporary* investment tax credit is in effect, would be higher than the rate of investment that would occur over the same period during which a *permanent* credit of the same magnitude was in effect. Why? If firms knew the investment tax credit were temporary, they would advance the timing of their planned investments in order to take advantage of the higher credit during the current period. If there were a permanent change in the investment tax credit, then the desired capital stock would rise and there would on that account be more investment, but there would not be a bunching of investment.

It is for this reason that temporary changes in the investment tax credit have been suggested as a highly effective countercyclical policy measure. However, this is not a simple policy tool, as expectations about the timing and duration of the credit might conceivably worsen the instability of investment.

Summary on the Neoclassical Theory of Business Fixed Investment

The main conclusions of the theory of business fixed investment as developed here are as follows:

1. Over time, net investment spending is governed by the discrepancy between actual and desired capital.
2. Desired capital depends on the rental (user) cost of capital and the expected level of output. Capital demand rises with expected output and the investment tax credit, and declines with an increase in *real* interest rates.
3. Monetary and fiscal policies exert effects on investment via the desired capital stock, although the short-run impact is likely to be minor. The longer-run effects are larger. The lags with which these investment effects occur are important to bear in mind in shaping stabilization policy.
4. Investment theory, like consumption theory, emphasizes the role of expected or permanent income or output as a determinant of capital demand.

9-3 BUSINESS FIXED INVESTMENT: ALTERNATIVE APPROACHES AND EMPIRICAL RESULTS

In this section we briefly discuss the way a firm approaches its investment decisions and also describe the standard *accelerator theory of investment*. Then we go on to examine some empirical evidence on investment.

The Business Investment Decision: The View from the Trenches

Business people making investment decisions typically use *discounted cash flow analysis.* The principles of discounting are described in the appendix to this chapter. Consider a business person deciding whether to build and equip a new factory. The first step is to figure out how much it will cost to get the factory into working order, and how much revenue the factory will bring in each year after it starts operation.

For simplicity we consider a very short-lived project, one that costs $100 in the first year to set up and that then generates $50 in revenue (after paying for labour and raw materials) in the second year and a further $80 in the third year. By the end of the third year the factory has disintegrated.

The manager wants to know whether to undertake such a project. Discounted cash flow analysis says that the revenues received in later years should be *discounted* to the present in order to calculate their present value. As the appendix on discounting shows, if the interest rate is 10 percent, $110 a year from now is worth the same as $100 now. Why? Because if $100 were lent out today at 10 percent, a year from now the lender would end up with $110. Thus to calculate the value of the investment project, the businessperson calculates its present discounted value at the interest rate at which the business can borrow. If the present value is positive, then the project is undertaken.

Suppose that the relevant interest rate is 12 percent.[16] The calculation of the present discounted value of the investment project is shown in Table 9-3. The $50 received in year 2 is worth only $44.50 today: $1 a year from now is worth $1/1.12 = 0.893 today, and so $50 a year from now is worth $44.60. The pres-

TABLE 9-3   DISCOUNTED CASH FLOW ANALYSIS AND PRESENT VALUE ($)

	Year 1	Year 2	Year 3	Present discounted value
Cash or revenue	−100	+50	+80	
Present value of $1	1	$1/1.12$ = 0.893	$(1/1.12^2)$ = 0.797	
Present value of costs or revenue	−100	50×0.893 = 44.60	80×0.797 = 63.76	(−100 + 44.60 + 63.76) = 8.36

[16] The interest rate here is nominal, because we are calculating the present value of dollars to be received in the future.

ent value of the $80 received in year 3 is calculated similarly. The table shows that the present value of the net revenue received from the project is positive ($8.36) and thus that the firm should undertake the project.

Note that if the interest rate had been much higher — say, 18 percent — the decision would have been *not* to undertake the investment decision. We thus see how the interest rate affects the investment decision of the typical firm. The higher the interest rate, the less likely the firm will be to undertake any given investment project.

Each firm has at any time an array of possible investment projects, and estimates of the costs and the revenues from those projects. Depending on the level of the interest rate, it will want to undertake some of the projects and not undertake others. Taking all firms in the economy together and adding their investment demands, we obtain the total demand for investment in the economy at each interest rate.

This approach to the investment decision, which, of course, can be applied to investment projects of any duration and complexity, seems far from the description of Section 9-2 in terms of a desired capital stock and rate of adjustment.

Actually, the two approaches are quite consistent. First, we should think of the desired capital stock as being the stock of capital that will be in place when the firms have their factories and new equipment on-line. Second, the adjustment speed tells us how rapidly firms on average succeed in installing that capital.

We started with the formulation in terms of the desired capital stock because the framework provides a very clear way of including the different factors that affect investment. For instance, it is easy to see how expectations of future output and taxes affect investment.

However, since the two approaches are consistent, the same factors could be included using discounted cash flow analysis. The effects of expectations of future output can be analyzed using the discounted cash flow approach by asking what determines the firms' projections of their future revenues (corresponding to the $50 in year 2 and $80 in year 3 in the example above); expected demand for their goods and their output must be relevant. Similarly, taxes can be embodied by analyzing how taxes affect the amount of revenue the firm has left after taxes in each future year; the investment tax credit reduces the amount the firm has to lay out in the early years when it is actually building the project —because the government provides a refund of part of the cost of the project through taxes.

Finally, the firm makes decisions about the speed of adjustment by considering the cash flows associated with building the project at different speeds. If the project can be built more rapidly, the firm will decide on the speed with which it wants the project brought on-line by considering the present discounted costs and revenues associated with speeding it up.

The Accelerator Model of Investment

The *accelerator model of investment* asserts that the rate of investment is proportional to the *change* in the economy's output. To derive the accelerator model of investment, assume that there is complete adjustment of the capital stock to its desired level within one period (that is, that $\lambda = 1$), so that $K = K^*$; that there is no depreciation, so that $d = 0$; and that the desired capital-output ratio is a constant, independent of the rental cost of capital:

$$K^* = vY \tag{9}$$

In equation (9), v is a constant equal to the desired capital-to-output ratio. Substituting equation (9) into equation (8), setting $\lambda = 1$, and noting that $K_{-1} = K^*_{-1}$, we obtain

$$I = v(Y - Y_{-1}) \tag{10}$$

which is precisely the accelerator model of investment.

The accelerator model creates the potential for investment spending to fluctuate a good deal. If investment spending is proportional to the *change* in output, then when the economy is in a recovery, investment spending is positive, and when the economy is in a recession, investment will be negative.[17] Thus the accelerator model predicts that investment will fluctuate considerably, as Figure 9-1 shows it does.

Empirical Results

We now examine how the investment models we have developed, particularly the neoclassical model summarized in equation (8), perform empirically.

To use equation (8), it is necessary to substitute some specific equation for K^*, the desired capital stock. Frequently the Cobb-Douglas form is chosen. Using equation (3) in equation (8) yields a (net) investment function of the form

$$I = \lambda\left(\frac{\lambda Y}{rc} - K_{-1}\right) \tag{11}$$

The rental cost of capital, rc in equation (11), is as in equation (5), but adjusted for taxes.

---

[17] The accelerator is not in practice a complete model of investment, for gross investment spending cannot be negative.

Early empirical evidence, in particular that of Dale Jorgenson and his associates,[18] showed that an investment function including the variables in equation (11) provided a reasonable explanation of the behaviour of business fixed investment. However, the form shown in equation (11) could be improved upon by allowing more scope for investment to respond slowly to changes in output. The empirical evidence suggests that the adjustment of investment to output takes the bell-shaped form in Figure 9-6. The major impact of a change in output on actual investment occurs with a 2-period (year) lag. The impact in the first year is less than the impact 2 years later.

There are two, not mutually exclusive, explanations for the behaviour shown in Figure 9-6, corresponding to the two sources of dynamic behaviour in equation (8) that we discussed above. The first possibility is that the lag pattern of Figure 9-6 reflects the way in which expectations about future output, and thus the long-run desired capital stock, are formed. In that view, only a sustained

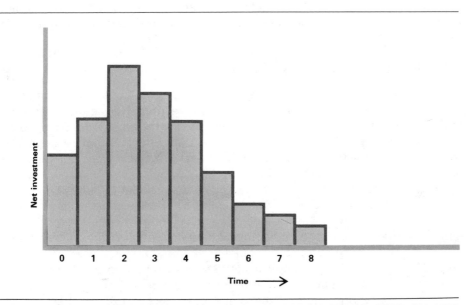

FIGURE 9-6 EFFECTS OF AN INCREASE IN OUTPUT IN PERIOD ZERO ON NET INVESTMENT IN SUBSEQUENT PERIODS (YEARS)

[18] See Dale W. Jorgenson, "Econometric Studies of Investment Behavior: A Survey," *Journal of Economic Literature*, December 1971. For an application of the theory with Canadian data, see G.O. Gaudet, J.D. May, and D.G. McFetridge, "Optimal Capital Accumulation: The Neoclassical Framework in a Canadian Context," *Review of Economics and Statistics*, August 1976.

increase in output will persuade firms that the capital stock should be increased in the long run. Figure 9-6 would then imply that it takes about 2 years for changes in the variables that determine the desired capital stock to have a major impact on expectations.

The second explanation relies less on expectations and more on the physical delays in the investment process. That interpretation would be that Figure 9-6 reflects the long time it takes for a change in the desired capital stock to be translated into investment spending. In industries in which investment can be undertaken quickly, there may be some response within a year. In other industries there may be long lags between the time machinery is ordered and the time it is ready to be delivered. In the economy as a whole, the maximum impact on investment of a change in the desired capital stock happens only 2 years after the change in the desired stock.

For many purposes, it does not matter which explanation of the form of Figure 9-6 is correct, and it is difficult to tell the explanations apart empirically. It is undoubtedly true that both explanations are relevent. The important point is that lags in the determination of the level of business fixed investment are long.

The Accelerator Model and Cost of Capital Effects

Controversy about the determinants of investment continues. Note from equation (11) that the neoclassical model relates investment to the ratio of output to the rental cost of capital (Y/rc). Thus, by the way the equation is set up, both output and the rental cost of capital have similar effects on investment. The issue is whether the rental cost of capital matters in fact as much for investment as the neoclassical model implies.

Some research[19] suggests that the accelerator model of equation (10) — somewhat expanded — does about as good a job of explaining investment behaviour as the neoclassical model. The accelerator model is expanded in empirical work to make the rate of investment depend not only on the change in income this period but also on the change in income in earlier periods. In empirical applications this simple accelerator model therefore differs from the neoclassical model mainly in that it omits the cost of capital.

There are also findings that the rental cost of capital does affect investment.[20] It is clear from the conflicting findings that the evidence is not strong

---

[19] Peter K. Clark, "Investment in the 1970's: Theory, Performance and Predictions," *Brookings Papers on Economic Activity*, 1979:1.

[20] For example, Martin Feldstein, "Inflation, Tax Rules and Investment: Some Economic Evidence," *Econometrica*, July 1982, and Ben Bernanke, "The Determinants of Investment: Another Look," *American Economic Review*, Papers and Proceedings, May 1983.

enough to decide the precise relative roles of the cost of capital and expectations of future output. No doubt both are major determinants of investment spending. Certainly theory suggests that the rental cost of capital should play an important role in affecting investment.

We now discuss some other aspects of investment behaviour.

Sales and Profits as Determinants of Investment

Some studies find either the level of sales or total profits to be factors explaining the level of investment. The level of sales could be interpreted as affecting expectations of future output and thus affecting the desired capital stock. Note that output and sales differ by the amount of inventory accumulation.

The role of profits can be interpreted similarly. High profits may provide an indication of future demand for the firm's product, and thus of future output. Alternatively, it is often argued that firms prefer to use retained profits to finance investment, rather than borrow. The preference might result from the expense of having to raise outside funds relative to using inside funds. However, in using its retained profits to finance investment rather than borrow, the firm has also to consider the possibility of paying out its profits to the firm's owners, who can invest in other firms. Thus even when using retained earnings, firms have to take into account the level of interest rates—as a measure of the returns their owners could receive if the earnings were paid out.

Why Does Investment Fluctuate?

The facts with which we started this chapter show that investment fluctuates much more than consumption spending. The accelerator model provides one explanation of these fluctuations. There are two other basic explanations: the uncertain basis for expectations and the flexibility of the timing of investment.

Uncertain Expectations

Keynes, in the *General Theory*, emphasized the uncertain basis on which investment decisions are made. In his words, ". . . we have to admit that our basis of knowledge for estimating the yield ten years hence of a railway, a copper mine, a textile factory, the goodwill of a patent medicine . . . amounts to little and sometimes to nothing. . . ."[21] Thus, he argued, investment decisions are very much affected by how optimistic or pessimistic the investors feel.

---

[21] J.M. Keynes, *The General Theory of Employment, Interest and Money* (New York: Macmillan, 1936), pp. 149–150.

The term "animal spirits" is sometimes used to describe the optimism or pessimism of investors, where "animal spirits" indicates that there may be no good basis for the expectations on which investors base their decisions. If there is no good basis for the expectations, then they could change easily—and the volume of investment along with the expectations.

The Timing of Investment Decisions

The second possible reason for fluctuations in investment is that investment decisions can be delayed if the project will take a long time to come on-line. Suppose a firm has an investment project it would like to undertake, but the economy is currently in a recession and the firm is not sure when the recession will end. Further, at the current time it cannot even usefully fully employ all the capital it already has. Such a firm might choose to wait until the prospects for the economy look better — when the recovery gets under way — before deciding to start the investment project.

Either or both of these factors could help account for the substantial fluctuations that are seen in business investment spending. Indeed, they may also explain the success of the accelerator theory of investment, for if firms wait for a recovery to get under way before investing, their investment will be closely related to the change in GDP.

9-4   RESIDENTIAL CONSTRUCTION

We study residential construction separately from other fixed investment both because somewhat different theoretical considerations are relevant[22], and because institutional features of the economy make residential construction especially sensitive to changes in interest rates.

Figure 9-7 shows residential construction spending in constant (1981) dollars for the period 1966–1986. Residential construction declines in recession periods such as 1970, 1974–75, 1980, and 1982.

Theory

Residential construction consists of the building of single-family and multi-family dwellings which we shall call housing. Housing is distinguished as an asset by its long life. Consequently, investment in housing in any one year tends

---

[22] In the concluding section of this chapter, we explain why slightly different theoretical models are used in explaining business fixed investment and residential construction.

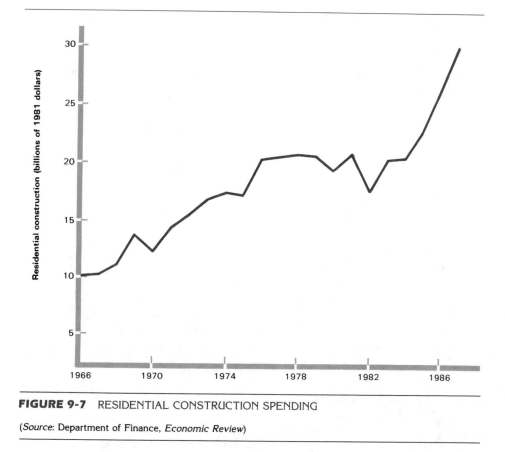

FIGURE 9-7   RESIDENTIAL CONSTRUCTION SPENDING

(*Source*: Department of Finance, *Economic Review*)

to be a very small proportion of the existing stock of housing—about 3 percent. The theory of residential investment starts by considering the demand for the existing stock of housing. Housing is viewed as one among the many assets that a wealth holder can own.

In Figure 9-8a we show the demand for the stock of housing in the downward-sloping DD_0 curve. The lower the price of housing (P_H), the greater the quantity demanded. The position of the demand curve itself depends on a number of economic variables. First, the greater wealth is, the greater the demand for housing. The more wealthy individuals are, the more housing they desire to own. Thus an increase in wealth would shift the demand curve from DD_0 to DD_1. Second, the demand for housing as an asset depends on the real return available on other assets. If returns on other forms of holding wealth—such as bonds—are low, then housing looks like a relatively attractive form in which to hold wealth. The lower the return on other assets, the greater the demand

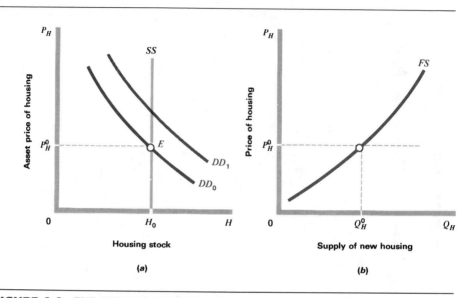

FIGURE 9-8   THE HOUSING MARKET: DETERMINATION OF THE ASSET PRICE OF HOUSING AND THE RATE OF HOUSING INVESTMENT. The supply and demand for the stock of housing determine the asset price of housing (P_H^0) in panel **(a)**. The rate of housing investment (Q_H^0) is determined by the flow supply of housing at price P_H^0, in panel **(b)**.

for housing. A reduction in the return on other assets, such as bonds or common stock, shifts the demand curve from DD_0 to DD_1.

Third, the demand for the housing stock depends on the net real return obtained by owning housing. The gross return — before taking costs into account — consists of rent, if the housing is rented out, or the implicit return that the homeowner receives by living in the home, plus capital gains arising from increases in the value of the housing. In turn, the costs of owning the housing consist of interest costs, typically the mortgage interest rate, plus any real estate taxes, and depreciation. These costs are deducted from the gross return and, after tax adjustments, constitute the net return. An increase in the net return on housing, caused, for example, by a reduction in the mortgage interest rate, makes housing a more attractive form in which to hold wealth and shifts up the demand curve for housing from DD_0 to DD_1.

The price of housing is determined by the interaction of this demand with the stock supply of housing. At any time the stock supply is fixed — there is a given stock of housing that cannot be adjusted quickly in response to price changes. The supply curve of the stock of housing is the SS curve of Figure 9-8a. The equilibrium *asset price of housing*, P_H^0, is determined by the intersection of the supply and demand curves. The asset price of housing is the price of a typical house or apartment. At any one time, the market for the stock of housing determines the asset price of housing.

The Rate of Investment

We now consider the determinants of the rate of investment in housing, and for the purpose turn to Figure 9-8b. The curve FS represents the supply of new housing as a function of the price of housing. This curve is the same as the regular supply curve of any industry. The supply curve shows the amount of a good that suppliers want to sell at each price. In this case, the good being supplied is new housing. The position of the FS curve is affected by the costs of factors of production used in the construction industry and by technological factors affecting the cost of building.

The curve FS is sometimes called the flow supply curve, since it represents the *flow* of new housing into the market in a given time period. In contrast, the *stock* supply curve SS represents the total amount of housing in the market at a moment of time.

Given the price of housing established in the asset market, P_H^0, building contractors supply the amount of new housing, Q_H^0, for sale at that price. The higher the asset price, the greater the supply of new housing. Now the supply of new housing is nothing other than gross investment in housing—total additions to the housing stock. Figure 9-8 thus represents our basic theory of the determinants of housing investment.

Any factor affecting the demand for the existing stock of housing will affect the asset price of housing, P_H, and thus the rate of investment in housing. Similarly, any factor shifting the flow supply curve FS will affect the rate of investment. We have already investigated the major factors shifting the DD demand curve for housing, but will briefly repeat that analysis.

Suppose the interest rate — the rate potential homeowners can obtain by investing elsewhere — rises. Then the asset demand for housing falls and the price of housing falls; that, in turn, induces a decline in the rate of production of new housing, or a decline in housing investment. Alternatively, suppose that the mortgage interest rate rises: once again there is a fall in the asset price of housing and a reduction in the rate of construction.

Because the existing stock of housing is so large relative to the rate of investment in housing, we can ignore the effects of the current supply of new housing on the price of housing in the short run. However, over time, the new construction shifts the SS curve of the left-hand panel to the right as it increases the housing stock. The long-run equilibrium in the housing industry would be reached, in an economy in which there was no increase in population or wealth over time, when the housing stock was constant. Constancy of the housing stock requires gross investment to be equal to depreciation, or net investment to be equal to zero. The asset price of housing would have to be at the level such that the rate of construction was just equal to the rate of depreciation of the existing stock of housing in long-run equilibrium. If population or income and wealth were growing at a constant rate, the long-run equilibrium would be one in which the rate of construction was just sufficient to cover depreciation and the steadily growing stock demand. In an economy subjected to continual nonsteady changes, that long-run equilibrium is not necessarily ever reached.

Minor qualifications to the basic theoretical structure arise chiefly because new housing cannot be constructed immediately in response to changes in P_H; rather, it takes a short time for that response to occur. Thus, the supply of new housing responds, not to the actual price of housing today, but to the price expected to prevail when the construction is completed. However, the lags are quite short; it takes less than a year to build a typical house. Another qualification stems from that same construction delay. Since builders have to incur expenses before they sell their output, they need financing over the construction period, and hence the position of the flow supply curve is affected by the interest rate.

The Q Theory of Investment

We digress for a moment to note that the model of the housing market which emphasizes the asset market and the rate of addition to the stock can similarly be used to analyze business fixed investment. Indeed, an increasingly used view of business fixed investment is the q theory that focusses on the stock market (see footnote 12). It can be cast in terms very similar to that of the housing model. At any one moment all the shares in the economy are in inelastic supply, just like the housing stock. Stock market investors place a value on those shares, with the price of shares in the stock market corresponding to P_H in Figure 9-8.

The price of a share in a company is the price of a claim on the capital in the company. The managers of the company can then be thought of as responding to the price of the stock by producing more new capital — that is, investing — when the price of shares is high and producing less new capital or not investing at all when the price of shares is low.

What is q? It is an estimate of the value the stock market places on a firm's assets relative to the cost of producing those assets. When the ratio is high, firms will want to produce more assets, so that investment will be rapid. Similarly, P_H can be thought of as the price of an existing house relative to the cost of building a new one. When that ratio is high, there will be lots of building.

Monetary Policy and Residential Construction

Monetary policy has powerful effects on the housing market. Most of the loans obtained to finance new construction are mortgages provided by financial institutions, particularly life insurance companies, trust companies, mortgage loan companies, and chartered banks. When interest rates rise, the supply of mortgage funds is affected in two ways. First, the interest cost to financial institutions of attracting deposits rises as the return on alternative investments increases. Second, the proportion of their assets channelled into mortgages falls as the yields on other securities rise.

The demand for housing is sensitive to interest rates, and the reason for this can be seen in Table 9-4. It shows the monthly payment that has to be made to repay a $50 000 mortgage with a 25 year amortization period at various interest rates. The monthly payment approximately doubles when the interest rate doubles. Thus an essential component of the cost of owning a house rises almost proportionately with the interest rate. It is therefore not surprising that the demand for housing is very sensitive to the interest rate.

TABLE 9-4   MONTHLY PAYMENTS ON MORTGAGES

Interest rate	5%	10%	15%
Monthly payment	$292	$454	$640

Note: The assumed mortgage is a loan for $50 000, paid back over 25 years, with equal monthly payments for those 25 years.

The above statement has to be qualified, since we should be concerned with the *real* and not the nominal interest cost of owning a house — and certainly much of the rise of the mortgage interest rate is a result of increases in the expected rate of inflation. However, the *nominal* interest rate also affects the homeowner. This results from the fact that a mortgage contract typically requires that the borrower pay a fixed amount each month over the lifetime of the mortgage. Even if the interest rate rises only because the expected rate of inflation has risen—and thus the real rate is constant—the payments that have to be made *today* by a borrower go up, but the inflation has not yet happened. Thus the real payments made today by a borrower rise when the *nominal* interest rate rises, even if the real rate does not rise.[23] Given the higher real monthly payments when the *nominal* interest rate rises, we should expect the nominal interest rate also to affect housing demand.

[23] How can the real payments rise if the real interest rate stays the same? The explanation is that today's real payments rise, but the real present value of future payments falls: the repayment stream tilts toward the present. For more on this feature, see Franco Modigliani and Donald Lessard (eds.), *New Mortgage Designs for Stable Housing in an Inflationary Environment*, Federal Reserve Bank of Boston, Conference Series #14, 1975.

9-5   CONCLUDING REMARKS

We have presented several different models to explain the different categories of investment behaviour in this chapter. Nonetheless, there is a basic common element in the models, the interaction of the demand for the stock of capital with investment. In each case we started by examining the determinants of the desired stock — capital or housing. The discussion of inventory investment started by examining the determinants of the desired inventory-sales ratio. Then, in each case, we went on to analyze or describe the determinants of the rate per year of that type of investment.

We come now to the question of why there is a difference between the theoretical models used to explain the level of business fixed investment and residential construction. The fundamental difference arises from the degree of standardization of the capital and the associated question of the existence of a good market for the used capital goods. Much of business fixed investment is in capital that is specifically designed for a given firm and is not of much use to other firms. It is, accordingly, difficult to establish a market price for the stock of that type of capital, and the theory used in discussing residential construction would be difficult to apply in that case. Although housing, too, varies a good deal, it is, nonetheless, possible to talk of a price of housing. Further, used housing is a very good substitute for new housing, whereas that is less often true for many capital goods.

To look ahead, note that the emphasis in this chapter has been on investment as a component of aggregate demand. However, the definition of investment as adding to the capital stock suggests that it is also a key in understanding aggregate supply. We turn to the supply-side aspect of investment in Chapter 20.

9-6   SUMMARY

1. Investment constitutes about 20 percent of aggregate demand, but fluctuations in investment account for a large share of business cycle movements in GDP. We analyze investment in three categories: business fixed investment, residential construction, and inventory investment.

2. Investment is spending that adds to the capital stock.

3. Inventory investment fluctuates proportionately more than any other class of investment. Firms have a desired inventory-to-sales ratio. The actual ratio may get out of line if sales are unexpectedly high or low, and then firms change their production levels to adjust inventories. For instance, when aggregate demand falls at the beginning of a recession,

inventories build up. Then when firms cut back production, output falls even more than did aggregate demand. This is the inventory cycle.

4. The neoclassical theory of business fixed investment sees the rate of investment being determined by the speed with which firms adjust their capital stocks toward their desired levels. The desired capital stock is larger the more output the firm expects to produce, and the smaller is the rental or user cost of capital. Since investment is undertaken for *future* production, it is expected future (permanent) output that determines the desired capital stock.

5. The real interest rate is the nominal (stated) interest rate minus the inflation rate.

6. The rental cost of capital is higher, the higher the real interest rate, the lower the price of the firm's stock, and the higher the rate of depreciation of capital. Taxes also affect the rental cost of capital, in particular through the investment tax credit. The investment tax credit is, in effect, a government subsidy for investment.

7. In practice, firms decide how much to invest using discounted cash flow analysis. This analysis gives answers that are consistent with those of the neoclassical approach.

8. The accelerator model of investment is a special case of the gradual adjustment model of investment. It predicts that investment demand is proportional to the *change* in output.

9. Empirical results show that business fixed investment responds with long lags to changes in output. The accelerator model, which does not take into account changes in the rental cost of capital, does almost as good a job of explaining investment as the more sophisticated neoclassical model.

10. The theory of housing investment starts from the demand for the *stock* of housing, affected by wealth, the interest rates available on alternative investments, and the mortgage rate. Increases in wealth increase the stock demand for housing; increases in either the interest rate on alternative assets or the mortgage rate reduce the stock demand. The price of housing is determined by the interaction of the stock demand and the given stock supply of housing available at any given time.

11. The rate of housing investment is determined by the rate at which builders supply housing at the going price.

12. Housing investment is affected by monetary policy because housing demand is sensitive to the interest rate (real and nominal), and also because it affects the supply of mortgage funds.

13. We now summarize the common elements of the different models. First, aggregate investment is the sum of the different types of investment spending. Thus any variable that affects any of the categories of investment analyzed also affects aggregate investment. Second, monetary and fiscal policy both affect investment, particularly business fixed investment and housing investment. The effects take place through changes in the real (and nominal in the case of housing) interest rates and through tax incentives for investment. Third, there are substantial lags in the adjustment of investment spending to changes in output and other determinants of investment. This is true particularly for business fixed investment and inventory investment. Such lags are likely to increase fluctuations in GDP.

KEY TERMS

Business fixed investment	Real interest rate
Residential construction	Gradual adjustment hypothesis
Inventory investment	Discounted cash flow analysis
Desired capital stock	Accelerator model of investment
Marginal product of capital	Inventory cycle
Rental (user) cost of capital	Present discounted value
Cobb-Douglas production function	q theory

PROBLEMS

1. (a) Explain how final sales and output can differ.
    (b) Point out from Figure 9-2 periods of planned and unplanned inventory investment and decumulation.
    (c) During a period of slow but steady growth, how would you expect final sales and output to be related? Explain. Draw a hypothetical figure like Figure 9-2 for such a period.

2. We have seen in Chapters 8 and 9 that *permanent* income and output, rather than current income and output, determine consumption and investment.
    (a) How does this affect the *IS-LM* model built in Chapter 4? (Refer to Figure 8-4.)
    (b) What are the policy implications of the use of "permanent" measures?

3. In Chapter 4 it was assumed that investment rises during periods of low interest rates. That, however, was not the case during the 1930s, when

investment and interest rates were both very low. Explain how this can occur. What would have been appropriate fiscal policy in such a case?

4. According to the description of business fixed investment in this chapter, how would you expect a firm's investment decisions to be affected by a sudden increase in demand for its product? What factors would determine the speed of its reaction?

5. It is often suggested that investment spending is dominated by "animal spirits"—the optimism or pessimism of investors. Is this argument at all consistent with the analysis of Sections 9-2 and 9-3?

6. Here are the cash flows for an investment project:

Year 1	Year 2	Year 3
−200	100	120

Should this firm undertake the project:
(a) If the interest rate is 5 percent?
(b) If the interest rate is 10 percent?

7. Is there any relation between the neoclassical theory of investment and the way firms make their investment decisions in practice?

8. Explain how the two panels of Figure 9-8 react together over time. What would happen if the demand for housing stock (DD) shifts upward and to the right over time?

9. Trace carefully the step-by-step effects on the housing market (using Figure 9-8) of an increase in interest rates. Explain each shift and its long-run and short-run effects.

10. Suppose that an explicitly temporary tax credit is enacted. The tax credit is at the rate of 10 percent and lasts only 1 year.
(a) What is the effect of this tax measure on investment in the long run (say, after 4 or 5 years)?
(b) What is the effect in the current year and the following year?
(c) How will your answers under a and b differ if the tax credit is permanent?

*11. For this question use the Cobb-Douglas production function and the corresponding desired capital stock given by equation (3). Assume that $\gamma = 0.3$, $Y = 250$ million, and $rc = 0.15$.
(a) Calculate the desired capital stock K^*.
(b) Now suppose that Y is expected to rise to 300 million. What is the corresponding desired capital stock?

(c) Suppose that the capital stock was at its desired level before the change in income was expected. Suppose further that $\gamma = 0.4$ in the gradual adjustment model of investment. What will the rate of investment be in the first year after expected income changes? In the second year?

(d) Does your answer in c refer to gross or net investment?

*APPENDIX: INTEREST RATES, PRESENT VALUES, AND DISCOUNTING

In this appendix we deal with the relationships among bond coupons, interest rates and yields, and the prices of bonds. In doing so, we shall introduce the very useful concept of present discounted value (PDV).

Section 1

We start with the case of a perpetual bond, or perpetuity. Such bonds have been issued in a number of countries, including the United Kingdom, where they are called Consols. The Consol is a promise by the British government to pay a fixed amount to the holder of the bond every year and forever. Let us denote the promised payment per Consol by Q_c, the *coupon*.[24]

The *yield* on a bond is the return per dollar that the holder of the bond receives. The yield on a savings account paying 5 percent interest per year is obviously just 5 percent. Someone paying $25 for a Consol that has a coupon of $2.5 obtains a yield of 10 percent [($2.5/25) × 100%].

The yield on a Consol and its price are related in a simple way. Let us denote the price of the Consol by P_c and the coupon by Q_c. Then, as the above example suggests, the yield i is just

$$i = \frac{Q_c}{P_c} \tag{A1}$$

which says that the yield on a perpetuity is the coupon divided by the price. Alternatively, we can switch equation (A1) around to

$$P_c = \frac{Q_c}{i} \tag{A2}$$

---

[24] The *coupon rate* is the coupon divided by the face value of the bond, which is literally the value printed on the face of the bond. Bonds do not necessarily sell for their face value, though customarily the face value is close to the value at which the bonds are sold when they first come on the market.

which says that price is the coupon divided by the yield. So, given the coupon and the yield, we can derive the price, or given the coupon and the price, we can derive the yield.

None of this is a theory of the determination of the yield or the price of a perpetuity. It merely points out the relationship between price and yield. Our theory of the determination of the yield on bonds is presented in Chapter 4. The interest rate in Chapter 4 corresponds to the yield on bonds, and we tend to talk interchangeably of interest rates and yields.

We shall return to the Consol at the end of this appendix.

Section 2

Now we move to a short-term bond. Let us consider a bond which was sold by a borrower for $100, on which the borrower promises to pay back $108 after 1 year. This is a 1-year bond. The yield on the bond to the person who bought it for $100 is 8 percent. For every $1 lent, the lender obtains both the $1 principal and 8 cents extra at the end of the year.

Next we ask a slightly different question. How much would a promise to pay $1 at the end of the year be worth? If $108 at the end of the year is worth $100 today, then $1 at the end of the year must be worth $100/108, or 92.6 cents. That is the value today of $1 in 1 year's time. In other words, it is the present discounted value of $1 in 1 year's time. It is the present value because it is what would be paid today for the promise of money in 1 year's time, and it is discounted because the value today is less than the promised payment in a year's time.

Denoting the 1-year yield or interest rate by i, we can write that the present discounted value of a promised payment Q_1, 1 year from now, is

$$PDV = \frac{Q_1}{1 + i} \qquad \text{(A3)}$$

Let us return to our 1-year bond and suppose that the day after the original borrower obtained the money, the yield on 1-year bonds rises. How much would anyone *now* be willing to pay for the promise to receive $108 after 1 year? The answer must be given by the general formula (A3). That means that the price of the 1-year bond will fall when the interest rate or yield on such bonds rises. Once again, we see that the price of the bond and the yield are inversely related, given the promised payments to be made on the bond.

As before, we can reverse the formula for the price in order to find the yield on the bond, given its price and the promised payment Q_1. Note that the price P is equal to the present discounted value, so that we can write

$$1 + i = \frac{Q_1}{P} \qquad \text{(A4)}$$

Section 3

Next we consider a 2-year bond. Such a bond would typically promise to make a payment of interest, which we shall denote Q_1, at the end of the first year, and then a payment of interest and principal (usually the amount borrowed), Q_2, at the end of the second year. Given the yield i on the bond, how do we compute its *PDV*, which will be equal to its price?

We start by asking first what the bond will be worth 1 year from now. At that stage, it will be a 1-year bond, promising to pay the amount Q_2 in 1 year's time, and yielding i. Its value 1 year from now will accordingly be given by equation (A3), except that Q_1 in equation (A3) is replaced by Q_2. Let us denote the value of the bond 1 year from now by PDV_1, and note that

$$PDV_1 = \frac{Q_2}{1 + i} \tag{A5}$$

To complete computing the *PDV* of the 2-year bond, we can now treat it as a 1-year bond, which promises to pay Q_1 in interest 1 year from now, and also to pay PDV_1 1 year from now, since it can be sold at that stage for that amount. Hence, the *PDV* of the bond, equal to its price, is

$$PDV = \frac{Q_1}{1 + i} + \frac{PDV_1}{1 + i} \tag{A6}$$

or

$$PDV = \frac{Q_1}{1 + i} + \frac{Q_2}{(1 + i)^2} \tag{A6a}$$

As previously, given the promised payments Q_1 and Q_2, the price of the bond will fall if the yield rises, and vice versa.

It is now less simple to reverse the equation for the price of the bond to find the yield than it was before; that is because from equation (A6), we obtain a quadratic equation for the yield, which has two solutions.

Section 4

We have now provided the outline of the argument whereby the present discounted value of *any* promised stream of payments for any number of years can be computed. Suppose that a bond, or any other asset, promises to pay amounts Q_1, Q_2, Q_3 . . . , Q_n in future years, 1, 2, 3, . . . , n years away. By pursuing the type of argument given in Section 3, it is possible to show that the *PDV* of such a payments stream will be

$$PDV = \frac{Q_1}{1 + i} + \frac{Q_2}{(1 + i)^2} + \frac{Q_3}{(1 + i)^3} + \ldots + \frac{Q_n}{(1 + i)^n} \tag{A7}$$

As usual, the price of a bond with a specified payments stream will be inversely related to its yield.

Section 5

The formula (A7) is the general formula for calculating the present discounted value of any stream of payments. Indeed, the payments may also be negative. Thus in calculating the *PDV* of an investment project, we expect the first few payments, for example, Q_1 and Q_2, to be negative. Those are the periods in which the firm is spending to build the factory or buy machinery. Then in later years the Q_i become positive as the factory starts generating revenues.

Firms undertaking discounted cash flow analysis are calculating present values using a formula such as (A7).

Section 6

Finally, we return to the Consol. The Consol promises to pay the amount Q_c forever. Applying the formula, we can compute the present value of the Consol by

$$PDV = Q_c \left[\frac{1}{(1 + i)} + \frac{1}{(1 + i)^2} + \frac{1}{(1 + i)^3} + \ldots + \frac{1}{(1 + i)^n} + \ldots \right] \qquad \text{(A8)}$$

The contents of the parentheses on the right-hand side are infinite series, the sum of which can be calculated as $1/i$. Thus,

$$PDV = \frac{Q_c}{i} \qquad \text{(A9)}$$

This section casts a slightly different light on the commonsense discussion of Section 1 of this appendix. Equations (A8) and (A9) show that the Consol's price is equal to the *PDV* of the future coupon payments.

CHAPTER 10

The Demand for Money

Money is a means of payment or medium of exchange. Since money is used for purchasing goods, individuals are interested in the purchasing power of their money holdings—the value of their cash balances in terms of the goods the cash will buy. In other words, they are concerned with their *real balances* rather than their *nominal* money holdings. What this means in practice is that (1) *real* money demand is unchanged when the price level increases, but *all* real variables, such as the interest rate, real income and real wealth, remain unchanged; and (2) *nominal* money demand increases in proportion to the increase in the price level, given the constancy of the real variables just specified.[1]

We have a special name for behaviour that is not affected by changes in the price level, all real variables remaining unchanged. An individual is free from *money illusion* if a change in the level of prices, holding all real variables constant, leaves real behaviour, including real money demand, unchanged. By contrast, an individual whose real behaviour is affected by a change in the price level, all real variables remaining unchanged, is said to suffer from money illusion.

In Chapter 4, we also assumed that the demand for money increases with the level of real income and decreases with the nominal interest rate. Recall that

---

[1] Be sure you understand that (1) and (2) say the same thing in slightly different ways.

the response of the demand for money to interest rates is important in determining the effectiveness of fiscal policy. Changes in fiscal variables, such as tax rates or government spending, affect aggregate demand if the demand for money changes when the interest rate changes — if the demand for money is interest-elastic. If the demand for money does not react at all to changes in the interest rate, increases in government spending totally *crowd out* private spending and leave the level of income unaffected.

The demand for money has been studied very intensively at both the theoretical and empirical levels. There is by now almost total agreement that the demand should, as a theoretical matter, increase as the level of real income rises and decrease as the nominal interest rate rises. Empirical work bears out these two properties of the demand-for-money function.

10-1   COMPONENTS OF THE MONEY STOCK

The money supply definitions currently provided by the Bank of Canada are shown in Table 10-1.[2] The most widely used concept is M1 which includes currency and demand deposits. Currency consists of notes and coin in circulation outside the banking system, and demand deposits are chequing accounts at the chartered banks. M2 is a broader measure of the money supply that includes personal savings accounts and nonpersonal notice deposits.[3]

Although *M2* includes the major assets that serve as a means of payment, it does not encompass all chequing accounts. For example, it includes only deposits in the chartered banks and it can be argued that chequable deposits in other financial institutions such as trust companies and credit unions should be included. Similarly, there is a question as to whether credit cards should not be regarded as means of making payment. If so, and the argument is certainly compelling, we should probably count the amount that people are allowed to charge by using their credit cards as part of the money stock.

Historically, there have often been changes in the type of assets which can be used as means of payment, and simultaneous disagreements about what constitutes money in those circumstances. When cheques first began to be widely used in England early in the nineteenth century, there was a disagreement over whether demand deposits should be regarded as part of the money

---

[2] For a detailed description of the definitions, see *Bank of Canada Review*, Table E1 and the appended notes. Details concerning recent revisions are given in the February 1988 issue.

[3] A notice deposit is an account on which the bank reserves the right to require notice before a withdrawal can be made. Personal savings accounts have such a provision, but it is not normally enforced. (Look at the small print in your passbook!)

TABLE 10-1 COMPONENTS OF THE MONEY STOCK, JANUARY, 1988
(billions of dollars, average of Wednesdays)

(1) Currency	15.8
(2) Demand deposits	20.1
$M1$ = (1) + (2)	35.9
(3) Personal savings deposits	137.7
(4) Nonpersonal notice deposits	16.1
$M2$ = $M1$ + (3) + (4)	189.7
(5) Nonpersonal term deposits	35.5
(6) Foreign currency deposits*	6.4
$M3$ = $M2$ + (5) + (6)	231.6

*Deposits of residents booked in Canada.
Source: *Bank of Canada Review*

stock. Now that point is not disputed. We can expect there to be continuing changes in the financial structure over the years, with consequent changes in the definitions of the various money supply concepts.

Table 10-1 also shows the broader definition of the money supply, $M3$. $M3$ includes all Canadian dollar deposits in chartered banks and foreign currency deposits held by residents. The components of $M3$ that are not part of $M1$ or $M2$ are in general less *liquid* in that they cannot immediately and conveniently be used for making payments. However, they are assets that are close to being money in the sense that they are available with only a little difficulty for making payments.

In summary, there is no unique set of assets which will always constitute the money supply. At present, there are arguments for using a broader definition of the money stock than $M1$ and even arguments for using a less broad definition—should $1000 bills be included, for example? Further, over the course of time, the particular assets that serve as a medium of exchange, or means of payment, will certainly change further.

10-2 THE FUNCTIONS OF MONEY

Money is so widely used that we rarely step back to think how remarkable a device it is. It is impossible to imagine a modern economy operating without the use of money or something very much like it. In a mythical barter economy in which there is no money, every transaction has to involve an exchange of goods (and/or services) on both sides of the transaction. The examples of the difficulties of barter are endless. The economist wanting a haircut would have to find a barber wanting to listen to a lecture on economics; the actor wanting a suit would have to find a tailor wanting to watch movies; and so on. Without a medium of exchange, modern economies could not operate.

Money, as a medium of exchange, makes it unnecessary for there to be a "double coincidence of wants" in exchanges. By the double coincidence, we have in mind the above examples. The wants of two individuals would have to be identically matched for the exchange to take place. For instance, the man selling movie tickets would have to find a buyer whose goods he wanted to buy (the suit) while, at the same time, the woman selling suits would have to find a buyer whose goods she wanted to buy (the movie tickets).

There are four traditional functions of money, of which the medium of exchange is the first.[4] The other three are store of value, unit of account, and standard of deferred payment.

A *store of value* is an asset that maintains value over time. Thus, an individual holding a store of value can use that asset to make purchases at a future date. If an asset were not a store of value, then it would not be used as a medium of exchange. Imagine trying to use ice cream as money in the absence of refrigerators. There would hardly ever be a good reason for anyone to give up goods for money (ice cream) if the money were sure to melt within the next few minutes. If the seller were unwilling to accept the ice cream in exchange for his or her goods, then the ice cream would not be a medium of exchange. However, there are many stores of value other than money—such as bonds, stocks, and houses.

The *unit of account* is the unit in which prices are quoted and books kept. Prices are quoted in dollars and cents, and dollars and cents are the units in which the money stock is measured. Usually, the money unit is also the unit of account, but that is not essential. In the German hyperinflation of 1922–1923, dollars were the unit of account for some firms, whereas the mark was the medium of exchange.

Finally, as a *standard of deferred payment*, money units are used in long-term transactions, such as loans. The amount that has to be paid back in 5 or 10 years is specified in dollars and cents. Dollars and cents are acting as the standard of deferred payment. Once again, though, it is not essential that the standard of deferred payment be the money unit. For example, the final payment of a loan may be related to the behaviour of the price level, rather than being fixed in dollars and cents. This is known as an indexed loan.

The last two of the four functions of money are, accordingly, functions which money *usually* performs, but not functions that it *necessarily* performs. The store of value function is one that many assets perform.

---

[4] See W.S. Jevons, *Money and the Mechanism of Exchange* (London: Routledge & Kegan Paul, 1910).

There are fascinating descriptions of different types of money that have existed in the past that we do not have room to review here,[5] but there is one final point we want to emphasize. *Money is whatever is generally accepted in exchange.* However magnificently a piece of paper may be engraved, it will not be money if it is not accepted in payment. However unusual the material of which it is made, anything that is generally accepted in payment is money. The only reason money is accepted in payment is that the recipient believes that it can be spent at a later time. There is thus an inherent circularity in the acceptance of money. Money is accepted in payment because it is believed that it will also be accepted in payment by others.

10-3   THE DEMAND FOR MONEY: THEORY

In this section we review the three major motives underlying the demand for money. In doing so, we will concentrate on the effects of changes in income and changes in the interest rate on money demand.

The three theories we are about to review correspond to Keynes's famous three motives for holding money[6]: (1) the transactions motive, which is the demand for money arising from the use of money in making regular payments; (2) the precautionary motive, which is the demand for money to meet unforeseen contingencies; and (3) the speculative motive, which arises from the uncertainties about the money value of other assets that an individual can hold. In discussing the transactions and precautionary motives, we are mainly discussing M1, whereas the speculative motive refers more to M2, as we shall see.

Although we examine the demand for money by looking at the three motives for holding it, we cannot separate a particular person's money holdings, say, $500, into three neat piles of, say, $200, $200, and $100, that are being held from each motive. Money being held to satisfy one motive is always available for another use. The person holding unusually large balances for speculative reasons also has those balances available to meet an unexpected emergency, so that they serve too as precautionary balances. All three motives influence an individual's holdings of money, and as we shall see, each leads to the prediction that the demand for money should fall as the interest rate on other assets increases.

This final point is worth emphasizing. Money (M1) generally earns no interest (currency and some chequable deposits) or less interest than other assets. Any-

---

[5] See Paul Einzig, *Primitive Money* (New York: Pergamon Press, 1966).

[6] J.M. Keynes, *The General Theory of Employment, Interest and Money* (New York: Macmillan, 1936), Chap. 13.

one holding money is giving up interest that could be earned by holding some other asset, such as a savings deposit or a bond. The higher the interest loss from holding a dollar of money, the less money we expect the individual to hold. The demand for money will thus be higher, the greater the interest rate on money itself if interest is paid on demand deposits, and will be lower, the higher the interest rate on alternative assets. In practice, we can measure the cost of holding money as the difference between the interest rate paid on money (perhaps zero) and the interest rate paid on the most nearly comparable other asset, such as a savings deposit or, for corporations, a certificate of deposit or commercial paper.

For most of the remainder of the chapter, we shall write as if money earns no interest. This is true of much of the $M1$ stock. Further, it is easy to modify the analysis to take account of the payment of interest on other parts of $M1$. All that is necessary is to substitute the difference between the interest rate on the alternative asset and the interest rate on money in places we mention only the interest rate on the alternative asset.

The Transactions Demand

The transactions demand for money arises from the use of money in making regular payment for goods and services. In the course of each month, an individual makes a variety of payments for such items as rent or mortgage, groceries, the newspaper, and other purchases. In this section we examine how much money an individual would hold for such purchases.

In analyzing the transactions demand, we are concerned with a tradeoff between the amount of interest an individual forgoes by holding money and the costs and inconveniences of holding a small amount of money. To make the problem concrete, consider a man who is paid, say, $1800 each month. Assume that he spends the $1800 evenly over the course of the month, at the rate of $60 per day. Now at one extreme, the individual could simply leave his $1800 in cash (whether currency or demand deposits) and spend it at the rate of $60 per day. Alternatively, on the first day of the month the individual could take his $60 to spend that day and put the remaining $1740 in a daily-interest savings account. Then every morning he could go to the bank to withdraw that day's $60 from the savings account. By the end of the month he would have earned interest on the money he had each day in the savings account. This would be the *benefit* of keeping his money holdings down as low as $60 at the beginning of each day. The *cost* of keeping money holdings down is simply the cost and inconvenience of the trips to the bank to withdraw the daily $60. To decide on how much money to hold for transactions purposes, the individual has to weigh the costs of holding small balances against the interest advantage of doing so.

We now study the tradeoff in more detail and derive a formula for the demand for money. Suppose the nominal monthly income[7] of the individual is Y_N. We make the simplifying assumption that Y_N is paid to his or her savings account, rather than a chequing account, each month. The money is spent at a steady rate over the course of the month. To spend it, the individual has to get it out of the savings account and into cash, which may be currency or a chequing account. If left in the savings account, the deposit earns interest at a rate of i per month. It earns zero interest as cash. The cost to the individual of making a transfer between cash and the savings account (which we henceforth call bonds for convenience) is $\$tc$. That cost may be the individual's time, or it may be a cost that he or she explicitly pays someone else to make the transfer. For convenience we refer to it as a broker's fee.

The Inventory Approach

The approach we are describing to the demand for money is known as the *inventory-theoretic approach*.[8] Although we are describing an individual's trans-actions demand, similar considerations apply for firms deciding how to manage their money. You should think of the inventory-theoretic approach applying equally well, with small changes in terminology and assumptions, to firms and households.

The individual has to decide how many transactions to make between bonds and cash each month. If he or she makes just one transaction, transferring Y_N into cash at the beginning of the month, the cash balance over the course of the month will be as shown in Figure 10-1a. It starts at Y_N, is spent evenly over the month, and is down to zero by the end of the month, at which time a new payment is received by the individual and transferred into his or her chequing account. If the individual makes two withdrawals from the savings account, he or she first transfers $Y_N/2$ into cash at the beginning of the month, resulting in

---

[7] As a reminder, nominal income Y_N is defined as real income Y times the price level P: $Y_N \equiv PY$.

[8] The approach was originally developed to determine the inventories of goods a firm should have on hand. In that context, the amount Y_N would be the monthly sales of the good, tc the cost of ordering the good, and i the interest rate for carrying the inventory. The analogy between money as an inventory of purchasing power, standing ready to buy goods, and an inventory of goods, standing ready to be bought by customers, is quite close. The inventory-theoretical approach to the demand for money is associated with the names of William Baumol and James Tobin. (William Baumol, "The Transactions Demand for Cash: An Inventory Theoretic Approach," *Quarterly Journal of Economics*, November 1952; and James Tobin, "The Interest Elasticity of Transactions Demand for Cash," *Review of Economics and Statistics*, August 1956.) The most famous result of Baumol's and Tobin's work is the *square-root law* of the demand for money, which is presented later in Eq. (4).

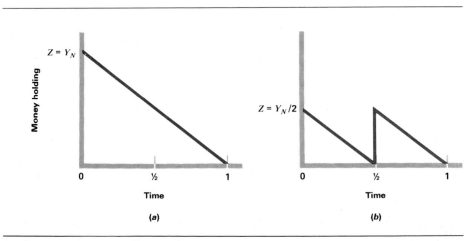

FIGURE 10-1 THE AMOUNT OF CASH HELD DURING THE MONTH RELATED TO THE NUMBER OF WITHDRAWALS. Panel **(a)** shows the pattern of money holding during the month when the individual makes just one transaction from the savings account to cash during the month. At the beginning of the month the individual transfers the entire amount to be spent Y_N, into cash, and then spends it evenly over the month. Panel **(b)** shows the pattern of money holding when there are two transactions, one at the beginning of the month and one in the middle of the month. In panel **(a)** average cash holdings for the month are $Y_N/2$; in panel **(b)** they are $Y_N/4$.

a cash balance that is run down to zero in the middle of the month, at which time another $Y_N/2$ is transferred into cash and spent evenly over the rest of the month.[9] Figure 10-1b shows the individual's cash holdings in that case.

We shall denote the size of a cash withdrawal from the bond portfolio (savings account) by Z and the number of withdrawals from the bond portfolio by n. Thus, n is the number of times the individual adds to the cash balance during the month. If he or she makes n equal-sized withdrawals during the month, transferring funds from the savings account to his or her chequing account, then the size of each transfer is Y_N/n, since a total of Y_N has to be transferred from the savings account into cash. For example, if Y_N is $1800, and n, the number of transactions, is 3, then Z, the amount transferred to cash each time, is $600. Accordingly, we can write

$$nZ = Y_N \tag{1}$$

---

[9] With simple interest being paid on the savings account, the individual's transactions between bonds and cash should be evenly spaced over the month. We leave the proof of that for the case where there are two transactions to the problem set.

Suppose that the amount Z is transferred from bonds to cash at each withdrawal. What then is the *average* cash balance over the course of the month? We want to find the size of the average cash balance in order to measure the interest that is lost as a result of holding cash; if that amount were not held as cash, it could be held as interest-earning bonds. In Figure 10-1a, the average cash balance held during the month is $Y_N/2 = Z/2$, since the cash balance starts at Y_N and runs down in a straight line to zero.[10] In the case of Figure 10-1b, the average cash balance for the first half of the month is $Y_N/4 = Z/2$, and the average cash balance for the second half of the month is also $Z/2$. Thus, the average cash balance for the entire month is $Y_N/4 = Z/2$. Similarly, if three withdrawals were made, the average cash balance would be $Y_N/6 = Z/2$. In general, the average cash balance is $Z/2$, as you might want to confirm by drawing diagrams similar to Figure 10-1 for $n = 3$ or other values of n.

The interest cost of holding money is the interest rate times the average cash balance, or $iZ/2$. From equation (1), that means the total interest cost is $iY_N/2n$. The other component of the cost of managing the portfolio is the brokerage cost, or the cost in terms of the individual's time and inconvenience in managing his money. That cost is just the number of withdrawals made, n, times the cost of each withdrawal, tc, and is thus equal to $n \times tc$. The total cost of managing the portfolio is the interest cost plus the total brokerage cost:

$$\text{Total cost} = n \times tc + \frac{iY_N}{2n} \qquad (2)$$

Equation (2) shows formally that the brokerage cost $n \times tc$ increases as the number of withdrawals (transactions between bonds and money) rises, and that the interest cost decreases as the number of withdrawals increases. It thus emphasizes the tradeoff faced in managing money, and suggests that there is an optimal number of withdrawals the individual should make to minimize the total cost of holding money to meet transactions requirements for buying goods.

To derive that optimal point, we want to find the point at which the benefit of carrying out another withdrawal is less than, or just equal to, the cost of making another transaction between bonds and money. If the benefit of making another transaction were greater than the cost, then another withdrawal should be made, and the original point could not have been optimal. The cost of making another transaction is always equal to tc. In Figure 10-2, we show the costs of making a further transaction by the marginal cost curve MC, which is horizontal at the level tc. The financial benefit from making another transaction

[10] The average cash balance is the average of the amount of cash the individual holds at each moment during the month. For instance, if he held $400 for 3 days and zero for the rest of the month, the average cash balance would be $40, or one-tenth (3 days divided by 30 days) of the month times $400.

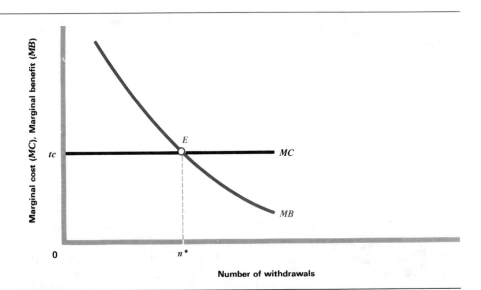

FIGURE 10-2   OPTIMAL CASH MANAGEMENT DETERMINING THE OPTIMAL NUMBER
OF WITHDRAWALS. The marginal cost of making another transaction is the constant amount,
tc, as shown by the *MC* curve. The marginal benefit of making another transaction is the amount
of interest saved by holding smaller money balances. The marginal benefit decreases as the
number of withdrawals from the savings account increases. Point *E* is the point at which the cost
of managing money holdings is minimized. Corresponding to point *E* is *n**, the optimal number
of transactions to make between the savings account and money.

is represented by the *MB* (marginal benefit) curve in Figure 10-2, which represents the interest *saved* by making another withdrawal and thus having a
smaller cash balance on average during the month.

The more transactions between money and bonds an individual makes, the
lower is the total interest cost, but the reduction of the interest cost obtained
by making more transactions falls off rapidly as the number of withdrawals
increases. There is a substantial saving in interest costs by making two withdrawals rather than one, but very little saving in interest costs by making thirty-
one transactions rather than thirty.

This suggests that the marginal benefit of making more withdrawals
decreases as the number of withdrawals becomes large. The *MB* curve in Figure
10-2 is, accordingly, downward-sloping.[11]

---

[11] Two points about Fig. 10-2: First, note that we have, for convenience, drawn the curves
as continuous, even though you will recognize that it is only possible to make an integral
number of transactions, and not, for example, 1.6 or 7.24 transactions. Second, if you
use the calculus, try to derive the equation of the marginal benefit curve from the
component of costs in Eq. (2) that is due to interest lost.

In Figure 10-2, the optimal number of transactions is given by n^*, the number at which the marginal benefit in terms of interest saved is equal to the marginal cost of making a transaction. Given the number of transactions and the individual's income, we also know the average cash balance M, using the relationship between average money holdings and the size of each transfer which we derived earlier:

$$M = \frac{Z}{2} = \frac{Y_N}{2n} \tag{3}$$

Properties of Money Demand

From Figure 10-2 we can see two important results. First, suppose the brokerage cost rises. That shifts the MC curve up, decreases the number of withdrawals n, and therefore [from equation (3), where M is inversely related to n] *increases* the average holding of money. Second, an increase in the interest rate shifts up the MB curve, therefore increases n, and thus [again, from equation (3)] reduces the holding of money: when the interest rate is higher, the individual is willing to make more trips to the bank to earn the higher interest now available. Figure 10-2 thus shows one of the key results we wanted to establish — that the demand for money is inversely related to the interest rate.

In the case of an increase in income, Figure 10-2 is unfortunately less useful. An increase in income shifts up the MB curve and increases the number of transactions, but from equation (3), we see that an increase in the number of transactions accompanying an increase in income does not necessarily imply that the demand for money rises, since it seems that n could increase proportionately more than Y_N. However, more complete algebraic analysis of the individual's optimal behaviour will show that the demand for money in this model rises when income rises.

The famous *square-root formula* for money demand, developed by William Baumol and James Tobin,[12] both makes the results of the graphical analysis of Figure 10-2 more precise and resolves the ambiguity about the effects of income on the demand for money. The formula gives the demand for money that is obtained as a result of minimizing the total costs in equation (2) with respect to the number of withdrawals and then using equation (3) to derive the cash balance.[13] The formula is

$$M^* = \sqrt{\frac{tc \times Y_N}{2i}} \tag{4}$$

---

[12] See the references in footnote 8.

[13] If you can handle calculus, try to derive Eq. (4) by minimizing total cost in Eq. (2).

Equation (4) shows that the transactions demand for money increases with the brokerage fee, or the cost of transacting, and with the level of income. The demand for money decreases with the interest rate.

Money Demand Elasticities

Equation (4) also shows that an increase in income raises the demand for money proportionately less than the increase in income itself. To put the same point somewhat differently, the ratio of income to money, Y_N/M, rises with the level of income. A person with a higher level of income than another holds proportionately less money than the other person. This point is sometimes put in different words by saying that there are *economies of scale* in cash management.

Yet another way of saying the same thing is that the income elasticity of the demand for money is less than 1 [it is equal to ½ in equation (4)]. The income elasticity measures the percentage change in the demand for money due to a 1 percent change in income. [14]

Similarly, equation (4) implies that the elasticity of the demand for money with respect to the brokerage fee is ½, and the elasticity with respect to the interest rate is $-½$.

What accounts for the fact that people can somehow manage with less cash per dollar of spending as income increases? The reason is that cash management is more effective at high levels of income because the average cost per dollar of transaction is lower with large-size transactions. In turn, the lower average cost of transactions results from the fixed brokerage fee per transaction; it costs as much to transfer $10 as $10 million, so that the average cost per dollar transferred is lower for large transfers.

However, in the case of households, we should recognize that the "brokerage cost" tc, the cost of making withdrawals from a savings account, is in part the cost of time and the nuisance of having to go to the bank. Since the cost of time to individuals is likely to be higher the higher their income, tc may rise with Y_N. In that case, an increase in income would result in an increase in the demand for money by more than the income elasticity of ½ indicates because tc goes up together with Y_N.

The Demand for Real Balances

We started this chapter by emphasizing that the demand for money is a demand for real balances. It is worth confirming that the inventory theory of the demand

---

[14] The income elasticity of demand is $\dfrac{\Delta(M/P)}{M/P} \Big/ \dfrac{\Delta Y}{Y}$. Similarly, the interest elasticity is

$\dfrac{\Delta(M/P)}{M/P} \Big/ \dfrac{\Delta i}{i}$.

for money implies that the demand for real balances does not change when all prices double (or increase in any other proportion). When all prices double, both Y_N and tc in equation (4) double — that is, both nominal income and the nominal brokerage fee double. Accordingly, the demand for nominal balances doubles, so that the demand for real balances is unchanged. The square-root formula does not imply any money illusion in the demand for money. Thus we should be careful when saying the income elasticity of demand for money implied by equation (4) is $\frac{1}{2}$. The elasticity of the demand for *real* balances with respect to *real* income is $\frac{1}{2}$. If income rises only because all prices (including tc) rise, then the demand for *nominal* balances rises proportionately.

Integer Constraints

So far we have ignored the important constraint that it is possible to make only an integral number of transactions, such as 1, 2, 3, etc., and that it is not possible to make 1.25 or 3.57 transactions. However, when we take account of this constraint, we shall see that it implies that many people do not make more than the essential one transaction between money and bonds within the period in which they are paid.[15] Consider our previous example of the person who received $1800 per month. Suppose, realistically, that the interest rate per month on savings deposits is $\frac{1}{2}$ percent. The individual cannot avoid making one initial transaction, since income initially arrives in the savings account. The next question is whether it pays to make a second transaction. That is, does it pay to keep half the monthly income for half a month in the savings account and make a second withdrawal after half a month? With an interest rate of $\frac{1}{2}$ percent per month, interest for half a month would be $\frac{1}{4}$ percent. Half the income would amount to $900, and the interest earnings would, therefore, be $900 $\times$ $\frac{1}{4}$ percent = $2.25.

Now if the brokerage fee exceeds $2.25, the individual will not bother to make more than one transaction. And $2.25 is not an outrageous cost in terms of the time and nuisance of making a transfer from the savings to the chequing account. Thus, for many individuals whose monthly net pay is below $1800, we do not expect formula (4) to hold exactly. Their cash balance would instead simply be half their income. They would make one transfer into cash at the beginning of the month; Figure 10-1a would describe their money holdings. For such individuals, the income elasticity of the demand for money is 1, since their demand for money goes up precisely in proportion with their income. The interest elasticity is zero, so long as they make only one transaction.

---

[15] If we had assumed that individuals were paid in cash, it would turn out that many people would not make any transactions between money and bonds in managing their transactions balances.

The very strong restrictions on the income and interest elasticities of the demand for money of equation (4) are not valid when the integer constraints are taken into account. Instead, the income elasticity is an average of the elasticities of different people, some of whom make only one transaction from bonds to money, and the elasticity is therefore between ½ and 1. Similarly, the interest elasticity is also an average of the elasticities across different individuals, being between — ½ and zero.[16] Because firms deal with larger amounts of money, they are likely to make a large number of transactions between money and bonds, and their income and interest elasticities of the demand for money are therefore likely to be close to the ½ and — ½ predicted by equation (4).

The Payment Period

Once the integer constraints are taken into account, it can also be seen that the transactions demand for money depends on the frequency with which individuals are paid (the payment period). If one examines the square-root formula (4), the demand for money does not seem to depend on how often a person is paid, since an increase in the payments period increases both Y_N and i in the same proportion. Thus the demand for money appears unaffected by the length of the period. However, consider a person who makes only one transaction from bonds to money at the beginning of each month. Her money demand is $Y_N/2$. If such a person were paid weekly, her demand for money would be only one-quarter of the demand with monthly payments. Thus we should expect the demand for money to increase with the length of the payment period.

Summary

The inventory-theoretic approach to the demand for money gives a precise formula for the transactions demand for money. The income elasticity of the demand for money is ½, and the interest elasticity is — ½. When integer constraints are taken into account, the limits on the income elasticity of demand are between ½ and 1, and the limits on the interest elasticity are between — ½ and zero. We have outlined the approach in terms of an individual's demand for money, but a similar approach is relevant for firms.

Some of the assumptions made in deriving the square-root formula are very restrictive. People do not spend their money evenly over the course of the month, and they do not know exactly what their payments will be. Their cheques are not paid into savings accounts, and so on. It turns out, though, that the

---

[16] See Robert J. Barro, "Integer Constraints and Aggregation in an Inventory Model of Money Demand," *Journal of Finance*, March 1976.

major results we have derived are not greatly affected by the use of more realistic assumptions. There is thus good reason to expect the demand for money to increase with the level of income and to decrease as the interest rate on other assets (or, generally, the cost of holding money) increases.

The Precautionary Motive

In discussing the transactions demand for money, we focussed on transactions costs and ignored uncertainty. In this section, we concentrate on the demand for money that arises because people are uncertain about the payments they might want to, or have to make.[17] Suppose, realistically, that an individual did not know precisely what payments he would be receiving in the next few weeks and what payments he would have to make. He might decide to have a hot fudge sundae, or need to take a cab in the rain, or have to pay for a prescription. If he did not have money with which to pay, he would incur a loss. The loss could be missing a fine meal, or missing an appointment, or having to come back the next day to pay for the prescription. For concreteness, we shall denote the loss incurred as a result of being short of cash by q. The loss clearly varies from situation to situation, but as usual we simplify.

The more money an individual holds, the less likely he or she is to incur the costs of illiquidity (that is, not having money immediately available), the more money he or she holds, the more interest he or she is giving up. We are back to a tradeoff situation similar to that examined in relation to the transactions demand. Somewhere between holding so little money for precautionary purposes that it will almost certainly be necessary to forgo some purchase (or to borrow in a hurry) and holding so much money that there is little chance of not being able to make any payment that might be necessary, there must be an optimal amount of precautionary balances to hold. That optimal amount will involve the balancing of interest costs against the advantages of not being caught illiquid.

Once more, we write down the total costs of holding an amount of money M.[18] This time we are dealing with expected costs, since it is not certain what the need for money will be. We denote the probability that the individual is illiquid during the month by $p(M, \sigma)$. The function $p(M, \sigma)$ indicates that the probability of the person's being illiquid at some time during the month depends on the level of money balances M being held and the degree of uncertainty σ about the net payments that will be made during the month. The probability of illiquidity is lower, the higher is M, and higher, the higher is the degree of uncertainty σ. The *expected cost* of illiquidity is $p(M, \sigma)q$—the probability of

---

[17] See Edward H. Whalen, "A Rationalization of the Precautionary Demand for Cash," *Quarterly Journal of Economics*, May 1966.

[18] This paragraph contains technical material that is optional and can easily be skipped.

illiquidity times the cost of being illiquid. The interest cost associated with holding a cash balance of M is just iM. Thus, we have

$$\text{Expected costs} = iM + p(M, \sigma)q \qquad (5)$$

To determine the optimal amount of money to hold, we compare the marginal costs of increasing money holding by $1 with the expected marginal benefit of doing so. The marginal cost is again the interest forgone, or i. That is shown by the MC curve in Figure 10-3. The marginal benefit of increasing money holding arises from the lower expected costs of illiquidity. Increasing precautionary balances from zero has a large marginal benefit, since that takes care of small, unexpected disbursements that are quite likely. As we increase cash balances further, we continue to reduce the probability of illiquidity, but at a decreasing rate. We start to hold cash to insure against quite unlikely events. Thus, the marginal benefit of additional cash is a decreasing function of the level of cash holdings—more cash on hand is better than less, but at a diminishing rate. The marginal benefit of increasing cash holdings is shown by the MB curve in Figure 10-3.

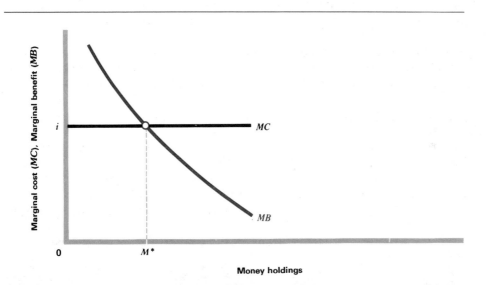

FIGURE 10-3 THE PRECAUTIONARY DEMAND FOR MONEY. The MC schedule shows the marginal cost of holding an extra dollar of money: holding an extra dollar means losing interest, and so the MC curve is horizontal at a level equal to the interest rate (or, more generally, the difference between the interest rate on money and alternative assets). The marginal benefit (MB) of holding an extra dollar is that the consumer is less likely to be short of money when it is needed. The marginal benefit declines with the amount of money held. The optimal amount of money to hold is shown by M^*, where marginal cost is equal to marginal benefit.

The optimal level of the precautionary demand for money is reached where the two curves intersect. That level of money is shown as $M*$ in Figure 10-3. Now we can use Figure 10-3 to examine the determinants of the optimal level of the precautionary demand. It is, first, apparent that precautionary balances will be larger when the interest rate is lower. A reduction in the interest rate shifts the MC curve down and increases $M*$. The lower cost of holding money makes it profitable to insure more heavily against the costs of illiquidity. An increase in uncertainty leads to increased money holdings because it shifts up the MB curve. With more uncertainty about the flow of spending, there is more scope for unforeseen payments and thus a greater danger of illiquidity. It therefore pays to insure more heavily by holding larger cash balances. Finally, the lower the costs of illiquidity, q, the lower the money demand. A reduction in q moves the MB curve down. Indeed, if there were no cost to illiquidity, no one would bother to hold money. There would be no penalty for not having it, while at the same time, holding it would mean a loss of interest.

The model of precautionary demand can be applied to goods other than money. It is a broad theory that applies to any commodity inventory that is held as insurance against contingencies. For instance, cars carry spare tires. You can work out circumstances under which one would want to have more than one spare tire in a car, and even circumstances in which zero would be the optimal number. The idea of the precautionary demand for money or for goods is quite general. So, too, are the determinants of the precautionary demand: the alternative cost in terms of interest forgone, the cost of illiquidity, and the degree of uncertainty that determines the probability of illiquidity.

The Speculative Demand for Money

The transactions demand and the precautionary demand for money emphasize the medium of exchange function of money, for each refers to the need to have money on hand to make payments. Each theory is more relevant to the $M1$ definition of money than any other, though the precautionary demand could certainly explain part of the holding of savings accounts and other relatively liquid assets which are part of $M2$. Now we move over to the store of value function of money and concentrate on the role of money in the investment portfolio of an individual.

An individual who has wealth has to hold that wealth in specific assets. Those assets make up a *portfolio*. One would think an investor would want to hold the asset which provides the highest returns. However, given that the return on most assets is uncertain, it is unwise to hold the entire portfolio in a single *risky asset*. You may have the hottest tip that a certain stock will surely double within the next 2 years, but you would be wise to recognize that hot tips are far from infallible, and that you could lose a lot of money in that stock as well as make money. A prudent, risk-averse investor does not put all his or her eggs in one basket. Uncertainty about the returns on risky assets leads to a diversified portfolio strategy.

As part of that diversified portfolio, the typical investor will want to hold some amount of a safe asset as insurance against capital losses on assets whose prices change in an uncertain manner. The safe asset would be held precisely because it is safe, even though it pays a lower expected return than risky assets. Money is a safe asset in that its nominal value is known with certainty.[19] In a famous article, James Tobin argued that money would be held as the safe asset in the portfolios of investors.[20] The title of the article, "Liquidity Preference as Behaviour towards Risk," explains the essential notion. In this framework the demand for money, the safest asset, depends on the expected yields, as well as on the riskiness of the yields, on other assets. The riskiness of the return on other assets is measured by the variability of the return. Using reasonable assumptions, Tobin shows that an increase in the expected return on other assets—an increase in the opportunity cost of holding money (that is, the return lost by holding money)—lowers money demand. By contrast, an increase in the riskiness of the returns on other assets increases money demand.

An investor's aversion to risk certainly generates a demand for a safe asset. The question we want to consider is whether that safe asset is money. That is, we want to ask whether considerations of portfolio behaviour do generate a demand for money. The relevant considerations in the portfolio are the returns and the risks on assets. From the viewpoint of the yield and risks of holding money, it is clear that term or savings deposits have the same risks as currency or chequable deposits. However, they generally pay a higher yield. The risks in both cases are the risks arising from uncertainty about inflation. Given that the risks are the same, and with the yields on time and savings deposits higher than on currency and demand deposits, portfolio diversification explains the demand for assets such as time and savings deposits better than the demand for $M1$. We therefore regard the speculative demand as applying primarily to $M2$.

The implications of the speculative, or risk-diversifying, demand for money are similar to those of the transactions and precautionary demands. An increase in the interest rate on nonmoney assets, such as long-term bond yields or equity yields, will reduce the demand for $M2$. An increase in the rate paid on savings accounts will increase the demand for savings accounts, perhaps even at the

---

[19] Of course, when the rate of inflation is uncertain, the real value of money is also uncertain, and money is no longer a safe asset. Even so, the uncertainties about the values of equity are so much larger than the uncertainties about the rate of inflation that money can be treated as a relatively safe asset.

[20] James Tobin, "Liquidity Preference as Behaviour towards Risk," *Review of Economic Studies*, February 1958.

cost of the demand for M1, as people take advantage of the higher yields they can earn on their investment portfolios to increase the size of those portfolios. One important difference between the speculative and the other two categories of demand is that here the level of wealth is clearly relevant to the demand for M2. The level of wealth determines the size of the total portfolio, and we expect that increases in wealth lead to increases in the demand for the safe asset, and thus in M2 demand.

One final point on the speculative demand. Many individuals with relatively small amounts of wealth will indeed hold part of that wealth in savings accounts in order to diversify their portfolios. However, bigger investors are sometimes able to purchase other securities which pay higher interest and also have fixed (that is, risk-free) nominal values. Large term deposits (in excess of $100 000) are sometimes an example of such assets, as are treasury bills on occasion. For such individuals or groups, the demand for a safe asset is not a demand for money.

10-4   EMPIRICAL EVIDENCE

This section examines the empirical evidence—the studies made using actual data — on the demand for money. We know that the *interest elasticity* of the demand for money plays an important role in determining the effectiveness of monetary and fiscal policies. We showed in Section 10-3 that there are good theoretical reasons for believing the demand for real balances should depend on the interest rate. The empirical evidence supports that view very strongly. Empirical studies have established that the demand for money is responsive to the interest rate. An increase in the interest rate reduces the demand for money.

The theory of money demand also predicts that the demand for money should depend on the level of income. The response of the demand for money to the level of income, as measured by the *income elasticity* of money demand, is also important from a policy viewpoint. The income elasticity of money demand provides a guide to the Bank of Canada as to how fast to increase the money supply to support a given rate of growth of GDP without changing the interest rate.

Suppose that the aim is for GDP growth of 10 percent, 6 percent real growth and 4 percent inflation. If the Bank of Canada wants to provide a sufficient growth rate of money to prevent interest rates from rising, it has to know the income elasticity of the demand for real balances. Suppose the real income elasticity is ½. Then we would require monetary growth of 7 percent to prevent an increase in interest rates. Why? First, the demand for nominal money increases in proportion to the price level, since money demand is a demand for real balances. Thus 4 percent growth in money is needed to meet the increased demand from the 4 percent increase in the price level. The 6 percent growth in real income would increase the demand for real balances by 3 percent (= 6 percent × ½), given the real income elasticity of ½ Hence, the needed 7 percent (= 4 + 3) growth in the nominal money supply to meet the increased demand arising from the increase in income.

Lagged Adjustment

The empirical work on the demand for money has introduced one complication that we did not study in the theoretical section — that the demand for money adjusts to changes in income and interest rates *with a lag*. When the level of income or the interest rate changes, there is first only a small change in the demand for money. Then, over the course of time, the change in the demand for money increases, slowly building up to its full long-run change. Reasons for this lag are not yet certain. The two usual possibilities exist in this case too. The lags may arise because there are costs of adjusting money holdings, or they may arise because money holders' expectations are slow to adjust. If people believe that a given change in the interest rate is temporary, they may be unwilling to make a major change in their money holdings. As time passes and it becomes clearer that the change is not transitory, they are more willing to make a larger adjustment.

Empirical Results

There are several published studies of the demand for money in Canada using postwar quarterly data.[21] The results of the most recent one are fairly typical and are summarized in Table 10-2. The table shows the elasticities of the demand for real balances with respect to real income Y (real GNP) and the rate on commercial paper i. This interest rate is relevant to the demand for money

TABLE 10-2   ELASTICITIES OF REAL MONEY DEMAND (M1)

	Y	i
Short run	0.22	−0.054
Long run	0.73	−0.18

Source: S. Poloz, "Simultaneity and the Demand for Money in Canada," *Canadian Journal of Economics*, August 1980, p. 413.

[21] See for example K. Clinton, "The Demand for Money in Canada, 1955–70." *Canadian Journal of Economics*, February, 1973; N. Cameron, "The Stability of Canadian Demand for Money Functions," *Canadian Journal of Economics*, May, 1979; S. Poloz, "Simultaneity and the Demand for Money in Canada," *Canadian Journal of Economics*, August 1980.

because commercial paper is an asset which is very liquid for corporations that hold it instead of money for short periods of time.

In the short run (one quarter), the elasticity of demand with respect to real income is 0.22. This means that a 1 percent increase in real income raises money demand by 0.22 percent, which is considerably less than proportionately. The table shows that the interest elasticity of money demand with respect to interest rates is negative: an increase in interest rates reduces money demand. The short-run interest elasticity is quite small. An increase from 8 percent to 10 percent, that is, a 25 percent increase (10/8 = 1.25), reduces the demand for money by only 1.35 percent (= 0.054 × 25 percent).

The long-run elasticities exceed the short-run elasticities by a factor of more than 3, as Table 10-2 shows. The long-run real income elasticity is 0.73, meaning that in the long run the increase in real money demand occurring as a result of a given increase in real income is only 73 percent as large as the increase in income. Real money demand thus rises less than proportionately to the rise in real income. The long-run interest elasticity is −0.18, meaning that an increase in i from 8 to 10 percent would reduce the demand for money by 4.5 percent.

How long is the long run? That is, how long does it take the demand for money to adjust from the short-run elasticities of Table 10-2 to the long-run elasticities shown in the table? Actually, it takes forever for the full long-run position to be reached. Table 10-3, however, shows the elasticities of the demand for real balances in response to changes in the level of income and interest rates after one, two, three, four, and eight quarters. Three-fourths of the adjustment is complete within the first year, and over 90 percent of the adjustment is complete within the first two years.

TABLE 10-3 DYNAMIC PATTERNS OF ELASTICITIES OF MONEY DEMAND WITH RESPECT TO REAL INCOME AND INTEREST RATES

Quarters elapsed	Y	i
1	0.22	−0.054
2	0.37	−0.092
3	0.48	−0.119
4	0.55	−0.138
8	0.69	−0.172
Long run	0.73	−0.182

Source: Calculated using the elasticities shown in Table 10-2 and reported by Poloz, op. cit.

In summary, we have so far described three essential properties of money demand:

1. The demand for real money balances responds negatively to the rate of interest. An increase in interest rates reduces the demand for money.

2. The demand for money increases with the level of real income. However, the income elasticity of money demand is less than 1 so that money demand increases less than proportionately with income.
3. The short-run responsiveness of money demand to changes in interest rates and income is considerably less than the long-run response. The long-run elasticities are estimated to be over three times the size of the short-run elasticities.

There is one more important question to be considered. This is the question of how money responds to an increase in the level of prices. Here a number of researchers have found strong evidence that an increase in prices raises nominal money demand in the same proportion. We can add, therefore, a fourth conclusion:

4. The demand for nominal money balances is proportional to the price level. There is no money illusion; in other words, the demand for money is a demand for *real* balances.

Financial Innovation and Money Demand

Over the past fifteen years there have been a number of innovations in Canadian financial markets that have affected the demand for money.[22] Some of these have affected individual depositors and others have affected the banking arrangements of businesses.

For individual depositors, the major change has been the introduction of daily interest accounts. Prior to 1979, the standard savings account in a chartered bank paid interest on the minimum balance held over each calendar month. Most individuals were unable to earn interest on funds available for periods of less than a month and thus were likely to keep funds received from salary payments in chequing accounts. The introduction of savings accounts which pay interest on daily balances provided a new option which reduced the demand for M1.

In 1981, banks and other financial institutions began offering daily interest chequing accounts. Typically these accounts pay a higher interest rate on balances above some minimum such as $2000 and a much lower rate on balances below the minimum. Similarly, businesses were induced to shift from non-interest bearing chequing accounts to nonpersonal term deposits. The Bank of Canada attempted to allow for the effect of these deposits by including them in the M1A definition of the money supply.

Another innovation affecting business depositors has been the provision of more cash management services that enable the banks' customers to reduce their holdings of transactions balances and earn more interest. For example,

---

[22] See C. Freedman, "Financial Innovation in Canada: Causes and Consequences," *American Economic Review*, May 1983 and *Bank of Canada Review*, Feb. 1987, pp. 3–16.

there are arrangements under which surplus funds are automatically shifted at the end of each day to higher interest accounts. Such practices further reduce the demand for $M1$.

10-5 THE INCOME VELOCITY OF MONEY AND THE QUANTITY THEORY

The *income velocity of money* is the number of times the stock of money is turned over per year in financing the annual flow of income. Thus in 1986 GDP was $509.9 billion, the money stock ($M1$) averaged 31.4 billion, and velocity was therefore about 16. The average dollar of money balances financed $16 of spending on final goods and services, or the public held on average just under $0.06 of $M1$ per dollar of income. While we usually calculate velocity for the economy as a whole, we can also calculate it for an individual. For instance, for someone earning $20 000 per year, who has average money balances during the year of $2000, the income velocity of money holdings is 10.[23]

Income velocity (from now on we shall refer to velocity rather than income velocity) is defined as

$$V \equiv \frac{Y_N}{M} \tag{6}$$

the ratio of nominal income to nominal money stock. An alternative way of writing equation (6) recognizes that Y_N, nominal GDP, is equal to the price level P times real income Y. Thus

$$M \times V = P \times Y \tag{7}$$

The Quantity Theory

Equation (7) is the famous *quantity equation*, linking the product of the price level and the level of output to the money stock. The quantity equation became

---

[23] Why do we say income velocity and not plain velocity? There is another concept, transactions velocity, that is, the ratio of total transactions to money balances. Total transactions far exceed GDP for two reasons. First, there are many transactions involving the sale and purchase of assets that do not contribute to GDP. Second, a particular item in final output typically generates total spending on it that exceeds the contribution of that item to GDP. For instance, 1 dollar's worth of wheat generates transactions as it leaves the farm, as it is sold by the miller, as it leaves the baker for the supermarket, and then as it is sold to the household. One dollar's worth of wheat may involve several dollars of transactions before it is sold for the last time. Transactions velocity is thus higher than income velocity.

the (classical) *quantity theory of money* when it was argued that both V, the income velocity of money, and Y, the level of output, were fixed. Real output was taken to be fixed because the economy was at full employment, and velocity was assumed not to change much. Neither of these assumptions holds in fact, but it is, nonetheless, interesting to see where they lead. *If both V and Y are fixed, then it follows that the price level is proportional to the money stock. Thus the classical quantity theory was a theory of inflation.* The classical quantity theory argued that the price level was proportional to the money stock:

$$P = V\frac{M}{Y} \tag{7a}$$

The classical quantity theory applies in the *classical case* supply function examined in Chapter 7. Recall that in that case, with a vertical aggregate supply function, changes in the quantity of money result in changes in the price level, with the level of output remaining at its full employment level. When the aggregate supply function is not vertical, increases in the quantity of money increase both the price level and output, and the price level is therefore not proportional to the quantity of money. Of course, if velocity is constant, *nominal GDP* (the price level times output) is proportional to the money stock.

Velocity and Policy

Velocity is a useful concept in economic policy making. We see how to use it by rewriting (6) as

$$Y_N \equiv VM \tag{6a}$$

Given the nominal money stock (M) and given velocity, we know the level of nominal GDP. Thus if we can predict the level of velocity, we can predict the level of nominal income, given the money stock.

Further, *if velocity were constant, changing the money supply would result in proportionate changes in nominal income.* Any policies, including fiscal policies, that did not affect the money stock would not affect the level of income. You will probably now recognize that we have previously discussed a case of constant velocity. In Chapter 4, we discussed the effectiveness of fiscal policy when the demand for money is not a function of the interest rate and the *LM* curve is therefore vertical. The vertical *LM* curve is the same as the assumption of constant velocity.

Velocity and the Demand for Money

The discussion of constant velocity is closely related to the behaviour of the demand for money. Indeed, the notion of velocity is important because it is a convenient way of talking about money demand.

We now examine the relationship between velocity and the demand for money. Let the demand for real balances be written $L(i, Y)$, consistent with Chapter 4. Recall that Y is real income. When the supply of money is equal to the demand for money, we have

$$\frac{M}{P} = L(i, Y) \tag{8}$$

or $M = PL(i, Y)$. Now we can substitute for the nominal money supply into equation (6) to obtain

$$V = \frac{Y_N}{PL(i, Y)} = \frac{Y}{L(i, Y)} \tag{6b}$$

where we have recognized that Y_N/P is the level of real income. Income velocity is the ratio of the level of real income to the demand for real balances.

From equation (6b) we note that velocity is a function of real income and the interest rate. Consider first the effects of a change in the interest rate on velocity. An increase in the interest rate reduces the demand for real balances and therefore increases velocity: when the cost of holding money increases, money holders make their money do more work and thus turn it over more often.

The way in which changes in real income affect velocity depends on the income elasticity of the demand for money. If the income elasticity of the demand for real balances were 1, then the demand for real balances would change in the same proportion as income. In that case, changes in real income would not affect velocity. Suppose that real income Y increased by 10 percent. The numerator Y in equation (6b) would increase by 10 percent, as would the denominator, and velocity would be unchanged. However, we have seen that the income elasticity of the demand for money is less than 1. That means that velocity *increases* with increases in real income. For example, suppose that real income rose 10 percent, and the demand for real balances increased only by 7.3 percent ($= 0.73 \times 10$ percent), as Poloz's results suggest. Then the numerator of Equation (6b) would increase by more than the denominator, and velocity would rise.

BOX 10-1   MONEY DEMAND AND HIGH INFLATION

The demand for real balances depends on the alternative cost of holding money. That cost is normally measured by the yield on alternative assets, say treasury bills, commercial paper, or term deposits, but there is another margin of substitution. Rather than holding their wealth in financial assets, households or firms can also hold real assets: stocks of food, or houses, or machinery. This margin of substitution is particularly important in countries where inflation is very high and capital markets do not function well. In that case it is quite possible that the return on holding goods can even be higher than that on financial assets.

Consider a household deciding whether to hold $100 in currency or a demand deposit or else to hold it in the form of groceries on the shelf. The advantage of holding groceries is that, unlike money, they maintain their real value. Rather than having the purchasing power of money balances eroded by inflation, the household gets rid of money, buying goods and thus avoiding a loss.

This "flight out of money" occurs systematically when inflation rates become high. In a famous study of hyperinflations (defined in the study as inflation rates of more than 50 percent *per month*) Phillip Cagan of Columbia University found large changes in velocity taking place as inflation increased. In the most famous hyperinflation, in Germany in 1922–1923*, the quantity of real balances at the height of the hyperinflation had fallen to one-twentieth of its preinflation level. The increased cost of holding money leads to a reduction in real money demand and with it to changes in the public's payments habits as everybody tries to pass on money like a hot potato. We shall see more on this in Chapter 17 where we study money and inflation.

In well developed capital markets interest rates will reflect expectations of inflation and hence it will not make much difference whether we measure the alternative cost of holding money by interest rates or inflation rates. However, when capital markets are not free because interest rates are regulated or have ceilings, it is often appropriate to use inflation, not interest rates as the measure of the alternative cost. Franco Modigliani has offered the following rule of thumb: The right measure of the opportunity cost of holding money is the higher of the two, interest rates or inflation.

---

* Phillip Cagan, "The Monetary Dynamics of Hyperinflation," in Milton Friedman (ed.), *Studies in the Quantity Theory of Money* (Chicago: The University of Chicago Press, 1956).

The empirical work reviewed in Section 10-4 makes it clear that the demand for money and, therefore, also velocity do react systematically to changes in interest rates and the level of real income. The empirical evidence therefore decisively refutes the view that velocity is unaffected by changes in interest rates and that fiscal policy is, accordingly, incapable of affecting the level of nominal income. In terms of Equation (6b), and using the analysis of Chapter 4, expansionary fiscal policy can be thought of as working by increasing interest rates, thereby increasing velocity, and thus making it possible for a given stock of money to support a higher level of nominal GDP.

Velocity in Practice

The empirical evidence we reviewed in Section 10-4 is useful in interpreting the behaviour of velocity shown in Figure 10-4. The figure shows a striking and steady increase in velocity. The velocity of $M1$ has increased from under 8 in the early sixties to 16 in 1986. The average dollar finances twice the income flow now than it did in the early sixties. This increase in velocity can of course

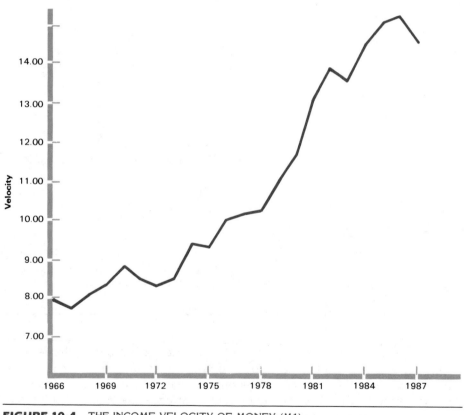

FIGURE 10-4   THE INCOME VELOCITY OF MONEY ($M1$)

(*Source*: Adapted from *Bank of Canada Review*)

be explained by the same factors that explain the demand for money. Velocity has risen because income has risen (since the income elasticity of demand is less than 1) and because interest rates have risen.

10-6 SUMMARY

1. The demand for money is a demand for real balances. It is the purchasing power, not the number, of their dollar bills that matters to holders of money.

2. The money supply (M1) is made up of currency and demand deposits. M2 and M3 are broader measures that include savings accounts, and term and notice deposits.

3. The chief characteristic of money is that it serves as a means of payment.

4. There are two broad reasons why people hold money and thus forgo interest that they could earn by holding alternative assets. These reasons are transactions costs and uncertainty.

5. Transactions costs are an essential aspect of money demand. If it were costless to move (instantaneously) in and out of interest-bearing assets, nobody would hold money. Optimal cash management would involve transfers from other assets (bonds or saving deposits) just before outlays, and it would involve immediate conversion into interest-bearing form of any cash receipts. The existence of transactions costs—brokerage costs, fees, and time costs—makes it optimal to hold some money.

6. The inventory-theoretic approach shows that an individual will hold a stock of real balances that varies inversely with the interest rate but increases with the level of real income and the cost of transactions. The income elasticity of money demand is less than unity, implying that there are economies of scale.

7. Transactions costs, in combination with uncertainty about payments and receipts, give rise to a precautionary demand for money. Money holdings provide insurance against illiquidity. Optimal money holdings are higher, the higher the variability of net disbursements and the higher the cost of illiquidity. Since holding money implies forgoing interest, optimal money holdings will vary inversely with the rate of interest.

8. Portfolio diversification involves the tradeoff between risk and return. Saving accounts form part of an optimal portfolio because they are not

risky — their nominal value is constant. Savings accounts dominate currency or demand deposits, which are also safe nominal assets, because they bear interest. Thus the speculative portfolio demand for money is a demand for saving or term deposits.

9. The empirical evidence provides strong support for a negative interest elasticity of money demand and a positive income elasticity. Because of lags, short-run elasticities are much smaller than long-run elasticities. The long-run income elasticity is about 0.7, and the long-run interest elasticity is about −0.2.

10. Over the past ten years the demand for money ($M1$) declined as a result of both the introduction of new assets and improvements in cash management methods.

11. The income velocity of money is defined as the ratio of income to money or the rate of turnover of money. Since the sixties, velocity has increased to a level of about 16.

12. The empirical evidence implies that an increase in real income raises velocity, as does an increase in the rate of interest. At higher levels of income or at higher interest rates, there is a lower demand for money in relation to income. Higher interest rates lead people to economize on cash balances.

13. Inflation implies that money loses purchasing power, and inflation thus creates a cost of holding money. The higher the rate of inflation, the lower the amount of real balances that will be held. Hyperinflations provide striking support for this prediction. Under conditions of very high expected inflation, money demand falls dramatically relative to income. Velocity rises as people use less money in relation to income.

KEY TERMS

Real balances	Transactions demand
Money illusion	Inventory-theoretic approach
M1	Square-root formula
M2	Precautionary demand
Liquidity	Speculative demand
Medium of exchange	Income velocity of money
Store of value	Quantity equation
Unit of account	Quantity theory of money
Standard of deferred payments	Hyperinflation

PROBLEMS

1. To what extent would it be possible to design a society in which there was no money? What would the problems be? Could currency at least be eliminated? How? (Lest all this seems too unwordly, you should know that some people are beginning to talk of a "cashless economy" in the next century.)

2. Evaluate the effects of the following changes on the demand for $M1$ and $M2$. Which of the functions of money do they relate to?
   (a) "Instant cash" machines which allow 24-hour withdrawals from savings accounts at banks.
   (b) The employment of more tellers at your bank
   (c) An increase in inflationary expectations
   (d) Widespread acceptance of credit cards
   (e) Fear of an imminent collapse of the government
   (f) A rise in the interest rate on nonchequable savings deposits

3. (a) Determine the optimal strategy for cash management for the person who earns $1600 per month, can earn 0.5 percent interest per month in a savings account, and has a transaction cost of $1.
   (b) What is the individual's average cash balance?
   (c) Suppose income rises to $1800. By what percentage does the person's demand for money rise? (Pay attention to the integer constraints.)

4. Discuss the various factors that go into an individual's decision regarding how many traveller's cheques to take on a vacation.

5. In the text, we said that the transactions demand-for-money model can also be applied to firms. Suppose a firm sells steadily during the month and has to pay its workers at the end of the month. Explain then how it would determine its money holdings.

6. This chapter emphasizes that the demand for money is a demand for real balances. Thus the demand for nominal balances rises with the price level. At the same time, inflation causes the real demand to fall. Explain how these two assertions can both be correct.

7. "Muggers favor deflation." Comment.

*8. The assumption was made in the text that, in the transactions demand for cash model, it is optimal to space transactions evenly throughout the month. Prove this as follows in the case where $n = 2$. Since one transaction must be made immediately, the only question is when to make the second one. For simplicity, call the beginning of the month $t = 0$ and the end of the month $t = 1$. The consider a transaction strategy which performs the second transaction at the time t_0. If income is Y_N, then this will require moving $t_0 Y_N$ into cash now and $(1 - t_0) Y_N$ at time t_0. Calculate the total cost incurred under this strategy, and try various values of t_0 to see which is optimal. (If you are familiar with calculus, prove that $t_0 = \frac{1}{2}$ minimizes total cost.)

*9.   For those students familiar with calculus, derive equation (4) from equation (2) by minimizing total costs with respect to n.

CHAPTER

The Money Supply Process

We have so far taken the money supply to be given and determined by the Bank of Canada. By and large, the Bank is indeed able to determine the money supply quite accurately, but it does not set it directly. In this chapter we study the ways in which the actions of the Bank of Canada, the chartered banks, and the public interact in determining the stock of money.

In conducting monetary policy, the Bank of Canada pays attention to the behaviour of both interest rates and the money supply. We will show that the Bank of Canada cannot simultaneously set both the money supply and the interest rate at whatever level it wants, though it can set either the money supply or the interest rate. In addition, we shall examine in some detail the way in which the Bank of Canada operates monetary policy.

11-1 DEFINITIONS

We noted in Chapter 10 that the money supply measure $M1$ is the sum of demand deposits, DD, and currency held by the public, CU.

$$M1 = DD + CU \tag{1}$$

A broader measure of the money supply is $M2$, which includes personal savings and nonpersonal notice deposits, SD.

$$M2 = M1 + SD \tag{2}$$

Table 11-1 summarizes the data in Table 10-1 and shows the components of the money stock in January 1988. $M1$ was $35.9 billion of which about 44 percent was currency. $M2$ was over five times as large with personal savings deposits making up the major portion of the difference between $M1$ and $M2$.

TABLE 11-1   COMPONENTS OF THE MONEY STOCK, JANUARY 1988
(millions of dollars, average of Wednesday)

(1) Currency	(2) Demand deposits	(3) $M1 =$ (1) + (2)	(4) Personal savings & nonpersonal notice dep.	(5) $M2 =$ (3) + (4)
15 815	20 123	35 938	153 825	189 763

Source: *Bank of Canada Review*

Since these deposits have been growing more rapidly than $M1$, $M2$ has been growing more rapidly than $M1$. This can be seen in Figure 11-1 which shows the behaviour of these aggregates since 1968.

For simplicity, we shall now ignore the distinction between demand and savings deposits and consider the money supply process as if there were only a uniform class of deposits D. Using that simplification, we define money as deposits plus currency:

$$M \equiv CU + D \tag{3}$$

Starting from Equation (3), we now begin to develop the details of the process of money stock determination. It is apparent from Equation (3) that both the public and the chartered banks have an influence on the determination of the money supply. The public has a role because its demand for currency affects the currency component CU. The banks have a role because the other component of the money stock, deposits D, is a liability of the banks, that is, a debt the banks owe their customers. We know too that the Bank of Canada has a part (the most important) in determining the money supply. The interactions among the actions of the public, the chartered banks, and the Bank of Canada determine the money supply, and we shall summarize their behaviour in the money supply process by three separate variables.

The Public

From the viewpoint of money supply determination, the variable on which we concentrate as representing the behaviour of the public is the *currency-deposit ratio* (*cu*), that is, the ratio of the public's holdings of currency (CU) to their

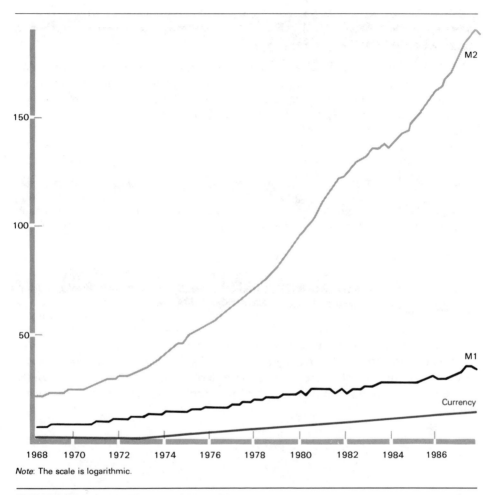

150 —

100 —

50 —

M2

M1

Currency

1968   1970   1972   1974   1976   1978   1980   1982   1984   1986

Note: The scale is logarithmic.

FIGURE 11-1   MONETARY AGGREGATES

(*Source:* Adapted from *Bank of Canada Review*)

holdings of deposits (*D*). Using the broader definition of the money supply (*M2*), the value of this ratio in January 1988 was 0.091 (equals $15.8 billion of currency divided by $174 billion of deposits).

The Chartered Banks

The behaviour of the chartered banks is summarized by the *cash reserve ratio.* Cash reserves are assets held by the chartered banks to meet (1) the demands of their customers for currency and (2) payments their customers make by cheques which are deposited in other banks. Cash reserves consist of notes held by the chartered banks (till money) and also of deposits held by the chartered banks at the Bank of Canada.

The chartered banks have accounts at the Bank of Canada which they can use to make payments among themselves. Thus, when my bank has to make a payment to your bank because I paid you with a cheque drawn on my bank account, it makes the payment by transferring money from its account to your bank's account at the Bank of Canada.[1]

We examine the determinants of the banks' demand for cash reserves, RE, in more detail in Section 11-5, but in the meantime we summarize that behaviour by the ratio of cash reserves to deposits, $re \equiv RE/D$. The cash reserve ratio is less than 1 since banks hold other assets such as securities and loans they make to individuals and firms. In January 1988, the chartered banks held cash reserves of $5.2 billion so that the cash reserve ratio was $5.2/174 = 0.030$.

The Bank of Canada

The Bank of Canada's behaviour is summarized by the stock of *high-powered money*, or the *monetary base*, H. High-powered money consists of currency and deposits of the chartered banks at the Bank of Canada. Part of the currency is held by the public—the $15.8 billion previously referred to. The remainder is held by the chartered banks as till money. The notes that constitute most of the outstanding stock of currency are issued by the Bank of Canada, and the cash reserves held by chartered banks as Bank of Canada deposits are a liability of the Bank of Canada, that is a debt of the Bank of Canada to the chartered banks.

11-2 THE MONEY MULTIPLIER

In this section we develop a simple approach to money stock determination. The approach is organized around the supply of and the demand for *high-powered money*. The Bank of Canada can control the *supply* of high-powered money. The total *demand* for high-powered money comes from the public, who want to use it as currency, and the chartered banks, who need it as cash reserves. Because the public has a preferred ratio of currency to deposits and because the banks have a desired ratio of reserves to deposits, we can calculate the total money stock that can be supported by any given stock of high-powered money.

---

[1] Since the establishment of the Canadian Payments Association in 1980, other financial institutions such as trust companies have also been able to participate in the cheque clearing system by maintaining deposits at the Bank of Canada.

Before we go into the details, we want to think briefly about the relationship between the money stock and the stock of high-powered money (Figure 11-2). At the top of the figure we show the stock of high-powered money. At the bottom we show the stock of money. They are related by the *money multiplier.* The money multiplier is the ratio of the stock of money to the stock of high-powered money.

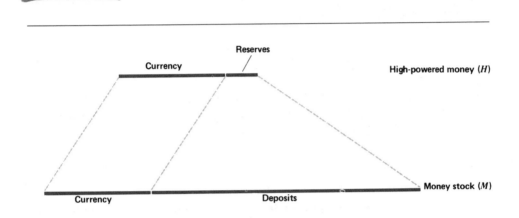

FIGURE 11-2 THE MONEY MULTIPLIER. The money multiplier is the ratio of the money stock (the base of the diagram) to high-powered money. The multiplier is larger than 1. It is larger, the smaller the ratio of currency to deposits and the smaller the ratio of cash reserves to deposits.

The money multiplier is larger than 1. It is clear from the diagram that the multiplier is larger the larger are deposits as a fraction of the money stock. That is because currency uses up 1 dollar of high-powered money per dollar of money. Deposits, by contrast, use up only the amount *re* of high-powered money (in reserves) per dollar of money stock. For instance, if the reserve ratio *re* is 10 percent, every dollar of the money stock in the form of deposits uses up only 10 cents of high-powered money.

It is thus clear that (1) *the money multiplier is larger, the smaller is the reserve ratio re.* In addition, (2) *the money multiplier is larger, the smaller is the currency deposit ratio cu.* That is because the smaller is *cu*, the smaller the proportion of the high-powered money stock that is being used as currency (which translates high-powered money only one for one into money) and the larger the proportion that is available to be reserves (which translate much more than one for one into money).

The precise relationship between the money stock *M*, the stock of high-powered money *H*, the reserve-deposit ratio *re*, and the currency-deposit ratio *cu* is derived in the Appendix to this chapter. Here we present the resulting expression for the money supply expressed in terms of its principal determinants, re, cu, and H:

$$M = \frac{1 + cu}{re + cu} H \equiv mm \cdot H \tag{4}$$

where mm is the money multiplier given by

$$mm \equiv \frac{1 + cu}{re + cu} \tag{5}$$

Careful examination of the formula for the money multiplier (5) shows that the multiplier is higher the smaller the reserve ratio and the smaller the currency-deposit ratio—as our earlier discussion suggested.

Numerical Example

We can calculate the money multiplier as given by Equation (5) using the actual values of the two ratios that existed in January 1988. For M2, we have $cu = 0.091$ and $re = 0.030$, so that

$$mm = \frac{1 + 0.091}{0.030 + 0.091} = 9.0$$

The same result can be obtained by taking the ratio of the M2 money stock ($189.8 billion) to the sum of currency ($15.8 billion) and reserves ($5.2 billion).

Graphical Analysis

Figure 11-3 shows graphically how the money multiplier works. The supply of high-powered money, H, is shown by the horizontal black line. The demand for high-powered money, HD, is an upward-sloping line with slope equal to 1 over the money multiplier. The intersection point E is the point at which the demand for high-powered money is equal to the supply. The corresponding money supply is shown by M_0.

Now suppose the stock of high-powered money increases to H'. The $\overline{HH}$ schedule moves up by amount ΔH to $\overline{HH'}$. The money supply increases until we reach point E', with new money stock M'. Because the slope of the HD schedule is less than 1, the distance between M_0 and M' is greater than ΔH.

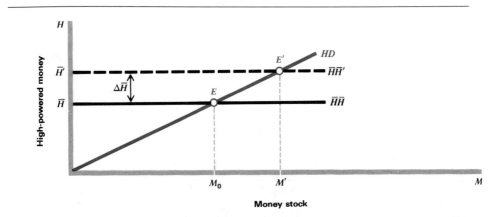

FIGURE 11-3   THE MONEY MULTIPLIER AND AN INCREASE IN THE MONETARY BASE. The HD schedule shows the demand for high-powered money, as related to the money stock M. The slope of the HD schedule is 1 over the money multiplier [see Equation (4)]. The supply of high-powered money is shown by the $\overline{HH}$ schedule. At point E the demand for high-powered money is equal to supply. The corresponding money supply is M_0. An increase in the stock of high-powered money by $\Delta\overline{H}$ shifts the $\overline{HH}$ schedule up to $\overline{HH}'$, resulting in a new equilibrium money stock M'. The ratio of the distance $(M' - M_0)$ (the increase in the money stock) to $\Delta\overline{H}$ (the increase in the base) is equal to the money multiplier.

Indeed, the ratio of the distance $(M' - M_0)$, which is the increase in the money stock, to $\Delta\overline{H}$ is equal to the money multiplier.[2]

The Multiplier in Practice

The behaviour of the money multipliers over the period 1968 to 1987 is shown in Figure 11-4. A glance at this chart shows that they are far from constant. Since the Bank of Canada controls $\overline{H}$, *it would be able to control M exactly* if the multiplier were constant or fully predictable. However, the money multiplier varies, not entirely predictably, and the Bank of Canada cannot always set the money supply at precisely the level it wants. In the rest of this chapter we take a closer look at the reasons the money multiplier varies.

---

[2] In problem 1, we ask you to use Fig. 11-3 to show the effects of increases in the currency-deposit ratio (cu) and the reserve-deposit ratio (re) on the money multiplier and the money stock. Changes in these ratios change the slope of the HD line in Fig. 11.3.

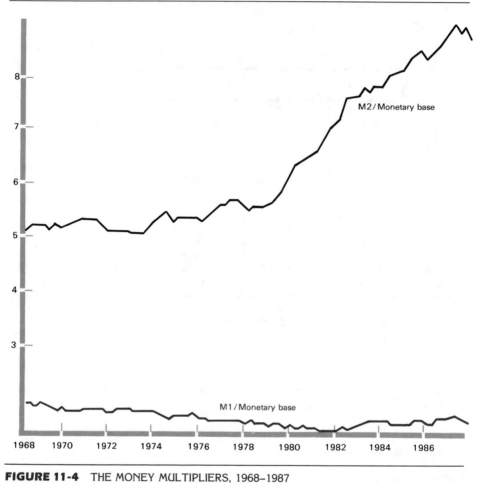

FIGURE 11-4   THE MONEY MULTIPLIERS, 1968–1987

(*Source:* Adapted from *Bank of Canada Review*)

11-3   THE STOCK OF HIGH-POWERED MONEY

Table 11-2 shows the balance sheet of the Bank of Canada. The components of the monetary base appear on the liability side and high-powered money is created when the Bank of Canada acquires assets or reduces its liability in the form of Government of Canada deposits.

TABLE 11-2   BALANCE SHEET OF THE BANK OF CANADA, JANUARY 1988
(millions of dollars)

ASSETS		LIABILITIES	
Government of Canada		Notes in circulation	
securities	19 270	Held by Chartered Banks	3 626
Advances	366	Other	14 460
Net foreign currency		Chartered bank deposits	1 608
assets	160	Government of Canada	
Other assets, net	16	deposits	118
Total assets	19 812		19 812

Source: *Bank of Canada Review*

Open Market Operations

The major means by which the Bank of Canada changes the monetary base is *open market operations.* We will examine the mechanics of an open market *purchase,* an operation in which the Bank of Canada buys, say, $1 million of government bonds from individuals or businesses which comprise the nonbank private sector. The accounting for the open market purchase is shown in Table 11-3. The Bank of Canada's holdings of government securities rise by $1 million and the nonbank private sector's holdings fall by the same amount. How does the Bank of Canada pay for the bonds? It writes a cheque on itself and the seller deposits the cheque in a chartered bank which in turn sends the cheque to the Bank of Canada. Thus, chartered bank reserves held in the form of Bank of Canada deposits increase by $1 million. The Bank of Canada owns more government securities, and the stock of high-powered money has been increased

TABLE 11-3   EFFECTS ON BALANCE SHEETS OF AN OPEN MARKET PURCHASE FROM THE NONBANK PRIVATE SECTOR

NONBANK PRIVATE SECTOR

ASSETS		LIABILITIES	
Government securities	− 1		
Deposits	+ 1		

CHARTERED BANKS

ASSETS		LIABILITIES	
Cash reserves	+ 1	Deposits	+ 1

BANK OF CANADA

ASSETS		LIABILITIES	
Government securities	+ 1	Chartered bank deposits	+ 1

by the amount of the open market purchase. That increase in high-powered money shows up as an increase in chartered bank deposits at the Bank of Canada. Later, as the money stock increases, the demand for currency will rise, and part of the increase in $\bar{H}$ will show up on the Bank of Canada's balance sheet as currency. Chartered bank deposits will fall by the amount that currency rises on the ("Liabilities") side of Table 11-3. You should now trace the way in which an open market sale reduces the stock of high-powered money.

The only strange part of the story of the open market purchase is that the Bank of Canada can write cheques on itself. The cheque instructs the Bank to pay $1 million to the order of the seller on the bond. The payment is made by giving the eventual owner of the cheque a deposit at the Bank of Canada. That deposit can be used to make payments to other banks, or it can be exchanged for currency. Just as the ordinary deposit holder at a chartered bank can obtain currency in exchange for deposits, the chartered bank deposit holder at the Bank of Canada can acquire currency in exchange for deposits. When the Bank of Canada pays for the bond with a deposit, it creates high-powered money with a stroke of the pen. Further, since it is the issuer of currency, it also creates high-powered money by simply printing it. In either event, the Bank of Canada can create high-powered money at will merely by buying assets, such as government bonds, and paying for them with its liabilities.

We have assumed so far that the open market purchase is made from the nonbank private sector. What will happen if the seller is a chartered bank? This case is illustrated in Table 11-4. The chartered bank receives a cheque from the Bank of Canada and exchanges it for a deposit. Thus chartered bank cash reserves and the stock of high-powered money increase as in the previous case, but the transaction has no direct effect on the nonbank private sector.

TABLE11-4 EFFECTS ON BALANCE SHEETS OF AN OPEN MARKET PURCHASE FROM A CHARTERED BANK

CHARTERED BANKS		
ASSETS		LIABILITIES
Government Securities	− 1	
Cash reserves	+ 1	

BANK OF CANADA		
ASSETS		LIABILITIES
Government securities	+ 1	Chartered bank deposits + 1

Government of Canada Deposits and the Base

As shown in Table 11-2, the Government of Canada maintains deposits with the Bank of Canada and it uses this account for government receipts and payments. If this were the only bank account maintained by the government, fluctuations in government revenues and expenditures would be reflected in fluctuations in the stock of high-powered money. For example, in a period in which the government receives more than it spends, there would be a transfer of deposits from the chartered banks to the government's account at the Bank of Canada so that cash reserves would be reduced. To avoid these effects, the Government of Canada maintains deposits with the chartered banks as well as with the Bank of Canada. Transfers of these deposits between the chartered banks and the Bank of Canada can then be used to offset the effects of government transactions and provide an alternative means of controlling the stock of high-powered money.

Borrowed Reserves

The chartered banks can increase their cash reserves by borrowing from the Bank of Canada at a rate of interest known as the *bank rate*. This arrangement is designed to provide a "lender of last resort" and advances are made to the chartered banks only occasionally. Rather than relying on advances from the Bank of Canada, the chartered banks typically meet their cash requirements by varying their holdings of interest-earning liquid assets or bidding for blocks of funds available for investment by large corporations. Earning liquid assets consist of treasury bills, Government of Canada bonds, day-to-day loans and other short-term loans.

Purchase and Resale Agreements

When a chartered bank varies its holdings of *day-to-day loans* for the purpose of managing its cash position, there can be an indirect effect on the monetary base. These loans are made to a group of investment dealers who carry inventories of Government of Canada securities. When necessary, these dealers can in turn obtain financing from the Bank of Canada under *purchase and resale agreements (PRA)*; that is, they can sell securities to the Bank of Canada with an agreement to repurchase them within a stated maximum time period. Thus, when chartered banks reduce their day-to-day loans they may induce an increase in PRA, so that the end result is the same as if the banks had borrowed from the Bank of Canada directly. During 1987 an average of $68 million of government securities were held by the Bank of Canada under PRA.

11-4 THE SIZE OF THE MONEY MULTIPLIER

As we have seen, the size of the money multiplier depends on the currency-deposit ratio and the cash reserve ratio. We now consider the determinants to these two ratios.

The Currency-Deposit Ratio

The currency-deposit ratio reflects the behaviour of the public and is determined primarily by payment habits. It has a strong seasonal pattern and is highest around Christmas. It increases when the ratio of consumption to GDP increases, since currency demand is more closely linked to consumption than GDP, while deposit demand is more closely linked to GDP.

The ratio of currency to demand deposits has shown a rising trend and this accounts for some of the decline in the $M1$ multiplier shown in Figure 11-4.

The Cash Reserve Ratio

The banking system affects the money multiplier through the ratio of cash reserves to deposits. The major determinants of this ratio are the *minimum required cash reserve ratios* prescribed under the Bank Act. Under the provisions of the 1980 changes to the Bank Act, the ratio for demand deposits is currently set at 10 percent. For notice deposits, the ratio is 2 percent for the first $500 million of deposits in each bank, and 3 percent for the remainder. The foreign currency component of $M3$ is also subject to a 3 percent minimum reserve ratio.

Excess Cash Reserves

A second factor affecting the cash-reserve ratio is the amount of *excess cash reserves* held by the chartered banks beyond the level of required cash reserves. In deciding how much excess reserves to hold, a bank's economic problem is very similar to the problem of the individual in deciding on a precautionary demand for money. Banks hold reserves to meet demands on them for currency or payments to other banks. The opportunity cost of holding excess cash reserves is the interest forgone and in principle we might expect the demand to depend on the rate of interest. However, since chartered bank holdings of excess cash reserves are typically very small (less than one-tenth of one percent of total deposits) this relationship is not of much importance in determining the money multiplier.

11-5   BANK LENDING AND THE MONEY MULTIPLIER

As can be seen from the balance sheet in Table 11-5, loans and investments make up a substantial fraction of chartered bank assets. In this section, we show how the process of bank lending plays an important role in the operation of the money multiplier and the determination of the money supply.

When banks make loans or purchase securities, they pay for the assets they acquire by creating deposits. A bank that makes a loan to a customer does not give the customer currency, but rather gives the loan in the form of a deposit

TABLE 11-5   BALANCE SHEET OF THE CHARTERED BANKS, JANUARY 1987
(billions of dollars)

ASSETS		LIABILITIES	
Bank of Canada notes		Demand deposits	20.4
and deposits	5.2	Personal savings deposits	137.7
Loans and investments		Nonpersonal term and	
Government of Canada		notice deposits	51.7
securities	14.5	Government of Canada	
Loans	208.4	deposits	1.6
Other securities	12.7	Other liabilities, net	29.4
Total Canadian dollar			
major assets	240.8		240.8

Source: *Bank of Canada Review*

at the bank and allows the customer to draw on the deposit either by taking out currency or writing a cheque on the account.

The Adjustment Process

For purposes of illustration we assume a currency-deposit ratio of 0.25 and a cash reserve ratio of 0.10. Suppose the stock of high-powered money has been increased by 1 dollar through an open market purchase. We start by considering the individual who sold the bond to the Bank of Canada. That person is paid with a cheque which he or she takes to the bank. Since this person, like all asset holders, has a currency-deposit ratio of cu, he or she will keep a fraction $cu/(1 + cu)$ as currency and deposit the balance. With $cu = 0.25$, he or she keeps 20 cents ($= 0.25/1.25$ dollars) as currency and deposits 80 cents.

At this stage the money stock has increased by only 1 dollar as a result of the increase in the stock of high-powered money. The effect of the deposit on the bank's balance sheet is shown in Table 11-6a. The bank has increased its

TABLE 11-6   EFFECTS OF LENDING ON BANK BALANCE SHEETS*

(a) ASSETS		LIABILITIES		(b) ASSETS		LIABILITIES	
Cash				Cash			
reserves	80	Deposits	80	reserves	8	Deposits	80
				Loans	72		

*In (a), reserves and deposits both increase by $1/(1 + cu)$. In (b), the bank lends out the fraction $1 - re$ of the reserves. The values of cu and re are 0.25 and 0.10 respectively.

cash reserves by 80 cents as a result of depositing at the Bank of Canada the cheque received from its customer and then paying out 20 cents in currency.

Now comes the crucial stage. The bank does not want to hold the *entire* extra 80 cents as cash reserves. The bank's reserve ratio is only *re*, so that it will hold only *re* of an extra dollar of deposits it receives in the form of cash reserves and lend out the rest to earn interest. Given *re* = 0.10, it will lend out 72 cents (= 0.90 × 80 cents).

This loan is shown in Table 11-6*b*. For simplicity we assume the borrower receives the loan of 72 cents in the form of currency. *It is at this stage that the bank's lending activities have increased the money supply by more than the increase in high-powered money.* The person who sold the bond to the Bank of Canada has 1 more dollar of money, but the person who borrowed from the bank also has more money holdings—the 72 cents lent by the bank. The money supply has increased by $1.72.

The person receiving the 72 cents will now want to hold a fraction $cu/(1 + cu)$ as bank deposits, but when this amount is deposited in a bank, the bank will want to lend out a fraction $1 - re$.

Clearly this process can keep going through many stages. As we show in the Appendix to this chapter, when we add up the increases in currency and deposits, we get the multiplier expression given in Equation (5). In our numerical example the increases in the money stock add up to:

$$\frac{1 + 0.25}{0.25 + 0.10} = 3.571$$

Multiple Expansion of Bank Deposits

The process described above is known as the *multiple expansion of bank deposits.* It shows how an increase in deposits leads to further deposits, and therefore shows how the money multiplier works. There is one further interesting aspect of the multiplier. It is possible to say that the banking system creates money in the sense that if there were not a banking system, a $1 increase in H would increase the money stock by only $1. With the banking system, the $1 increase in H leads to more than a $1 increase in M.[3]

The interesting point is that at each stage of the process, no one bank believes it is, or can be said to be, creating money. At each stage, each bank in the process is only lending out money that has been deposited with it. Each bank

---

[3] Bank loans and purchases of securities are described as *bank credit.* It is the existence of bank credit that makes the money stock larger than the stock of high-powered money. If banks did not extend credit (that is, did not make loans or buy securities), the entire multiple expansion process would never get off the ground, and we would have $M = H$.

manager would rightly, and no doubt vehemently, deny that the bank is creating money. The system as a whole, though, is creating money through the successive rounds of loans and subsequent further bank deposits.

11-6   CONTROL OF THE MONEY STOCK AND CONTROL OF THE INTEREST RATE

We make a simple but important point in this section: The Bank of Canada cannot simultaneously set both the interest rate and the stock of money at any given target levels that it may choose. If the Bank of Canada wants to achieve a given interest rate target, such as 8 percent, it has to supply the amount of money that is demanded at that interest rate. If it wants to set the money supply at a given level, say $40 billion in the month of June 1988, it has to allow the interest rate to adjust to equate the demand for money to that supply of money.

Figure 11-5 illustrates the point. Suppose that the Bank of Canada, for some reason, decides that it wants to set the interest rate at a level i^* and the money

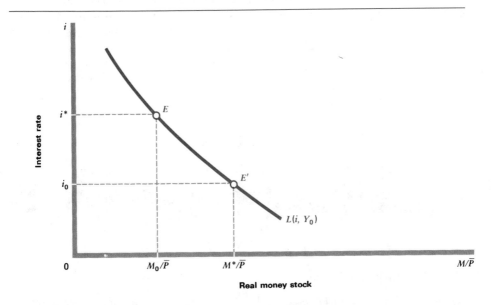

FIGURE 11-5   CONTROLLING THE MONEY STOCK AND INTEREST RATES. The Bank of Canada cannot simultaneously set both the interest rate and the money stock levels it wants. Suppose it wanted the interest rate to be i^* and the money stock to be M^*. These two levels are inconsistent with the demand for money. If the Bank insists on the interest rate level i^*, it will have to accept a money stock equal to M_0. If instead the Bank wants to set the money stock at M^*, it will end up with an interest rate equal to i_0.

stock at the level M^*, but that the demand for money function is as shown in $L(i, Y_0)$. The Bank is able to move the money supply around but it is not able to move the money demand function around. It therefore has to accept that it can set only the combinations of the interest rate and the money supply that lie along the money demand function. At the interest rate i^*, it can have the money supply $M_0/\overline{P}$. At the target money supply $M^*/\overline{P}$, it can have the interest rate i_0. It cannot have both $M^*/\overline{P}$ and i^*.

The point is sometimes put more dramatically as follows. When the Bank of Canada decides to set the interest rate at some given level and keep it fixed — a policy known as *pegging* the interest rate — it loses control over the money supply. It has to supply whatever amount of money is demanded at that interest rate. If the money demand curve were to shift, because of income growth, say, the Bank would have to increase the stock of high-powered money to increase the money supply.

As an operational matter, the Bank of Canada in its day-to-day operations can more easily control interest rates exactly than it can control the money stock exactly. The Bank buys and sells government securities—primarily treasury bills—on a regular basis. If the Bank of Canada wants to raise the price of government securities (lower the interest rate), it can buy the securities at the price it wants. If it wants to reduce the price of government securities (raise the interest rate), it can sell a sufficient amount of securities from its large portfolio. Thus, on a day-to-day basis, the Bank can determine interest rates quite accurately.

11-7   OTHER INSTRUMENTS OF MONETARY POLICY

The above discussion has focussed on the operation of monetary policy through control of the monetary base using open market operations. The Bank of Canada also makes use of changes in the bank rate and *secondary reserve requirements* to influence credit markets.

Changes in the Bank Rate

As indicated in Section 11-3 above, the bank rate is the rate of interest at which the Bank of Canada makes advances to the chartered banks. In principle, an increase in the bank rate can affect the money supply by raising the chartered bank's demands for excess cash reserves. Banks might be induced to maintain a larger cushion in view of the higher cost of borrowing if they suffer a loss of cash and are forced to seek accommodation from the Bank of Canada to meet their reserve requirements. It is not likely that this mechanism is of much importance in Canada, since the chartered banks rarely borrow from the Bank of Canada. On the other hand, the bank rate still plays a role as a signal of the Bank's view concerning the appropriate level of interest rates and its intentions with regard to monetary tightness or ease. These "announcement effects" of bank rate changes can be used to reinforce changes in other instruments of monetary policy.

The Floating Bank Rate

During the period 1956–1962 and more recently beginning in March 1980, the Bank of Canada has used a floating bank rate system under which the rate is automatically set each week at one-quarter of one percent above the rate of interest on 91-day treasury bills. At other times the bank rate has been fixed at the discretion of the Bank of Canada.

The main advantage of the floating rate is that it automatically maintains a small penalty cost to a chartered bank that makes use of Bank of Canada advances to replenish its cash reserves rather than selling some of its earning liquid assets. However, this system has been a subject of considerable controversy in the financial community. The objections are misguided to the extent that they are based on the notion that the Bank of Canada can control interest rates as a separate objective of policy while at the same time independently controlling the money supply. As we saw in the previous section, this is clearly not possible.

A legitimate argument is that the floating bank rate eliminates the information concerning Bank of Canada intentions provided by announced changes. On the other hand, these announcement effects are a somewhat clumsy and inefficient means of transmitting information. In periods of rapidly changing interest rates, bank rate changes have frequently followed rather than led changes in market rates. The volatility of interest rates during 1980 is cited by the Bank of Canada as the major reason for the return to a floating rate.[4]

Secondary Reserve Requirements

At times when the Bank of Canada is attempting to restrain inflationary forces, it may wish to dampen expenditures not only through higher interest rates but also through some form of direct control over the expansion of bank loans. Restricting the supply of cash reserves will not restrain the banks from extending credit if they have substantial quantities of liquid assets that can be sold off to finance new loans. The Bank of Canada is empowered to restrict the

---

[4] See *Annual Report* of the Bank of Canada for 1980, p. 9, 34.

ability of the chartered banks to expand their loans through the imposition of a required minimum secondary reserve ratio within the range of 0 to 12 percent of deposits. Secondary reserves are defined as holdings of treasury bills, day-to-day loans, and excess cash reserves.

A required minimum ratio of 9 percent was set in July 1970. Over the period 1971 to 1981, it was lowered in stages to 4 percent and it has remained at that level since.

*11-8   SHORT-RUN CONTROL OF THE MONEY SUPPLY

The discussion of bank deposit expansion given above neglected some institutional features of reserve requirements that influence the short-run response of the banking system to changes in the supply of high-powered money.[5]

Reserve Average Period

An individual bank is subject to erratic day-to-day fluctuations in its cash position as cheques are cleared and deposits are transferred from one bank to another. In view of this, the required reserve ratios apply not to each day's holdings of cash reserves, but to the average level over some specified period. Since 1969, this reserve averaging period has been two weeks. Thus, banks do not need to adjust to changes in their cash reserves on a particular day unless they are approaching the end of a two-week period with an average level of reserves below the minimum requirement.

Furthermore, the level of required cash reserves in effect at any time is not based on the current volume of deposits, but rather on the average volume of deposits during the *preceding* month. Thus, an expansion of loans and deposits will not affect total excess reserves during the current month, but will increase the level of required reserves that must be held in the following month. Of course, to the extent that the banks are not all expanding their loans at the same rate, deposits and cash will be redistributed, so that the faster growing banks will tend to lose reserves to the slower growing ones.

Chartered bank holdings of Bank of Canada notes that can be counted towards reserve requirements are also calculated as an average over the preceding month. This means that changes in the public's demand for currency have no effect on a bank's reserve position in the current month unless they induce the bank to reduce or replenish its till money by respectively increasing or running down its deposits at the Bank of Canada.

---

[5] For a detailed description of the requirements under the Bank Act, see *Bank of Canada Review,* notes to Table C10.

Actual Versus Desired Excess Cash Reserves

Under the circumstances described above, the Bank of Canada can control not only the total base, but also the reserve component of the base. Further, since required cash reserves are determined by deposits in the preceding month, effective control can be exercised over the excess cash reserves of the chartered banks.

The method by which the Bank of Canada induces changes in the money supply is to cause the actual level of excess reserves to diverge from the level which the banks find it desirable to maintain.[6] Suppose that the Bank of Canada wishes to bring about a contraction of the money supply. By setting the level of excess cash reserves below the level regarded by the banks as a minimum acceptable one, it will induce the banks to sell liquid assets in an attempt to increase their holdings of cash. However, the banking system as a whole will be frustrated in this attempt, since the assets it sells will be paid for by cheques drawn on the banks; assets and deposits will fall but cash reserves will remain the same. In addition, interest rates will rise since the banks will have to offer increased yields to induce nonbank investors to increase their holdings of securities at the expense of their holdings of bank deposits. As long as the supply of excess cash reserves is kept below the level desired by the banks, the money supply will continue to fall and interest rates will continue to rise.

Thus, if the Bank of Canada wishes to reduce the money supply by some target amount, it keeps the banks in a tight cash position until the target is achieved, and then restores the supply of cash reserves to the level desired by the banks. Similarly, an increase in the money supply is brought about by injecting additional cash into the banking system and inducing the banks to bid for additional liquid assets. In practice, this control of the money supply through cash reserve management by the Bank of Canada is a process of successive approximation, because the level of cash desired by the banks varies and cannot easily be predicted. By testing the reaction of the banks to a particular supply of cash, the Bank of Canada can estimate the target levels of cash that the banks are attempting to achieve and adjust the supply accordingly.

11-9   SUMMARY

1. The stock of money is determined by the Bank of Canada through its control of the monetary base (high-powered money); the public through its preferred currency-deposit ratio; and the chartered banks through the cash reserve ratio.

---

[6] For a detailed discussion of this mechanism, see J.F. Dingle, G.R. Sparks and M.A. Walker, "Monetary Policy and the Adjustment of Chartered Bank Assets," *Canadian Journal of Economics,* Nov., 1972.

2.   The money multiplier is the ratio of the money stock to high-powered money. It is larger the smaller the cash reserve ratio and the smaller the currency-deposit ratio. The major determinants of the cash reserve ratio are the minimum required cash reserve ratios.

3.   The Bank of Canada controls the money supply primarily through open market operations. These are purchases and sales of government securities that have a direct affect on the stock of high-powered money.

4.   The adjustment to a change in the stock of high-powered money takes place in stages as banks lend out the excess reserves which arise from deposit creation at the previous stage.

5.   The Bank of Canada cannot set both the interest rate and the stock of money at independently chosen target levels. It chooses only those combinations that are consistent with the demand for money.

6.   Other instruments of monetary policy are changes in the bank rate and secondary reserve requirements. Beginning in 1980, the Bank of Canada adopted a floating bank rate which is automatically set each week at one-quarter of one percent above the treasury bill rate.

7.   Since required cash reserves depend on average deposits in the preceding month, the Bank of Canada can exercise control over the money supply in the short run by setting the supply of excess cash reserves. Changes in the money supply are induced by purchases or sales of liquid assets by the chartered banks in response to deviations of actual cash reserves from the desired level.

KEY TERMS

Currency-deposit ratio	Bank rate
Cash reserve ratio	Excess cash reserves
High-powered money (monetary base)	Multiple expansion of bank deposits
Money multiplier	Secondary reserve requirements
Open market operation	Floating bank rate

APPENDIX

We derive the equilibrium money stock and the multiplier by looking at the demand and supply of money and of high-powered money. Consider, first, equilibrium between the supply of money and the demand for money, which, in turn, equals currency plus deposits:

$$M = CU + D \equiv (cu + 1)D \qquad \text{(A1)}$$

where we have substituted for $CU = cuD$, noting the public's desired ratio of currency to deposits cu.

Equilibrium between the supply of high-powered money and the demand for high-powered money which equals currency plus reserves implies:

$$\overline{H} = CU + RE \equiv (cu + re)D \qquad \text{(A2)}$$

Again we have expressed the demand side in terms of the desired ratio of currency to deposits and of the banks' cash reserve ratio re. When (A1) and (A2) both hold, we are in monetary equilibrium because people hold the composition of their money balances in the preferred ratio and banks hold just the right ratio of reserves to deposits.

Dividing (A2) by (A1) yields an expression for the money multiplier:

$$M/\overline{H} = mm \equiv \frac{1 + cu}{cu + re} \qquad \text{(A3)}$$

The money multiplier thus depends on the cu ratio and the re ratio. We can also use (A3), multipling both sides by $\overline{H}$, to obtain the money supply in terms of the principal determinants mm and $\overline{H}$:

$$M = mm\,\overline{H} \qquad \text{(A4)}$$

In writing (A4) we remember that mm is dependent on the currency-deposit preferences of the public and the cash reserve ratio of banks. It thus takes into account preferences about the composition of balance sheets.

The Multiplier Process

Table A11-1 shows the successive steps by which the money multiplier builds up following an increase in the stock of high-powered money by $1. Round 1 is the process described in Table 11-6, ending with the bank making a loan. Round 2 starts when the borrower spends the loan, and the person receiving the proceeds holds some of that amount as currency and deposits the rest in a bank. Round 2 ends once again with a bank loan and so forth.

We can now add up the increases in currency, deposits, reserves and bank credit occurring over all the rounds together, that is, during the entire process.

TABLE A11-1 MULTIPLE EXPANSION OF BANK DEPOSITS, BANK LOANS, AND THE MONEY MULTIPLIER

Increase in H	Increase in currency	Increase in deposits	Increase in reserves	Increase in bank loans	Stage
1	$\dfrac{cu}{1+cu}$	$\dfrac{1}{1+cu}$	$\dfrac{re}{1+cu}$	$\dfrac{1-re}{1+cu}$	Round 1
	$\dfrac{cu}{1+cu}\left(\dfrac{1-re}{1+cu}\right)$	$\dfrac{1}{1+cu}\left(\dfrac{1-re}{1+cu}\right)$	$\dfrac{re}{1+cu}\left(\dfrac{1-re}{1+cu}\right)$	$\dfrac{1-re}{1+cu}\left(\dfrac{1-re}{1+cu}\right)$	Round 2
	$\dfrac{cu}{1+cu}\left(\dfrac{1-re}{1+cu}\right)^2$	$\dfrac{1}{1+cu}\left(\dfrac{1-re}{1+cu}\right)^2$	$\dfrac{re}{1+cu}\left(\dfrac{1-re}{1+cu}\right)^2$	$\dfrac{1-re}{1+cu}\left(\dfrac{1-re}{1+cu}\right)^2$	Round 3
	$\dfrac{cu}{1+cu}\left(\dfrac{1-re}{1+cu}\right)^n$	$\dfrac{1}{1+cu}\left(\dfrac{1-re}{1+cu}\right)^n$	$\dfrac{re}{1+cu}\left(\dfrac{1-re}{1+cu}\right)^n$	$\dfrac{1-re}{1+cu}\left(\dfrac{1-re}{1+cu}\right)^n$	Round $n+1$
	$\dfrac{cu}{1+cu}\,SUM$	$\dfrac{1}{1+cu}\,SUM$	$\dfrac{re}{1+cu}\,SUM$	$\dfrac{1-re}{1+cu}\,SUM$	Total*
	$\dfrac{cu}{cu+re}$	$\dfrac{1}{cu+re}$	$\dfrac{re}{cu+re}$	$\dfrac{1-re}{cu+re}$	After substituting for *SUM* from Equation (7)

* *SUM* is defined by Equation (A5).

As in the case of the expenditure multiplier in Chapter 3, we have the sum of an infinite series, denoted here as *SUM* and given by[7]

$$SUM = 1 + \left(\frac{1-re}{1+cu}\right) + \left(\frac{1-re}{1+cu}\right)^2 + \left(\frac{1-re}{1+cu}\right)^3 + \dots \tag{A5}$$

$$= \frac{1+cu}{cu+re}$$

We use Equation (A5) in arriving at the bottom row of Table A11-1, which shows that currency increases by the fraction $[cu/(cu + re)]$ of $1 following the increase in H of $1, that deposits increase by $[1/(cu + re)]$, that reserves increase by $[re/(cu + re)]$, and finally, that credit increases by $[(1 - re)/(cu + re)]$.

Adding the increases in currency and deposits, we discover that the two together have risen by the amount $[(1 + cu)/(cu + re)]$, which is nothing other than the money multiplier. Table A11-1 thus provides another way of thinking about the money multiplier. The table also shows how, and by how much, the banking system creates loans (or buys securities) when the central bank increases high-powered money.

In the numerical example given in Section 11-5, currency increases by $0.714 $[cu/(cu + re)]$, deposits by $2.857 $[1/(cu + re)]$, reserves by $0.286 $[re/(cu + re)]$, and bank loans by $2.571 $[(1 - re)(cu + re)]$. The money stock increases by $3.571 or 3.571 times the increase in the stock of high-powered money. This is the value that can be obtained directly from the sum of the infinite series shown in Equation (A5).

PROBLEMS

1. Use Figure 11-3 to show how (a) an increase in the currency-deposit ratio and (b) an increase in the cash reserve ratio affect the money stock, given the monetary base.

2. Show the effects on the balance sheets of the Bank of Canada and the chartered banks of a change in the monetary base brought about by a

---

[7] *Technical note*: The formula for the sum of a geometric series, which can in general be written

$$SUM = 1 + a + a^2 + \dots .$$

where a is a number between minus and plus 1, is

$$SUM = \frac{1}{1-a}$$

If you have not met geometric series before, you may want to take an example, say, $a = 1/4$, and start adding the terms in the first formula in the footnote. You will soon find your answer coming close to $4/3$, which is the answer given by the second formula in the footnote.

transfer of government deposits from the chartered banks to the Bank of Canada.

3. Table 11-3 shows the initial impact on the Bank of Canada's balance sheet of an open market purchase. As noted in the text, at the end of the process both currency and chartered bank deposits at the Bank of Canada rise. What is the final increase in currency? Use the ratios cu and re in arriving at your answer.

4. A proposal for "100 percent banking" involves a reserve-deposit ratio of unity. Such a scheme has been proposed in order to enhance control over the money supply. Indicate (a) why such a scheme would help monetary control and (b) what bank balance sheets would look like under this scheme. (c) How would banking remain profitable, under 100 percent money?

5. Suppose a bank has excess reserves and makes a loan to someone who immediately withdraws the deposit the bank has given him and holds it as currency. Why does the bank's granting of the loan increase the money supply?

6. Discuss the impact of credit cards on the money multiplier.

7. This problem extends the analysis of the chapter by further distinguishing between M1 and M2. Assume a currency-demand deposit ratio cu and a desired ratio of demand to notice deposits of the public, $d = DD/ND$. Assume, too, that banks have reserve ratios, described by r_d and r_n with respect to demand and notice deposits, where the reserve ratio for notice deposits r_n is lower than that for demand deposits r_d.
   (a) Use the definition of M1 and the ratios d, r_d and r_n to derive an expression for the equilibrium stock of M1.
   (b) Use the definition of M2 and the ratios to derive an expression for the equilibrium stock of M2.
   (c) Show the effects of an increase in the demand-notice deposit ratio on credit.

8. Use Figure 11-3 and an IS-LM diagram to show the effect of an increase in required reserves on:
   (a) The equilibrium money supply
   (b) Interest rates
   (c) The equilibrium level of income

9. The Canada Deposit Insurance Corporation insures chartered bank deposits against bank default. Discuss the implications of that deposit scheme for the money multiplier.

10. Assume required reserves were zero. Would banks hold any reserves?

CHAPTER

Problems of Stabilization Policy

Figure 12-1, which shows the unemployment rate over the period1931–1987, gives the clear impression that stabilization policy has left something to be desired. Standing out is the disaster of the Great Depression decade of the thirties, when the unemployment rate reached nearly 20 percent of the labour force. Unemployment has also at times been high in the post–World War II period, as in the recession of 1982–1983.

The historical record forcefully raises the question of why the economy has not done better. The preceding chapters have laid out a clear body of theory that seems to show exactly the measures that can be used to maintain full employment. High unemployment, or a large GDP gap, can be reduced by expansionary monetary or fiscal policy. Similarly a boom and inflation can be contained by restrictive monetary or fiscal policies.

The policies needed to prevent the fluctuations in unemployment seen in Figure 12-1 accordingly appear to be simple. The policy maker knows the full-employment level of output. If there is unemployment, a model such as the *IS-LM* model can be used to calculate the level of government spending or taxes needed to get income to the full employment level. If it is all so simple, how did the fluctuations in Figure 12-1 occur?

The answer must be that policy making is far from simple. Part of the difficulty arises from the possible conflict between the maintenance of full employment and the target of low inflation. That important issue is discussed in Chapter 15 and 16. Other difficulties are described in this chapter.

We begin by discussing the types of disturbance that cause the economy to move away from the full-employment level of output in the first place. Then we briefly describe *econometric models,* models of the economy with specific numerical values for parameters and multipliers, that can be used to assist policy making. The bulk of the chapter is taken up by a discussion of three

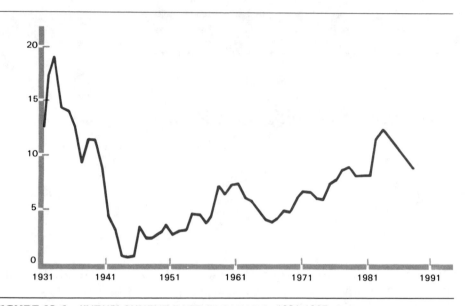

FIGURE 12-1 UNEMPLOYMENT RATE IN CANADA, 1931-1987

(*Source*: Adapted from Statistics Canada, 11-505; Department of Finance, *Economic Review*)

factors that in large measure account for the failure of policy continually to achieve its targets. The three *handicaps of policy making* are

1. lags in the effects of policy;
2. the role of expectations in determining private sector responses to policy;
3. uncertainty about the effects of policy.

In a nutshell, we are going to argue that a policy maker who (1) observes a disturbance, (2) does not know whether it is permanent or not, (3) takes time to develop a policy which (4) takes still more time to affect behaviour and (5) has uncertain effects on aggregate demand is very poorly equipped to do a perfect job of stabilizing the economy.

12-1 ECONOMIC DISTURBANCES

Before identifying in detail the obstacles in the way of successful policy making, we discuss economic disturbances in terms of their sources, persistence, and importance for policy. Disturbances are shifts in aggregate demand or aggregate supply that cause output, interest rates, or prices to diverge from their target paths.

We return to the *IS-LM* model as the framework for the discussion of economic disturbances in this chapter. In Figure 12-2 we show the *IS* and *LM* schedules and also the full-employment level output, Y^*. The economy is initially at full employment at point E. Now what disturbances might cause the economy to move away from full employment? Obviously, anything that shifts the *IS* and/or *LM* curves would disturb the economy and move it away from E.

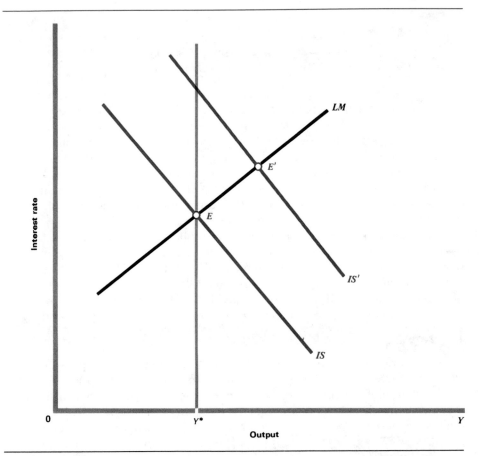

FIGURE 12-2 AN AGGREGATE DEMAND DISTURBANCE. The economy is initially in equilibrium at point E, with level of output Y^*. An increase in government spending shifts the *IS* curve to *IS'*. This disturbance tends to raise the level of output above the full-employment level. Monetary and/or fiscal policy, or even rationing, may be used to keep the level of demand in check, shifting the *IS'* curve back to *IS* and/or shifting the *LM* curve up and to the left.

In terms of overall economic impact, the major disturbances to the economy — the forces moving the *IS* and *LM* curves — have typically been wars. The effects of the increases in government spending associated with World War II and the Korean War can be seen in Figure 12-1 in the very low unemployment rates in those periods. Of these, World War II had the largest impact on the economy. At the height of the war, in 1944, federal government spending exceeded 40 percent of income.

As shown in Figure 12-2, an increase in government spending would shift the *IS* schedule upward and therefore lead to an excess demand for goods. To contain aggregate spending to the full-employment level of output, increased government spending would have to be offset by a reduction in private demand, that is, a reduction in investment and/or consumption spending. Investment spending can be reduced by allowing the interest rate to rise, and consumption spending can be reduced by increasing income taxes. These conventional economic policies may not be sufficient in wartime, however. In World War II more direct methods of reducing investment and consumption were used. A system was set up in which investment projects had to be approved. That system served to reduce the overall rate of private investment and also to direct investment toward areas helpful for the war effort. There was also some rationing of consumption goods, which reduced consumption expenditure as some of the rationed demand spilled over into increased saving rather than being diverted toward other goods. Thus, the aggregate level of consumption spending was reduced by using rationing to reduce the consumption of various goods essential for the war effort (gasoline, tires, shoes, etc.).[1]

Changes in government spending or tax policies not connected with wars may also constitute economic disturbances. Government spending or taxes may be increased or reduced for reasons which have to do with the government's view of desirable social policies. Those changes too may affect the level of aggregate demand if not accompanied by appropriate monetary and fiscal policies. In a country like Canada that is heavily dependent on foreign trade, changes in foreign demand for our exports may be an important source of disturbances.

Other economic disturbances that lead to changes in aggregate demand, which originate in the private sector, are shifts in the consumption or investment function. If consumers decide to consume more out of their disposable income at any given level of income, the *IS* curve of Figure 12-2 shifts upward, tending to increase the level of income. If there is no economic explanation for the shift in the consumption function, then it is attributed to a change in the

---

[1] In passing, it is worth considering for a moment why partial rationing might work as a macroeconomic policy, that is, as a policy reducing aggregate demand. The reason must be that part of the expenditure that is precluded by rationing does not shift to other goods but instead increases saving, that is, future consumption.

tastes of consumers between consumption and saving. In such a case, we describe the shift as a disturbance.

Similarly, if investment spending increases for no apparent economic reason, then we attribute the increase to an unexplained change in the optimism of investors about the returns from investment. Again, we regard that change in investment behaviour as a disturbance to the system. Changes in the optimism of investors are sometimes described as changes in their *animal spirits*—a term that suggests that there may be little rational basis for those spirits.[2] Some shifts in the investment function are caused by new inventions that require large amounts of investment for their successful marketing, such as the development of the railways in the nineteenth century and the spread of the automobile in the 1920s.

Shifts in the demand for money may affect the interest rate, and thus indirectly affect the rate of investment. Another source of disturbances is changes in supply conditions, such as the oil price increases of 1973–1974 and 1979–1980 and the oil price decrease of 1985–1986. In addition, the behaviour of wages may constitute a source of economic disturbances.

Finally, there is the interesting possibility that disturbances may be caused by the policy makers themselves. There are two different arguments concerning this possibility. First, since policy making is difficult, it is entirely possible that the attempts of policy makers to stabilize the economy could be counterproductive. Indeed, a forcefully stated and influential view of the causes of the Great Depression[3] argues that an inept monetary policy in the United States was chiefly responsible for the severity of the depression. The argument of Friedman and Schwartz is basically that the officials in charge of the American central bank in the early 1930s did not understand the workings of monetary policy and therefore carried out a policy that made the depression worse rather than better.

The second argument that policy makers themselves may be responsible for economic disturbances arises from the relationship between election results and economic conditions in the period before the election. If it appears that incumbents tend to be reelected when economic conditions, primarily the unemployment rate, are improving in the year before the election, it is tempting for them to try to *improve* economic conditions in the period before the election; their efforts may involve tax reductions or increases in government spending. It is now quite common to talk of the *political business cycle*. The political

---

[2] Keynes, in particular, argued that shifts in the investment function were a major cause of fluctuations in the economy. See J.M. Keynes, *The General Theory of Employment, Interest and Money* (New York: Macmillan, 1936), Chap. 22.

[3] See Milton Friedman and Anna J. Schwartz, *The Great Contraction* (Princeton, N.J.: Princeton University Press, 1965). We review the argument in Chapter 13.

business cycle consists of economic fluctuations produced by economic policies designed to help win elections.

While some evidence supports the notion of a political business cycle, the argument should be regarded as tentative because the link between economic conditions and election results is not yet firmly established.

We proceed next to discuss economic models and the three factors that make the task of policy makers far more difficult than an over literal interpretation of the simple *IS-LM* model in Figure 12-2 might suggest.

12-2 ECONOMETRIC MODELS FOR POLICY MAKING AND FORECASTING

In Figure 12-3 we show the typical situation facing economic policy makers. Something has happened that created a recession. Output is a level Y_0 rather than full-employment level Y^*. How should policy makers react if they want to get output back to the full-employment level? The *IS-LM* model gives a number

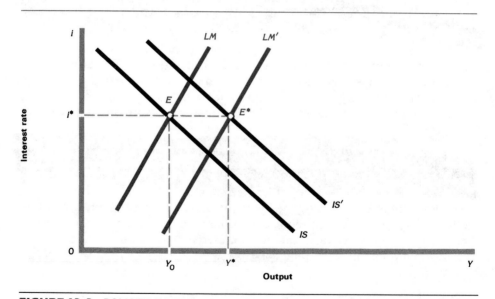

FIGURE 12-3 POLICIES TO END A RECESSION. The economy is in a recession at point E. Policy makers plan to return to full-employment output at the interest rate i^*, at point E^*. The *IS* curve has to be shifted to *IS'* and the *LM* curve to *LM'*. This requires expansionary fiscal and monetary policy. The precise amounts to increase government spending and the money stock can be calculated from the government spending and monetary policy multipliers.

of choices. One possibility is to increase the money stock; or taxes could be reduced, or government spending increased.

Suppose the decision has been made to attempt to return to full employment at point E^*, with the interest rate remaining at i^*. Suppose also that the plan is to do this by increasing government spending and at the same time expanding the money supply. The IS curve has to be shifted to IS' and the LM curve to LM'.

Such plans are, however, not detailed enough. The policy makers need to know not only in what direction to shift government spending and the money stock, but also *how much* to change them. If government spending should be increased by $5 billion, it will not do much good to increase it by $1 billion. On the other hand, if it should be increased by only $1 billion, an increase in government spending of $5 billion will push the economy well beyond the point of full employment and create inflationary pressures. The policy makers have to know not only the medicines to prescribe, but also the right doses.

In other words, they have to know the *multipliers*, associated with monetary and fiscal policy. To calculate these multipliers, they typically rely on *econometric models*. An econometric model is an equation or a set of equations with numerical values for parameters, based on the past behaviour of the economy, describing the behaviour of some specific sectors of the economy or the economy as a whole.

Econometric Models of Canada

A considerable number of econometric models of the Canadian economy have been constructed and are used regularly for forecasting and policy analysis. Within the federal government, there are models at the Bank of Canada, Department of Finance and the Economic Council of Canada. Models are also maintained by John Helliwell at the University of British Columbia and the Institute of Policy Analysis at the University of Toronto. Models are operated as private commercial enterprises by Chase Econometrics, Data Resources of Canada and Informetrica.

These models describe aggregate demand using an extended *IS-LM* framework. Equations are estimated for the components of aggregate demand using theories similar to those described in Chapters 8-11. The consumption function, for instance, would be similar to the sophisticated function we discussed in Chapter 8, although in most cases it would be disaggregated into several components.

To be useful, the models must also include equations to predict the rate of inflation as well as output. For this purpose the models have aggregate supply sectors along the lines described in Chapters 14 to 16.

Fiscal and monetary policy multipliers for two of the Canadian models are shown in Table 12-1. CANDIDE is the Economic Council of Canada model and

TABLE 12-1 REAL INCOME MULTIPLIERS FROM TWO ECONOMETRIC MODELS

Policy change		Year			
		1	3	5	10
Fiscal policy: increase in government spending (multiplier effect)	CANDIDE	1.98	2.25	1.85	0.77
	RDXF	1.09	0.58	0.34	0.06
Monetary policy: 1 percent decrease in money supply (percent change in output)	CANDIDE	0	−0.17	−0.33	−0.21
	RDXF	−0.22	−0.13	−0.06	−0.06

Source: B.O'Reilly, G. Paulin, and P. Smith, *Responses of Various Econometric Models to Selected Policy Shocks,* Bank of Canada Technical Report 38, July 1983. CANDIDE and RDXF are models constructed by the Economic Council of Canada and the Bank of Canada, respectively.

RDXF is one of the models at the Bank of Canada. The table shows *dynamic multiplier* effects which take place in stages over time and reflect the various lags built into models. For fiscal policy, the CANDIDE model shows a larger effect on real income in the third year compared with the initial year, while the RDXF model shows declining multiplier effects. In both cases we see crowding out occurring so that by the tenth year the changes in output are much smaller.

For policy changes, the multiplier effects are quite different in magnitude and lag pattern between the two models. This reflects differences in size and degree of disaggregation between the two models as well as differences in the theoretical assumptions used in constructing the equations. At the present time there is clearly no consensus on the exact structure of the economy and thus there is considerable variation among the models.

12-3 LAGS IN THE EFFECTS OF POLICY

Suppose that the economy was at full employment and has been affected by an aggregate demand disturbance that reduces the equilibrium level of income below full employment in Figure 12-3 toward point *E*. Suppose further that there was no advance warning of this disturbance and that, consequently, no policy actions were taken in anticipation of its occurrence. Policy makers now have to decide *whether at all* and *how* to respond to the disturbance.

The first concern, and the first difficulty, should be over the permanence of the disturbance and its subsequent effects. Suppose the disturbance is only transitory, such as a one-period reduction in consumption spending. When the disturbance is transitory so that consumption rapidly reverts to its initial level, the best policy may be to do nothing at all. Provided suppliers or producers do not mistakenly interpret the increase in demand as permanent but, rather, perceive it as transitory, they will absorb it by production and inventory changes rather than capacity adjustments. The disturbance will affect income in this period but will have very little permanent effect. Policy actions generally do not affect the economy immediately. Any policy actions taken to offset the disturbance this period, for example, a tax reduction, will have their impact on spending and income only over time. In later periods, however, the effects of the initial fall in demand on the level of income will be very small, and without the policy action the economy would tend to be very close to full employment. The effects of a tax cut, therefore, would be to raise income in later periods and move it away from the full-employment level. Thus, if the disturbance is temporary and it has no long-lived effects and policy operates with a lag, then the best policy is to do nothing.

Figure 12-4 illustrates the main issue. Assume an aggregate demand disturbance reduces output below potential, starting at time t_0. Without active policy intervention output declines for a while but then recovers and reaches the full-employment level again at time t_2. Consider next the path of GDP under an active stabilization policy, but one that works with the disadvantage of lags.

FIGURE 12-4   LAGS AND DESTABILIZING POLICY. A disturbance at time t_0 reduces output below the full-employment level. It takes until t_1 before policy responds, and there is a further lag until the policy starts working. By the time the full effects of the policy are evident, output would already have returned to the full-employment level even without policy. However, because a policy action has been taken, output now rises *above* the full-employment level and then fluctuates around Y^*. The lags in policy thus have made policy a source of fluctuations in output that would not otherwise have happened.

Thus, expansionary policy might be initiated at time t_1 and start taking effect some time after. Output now tends to recover faster as a consequence of the expansion and, because of poor dosage and/or timing, actually overshoots the full-employment level. By time t_3, restrictive policy is initiated, and some time after, output starts turning down toward full employment and may well continue cycling for a while. If this is an accurate description of the potency or scope of stabilization policy, then the question must seriously arise whether it is worth trying to stabilize output or whether the effect of stabilization policy is, in fact, to make things worse. Stabilization policy may actually *destabilize* the economy.

One of the main difficulties of policy making is in establishing whether or not a disturbance is temporary. It was clear enough in the case of World War II that a high level of defence expenditures would be required for some years. However, in the case of the Arab oil embargo of 1973–1974, it was not clear at all how long the embargo would last or whether the high prices for oil that were established in late 1973 would persist. At the time, there were many who argued that the oil cartel would not survive and that oil prices would soon fall — that is, the disturbance was temporary. "Soon" turned out to be 12 years. Let us suppose, however, that it is known that the disturbance will have effects that will last for several quarters, and that the level of income will, without policy, be below the full-employment level for some time. What lags do policy makers encounter?

We now consider the steps required before a policy action can be taken after a disturbance has occurred, and then the process by which that policy action affects the economy. There are delays, or lags, at every stage. It is customary and useful to divide the lags into an *inside* lag, which is the time period it takes to undertake a policy action — such as a tax cut, or an increase in the money supply — and an *outside* lag, which describes the timing of the effects of the policy action on the economy. The inside lag, in turn, is divided into recognition, decision, and action lags.

The Recognition Lag

The *recognition lag* is the period that elapses between the time a disturbance occurs and the time the policy makers recognize that action is required. This lag could in principle be *negative* if the disturbance could be predicted and appropriate policy actions considered *before* it even occurs. For example, we know that seasonal factors affect behaviour. Thus it is known that at Christmas the demand for currency is high. Rather than allow this to exert a restrictive effect on the money supply, the Bank of Canada will accommodate this seasonal demand by an expansion in high-powered money. In other cases the recognition lag has been positive, so that some time has elapsed between the disturbance and recognition that active policy was required.

The major reason that there is any recognition lag at all, apart from the delay in collecting statistical data, is that it is never certain what the consequences of a disturbance will be. That uncertainty in turn is a result of economists' lack of knowledge of the workings of the economy (which was discussed above) as well as political uncertainties.

The Decision and Action Lags

The recognition lag is the same for monetary and fiscal policy. The Bank of Canada and the Department of Finance are in constant contact with one another and share their predictions about the future course of the economy. For the *decision* lag — the delay between the recognition of the need for action and a policy decision — by contrast there is a difference between monetary and fiscal policy. Once the need for a policy action has been recognized by the Bank of Canada, the decision lag for monetary policy is short. Further, the action lag — the lag between the policy decision and its implementation — for monetary policy is also short.

However, fiscal policy actions are less rapid. Once the need for fiscal policy action has been recognized, the government has to prepare legislation for that action. Next, the legislation has to be considered and approved by Parliament before the policy change can be made. Even after the legislation has been approved, the policy change has still to be put into effect. If the fiscal policy takes the form of a change in tax rates, it may be some time before the changes in tax rates begin to be reflected in pay-cheques — that is, there may be an action lag.

Built-In Stabilizers

The existence of the inside lag of policy making focusses attention on the built-in or automatic stabilizers that we discussed in Chapter 3. One of the major benefits of automatic stabilizers is that their inside lag is zero. Recall from Chapter 3 that the most important automatic stabilizer is the income tax. It stabilizes the economy by reducing the multiplier effects of any disturbance to aggregate demand. The multiplier for the effects of changes in autonomous spending on GDP is inversely related to the income tax rate. The higher the tax rate, the smaller the effects of any given change in autonomous demand on GDP. Similarly, unemployment compensation is another automatic stabilizer. When workers become unemployed and reduce their consumption, that reduction in consumption demand tends to have multiplier effects on output. Those multiplier effects are reduced when a worker receives unemployment compensation because disposable income is reduced by less than the loss in earnings.

Although built-in stabilizers have desirable effects, they cannot be carried too far without also affecting the overall performance of the economy. The multiplier could be reduced to 1 by increasing the tax rate to 100 percent, and that would appear to be a stabilizing influence on the economy. However, with 100 percent marginal tax rates, the desire to work and consequently the level of GDP, would be reduced. Thus there are limits on the extent to which automatic stabilizers are desirable. Nonetheless, automatic stabilizers play an important role in the economy; it has been argued that the absence of significant unemployment compensation in the 1930s was one of major factors making the Great Depression so severe, and that the existence of the stabilizers alone makes the recurrence of such a deep depression unlikely.

The Outside Lag

The inside lag of policy is a *discrete* lag in which policy can have no effect on the economy until it is implemented. The outside lag is generally a *distributed* lag: once the policy action has been taken, its effects on the economy are spread over time. There is usually a small immediate effect of a policy action, but other effects occur later.

The idea that policy operates on aggregate demand and income with a distributed lag is shown in Figure 12-5. The process illustrated is the same as that represented by the numerical results from the econometric models shown in Table 12-1.

Suppose that we are considering a once-for-all increase in high-powered money in period 1, as shown in Figure 12-5a. This increase in high-powered money, by affecting interest rates and therefore aggregate spending, changes the level of income in subsequent periods by the amounts indicated in Figure 12-5b. The height of the bars shows the amount by which GDP exceeds the level that it would have had in the absence of the policy change. The main point to be made is that monetary or fiscal actions taken now affect the economy over time.

If we measure time in quarters, the impact in the initial period is likely to be relatively small with most of the affect coming later in the adjustment period as illustrated in Figure 12-5b. Thus if it were necessary to increase the level of employment rapidly to offset a demand disturbance, a large policy change would be necessary. However, in later quarters large effects on GDP would be built up so that there would probably be an overcorrection of the unemployment leading to inflationary pressures. It would then be necessary to reverse policy and undertake contractionary actions to avoid the inflationary consequences of the initial expansionary policy.

It should thus be clear that when policy acts slowly, with the impacts of policy building up over time, considerable skill is required of policy makers if their own attempts to correct an initially undesirable situation are not to lead to problems that themselves need correcting. Recall also that we have been talking here about the *outside* lag, and that the policy action we are considering

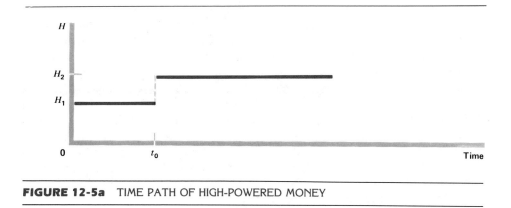

FIGURE 12-5a TIME PATH OF HIGH-POWERED MONEY

would be taken only six months after the initial disturbance if the inside lag is six months long.

Why are there such long outside lags? We have already discussed some of the reasons for these lags in Chapter 8 on the consumption function, where current consumption depends on lagged income, and also in Chapter 9 on investment, where the accelerator models imply that investment depends on lagged and current income. Similar lags are also present in the financial sector of the economy, where the demand for money depends on lagged income. Each of these sources of lags creates an outside lag, and their interaction generally produces longer lags than each of the underlying lags.

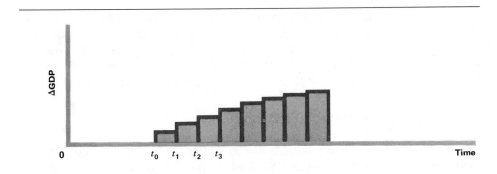

FIGURE 12-5b DYNAMIC MULTIPLIERS FOR THE EFFECTS OF A CHANGE IN HIGH-POWERED MONEY ON GDP. An increase in the stock of high-powered money causes GDP to increase by successively larger amounts as we move through time. The height of the bars shows the amount by which GDP exceeds the level that it would have been in the absence of the policy change.

Because the point is so important, let us describe in more detail how the lags of monetary policy arise. Suppose the Bank of Canada conducts an open market purchase. Because aggregate demand depends heavily on lagged values of income, interest rates, and other economic variables, the open market purchase initially has effects mainly on short-term interest rates and not on income. Short-term interest rates, such as the treasury bill rate, affect long-term interest rates with a lag. The long-term interest rates in turn affect investment with a lag , and also affect consumption by affecting the value of wealth.[4] Then when aggregate demand is affected by the initial open market purchase, the increase in aggregate demand itself produces lagged effects on subsequent aggregate demand through the fact that both consumption and investment depend on past values of income. So the effects of an initial open market purchase will be spread through time, as in Figure 12-5.

Monetary and Fiscal Policy Lags

The discussion in the previous paragraph suggests that fiscal policy and certainly changes in government spending, which act directly on aggregate demand, may affect income more rapidly than monetary policy. This is indeed the case. However, the fact that fiscal policy acts faster on aggregate demand than monetary policy must not lead us to overlook the fact that fiscal policy has a considerably longer inside lag. Moreover, the inside lag for government spending is longer than that for taxes because, when the government purchases goods and services, it has to decide what goods to buy, have bids for the sale of those goods submitted by the private sector, and then decide on the award of the contracts. In summary, therefore, fiscal policy is attractive because of the short outside lag, but that advantage is more than offset by a potentially long inside lag.

Our analysis of lags indicates clearly one difficulty in undertaking stabilizing short-term policy actions: it takes time to set the policies in action, and then the policies themselves take time to affect the economy. But that is not the only difficulty. Further difficulties considered in Sections 12-4 and 12-5 arise from uncertainty about the exact timing and magnitude of the effects of policy.

12-4 THE ROLE OF EXPECTATIONS

We have discussed the two basic sources of lags in economic behaviour in earlier chapters. The first source is the costs of rapid adjustment. For example,

---

[4] Recall that in Chapter 8 we discussed the life-cycle model of consumption demand, in which consumption is affected by the level of wealth. Part of wealth is the value of stock market assets; the value of stock market assets rises when the long-term interest rate falls. Thus, interest rates affect consumption through a wealth effect.

in Chapter 9 we showed how the costs of adjusting the actual capital stock to the desired capital stock led to lags in the investment function. The second source of lags is expectations. In this section we focus on expectations, their formation, and the effects they have on policy and its effectiveness.

While it is undoubtedly true that the past behaviour of a variable influences expectations about its future behaviour, it is aslo true that consumers and investors will sometime use more information than is contained in the past behaviour of a variable when trying to predict its future behaviour.

Consider, for example, forecasts of permanent income — long-run average income. In Chapter 8, as in Friedman's original work on the consumption function, permanent income is estimated as an average of income in the recent past. Suppose, however, that you were a resident of a small country that had just discovered vast gold deposits. You would then take the information about the gold discovery into account in forming an estimate of your permanent income. You would *immediately* estimate a permanent income substantially higher than your historical average income. Alternatively, suppose that you have been estimating the expected rate of inflation as an average of past rates of inflation, at a time when the inflation rate is high and a new government is elected on a strictly anti-inflationary platform. Then you would lower your estimate of the inflation rate; that is, you would use more information in predicting it than is contained solely in its past behaviour.

It is, in general, very difficult to incorporate all relevant information that is used by economic agents within a simple econometric model. That means that there will inevitably be errors in what the models predict for the consequences of various policy actions, meaning, in turn, that it is dicfficult to control the economy precisely.

Expectations and Policy

It is particularly important to consider the effects of a given policy action itself on expectations, since it is possible that a new type of policy will affect the way in which expectations are formed.[5] Suppose that the Bank of Canada announced a new monetary policy designed to stabilize the average level of income and avoid booms and recessions. The new policy would be to reduce the money supply whenever the income level rose and to increase the money supply whenever the income level fell. Such a counter-cyclical rule has implications for expectations. Clearly, it would be inappropriate in the presence of

---

[5] The interactions of policy and expectations have been the focus of the rational expectations approach to macroeconomics. We have mentioned rational expectations in earlier chapters. Chapter 18 provides a full treatment. For an early statement, see Thomas J. Sargent and Neil Wallace, "Rational Expectations and the Theory of Economic Policy," *Journal of Monetary Economics,* April 1976, and William Fellner, *Towards a Reconstruction of Macroenonomics* (American Enterprise Institute, 1976).

such monetary policy to use an expectations mechanism that implies that an increase in income will persist. The monetary policy rule implies that the money supply should be reduced following an increase in income, and one expects the reduction in money to exert at least a dampening effect on income.

While correct expectations mechanisms must therefore use information about policy responses to disturbances, such care is difficult to apply in practice. Most expectations mechanisms embodied in econometric models of the economy and used for the assessment of policies assume that expectations affecting consumption and investment spending are based entirely on past values.

Econometric Policy Evaluation

The preceding discussion of the effects of a change in policy on expectations is part of a wider *econometric policy evaluation critique* formulated by Robert E. Lucas, of the University of Chicago, intellectual leader of the rational expectations approach to macroeconomics.[6] Lucas argues that existing macroeconometric models cannot be used to study the effects of policy changes *because the way private agents (firms and consumers) respond to changes in income and prices depends on the types of policy being followed.*

For example, suppose there is a change in income this period. How does consumption react? If policy is successful in keeping income always very close to potential, the change in income will be viewed as transitory, and there will be almost no change in consumption. But if policy is such that deviations of output from potential are typically prolonged, the change in income will be regarded as more permanent and the consumption response will be large. The key point is that the consumption response to changes in income depends on the types of policy being followed. Therefore one cannot use a consumption function which does not allow for this change in behaviour to examine the effects of policy changes.

Lucas argues that problems of this sort are pervasive in macroeconometric models. He does not argue that it will never be possible to use econometric models to study policy, only that existing models cannot be used for that purpose.

Accordingly, the Lucas critique is not one that rules out the use of econometric models. It suggests rather that very careful modelling of the responses of consumers and firms to changes in income and prices is necessary. For instance, the consumption example above would not be impossible to handle, so long as permanent income were estimated as a weighted average of past incomes that changed appropriately as the behaviour of income itself changed with policy.

---

[6] See "Econometric Policy Evaluation: A Critique," in R.E. Lucas, Jr., *Studies in Business Cycle Theory* (Cambridge, Mass.: M.I.T. Press, 1981).

Summary

This section has made two important points about the role of expectations in explaining the difficulties of policy making. First, the general point is that the difficulties of modelling the way in which expectations are formed will inevitably lead to errors in economists' forecasts of the effects of particular policy actions on the economy. The second point, a particular one, is that expectations themselves are likely to be affected by policy measures, and that failure to take account of the effects of policy on expectations will lead to mistaken predictions of the effects of those policies.

12-5 UNCERTAINTY AND ECONOMIC POLICY

So far in this chapter we have described the disturbances that affect the economy, econometric models that are used in policy making, the difficulties of making policy when there are long lags in the effects of policy, and the problem of modelling expectations. We can summarize most of the implied problems for policy making by saying that it is impossible to predict the effects of any given policy action exactly.

How should a policy maker react in the face of these uncertainties? We want to distinguish here between uncertainty about the correct model of the economy and uncertainty about the precise values of the parameters or coefficients within a given model of the economy, even though the distinction is not watertight.

First, there is considerable disagreement and therefore uncertainty about the correct model of the economy, as shown by the large number of macroeconometric models. Reasonable economists can and do differ about what theory and empirical evidence suggest are the correct behavioural functions of the economy. Generally, each economist will have reasons for favouring one particular form and will use that form. But, being reasonable, the economist will recognize that the particular formulation being used may not be the correct one, and will thus regard its predictions as subject to a margin of error. In turn, policy makers will know that there are different predictions about the effects of a given policy, and will want to consider the range of predictions that are being made in deciding on policy.

Second, as we noted in Section 12-2, even within the context of a given model there is uncertainty about the values of parameters and multipliers. The statistical evidence does allow us to say something about the likely range of parameters or multipliers,[7] so that at least we can get some idea of the type of errors that could result from a particular policy action.

---

[7] We are discussing here *confidence intervals* about estimates of parameters; see Robert S. Pindyck and Daniel L. Rubinfeld, *Econometric Models and Economic Forecasts* (New York: McGraw-Hill, 1976), for further discussion.

Uncertainty about the size of the effects that will result from any particular policy action is known as *multiplier uncertainty.* For instance, our best estimate of the multiplier of an increase in government spending might be 1.2. If GDP has to be increased by $6 billion, we would increase government spending by $5 billion, but the statistical evidence might be better interpreted as saying only that we can be quite confident the multiplier is between 0.9 and 1.5. In that case, when we increase government spending by $5 billion, we expect GDP to rise by some amount between $4.5 and $7.5 billion.

What is optimal behaviour in the face of such multiplier uncertainty? The more precisely policy makers are informed about the relevant parameters, the more activist the policy can afford to be. Conversely, if there is a considerable range of error in the estimate of the relevant parameters—in our example, the multiplier—then policy should be more modest. With poor information, very active policy runs a large danger of introducing unnecessary fluctuations in the economy.

12-6   ACTIVIST POLICY

We started this chapter asking why there are any fluctuations in the economy when the policy measures needed to iron out those fluctuations seem to be so simple. The list of difficulties in the way of successful policy making that we have outlined may have raised a different question: Why should one believe that policy can do anything to reduce fluctuations in the economy?

Indeed, considerations of the sort spelled out in the previous four sections have led Milton Friedman and others to argue that there should be no use of active countercyclical monetary policy,[8] and that monetary policy should be confined to making the money supply grow at a constant rate. The precise value of the constant rate of growth of money, Friedman suggests, is less important than the fact that monetary growth be constant and that policy should *not* respond to disturbances. At various times, he has suggested growth rates for money of 2 percent or 4 percent or 5 percent. As Friedman has expressed it, "By setting itself a steady course and keeping to it, the monetary authority could make a major contribution to promoting economic stability. By making that course one of steady but moderate growth in the quantity of money, it would make a major contribution to avoidance of either inflation or deflation of prices."[9] Friedman thus advocates a simple monetary rule in which the central bank does not respond to the condition of the economy. Policies that

---

[8] See Milton Friedman, *A Program for Monetary Stability* (New York: Fordham University Press, 1959).

[9] Milton Friedman, "The Role of Monetary Policy," *American Economic Review,* March 1968.

respond to the current or predicted state of the economy are called *activist policies.*

In discussing the desirability of active monetary and fiscal policy, we want to distinguish between policy actions taken in response to major disturbances to the economy and *fine tuning* in which policy variables are continually adjusted in response to small disturbances to the economy. We see no case for arguing that monetary and fiscal policy should not be used actively in the face of major disturbances to the economy. Most of the considerations of the previous sections of this chapter indicate some uncertainty about the effects of policy, but there are still clearly definable circumstances in which there can be no doubt that the appropriate policy is expansionary or contractionary. A government coming to power in 1933 should not have worried about the uncertainties associated with expansionary policy that we have outlined. The economy does not move from 20 percent unemployment to full employment in a short time (precisely because of those same lags that make policy difficult). Thus, expansionary measures, such as a rapid growth of the money supply, or increased government expenditures, or tax reductions, or all three, would have been appropriate policy since there was no chance they would have an impact only after the economy was at full employment. Similarly, contractionary policies for private demand are called for in wartime. In early 1982, with unemployment over 10 percent and rising rapidly and forecasts of unemployment for the next two years being very high, policies designed to reduce unemployment were appropriate.[10] In the event of large disturbances in the future, active monetary and/or fiscal policy should once again be used.[11]

Fine tuning presents more complicated issues. In the case of fiscal policy, the long inside lags make discretionary fine tuning virtually impossible, though automatic stabilizers are in fact fine tuning all the time. On the other hand, with monetary policy decisions being made frequently, fine tuning of monetary policy is indeed possible. The question then is whether a small increase in the unemployment rate should lead to a small increase in the growth rate of money, or whether policy should not respond until the increase in unemployment becomes large, say more than 1.0 percent.

The problem is that the disturbance that caused the increase in unemployment may be either transitory or permanent. If transitory, nothing should be done. If permanent, policy should react to a small disturbance in a small way. Given uncertainty over the nature of the disturbance, the technically correct

---

[10] Because the inflation rate was high in 1982, policy making then required some judgment about the costs of inflation compared with those of unemployment, a topic discussed in Chapter 16. Policy making in 1982 was thus more difficult than policy making in 1933.

[11] Interestingly, in the article cited in footnote 9, Friedman argues for the use of active policy in the face of major disturbances.

response is a small one, between the zero that is appropriate for a transitory shock and the full response that would be appropriate for a permanent disturbance. Accordingly we believe that fine tuning is appropriate provided that policy responses are always kept small in response to small disturbances.

However, we should emphasize that the argument for fine tuning is a controversial one. The major argument against it is that in practice policy makers cannot behave as suggested — making only small adjustments to small disturbances. Rather, it is argued, they tend to try to do too much, if allowed to do anything. Instead of merely trying to offset disturbances, they attempt to keep the economy always at full employment and therefore undertake inappropriate large policy actions in response to small disturbances.

The major lesson of the previous sections is not that policy is impossible, but that policy that is too ambitious in trying to keep the economy always at full employment (with zero inflation) is impossible. The lesson is to proceed with extreme caution, always bearing in mind the possibility that policy itself may be destabilizing. We see no reason why the Bank of Canada should try to keep the money supply always growing at the same rate; we believe, on the contrary, that the stability of the economy would be improved by its following a careful counter-cyclical policy. Similarly, if fiscal policy were not subject to a long inside lag, we would believe it possible for cautiously used active fiscal policy to be stabilizing.

Rules versus Discretion

Finally, in this chapter, we want to discuss the issue of "rules versus discretion." The issue is whether the monetary authority and also the fiscal authority should conduct policy in accordance with a preannounced rule that describes precisely how their policy variables will be determined in all future situations, or whether they should be allowed to use their discretion in determining the values of the policy variables at different times.

One example is the constant growth rate rule, say, at 4 percent, for monetary policy. The rule is that no matter what happens, the money supply will be kept growing at 4 percent. Another example would be a rule stating that the money supply growth rate will be increased by 2 percent per year for every 1 percent unemployment in excess of, say, 5 percent. Algebraically, such a rule would be expressed as

$$\frac{\Delta M}{M} = 4.0 + 2(u - 5.0) \tag{1}$$

where the growth rate of money $\Delta M/M$ is at an annual percentage rate, and u is the percentage unemployment rate.

The activist monetary rule of Equation (1) is shown in Figure 12-6. On the horizontal axis, we show the unemployment rate, and on the vertical axis, the

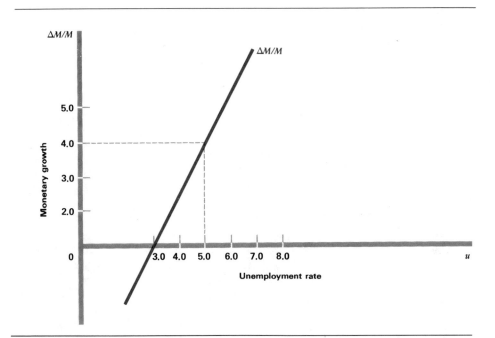

FIGURE 12-6   AN ACTIVIST MONETARY RULE. The figure describes an activist monetary rule. The growth rate of money is high when the unemployment rate is high and is low when unemployment is low. That way monetary policy is expansionary at times of recession and contractionary in a boom.

growth rate of the money stock. At 5 percent unemployment, monetary growth is 4 percent. If unemployment rises above 5 percent, monetary growth is *auto-matically* increased. Thus, with 7 percent unemployment, monetary growth would be 8 percent. Conversely, if unemployment dropped below 5 percent, monetary growth would be lowered below 4 percent. The rule therefore gears the amount of monetary stimulus to an indicator of the business cycle. By linking monetary growth to the unemployment rate, an activist, anti-cyclical monetary policy is achieved, but this is done without any discretion.

BOX 12-1   DYNAMIC INCONSISTENCY AND RULES VERSUS DISCRETION

In the last decade economists have developed an intriguing argument in favour of rules rather then discretion. The argument is that policy makers who have discretion will in the end not act consistently, even though it would be better for the economy in the long run if they were consistent.*

How can that be? Here is a noneconomic example. By threatening to punish their children, parents can generally make the children behave better. So long as the children behave well, all is well, but when a child misbehaves, the parent has a problem, since punishing the child is unpleasant for both parent and child. One solution is not to punish but to threaten to punish next time. However, if there was no punishment this time, there is unlikely to be punishment next time either, and the threat loses its beneficial effect. The dynamically consistent parent should use punishment each time the child misbehaves, thereby producing better behaviour in the long run despite its short-run cost.

What does this have to do with economics? Suppose the inflation rate has risen because of a supply shock. The central bank is considering whether to accommodate it by expanding the money supply or not. If it accommodates, prices will rise more now, but there will be less unemployment, so that seems like a good thing to do. This is the equivalent of not punishing the misbehaving child. However — warn those in favour of rules who worry about dynamic consistency — if the central bank accommodates every inflationary pressure because it fears unemployment, people will soon come to expect it to do that, and they will build an allowance for expected inflation into the wages they set. The central bank will lose whatever reputation it had as an inflation fighter, and the economy will develop an inflationary bias with the inflation rate creeping up over time.

Much better, says the dynamic consistency approach, that the central bank should have a rule that prevents it from making responses that are right from the short-run viewpoint but wrong from the long-run perspective. Those who nonetheless favor discretion for the central bank emphasize the importance of preserving flexibility for monetary policy. To the dynamic inconsistency argument, they counter that as long as the central bank is aware that having a good reputation helps it keep the inflation rate low, it will take any loss of reputation in account when it decides how to respond to particular shocks, and thus will not be dynamically inconsistent.

---

* The basic reference is Finn Kydland and Edward Prescott, "Rules Rather than Discretion; The Inconsistency of Optimal Plans, *Journal of Political Economy*, June 1977. This is very difficult reading.

The issue of rules versus discretion has been clouded by the fact that most proponents of rules have been nonactivists, whose preferred monetary rule is a constant growth rate rule. Consequently, the argument has tended to centre on whether activist policy is desirable or not. The fundamental point to recognize is that we can design *activists rules*. We can design rules that have counter-cyclical features without at the same time leaving any discretion in their actions to policy makers. The point is made by Equation (1), which is an activist rule because it expands money when unemployment is high and reduces it when unemployment is low. It leaves no room for policy discretion and in this respect is a rule.

Given that the economy and our knowledge of it are both changing over time, there is no case for stating permanent policy rules that would tie the hands of the monetary and fiscal authorities permanently. The practical issue in rules versus discretion then becomes that of whether the policy makers should announce in advance what policies they will be following for the foreseeable future. This would seem to be a desirable development in that it would aid private individuals in forecasting the future course of the economy.

*12-7   TARGETS AND INSTRUMENTS OF MONETARY POLICY

We conclude this chapter with a discussion of some operational problems in the implementation of monetary policy that arise from the existence of uncertainty. We begin with the issue of money supply targets.

Interest Rate Versus Money Supply Targets

Prior to the early 1970s, the Bank of Canada's monetary policy was formulated primarily in terms of target levels of interest rates and other measures of the cost and availability of credit. By 1973, the Bank had become dissatisfied with this approach and was beginning to move towards greater emphasis on control of the money supply. In his Annual Report for 1973, Governor Gerald Bouey commented as follows (page 7):

> Looking back on the experience of Canada and other countries over a longer period, . . . there have been more substantial and persisting departures from reasonable steady monetary growth than would appear in retrospect to have been desirable. Since the lags associated with monetary policy are rather long, the full effects of such departures do not become apparent until well after the event. . . . In the light of these considerations, I have a certain amount of sympathy with the case that is often made for more stable monetary growth over time. . . . The Bank of Canada certainly has no intention of basing its operations on any mechanistic formula, but . . . it has been giving considerable weight to underlying rates of monetary growth.

Although the governor had rejected the idea of a "mechanistic formula" for monetary growth in 1973, two years later the Bank of Canada announced that it would henceforth follow the practice of establishing target ranges for the rate of growth of the narrowly defined money supply (M1). The initial target was established in late 1975 at 10 to 15 percent a year. As can be seen in Table 12-2, the target was subsequently reduced in stages to the range of 4 to 8 percent which was announced in February 1981. The practice of announcing target ranges was discontinued in 1982.[12]

TABLE 12-2 BANK OF CANADA TARGET GROWTH RATES OF $M1$ 1975–1981

Base Period	Target Band	Base Period	Target Band
2nd Qtr. 1975	10–15%	June 1978	6–10%
Feb.–Apr. 1976	8–12	2nd Qtr.1979	5–9
June 1977	7–11	Aug.–Oct. 1980	4–8

Targets in the *IS-LM* Framework

Let us assume that the Bank of Canada's policy objective is to maintain a particular level of output. The question is whether it can do that more accurately by targeting the money stock or by fixing interest rates.[13] We should think of the analysis as applying to a time horizon of 3 to 6 months over which the Bank of Canada could achieve money supply targets with a small margin of error.

Figure 12-7a starts with the *IS* and *LM* curves. Recall that the *LM* curve shows combinations of the interest rate and output at which the money market is in equilibrium. The *LM* curve labelled *LM(M)* is the *LM* curve that exists when the Bank of Canada fixes the money stock. The *LM* curve labelled *LM(i)* describes money market equilibrium when the Bank fixes the interest rate. It is horizontal at the chosen level of the interest rate i^*.

The problem for policy is that the *IS* and *LM* curves shift as a result of disturbances that cannot be predicted. When they shift, output ends up at a level different from the target level. In figure 12-7a we show two alternative positions for the *IS* curve, IS_1 and IS_2. We assume that the Bank does not know in advance which *IS* curve will obtain: the position depends, for instance, on investment demand, which is difficult to predict. The Bank's aim is to have income come out as close as possible to the level Y^*.

[12] The targets were abandoned because of instability in the demand for money associated with the financial innovations discussed in Section 10-4 of Chapter 10. See Bank of Canada *Annual Report* for 1982, pp. 25–29.

[13] The analysis presented here is based on William Poole, "Optimal Choice of Monetary Policy Instruments in a Simple Stochastic Macro Model," *Quarterly Journal of Economics,* May 1970.

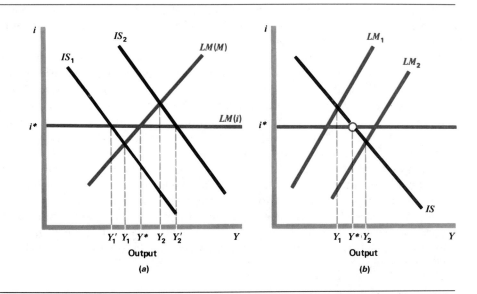

FIGURE 12-7   MONEY AND INTEREST RATE TARGETS. In panel (**a**), the *IS* curve shifts. If the Bank of Canada targets the money stock, the *LM* curve is shown by *LM(M)*. *LM(i)* is the *LM* curve when the interest rate is held constant. The aim of policy is to hit output level *Y**. If the *LM* curve is *LM(M)*, the output levels will be either Y_1 or Y_2, depending on where the *IS* curve turns out to be. In the case of an interest rate target, the corresponding levels of output are Y_1' and Y_2', both further from the desired level of output *Y**. Thus monetary targeting leads to more stable output behaviour. In panel (**b**) it is the *LM* curve that is shifting, because of shifts in the demand for money. With *LM* shifting and the *IS* curve stable, output will be at the target level *Y** if the interest rate is held constant at *i**, but will be at either Y_1 or Y_2 if the money stock is held constant. Therefore the Bank should target the interest rate if the demand-for-money function is unstable.

In Figure 12-7a we see that the level of output stays closer to *Y** if the *LM* curve is *LM(M)*. In that case the level of output will be Y_1 if the *IS* curve is IS_1 and Y_2 if the *IS* curve is IS_2. If policy had kept the interest rate constant, we would in each case have a level of income that is further from *Y**: Y_1' instead of Y_1, and Y_2' instead of Y_2.

Thus we have our first conclusion: If output deviates from its equilibrium level mainly because the *IS* curve shifts about, then output is stabilized by keeping the money stock constant. The central bank should, in this case, have monetary targets.

We can see from Figure 12-7a why it is more stabilizing to keep *M* than *i* constant. When the *IS* curve shifts to the right and the *LM(M)* curve applies, the interest rate rises, thereby reducing investment demand and moderating the effect of the shift. On the other hand, if the *LM(i)* curve applies, there is no resistance from monetary policy to the effects of the *IS* shift. Monetary policy is thus automatically stabilizing in Figure 12-7a when the *IS* curve shifts, and the money stock is held constant.

In Figure 12-7b we assume that the *IS* curve is stable. Now the uncertainty about the effects of monetary policy results from shifts in the *LM* curve. Assuming that the Bank of Canada can fix the money stock, the *LM* curve shifts because the money demand function shifts. The Bank does not know when it sets the money stock what the interest rate will be. The *LM* curve could end up being either LM_1 or LM_2. Alternatively the Bank could simply fix the interest rate at level i^*. That would ensure that the level of output is Y^*.

If the Bank were to fix the money stock, output could be either Y_1 or Y_2. If it fixes the interest rate, output will be Y^*. Thus we have our second conclusion: If output deviates from its equilibrium level mainly because the demand-for-money function shifts about, then the central bank should operate monetary policy by fixing the interest rate. That way it automatically neutralizes the effects of the shifts in money demand. In this case the central bank should have interest rate targets.

Implications for Bank of Canada Policy

The above analysis indicates that the shift to money supply targeting by the Bank of Canada was appropriate if the main source of disturbances is thought to be the goods market rather than the money market.[14] However, the argument depends on the existence of a stable demand for money. During the late 1970s and early 1980s, the financial innovations discussed in Chapter 10 caused a breakdown in the stability of this relationship and ultimately led to the abandonment of monetary targeting by the Bank of Canada.

BOX 12-2   RESEARCH STUDIES OF THE ROYAL COMMISSION ON THE ECONOMIC UNION AND DEVELOPMENT PROSPECTS FOR CANADA

Targets and Instruments

For a discussion of this issue, see the following studies published in J. Sargent (ed.), *Fiscal and Monetary Policy,* (vol. 21), University of Toronto Press, 1986.

---

[14] Another argument for money targeting arises from the distinction between real and nominal interest rates. The nominal interest rate can rise because inflation is expected. If the Bank fights this increase in the nominal rate by increasing the money stock, it is only feeding the inflation. We examine this argument in more detail in Chapter 15.

G.R. Sparks, "The Theory and Practice of Monetary Policy in Canada: 1945–83", pp. 139-41.

J.M. Dufour and D. Racette, "Monetary Control in Canada."

The Instrument Problem

The above analysis focusses on a 3 to 6 month time horizon over which the Bank of Canada can achieve money supply targets. As we argued in Chapter 11, the Bank cannot control the money supply in the short run. The variables over which the Bank of Canada does have direct control are called policy instruments and the choice of the appropriate variable to control in the face of unpredictable disturbances is known as the instrument problem.

The short-run operating problem can be described as follows. Having chosen its money supply target, should the Bank of Canada implement its policy by setting the level of the interest rate or the monetary base? The analysis of Figure 12-7 can be applied in this context by assuming that the upward sloping LM curve in Figure 12-7a is drawn for a given level of the monetary base H, rather than the money supply. The shifts in the LM curve shown in Figure 12-7b then reflect shifts in the money multiplier as well as the demand for money.

The conclusions from the analysis become:

1. If the demand for money and the money multiplier are stable, then the Bank of Canada should use H as the instrument and allow interest rates to fluctuate in response to shifts in the IS curve.
2. If the IS curve is stable, then the Bank should use the interest rate as the instrument and allow H to fluctuate in response to shifts in the demand for money and the money multiplier.

The Bank of Canada's Operating Procedure

During the period 1975 to 1982 when the Bank of Canada was setting targets for the money supply, its operating procedure was as follows. Having set its money target, a projection was made for income and the price level, and a money demand function was used to infer the appropriate setting for the interest rate.[15] Thus the Bank used the interest rate as the instrument.

The rationale for this procedure is that the goods market is relatively predictable in the short run but the money market is not. In particular, as we argued in Section 11-8 of Chapter 11, the money multiplier is likely to be unstable in the short run.

---

[15] In algebraic terms the value for the interest rate was obtained using an LM equation of the form shown in Equation 11a of Chapter 4.

12-8   SUMMARY

1. Despite the apparent simplicity of policies needed to maintain continuous full employment, the historical record of the behaviour of unemployment, shown in Figure 12-1, implies that successful stabilization policy is difficult to carry out.

2. Many of the complications in the execution of stabilization policy are a result of the tradeoff between inflation and unemployment in the short run. This important topic is deferred to Chapter 15. The present chapter concentrates on other sources of difficulty for stabilization policy.

3. The potential need for stabilizing policy actions arises from economic disturbances. Some of these disturbances, such as changes in money demand, consumption spending, or investment demand, arise from within the private sector. Others, such as wars, may arise for non-economic reasons.

4. Inappropriate economic policy may also tend to move the economy away from full employment. Policy may be inappropriate because policy makers make mistakes or because policy is manipulated for political reasons, leading to the political business cycle.

5. Policy makers work with econometric models in predicting the effects of their policy actions. Econometric models are typically statistical descriptions of the types of model we have worked with in earlier chapters and also include an aggregate supply sector. Existing econometric models vary considerably in structure and thus imply widely varying numerical values for policy multipliers.

6. The first difficulty of carrying out successful stabilization policy is that policy works with lags. The inside lag — divided into recognition, decision, and action lags — is the period between which an action becomes necessary and when it is taken. The outside lag is the period between which a policy action is taken and when it affects the economy. The outside lag is generally a distributed lag: the effects of a policy action build up over the course of time.

7. The behaviour of expectations is a further source of difficulty for policy making. First, it is difficult to know exactly what determines expectations and to capture those factors in a simple formula. Second, policy actions themselves are likely to affect expectations.

8. More generally, there is always uncertainty about the effects of a given policy action on the economy. Economists are not agreed on the "correct" model of the economy, and evidence is not likely to be at hand soon to decisively settle disagreements over some behavioural functions — such

as the consumption function. Even if we did know the form of the behavioural functions, the statistical evidence would be insufficient to pinpoint the values of the relevant parameters.

9. There are clearly occasions on which active monetary and fiscal policy actions should be taken to stabilize the economy. These are situations in which the economy has been affected by major disturbances.

10. Fine tuning — continuous attempts to stabilize the economy in the face of small disturbances—is more controversial. If fine tuning is undertaken, it calls for small policy responses in an attempt to moderate the economy's fluctuations, rather than to remove them entirely. A very active policy in response to small disturbance is likely to destabilize the economy.

11. The real issue in rules versus discretion is whether policy actions should be announced as far in advance as possible. Such announcements are desirable in that they aid private individuals in forecasting the future behaviour of the economy.

12. During the period 1975 to1981, the Bank of Canada operated monetary policy using target rates of growth of the money supply. This is an appropriate strategy if the money market is stable and the goods market is subject to substantial disturbances.

KEY TERMS

Economic disturbances	Multiplier uncertainty
Political business cycle	Activist policy
Econometric models	Policy rule
Inside lag	Fine tuning
Recognition lag	Rules versus discretion
Decision lag	Dynamic consistency
Action lag	Targets and instruments of monetary
Outside lag	policy

PROBLEMS

1. Suppose the GDP is $4 billion below its potential level. It is expected that next period GDP will be $2 billion below potential, and two periods from now it will be back at its potential level. You are told that the multiplier for government spending is 2, and that the effects of the increased government spending are immediate. What policy actions can be taken to put GDP back on target each period?

2. The basic facts about the path of GDP are as above. But there is now a one-period outside lag for government spending. Decisions to spend today are translated into actual spending only tomorrow. The multiplier for government spending is still 2 in the period that the spending takes place.
   (a) What is the best that can be done to keep GDP as close to target as possible each period?
   (b) Compare the path of GDP in this question with the path in problem (1), after policy actions have been taken.

3. Life has become more complicated. Government spending works with a distributed lag. Now when $1 billion is spent today, GDP increases by $1 billion this period and 1.5 billion next period.
   (a) What happens to the path of GDP if government spending rises enough this period to put GDP back to its potential level this period?
   (b) Suppose fiscal policy actions are taken to put GDP at its potential level this period. What fiscal policy will be needed to put GDP on target next period?
   (c) Explain why the government has to be so active in keeping GDP on target in this case.

4. Suppose that you knew that the multiplier for government spending was between 1 and 2.5, but that its effects were all over in the period that spending was increased. How would you run fiscal policy if GDP would, without policy, behave as in problem 1?

5. Explain why monetary policy works with a distributed lag, as in Figure 12-5.

6. Evaluate the argument that monetary policy should be determined by a rule rather than discretion. How about fiscal policy?

7. Evaluate the arguments for a constant growth rate rule for money.

8. (a) What is the unemployment rate at the time you are reading this?
   (b) Should either fiscal or monetary policy be changed to enable the economy to return more rapidly to full employment?

9. Use Figure 12-7 to analyze the short-run problem of instrument choice. What conclusions can you draw for the validity of the Bank of Canada's strategy of using the interest rate as the instrument?

CHAPTER 13

Fiscal Policy and Public Finance

This chapter is intended to serve two purposes. The first is to review the experience of the 1930s and the postwar period. The Great Depression is worth studying for purely historical interest, but of equal importance is the fact that the thirties and the war that followed molded many of the institutions and views of the modern economy. The role of government expanded markedly, and it was the experience of the thirties that led to the view, now taken for granted in practice, that the government has primary responsibility for satisfactory economic performance.

The second purpose of the chapter is to discuss a number of questions connected with the budget, government spending and taxes. In Section 13-3 we described the financing of the federal government budget deficit, that is, how the government pays for the excess of its spending over its income from taxes. The issue of the burden of the debt is taken up at the conclusion of the chapter.

13-1 THE GREAT DEPRESSION

In this section we describe the experience of the 1930s and review the controversy over the causes of the depression. Data describing the performance of the Canadian economy are shown in Figure 13-1 and Table 13-1. As can be seen from the chart, between 1929 and 1933, real income fell by 30 percent and the price level fell by 20 percent. Investment collapsed; indeed *net* investment was negative from 1932 to 1936. The unemployment rate rose to nearly

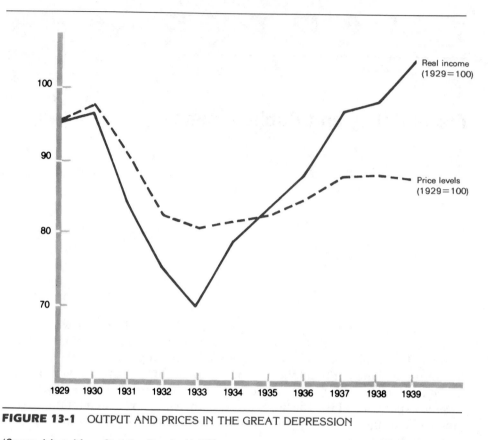

FIGURE 13-1 OUTPUT AND PRICES IN THE GREAT DEPRESSION

(*Source*: Adapted from Statistics Canada, 11-505)

20 percent in 1933 and remained above 11 percent through the thirties, with the exception of 1937 when it dipped close to 9 percent. By 1933 the stock market had fallen almost to one-third of its 1929 value.

Events in Canada closely mirrored those in the United States and the economic collapse in the U.S. was a major cause of the decline in Canada. The sharp fall in our exports, shown in Table 13-1 resulted from the fall in income in the U.S. and other countries and the psychological impact was an important factor in the collapse of investment. In view of this it is necessary to examine events in the U.S. in order to obtain clues as to the causes of the depression.

American Experience in the 1930s

The depression and the stock market crash of October 1929 are popularly thought of as almost the same thing. In fact, the U.S. economy started turning

TABLE 13-1   THE GREAT DEPRESSION IN CANADA

	GNP	Govt. Exp.	Exports	GNE Deflator (1961 = 100)	Gross Investment	Budget Surplus	Unemployment Rate (%)	Stock Market Index (1961 = 100)
	(billions of 1961 dollars)				(% of GNP)			
1929	12.24	1.70	3.10	50.2	22.2	0.2		49.0
1930	11.71	1.93	2.70	48.8	18.9	−3.9		35.0
1931	10.23	1.94	2.41	45.9	15.5	−6.6	11.6	21.9
1932	9.17	1.79	2.24	41.6	8.8	−7.3	17.6	14.2
1933	8.56	1.47	2.26	40.8	6.8	−5.0	19.3	17.6
1934	9.59	1.58	2.55	41.4	7.7	−4.7	14.5	22.1
1935	10.34	1.68	2.81	41.6	8.6	−4.0	14.2	23.6
1936	10.80	1.67	3.38	42.9	10.0	−0.7	12.8	30.7
1937	11.89	1.79	3.46	44.1	11.8	−0.6	9.1	32.6
1938	11.98	1.93	3.12	44.0	11.3	−2.8	11.4	26.8
1939	12.87	2.02	3.44	43.7	10.3	−0.8	11.4	25.8

Source: Statistics Canada, 11-505.

down before the stock market crash. The peak of the business cycle is estimated to have been in August 1929, and the stock market itself peaked in September 1929. Using September 1929 as the base period, Standard & Poor's composite stock price index fell from 100 in September to 66 in November. It rose again through March 1930, but then the collapse continued until the index fell to 15 in June 1932.

By early 1931, the U.S. economy was suffering from a very severe depression, but not one that was out of the range of the experience of the previous century.[1] It was in the period from early 1931 until Franklin Roosevelt became President in March 1933 that the depression became "Great."

Economic Policy

What was economic policy during this period? The money stock fell from 1929 to 1930, and then fell rapidly in 1931 and 1932 and continued falling through April 1933. At the same time, the composition of the money stock changed.

---

[1] Milton Friedman and Anna J. Schwartz, in *A Monetary History of the United States 1867–1960* (Princeton, N.J.: Princeton University Press, 1963), give a very detailed account of the great depression, comparing it with other recessions and emphasizing the role of the Fed. For a more general economic history of the period see Robert A. Gordon, *Economic Instability: The American Record* (New York: Harper & Row, 1974), Chapter 3.

In March 1931 the currency-demand deposit ratio was 18.5 percent; 2 years later, it was 40.7 percent.

The fall in the money stock was the result of large-scale bank failures. Banks failed because they did not have the reserves with which to meet customers' cash withdrawals, and in failing they destroyed deposits and hence reduced the money stock. But the failures went further in reducing the money stock, because they led to a loss of confidence on the part of depositors and hence to an even higher desired currency-deposit ratio. Furthermore, banks that had not yet failed adjusted to the possibility of a run by holding increased reserves relative to deposits. The rise in the currency-deposit ratio and the reserve-deposit ratio reduced the money multiplier and hence sharply contracted the money stock.

The American central bank, commonly referred to as the Fed (Federal Reserve System), took very few steps to offset the fall in the money supply; for a few months in 1932 it did undertake a program of open market purchases, but otherwise seemed to acquiesce in bank closings and certainly failed to understand that the central bank should act vigorously in a crisis to prevent the collapse of the financial system.[2]

Canadian experience was similar but for quite different reasons. There was little scope for monetary policy in Canada during the early years of the depression as there was no central bank (the Bank of Canada began operations in 1935). As in the U.S., the money supply fell sharply after the 1929 crash, but there were no bank failures. However, the monetary base fell as a result of the institutional arrangements at the time under which the volume of bank reserves was determined primarily at the initative of the chartered banks through a form of borrowing.[3] With the onset of the depression, the demand for loans by credit-worthy borrowers collapsed and the chartered banks responded by contracting their operations.

Fiscal policy in the U.S. was also not very vigorous. The natural impulse of politicians then was to balance the budget in times of trouble, and much rhetoric was devoted to that proposition. The presidential candidates in 1932 campaigned on balanced budget platforms. In fact, the federal government ran enormous deficits, particularly for that time, averaging 2.6 percent of GNP from 1931 to 1933, and even more later. The belief in budget balancing was more than rhetoric, however, for state and local governments raised taxes to match their expenditures, as did the federal government, particularly in 1932 and 1933. President Roosevelt tried seriously to balance the budget — he was no

---

[2] Friedman and Schwartz speculate on the reasons for the Fed's inaction; the whodunit or "who didn't do it" on pp. 407 to 419 of their book (cited in footnote 1) is fascinating.

[3] See T.J. Courchene, "An Analysis of the Canadian Money Supply: 1925–1934." *Journal of Political Economy,* May/June 1969.

Keynesian. The full-employment surplus shows fiscal policy (combined state, local, and federal) as most expansionary in 1931, and moving to a more contractionary level from 1932 to 1934. In fact, the full-employment surplus was positive in 1933 and 1934, despite the actual deficits. Of course, the full-employment surplus concept had not been invented in the 1930s.

Economic activity recovered in the period from 1933 to 1937, with fiscal policy becoming more expansionary and the money stock growing rapidly. The growth of the money stock was based on an inflow of gold from Europe which provided an increase in high-powered money. This period also saw a program of legislative action to aid recovery known as the *New Deal*.

International Aspects

Another important aspect of the depression deserves mention: it was virtually worldwide. To some extent, this was the result of the collapse of the international financial system.[4] It resulted too from the mutual adoption of high tariff policies by many countries, keeping out foreign goods to protect domestic producers. Of course, if each country keeps out foreign goods, the volume of world trade declines, providing a contractionary influence on the world economy.

The experience of the thirties varied internationally. Sweden suffered its depression in the twenties and benefited from expansionary policies in the thirties. Britain's economy too suffered more in the twenties than in the thirties. Germany grew rapidly after Hitler came to power and expanded government spending. China escaped the recession until after 1931, essentially because it had a floating exchange rate. As always, there is much to be learned from the exceptions.

13-2 THE GREAT DEPRESSION: THE ISSUES AND IDEAS

What caused the great depression, could it have been avoided, and could it happen again? The question of what caused the depression seems purely academic, but it is much more than that. The depression was the greatest economic crisis the Western world had experienced.

The classical economics of the time had no well-developed theory that would explain persistent unemployment, nor any policy prescriptions to solve the

---

[4] This aspect of the depression is emphasized by Charles Kindleberger. *The World in Depression, 1929–1939* (Berkeley: University of California Press, 1973), and Gottfried Haberler, *The World Economy, Money and the Great Depression* (Washington, D.C.: American Enterprise Institute, 1976).

problem. Many economists of the time did, in fact, recommend government spending as a way of reducing unemployment, but they had no macroeconomic theory by which to justify their recommendations.

Keynes wrote his greatest work, *The General Theory of Employment, Interest and Money* in the 1930s, after Britain had suffered during the 1920s from a decade of double-digit unemployment and while the United States was in the depths of its depression. He was fully aware of the seriousness of the issues. As Don Patinkin of the Hebrew University put it:

> . . . the period was one of fear and darkness as the Western world struggled with the greatest depression that it had known . . . [T]here was a definite feeling that by attempting to achieve a scientific understanding of the phenomenon of mass unemployment, one was not only making an intellectual contribution, but was also dealing with a critical problem that endangered the very existence of Western civilization.[5]

Keynesian theory explained what had happened, what could have been done to prevent the depression, and what could be done to prevent future depressions. The explanation soon became accepted by most macroeconomists, in the process described as the Keynesian revolution.

The Keyesian Explanation

The essence of the Keynesian explanation of the great depression is based on the simple aggregate demand model developed in Chapter 3. Growth in the twenties, in this view, was based on the mass production of the automobile and radio and was fueled by a housing boom. The collapse of growth in the thirties resulted from the drying up of investment opportunities and a downward shift in investment demand. Some researchers also believe there was a downward shift in the consumption function in 1930.[6] Poor fiscal policy, as reflected in the perverse behaviour of the full-employment surplus from 1931 to 1933, shares the blame, particularly for making the depression worse.

What does this view have to say about the monetary collapse? The Fed argued in the thirties that there was little it could have done to prevent the depression, because interest rates were already as low as they could possibly go. A variety of sayings of the type, "You can lead a horse to water but you can't make it drink," were used to explain that further reductions in interest rates would have

---

[5] In "The Process of Writing *The General Theory*: A Critical Survey," in Don Patinkin and J. Clark Leith (eds.), *Keynes, Cambridge and the General Theory* (Toronto: University of Toronto Press, 1978), p. 3. For a short biography of Keynes, see D.E. Moggridge, *John Maynard Keynes* (New York: Penguin Books, 1976).

[6] Peter Temin, *Did Monetary Forces Cause the Great Depression?* (New York: Norton, 1976).

had no effect if there was no demand for investment. Investment demand was thought to be very unresponsive to the rate of interest — implying a very steep IS curve. At the same time, the LM curve was believed to be quite flat, though not necessarily reaching the extreme of a liquidity trap. In this situation, as we saw in Chapter 4, monetary expansion would be relatively ineffective in stimulating demand and output.

It was also widely believed that the experience of the depression showed that the private enonomy was inherently unstable in that it could self-depress with no difficulty if left alone. The experience of the thirties, implicitly or explicitly, was the basis for the belief that an active stabilization policy was needed to maintain good enonomic performance.

The Keynesian model not only offered an explanation of what had happened, but also suggested policy measures that could have been taken to prevent the depression, and that could be used to prevent future depressions. Vigorous use of counter-cyclical fiscal policy was the preferred method for reducing cyclical fluctuations. If a recession ever showed signs of deteriorating into a depression, the cure would be to cut taxes and increase government spending. And those policies would, too, have prevented the depression from being as deep as it was.

There is nothing in the IS-LM model developed in Chapter 4 that suggests fiscal policy is more useful than monetary policy for stabilization of the economy. Nonetheless, it is true that until the 1950s, Keynesians tended to give more emphasis to fiscal than to monetary policy.

The Monetarist Challenge

The Keynesian emphasis on fiscal policy, and its downplaying of the role of money, was increasingly challenged by Milton Friedman and his co-workers[7] during the 1950s. During this period Friedman was developing much of the analysis and evidence that provided the basis for monetarism, which we describe in detail in Chapter 18. The main thrust was a heavy emphasis on the role of monetary policy in determining the behaviour of both output and prices.

If monetary policy was to be given an important role, though, it was necessary to dispose of the view that monetary policy had been tried in the great depression and had failed. In other words, the view that "You can lead a horse to the water, etc.," had to be challenged.

The view that monetary policy in the thirties had been impotent was attacked in 1963 by Friedman and Schwartz in their *Monetary History*. They argued that the depression, far from showing that money does not matter, "is in fact a tragic

---

[7] See, in particular, Milton Friedman (ed.), *Studies in the Quantity Theory of Money* (Chicago: University of Chicago Press, 1956).

testimonial to the importance of monetary factors."[8] They argued, with skill and style, that the failure of the Fed to prevent bank failures and the decline of the money stock from the end of 1930 to 1933 was largely responsible for the recession being as serious as it was. This monetary view, in turn, came close to being accepted as the orthodox explanation of the depression.[9]

Synthesis

Both the Keynesian and the monetarist explanations of the great depression fit the facts, and both provide answers to the question of why it happened, and how to prevent it from happening again. Inept fiscal and monetary policies both made the great depression severe. If there had been prompt, strong, expansive monetary and fiscal policy, the economy would have suffered a recession but not the trauma it did.

On the question of whether it could happen again, there is agreement that it could not, except, of course, in the event of truly perverse policies. These are less likely now than they were then. For one thing, we have history to help us avoid its repetition. Taxes would not again be raised in the middle of a depression, nor would attempts be made to balance the budget. The Bank of Canada would seek actively to keep the money supply from falling. In addition, the government now has a much larger role in the economy than it did then. The higher level of government spending, which is relatively slow to change, and automatic stabilizers, including the income tax,[10] unemployment insurance, and social insurance, give the economy more stability than it had then.[11]

There is no inherent conflict between the Keynesian and monetarist explanations of the great depression. The *IS-LM* model, augmented by the supply-side analysis of wage and price adjustment, discussed in Chapter 7, easily combines both explanations. Why, then, has there been controversy over the causes of the great depression? The reason is that the thirties are seen as the period that set the stage for massive government intervention in the economy. Those opposed to an active role for government have to explain away the debacle of the economy in the thirties. If the depression occurred because of, and not despite, the government, the case for an active government role in economic

---

[8] Friedman, and Schwartz, *op. cit,*. p. 300.

[9] Ben Bernanke, in "Nonmonetary Effects of the Financial Crisis in the Propagation of the Great Depression," *American Economic Review,* June 1983, takes issue with the monetary view, arguing instead that the destruction of the financial system made it difficult for borrowers to obtain funds needed for investment.

[10] Recall from Chap. 3 that a proportional income tax reduces the multiplier.

[11] See Martin Baily, "Stabilization Policy and Private Economic Behavior," *Brookings Papers on Economic Activity,* 1978:1 (Washington, D.C.: The Brookings Institution, 1978).

stabilization is weakened. Further, the thirties are a period in which the economy behaved in such an extreme way that competing theories have to be subjected to the test of whether they can explain that period. Those are the main reasons the dispute over the causes of the great depression continues more than 50 years after it began.

13-3   FISCAL POLICY IN THE POSTWAR PERIOD

The experience of the Great Depression and World War II resulted in a fundamental change in the role of government expenditures and taxes as instruments of government policy. The 1945 White Paper on Employment and Income established the principle that the federal government had a responsibility to maintain high and stable levels of employment and income. Since then, consideration of the desired degree of fiscal stimulus or restraint has become an important element in the budgets presented to Parliament.

Both the achievements and failures of economic policy in the postwar period can be seen in Figure 13-2. In comparison with earlier eras, the fifties and sixties

FIGURE 13-2   INFLATION AND UNEMPLOYMENT, 1953-1987

(*Source*: Adapted from Statistics Canada 11-206, 11-505, 71-201)

were years of prosperity and steady growth. The first prolonged slump occurred during the years 1958 to1961 when the unemployment rate reached a peak of 7.1 percent. By 1965, the economy was operating at or near potential, but in retrospect, it appears that policy makers misjudged the situation. As can be seen in Figure 13-3, rising income had moved government budgets into a surplus position, but some of the restraining effects of the built-in stablizers were offset by tax cuts introduced in the federal budget of April 1965. As a result, the cyclically adjusted federal budget moved to a deficit position. Tax increases and some expenditure cuts were imposed in the years 1966–1968, but fiscal restraint came too late to prevent the entrenchment of inflationary forces. The rate of inflation had crept up steadily during the sixties and by 1969 had reached 4.6 percent.

FIGURE 13-3   ACTUAL AND CYCLICALLY ADJUSTED BUDGET BALANCE AS A PERCENTAGE OF GDP

(*Source*: Department of Finance, *Economic Review*, The Fiscal Plan, Feb., 1986)

Perspectives on economic policy in the sixties appear to differ widely. It was a period in which faith in the efficacy of activists fiscal policy reached a peak. Although the analytical approach consisted basically on the Keynesian tools we have outlined in previous chapters, fiscal activism became known as the

"New Economics" in the United States.[12] In one view, the period was one of high employment and prosperity, thanks to the activist stance of policy. An alternative view is that overexpansionist policies in that period were responsible for the inflation that was to prove to be the economic policy problem of the seventies. Actually, both views are correct. Policy in the early sixties was indeed successful, and economic policy in the second half of the period was overexpansionary or, equivalently, not sufficiently contractionary, in the face of increases in spending to a large extent related to the Vietnam war. Government spending in the U.S. rose rapidly, and rising income in the U.S. stimulated demand for Canadian exports, thereby contributing to inflationary pressure in Canada.

The decade of the 1970s began with the federal government in a surplus position, but there was a shift to an expansionary policy in view of the steep rise in unemployment that had occurred. With an unemployment rate in excess of 6 percent during most of 1971 and 1972, the federal budget was maintained in a deficit position. In 1974 the emphasis shifted to moderating the inflationary pressures that were building up. At midyear the unemployment rate was down around 5 percent and the consumer price index was rising at a rate in excess of 10 percent. However, toward the end of the year there was a significant worsening of the outlook. Slower growth and rising unemployment occurred in Canada while the United States experienced a substantial *decline* in real output. In view of these conditions, an expansionary budget was brought down late in the year which provided for a reduction in personal income taxes of about $1.5 million in 1975.

As can be seen for Figure 13-3, the federal budget moved to a substantial deficit position in 1975 and 1976. This resulted from both the automatic response to tax revenues and unemployment insurance benefits, to relatively low levels of economic activity, and the effects of discretionary policy as reflected in the cyclically adjusted federal balance. Further tax cuts were introduced in 1977 and 1978 in response to rising unemployment rates, but policy decisions were complicated by the emergence of two major dilemmas.

First, although the unemployment rate rose above 8 percent in 1977 for the first time since the 1930s, the rate of inflation continued at an unacceptably high level. By 1981, the consumer price index was rising at a 12 percent rate and unemployment was still over 7 percent of the labour force. In the third

---

[12] See the history of the New Economics in W.W. Heller, *New Dimensions of Political Economy* (New York: Norton, 1967). Walter Heller, now a professor at the University of Minnesota, was one of the chief architects of the economic policies of the Kennedy-Johnson administration. With him, as members of the Council of Economic Advisers or staff economists, were highly distinguished economists: James Tobin, Kenneth Arrow, Robert Solow, Otto Eckstein, Gardner Ackley, and the late Arthur Okun. Paul A. Samuelson served as an unofficial adviser.

quarter of 1981 Canada plunged into the worst recession of the postwar period and the inflation rate finally eased as the unemployment rate reached 12 percent at the trough. At the end of 1987, unemployment was still above 8 percent while the inflation rate had come down to 4 percent. The problem of coexistent high unemployment and high inflation was still with us.

The second dilemma that arose in the late 1970s was the rapid growth of the govenment deficit. This growth was accelerated by the 1981–1982 recession but as can be seen in Figure 13-3, much of it was a cyclically adjusted or *structural deficit* arising from an imbalance between tax rates and expenditure programs. By 1984 the structural deficit of the federal government had risen above 6 percent of GDP as compared with an average of less than .1 percent over the period 1953 to 1974. The issue of large deficits and a rising national debt are taken up in Section 13-4 below. We conclude this section with a look at government revenue and expenditure.

BOX 13-1   RESEARCH STUDIES OF THE ROYAL COMMISSION ON THE ECONOMIC UNION AND DEVELOPMENT PROSPECTS FOR CANADA

Fiscal Policy in Canada

For a discussion of fiscal policy, see the following studies published in J. Sargent (ed.), *Fiscal and Monetary Policy*, (Vol. 21), Toronto, University of Toronto Press, 1986.

D. Purvis and C. Smith, "Fiscal Policy in Canada: 1963–84."
N. Bruce and D. Purvis, "Consequences of Government Budget Deficits.
J.Bossons, "Issues in the Analysis of Government Deficits."
R. Boadway and S. Clark, "The Government Budget, the Accumulation of Capital, and Long-run Welfare."

Government Revenue and Expenditure

Table 13-2 shows the pattern of federal government revenues and expenditures over the period 1970 to 1986. Revenues grew faster than GDP from 1970 to 1975, but grew more slowly thereafter as a result of a slowing down of income growth and the introduction of various tax reductions. As estimated by the Department of Finance, the cumulative effect of the tax changes made in the

TABLE 13-2   FEDERAL GOVERNMENT REVENUE AND EXPENDITURE
(billions of dollars)

REVENUE	1970	1975	1980	1985	1986
Personal income and other					
direct taxes	7.4	15.2	23.5	42.7	49.0
Corporation taxes	2.6	5.8	9.4	12.5	11.4
Indirect taxes	4.0	8.0	12.3	18.9	20.7
Other revenue	1.5	2.8	5.5	9.6	10.2
Total revenue	15.5	31.8	50.7	83.7	91.3
(percent of GDP)	(17.4)	(18.5)	(16.3)	(17.5)	(17.9)
EXPENDITURE					
Goods and services	5.0	9.4	14.9	26.0	26.2
Transfers to persons	4.0	10.6	16.5	31.7	33.3
Transfers to provinces					
and municipalities	3.4	7.7	12.8	21.7	21.1
Interest on the public					
debt	1.9	3.7	9.9	25.3	26.4
Other transfers	1.0	4.2	7.2	11.0	9.0
Total expenditure	15.3	35.6	61.3	115.7	116.0
(percent of GDP)	(17.2)	(20.8)	(19.8)	(24.1)	(22.8)
SURPLUS OR DEFICIT (−)	0.2	− 3.8	− 10.6	− 32.0	− 24.7

Source: Dept. of Finance, *Quarterly Economic Review,* Annual Reference Tables

budgets over the period 1972 to 1981 was a reduction of revenue in the 1982–83 fiscal year of nearly $25 billion.[13]

On the expenditure side, the most rapid growth has been in interest on the public debt and transfer payments. Between 1980 and 1985, total expenditure more than doubled and the size of the federal deficit tripled. A substantial slowdown in the growth of expenditures was achieved in 1986.

Provincial and Municipal Governments

Table 13-3 shows the budgetary position of the provincial and municipal governments. Their expenditures grew at about the same rate as federal outlays during the 1970s but their revenues grew at a faster rate, and as a result their budget balance improved.

---

[13] See Department of Finance, *The Federal Deficit in Perspective,* 1983, Annex D. About three-fifths of this revenue loss was attributable to indexation of the personal income tax. Indexation is discussed in Chapter 16.

TABLE 13-3 PROVINCIAL AND MUNICIPAL REVENUE AND EXPENDITURE
(billions of dollars)

	1970	1975	1980	1985	1986
REVENUE					
Own sources	14.9	29.6	60.0	97.8	104.0
Federal cash transfers	3.4	7.6	12.6	21.4	20.8
Total revenue	18.3	37.2	72.6	119.2	124.8
(percent of GDP)	(20.5)	(21.7)	(23.4)	(24.9)	(24.5)
EXPENDITURE					
Goods and services	14.6	30.1	52.6	82.9	87.5
Transfers to persons	2.8	5.7	11.4	20.3	21.3
Interest on the public debt	1.4	2.8	6.9	15.3	16.0
Other transfers	0.3	1.1	2.9	5.9	6.5
Total expenditure	19.1	39.7	73.8	124.4	131.3
(percent of GDP)	(21.4)	(23.1)	(23.8)	(25.9)	(25.8)
SURPLUS OR DEFICIT (−)	−0.8	−2.5	−1.2	−5.2	−6.5

Source: Dept. of Finance, *Quarterly Economic Review,* Annual Reference Tables

One of the principal contributions to the growth of revenues has been natural resource royalties. By 1980, these accounted for over 7 percent of total revenues, as compared with less than 2 percent in 1970. Almost all of this revenue goes to Alberta, Saskatchewan, and British Columbia and the surplus for provincial and municipal governments in 1980 arose from the net effect of a substantial surplus in these three provinces and a substantial deficit in the remainder. As in the case of the federal government, the low level of economic activity in the early 1980s led to a marked deterioration in the financial position of the provinces and municipalities.

13-4 GOVERNMENT DEFICITS AND THE NATIONAL DEBT

As we indicated in the preceding section, the mounting structural deficit was a major problem in the early 1980s. Beginning with the budget of November 1984 the Minister of Finance adopted a strategy of gradual reduction of the deficit primarily through a slowdown in the growth of expenditures. The objective was to halt the growth of the debt-income ratio by the end of the decade.

A similar problem existed in the U.S. as a result of substantial tax cuts introduced in 1981 as part of the "supply-side" program of the Reagan administration (see Box). Many economists on both sides of the border were expressing concern about the implications for the future. There was a fear that continued massive government borrowing would cause interest rates to rise and crowd out private investment. An alternative danger was that rising interest rates would induce the central banks to intervene to hold them down. This would involve increasing the money supply and creating inflationary pressure.

The emergence of unprecedented deficits raises a number of questions that we have not yet considered. We begin this section by examining the relationship between the federal government's deficit and changes in the stocks of money and government debt.

BOX 13-2   THE LAFFER CURVE

Arthur Laffer, of Pepperdine University, is among the best known of the supply-side economists. Figure 1 shows the *Laffer curve*, relating tax revenues to the tax rate. The curve shows total tax revenue first increasing as the tax rises and then eventually decreasing.

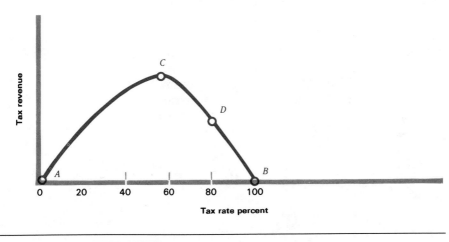

FIGURE 1   THE LAFFER CURVE

The argument supporting the shape of the curve is as follows. Assume that we are discussing the income tax rate. When the tax rate is zero, government tax revenue is certainly zero. Hence we have point *A* on the curve. Further, suppose the tax rate were 100 percent. Then the government would be taking all the income that people earn. There would be no point in working if the government took all earnings, and so income in that case too would be zero. Then tax revenue would be zero. Accordingly, point *B* is also a point on the Laffer curve.

Between A and B, though, the government certainly takes in some revenue from taxes. Thus we expect the curve to start to rise from point A as the tax rate is increased from zero to some very small rate, such as 3 percent. Eventually, though, the curve has to come back down to B. Thus at some point it will turn around — perhaps at a tax rate of 60 percent, as shown in Figure 1. Point C is the dividing line: at tax rates below 60 percent, any increase in the tax rate *raises* total tax revenue. At tax rates above 60 percent, any increase in the tax rate *reduces* total revenue. Looking at the same relationship in the opposite direction, we find that at any tax rate above 60 percent a *cut* in the tax will *increase* total tax revenue.

Supply-siders were thus arguing in 1981 that the American economy was to the right of the point where the Laffer curve turns down — say, at some point such as D. There was no evidence to support this assertion, and it does not appear to have been right, although it is a theoretical possibility.

Supply-siders made a similar claim about the effects of cuts in taxes on saving. When tax rates on saving are cut, the after-tax rate of return rises. For instance, suppose someone is earning 9 percent before tax on savings. The tax rate is 25 percent, implying an after-tax rate of return on savings of 6.75 percent (= 0.75 × 9 percent). Now suppose the tax rate is cut to 20 percent. The after-tax rate of return rises to 7.2 (= 0.8 × 9 percent). Surely, supply-siders argued, such a person will save more.* Then there will be more investment, a larger capital stock, and high output. With output higher, total tax revenue could be higher despite the cut in the tax rate.

Whatever the theoretical possibilities, the 1981 tax cuts did not lead to an increase in government revenue in the U.S. This excessively optimistic element in supply-side economics was never believed by any but a small minority of economists, and is now totally dismissed.† The emphasis on the role of incentives, though, is a valuable component of supply-side analysis and is discussed further in Chapter 18.

---

* There are conflicting income and substitution effects at work in this case, too, and the theoretical effect of the cut in the tax rate on saving is uncertain.

† On the supply-side story, see Jude Wanniski, *The Way the World Works* (New York: Touchstone, 1978); Paul Craig Roberts *The Supply-Side Revolution,* Harvard University Press, 1984; and Richard H. Fink (ed.) *Supply-Side Economics* (University Publications of America, 1982). For a critical view, see Robert Lekachman, Greed Is Not Enough: Reganomics (New York: Pantheon, 1982).

The Mechanics of Financing the Deficit

How does the government pay for its spending? Directly, it pays for most of its spending with cheques, drawn on the Bank of Canada. Aside from the fact that the cheque is drawn on a bank in which private individuals do not have accounts, a payment made by the government looks much like a cheque payment made by anyone else. Like an individual, the federal government must have funds in the account on which it writes cheques. So the question of how the federal government finances its spending is the same as the question on how it makes sure that it has funds in the bank account (at the Bank of Canada) on which in writes its cheques.

The federal government receives the bulk of its revenues from taxes and in some years taxes are less than expenditures so that it runs a budget deficit. Total government expenditures consist of expenditures on goods and services, G, and transfers, TR. Denoting taxes by TA and the deficit by BD we know that

$$BD \equiv (G + TR) - TA \equiv - BS \qquad (1)$$

Equation (1) reminds us that the deficit, BD is just the negative of the surplus, BS.

Now, how does the government make payments when its tax receipts are insufficient to cover its expenditures? The answer is that it has to borrow either from the public or the Bank of Canada. When the government finances its deficit by borrowing from the private sector, it is engaged in debt financing. It sells securities or debt to the private sector and, in return, receives cheques from individuals and firms (including banks) in exchange for the securities it sells them. The cheques are deposited in government accounts at the chartered banks or at the Bank of Canada, and can then be spent in the same way as tax receipts.

Alternatively, the government can borrow from the Bank of Canada by selling securities to the Bank. However, there is a major difference between government borrowing from the public and the Bank of Canada. When the Bank of Canada lends to the government by buying securities, it pays for them by giving the government a cheque on the Bank of Canada, that is, by creating high-powered money. When the government spends the deposit it has received at the Bank of Canada in exchange for its debt, it leaves the private sector with larger holdings of high-powered money. By contrast, when the government borrows from the public, it receives and then spends high-powered money, thus leaving the amount of high-powered money in the hands of the public unchanged, except for a brief transition period between the sale of securities and expenditures by the government. Since the stock of high-powered money is an important macroeconomic variable, the distinction between selling debt to the public and selling it to the Bank of Canada is in fact essential.

When the government borrows from the central bank to finance its deficit, it is engaged in money financing. Alternatively, the sale of securities to the Bank of Canada is referred to as monetizing the debt, meaning that the Bank creates (high-powered) money to finance the debt purchase. Another way of looking at the difference between sales to (borrowing from) the Bank of Canada and the public is to ask: What is the net change in the private sector's portfolio after the government has made *and* financed its expenditures? Consider first the case of borrowing from the public or selling debt to the public. In this case, the public holds more debt and an unchanged quantity of high-powered money, since the government spends the money it obtains from the debt sale to cover its deficit. Consider next the case where the deficit is financed by sale of debt to the Bank of Canada. In this event, the private sector's debt holding is unchanged while its holding of high-powered money is increased. The reason is that expenditures were financed by the creation of high-powered money by the Bank of Canada.

The Government Budget Constraint

We have seen that the government deficit can be financed in two ways: by sales of securities to the private sector and by borrowing from the Bank of Canada. Let ΔB_p and ΔB_b be the change in the value of government bonds held by the private sector and the Bank of Canada, respectively. Writing H for the stock of high-powered money, we have

$$BD = \Delta B_b + \Delta B_p = \Delta H + \Delta B_p \qquad (2)$$

Equation (2) is called the government budget constraint. It states that the budget deficit is financed by borrowing either from the Bank of Canada or from the private sector. The change if Bank of Canada holdings of debt causes a corresponding change in high-powered money (ΔH), so that we can say that the budget deficit is financed either by selling debt to the public or by increasing the stock of high-powered money. It is in this sense that the Bank of Canada "monetizes" the debt.[14]

The view that the deficit is financed either by selling debt to the public or by increasing the stock of high-powered money looks at the government sector as a whole, including or "consolidating" the Bank of Canada along with the government in the government sector. When one thinks of the government sector as a whole, relative to the private sector, the transactions in which the Bank of Canada buys debt from or lends to the government are seen as mere bookkeeping entries within the government sector.

Although this consolidation is useful for some purposes, it is important to recognize that the institutional arrangements provide for a clear division of responsibility under which the Bank of Canada determines the devision of the total deficit BD, in Equation (2), between the change in high-powered money

---

[14] Note that the government budget constraint (2) also shows that for a given value of the deficit, changes in the stock of high-powered money are matched by offsetting changes in the public's holdings of government debt. A positive ΔH matched by a negative ΔB_p is nothing other than an open market purchase.

and the change in government debt held by the private sector. There is no *necessary* association between the size of the government deficit in Canada and increases in the stock of high-powered money. If the Bank of Canada does not purchase securities when the government is borrowing, the stock of high-powered money is not affected by the deficit. On the other hand, there will be a more or less automatic association between Bank of Canada purchases of securities and government borrowing if the Bank of Canada commits itself to maintaining interest rates on government bonds at a constant level. As we saw in Chapter 4, an increase in the government deficit tends to increase the interest rate. If the Bank of Canada wishes to prevent this it must intervene in the market and purchase securities.

Prior to 1975, the Bank of Canada's policy focussed primarily on target interest rates, which could change from time to time, so that there was a link between deficits and Bank of Canada purchases of securities. Between 1975 and 1982 the Bank operated a policy which concentrated on the behaviour of the money supply. A commitment to bring about a given money stock breaks the link between government deficits and the creation of high-powered money. If the Bank of Canada creates high-powered money at a rate that should result in money's growing at the target rate, the change in the stock of high-powered money is not directly associated with the size of the government deficit.

Deficits and the National Debt

It follows from Equation (2) that when the budget is not balanced, the government changes the net amount of claims on it held by the private sector and the Bank of Canada. Those claims are the securities sold to the private sector and the Bank of Canada, and they represent claims for future interest payments. The total stock of government bonds (or claims on the government) outstanding constitutes the national, or public, debt. When the budget is in deficit, the national debt increases—the stock of claims against the government increases. When the budget is in surplus, the national debt decreases. The government takes in more taxes than it pays out, and can use the excess to retire (or buy back) previously issued debt.

The national debt is thus a direct consequence of past deficits in the federal budget. The way the national debt is divided between private sector claims on the government and high-powered money depends on past monetary policy. If the Bank of Canada has financed only a small part of each deficit in the past, then the ratio of high-powered money to national debt is small.

The government sells securities more or less continuously. There is, for instance, a weekly treasury bill auction, at which prospective buyers of treasury bills (lenders to the federal government) submit sealed bids specifying how much they are prepared to lend at different interest rates. The government sells the amount of treasury bills it has offered at the auction to the bidders who offer the highest prices, or the lowest interest rates.[15] Longer-term debt issues are less frequent. Issues of government debt are not all made for the purpose of financing the budget deficit. Most debt issues are made to refinance parts of the national debt that are maturing. For example, the government has to pay the amount it borrowed to a treasury bill holder when the treasury bill matures. Six months after a 180-day treasury bill is issued, the government has to pay the face amount of the treasury bill to the holder. Typically, the government obtains the funds to make those payments by further borrowing. The process by which the government (with the help and advice of the Bank of Canada) finances and refinances the national debt is known as *debt management.* Only a part of debt management is concerned with financing the current budget deficit. Most of it is concerned with the consequences of past budget deficits.

Interest Payments and Deficits

It is useful to distinguish between two components of the budget deficit: The *primary* or *noninterest deficit* and interest payments on the public debt.

$$\text{Total deficit} = \text{primary deficit} + \text{interest payments} \qquad (3)$$

The primary deficit represents all government spending, except interest payments, less government revenue.

$$\text{Primary deficit} = \text{noninterest expenditure} - \text{total revenue} \qquad (4)$$

The distinction between the two components highlights the role of the public debt in the budget. Interest has to be paid when there is debt outstanding. The overall budget will be in deficit unless the interest payments on the debt are matched by a primary surplus. Table 13-4 shows the total deficit and the two components.

Consider first the period 1970–1974. Interest payments averaged $2.3 billion, but there was an overall surplus of $1.3 billion. The primary surplus of $3.6 billion was enough to cover the interest payments and allow some reduction in the stock of debt. By contrast in 1980–1984 interest payments were over six times as large and there was a primary deficit. In 1985, the primary deficit reached 1.4 percent of GDP and the total deficit was 6.7 percent of GDP.

---

[15] Technically, there is no interest paid on treasury bills. Instead, a treasury bill is a promise to pay a given amount on a given date, say $100 on June 30. Before June 30, the treasury bill sells for a *discount* at less than $100, with the discount implying a rate of interest. For instance, if the treasury bill just described sold for $97.50 on January 1, the holder of the bill for six months would earn a little more than 5 percent per annum, or 2.5 percent for six months.

TABLE 13-4   INTEREST ON THE PUBLIC DEBT AND THE PRIMARY DEFICIT
(billions of dollars, period averages)

	Primary Deficit	Interest on Public Debt	Total Deficit	Primary Deficit (percent of GDP)
1970–74	−3.6	2.3	−1.3	−3.1
1975–79	1.4	5.6	7.0	0.6
1980–84	2.9	15.8	18.7	0.8
1985	6.7	25.3	32.0	1.4
1986	−1.6	26.4	24.8	−0.3

Source: Dept. of Finance, *Quarterly Economic Review,* Annual Reference Tables

Table 13-4 draws attention to a key problem in deficit financing. *If there is a primary deficit, then the total deficit will keep growing as the debt grows because of the deficit, and interest payments rise because the debt is growing.* The problem is exactly the same for an individual as for a country: someone who is spending more than he or she earns, and borrowing to cover the difference, will find a need to borrow more and more each year just because the interest on past borrowing keeps rising.

Deficits in a Growing Economy

The impossibility of running a permanent debt-financed primary deficit is a dramatic conclusion that certainly seems to justify concern over the massive deficits the Canadian economy faces for the next decade. However, the problem is less serious in a growing economy.

As can be seen in Figure 13-4, the national debt in Canada has risen for most of the past 30 years. Does this mean the government budget is bound to get out of control, with interest payments rising so high that taxes have to keep rising until eventually something terrible happens? The answer is "no" because the economy has continued growing. Figure 13-5 shows that the ratio of the debt to GDP declined until 1975 because GDP grew more rapidly than the debt.

Why is it useful to look at the ratio of debt to income rather than at the absolute value of the debt? The reason is that GDP is a measure of the size of the economy, and the debt-GDP ratio is thus a measure of the magnitude of the debt relative to the size of the economy.

We can formalize this discussion by writing the equation for the debt-income ratio and considering explicitly how it changes over time. We define the following symbols:

r = real or inflation adjusted interest rate
x = primary deficit as a fraction of nominal income
y = growth rate of real income
b = debt to income ratio

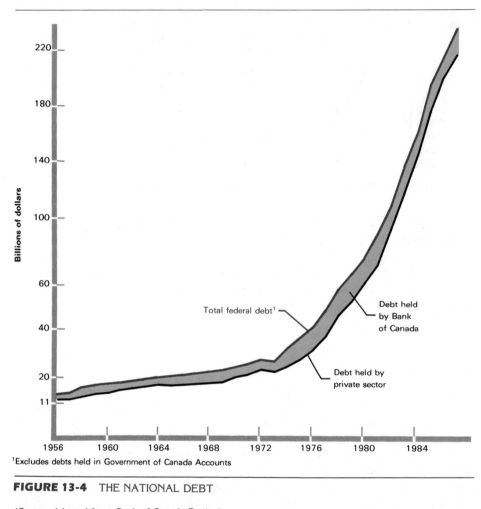

FIGURE 13-4   THE NATIONAL DEBT

(*Source*: Adapted from *Bank of Canada Review*)

In the appendix we show that the debt-income ratio rises over time if

$$b(r - y) + x > 0$$

The evolution of the debt-income ratio depends on the relationship between the real interest rate and the growth rate of output, and the noninterest budget surplus. The higher the interest rate and the lower the growth rate of output, the more likely the debt-income ratio is to be rising. A large noninterest surplus tends to make the debt-income ratio fall.

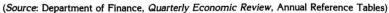

FIGURE 13-5 THE NATIONAL DEBT AS A PERCENTAGE OF GDP

(*Source*: Department of Finance, *Quarterly Economic Review*, Annual Reference Tables)

The above relationship brings out why over the early 1970s the debt-income ratio was falling. The real interest rate was practically zero, output grew steadily, and the noninterest budget was in surplus or near balance. In these circumstances debt grows less rapidly than nominal income and hence the debt-income ratio fell. By contrast, in the 1980s the opposite is the case. Real interest rates are very high, growth is sluggish, and the noninterest budget is in deficit. As a result the debt-income ratio is rising. In a period of slow growth and high real interest rates deficits therefore translate into a rapidly rising debt-income ratio.

What would happen if the deficit were too large, so that debt grows relative to income seemingly without bounds? Such a process can really not go on forever. Ultimately the public debt totally overshadows and displaces other assets, and crowding out becomes so pervasive that the public comes to expect *some* action to balance the budget. This might involve inflation,[16] special taxes, or cuts in government spending to balance the budget.

---

[16] See T. Sargent and N. Wallace, "Some Unpleasant Monetarist Arithmetic," Federal Reserve Bank of Minnesota, *Quarterly Review,* Fall 1981. As the title suggests, the treatment is technical. The main point the authors make is that debt problems ultimately become inflation problems. We return to this issue in Chapter 17.

How does inflation help solve the deficit problem? It does so because a large *unanticipated* inflation will reduce the real value of the out-standing stock of government debt. The national debt in most countries is *nominal*, meaning that the government is obliged to pay only a certain number of dollars to the holders of the debt. A policy that raises the price level thus reduces the real value of the payments the government is obliged to make. The debt can therefore virtually be wiped out by a large enough unanticipated inflation — so long as the debt is a nominal debt.

It is important to have some perspective on the relevance of these extreme conditions to the world today. Canada in the mid-1980s was not close to facing a massive debt crisis in which the national debt was so large as to overshadow other macroeconomic problems and in which the government could not finance its deficit by borrowing from the public. However, it did face the prospect of a rapid rise in the ratio of debt to income, back to levels it had been in the 1950s.

There are, though, a number of countries even today where many years of deficits have cumulated into a large public debt that ultimately becomes unmanageable. Often that outcome is clearly visible ahead of time, but on occasion a sharp increase in real interest rates together with a major loss in tax revenues, perhaps because of a world recession, can suddenly make the debt problem much more immediate. In particular, that problem faced many developing countries that had borrowed abroad during the seventies and in 1980–1981 when the real interest rate was still low. When the real interest rate rose, their heavy indebtedness meant that they had to make large interest payments to foreigners, which for many of the countries was extremely difficult to do. The result was the world debt crisis of 1982–1986.

The Burden of the Debt

To what extent is the national debt a burden? It must be recognized of course that corresponding to the liability that we all have as our share of the national debt, there are assets in the form of government securities held by Canadians. With the exception of debt held by foreigners, we owe the national debt to ourselves. Each individual shares in the public debt, but many individuals own claims on the government that are the other side of the national debt. If there is a debt for individuals taken together, it arises from prospective taxes to pay off the debt. The taxes that different individuals would pay to retire the debt would also vary among the population. To a first approximation, one could think of the liability that the debt represents as cancelling out the asset that the debt represents to the individuals who hold claims on the government. The question at issue then is whether the debt is counted as part of wealth for the population as a whole.

Are Bonds Wealth? The Barro-Ricardo Problem

It is possible that individuals in the economy calculate their wealth by taking into account the tax payments they will have to make in the future. Suppose that everyone believed that the national debt would eventually be paid off. Then everyone would know that at some point in the future the federal government would have to run a surplus. Individuals might think the federal government would at some future date have to raise taxes in order to pay off the debt. In this case an increase in the debt would increase their wealth and at the same time suggest to them that their taxes would be higher in the future. The net effect on aggregate demand might then be zero. The issue raised by this argument is sometimes posed by the question: Are government bonds wealth?

The question whether government bonds are net wealth goes back at least to the classical English economist David Ricardo. It has been given prominence in the work of the new classical economists, in particular Robert Barro.[17] Hence it is known as the *Barro-Ricardo equivalence proposition*. The proposition is that debt finance by bond issue merely postpones taxation, and therefore, in many instances is strictly equivalent to current taxation.

The strict Barro-Ricardo proposition that government bonds are not net wealth turns on the argument that people realize their bonds will have to be paid off with furture increases in taxes. (Incidentally, after raising this as a theoretical possibility, Ricardo rejected its practical significance.) If so, an increase in the budget deficit unaccompanied by cuts in government spending should lead to an increase in saving that precisely matches the deficit.

When the government reduces taxes to run a deficit, the public recognizes their taxes will be higher in the future. Their permanent income is thus unaffected by the government's switch from taxes today to taxes tomorrow. Their consumption is accordingly also unchanged. Since the tax cut increased disposable income, but consumption has not risen, saving must rise. The Barro-Ricardo proposition thus implies that a cut in current taxes that carries with it an implied increase in future taxes should lead to an increase in saving.

Empirical research continues in an attempt to settle the issue of whether the debt is wealth.[18] The issue is not yet closed. The theoretical arguments are not

---

[17] See Robert Barro, "Are Government Bonds Net Wealth?," *Journal of Political Economy*, December 1974. A recent theoretical challenge to the Barro-Ricardo view is Oliver Blanchard's "Debt, Deficits and Finite Horizons," *Journal of Political Economy*, April 1985.

[18] Intensive empirical work on this issue is taking place. For examples and reviews see David Aschauer, "Fiscal Policy and Aggregate Demand," *American Economic Review*, March 1985; Roger Kormendi, "Government Debt, Government Spending and Private Sector Behavior," *American Economic Review*, December 1983; James Barth, George Iden, and Frank Russek, "Do Federal Deficits Really Matter?," *Contemporary Policy Issues*, Fall 1984; John Tatom, "Two Views of the Effects of Government Deficit in the 1980s," *Federal Reserve Bank of St. Louis, Review*, October 1985.

conclusive, and it is difficult to isolate the effects of changes in debt on consumption demand in empirical studies. We believe the evidence to date is on balance unfavourable to the Barro-Ricardo proposition, but recognize that the issue has not yet been decisively settled.

Intergenerational Fairness

To the extent that debt does involve some burden, a government that runs a deficit and creates a larger debt shifts the cost of financing current spending to future generations. There are two reasons to suppose that this may happen.

First, even if Barro-Ricardo equivalence does hold we have to take into account that part of the debt is owned by foreigners. In that case, for the Canadian economy as a whole, part of the asset represented by the debt is held by foreigners, while the future tax liability accrues entirely to residents. Thus the part of the debt held by foreigners represents a burden on the future.

Second, if Barro-Ricardo equivalence does not hold, then it can be argued that the national debt creates a burden on future generations by reducing their capital stock. Since debt financing increases the interest rate and reduces investment, the capital stock would be lower with debt financing than otherwise. If individuals regard the debt as part of their wealth, they increase their consumption at a given level of income and this results in a smaller proportion of GDP being invested.

BOX 13-3 OPTIMAL DEFICITS AND INTERTEMPORAL TAX DISTORTIONS

Until recently the typical pattern has been that the debt-income ratio increases in wartime and declines in peacetime. This seems to be a sensible way to proceed although under the Barro-Ricardo hypothesis, current and future taxation have the same effects so that it does not matter how the deficit is financed. If the hypothesis does not hold, then debt finance represents a means of giving future generations a share in the economic burden of the war.

An alternative theory of optimal deficits, developed by Finn Kydland of Carnegie-Mellon University and Edward Prescott of the University of Minnesota,* focusses on tax distortions, or *tax wedges*. These distortions occur because taxes create a difference between the market price on commodities and their

---

* "A Competitive Theory of Fluctuations and the Feasibility and Desirability of Stabilization Policy," in Stanley Fischer (ed.), *Rational Expectations and Economic Policy*, University of Chicago Press, 1980.

value to consumers and producers. For instance, the income tax means that workers, who take home only an after-tax wage, place a lower value on their work than the employer, who has to pay a pretax wage.

In order to minimize these distortions over time, Kydland and Prescott show that tax *rates* should be kept constant. To see why, suppose that on the contrary taxes were high during war and low during peace. Then according to this theory, which is a supply-side theory, individuals would work less during the war and more during peace. Rather than have labour supply moving perversely in that way, Kydland and Prescott show that under their assumptions tax rates should be kept constant.

The government budget constraint says that the present value of government spending has to be equal to the present value of taxes. If tax rates are constant, deficits will be high when government spending is *temporarily* high and surpluses will occur when government spending is temporarily low. The reason is that on average the budget has to be balanced. If tax rates are kept constant, then revenues will change relatively little. Government spending can fluctuate more, and when it is high there will be a deficit.

This tax-smoothing argument indeed suggests that the typical pattern of large wartime deficits is the correct one.

13-5 SUMMARY

1. The great depression shaped both macroeconomics and many of the economy's institutions. The extremely high unemployment and the length of the depression led to the view that the private economy was unstable and that government intervention was needed to maintain high employment levels.

2. Keynesian economics succeeded because it seemed to explain the causes of the great depression—a collapse of investment demand—and because it pointed to expansionary fiscal policy as a means of preventing future depressions.

3. Federal government spending is financed through taxes and through borrowing, which is necessary when the budget is in deficit.

4. Borrowing may be from the private sector or from the Bank of Canada.

5. Lending to the government by the Bank of Canada changes the stock of high-powered money, whereas lending by the private sector to the government to finance the deficit does not affect the stock of high-powered money.

6. The stock of claims held by the Bank of Canada and the private sector against the government — the national debt — changes with the budget deficit. The national debt increases when there is a budget deficit and decreases when there is a budget surplus.

7. Because the deficit can be financed in two ways, there is no *necessary* connection between the budget deficit and changes in the stock of high-powered money. Equation (2), the government budget constraint, says only that the *sum* of changes in the stock of debt and changes in high-powered money is approximately equal to the budget deficit.

8. The Barro-Ricardo equivalence proposition notes that debt represents future taxes. Accordingly it asserts that debt-financed tax cuts will not have any effect on aggregate demand.

9. The debt-income ratio rises if the growth rate of debt — determined by interest payments and the primary deficit — exceeds the growth rate of nominal income.

10. Debt financing of a permanent increase in government spending is not viable if the economy is not growing. The interest payments on the debt would continually increase, making for a rising deficit that has to be funded by ever-increasing borrowing. In a growing economy, small deficits can be run permanently without causing the debt-GDP ratio to rise.

11. With the exception of debt held by foreigners, the national debt is not a burden since we owe it to ourselves. However, the debt may be a burden in the long run because it leads to a decline in the capital stock.

KEY TERMS

Structural deficit   Debt-income ratio
Debt finance   Laffer curve
Money finance   Barro-Ricardo equivalence
Monetizing the debt   Primary deficit
Government budget constraint Burden of the debt
National Debt

PROBLEMS

1. Using *IS-LM* curves, describe the competing "autonomous spending" and "monetary" explanations for the Great Depression.

2. Explain why many people believe the inflationary problems of the 1970s have their roots in the 1960s. How can this be so? What would be the cause? What could have been done to avoid such "heating up" of the economy, in this view?

3. Government budget deficits are often a source of public concern. What would be the implications for stabilization policy of a commitment to a balanced budget every year?

4. Discuss the notion of the monetary-fiscal policy mix. What determines the mix that is chosen? Illustrate, using a *IS-LM* diagram, how the effects of the mixes of 1971 and 1981 differ, given the information below. (Ignore changes in the level of income.)

	1971	1981
Cyclically adjusted federal deficit (% of GNP)	0	−1.7
Increase in the treasury bill rate (percent)	−2.5	5.0

5. What effect does a federal government surplus have on the stock of money and the stock of debt? Explain in detail the mechanics of how the stocks of money and bonds are affected.

6. Suppose the government issues $1 billion in treasury bills which are bought by the public. Then the Bank of Canada conducts open market purchases of $300 million. Effectively, how has the debt been financed?

7. Under what circumstances are fiscal and monetary policy related rather than existing as two completely independent instruments in the hands of the government?

8. Some people say that a huge government debt is a burden while others point out that a large debt means individuals own large amounts of government securities and thus are wealthier. Who is right?

9. Suppose the real interest rate is 3 percent, output growth is 7 percent, the debt-income ratio is 50 percent, and the primary deficit is 7 percent of GDP. Will the debt-income ratio increase or fall?

10. Explain in words why a high growth rate of output will tend, other things being equal, to reduce the debt-income ratio. How does your answer help explain Figure 13-5?

11. "Canada faces a fiscal crisis because mounting deficits are driving the debt-income ratio far beyond the range that this country has experienced. From these high debt levels there is no return except by years of high taxes to pay off the debt." Comment on this statement.

APPENDIX: THE POTENTIAL INSTABILITY OF DEBT FINANCE

In this appendix we develop a framework to assess the instability problem associated with debt finance. We focus on the debt-income ratio and ask under what conditions the debt-income ratio will rise over time. Instability arises if the debt-income ratio rises year after year without limits.[19]

The derivation uses definitions, addition and subtraction and avoids calculus. Its main purpose is for you to see where the formula in the text comes from.

B = nominal stock of debt outstanding
i = nominal interest rate
r = real interest rate
P = price level
Y = level of real output
x = noninterest or primary budget deficit (relative to income)
b = debt-income ratio
y = growth rate of output

The debt-income ratio is defined as the ratio of debt outstanding relative to nominal income.

$$\text{Debt-income ratio} = b \equiv \frac{B}{PY} \tag{A1}$$

The increase in debt from one year to the next is the result of the budget deficit. It therefore is equal to interest payments, which are equal to the debt outstanding, times the interest rate, iB, plus the noninterest deficit, xPY:

$$B_{t+1} - B_t \equiv \Delta B = iB_t + xP_tY_t \tag{A2}$$

Over time the debt-income ratio changes by Δb. From equation (A1) the change over time can be calculated as

$$\Delta b = \frac{B_{t+1}}{P_{t+1}Y_{t+1}} - \frac{B_t}{P_tY_t} = \frac{B_t + \Delta B}{P_tY_t(1 + y)(1 + \pi)} - b_t \tag{A3}$$

---

[19] The discussion of debt-income ratios draws on James Tobin, "Budget Deficits, Federal Debt and Inflation in the Short and Long Run," in The Conference Board, *Toward a Reconstruction of Federal Budgeting*, 1982; Robert Eisner and Paul Pieper, "A New View of the Federal Debt and Budget Deficits," *American Economic Review*, March 1984; Willem Buiter, "A Guide to Public Sector Debt and Deficits," *Economic Policy*, November 1985; and Congressional Budget Office, *The Economic Outlook*, February 1984.

where we have simply used the definitions of the growth rate $Y_{t+1} \equiv Y_t(1 + y)$ and inflation rate $P_{t+1} \equiv P_t(1 + \pi)$ and (A1). Note that the growth rate of nominal income appears in (A3) as the term $(1 + y)(1 + \pi)$. To simplify notation we use the definition $q \equiv 1/(1 + y)(1 + \pi)$ to denote the reciprocal of the growth rate of nominal income.

Equation (A3) can be simplified to the following form:

$$\Delta b = b\left[\frac{1 + \Delta B/B}{(1 + y)(1 + \pi)} - 1\right] = qb\left[\left(1 + \frac{\Delta B}{B}\right) - (1 + y)(1 + \pi)\right] \quad \text{(A3a)}$$

which states that if the growth rate of debt $(1 + \Delta B/B)$ exceeds the growth rate of nominal income $(1 + y)(1 + \pi)$ the debt-income ratio must increase.

Our next task is to relate the change in the debt-income ratio to interest rates and the primary deficit. Substituting the expression for the change in nominal debt from (A2) into (A3a) yields

$$\Delta b = qb[(1 + i) - (1 + y)(1 + \pi)] + qx \quad \text{(A4)}$$

Using the approximation $(1 + y)(1 + \pi) \approx 1 + y + \pi$ and the definition of the real interest rate, $r = i - \pi$, we get the final form of the equation:[20]

$$\Delta b = q[(r - y)b + x] \quad \text{(A5)}$$

This equation states that the debt-income ratio will be rising if the expression in square brackets is positive. The expression *must* be positive if the real interest rate exceeds the growth rate *and* there is a noninterest deficit $(x > 0)$. It must be falling if the real interest rate is less than the growth rate *and* there is a noninterest surplus. In between there are different possibilities. The important point to recognize is that a shift in the economy toward high real interest rate and low growth rates, combined with a noninterest deficit cannot but cause the debt-income ratio to be rising.

---

[20] The approximation $(1 + y)(1 + \pi) \approx 1 + y + \pi$ neglects the term $y\pi$. If both the growth rate of output and the inflation rate are small fractions, say 0.05 and 0.11, the product is only a small quantity and can be ignored. But if inflation is large, say 500 percent, the interaction term $y\pi$ cannot be neglected.

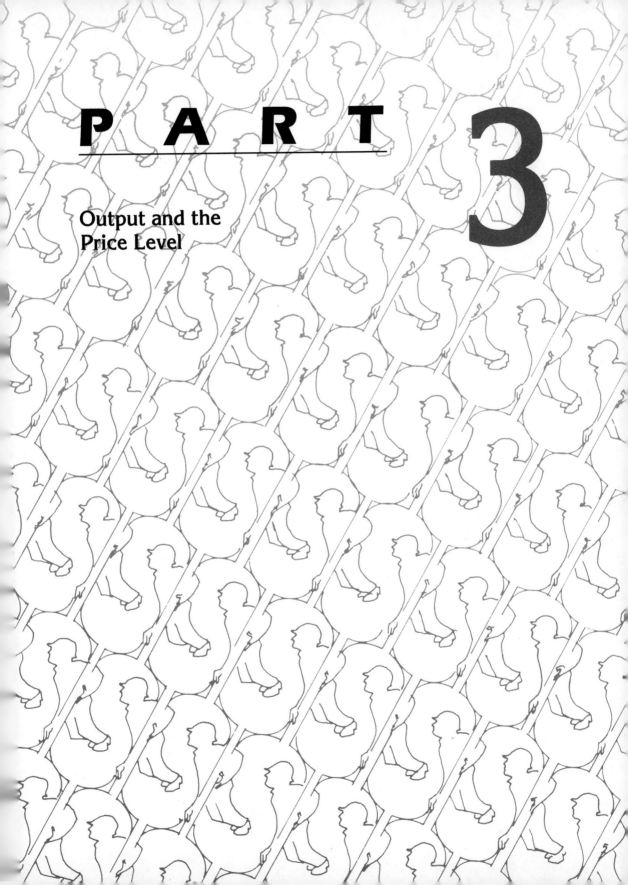

P A R T

3

**Output and the
Price Level**

CHAPTER 14

Aggregate Supply: Wages, Prices, and Employment

In this chapter and the next we develop the aggregate supply side of the economy. We show the links between wages, prices, and employment, and the adjustment process to disturbances in aggregate demand—monetary or fiscal policy changes or autonomous changes in spending. The development of the aggregate supply side of the economy also allows us to study how the economy adjusts to *supply shocks*, such as the increases in oil prices in 1973–1974 and 1979–1980, or the decline in oil prices in 1985–1986.

The supply side of the economy is an essential part of the *dynamics* of prices (inflation) and output, that is, of the adjustment of prices and output over-time when the economy is hit by a disturbance. Investing time in studying aggregate supply is worthwhile because the theory is needed to understand inflation and, in particular, the policy dilemma that comes from the existence of a short-run tradeoff between inflation and unemployment.

The theory of aggregate supply is one of the least settled areas in macroeconomics. The difficulty arises from the contrast between an idealized world in which output is always at the full employment level, and the fact that the labour market in particular seems to adjust slowly to changes in aggregate demand. We start with the frictionless neoclassical model of the labour market to illustrate how the labour market might work in an idealized model. Then, in Section 14-2 we present the Phillips curve, which shows the basic fact that wages adjust slowly to changes in aggregate demand. This fact is explained in terms of wage-setting behaviour in Section 14-3. In Sections 14-4 and 14-5 we develop a theory of aggregate supply that is consistent with and accounts for the behaviour of wages seen in the Phillips curve. We use that theory in Section 14-6 to study the responses of the economy to supply shocks.

14-1 THE FRICTIONLESS NEOCLASSICAL MODEL OF THE LABOUR MARKET

We have already shown the vertical aggregate supply curve of the classical case that exists when the labour market clears continuously and immediately in response to shocks (Chapter 7). In this section we derive this classical aggregate supply curve starting from micro foundations.

Figure 14-1 presents a microeconomic analysis of the labour market. There is a downward-sloping demand curve for labour, *ND*: the quantity of labour demanded is greater the lower is the real wage. The real wage is the ratio of the wage rate to the price level, or the amount of goods that can be bought with an hour of work. Also shown is an upward-sloping supply curve of labour

FIGURE 14-1 LABOUR MARKET EQUILIBRIUM AND FULL EMPLOYMENT. The labour supply curve *NS* shows the quantity of labour supplied increasing with the real wage. Along *ND* a reduction in the real wage causes an increase in the quantity of labour demanded. The labour market is in equilibrium at point *E*.

NS, indicating that as the real wage rises more workers come into the labour force seeking work.[1]

The full derivation of the demand curve for labour in Figure 14-1 is presented in the appendix to this chapter. The demand curve slopes downward because it is assumed that the marginal productivity of labour decreases as more labour is employed. Firms are competitive and are therefore willing to pay a real wage equal to the value of the marginal product of labour. There is a fixed amount of capital. As more labour is added, each new workers has less machinery with which to cooperate than the previous workers, and therefore the amount the new worker adds to output (the marginal product of labour) is lower than the amount added by the previous workers. The marginal productivity of labour is thus declining, and the demand curve slopes downward.

The labour supply and demand curves intersect at point *E*, with a corresponding level of labour input or employment *N** and an equilibrium real wage *(W/P)**. *N** is the *full-employment level of employment*. In this idealized frictionless neoclassical model, everyone is working precisely the amount he or she wants to at the going wage, *(W/P)** at point *E*, and firms are hiring precisely the amount of labour they want at the real wage *(W/P)** at point *E*. There is always full employment in the frictionless neoclassical world.[2]

Corresponding to the full-employment level of employment *N** is the full-employment level of output *Y**. That is the level of output that is produced using the existing amounts of other factors (the capital stock, land, raw materials) and the full-employment amount of labour *N**.

A Change in the Quantity of Money

In Figure 14-2 we show the labour supply and demand curves with the *nominal* wage on the vertical axis. The price level is assumed to be at a given level, say P_0. With a constant price level, a change in the nominal wage is also a change

---

[1] If you have studied microeconomics, you have probably seen the "backward-bending" labour supply curve, which is negatively sloped at high wages. That occurs because when the wage rises, individuals can both work less and earn more income. They may choose to respond to higher wages by working less. Although the labour supply curve may well slope backward in the long run (we work fewer hours than our grandparents and have much higher wages than they did) the supply curve of labour *for the economy* in the short run of a few years is positively sloped. That is because as the wage rises, people who were not working decide it is worthwhile to take a job rather than work at home, and they enter the labour force. Further, people already on the job may in the short run want to work longer hours when the real wage rises.

[2] In our description here, technology and the stock of capital are given but these can change and, as a result, the full-employment level of output will change too. For example, an increase in the capital stock will raise full-employment output, as does an improvement in technology.

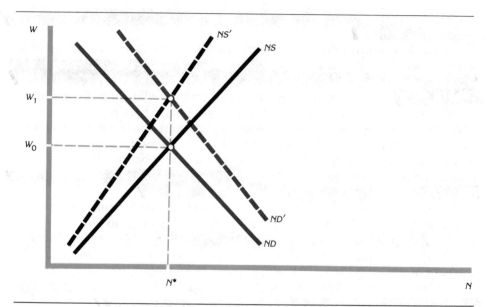

FIGURE 14-2   THE EFFECTS OF A CHANGE IN THE PRICE LEVEL ON THE LABOUR MARKET. Labour supply and demand curves NS and ND are shown for a constant price level. An increase in the price level shifts both curves upward in the same proportion, to NS' and ND', respectively. The equilibrium level of employment N* is unaffected by the change in the price level.

in the real wage, and the labour supply and demand curves thus look exactly as they do in Figure 14-1. The equilibrium nominal wage is W_0.

Now suppose there is an increase in aggregate demand, say because the central bank increases the quantity of money. At the existing price and wage levels the real money stock M/P is higher and interest rates are lower. Hence more goods will be demanded. Suppose that the increase in the demand for goods raises the price level above P_0. Then both the labour demand and supply curves in Figure 14-2 will shift up to ND' and NS', respectively.

The two curves shift upward by exactly the same proportion since, at each level of the nominal wage, the real wage is now lower in the same proportion as the price level has risen. When the two curves shift upward by the same proportion, they intersect at the same level of employment N. Thus the level of employment will remain at N despite the increase in the price level. The nominal wage rises, in Figure 14-2 to the level W_1, but the real wage remains unchanged. Indeed, any increase in the price level will simply shift both curves by the same vertical distance, leaving the level of employment unaffected. Only when the price level has risen in the same proportion as the money stock, will the economy be back in equilibrium with the same real balances, the same real wage, and the same level of employment. Money is neutral in this frictionless neoclassical world, as we saw at the end of Chapter 7.

Frictional Unemployment and the Natural Rate of Unemployment

Taken literally the frictionless neoclassical model implies that there is no unemployment, but by including frictions, the theory can account for some unemployment of labour. The frictions occur because the labour market is always in a state of flux. Some people are retiring from their jobs, other people are looking for jobs for the first time, some firms are expanding and are hiring new workers, others have lost business and have to contract, firing workers.

Because it takes time for an individual to find the right new job, there will always be some *frictional* unemployment as people search for jobs. Frictional unemployment is the unemployment that exists as a result of individuals shifting between jobs and looking for new jobs.

There is some amount of frictional employment associated with the full-employment level of employment N^* and full-employment level of output Y^*. That amount of unemployment is called the *natural rate*. The natural rate of unemployment is the rate of unemployment arising from labour market frictions that exists when the labour market is in equilibrium.

We do not go into the determinants and estimates of the natural rate of unemployment here, reserving that for Chapter 16. The important point is that the existence of some unemployment is not necessarily inconsistent with the neoclassical model of the labour market in which the economy is always at the full employment level of output.

14-2   WAGES, PRICES, AND OUTPUT: THE FACTS

Two major implications of the neoclassical theory of the labour market are at odds with the facts. First, the rate of unemployment fluctuates far more than is consistent with the view that all unemployment is frictional. Figure 14-3 shows the unemployment rate for the period since 1965. It cannot be that the 12 percent unemployment seen in 1982 is equal to the natural rate. Thus it cannot be that the labour market was always in equilibrium at full employment over the period since 1965. Much less can it be believed that the labour market was at the full-employment level of employment in 1933 when the unemployment rate was nearly 20 percent of the labour force.

The Phillips Curve

The second fact that is inconsistent with the neoclassical theory is that the wage appears to adjust slowly in response to shifts in aggregate demand. The notion

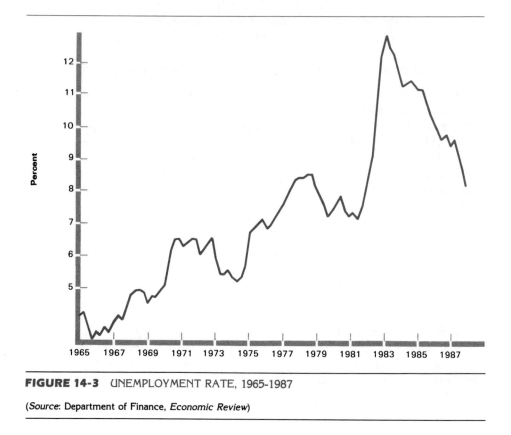

FIGURE 14-3 UNEMPLOYMENT RATE, 1965-1987

(*Source*: Department of Finance, *Economic Review*)

that an increase in aggregate demand will first affect output and employment, and only then wages and prices, is an old one.

The notion is made precise in the *Phillips curve*. In 1958, A. W. Phillips, then a professor at the London School of Economics, published a comprehensive study of wage behaviour in the United Kingdom for the years 1861–1957.[3] The main finding is summarized in Figure 14-4, reproduced from his article:

The Phillips curve is an inverse relationship between the rate of unemployment and the rate of increase of money wages: The higher the rate of unemployment, the lower the rate of wage inflation. In other words, there is a tradeoff between wage inflation and unemployment.

The Phillips curve shows that the rate of wage inflation decreases with the unemployment rate. Letting W be the wage this period, and W_{-1} the wage last period, the rate of wage inflation gW is defined as

---

[3] A. W. Phillips, "The Relation between Unemployment and the Rate of Change of Money Wages in the United Kingdom, 1861–1957," *Economica*, November 1958.

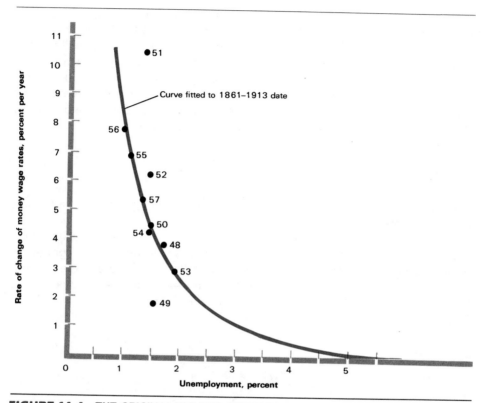

FIGURE 14-4 THE ORIGINAL PHILLIPS CURVE FOR THE UNITED KINGDOM

(*Source*: A.W. Phillips, "The Relation between Unemployment and the Rate of Change of Money Wages in the United Kingdom, 1861–1957," *Economica*, November 1958.)

$$gW = \frac{W - W_{-1}}{W_{-1}} \tag{1}$$

With u^* representing the natural rate of unemployment we can write the simple Phillips curve as

$$gW = -\epsilon(u - u^*) \tag{2}$$

This equation states that wages are falling when the unemployment rate exceeds the natural rate, $u > u^*$, and rising when unemployment is below the natural rate.

The Phillips curve implies that wages and prices adjust slowly to changes in aggregate demand. Why? Suppose the economy is in equilibrium with prices stable and unemployment at the natural rate. Now there is an increase in the money stock by say 10 percent. Prices and wages both have to rise by 10 percent for the economy to get back to equilibrium, but the Phillips curve shows that for wages to rise by an extra 10 percent, the unemployment rate will have to fall. That will cause the rate of wage increase to go up. Wages will start rising, prices too will rise, and eventually the economy will return to the full-employ-ment level of output and unemployment. In the meantime the increase in the money stock caused a reduction in unemployment. This point can be readily seen by rewriting (2) (using the definition of the rate of wage inflation) to look at the level of wages today relative to the past level:

$$W = W_{-1}[1 - \epsilon(u - u^*)] \tag{2a}$$

For wages to rise above their previous level, unemployment must fall below the natural rate.

Although Phillips' own curve relates the rate of increase of wages or wage inflation to unemployment as in (2) above, the term "Phillips curve" gradually became used to describe either the original Phillips curve *or* a curve relating the rate of increase of *prices*—the rate of inflation—to the unemployment rate. Figure 14-5 shows inflation and unemployment data for Canada. The obser-

Note: Inflation is the rate of change over the year of the Consumer Price Index.

FIGURE 14-5   INFLATION AND UNEMPLOYMENT

(*Source:* Adapted from Statistics Canada, 11-003, 11-206, 11-505, 71-201) vations for 1963 and 1966 display a Phillips curve tradeoff with the shape of the original Phillips curve of Figure 14-4.

The Policy Tradeoff

The Phillips curve rapidly became a cornerstone of macroeconomic policy analysis. It suggested that policymakers could choose different combinations of unemployment and rates of inflation. For instance, they could have low unemployment as long as they put up with high inflation as in 1966, or they could maintain low inflation by having high unemployment, as in 1963.

However, this simple Phillips curve has not held up well in retrospect. Figure 14-5 shows that the relationship observed in the 1960s clearly does not describe the experience of the 1970s.

The Friedman-Phelps Amendment

Remarkably, the death of the simple Phillips curve was predicted in the late sixties by Professors Milton Friedman, then of the University of Chicago, and Edmund Phelps of Columbia.[4] Friedman and Phelps argued that the simple Phillips curve would shift over time as workers and firms became used to and began to expect continuing inflation.

On the basis of economic theory[5] they concluded that the notion of a long-run tradeoff between inflation and unemployment was illusory. The Friedman-Phelps proposition is: *In the long run the economy will move to the natural rate of unemployment whatever the rate of change of wages and the inflation rate.*

The argument was based on the definition of the natural rate of unemployment as the rate of frictional unemployment consistent with the labour market being in equilibrium. As long as unemployment is above the natural rate, more people are looking for jobs than is consistent with equilibrium in the labour market. This excess unemployment should cause the real wage to fall, so that firms want to hire more workers and fewer want to work, reducing the unemployment rate back to the natural rate. Similarly, when unemployment is below the natural rate, there are too few people available for firms to fill jobs as rapidly as they do normally. The real wage should rise, leading firms to want to employ fewer workers and attracting more people into the labour force. The unemployment rate would rise back to the natural level. Thus there is no long-run tradeoff between inflation and unemployment.

---

[4] Milton Friedman, "The Role of Monetary Policy," *American Economic Review*, March 1968, and Edmund Phelps, *Inflation Policy and Unemployment Theory*, Norton, 1972.

[5] Remember that at the time they were writing (Phelps first made the argument in the 1960s) the facts appeared to support the Phillips curve as a long-run tradeoff—after all Phillips' own data covered a period of nearly a century.

14-3 WHY ARE WAGES STICKY?

The assumption that wages are slow to adjust to shifts in demand is essential in our derivation of an aggregate supply curve that produces a gradual rather than an instantaneous adjustment of the economy to disturbances. With gradual adjustment of wages, a monetary or fiscal expansion has an extended effect on output and employment. The key question in the theory of aggregate supply is why the nominal wage adjusts slowly to shifts in demand, or why wages are *sticky*. Wages are sticky, or wage adjustment sluggish, when wages move slowly over time, rather than being fully and immediately flexible so as to assure full employment at every point in time.

To clarify the assumptions that we make about wage stickiness, we translate the Phillips curve in (2) into a relationship between the rate of change of wages gW and the level of employment. There is a need to distinguish three different employment concepts: (1) actual employment denoted by N, (2) the equilibrium employment level that occurs in a neoclassical labour market, N^* (that is, the employment level consistent with unemployment being at the natural rate), and (3) the level of employment, LF, that would exist if there were zero unemployment and everyone was working. Thus LF stands for the total labour force.[6]

With these definitions we can move between the concepts of employment and unemployment. We use the definition of the actual unemployment rate as the fraction of the total labour force (LF) that is not employed:[7]

$$u = \frac{LF - N}{LF} \tag{3}$$

Substituting (3) into (2), we obtain the Phillips curve relationship between the level of employment and the rate of change in wages:

$$gW \equiv \frac{W - W_{-1}}{W_{-1}} = -\epsilon \left(\frac{N^* - N}{LF} \right) \tag{2b}$$

or, rewriting the equation, we show the Phillips curve as a relationship between the wage this period, last period's wage, and the actual level of employment:

---

[6] With a positively sloped labour supply curve, the full-employment level of the labour force depends on the real wage. We mean by N^* the equilibrium level of N when the labour market is in its neoclassical equilibrium shown in Fig. 14-1, adjusted for frictional unemployment.

[7] Note that the total labour force (LF) exceeds the full-employment level of employment N^* because it is normal for some people to be unemployed while they search for jobs. The definition of the natural unemployment rate is $u^* = (LF - N^*)/LF$, and the actual unemployment rate is $u = (LF - N)/LF$.

$$W = W_{-1}\left[1 + \epsilon\left(\frac{N - N^*}{LF}\right)\right] \qquad (4)$$

Equation (4), the wage-employment relation, WN, is shown in Figure 14-6. The wage this period is equal to the wage that prevailed last period (say, last quarter), but with an adjustment for the level of employment. At full employment ($N = N^*$) the wage this period is equal to last period's wage. If employment is above the full-employment level, the wage increases above last period's wage. If employment is below the full employment level, the wage this period falls below last period's wage. The extent to which the wage responds to employment depends on the parameter ϵ. If ϵ is large, unemployment has large effects on the wage and the WN line is steep.

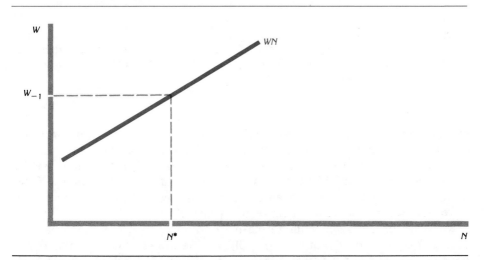

FIGURE 14-6   THE WAGE-EMPLOYMENT RELATION. Within a period, the wage increases with the level of employment, as shown by WN. If employment is at its neoclassical equilibrium level, N^*, the wage level in this period is equal to the wage last period.

The Phillips curve relationship in (4) also implies that the WN relationship shifts over time, as in Figure 14-7. If there is overemployment this period, the WN curve will shift upward next period to WN'. If there is less than full employment this period, the WN curve will shift downward next period to WN'' Thus changes in aggregate demand that move the rate of unemployment this period will have effects on wages in subsequent periods. In other words, the adjustment to a change in employment is dynamic, that is, it takes place over time.

The central element in any explanation of wage stickiness is the fact that the labour market involves long-term relations between firms and workers. Most

FIGURE 14-7   THE SHIFTING WAGE-EMPLOYMENT RELATION. The *WN* curve shifts over time if employment differs from the full-employment level N^*. If N exceeds N^* this period, the *WN* curve will shift upward to *WN'* next period.

of the labour force expects to continue in its current job for some time. Working conditions, including the wage, are renegotiated periodically, but not frequently. That is because it is costly to negotiate frequently if the wage is set by negotiation; and costly to obtain information about alternative wages if the wage is supposed to be set by market conditions. Typically, firms and workers reconsider wages and adjust them once a year.[8]

Wages are usually set in dollar terms in economies with low rates of inflation.[9] Thus the agreement is that the firm will pay the worker so many dollars per hour or per month, for the next quarter or year. Some formal union labour contracts last 2 or 3 years and may fix nominal wages for the period of the contract. Frequently union contracts include separate wage rates for overtime hours, which implies that the wage rate paid by firms is higher the more labour

---

[8] The frequency with which wages (and prices) are reset depends on the stability of the level of output and prices in the economy. In extreme conditions, such as hyper-inflations, wages might be reset daily or weekly. The need to reset prices and wages frequently is indeed seen as one of the costs of high and unstable rates of inflation.

[9] In economies with high inflation, wages are likely to be *indexed* to the price level, that is, adjusted for changes in prices. Even in Canada some long-term labour contracts contain indexing clauses where the wage is increased to compensate for past price increases. The indexing clauses typically adjust wages once a quarter (or once a year) to compensate for price increases in the past quarter (or year).

is employed. That is one reason the WN curve in Figure 14 — 6 is positively sloped.

At any moment of time, firms and workers will have agreed, explicitly or implicitly, on the wage schedule that is to be paid to currently employed workers. There will be some base wage, corresponding to a given number of hours of work per week, and depending on the type of job, perhaps a higher wage for overtime. The firm then sets the level of employment each period. If demand is high, employment will be high, and the nominal wage with it.

Now consider how wages adjust when the demand for labour shifts and firms increase hours of work. In the short run, wages rise along the WN curve. With demand up, workers will press for an increase in the base wage at the next labour negotiation. However, not all wages are negotiated simultaneously. Rather wage-setting dates are *staggered*, that is, they overlap.[10] Assume that wages for half the labour force are set in January and the other half in July. Suppose the money stock went up in September. When the time comes to renegotiate half the contracts in January, both the firms and the workers negotiating know that other wages will not change for the next 6 months.

Workers do not adjust their base wage all the way to the level that will take the economy to the long-run equilibrium because, if they do, their wages will be very high relative to other wages for the next 6 months. Firms will prefer to employ workers whose wages have not yet risen; there is thus a danger of unemployment to the January wage-setting workers if the renegotiated wages go too high. They are therefore adjusted only part-way toward equilibrium.

Then in July, when the time comes to reset the other half of the wages, those too are not driven all the way to the equilibrium level because the January wages will then be relatively lower. So the July wages will go above the January wages, but still only part way to the full-employment equilibrium base wage.

This process keeps on going, with the supply curve rising from period to period as wages leapfrog each other with first one wage and then another being renegotiated. The position of the aggregate supply curve in any period will depend on where it was last period, because each unit renegotiating wages has to consider the level of its wage relative to the wages that are not being reset. The level of the wages that are not being reset is reflected in last period's wage rate and that is why there is a W_{-1} term on the right-hand side of the Phillips curve equation (4).

During this adjustment process, firms will also be resetting prices as wages (and thus firms' costs) change. The process of wage and price adjustment continues until the economy is back at the full-employment equilibrium with the same real balances. The real-world adjustment process is more complicated than the January-July example because wages are not reset quite as regularly

---

[10] The adjustment process we present here is based on John Taylor, "Aggregate Dynamics and Staggered Contracts," *Journal of Political Economy*, February 1980.

as that, and also because not only wage but also price adjustments[11] have to be taken into account. However, the January-July example gives the essence of the adjustment process.

This account of slow wage and price adjustment raises at least two serious questions. The first is why firms and workers do not readjust wages more frequently when clearly understandable disturbances affect the economy. If they did, then perhaps they could adjust wages so as to maintain full employment. Recent research emphasizes that comparatively small costs of resetting wages and prices can keep adjustment processes from operating fast.[12] In any event the problems of coordinating wage and price adjustments to move back rapidly to equilibrium in a large economy where there are many different forces affecting supply and demand in individual markets are also formidable.

The second is why firms and unemployed workers do not get together when there is high unemployment, with the firms giving jobs to the unemployed at wages below those their current workers receive. Such practices are probably bad for the morale of the labour force on the job, but even so this pattern has to a limited extent been seen in the United States in the period since 1982 in the so-called *two-tier* wage system. In this system veterans are on one wage schedule and new employees on a much lower schedule. However, — and this is precisely the point of this section — the introduction of the two-tier system did not happen immediately as unemployment developed, but rather took place slowly over a period of years. That pattern is consistent with the sluggish adjustment of wages.

To summarize, the combination of the assumptions that wages are preset and wage adjustment staggered generates the type of gradual wage and output adjustment we observe in the real world. That accounts for the dynamics. The upward-sloping aggregate supply curve to which we now turn is accounted for by overtime wages for some workers, and by the fact that wages in those contracts that are renegotiated within the period (such as a quarter) do respond to market conditions.

14-4 THE AGGREGATE SUPPLY CURVE

We derive the aggregate supply curve in four steps. First, we relate output to employment. Second, we relate the prices firms charge to their costs, and third, we use the Phillips curve relationship between wages and employment. Then

---

[11] For an interesting study of the frequency of price adjustments (for newspapers) see Stephen G. Cecchetti, "Staggered Contracts and the Frequency of Price Adjustment," *Quarterly Journal of Economics*, Supplement, 1985.

[12] These theories are at the frontier of research. For the flavour of the argument, see N. Gregory Mankiw, "Small Menu Costs and Large Business Cycles: A Macroeconomic Model of Monopoly," *Quarterly Journal of Economics*, May 1985.

we put the three components together to derive an upward-sloping aggregate supply curve, a relationship between the price level and output, of the type used in Chapter 7.

The Production Function

The production function links the level of employment of labour to the level of output. The simplest production function is one in which output is proportional to the input of labour:

$$Y = aN \tag{5}$$

Here Y is the level of output produced, and N is the amount of labour input or employment (measured in hours of work, for example).

The coefficient a is called the input coefficient or *labour productivity*. Labour productivity is the ratio of output to labour input, Y/N, that is, the amount of output produced per unit of labour employed. For instance, if a is equal to 3, then one unit of labour (1 hour of work) will produce three units of output.

The assumption in equation (5) is that the productivity of labour is constant. In fact labour productivity changes over time. It tends to grow over long periods, as workers become better trained, educated, and equipped with more capital. It also changes systematically during the business cycle. Productivity tends to begin to fall before the start of a recession and then to start recovering either during the recession or at the beginning of the recovery. This productivity behaviour is explained in Box 14-1.

We simplify by assuming that labour productivity is constant. An important point to notice though is that labour productivity is *not* inversely related to the level of output. The neoclassical demand function for labour shown in Figure 14-1 is built on the assumption that the marginal product of labour decreases as employment increases. If that were so for all levels of output, the average product of labour would also decrease as output increased, but it does not. That is one reason the neoclassical analysis is not an accurate description of the behaviour of wages and prices over the business cycle.[13]

---

[13] A major reason is that the assumption of the neoclassical analysis that capital remains fully employed throughout is not correct. Note from the appendix to this chapter that the diminishing marginal product of labour follows from the assumption that, because the capital stock is fixed in the short run, each succeeding worker has less capital with which to work. However, the use of capital also varies over the cycle, with capital being unemployed in recessions and heavily employed during booms. For instance, factories may run on three shifts a day during booms, using the capital all the time, and only one shift a day during recessions. Data on the use of capital, so-called capacity utilization data are imperfect, but suggest that, if anything, the capital-in-use to labour ratio may be higher during booms than in recessions. In that case neoclassical theory would not predict that the marginal productivity of labour is lower in booms, as it does in Fig. 14-1.

BOX 14-1   THE CYCLICAL BEHAVIOUR OF PRODUCTIVITY

In developing the sticky wage macroeconomic model we made a strong assumption about the link between output and employment, namely, $Y = aN$. According to our assumption, labour productivity Y/N is equal to a constant a.

That assumption is readily testable by looking at the cyclical behaviour of labour productivity or output per worker, Y/N. The data given in Table 1 shows that productivity falls as the economy moves into a recession and increases during the recovery. How do we explain these facts, and what implications do they have for our model? Firms maintain long-term relations with their labour force. Part of that long-term relation is that during recessions firms are slow to dismiss personnel, especially highly specialized workers that the firm does not want to risk losing permanently. This applies also to managers, because even if the firm produces only half the normal level of output, it is difficult to reduce management by half.

TABLE 1   THE CYCLICAL BEHAVIOUR OF PRODUCTIVITY

Recession (peak to trough)	Percent change peak to trough		Percent change in four quarters following trough	
	Output	Productivity	Output	Productivity
1974:1-74:3	−0.6	−2.3	1.8	0.3
1979:4-80:2	−1.5	−1.9	5.5	1.9
1981:2-82:4	−7.5	−2.6	7.1	3.7

Source: Department of Finance, *Economic Review*

Thus employment tends to fluctuate *less* than output or production. During a recession output falls, but employment falls relatively less. Hence productivity — the ratio of output to employment — falls. Conversely, in a recovery production rises, but because the firm has kept on or *hoarded* a lot of the work force, employment increases less. Thus productivity rises in a recovery.

The effects we have just described are reinforced by the fact that the firm bases its hiring and firing on expectations about future production. A firm will hire more workers and incur the expense of increasing employment only if there is an expectation that production and output will be higher for some time. Otherwise, paying overtime to the existing labour force would be a cheaper solution. Conversely, firms will lay off or dismiss workers only if they believe the decline in demand will last some time. Here then is another source of discrepancy between current employment and current production. Current production may be low but employment high because firms believe demand has declined only transitorily.

By assuming a tight link between output and employment, our model thus simplifies the complex relationships between a firm's production decisions and its employment decisions. For purposes of understanding aggregate supply, the simplification is justifiable, since output and employment do, in practice, move in the same direction, even if not exactly in lockstep.

Costs and prices

The second step in developing the theory of supply is to link firms' prices to their costs. Labour costs are the main component of costs. The guiding principle here is that a firm will supply output at a price that at least covers its costs. Of course, firms would like to charge far more than cost, but competition from existing firms, and firms that might enter the economy to capture some of the profits, prevent prices from getting far out of line with costs.

We assume that firms base price on the labour cost of production. Since each unit of labour produces a units of output, the labour cost of production per unit is W/a. For instance if the wage is $15 per hour and a is 3, then the labour cost is $5 per unit. The ratio W/a is often called *unit labour cost*.

Firms set price as a *markup, z*, on labour costs:

$$P = \frac{(1 + z)W}{a} \tag{6}$$

The markup over labour costs covers the cost of other factors of production that the firm uses, such as capital and raw materials, and includes an allowance for the firm's normal profits. If competition in the industry is less than perfect, then the markup will also include an element of monopoly profit.[14]

Employment and Wages and the Aggregate Supply Curve

The three components of the aggregate supply curve are the production function (5), the price-cost relation (6), and the Phillips curve (4). The price level is

---

[14] Students who have taken microeconomics will realize that in competitive industries price is assumed to be determined by the market, rather than set by firms. That is quite consistent with equation (2), for if the industry were competitive, z would cover only the costs of other factors of production and normal profits, and the price would thus be equal to the competitive price. Equation (2) is slightly more general, because it allows also for price setting by firms in industries that are less than fully competitive.

proportional to the wage [from equation (6)], but today's wage is linked through the Phillips curve in (4) to the level of employment and to past wages. We can use that wage equation and replace the wage in (6) to obtain a link between the level of employment and the price level:

$$P = (1 + z)aW_{-1}\left[1 + \epsilon\left(\frac{N - N^*}{LF}\right)\right] \tag{7}$$

which, noting that $P_{-1} = (1 + z)aW_{-1}$ reduces to

$$P = P_{-1}\left[1 + \epsilon\left(\frac{N - N^*}{LF}\right)\right] \tag{7a}$$

Further, the level of output is proportional to employment [from the production function, equation (5)]. Thus we can replace N, N^*, and LF in equation (7a) by Y/a, Y^*/a, and YF/a, respectively, where YF is the level of output that would occur if the entire labour force were employed. Making that change, we obtain

$$P = P_{-1}\left[1 + \epsilon\left(\frac{Y - Y^*}{YF}\right)\right]$$

Finally, defining $\lambda \equiv \epsilon/YF$, we obtain the *aggregate supply curve*

$$P = P_{-1}[1 + \lambda(Y - Y^*)] \tag{8}$$

Figure 14-8 shows the aggregate supply curve implied by equation (6). The supply curve is upward-sloping. Like the WN curve on which it is based, the AS curve shifts over time. If output this period is above the full-employment level Y^*, then next period the AS curve will shift up to AS'. If output this period is below the full-employment level, the AS curve next period will shift down to AS''. Thus the properties of the AS curve are those of the WN curve. This is both because the markup is fixed at z and because output is proportional to employment.

The AS curve is the aggregate supply curve under conditions where wages are less than fully flexible. Prices increase with the level of output because increased output implies increased employment, reduced unemployment, and therefore increased labour costs. The fact that prices rise with output is entirely a reflection of the adjustments in the labour market where higher employment increases wages.[15] Firms pass on these wage increases by raising prices, and for that reason prices rise with the level of output.

---

[15] Note an important implication of markup pricing in (6). Because firms are assumed to maintain a constant markup of price over cost, the *real wage* does not change with

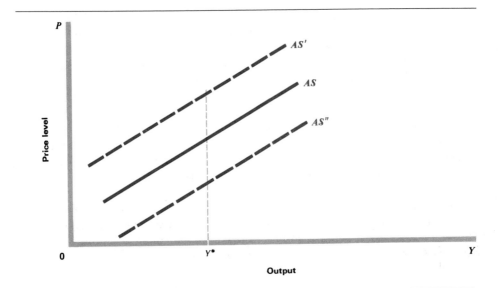

FIGURE 14-8   THE AGGREGATE SUPPLY CURVE. The aggregate supply curve *AS* is derived from the *WN* curve, with the added assumptions that output is proportional to employment, and that prices are set as a markup on labour costs. The *AS* curve, too, shifts over time, depending on the level of output. For instance, if output this period is above the full employment level *Y**, the *AS* curve will shift upward to *AS'* next period.

Properties of the Aggregate Supply Curve

We have now derived the aggregate supply schedule *AS* used in Chapter 7 and can, with the help of (8), explore its properties more closely. We emphasize three points:

1.   The aggregate supply schedule is flatter the smaller the impact of output and employment changes on current wages. If wages respond very little to

the level of employment in the theory developed in this chapter. Because different theories of aggregate supply have different implications about the cyclical behaviour of real wages, that behaviour has been studied intensively. For instance, some theories suggest that the level of employment is determined by the neoclassical labour demand curve *ND* in Fig. 14-1. In that case the real wage would be high in recessions and low in booms. Empirical evidence shows however that wages and employment are essentially independent over the cycle. For a study based on data from twelve countries that reaches that conclusion, see P. T. Geary and J. Kennan, "The Employment — Real Wage Relationship: An International Study," *Journal of Political Economy*, August 1982. It is because the data show no clear pattern that we assume in our theoretical development that the real wage is independent of the level of employment.

changes in unemployment, then the *AS* schedule in Figure 14-8 will be very flat. The coefficient λ in equation (8) captures this employment-wage change linkage.

2. The position of the aggregate supply schedule depends on the past level of prices. The schedule passes through the full employment level of output Y^* at $P = P_{-1}$. For higher output levels there is overemployment, and hence prices today are higher than those last period. Conversely, when unemployment is high, prices today will be below those last period.

3. The aggregate supply schedule shifts over time. If output is maintained above the full employment level Y^*, then over time wages continue to rise and the wage increases are passed on as increased prices.

Rather than discuss these three points in the abstract, we use the aggregate supply curve to examine the effects of a monetary expansion in Figure 14-9. This will give us a full understanding of both the short-run and long-run implications of the wage-price aggregate supply model.

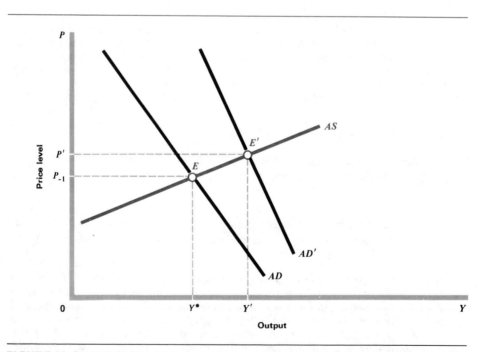

FIGURE 14-9 THE SHORT-RUN EFFECT OF AN INCREASE IN THE MONEY STOCK. The initial equilibrium at *E* is disturbed by an increase in the money stock that shifts the aggregate demand curve from *AD* to *AD'*. Short-run equilibrium is at *E'* where both the price level and output have increased. Prices are higher because the output expansion has caused an increase in wages, which are passed on into prices. The *AS* schedule is drawn quite flat, reflecting the assumption that wages are quite sticky.

14-5   THE EFFECTS OF A MONETARY EXPANSION

In Figure 14-9 we show the economy in full-employment equilibrium at point
E. The aggregate supply schedule AS is drawn for a given past price level P_{-1}.
It passes through the full-employment output level Y^* at the price level P_{-1}
because when output is at the full-employment level, there is no tendency for
wages to change, and hence costs and prices too are constant from period to
period. The aggregate supply schedule is drawn relatively flat, suggesting a
small effect of output and employment changes on wages.

Short-Run Effects

Suppose now that the nominal money stock is increased. At each price level
real balances are higher, interest rates are lower, and hence the demand for
output rises. The AD schedule shifts upward and to the right, to AD'. At the
initial price level $P = P_{-1}$ there is now an excess demand for goods. Firms find
that their inventories are running down and accordingly hire more labour and
raise output until point E', the short-run equilibrium, is reached. Note that at
E' both output and prices have risen. A monetary expansion has led to a short-
run increase in output. The rise in prices is due to the increase in labour costs
as production and employment rise.

Compare now the short-run result with the Keynesian and classical models
of Chapter 7 and the neoclassical model of this chapter. Our new equilibrium
at E' has a feature of each: output is higher, and prices have risen. Whether we
are more nearly in the classical or Keynesian situation depends entirely on the
slope of the aggregate supply schedule, that is, on the coefficient λ that translates employment changes into wage changes.

Medium-Term Adjustment

The short-run equilibrium at point E' is not the end of the story. At E' output is
above normal. Therefore, from (7) prices *will keep on rising*. Consider now in
Figure 14-10 what happens in the second period. Once we are in the second
period, looking back, the price in the preceding period was P' at point E'.
Therefore the second-period supply curve passes through the full- employment
output level at a price equal to P' We show this by shifting the aggregate supply
schedule up to AS', reflecting the increase in wages that has taken place since
last period in response to the high level of employment.

With the new aggregate supply schedule AS', and with the aggregate demand
schedule unchanged at the higher level AD', the new equilibrium is at E''. Comparing E' and E'' we note that output now has fallen compared with the first
period and prices have risen further. The increase in wages has been passed on
by firms as an upward shift of the AS schedule, and the resulting price increase

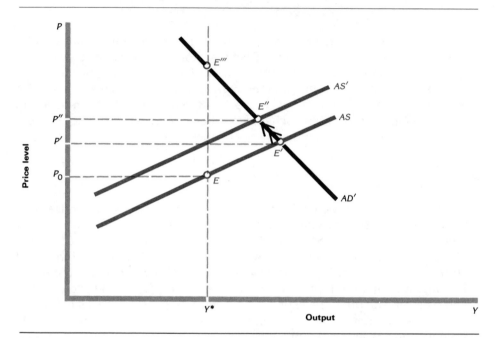

FIGURE 14-10 THE LONGER-TERM EFFECTS OF AN INCREASE IN THE MONEY STOCK. The increase in the money stock led to a short-run equilibrium at E'. But because output is above the full-employment level, wages are rising, and the AS curve is shifting upward. In the next period the AS curve shifts to AS', leading to equilibrium in that period being at E'', with a higher price level than in the previous period, but lower output. The adjustment from E to E' reflects cost pressures that arise in an overemployed economy. Prices continue to rise and output to fall until the economy reaches E''', at which point prices have risen in the same proportion as the money stock and output is back at Y^*.

reduces real balances, raises interest rates, and lowers equilibrium income and spending. Thus, starting in the second period, we enter a phase of the adjustment process in which the initial expansion begins to be reversed. We continue this process by looking at the long-term adjustment.

Long-Term Adjustment

As long as output is above normal, employment is above normal, and therefore wages are rising. Because wages are rising, firms experience cost increases, and these are passed on, at each output level, as an upward shift of the aggregate supply schedule. As long as the short- and medium-term equilibrium positions of the economy (points E', E'', etc.) lie to the right of Y^*, the AS schedule is shifting upward and to the left. As a result, ouput will be declining toward the full-employment level and prices will keep rising. This adjustment is shown in Figure 14-10.

Figure 14-10 shows that the upward-shifting AS schedule gives us a series of equilibrium positions on the AD schedule, starting with E' and moving up toward E'''. During the entire adjustment process, output is above the full-employment level, and prices are rising, but there is a long-run equilibrium at E''' in which the economy has returned to full employment.

Once prices have risen in the same proportion as the nominal money stock, the real money stock M/P is again at the initial level. This happens at E'''. When real balances and therefore interest rates are again at the initial level, so are aggregate demand, output, and employment. In the long run, once wages and prices have had time to adjust fully, the model has the same predictions as the classical case of Chapter 7 and Section 14-1. *The difference is only the adjustment process.* In the classical case a monetary expansion leads immediately to an equiproportionate rise in prices with no real expansion. Here output and prices *both* rise in the short and medium term, and only in the long run do we reach the classical case. In the short run the predictions of our model more closely resemble the Keynesian case of Chapter 7, and the more slowly that wages adjust to changes in employment, the greater the resemblance.

Because the adjustments of wages and prices are in fact slow, the short- and medium-term adjustments are an important aspect of macroeconomics.

We now conclude the chapter by using the aggregate supply-demand apparatus to study the effects of supply shocks.

14-6 SUPPLY SHOCKS

From the 1930s to the late 1960s, it was generally assumed that movements in output and prices in the economy were caused by shifts in the aggregate demand curve — by changes in monetary and fiscal policy (including wars as fiscal expansions) and investment demand. But the macroeconomics story of the 1970s was largely a story of *supply shocks.*

A supply shock is a disturbance to the economy whose first impact is to shift the aggregate supply curve. The two major supply shocks in the 1970s were the increases in the price of oil in 1973–1974 and 1979–1980. The real price of oil (defined as the world crude oil price in U.S. dollars deflated by the U.S. price level) is shown in Figure 14-11. The first OPEC shock, which produced a quadrupling of the real price of oil during 1973 and 1974, depressed the level of economic activity in the major industrial countries. The second OPEC price increase, which doubled the price of oil, intensified inflationary pressures. It also left the price of oil so high that many new sources of supply were developed, the OPEC cartel was weakened and in early 1986 the price of oil fell back to

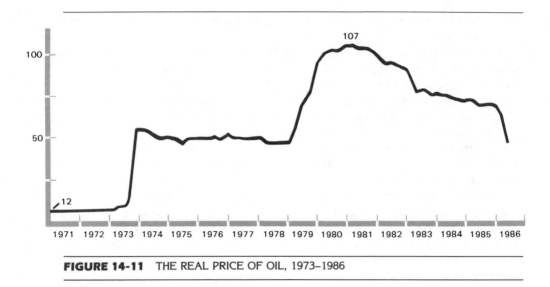

FIGURE 14-11 THE REAL PRICE OF OIL, 1973–1986

the level it had been in 1978. From the point of view of oil consumers that was a favourable oil price shock but it was of course bad news for oil producing regions including western Canada.

We start examining the effects of supply shocks by incorporating materials prices into the aggregate supply curve.

Incorporating Materials Prices in the Analysis

In Equation (6) labour costs (and the markup) were the only determinants of output prices. Materials such as energy or copper or cotton were entirely neglected. But clearly the manufacturing sector does use these inputs whose prices have an impact on the prices of final goods.

We incorporate materials prices in our analysis by modifying the price equation to include not only labour costs and the markup, but also *materials prices*, which we denote by P_m:

$$P = \frac{W(1 + z)}{a} + \theta P_m \qquad (9)$$

In (9) the term θ denotes the material requirement per unit output, and hence θP_m is the component of unit costs that comes from materials inputs.

The wage rate, we recall, increases with the level of output. Hence from equation (9) we still get an upward-sloping supply curve. Further, any increase in the price of materials will increase the price level as of a given W. Thus an increase in P_m shifts the AS curve upward, as in Figure 14-12.

We can alternatively write the price equation in terms of the *relative* or *real* price of materials, which we denote by the lowercase p_m. The relative price is given by

$$p_m = \frac{P_m}{P} \tag{10}$$

Substituting from (10) in (9) gives us a modified equation linking wages and prices:

$$P = \frac{1 + z}{1 - \theta p_m} \frac{W}{a} \qquad 1 > \theta p_m \tag{11}$$

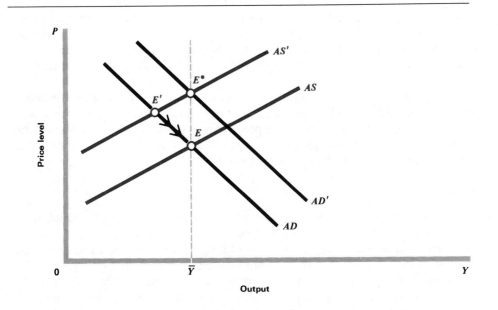

FIGURE 14-12 AN ADVERSE SUPPLY SHOCK. An increase in the real price of oil shifts the aggregate supply schedule upward and to the left, because the cost of production is now higher at each level of output. Because wages do not adjust enough in the short run, the economy moves into an unemployment equilibrium at E'. Prices are higher and output is lower because of the reduction in real balances. Over time, wages decline because of unemployment and the economy returns to the initial equilibrium at E. Accommodating monetary or fiscal policies could shift the AD schedule to AD', reducing the unemployment effects of the supply shock, but increasing its inflationary impact.

Equation (11) shows that for given wages, profit margins, and labour productivity an increase in the real price of commodities will increase prices simply because it raises costs.

An Adverse Supply Shock

An *adverse supply shock* is one that shifts the aggregate supply curve up. Figure 14-12 shows the effects of such a shock. The *AS* curve shifts upward to *AS'*, and the equilibrium of the economy moves from *E* to *E'*. The immediate effect of the supply shock is thus to raise the price level and reduce the level of output. An adverse supply shock is doubly unfortunate: it causes *higher* prices and *lower* output.

There are two points to note about the impact of the supply shock. First, the shock is best thought of as an increase in the price of a raw material used in production. The *AS* curve shifts upward because it now costs firms more to produce each unit of output. Second, we are assuming that the supply shock does not affect the level of potential output, which remains at Y^*.

What happens after the shock has hit? In Figure 14-12, the economy moves, from *E'* back to *E*. The unemployment at *E'* forces wages and thus the price level down. The adjustment is slow because wages are slow to adjust. The adjustment takes place along the *AD* curve, with wages falling until *E* is reached.

At *E* the economy is back at full employment, with the price level the same as it was before the shock. However, the nominal wage rate is lower than it was before the shock, because the unemployment in the meantime has forced the wage down. Thus the *real* wage too is lower than it was before the shock: the adverse supply shock reduces the real wage.

Accommodation of Supply Shocks

Could the unemployment required to bring down the wage rate be avoided by expansionary monetary and fiscal policy?

To answer that question, we look at Figure 14-12. If at the time of the oil price increase, aggregate demand could be increased by enough to move the economy to E^* rather than *E'*, prices would rise to the full extent of the upward shift in the aggregate supply curve. Money wages would remain unchanged, and the economy would have stayed at full employment. Of course, the real wage would be lower, but it must fall in any case.

The monetary and fiscal policies that shift the *AD* curve to *AD'* in Figure 14-12 are known as *accommodating* policies. There has been a disturbance that requires a fall in the real wage. Policy is adjusted to make possible, or accommodate, that fall in the real wage *at the existing nominal wage*. Accommodation involves a tradeoff between the inflationary impact of a supply shock and its recessionary effects. The more accommodation there is, the greater the inflationary impact and the smaller the unemployment impact.

14-7 SUMMARY

This chapter has covered a lot of hard ground. The major point to be established was that output variations along the short-run aggregate supply schedule are accompanied by only moderate price changes. In the short run, the price level varies little with the level of output. Over time, however, wages, costs, and prices will keep rising if output is above normal and keep falling if output is below normal.

We summarize the contents of the chapter as follows:

1. With wages and prices freely flexible, the equilibrium level of employment is determined in the labour market. The labour market is continuously in equilibrium at the full-employment level of employment. Aggregate supply would therefore be the amount of output produced by that amount of labour. Given that the labour market is always in equilibrium, the aggregate supply curve is vertical at the full-employment level of output.

2. The frictions that exist in real-world labour markets as workers enter the labour market and look for jobs, or shift between jobs, mean that there is always some frictional unemployment. The amount of frictional unemployment that exists at the full-employment level of employment is the *natural rate* of unemployment.

3. The labour market does not adjust quickly to disturbances. Rather the adjustment process takes time. The Phillips curve shows that nominal wages change slowly in accordance with the level of employment. Wages rise when employment is high and fall when employment is low.

4. We assume that the productivity of labour is constant over the business cycle, and that prices are based on costs of production. Thus when wages rise because the level of employment is high, prices are increased too.

5. Together the Phillips curve, the assumption that output is proportional to employment, and the proportionality of price to costs imply an upward sloping aggregate supply curve that shifts over time. A shift in the aggregate demand curve increases the price level and output. The increase in output and employment increases wages somewhat in the current period.

6. The full impact of changes in aggregate demand on prices occurs only over the course of time. High levels of employment generate increases in wages that feed into higher prices. As wages adjust, the aggregate supply curve shifts until the economy returns to equilibrium.

7. The aggregate supply curve is derived from the underlying assumptions that wages (and prices) are not adjusted continuously and that they are not all adjusted together. The positive slope of the aggregate supply curve is a result of some wages being adjusted in response to market conditions

and of previously agreed overtime rates coming into effect as employ-ment changes. The slow movement of the supply curve over time is a result of the slow and noncoordinated process by which wages and prices are adjusted.

8. Materials prices, along with wages, are a determinant of costs and prices. Changes in materials prices are passed on as changes in prices and there-fore changes in real wages. Materials price changes have been an important source of aggregate supply shocks.

9. Supply shocks, such as a material price increase, pose a difficult problem for macroeconomic policy. They can be accommodated through an expan-sionary aggregate demand policy with the effect of increased prices but stable output. Alternatively, they can be offset so that prices remain stable because of deflationary aggregate demand policy, but then output falls.

KEY TERMS

Frictionless neoclassical model   Unit labour cost
Frictional unemployment   Markup
Natural rate of unemployment   Sticky wages
Phillips curve   Adverse supply shock
Labour productivity   Accommodation of supply shocks

PROBLEMS

1. In the frictionless neoclassical model, assume that labour becomes more productive, with the labour demand curve shifting upward and to the right.
    (a) What is the effect of this change on the full-employment levels of employment and output?
    (b) What is the effect on the full-employment real wage?
    (c) How would your answers to (a) and (b) be affected if the labour supply curve were vertical?

2. What is the effect of an increase in the productivity of labour on the equilibrium price level in the frictionless neoclassical model? (Recall from Chapter 7 the type of aggregate supply curve implied in this case.)

3. Using Figures 14-9 and 14-10, analyze the effects of a reduction in the money stock on the price level and on output when the aggregate supply curve is positively sloped and wages adjust slowly over time.

4. In problem 3, what happens to the level of real balances as a result of the reduction in the nominal money stock?

5.   Suppose that the productivity of labour rises, that is, that the coefficient *a* in equation (1) increases. What are the short- and long-run impacts on prices, output, and the real wage? Compare your answer here with the answers to problems 1 and 2 above.

6.   Discuss the short-run and long-run adjustments to an increase in government spending using diagrams similar to Figures 14-9 and 14-10.

7.   Suppose the economy is in a recession. How can monetary and fiscal policies speed up the recovery? What would happen in the absence of these policies?

8.   The government increases income taxes. What are the effects on output, prices, and interest rates (a) in the short run and (b) in the long run?

9.   Discuss why wages move only sluggishly.

10.   Use the aggregate supply and demand framework to show the effect of a decline in the real price of materials. Show the effects (a) in the short run and (b) in the long run. .

11.   Suppose a policy could be found to shift the *AS* curve down.
      (a) What are the effects?
      (b) Why do you think there is great interest in such policies? [In Chapter 16 we discuss TIP (tax-based incentive programs) that are intended to shift the *AS* schedule down.]

12.   Suppose that an increase in materials prices is accompanied by a fall in the level of potential output. There is no change in monetary or fiscal policy, and so the *AD* curve does not shift.
      (a) What is the long-run effect of the disturbance on prices and output? Compare the effect with the case in the text where potential output does not fall.
      (b) Assume the upward shift of the *AS* schedule leads initially to a decline in output below the new potential level. Then show the adjustment process by which output and prices reach the new long-run equilibrium.

APPENDIX: THE NEOCLASSICAL MODEL OF THE LABOUR MARKET

The frictionless classical model is an idealized case where wages and prices are *fully* flexible, where there are no costs either to workers in finding jobs or to firms in increasing or reducing their labour force, and where firms behave competitively and expect to sell all they produce at prevailing prices. That case both serves as a benchmark for the discussion of more realistic cases and also allows us to introduce such useful concepts as the production function and the demand for labour. Throughout, we assume that labour is the only *variable* factor of production in the short run and that the capital stock is given.

The Production Function

A production function provides a relation between the quantity of factor inputs, such as the amount of labour used, and the maximum quantity of output that can be produced using those inputs. The relation reflects only technical efficiency. In equation (A1) we write the production function

$$Y = F(N, \ldots) \qquad (A1)$$

where Y denotes real output, N is labour input, and the dots denote other cooperating factors (capital, for example) that are in short-run fixed supply. The production function is shown in Figure 14A1. The production function exhibits

FIGURE 14-A1   THE PRODUCTION FUNCTION AND THE MARGINAL PRODUCT OF LABOUR. The production function links the amount of output produced to the level of labour input, given other factors of production such as capital. The schedule shows diminishing returns. Successive increases in labour yield less and less extra output. The marginal product of labour is shown by the slope of the production function, $\Delta Y/\Delta N$, that is, the increase in output per unit increase in employment. The flattening of the slope shows that the marginal product of labour is declining.

diminishing returns to labour, which means that the increase in output resulting from the employment of one more unit of labour declines as the amount of labour used increases.

Diminishing returns are shown in the production function by the fact that it is not a straight line through the origin (constant returns) or an upward-curling line (increasing returns). Diminishing returns are explained by the fact that as employment increases and other inputs remain constant, each labourer on the job has fewer machines with which to work and therefore becomes less productive. Thus, increases in the amount of labour progressively reduce the addition to output that further employment can bring. An increase in the labour force will always raise output, but progressively less so as employment expands. The marginal contribution of increased employment is indicated by the slope of the production function, $\Delta Y/\Delta N$. It is readily seen that the slope flattens out as we increase employment, thus showing that increasing employment makes a diminishing, but still positive, contribution to output.

Labour Demand

From the production function we proceed to the demand for labour. We are asking how much labour a firm would want to hire. The rule of thumb is to hire additional labour and expand production as long as doing so increases profits. A firm will hire additional workers as long as they will bring in more in revenue than they cost in wages.

The contribution to output of additional labour is called the *marginal product of labour*. It is equal, in Figure 14A1, to the slope of the production function. The marginal product, as we have seen, is both positive — additional labour is productive — and diminishing, which means that additional employment becomes progressively less productive. *A firm will employ additional labour as long as the marginal product of labour, MPN for short, exceeds the cost of additional labour.* The cost of additional labour is given by the real wage, that is, the nominal wage divided by the price level. The real wage measures the amount of real output the firm has to pay each worker. Since hiring one more worker results in an output increase of *MPN* and a cost to the firm of the real wage, firms will hire additional labour if the *MPN* exceeds the real wage. This point is formalized in Figure 14A2, which looks at the labour market.

The downward-sloping schedule in Figure 14A2 is the demand for labour schedule, which is the *MPN* schedule; firms hire labour up to the point at which the *MPN* is equal to the real wage. The *MPN* schedule shows the contribution to output of additional employment. If follows from our reasoning that the *MPN* is positive but that additional employment reduces it, so that the *MPN* schedule is negatively sloped.

Now consider a firm that currently employs a labour force, N_1, and assume the real wage is $(W/P)_0$, where W is the money wage and P the price of output. At an employment level N_1 in Figure 14A2, the firm is clearly employing too

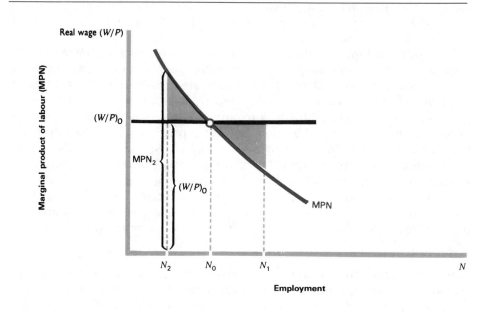

FIGURE 14-A2　THE OPTIMAL EMPLOYMENT CHOICE FOR A GIVEN REAL WAGE. The marginal product of labour *MPN* is a declining function of the level of employment because of diminishing returns. Given a real wage $(W/P)_0$, the optimal employment choice is N_0. At N_1 the marginal product of labour is less than the real wage, so that the firm would save by reducing employment. Conversely, at N_2 the marginal product exceeds the real wage, so that the firm would gain by hiring an additional worker.

much labour since the real wage exceeds the *MPN* at that level of employment. What would happen if the firm should reduce employment by one unit? The reduction in employment would decrease output by the *MPN*, and therefore reduce revenue to the firm. On the other side of the calculation, we have the reduction in the wage bill. Per unit reduction in employment, the wage bill would fall at the rate of the real wage $(W/P)_0$. The net benefit of a reduction in the employment level is thus equal to the vertical excess of the real wage over the *MPN* in Figure 14-A2. It is apparent that at the level of employment N_1, the excess is quite sizable, and it pays the firm to reduce the employment level. Indeed, it pays to reduce employment until the firm gets to point N_0. Only at that point does the cost of additional labour — the real wage — exactly balance the benefit in the form of increased output.

The same argument applies to the employment level N_2. Here employment is insufficient because the contribution to output of additional employment, MPN_2, exceeds the cost of additional employment, and it therefore pays to expand the level of employment. It is readily seen that with a real wage $(W/P)^0$, the firm's profits are maximized when employment is N_0. In general, given *any* real wage, the firm's demand for labour is shown by the *MPN* curve.

The firm's optimal employment position is formalized in equation (A2). At the optimal employment level the marginal product of labour (which is a declining function of employment) $MPN(N)$ is equal to the real wage:

$$MPN(N) = \frac{W}{P} \tag{A2}$$

Equilibrium in the Labour Market

We have now developed the relation between output and employment (the production function) and the optimal employment choice for a given real wage that is implied by the demand for labour. It remains to consider the determination of the real wage as part of labour market equilibrium. This process is illustrated in Figure 14-A3.

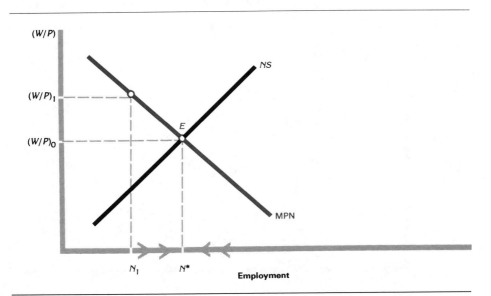

FIGURE 14-A3   EQUILIBRIUM IN THE LABOUR MARKET. The labour supply curve is *NS*. The demand for labour is the marginal product schedule *MPN*. Labour market equilibrium obtains at a real wage $(W/P)_0$. At that real wage the demand for labour equals the quantity of labour supplied. At a lower real wage there is an excess demand for labour; at a higher real wage there is an excess supply or unemployment.

We assume that labour supply increases with the real wage (W/P). The labour supply curve, NS, intersects the labour demand curve, MPN, at E. The equilibrium real wage is $(W/P)_0$, and the equilibrium level of employment is N^*.

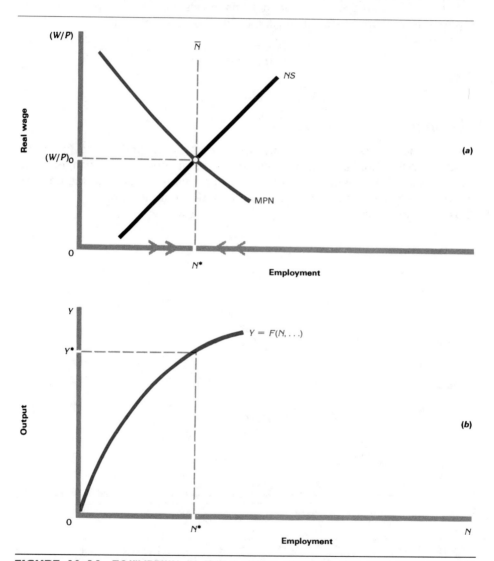

FIGURE 14-A4 EQUILIBRIUM IN THE LABOUR MARKET AND FULL-EMPLOYMENT OUTPUT. Part **(a)** of the diagram repeats the labour market equilibrium of Figure 14-A3. Part **(b)** shows the production function. The equilibrium employment level N^*, also the full-employment level, leads to an output Y^*, which is the full-employment level of output.

How would the labour market get to that equilibrium? Suppose that the real wage fell whenever there was an excess supply of labour and that it rose whenever there was an excess demand. In terms of Figure 14-A3 this would mean that the real wage would decline whenever it was above $(W/P)_0$. At $(W/P)_1$, for example, labour demand is only N_1 and thus falls short of the labour supply. This would put downward pressure on the real wage, cause the real wage to fall, and make it profitable to expand employment. Exactly the reverse argument holds for real wages lower than $(W/P)_0$, where there is an excess demand for labour.

From Figure 14-A3 we see that adjustment of the real wage would bring the labour market into full-employment equilibrium at a real wage $(W/P)_0$ and an employment level equal to N^*. Figure 14-A4 summarizes the complete equilibrium in the labour market and the corresponding level of *full-employment output Y^**, which is the level of output associated with employment equal to the given labour supply.

CHAPTER 15

Inflation and Unemployment

> I know of no example of a country that has cured substantial inflation without
> going through a transitional period of slow growth and unemployment.
>
> Milton Friedman.[1]

From the mid 1960s through the end of the 1970s, the inflation rate exhibited
a rising trend in both Canada and the United States. In late 1979, there was a
sharp change in monetary policy in the U.S. designed to reverse this trend. The
Bank of Canada followed suit and there was a sharp rise in interest rates in both
countries.

The decision was dramatic because there was little disagreement among
economists of widely different macroeconomic persuasions that the move
toward tight money would cause a recession along with a reduction in the
inflation rate.

There was indeed a sharp contraction in 1981 and 1982 with the unemployment rate in Canada rising above 12 percent. The rate of inflation subsequently
came down and, in the second half of the 1980s, the question is whether the
inflationary bias of the sixties and seventies has finally been broken.

In this chapter we address the problem of inflation and unemployment,
extending the analysis of Chapter 14, which focussed on the determinants of
the price level, to examine the inflation rate. We develop the short- and long-
run aggregate supply curves, emphasizing the role of inflationary expectations
in shifting the supply curve, and we extend the aggregate demand curve to take
account of ongoing inflation.

A key question is why is it apparently inevitable that inflation stabilization
should bring about unemployment and recession? The distinction between the

---

[1] *Bright Promises, Dismal Performances* (New York: Harcourt, Brace, Jovanovich, 1983),
p. 202.

short- and long-run aggregate supply curves is essential here. In the short run inflation cannot be reduced without creating a recession; in the long run, though, there is no tradeoff between inflation and unemployment.

We develop the analysis of the determination of output and inflation in Sections 15-1 to 15-6. This material includes the analysis of adjustments to changes in money growth and to fiscal policy changes. The chapter concludes with an important application of the dynamic model, the examination of alternative strategies for reducing inflation.

15-1 INFLATION, EXPECTATIONS, AND THE AGGREGATE SUPPLY CURVE

The aggregate supply curve in Chapter 14 shows the price level at which firms are willing to produce and sell different levels of output. The aggregate supply curve is

$$P = P_{-1}[1 + \lambda(Y - Y^*)] \tag{1}$$

where P is the price level, Y the level of output, and Y^* the full-employment level of output.

Recall now that the aggregate supply curve builds on three foundations:

- The Phillips curve, which shows that wages increase more rapidly the lower the level of unemployment
- The relationship between the unemployment rate and the level of output, with output being higher the lower the unemployment rate
- The assumption of *markup pricing*, that firms' prices are based on labour costs, being higher the higher the wage

The Phillips curve in turn is the result of market pressures on wages. When the unemployment rate is low, firms find it difficult to obtain the labour they demand and accordingly offer higher wages to attract workers. Thus wages rise more rapidly when unemployment is low. When the unemployment rate is high, jobs are difficult to find and firms can fill any vacancies they might have without raising wages — indeed wages may even be falling as workers compete for scarce jobs.

In this chapter we develop the aggregate supply curve in two directions. First, we modify it to take account of *expected inflation:* firms and workers take account of expected increases in the price level when they are fixing wages. Second, we transform the aggregate supply curve into a relationship between output and the *inflation rate* rather than the price level. That way we can use the aggregate supply curve to model ongoing inflation, that is, continuing changes in the price level.

Wage Setting and Expected Inflation

In setting wages, firms and workers react to conditions in the labour market. Thus, when output and employment are high, wages tend to rise fast. When output and employment are low, wages do not rise fast and may even fall. The *wage*-Phillips curve summarizes the link between wage inflation and the output gap. Let $gW = (W - W_{-1})/W_{-1}$ be the rate of wage inflation. Then we can write the wage-Phillips curve as

$$gW = \lambda(Y - Y^*) \tag{2}$$

which states that the rate of wage increase is larger the higher the level of output.

Friedman and Phelps pointed out[2] one major flaw in the wage-Phillips curve, equation (1): it ignores the effects of expected inflation on wage setting. Workers are interested in *real* wages, the amount of goods they can buy with their wages, not *nominal* wages, the dollar value of wages. Firms as well are concerned with the *real* wage, the dollar wage relative to the price at which they can sell their output.

It is clear that workers, who are concerned with the real wage they receive, will want the nominal wage to fully reflect inflation that they expect during the period between the time the wage is fixed and the time the wage is actually paid. In other words, quite independent of the effects of the level of employment on wage bargaining, workers will want compensation for expected inflation.

What about the other side? Why do firms agree to raise wages more rapidly when they expect higher prices? The reason is that they can afford to pay higher nominal wages if they will be able to sell their goods at higher prices. If all prices are rising, each firm can expect to be able to sell its output for a higher price because the prices of competing goods are increasing. Indeed, when wages and prices are rising at the same rate, both firms and workers are in the same position as they would be if there were no inflation and the real wage were constant.

When inflation is expected, the wage-Phillips curve becomes

$$gW = \pi^e + \lambda(Y - Y^*) \tag{3}$$

---

[2] See footnote 4 in Chapter 14. Another flaw that we have already seen in Chapter 14 is that the simple aggregate supply curve omits changes in the prices of factors of production other than labour, such as raw materials. We will leave those factors out here too.

Here π^e is the expected inflation rate. Equation (3) is called the *expectations-augmented* wage-Phillips curve, that is, it is the original Phillips curve augmented or adjusted to take account of expected inflation. At any given level of output, wages rise more the higher the expected rate of inflation: indeed, the assumption is that nominal wages rise 1 percent faster for each extra 1 percent of inflation that is expected.

The Aggregate Supply Curve

The next step is to transform the expectations-augmented wage-Phillips curve into a relationship between the inflation rate and the level of output, which depends on the expected rate of inflation. Once again we assume that firms maintain a constant markup of prices over wages, but that implies that the rate of increase of prices will be equal to the rate of increase in wages. We already denoted the rate of wage increase by gW and now denote the rate of increase of prices or the rate of inflation as $\pi = (P - P_{-1})/P_{-1}$. With this notation the statement that inflation is equal to the rate of wage increase becomes

$$\pi = gW \tag{4}$$

substituting the rate of wage increase equation (3) in (4) yields the *dynamic aggregate supply curve:*

$$\pi = \pi^e + \lambda(Y - Y^*) \tag{5}$$

Equation (5) is one of the two building blocks of a model of the inflation process. It is the *expectations-augmented supply curve*, which we use in the remainder of this chapter to study the behaviour of output and inflation. The fundamental difference from the aggregate supply curve of Chapter 14 is the inclusion of the expected inflation rate. In addition, because equation (5) deals with the inflation rate rather than the price level, it is a convenient form of the supply curve for studying ongoing inflation.

15-2   SHORT- AND LONG-RUN AGGREGATE SUPPLY CURVES

Expectations-augmented aggregate supply curves are shown in Figure 15-1. There is an aggregate supply curve corresponding to each expected rate of inflation. For example, on *SAS* the expected inflation rate is 5 percent, as can be seen from the fact that when $Y = Y^*$, at point A on *SAS*, the inflation rate on the vertical axis is 5 percent. [Note from equation (5) that when $Y = Y^*$, $\pi = \pi^e$.] The short-run aggregate supply curve shows the relationship between

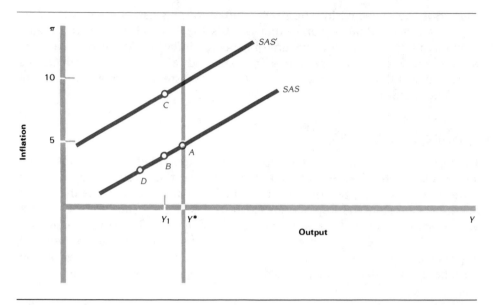

FIGURE 15-1   THE SHORT-RUN AGGREGATE SUPPLY CURVE. The expected inflation rate
is constant on a short-run aggregate supply curve: it is 5 percent on *SAS*, 10 percent on *SAS'*.
Each short-run aggregate supply curve is shown quite flat, reflecting the fact that, in the short
run, it takes a large change in output to generate a given change in inflation.

the inflation rate and the level of output when the expected rate of inflation is
held constant. The curves are called short-run because it is assumed that the
expected rate of inflation is constant (or at least does not change much) in the
short run of a few months or as much as a year.

   Given the expected inflation rate, the short-run aggregate supply curve shows
the inflation rate rising with the level of output: the higher the level of output,
the higher the rate of inflation. This is a reflection of the effect of higher output
levels on the rate of increase of wages and, through higher wages, on the rate
of increase of prices.

   The higher the expected inflation rate, the higher the aggregate supply curve.
Thus on *SAS'*, the expected inflation rate is 10 percent. And for any expected
inflation rate, there is a corresponding short-run aggregate supply curve, parallel to *SAS* and *SAS'*.

   On each short-run aggregate supply curve there is a tradeoff between inflation and output. To reduce the inflation rate it is necessary to reduce the level
of output, producing a recession, forcing the rate of wage increase down
through unemployment, and thus achieving a lower inflation rate.

   We show the short-run aggregate supply curves in Figure 15-1 as quite flat,
reflecting the evidence that in the short run—up to a year or even two—it takes

a large recession to bring about a substantial reduction in the inflation rate. That was the choice made for example in 1982 and 1983 when the inflation rate was reduced.

Changes in the Expected Inflation Rate

Each aggregate supply curve is drawn for a given expected rate of inflation. As the expected rate of inflation changes, the economy moves from one short-run aggregate supply curve to another. That means that the combination of the level of output and inflation rate that occurs depends on the expected inflation rate. For instance, the level of output of Y_1 in Figure 15-1 would be consistent with a low inflation rate at point B on SAS and a higher inflation rate at point C on SAS'.

If the economy moves from B to C as a result of an increase in expected inflation, we would find inflation rising without any increase in output. Going further, it is possible even for the inflation rate to increase and output to fall as the economy moves from one short-run aggregate supply curve to another. In these cases the usual tradeoff between inflation and output — more inflation produces higher output — totally disappears.

Changes in the expected rate of inflation help explain why the simple Phillips curve relationship seen in Figure 14-5 for 1963–1966 seemed to break down later. Through the end of the 1960s, there was relatively little awareness of inflation, and the economy was basically moving along an SAS curve. When, at the end of the sixties, people began to expect inflation to continue, the short-run aggregate supply curve began to shift, generating higher inflation at each given output level. The Friedman-Phelps analysis thus can explain why the simple Phillips curve of the sixties seemed to break down in the seventies — and recall that their analysis was made before the Phillips curve began to shift.

The conclusion of this section is the most important lesson economists and economic policy makers learned in the last 20 years. *The short-run aggregate supply curve shifts with the expected rate of inflation. The inflation rate corresponding to any given level of output therefore changes over time as the expected inflation rate changes. The higher the expected inflation rate, the higher the inflation rate corresponding to a given level of output.* That is why it is possible for the inflation rate and the unemployment rate to increase together, or for the inflation rate to rise while the level of output falls.

The Vertical Long-Run Aggregate Supply Curve

On each short-run aggregate supply curve, the expected inflation rate is constant and, except at points such as A where $Y = Y^*$, will turn out to be different from the actual inflation rate. For instance, at point D on SAS in Figure 15-1 the expected inflation rate is 5 percent, but the actual inflation rate is only 3 percent.

If the inflation rate remains constant for any long period, firms and workers will expect that rate to continue, and the expected inflation rate will become equal to the actual rate. The assumption is that $\pi = \pi^e$ distinguishes the *long-run* from the short-run aggregate supply curve. The long-run aggregate supply curve describes the relationship between inflation and output when actual and expected inflation are equal.

With the actual and expected inflation rates equal ($\pi = \pi^e$), the aggregate supply curve (5) shows that

$$Y = Y^* \qquad (6)$$

The long-run aggregate supply curve *LAS* in Figure 15-2 is a vertical line, joining points on short-run aggregate supply curves at which the actual and expected inflation rates are equal.

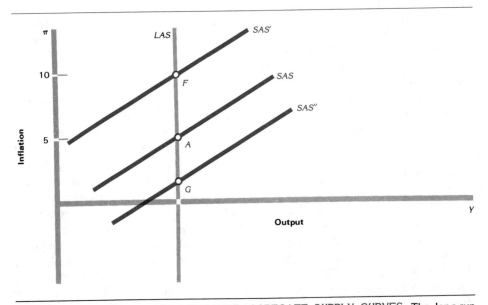

FIGURE 15-2   SHORT- AND LONG-RUN AGGREGATE SUPPLY CURVES. The long-run aggregate supply curve joins points on short-run aggregate supply curves at which expected inflation is equal to actual inflation. It is thus the vertical line *LAS*, at the level of output Y^*.

The meaning of the vertical long-run aggregate supply curve is that *in the long-run the level of output is independent of the inflation rate.* Note the important contrast between the short and the long run: in the short run, with a given expected rate of inflation, higher inflation rates are accompanied by higher output; in the long run, with the expected rate of inflation equal to the actual rate, the level of output is independent of the inflation rate.

15-3 THE ROLE OF EXPECTED INFLATION

Many of the controversies in macroeconomics are connected with the inclusion of expected inflation in the aggregate supply function. We therefore expand the discussion of the expectations-augmented Phillips curve in this section. There are three key questions. First, what exactly is the process by which expected inflation comes to be reflected in wages? Second, is it clearly *expected* inflation rather than compensation for *past* inflation that shifts the short-run aggregate supply curve? And third, what determines expected inflation?

Wage Adjustment

Wages are generally set before the work is done. Further, these are typically nominal, or dollar, wages. In some cases, particularly where there are union contracts, wages will be set for as much as 3 years ahead. In other cases, wages are adjusted once a year in an annual salary review.

It is in the adjustment of these wages that expected inflation makes its way into the wage. Wages will adjust both because prices are higher at the time the contract is negotiated than they were last time the wage was set and because inflation is expected between the time the wage is negotiated and the time it will actually be paid. Thus, as a process of inflation gets under way, wages fixed in each successive period are higher than they would otherwise have been.

Because some wages are preset for 1 or 2 years or even more, it takes time for expectations of inflation to work their way into wage adjustments. For instance, if a new policy that will produce higher inflation comes into effect in 1989, it may take until 1992 before all the wages eventually affected by that new policy are fully adjusted. And indeed, as we described in Chapter 14, if all wages are not adjusted at the same time, it may take much longer for all wages to come into line with a higher inflation rate, because the wage that is set in one firm or union or industry depends on the wages set elsewhere in the economy, not all of which are adjusting to the new conditions simultaneously.

Compensation for Past Inflation or Expected Inflation

We have described the adjustment for inflation in the expectations-augmented Phillips curve or aggregate supply curve as being for expected inflation. Another interpretation is that wage agreements compensate workers not only for expected inflation but also to some extent for past inflation.

The argument here is that when the inflation rate rises, workers who lost out because their real wages were low, want compensation for the losses. Note that this argument implies that compensation would be only for unexpected inflation, or inflation that was not taken into account when the previous contracts were negotiated.

In practice, at low inflation rates, an adjustment for expected inflation is very hard to distinguish from compensation for past inflation. If prices went up 10 percent last year, the firm is quite likely to raise wages this year. That may just be compensation for last year's inflation, or it may be compensation paid in advance for the inflation expected to take place during the coming year. Thus, it is very difficult to determine whether it is expected inflation or recent inflation that is represented by the π^e term in the expectations-augmented aggregate supply curve.

The confusion between whether it is compensation for past inflation or for expected inflation is illustrated by those contracts that contain formal *index* clauses, which adjust wages for inflation. These are called *COLA*, or cost-of-living adjustments, which are contained in many union contracts.[3] The typical COLA clause adjusts the wage once a year, or once every 3 months, by an amount that depends on the rate of inflation since the last adjustment. For instance, if the inflation rate in the last year was 8 percent, the wage rate may go up by 6 percent.

Now, is this compensation for past inflation or for future inflation? Because it is based on the past inflation rate, it looks like compensation for past inflation, but the wage that is to be paid is that for the *coming* year. Thus it may be compensation in advance for inflation in the coming year.

Why does it matter whether wage adjustments for inflation respond to yesterday's actual inflation or tomorrow's expected inflation? The difference is very important because the explanation has different implications for how quickly it takes for the inflation rate to change. If wages for next year reflect last year's inflation and prices are based on wages, as they are, then inflation today will reflect yesterday's inflation and inflation rates will change only gradually. If it is only expected inflation that matters for wage setting, then perhaps a radical change in policy that changes expectations can also change the inflation rate quickly.

Determinants of Expected Inflation

The question of whether it is compensation for past inflation or future inflation that affects wages is further complicated when we consider how people form their expectations of inflation.

Adaptive Expectations

One hypothesis that was used in the fifties and sixties, and that still commands some support, is that expectations are *adaptive*, based on the past behaviour of inflation. Thus under adaptive expectations the rate of inflation expected for next year might be the rate of inflation last year. Under this simplest adaptive expectations assumption, we would have

---

[3] See W.C. Riddell, *Dealing with Inflation and Unemployment in Canada*, Royal Commission Research Studies, Vol. 25, University of Toronto Press, 1986, pp. 133–135.

$$\pi^e = \pi_{-1} \tag{7}$$

Of course, the adaptive expectations assumption could be more complicated, for instance, if the expected inflation rate is the average of the last 3 years' inflation.

Note that if expectations are adaptive, it becomes virtually impossible to tell whether the π^e term in the aggregate supply curve represents expected inflation or compensation for past inflation. If $\pi^e = \pi_{-1}$, there is no difference between past inflation and expected inflation.

Rational Expectations

The rational expectations view is more general, arguing that for the determinants of expected inflation there can be no formula that is independent of the actual behaviour of inflation. The rational expectations hypothesis is the assumption that people base their expectations of inflation (or any other economic variable) on all the information economically available about the future behaviour of that variable.

The rational expectations approach to macroeconomics, associated primarily with the names of Robert Lucas of the University of Chicago and Thomas Sargent of the University of Minnesota, has been extremely influential. As we shall see in Chapter 18, the approach developed by Lucas, Sargent, and others involves much more than just a theory of expectations. For now, though, we concentrate on the expectations part of the theory.

The rational expectations hypothesis implies that people do not make systematic mistakes in forming their expectations. Systematic mistakes—for instance, always underpredicting inflation—are easily spotted. According to the rational expectations hypothesis, people correct such mistakes and change the way they form expectations accordingly. On average, according to the rational expectations hypothesis, expectations are correct because people understand the environment in which they operate. Of course people make mistakes from time to time, but they do not make *systematic* mistakes.

For much of this chapter we work with the simple adaptive expectations assumption (6) that the expected inflation rate is equal to the lagged inflation rate. The aggregate supply curve is thus[4]

$$\pi = \pi_{-1} + \lambda(Y - Y^*) \tag{8}$$

We use the aggregate supply curve (8), together with an aggregate demand curve to be introduced in the next section, to study the dynamic adjustment of

---

[4] Recall that with the assumption $\pi^e = \pi_{-1}$ in (8) we cannot distinguish the view that the π^e term represents expected inflation from the alternative view that it represents compensation for past inflation.

the economy to changes in policy. By way of contrast, we also use the rational expectations assumption and show just how radical are its implications.

15-4 DYNAMIC AGGREGATE DEMAND

The aggregate demand curve in Chapter 14 represents combinations of the *price level* and level of output at which the goods and assets markets are simultaneously in equilibrium. In this chapter, where we are studying continuing inflation, we work with an aggregate demand curve that shows the relationship between the level of output and the *inflation rate*. The dynamic aggregate demand curve shows the relationship between the rate of inflation and the rate of change of aggregate demand.

The dynamic aggregate demand curve used in this chapter, and which is derived in the appendix, is

$$Y = Y_{-1} + \varphi(m - \pi) + \sigma f \qquad (9)$$

In (8), m is the growth rate of the nominal money stock. Thus $(m - \pi)$ is the rate of change of real balances: when m exceeds π, the money stock is increasing faster than prices so real balances (M/P) are increasing. The other term, σf, denotes the impact on the increase of demand of a fiscal expansion.

The curve is most simply understood as saying that the *change* in aggregate demand $(Y - Y_{-1})$ is determined by the growth rate of real balances and by fiscal expansion. The higher the level of real balances, the lower the interest rate and the higher the level of aggregate demand; therefore, the more rapidly are real balances growing, the more rapidly is the interest rate falling, and the more rapidly is aggregate demand increasing. By the same line of argument an *increase* in government spending or a *cut* in taxes means an expansionary fiscal policy and hence an increase in demand over the previous period's level.

In the appendix to this chapter we show that the aggregate demand curve (8) is a simplified version of the aggregate demand curve obtained by using the full *IS-LM* model. The simplification is that we omit the expected rate of inflation that affects aggregate demand.[5] To start, we concentrate on presenting the aggregate demand schedule diagrammatically. For simplicity, we therefore suppress the term relating to fiscal policy changes. We return to fiscal policy changes later in the chapter.

---

[5] The expected rate of inflation enters because investment is affected by the *real* interest rate, whereas the demand for money is affected by the nominal interest rate. Thus when we say above that increases in real balances reduce interest rates, we should, to be more precise, say that while they reduce the nominal interest rate, whether they also reduce the real interest rate depends on how the expected inflation rate is changing.

In Figure 15-3 we plot the dynamic aggregate demand schedule (8), *DAD*. The shape of that schedule is most clearly seen by rewriting equation (9) as[6]

$$\pi = m - \frac{1}{\varphi}(Y - Y_{-1}) \qquad (10)$$

The schedule is drawn for a given growth rate of money and is downward sloping. Given the growth rate of money, a lower rate of inflation implies that real balances are higher and thus the interest rate is lower, and aggregate demand is higher. The negative slope results from this connection between lower inflation, implying higher growth in real balances, and hence higher spending.

The position of the aggregate demand curve depends on the level of output last period. The higher the level of output last period, the higher the inflation rate corresponding to any given level of current output on the aggregate demand curve.

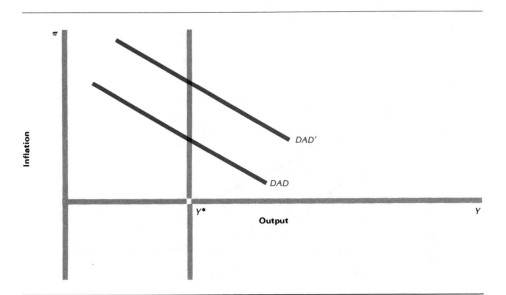

FIGURE 15-3 THE DYNAMIC AGGREGATE DEMAND SCHEDULE. The dynamic aggregate demand curve is downward-sloping and drawn for a given rate of growth of money and lagged output level. The growth rate of money is higher on *DAD'* than on *DAD*.

---

[6] As noted above we are now assuming $f = 0$ so that there is no fiscal policy change in the current period.

A change in the growth rate of money will shift the aggregate demand curve. As we see from equation (10), a change in the growth rate of money shifts the *DAD* curve vertically by precisely the same amount as the growth rate of money changes. Thus the dynamic aggregate demand curve *DAD'* in Figure 15-3 lies above *DAD* by the same distance as the growth rate of money has increased between *DAD* and *DAD'*.

15-5   DETERMINING THE INFLATION RATE AND OUTPUT LEVEL

The inflation rate and level of output are determined by aggregate demand and supply. Figure 15-4 shows the intersection of the upward-sloping aggregate supply curve and the downward-sloping aggregate demand curve at point *E*. The inflation rate this period is π_0, and the level of output is Y_0.

The current rate of inflation and the level of output clearly depend on the positions of the aggregate supply and demand curves. Thus changes in any of the variables that shift the aggregate supply and demand curves will affect the current inflation and output levels.

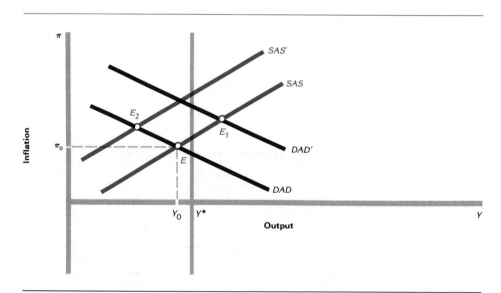

FIGURE 15-4   INFLATION AND OUTPUT IN THE SHORT-RUN. In the short run inflation and output are determined by the intersection of the aggregate supply and demand curves at point *E*. An upward shift of the aggregate demand curve raises both output and inflation. An upward shift of the aggregate supply curve increases the inflation rate while reducing the level of output.

The Inflation Rate and Output in the Short Run

Any upward shift in the aggregate demand curve causes an increase in both the rate of inflation and the level of output, as can be seen in the shift from E to E_1 when the *DAD* curve shifts upward to *DAD'*. Such a shift would be caused by an increase in the growth rate of money. It could also be caused by an increase in government spending or reduction in taxes, though we do not explicitly include those variables in the aggregate demand curve (8).[7] In addition, the position of the aggregate demand curve depends on the level of output last period. The higher the level of output last period (Y_{-1}) the higher the aggregate demand curve.

Given that an increase in the growth rate of money shifts the aggregate demand curve up by exactly the same amount as the growth rate of money rises, we see in Figure 15-4 that an increase in the growth rate of money causes both output and inflation to rise, but that the increase in inflation is less than the increase in the growth rate of money. Thus in the short run a 1 percent increase in money growth produces a less than 1 percent increase in inflation, because some of the effects of the increase in the money stock show up in producing higher output. This is exactly the same conclusion as we reached in Chapter 14, when we showed that in the short run an increase in the money stock causes both the price level and the level of output to increase.

Shifts in the aggregate supply curve also affect the rate of inflation and the level of output. An upward shift of the aggregate supply curve, such as the shift from *SAS* to *SAS'*, moves the equilibrium from E to E_2, raising the inflation rate and reducing the level of output. An increase in the expected rate of inflation would cause an upward shift such as that from *SAS* to *SAS'*. The reason is that the higher expected rate of inflation produces more rapid rises in wages that cause more rapid inflation.

Summarizing, we see that in the short run:

• An increase in the growth rate of money causes higher inflation and higher output, but inflation rises less than the growth rate of money.

• An increase in the expected rate of inflation causes higher inflation and lower output.

We also note, and leave to you to show, that the factors we have omitted here from the aggregate supply and demand curves change the inflation rate and output in the short run:

• A supply shock that shifts the aggregate supply curve upward causes higher inflation and lower output.

---

[7] Recall also that changes in expected inflation will shift the aggregate demand curve.

- An increase in expected inflation shifts the aggregate demand curve upward and to the right.[8] To understand this point, note from the appendix that the analysis in the text has omitted changes in inflationary expectations as another determinant of dynamic aggregate demand.

The Inflation Rate and Output in the Long Run

From the short run, we move to the hypothetical longest run, in which the growth rate of money is and will continue to be constant, in which expectations have adjusted to actual inflation, and in which output and inflation are constant. Such a situation is called a *steady state*, obviously because nothing is changing. Returning to the aggregate demand equation,

$$\pi = m - \frac{1}{\varphi}(Y - Y_{-1}) \tag{10}$$

we recognize that with output constant ($Y = Y_{-1}$), the inflation rate is equal to the growth rate of money. Thus, *in the steady state, the inflation rate is determined solely by the growth rate of money.*

On the aggregate supply side,

$$\pi = \pi^e + \lambda(Y - Y^*) \tag{5}$$

We set $\pi = \pi^e$ and recognize that output is at its potential level Y^*. Thus *in the steady state output is at its full-employment level.*

In the steady state, then, we have very simple relationships: the growth rate of money determines the inflation rate and output is at its potential level.

We want now to consider the real world importance of these steady-state relationships. The first thing to notice is that the economy never reaches a steady state. There are always disturbances affecting aggregate supply and demand: changes in expectations, or in the labour force, or in the prices of other factors of production, or in methods of production on the aggregate supply side; changes in fiscal policy, or in consumer tastes, or in monetary policy on the aggregate demand side. Thus in practice the economy will never

---

[8] When we include inflation in the aggregate demand curve, an increase in expected inflation causes both the aggregate supply and demand curves to rise, certainly increasing the inflation rate, but producing an uncertain effect on output. The net effect on output depends on whether the aggregate demand or supply curve moves up more. Typically the aggregate supply curve would shift up more, implying higher inflation and lower output — which corresponds with the conclusion reached above when we omit expected inflation from the aggregate demand curve.

reach a steady state: as it starts on the route toward a steady state, some shock or disturbance will come along to bump it off that route onto another path.

The steady-state relationships are useful, though, in indicating the long-run average behaviour of the economy. Over long periods, we can expect the economy on average to behave as if the steady-state relationships hold. On average, we expect output to be at its potential level,[9] and we expect the inflation rate to be determined by the growth rate of money. We take up the long-run relationship between inflation and output in more detail in the next chapter.

15-6 DYNAMIC ADJUSTMENT OF OUTPUT AND INFLATION

Many factors drive the inflation rate and the level of output in the short run, whereas in the steady state output is at its full-employment level and inflation is determined by the growth rate of money. In this section we ask how the economy moves toward the long-run equilibrium when a shock or disturbance affects aggregate supply or demand. To be specific, we examine the dynamic effects — that is, the effects that take place over time — of a change in the growth rate of money. We summarize here our two building blocks:

Dynamic aggregate supply:
$$\pi = \pi_{-1} + \lambda(Y - Y^*) \tag{8}$$

Dynamic aggregate demand:
$$\pi = m - \frac{1}{\varphi}(Y - Y_{-1}) \tag{10}$$

Note that we have made the adaptive expectations assumption that expected inflation is equal to last period's inflation rate.

In Figure 15-5, the economy is initially at point E, with output at its potential level Y^* and with inflation equal to the growth rate of money m_0, implying an initial inflation rate $\pi_0 = m_0$. Now suppose the growth rate of money increases, to a new higher level m_1. Refer to the period in which the growth rate of money changes as period 1.

The immediate short-run effect is a shift in aggregate demand from DAD_0 to DAD_1 so that the inflation rate and output both rise, to π_1 and Y_1, respectively. These changes in turn set off further adjustments. On the aggregate supply side, the increase in inflation causes expected inflation to increase, with the curve shifting to SAS_2. The new aggregate supply curve intersects the Y^* line

---

[9] Indeed, some economists define the natural rate of unemployment as the long-run average rate of unemployment. In that case by definition the unemployment rate is on average over long periods equal to the natural rate, to which the level of potential output corresponds.

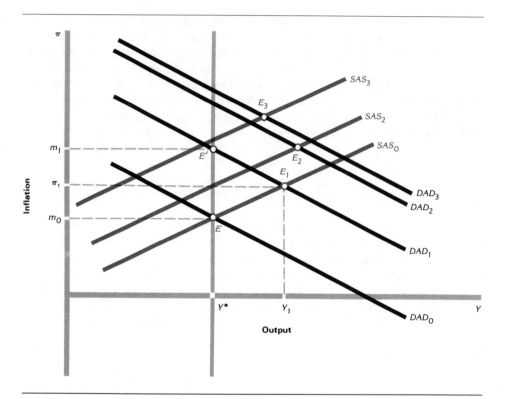

FIGURE 15-5 ADJUSTMENT TO A CHANGE IN THE GROWTH RATE OF MONEY. The increased growth rate of money shifts the aggregate demand curve up, from DAD_0 to DAD_1, raising the inflation rate and output. These changes in turn cause both the supply and demand curves to shift upward in the next period, raising the inflation rate. The process continues until the economy reaches the new steady state.

at the same rate of inflation as occurred in period 1, i.e., at π_1. The aggregate demand curve also shifts upward to DAD_2, because the level of output was higher the previous period.

The period 2 equilibrium is at point E_2. Because both the aggregate supply and aggregate demand curves have shifted upward, the inflation rate in period 2, π_2, is certainly higher than π_1. However, it is not clear whether the level of output in period 2, Y_2, is higher or lower than Y_1. That depends on whether the aggregate demand or supply curve shifted more from period 1 to period 2.[10]

---

[10] If $1 > \lambda\varphi$, then output rises in period 2 relative to period 1. If φ is small, the aggregate demand curve moves up a great deal, thereby tending to cause output in period 2 to be higher than Y_1.

In Figure 15-5 we show output higher in period 2 than in period 1. The process now continues, with the aggregate supply and demand curves moving yet further upward. We show the third-period equilibrium E_3 with a higher inflation rate and lower level of output than in the previous period.

It is not worth following the shifts of the aggregate supply and demand curves during the adjustment process in much further detail. Figure 15-6 shows the pattern of adjustment as the economy moves from E_1, the first-period equilibrium, to the eventual steady-state equilibrium at E'. So as to keep the diagram clear, we do not include the shifting supply and demand curves that underlie the pattern of adjustment shown, and we have, for convenience, smoothed the time path of adjustment. The first few points that we traced in Figure 15-5, E_1, E_2, and E_3, are also shown in Figure 15-6.

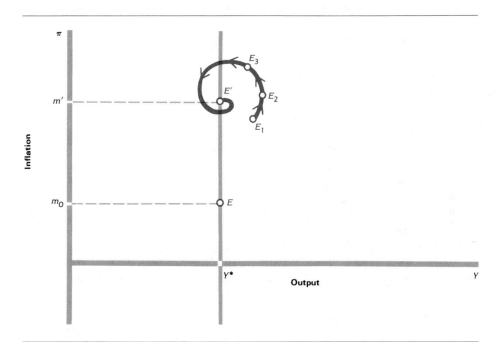

FIGURE 15-6   THE FULL ADJUSTMENT PATH. The full adjustment path moves from E_1 to E', but with fluctuations. During the adjustment process there are periods in which output is falling while inflation is rising.

Stagflation

Two special features of the adjustment process can be seen in Figure 15-6. First, there are times at which output decreases while the inflation rate increases. For instance, between E_2 and E_3 in Figures 15-5 and 15-6, the infla-tion rate increases while output decreases. This inverse relationship between the rate of inflation and output is a result of the shifts of the aggregate supply curve caused by changes in expected inflation.

The inverse relationship between the rate of inflation and output is important, for it often occurs in practice and is widely believed not to be consistent with accepted macroeconomics. This is *stagflation*. Stagflation occurs when infla-tion rises while output is either falling or at least not rising.

If one ignores the role of expected inflation in the Phillips curve, it is easy to conclude that periods in which output and inflation move in opposite directions — equivalently that increases in both inflation and unemployment at the same time — are impossible. Indeed, it is not only changes in expectations, but any supply shock, such as an increase in oil prices, that shifts the aggregate supply curve that can produce stagflation. Nonetheless, during periods of stagflation, such as 1975 and 1981, there are articles in the newspapers that the laws of economics are not working as they should because inflation is high or rising even as output is falling.

Overshooting

The most striking feature of Figure 15-6 is that the economy does not move directly to a new higher inflation rate following the increase in the growth rate of money. Rather, given the adaptive expectations assumption we are making, the level of output at some stages falls below Y^*. Similarly the inflation rate is sometimes above its long-run level m_1. In Figure 15-6 the economy fluctuates around the new long-run equilibrium at E'.

There is one more major lesson from this section. It is that the details of the adjustment process depend on the formation of expectations. Since the shifts in the supply curve are determined by shifting expectations, that point is easy to see in a general way. We make the point more specifically now, though, by replacing the adaptive expectations assumption by rational expectations.

Perfect Foresight Expectations

When there is no uncertainty, the rational expectations assumption is equiva-lent to the assumption of perfect foresight, namely, that firms and individuals correctly predict what will happen when policy changes. In that case we write

$$\pi^e = \pi \tag{11}$$

Under rational expectations, and without uncertainty, we assume that people understand how the economy works and have enough information to figure out what the inflation rate will be.

Substituting the perfect foresight assumption into the aggregate supply curve (5), we obtain

$$Y = Y^* \tag{12}$$

This is a radical result, for it means that, under perfect foresight, the economy is always at potential output. It is as if under rational expectations the long-run results take place in the short run.

How can that be? The underlying assumption of the Phillips curve mechanism that includes expected inflation is that firms and workers are trying to set wages at the level such that there will be full employment. In the Friedman-Phelps version of the Phillips curve, the only reason they might not achieve that is errors in expectations. If by assumption we remove errors in expectations, the economy will then always be at full employment.

Expected and Unexpected Changes in Monetary Policy

The timing of policy actions and the formation of expectations becomes very important under rational expectations. The Friedman-Phelps Phillips curve assumes that wages are set before the period begins. That would mean that wages cannot react to changes in the growth rate of money that are made after wages are set. So the rational expectations assumption would leave open the possibility that an *unexpected* change in monetary policy could affect output.

The logic of rational expectations implies that people base their expectations of inflation on the policies they believe the government is following. Suppose the growth rate of money has been m_0 for a long time. Then we will have under rational expectations $\pi^e = m_0$, as long as m_0 is the expected growth rate of money.

Then if the central bank unexpectedly changes the growth rate of money to m_1, the initial impact will be exactly as in Figure 15-5, with the economy moving to point E_1, because the terms of wage contracts have not yet been changed. However, one period later the adjustment under rational expectations will be very different from that in Figure 15-5. Namely, if everyone believes the central bank has indeed changed the growth rate of money, then the aggregate supply curve will move up by just that amount necessary for the economy to go back immediately to full employment, at Y^*.[11] One period later the economy will be in the steady state with output equal to Y^* and inflation equal to m_1.

---

[11] Using the aggregate supply and demand equations, it can be shown that the period 1 inflation rate under the perfect foresight assumption is given by the expression:

$$\pi_1 = \frac{m_0 + \lambda\phi m_1}{1 + \lambda\varphi}$$

The rational expectations assumption thus implies that monetary policy will not have real effects unless changes in monetary policy are unexpected. This remarkable conclusion is examined further in Chapter 18, where we discuss the rational expectations — equilibrium approach to macroeconomics at length.

At this point we should note that the issue of how π^e gets into the aggregate supply function is clearly crucial. If instead of expected inflation, the π^e term reflects compensation for past inflation, or if it takes a period of years for changed inflation rates to be reflected in labour contracts, then the adjustment pattern seen in Figures 15-5 and 15-6 is more representative of what will happen than is the rapid adjustment that takes place under rational expectations.

Summary

1.   If inflationary expectations are based on last period's inflation rate — or in general are adaptive, based on past inflation — an increase in the growth rate of money increases both the inflation rate and the level of output in the short run. Both the inflation rate and the level of output continue to fluctuate thereafter, tending eventually to move to the long-run equilibrium of the economy.

2.   In the adjustment process to a change in the growth rate of money, there are stages at which inflation and output move in opposite directions. This is because the aggregate supply curve is shifting. Stagflation occurs when output is falling while inflation stays high or rises.

3.   Adjustment patterns are radically different under rational expectations. A fully expected change in the growth rate of money does not affect the level of output at all, and only affects inflation. Even if the change in money growth was not expected, output is affected only until expectations adjust to the new growth rate of money. The question of how expectations translate into wages now becomes crucial to the dynamics. If it takes time for changed expectations to affect wages, then even with rational expectations, the adjustment process to a change in the growth rate of money will be lengthy.

15-7   THE ADJUSTMENT TO A FISCAL EXPANSION

In this section we consider how inflation and output respond to a permanent fiscal expansion. We saw in Chapter 14 that a sustained fiscal expansion leads to a cumulative increase in prices and a decline in the real money stock that raises interest rates until crowding out returns the economy to the initial equilibrium. We now establish exactly the same result in the dynamic framework.

Since we now focus on a fiscal expansion we return to (9) above and rewrite the equation, moving the inflation rate to the left-hand side:

$$\pi = m - \frac{1}{\varphi}(Y - Y_{-1}) + \frac{\sigma}{\varphi}f \qquad (10a)$$

This equation differs from (10) only in that it includes the current fiscal expansion as an extra term on the right-hand side of the equation. Given output and given the growth rate of money, a fiscal expansion ($f > 0$) will increase the rate of inflation or shift the aggregate demand schedule upward and to the left. Conversely, a current fiscal contraction ($f < 0$) shifts the aggregate demand schedule downward and to the left.

Suppose now that we have a given growth rate of money m_0 and that the economy is an initial steady state such that $Y = Y^*$ and $\pi = \pi^e = m$. Now a permanent fiscal expansion takes place. That means in the current period f in (10a) is a positive and for every period after it is zero because government spending now remains constant at the higher level. In Figure 15-7 we show the

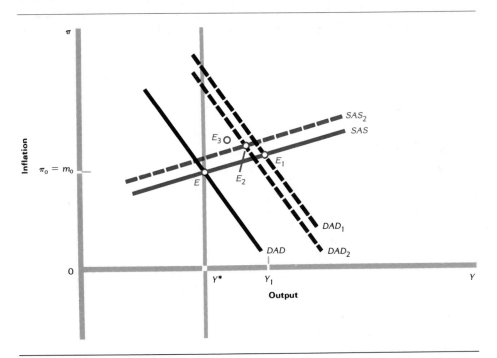

FIGURE 15-7   ADJUSTMENT TO A SUSTAINED FISCAL EXPANSION. Starting from the steady state at E, a fiscal expansion shifts aggregate demand to DAD_1 so that in the short run the economy moves to E_1. In the subsequent adjustment the aggregate demand schedule shifts back while the aggregate supply schedule shifts up and to the left as inflationary expectations increase. The economy thus suffers stagflation along a path shown by points E_2 and E_3.

fiscal expansion as the rightward shift of the aggregate demand schedule from DAD to DAD_1. In the short-run the economy moves to point E_1. Output unambiguously expands and inflation rises.

The subsequent adjustment process can be understood from (10a). Note that in the second period $f = 0$. Hence the aggregate demand schedule will shift downward to DAD_2. Because Y_1 exceeds Y, DAD_2 lies above DAD. On the supply side, using (8) the aggregate supply curve shifts upward to SAS_2. The new equilibrium, in period 2, already involves a return of output toward full employment. Inflation may be higher or lower than in period 1, depending on the relative shifts of the two schedules. This process continues over time, with the demand curve shifting inward and the aggregate supply curve shifting upward and to the left. The economy returns to full employment and then overshoots, as in Figure 15-6.

However, there is an important difference. In this case the growth rate of money is not changed and hence, in the long run, we return to the initial rate of inflation $\pi = m_0$. The typical path of the adjustment to a sustained fiscal expansion would then look like that shown in Figure 15-8. In the transition period inflation will have been higher than the growth rate of money and, as a result, real balances decline, interest rates rise, and real spending declines. The

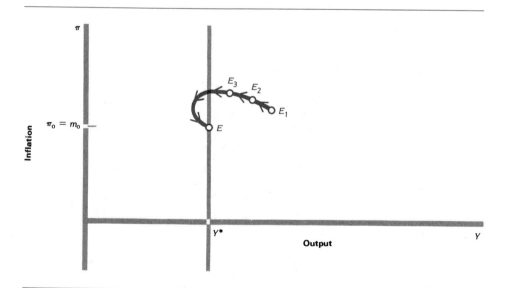

FIGURE 15-8   THE SMOOTHED ADJUSTMENT PATH FOR A SUSTAINED FISCAL EXPANSION. The smoothed adjustment path shows that following an initial expansion to point E_1 inflation rises further, but output falls. In the long run, following a period of unemployment, output returns to full employment Y^* and inflation to the level determined by the rate of money growth m_0.

fact that the economy returns to full-employment output, with government spending higher, means that private demand has been crowded out. Once again we note the stagflation syndrome. After the initial expansion, at point E_1 output is falling, but inflation is increasing. Thus fiscal expansion, just as much as increased monetary growth, cannot *permanently* raise output above normal. Of course, output will be above normal for a time, and that may be enough of a motive, at the right time, for a government to implement a fiscal expansion.

15-8 ALTERNATIVE STRATEGIES TO REDUCE INFLATION

Suppose the inflation rate in the economy is 10 percent, and the government decides to fight high inflation to try to get down to inflation rates of around 2 to 3 percent. The key question for any government contemplating disinflation is how to disinflate as cheaply as possible — that is, with as small a recession as possible. In this section we consider alternative strategies for disinflation. The basic method of disinflation should be clear from the previous section: it is to reduce the growth rate of aggregate demand, shifting the DAD curve downward. In the model we are using, that can be done by cutting back on money growth and, in the short run, by using fiscal policy. In this section we consider only monetary policy.

Gradualism

Figure 15-9 shows the choices. A policy of gradualism (in the left panel) attempts a slow and steady return to low inflation. The gradualist policy in Figure 15-9a begins with a small reduction in the money growth rate that shifts the aggregate demand curve down from DAD to DAD', moving the economy a little way along the short-run aggregate supply curve SAS, from E to E_1. In response to the lower inflation at E_1, the short-run aggregate supply curve shifts downward to SAS'. A further small cut in money growth moves the economy to E_2, the aggregate supply curve shifts down again, and the process continues.

Eventually output returns to its potential level at point E', at a lower inflation rate. There is no massive recession during the adjustment process, although unemployment is above normal throughout.

Cold Turkey

The right panel of Figure 15-9 shows the alternative. *The cold turkey strategy tries to cut the inflation rate fast.* The strategy starts with an immediate sharp cutback in money growth shifting the aggregate demand curve from DAD to DAD', moving the economy from E to E_1. There is a large recession, but because the aggregate supply curve is relatively flat, the reduction in inflation is small to begin with.

By creating a larger fall in the inflation rate than when gradualism is used, the cold turkey strategy causes the short-run supply curve to move down faster

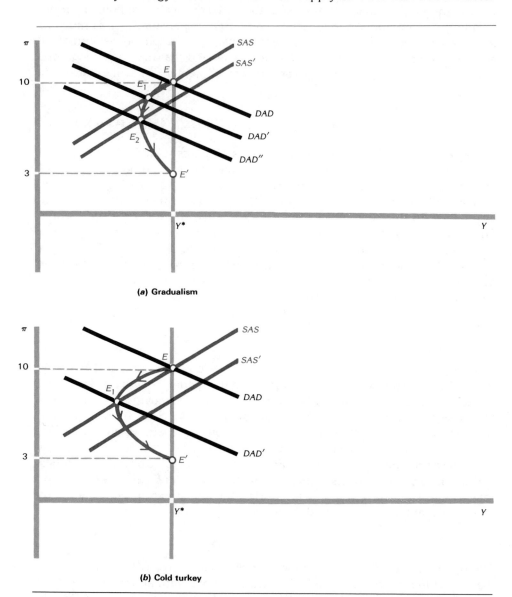

(a) Gradualism

(b) Cold turkey

FIGURE 15-9 ALTERNATIVE DISINFLATION STRATEGIES. In panel **(a)** policy reduces the inflation rate gradually from 10 to 3 percent, seeking to keep output from falling much below the potential level. In panel **(b)**, by contrast, the decision is made to try to end the inflation rapidly, by starting with a large cut in the growth rate of money that produces much lower inflation, at the cost of a large recession.

than it does in Figure 15-9a. The cold turkey strategy keeps up the pressure by holding the rate of money growth low. Eventually the rate of inflation falls enough that output and employment begin to grow again. The economy returns to point E' with full employment and a lower rate of inflation.

Gradualism versus Cold Turkey

Figure 15-10 presents the gradualist and cold turkey strategies in an alternative form. In the gradualist strategy the growth rate of money is initially reduced only slightly, and the economy never strays very far from the natural rate of unemployment, but the inflation rate comes down only slowly. The cold turkey strategy, by contrast, starts with a massive cut in the growth rate of money and a large recession. The recession is much worse than it ever is in the gradualist strategy, but the reduction in inflation is more rapid.

Which strategy should be chosen? Is moderate unemployment with higher inflation preferable to high unemployment with lower inflation? We cannot answer that before discussing the costs of inflation and unemployment in Chapter 16. In 1981–1982 a policy closer to cold turkey than to gradualism was chosen.

Credibility

The cold turkey strategy has one major point in its favour. It is clear in the case of cold turkey that a decisive policy change has been made, and that policy has the firm aim of driving down the inflation rate. The gradualist strategy, which takes a long time to be implemented, is more likely to be abandoned if it seems to be producing more unemployment than expected, or if the policy-making team changes.

Thus people forming their expectations rationally will be more likely to believe policy has changed under the cold turkey strategy than under gradualism. A belief that policy has changed will by itself drive down the expected rate of inflation and for that reason cause the short-run Phillips curve to shift down. A credible policy is one that the public believes will be kept up and succeed. The cold turkey policy gets a *credibility bonus* that gradualism does not.

Credibility and Rapid Deflation

Throughout the period of deflation, starting with the U.S. change in policy in October 1979, there has been strong emphasis on the credibility of policy. Some proponents of rational expectations even believed that if policy could only be made credible, it would be possible to disinflate practically without causing any recession at all.

The argument went like this. The expectations-augmented aggregate supply curve, equation (5), is

$$\pi = \pi^e + \lambda(Y - Y^*) \tag{5}$$

If policy is credible, people immediately adjust their expectations of inflation to the new policy, with its lower rate of growth of money. Thus the short-run aggregate supply curve will move down immediately when the new policy is announced. Accordingly, it is possible to move immediately from point *E* in Figure 15-9 to *E'*. In brief, the argument is that if policy is credible and if

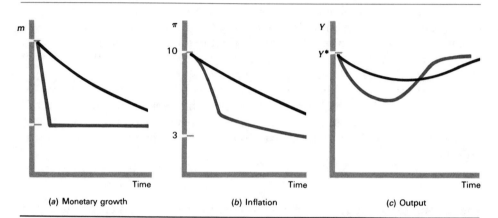

FIGURE 15-10 COLD-TURKEY VERSUS GRADUALISM. This is an alternative way of comparing the two strategies. Cold turkey (coloured curves) cuts the growth rate of money sharply, producing a massive but shorter recession. The gradualist strategy (black curves) produces much less unemployment, but also a much less rapid reduction in the inflation rate.

expectations are rational, the economy can move to a new long-run equilibrium immediately when there is a change in policy.

The experience of the United States and Canada in the early 1980s and even more, the experience of Britain in the same period when the Thatcher government was pursuing a resolute anti-inflationary policy that led to a 13 percent unemployment rate, casts doubt on this optimistic scenario. The reason the extreme credibility — rational expectations argument does not work is that it is not enough for people to believe a new policy will reduce the inflation rate. The expectations must also be incorporated into wage and other long-term contracts. The economy at any time has an overhang of past contracts, embodying past expectations, and it takes time for those to be renegotiated. Thus a rapid return to lower inflation in economies experiencing inflation rates in the 10 to 20 percent range is unlikely.

It is easiest to change the inflation rate when there are no long-term contracts in the economy. There will be few contracts of that kind if inflation is high and variable, for instance in a hyperinflation. Under such conditions no one will want to sign agreements in nominal terms because they will be gambling too much on the future behaviour of the price level. Long-term contracts disappear, and wages and prices are frequently reset. A credible policy will have rapid effects, but such rapid success cannot be expected in an economy where the structure of contracts has not yet been destroyed by extreme inflation.

It remains true, though, that whatever the structure of contracts, the more credible a policy that aims to disinflate the economy is, the more successful that policy will be.[12]

15-9 SUMMARY

1. The aggregate supply and demand curves introduced in this chapter differ from those of Chapter 14 by showing the relationship between output and the inflation rate rather than output and the price level.

2. The aggregate supply curve is modified further to include expected inflation. Wages increase more rapidly when inflation is expected, thus shifting the aggregate supply curve upward. Expected inflation enters prices through wages, which are changed as new wage terms are set. Thus the process through which a change in the expected inflation rate works its way into the aggregate supply curve may be quite slow.

3. The short-run aggregate supply curve, with constant expected rate of inflation, is positively sloped, and quite flat, because in the short run changes in output do not cause large changes in prices. In the short run there is a tradeoff between inflation and output. The long-run aggregate supply curve, with the actual and expected inflation rates equal, is vertical: there is no long-run tradeoff between inflation and output.

4. Under adaptive expectations, expected inflation is based on the recent behaviour of the inflation rate. For most of the chapter we make the particular adaptive expectations assumption that the expected inflation rate is equal to last period's inflation rate. Under rational expectations, there is

---

[12] The credibility issue is treated in several interesting papers in "Anti-inflation Policies and the Problem of Credibility," *American Economic Review* (Papers and Proceedings), May 1982.

no simple formula for determining expectations. Rather, people are assumed to form expectations using all the information that is available about the determinants of the inflation rate. Whereas under adaptive expectations a change in policy would not affect expectations until the actual inflation rate is affected; under rational expectations people knowing that policy will change will adjust their expectations immediately.

5. The dynamic aggregate demand curve is a negatively sloped relationship between the inflation rate and the level of output. Its position is determined by the growth rate of money, and by last period's level of output. The basic relationship follows from the link between aggregate demand and real balances: the more rapidly are real balances growing, the more rapidly is aggregate demand increasing. The dynamic aggregate demand curve is also shifted by changes in the aggregate demand curve and by fiscal policy changes.

6. The inflation rate and level of output are determined by the intersection of the aggregate supply and demand curves. In the short run changes in the growth rate of money affect both output and inflation. In the long run a change in the growth rate of money affects only the inflation rate.

7. During the adjustment process to a change in the growth rate of money, assuming adaptive expectations, there are periods of stagflation during which inflation is increasing while output falls. Typically, there is also overshooting of the new inflation rate, in the sense that on average during the adjustment process the increase in the inflation rate exceeds the increase in the growth rate of money.

8. The adjustment pattern is much more rapid under rational expectations. If the change in the growth rate of money is anticipated, then only the inflation rate changes when the money growth rate changes. If the change in monetary policy is unexpected, it does affect both the level of output and the inflation rate in the short run, but output returns to its potential level as soon as the new policy is understood.

9. There are two basic strategies to reduce the inflation rate. The gradualist strategy aims to bring the inflation rate down slowly, thereby avoiding any large recession. The cold turkey strategy cuts the growth rate of money by a large amount up front, thereby trying to reduce inflation fast at the cost of a larger recession. The cold turkey strategy may gain from a credibility bonus in that the government reduces expected inflation more rapidly by demonstrating its willingness to pay the price of disinflation.

KEY TERMS

Expectations-augmented aggregate
   supply curve
Short-run aggregate supply curve
Long-run aggregate supply curve
Adaptive expectations
Rational expectations

Stagflation
Overshooting
Gradualism
Cold turkey
Credibility

PROBLEMS

1. Explain why the expected rate of inflation affects the position of the expectations-augmented aggregate supply curve.

2. (a) Define the long-run aggregate supply curve.
   (b) Explain why the expectations-augmented long-run supply curve is vertical.
   (c) Does the economy ever reach the long run?

3. In Figures 15-5 and 15-6 we show how the economy reaches a higher rate of inflation. Starting at a steady state with 10 percent inflation, show how inflation would shift back to 4 percent if the growth rate of money were reduced immediately to 4 percent.

4. Consider the adjustment to a *transitory* fiscal expansion. For one period only government spending increases. In the next period it falls back to the initial level. Use (8) and (10a) to trace the adjustment path of inflation and of output. (*Note:* This is different from the analysis of Section 15-7. Here we have $f > 0$ in period 1 and $f < 0$ in period 2.)

5. Using the assumptions $\pi^e = \pi_{-1}$, $\lambda = 0.4$, and $\phi = 0.5$, and starting from a steady state with money growth equal to the inflation rate equal to 4 percent, calculate the inflation rate and output in the first three periods following an increase in the growth rate of money to 8 percent.

6. Suppose that in problem 5, expectations are rational instead of adaptive:
   (a) Suppose the change in money growth was announced before it happens, and everyone believes it will take place. What happens to inflation and output?
   (b) Suppose that money growth is unexpectedly increased from 4 percent to 8 percent in period 1, but that people believe from period 2 on that money growth will be 8 percent. Calculate the inflation rate in period 1 and in subsequent periods.

7. Consider an economy that experiences an adverse supply shock. We can model this by introducing in (8) a one-time shock which we denote by x:

$$\pi = \pi_{-1} + \lambda(Y - Y^*) + x$$

The term x is positive during the supply shock. Show the adjustment process to such a disturbance.

8. The economy finds itself in a recession as a result of an adverse supply shock. Show that both a fiscal expansion or increased monetary growth can speed the return of the economy to full employment.

9. Suppose that a new policy mix of fiscal expansion and a permanent reduction in money growth goes into effect.
    (a) What are the long-run effects on output and inflation?
    (b) How does the fiscal expansion affect the adjustment relative to that you discussed in answering problem 3?

APPENDIX: DYNAMIC AGGREGATE DEMAND

In the text we use the simplified dynamic aggregate demand curve

$$Y = Y_{-1} + \varphi(m - \pi) \tag{A1}$$

In (A1), m is the growth rate of the nominal money stock. In this appendix we derive the dynamic aggregate demand curve carefully from the *IS-LM* model of aggregate demand and show exactly where (A1) simplifies matters.

To derive the aggregate demand curve we return to the goods market equilibrium condition

$$Y = \overline{\alpha}(\overline{A} - br) \tag{A2}$$

where $\overline{A}$ denotes autonomous spending, $\overline{\alpha}$ is the multiplier, and r denotes the *real* rate of interest. Recall that investment demand is determined by the *real* and not the nominal interest rate.

Recognizing that the real interest rate is equal to the nominal interest rate i minus the expected rate of inflation, we rewrite (A2) as

$$Y = \overline{\alpha}(\overline{A} - bi + b\pi^e) \tag{A3}$$

In this form we recognize that goods market equilibrium depends on both the nominal interest rate *and* the expected inflation rate. Given the nominal interest rate, an increase in the expected rate of inflation increases aggregate demand — because it implies a lower real interest rate and larger investment demand.

Now we bring in the asset markets, by rewriting the condition that the supply of real balances is equal to the demand. Putting the interest rate on the left-hand side, as we did in equation (14) of Chapter 4,

$$i = \frac{1}{h}\left(kY - \frac{M}{P}\right) \tag{A4}$$

Substituting (A4) into (A3), we find that the level of output at which both the goods and assets markets are in equilibrium can be written as

$$Y = \bar{\alpha}\left(\bar{A} - \frac{b}{h}\left(kY - \frac{M}{P}\right) + b\pi^e\right)$$

or

$$Y = \gamma\left(\bar{A} + \frac{b}{h}\frac{M}{P} + b\pi^e\right) \tag{A5}$$

where

$$\gamma = \frac{\bar{\alpha}}{1 + (\bar{\alpha}bk/h)}$$

The aggregate demand curve (A5) shows that the *level* of aggregate demand is determined by autonomous demand (including fiscal policy), real balances, and the expected inflation rate. An increase in any of these three factors will increase the level of aggregate demand. Note that the only difference between the aggregate demand curve here and in the previous chapter is that we are now including the expected inflation rate — and that it enters because, given the nominal interest rate, a higher expected rate of inflation means a lower real interest rate.

It follows that the *change* in aggregate demand is determined by *changes* in autonomous demand, real balances, and the expected inflation rate. Assuming that the only change in autonomous demand comes from fiscal policy, we write

$$\Delta Y = \sigma f + \varphi(m - \pi) + \eta(\Delta\pi^e) \tag{A6}$$

where Δ indicates the change in a variable and f is the *change* in fiscal policy.

As described in the text, the term $(m - \pi)$ is the change in real balances, the difference between the growth rate of money and the rate of inflation: when money is growing faster than prices, real balances are increasing, and when money is growing more slowly than prices, real balances are decreasing.

Rewriting (A6) by recognizing that $\Delta Y = Y - Y_{-1}$,

$$Y = Y_{-1} + \sigma f + \varphi(m - \pi) + \eta(\Delta \pi^e) \tag{A7}$$

Equation (A7) is the complete aggregate demand relationship between the level of output and the inflation rate. Given last period's income, expectations, the change in fiscal policy, and the growth rate of money, higher inflation rates imply lower aggregate demand.

In the text we simplify by omitting the change in expected inflation, $\Delta \pi^e$.

CHAPTER

The Tradeoffs Between Inflation and Unemployment

In 1982 and 1983, the Canadian economy experienced the highest unemployment rate since the Great Depression. More than one person in ten in the labour force was unemployed. At the same time there was a sharp decline in the rate of inflation from 12 percent to 5 percent. This experience provided a clear example of the short-run tradeoff between inflation and unemployment. In this chapter we discuss this tradeoff and the cost-benefit analysis that policy makers must bear in mind when designing stabilization policy.

We start with a discussion of unemployment and develop the concept of the natural rate of unemployment. We then consider the costs of unemployment and inflation and conclude the chapter with a discussion of alternative policies for reducing the inflation rate.

16-1 THE ANATOMY OF UNEMPLOYMENT

An unemployed person is defined as one who is out of work and who (1) has either actively looked for work during the previous four weeks, or (2) is waiting to be recalled to a job after having been laid off, or (3) is waited to report to a new job within four weeks.[1]

In 1983, 11.9 percent of the labour force was unemployed. Table 16-1 shows a breakdown by age and sex of the unemployed at that time and four years

---

[1] For a detailed description of the definitions used and the data collection procedures, see notes at the end of Statistics Canada, 71–001.

TABLE 16-1   UNEMPLOYMENT RATES BY AGE AND SEX

Group	1979	1983	1987
Age 15–24	12.9	19.9	13.7
Men, 25 and over	4.5	9.2	7.0
Women, 25 and over	7.0	9.6	8.4
Total	7.4	11.9	8.9

Source: Statistics Canada, 11-003.

later when the overall rate had dropped to 8.9 percent. Table 16-2 and Figure 16-1 show a breakdown by region.

The tables reveal large differences in unemployment rates among groups. For instance, in 1983, the aggregate unemployment rate was 11.9 percent. For the age group 15–24 the rate was 19.9 percent, while for the group aged 25 and over it was 9.2 percent for men and 9.6 percent for women. The Atlantic provinces had the highest regional rate at 15 percent compared with the lowest rate of 9.7 percent in the prairie provinces. By 1987 unemployment had fallen but the rates for the age group 15–24 and the Atlantic region were still relatively high.

The tables also show the data for 1979 when unemployment was at the lowest level in the last 10 years. The unemployment rates for this year can be interpreted roughly as a measure of structural unemployment.[2] *Structural unemployment* is the unemployment that exists when the economy is at full employment. Structural unemployment corresponds to the *natural rate of*

TABLE 16-2   UNEMPLOYMENT RATES BY REGION

Region	1979	1983	1987
Atlantic provinces	11.6	15.0	14.1
Quebec	9.6	13.9	10.3
Ontario	6.5	10.4	6.1
Prairie provinces	4.3	9.7	8.7
British Columbia	7.6	13.8	12.0

Source: Bank of Canada *Review*.

---

[2] In 1979, the prairie provinces, particularly Alberta, were still in the midst of an oil and gas boom and thus had the lowest unemployment rates. By 1984, with the softening of resource markets, Ontario replaced the prairie provinces as the region with the lowest unemployment rate. Thus there was a shift in the regional distribution of structural unemployment.

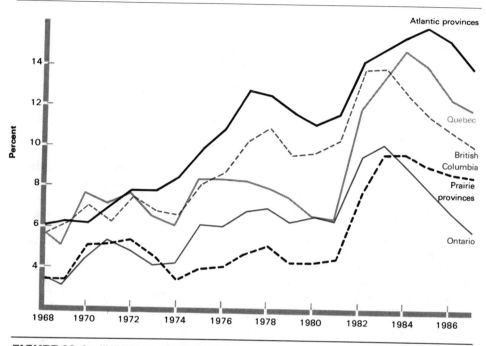

FIGURE 16-1   UNEMPLOYMENT RATES BY REGION

(*Source:* Adapted from *Bank of Canada Review*)

unemployment. Structural unemployment results from the structure of the labour market — from the nature of jobs in the economy and from the labour force participation patterns of workers. We discuss the determinants of structural unemployment in more detail below when we examine the natural rate of unemployment. *Cyclical unemployment* is unemployment in excess of structural unemployment; it occurs when output is below its full-employment level.

Characteristics of Canadian Unemployment

The anatomy of unemployment is built around three central facts of unemployment behaviour:

1.   There are substantial flows of individuals in and out of unemployment each month, and most people who become unemployed in any given month remain unemployed for only a short time.
2.   Much of the unemployment is constituted of people who will be unemployed for quite a long time.
3.   There is considerable variation of unemployment rates across different regions and groups in the labour force.

The first and second facts may seem contradictory. A numerical example should make it clear that there is no necessary contradiction. Suppose that the labour force consists of 100 people, and that five people become unemployed each month. Suppose that four of those people are unemployed for precisely one month, and one person will be unemployed for six months. Suppose also that the economy is in a steady state, so that this situation has repeated itself every month for years.

We ask first how many people are unemployed at any one time, say September 30. There will be five people who became unemployed September 1, one person who became unemployed August 1 (and who has been unemployed for two months), and so on, back to the person who became unemployed April 1, and whose six months of unemployment will end the next day, on October 1. In total, there will be ten people unemployed. So the unemployment rate is 10 percent. Of the ten, six will suffer a six-month spell of unemployment before they again become employed. This is consistent with the second fact, but remember that we started with five people becoming unemployed each month, four of whom remain unemployed for only a month. That is consistent with the first fact, that most people who become unemployed within a given month remain so for only a short time. We shall return to this example later in this section.

The third fact, variation of unemployment rates across different groups or regions in the labour force, can be examined using the relationship between the overall unemployment rate, u, and the unemployment rates, u_i, of groups within the labour force. The overall rate is a weighted average of the unemployment rates of the groups:

$$u = w_1 u_1 + w_2 u_2 + \ldots w_n u_n \tag{1}$$

The weights, w_i, are the fraction of the labour force that falls within the specific group, say, teenagers.

Equation (1) makes it clear that the overall unemployment rate may conceal the dramatic differences in unemployment rates among regions or groups alluded to in Fact 3. For instance, in 1983, the aggregate unemployment rate was 11.9 percent. For the age group 15–24 the rate was 19.9 percent, while for the group aged 25 and over it was 9.4 percent. In terms of Equation (1), we have

$$11.9\% = (0.24)\,19.9\% + (0.76)9.4\%$$

where the shares of the two groups in the labour force are 24 percent and 76 percent respectively.

We now turn to a more detailed examination of the three central facts about the anatomy of unemployment.

Flows In and Out of Unemployment

Figure 16-2 shows how people enter and leave the *unemployment pool*. A person may become unemployed for one of four reasons: (1) The person may be a new entrant into the labour force, looking for work for the first time or else be a reentrant — someone returning to the labour force after not having looked for more than four weeks. (2) A person may leave a job in order to look for other employment and be counted as unemployed while searching. (3) The person may be laid off. A *layoff* means that the worker was not fired but rather, will return to the old job if demand for the firm's product recovers. A firm will typically adjust to a decline in product demand by laying off some labour. A firm may also rotate layoffs among its labour force so that the individual laid-off worker may expect a recall even before product demand has fully recovered. (4) A worker may lose a job to which there is no chance of returning, either because he is fired or because the firm closes down.

These sources of inflow into the pool of unemployment have a counterpart in the outflow from the unemployment pool. There are essentially three ways of moving out of the pool of unemployment. (1) A person may be hired into a new job. (2) Someone laid off may be recalled. (3) An unemployed person may stop looking for a job and thus, by definition, leave the labour force. Such a person may plan to look for a job again soon.

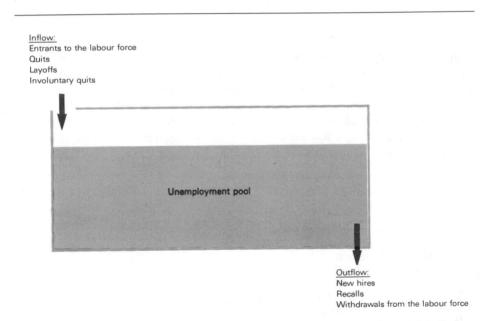

Inflow:
Entrants to the labour force
Quits
Layoffs
Involuntary quits

Unemployment pool

Outflow:
New hires
Recalls
Withdrawals from the labour force

FIGURE 16-2   FLOWS IN AND OUT OF THE UNEMPLOYMENT POOL

Table 16-3 shows the breakdown of the average flow into unemployment in 1987. Notice that a substantial fraction is accounted for by reentrants into the labour force. There is also a substantial flow from the unemployment pool out of the labour force. In June 1988, there were about 550 000 persons not in the labour force who had lost their jobs or had been laid off. This suggests that the distinction between being unemployed and being out of the labour force is not a very sharp one, and that individuals move quite easily in both directions — between being unemployed (meaning essentially that they looked for a job in the last four weeks) and not employed (out of the labour force).

TABLE 16-3   FLOWS INTO UNEMPLOYMENT, 1987

	Number (thousands)	Percent of labour force
Job losers	629	4.7
Job leavers	220	1.7
New entrants	46	0.4
Reentrants	272	2.1
	1 167	8.9

Source: Statistics Canada, 71-001, Dec. 1987.

The data in Table 16-4 illustrates the fact that there are substantial flows of individuals in and out of unemployment. On average in 1985 there were 12 639 000 persons in the labour force and an average of 10.5 percent were unemployed. However, this unemployment rate does not represent a constant group of individuals who were unemployed for the whole year. Of the 14 271 000 individuals who were in the labour force at some time during the year, 25.4 percent experienced a spell of unemployment with a duration that averaged less than a year.

TABLE 16-4   UNEMPLOYMENT RATE AND INCIDENCE OF UNEMPLOYMENT, 1985

Labour force and unemployment, annual average	
Total labour force (thousands)	12 639
Unemployed (thousands)	1 328
Unemployment rate (percent)	10.5
Incidence of unemployment	
In labour force at some time (thousands)	14 271
Unemployed at some time (thousands)	3 625
Incidence (percent)	25.4

Source: Statistics Canada, 71-001, Mar. 1986.

Consideration of the *duration* of spells of unemployment provides an alternative way of looking at flows in and out of unemployment. Given the unemployment rate, the shorter the average spell of unemployment — the time the individual is unemployed — the larger are the flows. For instance, in the example at the beginning of this section we had a 10 percent unemployment rate with five people becoming unemployed each month. We could also have a 10 percent unemployment rate if ten people became unemployed each month and each one remained unemployed for exactly one month. In the earlier example, the average spell is longer than a month, since four out of five spells end in a month, but one out of five lasts six months. (The average spell is thus two months.) The shorter the average duration, the larger the flows of labour through the unemployment pool, given the overall unemployment rate.

Table 16-5 shows the distribution of unemployment by duration in 1985. About one half of those surveyed had been unemployed for less than 14 weeks but nearly one quarter had been unemployed for more than six months. These data establish that despite the substantial flows in and out of unemployment, much of aggregate unemployment is accounted for by people who remain unemployed for a substantial time. Thus, if one believes that unemployment is a more serious problem when it affects only a few people intensely, rather than many people a little, these data suggest that unemployment is a more severe problem than the aggregate unemployment rate indicates.

TABLE 16-5   DURATION OF UNEMPLOYMENT, 1985

Number of weeks	Number (thousands)	Percent
1–4	911	25.1
5–13	1 070	29.5
14–26	796	21.9
27–39	450	12.4
40 and over	399	11.0
	3 625	100.0

Note: Duration here refers to duration up to the end of the week of the survey rather than completed spells of unemployment.
Source: Statistics Canada, 71-001, Mar. 1986.

16-2   THE NATURAL RATE OF UNEMPLOYMENT

The *natural rate of unemployment* is also called the full-employment level of unemployment, or the long-run equilibrium level of unemployment, or the structural unemployment rate. In this section, we discuss the determinants of the natural rate of unemployment and then examine estimates of changes in the natural rate since the fifties.

Figure 16-2 points to the factors causing the unemployment rate to change. Increases in the rate of entry to the labour force, or quits, or layoffs, or other job losses cause the unemployment rate to rise. Increases in hiring, or recalls, or withdrawals from the labour force, cause the unemployment rate to fall. Each of these factors is in part determined by economic variables, such as the level of aggregate demand and the actual and expected real wage rate. When aggregate demand rises (at a given real wage), firms increase their hiring. When aggregate demand falls, firms lay off workers. Thus there is an immediate link between the factors emphasized in Figure 16-2 and aggregate demand. However, it should be noted that the relationship between aggregate demand and the variables affecting the rate of unemployment is not unambiguous. For instance, an increase in the demand for labour increases quits at the same time as it reduces layoffs. A person thinking of leaving one job to search for another would be more likely to quit when the job market is good and demand is high than when there is heavy unemployment and the prospects of finding a good job quickly are low.

When the unemployment rate is constant, flows in and out of unemployment just balance each other. These flows can match at any level of unemployment. The *natural rate of unemployment*, however, is that rate of unemployment at which flows in and out of unemployment just balance,[3] *and* at which expectations of firms and workers as to the behaviour of prices and wages are correct.

The determinants of the natural rate of unemployment can be thought of in terms of the duration and frequency of unemployment. The *duration* of unemployment is the average length of time a person remains unemployed. The duration depends on (1) the organization of the labour market, in regard to the presence or absence of employment agencies, youth employment services, etc.; (2) the demographic makeup of the labour force; (3) the ability and desire of the unemployed to keep looking for a better job; and (4) the availability and types of jobs. If all jobs are the same, an unemployed person will take the first one offered. If some jobs are better than others, it is worthwhile searching and waiting for a good one. If it is very expensive to remain unemployed, say, because there are no unemployment benefits, an unemployed person is more likely to accept a job offer than to continue looking for a better one. If unemployment benefits are high, then it may be worthwhile for the unemployed

---

[3] We should recognize that when the labour force is growing and the unemployment rate is constant, the pool of unemployed grows over time. For example, with a labour force of 8 million and 5 percent unemployment, total unemployment is 400 thousand people. With a labour force of 10 million and 4.5 percent unemployment, there are 450 thousand unemployed, and the unemployment pool has grown by 50 thousand people.

person to continue looking for a better job rather than to accept a poor job when one is offered.

The behaviour of workers who have been laid off is also important when considering the duration of unemployment. Typically, a worker who has been laid off returns to the original job and does not search for another job. The reason is quite simple: once a worker, say, has been with a firm for a long time, he or she has special expertise in the way that firm works which makes the worker valuable to that firm but is not of great benefit to another employer. In addition, he or she may have built up seniority rights, including a pension. That means that such an individual could not expect to find as good a job if he or she searched for a new one. The best course of action may be to wait to be recalled.

Frequency of Unemployment

The *frequency of unemployment* is the average number of times, per period, that workers become unemployed. There are two basic determinants of the frequency of unemployment. The first is the variability of the demand for labour across different firms in the economy. The second determinant is the rate at which new workers enter the labour force: The more rapidly new workers enter the labour force the faster the growth rate of the labour force and the higher the natural rate of unemployment. Even when aggregate demand is constant, some firms are growing and some are shrinking. The shrinking firms lose labour and the growing firms hire more labour. The greater this variability of the demand for labour across different firms, the higher the unemployment rate. Further, the variability of aggregate demand itself will affect the variability of the demand for labour.

The four factors affecting duration and the two factors affecting frequency of unemployment are the basic determinants of the natural rate of unemployment.

You should note that the factors determining the level of the natural rate of unemployment are not immutable. The structure of the labour market and the labour force can change. The willingness of workers to remain unemployed while looking for, or waiting for, a new job can change. The variability of the demand for labour by different firms can shift. As Edmund Phelps has noted, the natural rate is not "an intertemporal constant, something like the speed of light, independent of everything under the sun."[4] Indeed, the natural rate is difficult to measure, and estimates of it have changed over the last few years from about 4 percent in the 1960s to 6 to 7 percent in the eighties.

---

[4] See E. Phelps, "Economic Policy and Unemployment in the Sixties," *Public Interest*, Winter 1974.

Estimates of the Natural Rate of Unemployment

Estimates of the natural rate of unemployment typically try to adjust for changes in the composition of the labour force, and perhaps for changes in the natural rate of unemployment of the various groups in the labour force. We can write an equation very similar to Equation (1) for the natural rate, $\bar{u}$;

$$\bar{u} = w_1\bar{u}_1 + w_2\bar{u}_2 + \ldots + w_n\bar{u}_n \tag{2}$$

Equation (2) says that the natural rate is the weighted average of the natural rates of unemployment of the subgroups in the labour force.

Figure 16-3 shows the natural rate of unemployment as estimated in a study by P. Fortin and L. Phaneuf, who consider four labour force groups on the basis of age and sex.[5] Table 16-6 shows the changing structure of the labour force as

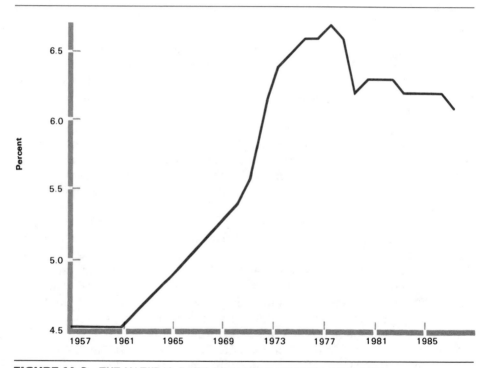

FIGURE 16-3   THE NATURAL RATE OF UNEMPLOYMENT, 1957–1987

(*Source:* See footnote 4.)

[5] See P. Fortin and L. Phaneuf, "Why is the Unemployment Rate So High in Canada?" Paper presented at the meetings of the Canadian Economics Association, May 1979. The estimates for 1979 and 1980 are from F. Reid and D. A. Smith, "The Impact of Demographic Changes on Unemployment," *Canadian Public Policy,* 1981.

reflected by the data for these groups. Over the period 1966 to 1975, the proportion of younger persons in the labour force grew and this is reflected in a rise in the overall natural rate of unemployment since this group has consistently experienced higher unemployment. The proportion of women in the labour force has grown steadily over the past 20 years as a result of growth in the female *participation rate* (the fraction of women who are in the labour force). Since the unemployment rate for females aged 25 and over rose during the 1970s, the increase in the participation rate for this group has contributed to the growth in the overall natural rate.

Unemployment Benefits

The sharp increase in the natural rate of unemployment in 1972 and 1973 reflects the estimated effects of liberalization of the benefits payable to the unemployed under the *Unemployment Insurance Act*. The effect of this program on the *measured* rate of unemployment depends on the replacement ratio, that is the ratio of after-tax income while unemployed to after-tax income while employed. There are three channels of influence.

TABLE 16-6 THE CHANGING STRUCTURE OF THE LABOUR FORCE AND UNEMPLOYMENT, 1966–1987

	Age Group 25 and over Males	Females	Age Group 15–24	Total
Proportion of Labour force				
1966	55.0	20.8	24.2	100.0
1970	52.2	22.4	25.4	100.0
1975	48.2	24.7	27.1	100.0
1980	45.7	27.8	26.5	100.0
1985	45.5	31.9	22.6	100.0
1987	45.3	33.3	21.4	100.0
Participation Rates				
1966	84.9	31.2	56.3	57.3
1970	83.3	34.5	55.9	57.8
1975	81.9	40.0	62.9	61.1
1980	80.7	46.4	67.2	64.1
1985	78.6	51.6	67.4	65.2
1987	77.9	53.7	69.2	66.2
Average unemployment rate				
1966–70	3.3	3.4	7.4	4.3
1971–75	3.9	5.5	10.5	6.0
1976–80	4.7	7.0	13.6	7.7
1981–85	7.9	8.8	17.3	10.4
1986–87	7.3	8.5	14.5	9.3

Source: Statistics Canada, 11-003.

First the presence of unemployment benefits allows longer job search. The higher the replacement ratio, the less urgent the need to take a job. The issue of the effect of unemployment compensation on unemployment rate is a major issue, particularly in Europe. Many observers of the very high levels of European unemployment see a major explanation in the fact that replacement ratios there are so high. Patrick Minford argues:

> The picture presented . . . is a grim one from the point of view of incentives to participate in employment. The replacement ratios are such that, should a person "work the system," incentives to have a job are, on the whole, rather small for a family man.[6]

The second channel through which unemployment benefits raise the *measured* unemployment rate is through *reporting effects*. To collect unemployment benefits people have to be "in the labour force," looking for work even if they do not really want a job. They therefore get counted as unemployed. In the absence of unemployment benefits some people might not be in the labour force, and hence measured unemployment rates would be lower.

The third channel is *employment stability*. With unemployment insurance, the consequences of being in and out of jobs are less severe, and accordingly, workers and firms do not find it as much in their interest to create highly stable employment. Further, the fact that a laid-off worker will not suffer a large loss from being unemployed makes it more attractive for an employer to lay off workers temporarily than to attempt to keep them on the job.[7]

There seems to be little doubt that unemployment compensation does add to the natural rate of unemployment. This does not imply, though, that unemployment compensation should be abolished. Individuals need time to do some searching if the economy is to allocate people efficiently among jobs. It would not make sense to put a skilled worker in an unskilled job the moment she loses her previous job, just because the worker cannot afford to search. Thus, even from the viewpoint of economic efficiency, zero is not the ideal level of unemployment benefits. Beyond that, society may be willing to give up some efficiency so that the unemployed can maintain a minimal standard of living. What is appropriate is a scheme that will create less incentive for firms to lay

---

[6] See Patrick Minford, *Unemployment, Causes and Cures* (Oxford: Blackwell, 1985), p. 39.

[7] An important issue here concerns *experience rating*. If the unemployment benefit scheme could be designed in such a way that firms that lay off workers end up having to pay the full cost of doing so, then there is no benefit to the firm of using layoffs in the way described in the text. Experience rating is used to some extent in the United States, but it is estimated that 30 percent of all layoffs are the result of imperfect experience rating. See Robert H. Topel, "On Layoffs and Unemployment Insurance," *American Economic Review*, September 1983.

off labour while at the same time ensuring that the unemployed are not exposed to economic distress. This is obviously difficult to carry off.

16-3 THE COSTS OF UNEMPLOYMENT

The costs of unemployment are so obvious that this section might seem superfluous. Society on the whole loses from unemployment because total output is below its potential level. The unemployed suffer as individuals both from their income loss while unemployed, and from the low level of self-esteem that long periods of unemployment cause.[8]

This section provides some estimates of the costs of forgone output resulting from unemployment, and clarifies some of the issues connected with the costs of unemployment and the potential benefits from reducing unemployment. We distinguish between cyclical unemployment, associated with short-run deviations of the unemployment rate from the natural rate and "permanent" or structural unemployment that exists at the natural rate.

Cyclical Unemployment

The fundamental cost of cyclical unemployment is the short-run loss of output. Are there any other costs of unemployment or, for that matter offsetting benefits? It is possible to imagine offsetting benefits. We do not discuss here the benefit arising from a temporary reduction in the inflation rate accompanying a temporary increase in unemployment, but rather, focus on the costs of unemployment taken by itself. A possible offsetting benefit occurs because the unemployed are not working and have more leisure. However, the value that can be placed on that leisure is small. In the first place, much of it is unwanted leisure.

Second, there is a fairly subtle issue that we shall have to explore. If a person were free to set his or her hours of work, he or she would work up to the point at which the individual judged the marginal value of leisure to be equal to the marginal return from working an extra hour. We would then be able to conclude that if the workday were slightly reduced, the overall loss would be extremely small. The reason is that the person acquires extra leisure from working less, at the cost of having less income, but he or she was previously at the point where the marginal value of leisure was equal to the after-tax marginal wage, so that the benefit of the increased leisure almost exactly offsets the private loss of income. However, the net marginal wage is less than the value of the

---

[8] See Robert J. Gordon, "The Welfare Cost of Higher Unemployment," *Brookings Papers on Economic Activity*, 1:1973 (Washington, D.C.: The Brookings Institution, 1973).

marginal product of an employed person to the economy. The major reason is that society taxes the income of the employed person, so that society as a whole takes a share of the marginal product of the employed person. When the employed person in our example stops working, he or she loses only the *net* of tax wage he or she has been receiving, but society also loses the taxes this person has been paying. The unemployed person values leisure at the net of tax wage, and that value is smaller than the value of his or her marginal product for society as a whole. Therefore, the value of increased leisure provides only a partial offset to the cost of cyclical unemployment.

Note that we do not count both the individual's personal loss of income and the foregone output as part of the cost of unemployment. The reason is that the foregone output implicitly includes the individual's own loss of income — it estimates the total loss of output to the economy as a whole as a result of the reduction of employment. That loss could in principle be distributed across different people in the economy in many different ways. For instance, one could imagine that the unemployed person continues to receive benefit payments totalling close to his or her previous income while employed, with the benefit payments financed through taxes on working individuals. In that case, the unemployed person would not suffer an income loss from being unemployed, but society would still lose from the reduction in total output available.

However, the effects of an increase in unemployment are, in fact, borne heavily by the unemployed themselves. There is thus an extra cost to society of unemployment that is very difficult to quantify. The cost arises from the uneven distribution of the burden of unemployment across the population. Unemployment tends to be concentrated among the poor, and that makes the distributional aspect of unemployment a serious matter. It is not one that we can easily quantify, but it should not be overlooked. Further, there are many reports of the adverse psychic effects of unemployment that, again, are not easy to quantify but should not be ignored.[9]

"Structural" Unemployment

The benefits of reducing the natural rate of unemployment are more difficult to estimate than the costs of cyclical unemployment. We cannot use the short-run output-employment relationship since the increase in output associated with cyclical changes in unemployment results in part from the fact that the labour put back to work in the short run is able to use capital that had not been fully utilized when unemployment was high. However, in the long run, which is relevant when considering a reduction in the natural rate of unemployment, it

---

[9] See Harry Maurer, *Not Working* (New York: Holt, Rinehart and Winston, 1979), and Kay L. Schlozman and Sidney Verba, *Injury to Insult* (Cambridge: Harvard University Press, 1979).

would be necessary to invest to provide for the capital with which the newly employed would work.

The available estimates of the social benefits of a reduction in long-run unemployment cannot be narrowed down to very solid numbers. Even more difficult is the estimate of an "optimal" long-run unemployment rate. Here we ask the question whether any — and, if so, how much — unemployment is desirable in the long run. A first guess at the answer to that question is that all unemployment is wasteful, since the unemployed labour could usefully be employed. However, that answer is not right. Those people who are unemployed in order to look for a better job are performing a valuable service not only for themselves. They are also performing a service for society by attempting to put themselves into a position in which they earn the most and are the most valuable.

Because the composition of demand shifts over time, we can expect always to have some firms expanding and some contracting. This is true even with a stable level of aggregate demand. Those who lose their jobs will be unemployed, and they benefit both society and themselves by not taking the very first job that comes along, but rather searching for the optimal employment. Accordingly, we can conclude that some unemployment is a good thing in an economy in which the composition of demand changes over time. It is one thing to recognize this and quite another to pin down the optimal rate of unemployment numerically.

16-4   THE COSTS OF INFLATION

The costs of inflation are much less obvious than those of unemployment. There is no direct loss of output from inflation, as there is from unemployment. In studying the costs of inflation, we again want to distinguish the short run from the long run. In the case of inflation, though, the relevant distinction is between inflation that is *perfectly anticipated* and taken into account in economic transactions, and *imperfectly anticipated*, or unexpected inflation. We start with perfectly anticipated inflation because that case provides a useful bench mark against which to judge unanticipated inflation.

Perfectly Anticipated Inflation

Suppose that an economy has been experiencing a given rate of inflation, say 5 percent, for a long time, and that it is correctly anticipated that the rate of inflation will continue to be 5 percent. In such an economy, all contracts would build in the expected 5 percent inflation. Borrowers and lenders will both know and agree that the dollars in which a loan will be repaid will be worth less than the dollars which are given up by the lender when making the loan. Nominal interest rates would be 5 percent higher than they would be in the absence of inflation. Long-term wage contracts will increase wages at 5 percent per year to take account of the inflation, and then build in whatever changes in real wages are agreed to. Long-term leases will take account of the inflation. In brief, any contracts in which the passage of time is involved will take the inflation into account. Inflation has no real costs in such an economy, except for a minor qualification.

That qualification arises because the interest rate that is paid on money might not adjust to the inflation rate. No interest is paid on currency, that is notes and coin, throughout the world, and no interest is paid on demand deposits in many countries. It is very difficult to pay interest on currency, so that it is likely that the interest rate on currency will continue to be zero, independent of the perfectly anticipated inflation rate. Interest can be, and in some cases is already, paid on demand deposits. Thus it is reasonable to expect that in a fully anticipated inflation, interest would be paid on demand deposits, and the interest rate paid on demand deposits would adjust to the inflation rate. If so, the only cost of perfectly anticipated inflation is that the inflation makes it more costly to hold currency.

The cost to the individual of holding currency is the interest forgone by not holding an interest-bearing asset. When the inflation rate rises, the nominal interest rate rises, the interest lost by holding currency increases, and the cost of holding currency therefore increases. Accordingly, the demand for currency falls. In practice, this means that individuals economize on the use of currency by carrying less in their wallets and making more trips to the bank to cash smaller cheques than they did before. The costs of these trips to the bank are often described as the "shoe-leather" costs of inflation. They are related to the amount by which the demand for currency is reduced by an increase in the anticipated inflation rate, and they are small.

We should add that throughout this discussion, we are assuming inflation rates that are not too high to effectively disrupt the payments system. This disruption was a real problem in some instances of hyperinflation, but it need not concern us here. We are abstracting, too, from the cost of "menu change." This cost arises simply from the fact that with inflation, as opposed to price stability, people have to devote real resources to marking up prices and changing pay telephones and vending machines as well as cash registers. These costs are there, but one cannot get too excited about them. On balance, the costs of fully anticipated inflation are small.

The notion that the costs of fully anticipated inflation are trivial does not square well with the strong aversion to inflation reflected in policy making and politics. The most important reason for that aversion is probably that inflations in Canada have not been steady, and that our inflationary experience is one of imperfectly anticipated inflation, the costs of which are substantially different from those discussed in this section.

There is a further line of argument that explains the public aversion to inflation, even of the fully anticipated, steady kind we are discussing here. The argument is that such a state is not likely to exist, that it is a mirage to believe that policy makers could and would maintain a steady inflation rate at any level other than zero. The argument is that policy makers are reluctant to use restrictive policy to compensate for transitory increases in the inflation rate. Rather than maintain a constant rate of inflation in the face of inflation shocks, the authorities would accommodate these shocks and therefore validate them. Any inflationary shock would add to the inflation rate rather than being compensated by restrictive policy. In this manner inflation, far from being constant, would in fact be rising as policy makers validate any and every disturbance rather than use policy to rigidly enforce the inflation target. Zero inflation, it is argued, is the only target that can be defended without this risk.[10]

Although there are many examples of countries with long inflationary histories, there does not appear to be any tendency for the inflation rate of those countries to increase over time. The argument thus seems weak. However, it is true that the inflation rate has been more stable in countries with low rates of inflation than in countries with inflation rates that are on average higher, perhaps providing a germ of validity to the notion.

Imperfectly Anticipated Inflation

The idyllic scene of full adjustment to inflation painted here does not describe economies that we actually know. Modern economies include a variety of institutional features representing different degrees of adjustment to inflation. Economies with long inflationary histories, such as those of Brazil and Israel, have made substantial adjustments to inflation through the use of indexing. Others in which inflation has been episodic, such as the Canadian economy, have made only small adjustments for inflation.

One of the important effects of inflation is to change the real value of assets fixed in nominal terms. A doubling of the price level, such as Canada experienced in the period from 1977 to 1987, cuts in half the purchasing power of all claims or assets fixed in money terms. Thus, someone who bought a 10-year government bond in 1977 and expected to receive a principal of, say, $100 in constant purchasing power at the 1987 maturity date, actually winds up with a $100 principal that has purchasing power of less than $50 in 1977 dollars. The doubling of the price level has effectively reduced the real value of the asset by one-half. It has transferred wealth from creditors — holders of bonds — to debtors. This effect operates with respect to all assets fixed in nominal terms, in particular, money, bonds, savings accounts, insurance contracts, and some

---

[10] See William J. Fellner, introductory essay in William J. Fellner (ed.), *Contemporary Economic Problems* (Washington, D.C.: American Enterprise Institute, 1973).

pensions. Obviously, it is an extremely important effect since it can certainly wipe out the purchasing power of a lifetime's saving that is supposed to finance retirement consumption.

These facts by themselves seem to explain the public concern over inflation. There appears to be a lot riding on each percentage-point change in the price level. That impression is slightly misleading. Many individuals are both debtors and creditors in nominal assets. Almost everyone has some money, and is thus a creditor in mominal terms. Many own housing, financed through mortgages whose value is fixed in nominal terms. Such individuals benefit from inflation because it reduces the real value of their mortgage. Other individuals have borrowed in nominal terms to buy consumer durables, such as cars, and to that extent have their real indebtedness reduced by inflation.

Table 16-7 shows the estimated impact of inflation on the relative net asset positions of households classified by age and income. Over the period 1969 to 1975, the young gained in relation to the old because they typically had much larger debts. The middle-income groups gained because they typically had assets in the form of real estate financed by mortgage debt. Fewer poor families had the means to buy property or to incur debt, while wealthier families naturally had a larger fraction of their wealth in financial assets.

In addition to the redistribution among households shown in Table 16-7, inflation brings about transfers among the household, corporate and government sectors. However, the gains and losses from these wealth transfers basically cancel out over the economy as a whole. When the government gains from inflation, the private sector may have to pay lower taxes later. When the corporate sector gains from inflation, owners of corporations benefit at the

TABLE 16-7   IMPACT OF INFLATION ON RELATIVE NET ASSET POSITIONS OF HOUSEHOLDS, 1969–1975

Age group in 1969					
Under 25	25–34	35–44	45–54	55–64	65 and over
(Percent)					
21.1	14.5	4.4	−7.2	−10.8	−11.6

Income group			
Less than $4 000	$4 000– 7 999	$8 000– 14 999	$15 000 and over
(Percent)			
−10.8	5.1	10.9	−10.0

Source: Economic Council of Canada, *Thirteenth Annual Review*, p. 22.

expense of others. If we really did not care about the distribution of wealth among individuals, the costs of unanticipated inflation would be negligible. Included in the individuals of the previous sentence are those belonging to different generations, since the current owners of the national debt might be harmed by inflation, to the benefit of future taxpayers.

Inflation redistributes wealth between debtors and creditors because changes in the price level change the purchasing power of assets fixed in money terms. There is room, too, for inflation to affect income positions by changing the distribution of income. A popular line of argument has always been that inflation benefits capitalists or recipients of profit income at the expense of wage earners. Unanticipated inflation, it is argued, means that prices rise faster than wages and therefore allow profits to expand. For Canada in the postwar period, there is no persuasive evidence to this effect. There is evidence that the real return on common stocks, that is the real value of dividends and capital gains on equity, is reduced by unanticipated inflation. Thus, equity holders appear to be adversely affected by unanticipated inflation.[11]

The fact that unanticipated inflation acts mainly to redistribute wealth, the net effects of which redistribution should be close to zero, has led to some questioning of the reasons for public concern over inflation. The gainers, it seems, do not shout as loudly as the losers. Since some of the gainers (future taxpayers) have yet to be born, this is hardly surprising. There is also a notion that the average wage earner is subject to an illusion when both the nominal wage and the price level increase. Wage earners are thought to attribute increases in nominal wages to their own merit rather than to inflation, while the general inflation of prices is seen as causing an unwarranted reduction in the real wage they would otherwise have received. It is hard to know how to test the validity of this argument. Nonetheless, it does appear that the redistributive effects of unanticipated inflation are large, and that, accordingly, some parts of the population could be seriously affected by it.

16-5   STRATEGIES TO DEAL WITH INFLATION

We have seen the costs of unemployment and the problems that arise from inflation. In this section we consider strategies to deal with inflation without incurring unacceptable costs in terms of unemployment. We begin with a discussion of wage indexation and then consider various policy measures to bring down the rate of inflation.

---

[11] See Charles R. Nelson, "Inflation and Rates of Return on Common Stocks," *Journal of Finance*, May 1976. See also Franco Modigliani and Richard Cohn, "Inflation, Rational Valuation and the Market," *Financial Analysts Journal*, March–April 1979, for a controversial view of the reasons why inflation affects the stock market.

BOX 16-1   RESEARCH STUDIES OF THE ROYAL COMMISSION ON THE ECONOMIC UNION AND DEVELOPMENT PROSPECTS FOR CANADA

An overview of the unemployment-inflation tradeoff and policies to deal with inflation are given in W.C. Riddell, *Dealing with Inflation and Unemployment in Canada*, (Vol. 25), University of Toronto Press, 1986.

See also the following studies in W.C. Riddell, *Work and Pay: The Canadian Labour Market*, (Vol. 17), University of Toronto Press, 1985.

W.C. Riddell, "Work and Pay: The Canadian Labour Market: An Overview"
S.F. Kaliski, "Trends, Changes and Imbalances: A Survey of the Canadian Labour Market."

For a discussion of indexation see the following paper in J. Sargent, *Postwar Macroeconomic Developments*, (Vol. 20), University of Toronto Press, 1986.

P. Howitt, "Indexation and the Adjustment to Inflation in Canada."

Indexation of Wages

In Chapter 15 we discussed the role of automatic cost of living adjustment (COLA) provisions in wage contracts. COLA provisions link increases in money wages to increases in the price level. The adjustment may be complete — 100 percent indexation — or only partial. Partial indexation takes one of two forms. There may be a *threshold* or a *cap*. A threshold specifies a minimum increase in the price level before indexation comes into play. This implies that small price increases are not compensated, while larger ones are. A cap puts a limit on the extent to which price increases are compensated, say, 10 percent per year. COLA clauses are designed to allow workers to recover purchasing power lost through price increases.

Why Indexation?

Indexation in some form is a quite common feature of labour markets in many countries. Indexation strikes a balance between the advantages of long-term wage contracts and the interests of workers and firms in not having *real* wages get too far out of line. Bargaining for wages is costly because workers (unions) and the firm have to devote time and effort to arrive at a settlement and often work is disrupted through strikes. It is in the common interest of workers and firms therefore to hold to a minimum the number of times these negotiations take place.

Thus wages are not negotiated once a week or once a month, but rather they are negotiated in the form of 2- or 3-year contracts. However, over the term of these contracts the evolution of prices — consumer prices and the prices at which firms sell their output—is not known with certainty. Therefore real wages paid by firms or received by workers are not known even if money wages are. To remedy this uncertainty, some provision is made to adjust wages for inflation. Broadly, there are two possibilities. One is to index wages to the CPI and in periodic reviews — say quarterly — increase wages by the increase in prices over the period. The other is to schedule periodic, preannounced wage increases based on the expected rate of price increase. If inflation were known with certainty, the two methods would come to the same thing, but since inflation can differ from expectations, there will be discrepancies. Prefixed wage increases may turn out to be high or low relative to actual inflation. On that account indexation on the basis of actual inflation offers greater assurance of stable real wages for workers than do scheduled increases.

Supply Shocks and Indexation

Suppose real material prices increase, and firms pass these cost increases on into higher prices of final goods. Consumer prices will rise, and under a system of 100 percent indexation, wages would rise. This leads to further price and material costs, and wage increases. Indexation here leads to an inflation spiral that would be avoided under a system of prefixed wage increases because then real wages could fall as a consequence of higher material prices.

The example makes it clear that we must distinguish two possibilities in considering the effects of wage indexing, monetary disturbances and real disturbances. In the case of a monetary disturbance (a shift in the *LM* schedule), there is a "pure" inflation disturbance, and firms can afford to pay the same real wages and therefore would not mind 100 percent indexation. In the case of adverse real disturbances, however, real wages must fall, and full indexation is entirely the wrong system because it stands in the way of downward real wage flexibility.

From the two cases it is apparent that neither completely prefixed wage increases nor complete indexation is likely to be optimal. The best arrangement will depend on the relative importance of monetary and real shocks. Countries that had practiced 100 percent indexation — for example, Italy and Brazil — have found in the 1970s that it is difficult to adjust to real shocks and that the indexation leads to a wage-price spiral that pushes up inflation with great speed.

Incomes Policy (or Wage and Price Controls)

In Chapter 15, we considered alternative strategies for bringing down the rate of inflation and concluded that the treatments for the inflation disease were painful. Inflation reduction takes time and involves unemployment because that is what is needed to get the rate of wage change down fast, either by law (wage-price controls) or by persuasion. *Incomes policies* are policies that attempt to reduce the rate of wage and price increases by direct action. Either wages and prices are controlled, or the government tries to persuade labour leaders and business to raise wages and prices more slowly than they otherwise would. Income policies, if successful, shift the short-run aggregate supply curve down.

A wage-price freeze certainly brings the inflation rate down, so why not get rid of inflation that way? The reason is that wages and prices have to change if resources are to be allocated efficiently in the economy. Anti-inflationary policy has to try to reduce the average rate of price increase without interfering with the role of prices in allocating resources. Over a short period, misallocations of resources from frozen wages and prices will be small and not costly, but if wages and prices are kept fixed for a long time, shortages of labour and particular goods will develop. The problem then is to find a way out of controls that does not reignite inflation.

One reason incomes policies have rarely been successful is that they are not combined with appropriate aggregate demand policies.[12] Incomes policies, or wage and price controls aim to move the aggregate supply curve down, thereby reducing the inflation rate. So long as the aggregate demand curve moves down at the same time, the inflation rate will fall and can stay low. However, if there is no accompanying change in the aggregate demand curve, the wage and price controls will only build up inflationary pressures that will eventually explode.

An interesting recent development is the use of wage and price controls as part of a complete package of economic policy measures taken to end extremely high inflation episodes. In 1985 in Argentina and Israel, and in 1986 in Brazil, policy packages were put into effect to reduce the inflation rate from several hundred percent per year to low double-digit per annum figures. In each case the policy measures involved cuts in the budget deficit and measures to control monetary growth. They also involved as central parts of the package controls on wages and prices. All three programs showed early signs of success. Whether they will ultimately succeed remains to be seen, but their initial success does suggest an important potential role for wage and price controls in rapidly ending inflation, *provided, of course, that the accompanying aggregate demand reduction measures are taken.*

Tip

Tax incentive plans (TIP) to reduce the inflation rate encourage workers and firms to keep wage and price increases low by providing tax incentives to do so.[13]

---

[12] For a careful account of wage and price controls see Hugh Rockoff, *Drastic Measures, A History of Wage and Price Controls in the United States* (London: Cambridge University Press, 1984). See, too, Robert Russell, *Can Chronic Inflation be Cured?* E. S. Woodward Lectures, Department of Economics, University of British Columbia, 1982.

[13] The *Brookings Papers on Economic Activity*, 2: 1978, contains several articles and discussions of TIP.

For instance, TIP might set a baseline rate of wage increase of 5 percent. Any firm that pays a higher rate of wage increase to its employees has its taxes increased. Any firm paying a lower rate of wage increase receives a tax break. Or the penalties and rewards might be placed directly on the workers. Any worker receiving an increase in excess of 5 percent would have his or her tax rate increased, and so forth.

The major problem with TIP is that it would be very difficult to administer. The aim is to discourage wage or price increases that are being made only to compensate for inflation. We would not, for instance, want to penalize a worker who has a large wage increase because he or she has worked hard and has been promoted, but how can the law discriminate between these two cases? If the law says anyone who is promoted is not penalized for receiving a rate of wage increase above the baseline rate, firms and workers who find it in their joint interest to raise the wage will do so by promoting people.

Both incomes policies and TIP run into the same difficulty. The difficulty is that relative wages and prices in the economy do have to change if the price mechanism is to work. Policies that operate directly on wages and prices have to try to prevent the overall price level from rising while relative prices are permitted to change. This is either impossible or extremely difficult over any extended period.

In the following chapter, we look at the policy choices that have been made by the policy authorities in Canada and consider the consequences for the Canadian economy.

16-7   SUMMARY

1. The anatomy of unemployment for Canada reveals frequent and short spells of unemployment. Nonetheless, a substantial fraction of unemployment is accounted for by those who are unemployed for quite a long time.

2. There is considerable variation of unemployment rates across different regions and groups in the labour force.

3. The concept of the natural rate of unemployment singles out that part of unemployment which would exist even at full employment. The unemployment arises in part because of a high frequency of job changes. The natural rate of unemployment is hard to conceptualize and even harder to measure. It has recently been estimated to be about 6 to 7 percent compared with 4 percent in the sixties.

4. The cost of unemployment is the psychic and financial distress of the unemployed as well as the loss of output. The loss of output is not compensated by the unemployed enjoying leisure. For one thing, a large part of unemployment is involuntary. For another, the social product of labour exceeds the wage rate because of income taxes.

5. The economy can adjust to perfectly anticipated inflation by moving to a system of indexed contracts and to nominal interest rates that reflect the expected rate of inflation. Thus there are no important costs to perfectly anticipated inflation. The only costs are those of changing price tags periodically and the cost of suboptimal holdings of currency.

6. Imperfectly anticipated inflation has important redistributive effects among sectors. Unanticipated inflation benefits monetary debtors and hurts monetary creditors. The government gains real tax revenue, and the real value of government debt declines.

7. Wage indexation links increases in money wages to increases in the price level. It prevents changes in real wages that would otherwise come about if the actual inflation rate differs from what was anticipated.

8. Alternative policies to reduce inflation include incomes policies (wage-price controls and less formal approaches) and tax incentive plans.

KEY TERMS

Unemployment pool
Duration of unemployment
Natural rate of unemployment
Structural unemployment

Perfectly anticipated inflation
Wage indexation
Tax incentive plans (TIP)

PROBLEMS

1. Discuss strategies whereby the government could reduce unemployment in or among:
    (a) Depressed industries
    (b) Unskilled workers
    (c) Depressed geographical regions
    (d) Teenagers
    Include comments on the *type* of unemployment you would expect in these various groups (that is, relative durations of unemployment spells).

2. Discuss how the following changes would affect the natural or structural rate of unemployment. Comment also on the side effects of these changes.
    (a) Elimination of unions
    (b) Increased participation of women in the labour market
    (c) Larger fluctuations in the *level* of aggregate demand
    (d) An increase in unemployment benefits
    (e) Elimination of minimum wages
    (f) Larger fluctuations in the *composition* of aggregate demand

3. Discuss the differences in unemployment between adults and youths. What does this imply about the types of jobs (on average) the different groups are getting?

4. Some people say that inflation can be reduced in the long run without an increase in unemployment, and so we should reduce inflation to zero. Others say a steady rate of inflation at, say, 6 percent is not so bad, and that should be our goal. Evaluate these two arguments and describe what, in your opinion, are good long-run goals for inflation and unemployment. How would these be achieved?

5. The following information is to be used for calculations of the unemployment rate. There are two major groups, adults and youths. Youths account for 25 percent of the labour force and adults for 75 percent. Adults are divided into men and women. Women account for 40 percent of the adult labour force. The following table shows the unemployment rates for the groups.

Group	Unemployment rate, u
Youths	15%
Adults:	
Men	7%
Women	8.5%

(a) How do the numbers in this table compare (roughly) with the numbers for the Canadian economy?
(b) Calculate the aggregate unemployment rate.
(c) Assume the unemployment rate for youths rises from 15 to 20 percent. What is the effect on female unemployment? (Assume 50 percent of the youths are men.) What is the effect on the aggregate unemployment rate?
(d) Assume the share of women in the adult labour force increases to 45 percent. What is the effect on the unemployment rate? What is the effect on the aggregate unemployment rate?
(e) Relate your answers to methods of estimating the natural rate of unemployment.

6. Use the data in Table 16-6 to calculate what 1975 and 1985 unemployment would have been if each group in 1975 and 1985 had the unemployment rate of the group in 1966. What does the answer tell you?

7. (a) What are the economic costs of inflation? Distinguish between anticipated and unanticipated inflation.
(b) Do you think anything is missing from the list of costs of inflation that economists present? If so, what?

CHAPTER 17

Money, Deficits, and Inflation

In this chapter we concentrate on the role of money growth in generating inflation and influencing interest rates and output. We take up four main topics.
First, we examine the monetarist proposition that inflation is a monetary phenomenon, which means that inflation is entirely, or at least primarily, due to
excessive money growth. Second, we study the linkages among interest rates,
inflation, and money growth. The question is whether increased money growth
raises or lowers interest rates. Third, we look at the links between budget deficits and money growth, and show how inflation can be viewed as a form of
taxation. Finally, we briefly describe hyperinflations and the role of money
growth in them.

We establish a few important, basic results in this chapter. The most important is that really high inflation is indeed primarily a monetary phenomenon in
the sense that inflation could not continue without continued money growth;
but typically in conditions of high inflation there are also high budget deficits
underlying the rapid money growth. Such was the case for instance in the
hyperinflations in 1984–1985 in Argentina, Bolivia, Brazil, or Israel. Similarly
in conditions of high inflation nominal interest rates become very high as
expected inflation becomes incorporated in nominal rates.

The real world application and significance of these results is quite striking
and can be seen in many high inflation countries around the world. However,
when inflation rates are lower, in the single-digit or low-double-digit range, real
disturbances like supply shocks may well be playing a relatively larger role,

and the simple results isolating the role of money become less dominant. Similarly, the role of the deficit in causing money growth becomes less definite: for instance, there was no acceleration in money growth in Canada in the early 1980s despite growing budget deficits.

We start out in Section 17-1 with the linkages between money growth and inflation. This section develops material covered in Chapter 14. Then we discuss evidence on the links between money and inflation, and between inflation and interest rates. In the third section we analyze the relationship between budget deficits and money growth and we conclude with a discussion of hyperinflation.

17-1 MONEY AND INFLATION

In this section we develop Chapter 15's analysis of the dynamics of inflation to show exactly the role played by money growth. Our task is to make sense of the monetarist claim that inflation is always and everywhere a monetary phenomenon.

To obtain a firm understanding of these points a double distinction has to be kept in mind. The first is between the short run and the long run. The second is the distinction between monetary and other disturbances (fiscal, for example, or oil shocks) to the economy.

Monetarists tend to concentrate on the long run and on economies where changes in money growth are the primary disturbances. Not surprisingly they tend to be right, *for this special case*, when they argue that money explains most of what is happening to inflation. However, as one moves away from the long run and from monetary disturbances, toward short-run inflation determination and alternative shocks, it becomes necessary to be much more eclectic. In the short run, disturbances other than changes in the money stock affect inflation and, conversely, changes in the money stock do have real effects. Even if the disturbances are purely monetary it will still generally take a while before they are fully reflected in inflation and only in inflation.

A key point in the distinction between the short run and the long run and in determining the dynamics of inflation is the role of expectations. Increased money growth will have real effects as long as inflationary expectations have not fully adapted. Milton Friedman has put this point as follows:

> Monetarist analysis goes on to say that any changes in the nominal quantity of money that are anticipated in advance will be fully embedded in inflationary and other expectations, but that unanticipated changes in the quantity of money will not be. An unanticipated increase or decrease in the quantity of money tends to affect total nominal spending some six to nine months later in countries like the United States, Japan or Great Britain. The initial effect is primarily on output rather than on prices. Prices tend to be affected only some

18 months to two years later. This does not mean that there is no further effect on real quantities. On the contrary, the delayed impact on prices means an overshooting of output—up or down depending on the initial stimulus—which will then require an overshooting in the opposite direction to allow the price level to reach its appropriate level. As a result the cyclical reaction pattern in both output and prices tend to last for a considerable period — years, not months. . . .[1]

We formalize these ideas by drawing on the model of Chapter 15. While using exactly the same model, we shift the exposition a little to focus on dynamics. Our task is to highlight a number of relationships involving money, interest rates, and inflation.

The Model

The starting point is the aggregate demand equation derived in Chapter 15. Aggregate demand and output will rise whenever real balances are increasing. Conversely, when real balances are falling, so, too, are aggregate demand and output.[2] We write this relation in equation (1) using the notation $\Delta Y = Y - Y_{-1}$, m = growth rate of money, π = inflation rate:

$$\Delta Y = f(m - \pi) \tag{1}$$

Assume now a given growth rate of money, m_0. In Figure 17-1a we show the schedule $\pi = m_0$ along which output is neither rising nor falling. Now we consider how output is changing at different points in Figure 17-1a. For points above the $\pi = m_0$ schedule, inflation exceeds the given growth rate of money. Hence real balances are falling and so, according to equation (1), is output. This is indicated by the arrow showing falling output. Conversely, below the schedule inflation is less than money growth, and hence real balances are increasing, interest rates are falling, and demand and output are growing.

The second relationship is the aggregate supply curve

$$\pi = \pi^e + \lambda(Y - Y^*) \tag{2a}$$

---

[1] See Milton Friedman, "Monetarism in Rhetoric and Practice," Bank of Japan *Monetary and Economic Studies*, October 1983, p. 2.

[2] In the appendix to Chapter 15 we developed the aggregate demand curve taking account of the role of inflationary expectations in determining the real interest rate. In that case there is an additional term in the aggregate demand relationship equation (1). Under the assumption to be made for much of this section that $\pi^e = \pi_{-1}$, i.e., that the expected inflation rate is equal to last period's inflation rate, current aggregate demand increases with the lagged inflation rate. In order to simplify, we do not include this term on the aggregate demand side in this section. The omission does not affect the general results obtained except possibly if the expectations effect on aggregate demand was very large.

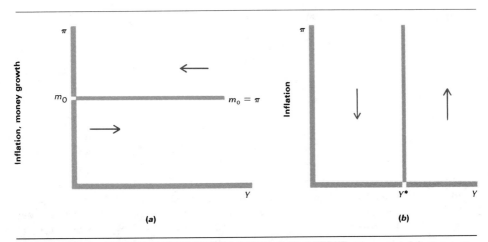

FIGURE 17-1 THE DYNAMICS OF INFLATION AND OUTPUT. The panel **(a)** shows the response of output to real balances. When inflation exceeds the growth rate of money, real balances are falling and hence demand and output are declining. Conversely, when inflation falls short of money growth, output is rising. The panel **(b)** shows that at output levels above Y^* inflation rises and at output levels below Y^* inflation declines.

In equation (2a) Y^* is the full-employment level of output, assumed in this section to be constant. For most of this section we make the simplest adaptive expectations assumption, that inflation expectations are given by last period's inflation rate, substituting $\pi^e = \pi_{-1}$.[3] Making that substitution in equation (2a), the change in inflation over time, denoted by $\Delta\pi = \pi - \pi_{-1}$, becomes a function of the output gap and is given by

$$\Delta\pi = \lambda(Y - Y^*) \tag{2}$$

Focussing again on dynamics, in Figure 17-1b we show the arrows that indicate the direction in which inflation is moving. When output is below the full-employment level, inflation is falling, and when output is above the full-employment level, inflation is rising.

Table 17-1 and Figure 17-2 combine the information in the two parts of Figure 17-1. The table shows the direction in which output and inflation are moving in each of the four regions in Figure 17-2. We use the arrows to show the combined movement or the path of inflation and output at each point.

Suppose the economy is at point A in region I. Because output is above the full-employment level, inflation is rising, but inflation is below money growth.

---

[3] We discuss behaviour under rational expectations of inflation later in this section.

TABLE 17-1 THE DETERMINANTS OF OUTPUT AND INFLATION

	$m > \pi$	$m < \pi$
$Y > Y^*$	I Y is ↑ π is ↑	II Y is ↓ π is ↑
$Y < Y^*$	III Y is ↑ π is ↓	IV Y is ↓ π is ↓

Therefore real balances are increasing, and hence demand and output are rising. Thus at point A output is rising as is inflation so that the economy moves in a northeastward direction. We can establish the direction of movement at points B, C, and D in a similar fashion. Note that point E is the only point in the diagram where *both* output and inflation are constant. This is the long-run equilibrium to which the economy ultimately converges.

In Figure 17-2 we complete the model by bringing in the *IS* schedule. On the vertical axis we show in the lower diagram the *real* or *inflation-adjusted* interest rate. Real aggregate demand, as we saw in the previous chapters, depends on the real interest rate. A higher real interest rate lowers aggregate demand and hence reduces equilibrium output as shown by the *IS* schedule. The lower part of Figure 17-2 helps us track the real interest rate in the adjustment process. For each level of output in the upper part we can find the corresponding equilibrium real interest rate on the *IS* schedule. Thus we can follow output, inflation, and the real interest rate all at the same time.

In Figure 17-2 we show a typical adjustment path starting at point A. The corresponding point is also labeled A in the lower part of Figure 17-2. At A inflation is rising because of overemployment. But because inflation is low relative to money growth, real balances are rising and hence demand and output are growing. The economy thus moves in a northeasterly direction. The driving force is the increasing level of real balances, which reduces interest rates and pushes up demand and output. Over time, as the economy cycles back to point E, the real interest rate first declines and then, as the economy enters region II, starts rising. The interest rate overshoots the long-run equilibrium level r^* (several times) before it ultimately settles at r^*.

An Increase in Money Growth

We now use this framework to examine once more the effects of a sustained increase in money growth. The conclusions are, of course, the same as those in Chapter 15. We start in long-run equilibrium at point E in Figure 17-3, where

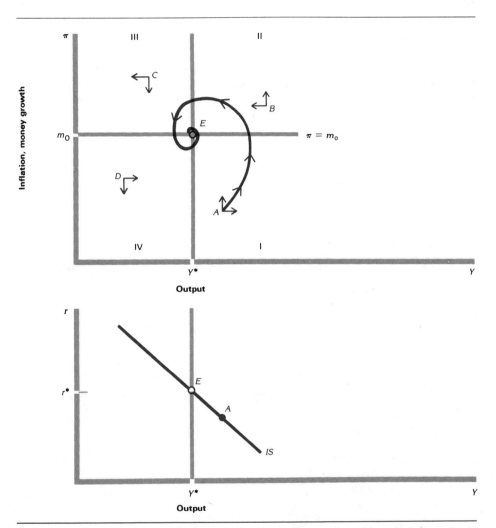

FIGURE 17-2   THE ADJUSTMENT PROCESS. The upper panel combines the information in Figure 17-1 to show how output and inflation evolve over time. The long-run equilibrium is at point E where inflation equals money growth and output is at the full-employment level. The lower panel shows the real rate of interest corresponding to each level of output along the IS curve. For example, if the economy is at point A in the upper panel, point A on the IS curve gives the corresponding real interest rate. The long-run equilibrium real interest rate is r^*.

money growth is initially m_0. The inflation rate is equal to the growth rate of money, and output is at its full-employment level. Now the growth rate of money is permanently raised to m'. The new $\pi = m'$ schedule lies above the previous one (which is not drawn to avoid cluttering up the diagram). The arrows in each region show the direction in which inflation and output are moving. The path starting at E shows the evolution of the economy.

At point E the growth rate of money m' now exceeds the initial inflation rate $\pi = m_0$. As a result, the real money stock is increasing. Interest rates are pushed down, and thus aggregate demand and output will be rising. At the very beginning of the adjustment process the economy therefore moves horizontally to

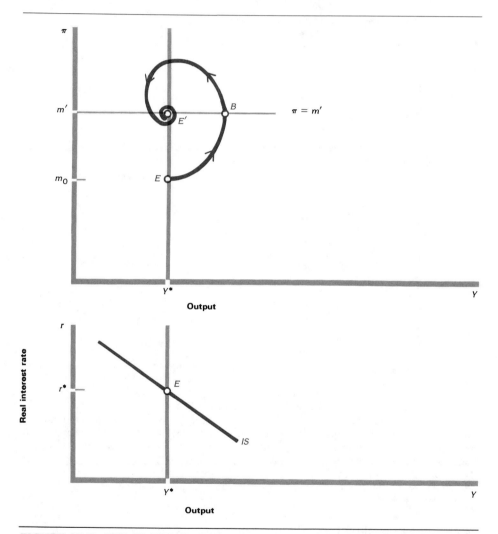

FIGURE 17-3   THE ADJUSTMENT TO AN INCREASE IN MONEY GROWTH. A sustained increase in money growth from m_0 to m' leads the economy along a path from E to E'. Output first expands, and inflation gradually builds up. In the long run, inflation rises to equal the growth rate of money. The economy returns to full employment at the real interest rate r^*.

the right with output rising, but the moment output starts exceeding the full-employment level, inflation increases. Now the path starts pointing in a north-easterly direction with rising output, because inflation remains low relative to money growth, and with inflation rising.

Over time the economy moves to point B. Here real balances are constant because now inflation has risen to the level of money growth, but output is above the full-employment level. Therefore inflation is still increasing, and the economy is thus pushed into region II. We do not describe the whole path, but it is apparent that the economy will cycle its way gradually to point E'.

Rational Expectations

The exact details of the adjustment path shown in Figure 17-3 depend on the assumptions about expectations. However, the general pattern—that increased monetary growth first raises output and ultimately is fully reflected in higher inflation—is valid for (almost) any assumption about expectations.

Only in a world of complete flexibility of wages and prices combined with rational expectations would the adjustment occur instantly without any dynamics whatsoever. In that case, if a change in the growth rate of money is expected, π^e in equation (2a) will be equal to m' at the time the growth rate of money changes, and output will remain at its full-employment level throughout.[4]

Once we move away from that extreme case—which requires both rational expectations and full flexibility of prices and wages—the pattern of adjustment is that shown in Figure 17-3. Alternative assumptions about expectations and the adjustment of wages and prices will primarily influence the speed of adjustment and the movement of nominal interest rates, but it will generally imply a slow adjustment pattern of the type seen in Figure 17-3.

Before going further we want to summarize the main results so far. There are four characteristics of the adjustment process and the new long-run equilibrium that are important to retain:

- A sustained increase in the growth rate of money will, in the long run when all adjustments have taken place, lead to an equal increase in the rate of inflation. If money growth rises by 5 percent, so, too, ultimately will the inflation rate.
- A sustained change in money growth will have no long-run effects on the level of output. Thus there is no long-run tradeoff between inflation and output.

---

[4] Remarkably, in this case the inflation rate would generally start to rise before the growth rate of money increases: that is because people expecting there to be inflation in the future reduce the quantity of real balances demanded and the price level therefore starts moving up.

- In the short run, during the adjustment process, increased monetary growth will affect the real interest rate, aggregate demand, and output. Specifically, in the initial stages there will be an expansion in output while inflation builds up.
- In the short run increased money growth will reduce the real interest rate, but in the long run, after all adjustments have taken place, the real interest rate will return to its initial level.

We ask you in Problem 1 at the end of the chapter to demonstrate the corresponding results for a sustained reduction in the growth rate of money. To complete our analysis, we now turn to the behaviour of real balances and the nominal interest rate.

The Fisher Equation

We have noted at various points in this book the relationship between nominal interest rates, real rates, and the expected rate of inflation. The (expected) real rate of interest is the nominal rate less the expected rate of inflation:

$$r^e = i - \pi^e \tag{3}$$

Equation (3) is the Fisher equation, so named after Irving Fisher (1867–1947), the most famous American economist of the first third of this century, who drew attention to the inflation–interest rate linkage.[5]

The Fisher equation immediately draws attention to a very important finding about money growth, inflation, and interest rates. We saw above that in the long run the real interest rate returns to the full-employment level r^*, and that actual and expected inflation converge. Using these two facts ($r^e = r^*$, $\pi^e = \pi$) we write the long-run relationship as

$$i = r^* + \pi \tag{4}$$

With r^* constant, equation (4) implies a central result: *In the long run when all adjustments have occurred, an increase in inflation is reflected fully in nominal interest rates.* Nominal interest rates rise one-for-one with the increase in infla-

---

[5] See Irving Fisher, *The Rate of Interest*, New York, Macmillan, 1907. Fisher taught at Yale and was an effective and sophisticated developer of the quantity theory of money. He had other interests too; he was the inventor of the card index file still used for keeping addresses, and was a health food enthusiast who wrote several books on the subject. Fisher was an early, if long forgotten, discoverer of the Phillips curve. See the reprinted version of his 1926 article "A Statistical Relation between Unemployment and Price Changes," under the heading "Lost and Found," *Journal of Political Economy*, March/April 1973, pp. 496–502.

tion. The reason we have such a strong inflation–nominal interest rate link is that in the long run the real interest rate is unaffected by purely monetary disturbances.

Of course, we already saw in Figure 17-3 that the constancy of the real interest rate holds only in long-run equilibrium. During the adjustment process the real interest rates does change, and hence changes in the nominal interest rate reflect both changes in real rates and changes in inflationary expectations.

Alternative Expectations Assumptions

The way in which expectations of inflation are formed will influence the adjust-ment path of the interest rate, real and nominal, to a change in money growth, though not the long-run implication of the Fisher equation. Depending on expectations, there are different paths for interest rates. The nominal rate may start out rising or it may first decline and then later rise.

Figure 17-4 shows a possible pattern, which has received considerable atten-tion in empirical work. In response to increased growth in nominal money, at time T_0 the real money stock grows and initially pushes down the nominal

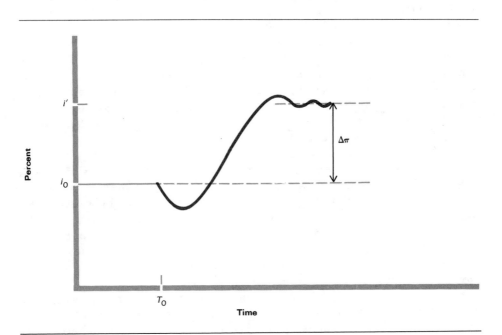

FIGURE 17-4 THE FISHER EFFECT. A sustained increase in money growth leads first to a reduction in nominal interest rates. Then, as output and inflation both increase, the interest rate gradually rises. In the long run it increases by the same amount as money growth and inflation.

interest rate. Then, as output rises and with it inflation, the nominal interest rate is pushed up until, ultimately, after some cycling it has increased by the full increase in money growth and inflation.

The declining phase of the nominal interest rate path is called the *liquidity effect* to denote the impact of increased real balances (liquidity) on the interest rate. The phase of increasing nominal interest rates just after the bottom is reached is called the *income effect*. In this phase increasing nominal income pushes up interest rates by increasing the quantity of real balances demanded. The long-run effect is called the *Fisher effect*, or *expectations effect*, to represent the impact of an increase in inflationary expectations, at a constant real interest rate, on the nominal interest rate. These names are suggestive of the three phases of adjustment as the economy is initially surprised by increased money growth and gradually adjusts to it.[6]

Real Balances and Inflation

In Figure 17-5 we present the demand for real balances as a function of the nominal interest rate. We now study the effect of a sustained change in the growth rate of money on the long-run equilibrium level of real balances.

For that purpose we simply combine two of our results. We saw that a sustained change in monetary growth changes, in the long run, the rate of inflation and the nominal interest rate in the same direction and by the same amount. A 3 percentage point increase in money growth raises the nominal interest rate by three percentage points in the long run. We therefore conclude from Figure 17-5 that *a sustained increase in money growth and in inflation ultimately leads to a reduction in the real money stock.*

This is a very important result that might seem a bit puzzling: increased *nominal* money growth reduces the long-run *real* money stock. Conversely, reduced nominal money growth raises the long-run real money stock. The reason is that higher inflation raises the nominal interest rate and hence raises the opportunity cost of holding money. Hence money holders will reduce the amount of real balances they choose to hold. This reduction in real balances is an important part of the adjustment process to an increase in money growth. It means that, *on average, in the adjustment period to an increase in money growth, prices must rise faster than money.*

Figure 17-6, which shows the time paths of inflation and money growth, helps explain the adjustment of real balances. At time T_0 money growth rises from m_0 to m'. At the very beginning, as we saw in Figure 17-3, nothing happens to inflation. Inflation builds up gradually until, with overshooting and cycling, it

---

[6] For an extensive discussion see Milton Friedman and Anna Schwartz, *Monetary Trends in the United States and the United Kingdom,* National Bureau of Economic Research, 1982, Chapter 10.

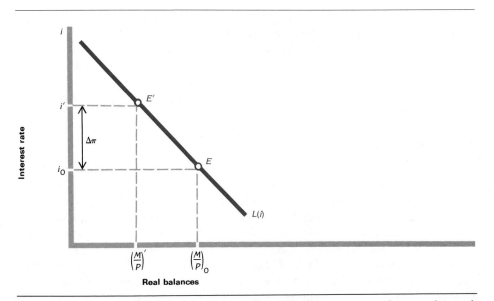

FIGURE 17-5   THE DEMAND FOR REAL BALANCES. An increase in inflation and accordingly in the nominal interest rate will reduce the equilibrium stock of real balances. As the interest rate increases in long-run equilibrium from i_0 to i', real balances decline from E to E'.

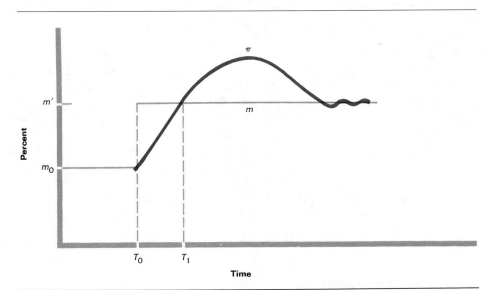

FIGURE 17-6   MONEY GROWTH AND INFLATION. An increase in money growth from m_0 to m' only gradually translates into increased inflation. In the adjustment process prices rise cumulatively more than money as shown by the overshooting of inflation. This implies that real balances will be reduced in the long run.

settles down at the higher level m'. In the phase up to time T_1 money growth exceeds inflation and real balances rise. Then in the following phase real balances are falling as the inflation rate exceeds money growth. The diagram is drawn to show that in the phase of decline, real balances fall more than they rise in the initial phase. This is the phase in which the economy adjusts in a major way to increased money growth as rising output and expectations push up the rate of inflation.

Alternative Expectations Assumptions

Once again, the long-run reduction in real balances in response to higher money growth is a general result. A sustained increase in money growth, *must* in the long run reduce the equilibrium level of real balances. The particulars of how expectations are formed determines the particular details of the path.

In the extreme case of full wage-price flexibility and rational expectations there would be an instant adjustment. The announcement of increased money growth would lead to an instant recognition that the opportunity cost of holding money is increased. The public would try to shift out of money because it is now expected to be more expensive to hold, but, of course, the economy in the aggregate cannot get rid of the existing nominal money stock. People trying to spend quickly to get rid of their real balances would cause prices to jump, thereby reducing real balances to the lower desired level. Following the jump, prices and money would start rising at the long-run equilibrium rate m' and the nominal interest rate would have increased to i'. All adjustments would occur literally in no time.

This full flexibility of wages and prices — rational expectations case may sound implausible, but it serves as a useful benchmark for comparison. On one side there is a world with only gradual adjustment of inflation and inflationary expectations. In that world, described by Friedman earlier, increased money growth takes time to find itself translated fully into inflation and interest rates. In the other world all adjustments are instant.

How exactly the real world adjustment takes place depends in good part on people's experience with inflation. In economies where inflation is the number one issue—because of a hyperinflation—it takes very little time for adjustment to occur, as we will see later in this chapter. However, in the Canadian economy, where inflation never became a complete way of life, the path of Figure 17-3 is a lot more likely.

17-2 EMPIRICAL EVIDENCE

We now turn to evidence on the links between money growth and inflation and between money growth and interest rates.

The Money-Inflation Link

To start we note the often-made statement that inflation is a monetary phenomenon. The claim that inflation is a monetary phenomenon means that sustained
high rates of money growth produce high inflation and that low rates of money
growth will eventually produce low rates of inflation. Further, the statement
that inflation is a monetary phenomenon means that high rates of inflation
cannot long continue without high rates of money growth. The view that inflation is a monetary phenomenon is the implication of the quantity theory of
money and is the backbone of monetarist macroeconomics.

Figure 17-7 presents evidence from Canada over the period since 1961, showing that the inflation rate and the growth rate of money have more or less moved
together. Although the relationship is clearly positive, it is also obvious that
the link between money growth and inflation is not precise.

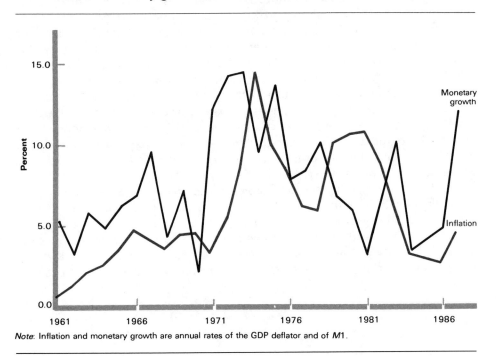

Note: Inflation and monetary growth are annual rates of the GDP deflator and of M1.

FIGURE 17-7   INFLATION AND MONETARY GROWTH IN CANADA

(Source: Adapted from Bank of Canada Review)

We expect to find a link between inflation and money growth because we
showed earlier that in the steady state the inflation rate is determined by money
growth. The aggregate demand curve was

$$\pi = m - \frac{1}{\varphi}(Y - Y_{-1}) \tag{5}$$

With $Y = Y_{-1} = Y^*$, that is with constant output, the inflation rate is equal to the growth rate of money. That is the basis for the view that inflation is in the long run a monetary phenomenon. We now want to expand the model slightly to recognize the growth of full-employment output over time. Suppose that output, instead of being constant, grows in the long run at the growth rate of potential output, g^*. In Canada g^* has been about 4 percent per annum. Some money growth is needed just to meet the increasing demand for real balances arising from growing income. Accordingly, the money growth rate will exceed the inflation rate in the long run.

The difference between money growth and inflation arises from the amount of money growth needed to meet the demand increases resulting from steadily rising income. How much money growth is that? Suppose the income elasticity of money demand is 0.7. Then for every 1 percent that income rises, the demand for real balances rises 0.7 percent. The 4 percent growth in potential output thus increases the demand for real balances by 2.8 percent a year.

If real money demand is rising—say, at the rate of 2.8 percent per year—as a result of income growth, then monetary equilibrium requires that the real money supply increase at the same rate. The growth rate of the real money stock is just the difference between the growth rate of the nominal money stock and the rate of inflation. For instance, if the nominal money stock is increasing at 10 percent and the rate of inflation is 7.9 percent, the real money stock is increasing at 2.1 percent per year.

If the real money supply has to be growing at 2.8 percent per year to maintain monetary equilibrium, then the rate of inflation has to be 2.8 percent less than the rate of money growth, or, in symbols, $\pi = m - 2.8$

More generally, with g^* as the growth rate of potential output and η as the income elasticity of the demand for real balances, the long-run relationship among the inflation rate, the growth rate of money, and the growth rate of output is

$$\pi = m - \eta g^* \tag{6}$$

Changes in Velocity and Inflation

Table 17-2 shows the inflation rate, the growth rate of $M1$, and the growth rate of real income for six countries over the period 1955–1984. According to equation (6), we should find that

$$\pi - (m - \eta g^*) = 0 \tag{6a}$$

TABLE 17-2   MONEY GROWTH AND INFLATION, 1955–1984

Country	(1) Inflation rate (CPI), π	(2) Growth rate of M1, m	(3) Growth rate of real GNP (or GDP), g^*	(4) $\pi - (m - g^*)$	(5) $\pi - (m - 0.7g^*)$
Canada	5.1	8.3	4.1	0.9	−0.3
Germany	3.5	8.3	4.0	−0.8	−2.0
Italy	8.4	15.3	4.2	−2.7	−4.0
Japan	5.7	12.5	6.8	0.0	−2.0
United Kingdom	7.4	7.7	2.3	2.0	1.3
United States	4.8	5.0	3.2	3.0	2.0

Source: International Financial Statistics.

In column (4) of Table 17-2 we calculate $\pi - (m - g^*)$, an amount which should be zero if the income elasticity of money demand is unity. Column (5) shows a similar calculation, assuming the income elasticity of money demand is 0.7.

The inflation experienced by Canada comes close to matching that predicted by Equation (8a). However, in the United Kingdom and the United States, inflation has been, on average, faster than predicted. In Italy, and, depending on the correct income elasticity, perhaps in Japan and Germany, inflation has been, on average, slower than predicted by equation (6).

In conclusion, the answer to the question, whether inflation is a monetary phenomenon in the long run, is yes. No major inflation can take place without rapid money growth, and rapid money growth will cause rapid inflation. Further, any policy that determinedly keeps the growth rate of money low will lead eventually to a low rate of inflation.

But at the same time the long-run link between money growth and inflation is not precise, as the data of Table 17-2 show. There are two reasons for that. First, increases in output increase the demand for real balances and reduce the inflation rate corresponding to a given rate of money growth. And second, financial institutions change, the definition of money changes, and the demand for money may shift over time.

Inflation and Interest Rates

The Fisher equation asserts a positive link between nominal interest rates and inflation. With the real interest rate approximately constant in the long run, and with expectations of inflation adjusting to actual inflation, the nominal interest rate adjusts to the prevailing rate of inflation.

Figure 17-8 shows quarterly averages of the nominal interest rate on 3-month treasury bills and the rate of inflation over the period for which the bills are outstanding. The *realized* real interest rate then is the difference between the nominal interest rate and the actual rate of inflation or, in symbols,

$$r = i - \pi \tag{7}$$

We do not have data on expected inflation and hence can reliably report only realized *actual* rates rather than expected real rates of interest. But in the short term, with inflation quite predictable there are no big discrepancies between expected and actual real rates.

Note from Figure 17-8 that in the 1970s there were several episodes of negative real rates, particularly in 1974–1975 when inflation increased sharply and exceeded the interest rate by a significant margin. By contrast, in the period since 1978 the real rate of interest has been *persistently* positive.

Note: Interest rate is the yield on 3 month Treasury bills. Inflation rate is the growth rate from the preceding year of the Consumer Price Index excluding food.

FIGURE 17-8   INTEREST RATES AND INFLATION

(*Source:* Adapted from *Bank of Canada Review*)

Table 17-3 shows international evidence on the interest rate–inflation link. The table conveys clearly the notion of a positive relationship between the nominal interest rate and inflation. The link is especially clear for a country like Brazil, which had both exceptionally high inflation rates and also extremely high interest rates. If that were not the case, real interest rates would be spectacularly negative.

TABLE 17-3 INTEREST RATES AND EXPECTED INFLATION, 1984*

Country	Interest rate % per annum	Average inflation rate, 1980–1984
Australia	12.2	8.7
Brazil	215.3†	132.5
Canada	11.1	8.3
France	11.7	10.5
Germany	5.5	4.3
Italy	17.3	14.9
Switzerland	4.7‡	4.5
United Kingdom	9.3	7.2
United States	9.6	6.0

*Interest rates are short-term market rates except as noted. The expected inflation rate is assumed to be the average of inflation rates over the previous 4 years.
†Bank rate.
‡Government bond yield.

Source: International Financial Statistics.

The evidence we have seen does tend to show that inflation and interest rates move together, within a country over time and across countries, but the evidence does not support a very strict Fisher equation. Year-to-year changes in inflation are not reflected one for one in nominal interest rates. The real rate does move, and hence the Fisher equation is primarily a guide to interest rates when inflationary disturbances are large relative to all other factors determining interest rates.

17-3 MONEY GROWTH AND THE INFLATION TAX

We have seen that a sustained increase in money growth ultimately translates into increased inflation. In this section we consider money creation as an alternative to explicit taxation for the purpose of financing government spending. Governments can — and some do — obtain significant amounts of resources year after year by printing money. This source of revenue is sometimes known as *seigniorage*, which means the government's ability to raise revenue through its right to create money.

When the government finances a deficit by creating money, it in effect keeps printing money, period after period, which it uses to pay for the goods and services it buys. This money is absorbed by the public; but why would the public choose to increase its holdings of nominal money balances period after period?

The only reason, real income growth aside, that the public would be adding to its holdings of nominal money balances is to offset the effects of inflation. Assuming there is no real income growth, in the long run the public will hold a constant level of *real* balances. However, if prices are rising, the purchasing power of a given stock of *nominal balances* is falling. To maintain the real value of its money balances constant, the public has to be adding to its stock of nominal balances, exactly at the rate that will offset the effects of inflation.

When the public is adding to its stock of nominal balances in order to offset the effects of inflation on holdings of real balances, it is using part of its income to increase holdings of nominal money. For instance, suppose someone has an income of $20 000 (nominal) this year. Over the course of the year, inflation reduces the value of that person's real balances. He or she therefore has to add, say, $300, to a bank account just to maintain the real value of his or her money holdings constant. That $300 is not available for spending. The person seems to be saving $300 in the form of money holdings, but in fact in real terms is not increasing his or her wealth by adding the $300 to nominal balances. All that person is doing is preventing his or her wealth from falling as a result of inflation.

Inflation acts just like a tax because people are forced to spend less than their income and pay the difference to the government in exchange for extra money.[7] The government thus can spend more resources, and the public less just as if the government had raised taxes to finance extra spending. When the government finances its deficit by issuing money, which the public adds to its holdings of nominal balances to maintain the real value of money balances constant, we say the government is financing itself through the inflation tax.[8]

How much revenue can the government collect through the inflation tax? The amount of revenue produced is the product of the tax rate (the inflation

---

[7] There is one complication in this analysis. The amount that is received by the government is the increase in the stock of *high-powered* money, because the central bank is buying debt with high-powered money. However, the public is increasing its holdings of both bank deposits and currency, and thus part of the increase in the public's holdings of money does not go to the government to finance the deficit. This complication in no way changes the essence of the analysis.

[8] Inflation is often referred to as the "cruelest tax." This does not refer to the above analysis of the inflation tax, but rather to the redistributions of wealth and income associated with unanticipated inflation, discussed in Chapter 16.

rate) and the object of taxation (the real monetary base). When real output is constant, inflation tax revenue is given by

$$\text{Inflation tax revenue} = \text{inflation rate} \times \text{real money base} \qquad (8)$$

The amount of revenue the government can raise through the inflation tax is shown by the curve AA in Figure 17-9. When the inflation rate is zero, the government gets no revenue from inflation.[9] As the inflation rate rises, the amount of inflation tax received by the government increases, but of course, as the inflation rate rises, people reduce their holdings of real balances, because it is becoming increasingly costly to hold money. Eventually the quantity of real balances falls so much that the total amount of inflation tax revenue received by the government falls. That happens starting at point C. This means there is a maximum amount of revenue the government can raise through the inflation tax: it is shown as amount IR^* in Figure 17-9. There is a corresponding inflation rate, denoted π^*, the steady-state inflation rate at which the inflation tax is at its maximum.

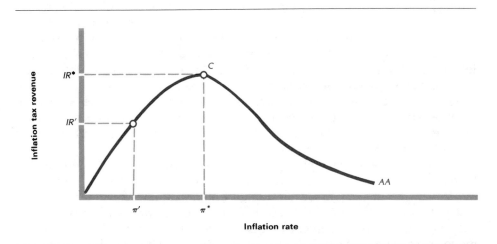

FIGURE 17-9 THE INFLATION TAX. At a zero inflation rate, the inflation tax revenue is zero. As the inflation rate rises, the government receives more revenue from inflation, up to point C, where the tax revenue reaches its maximum of IR^*. The corresponding inflation rate is π^*. Beyond point C the demand for real balances is falling so much as the inflation rate increases that total tax revenues decline.

[9] When the economy is growing, the government obtains some revenue from seigniorage even if there is no inflation. That is because when the demand for real monetary base is growing, the government can create some base without producing inflation.

We can look back to Figure 17-3 to study the long-run effects of money-financed deficits. We start at point E. Now the government cuts taxes and finances the deficit by printing money. We assume that the deficit is equal to amount IR' in Figure 17-9, and thus it can be financed entirely through the inflation tax. Now money growth has been permanently increased, and inflation will in the long run move to the rate π', corresponding to the inflation tax revenue IR'.

In the long run the economy reaches point E'. In that equilibrium expectations have fully adjusted to the inflation, and output is at the full-employment level. Inflation equals the growth rate of money,[10] and the inflation rate depends on the deficit size. The larger the deficit, the higher the inflation rate. Figure 17-9 raises the question of what happens if the government tries to finance a deficit larger than IR^* by printing money. That cannot be done. We take up that issue in the following section, on hyperinflations.

Inflation Tax Revenue

How much revenue can governments in practice obtain from the printing of money? The amount is quite small in developed economies in which the money base is small relative to the size of the economy. For instance, in Canada the base is about 4 percent of GDP even with the current low rates of inflation. At a 10 percent inflation rate the government would, from equation (9), be collecting about 0.4 percent of GDP in inflation tax revenue. That is not a trivial amount, but it is not a major source of government revenue either. It is hard to believe that the inflation rate in Canada is set with the revenue aspects of inflation as the main criterion. Rather the government chooses policies to influence the inflation rate on the basis of an analysis of the costs and benefits of inflation along the lines of Chapter 16.

In countries where the banking system is less developed and where people therefore hold large amounts of currency, the government obtains more revenue from inflation and is more likely to give high weight to the revenue aspects of inflation in setting policy. There have been cases where the government obtains as much as 10 percent of GDP in revenue from the creation of the money base. And, as we see in the next section, in conditions of high inflation where the conventional tax system breaks down, the inflation tax revenue may be the government's last resort to keep paying its bills.

Unpleasant Monetarist Arithmetic

In a well-known article, Thomas Sargent and Neil Wallace of the University of Minnesota have pointed to an important implication of the government budget

---

[10] Except for an adjustment that takes account of growth in real output.

constraint.[11] Specifically, *debt-financing of a deficit may in the long run be more inflationary than money financing.*

The argument turns on the fact that when a government finances a current deficit through debt, it incurs the obligation to pay interest on that debt in the future. In Chapter 13, the government budget constraint was defined as:

$$\text{Deficit} = \text{bond sales} + \text{increase in monetary base} \tag{9}$$

We also introduced a distinction between the primary deficit and the total deficit:

$$\text{Total deficit} = \text{primary deficit} + \text{interest payments} \tag{10}$$

Combining (9) and (10), we obtain:

$$\text{Bond sales} + \text{increase in monetary base} = \text{primary deficit} + \text{interest payments} \tag{11}$$

Consider now the choice between debt financing (bond sales) and money financing of a given deficit. If money financing is used, interest payments will be no larger in the future than they are now, but if the government turns to debt financing, it will have a larger deficit in the future. That in turn will have to be financed, either through money finance or debt finance.

Now imagine the following circumstances. The government has a given national debt today. The primary deficits today and in the future are, by assumption, given at some constant level, for example, the primary deficit may be zero. The government is considering whether to finance its current deficit by borrowing or by printing money. If it finances by borrowing, it intends to stop borrowing and switch to money financing in 5 years.

Under which alternative will the inflation rate ultimately be higher? The answer can be worked out from the following considerations. If the government starts money financing today, it will have to create money at a rate that finances the interest payments on the *existing* national debt. However, if it waits 5 years to start money financing, it will have to create money at a rate that finances the interest payments on the national debt that will exist 5 years from now. Because interest on the debt will have accumulated in the meantime, the debt will be larger 5 years from now, and therefore so will the inflation rate.

This example shows that, because of the accumulation of interest, short-run debt financing that ends in money financing will generally ultimately be more inflationary than immediate money financing of a given deficit.

---

[11] "Some Unpleasant Monetarist Arithmetic," *Federal Reserve Bank of Minneapolis, Quarterly Review*, Fall 1981.

The arithmetic is unpleasant for monetarists because it suggests that budget deficits may have more to do with the eventual inflation rate than the current growth rate of money.

The main question raised by this example is whether the government is eventually forced into money financing of a given deficit or whether it can continue debt finance forever. That depends on the relationship between the growth rate of output and the real interest rate. As we saw in Chapter 13, if the real interest rate is above the growth rate of output, and given a zero primary deficit, debt financing cannot continue forever, because the debt becomes a larger and larger part of GDP and interest payments keep mounting up. At some point, in that case, the government will have to turn to money financing. The turn to money financing will both provide some revenue, and, if the debt is nominal, perhaps reduce the value of the outstanding debt through unanticipated inflation.

If the real interest rate is below the growth rate of output, with a zero primary deficit, then the government can continue debt financing without the debt-GDP ratio rising. In that case debt finance is viable for the long term, and the hard choice posed by the Sargent-Wallace example can be avoided. Note also though that the tight link examined by Sargent and Wallace takes future primary deficits as given. If the government is willing to raise taxes at some future date to pay higher interest bills, there is no necessary link between current deficits and future money growth.

The Sargent-Wallace analysis does make clear why permanent deficits cause concern. If the national debt is growing relative to GDP, then ultimately the government will have to raise taxes or raise the inflation rate to meet its debt obligations. That is the long-run threat that leads people to worry about deficits. Of course the long run in this case may be decades away.

There is a further important point. The Sargent-Wallace concern is about *primary* deficits: if the total deficit is constant as a percentage of GDP, then ultimately the debt-GDP ratio will stabilize provided the economy is growing at all. For instance, a statement that the deficit in Canada would be 5 percent of GDP forever would not mean that the debt would explode as a percentage of GDP. Rather if the deficit were financed through debt, the debt-GDP ratio would eventually reach a steady state.[12] The explanation is that when the deficit is measured to *include* interest payments, a statement that the deficit will be

---

[12] This is a fairly technical but important point. If the total deficit is kept at a constant ratio to GDP, say 5 percent, that means that behind the scenes increasing interest payments are being met by higher taxes or lower government spending. Suppose that the debt-GDP ratio is denoted b, that GDP is growing at a real rate y, and that the total deficit as a percentage of GDP is denoted td. In steady state debt is being issued at just the rate that keps the debt-GDP ratio constant. That means that in steady state $td = y \cdot b$. Then the steady-state debt GDP ratio is just equal to td/y. For instance, if the deficit

constant forever means that behind the scenes the primary deficit or surplus is being adjusted to ensure that interest payments are being made without the debt-GDP ratio exploding.

17-4   HYPERINFLATION

Large budget deficits are inevitably part of the extreme inflations of 50 to 100 or even 500 percent per year that took place in the mid-80s in Latin America and Israel. They are also part of the even more extreme cases of *hyperinflation*. Although there is no precise definition of the rate of inflation that deserves the star ranking of hyper rather than high inflation, a working definition takes 1000 percent per annum as the rate that marks a hyperinflation.

In a hyperinflationary economy, inflation is so pervasive and such a problem that it completely dominates daily economic life. People spend significant amounts of resources minimizing the inflationary damage: they have to shop often, to get to the stores before the prices go up; their main concern in saving or investing is how to protect themselves against inflation; they reduce holdings of real balances to a remarkable extent to avoid the inflation tax, but have to compensate by going to the bank more often, daily or hourly instead of weekly, for example, to get currency.

The classic hyperinflations have taken place in the aftermath of wars. The most famous of all—though not the most rapid—was the German hyperinflation of 1922–1923. The average inflation rate during the hyperinflation was 322 percent *per month*. The highest rate of inflation was in October 1923, just before the end of the hyperinflation, when prices rose by over 29 000 percent.[13] In dollars that means that something that cost $1 at the beginning of the month would have cost $290 at the end of the month. The most rapid hyperinflation was that in Hungary at the end of World War II: the *average* rate of inflation from August 1945 to July 1946 was 19 800 percent per month, and the maximum monthly rate was 41.9 quadrillon percent.[14]

Keynes, in a masterful description of the hyperinflation process in Austria after World War I, tells of how people would order two beers at a time because

---

is 5 percent of GDP forever, and the growth rate of GDP is 4 percent, then the debt-GDP ratio will be 1.25, or 125 percent in steady state. At that point interest payments are a constant proportion of GDP.

[13] Data based on C. L. Holtferich, *Die Deutsche Inflation, 1914–1923* (New York: Walter de Gruyter, 1980).

[14] At least, so we think. The price level rose 41.9×10^{15} percent in July 1946. Data are from Phillip Cagan, "The Monetary Dynamics of Hyperinflation," in Milton Friedman (ed.), *Studies in the Quantity Theory of Money* (Chicago: University of Chicago Press, 1956). This classic paper contains data on seven hyperinflations.

they grew stale at a rate slower than the price was rising.[15] This and similar stories appear in all hyperinflations. They include the woman who carried her (almost worthless) currency in a basket and found that when she set it down for a moment, the basket was stolen but the money left behind. It was said it was cheaper to take a taxi than a bus because in the taxi you pay at the end of the ride and in the bus at the beginning.

Hyperinflationary economies are typically marked by widespread indexing, more to the foreign exchange rate than to the price level. That is because it becomes difficult to keep measuring prices on a current basis, when they change so fast. So prices might be specified in terms of dollars, and the actual amount of the local currency (marks in the German case) that has to be paid in each transaction is calculated from the dollar price and the exchange rate. Wages are paid very often at the end of hyperinflation, in the German case, several times a day.

Deficits and Hyperinflation

The hyperinflationary economies all suffered from large budget deficits and from rapid money printing. In several cases the origin of the budget deficit was wartime spending, which generated large national debts and also destroyed the tax-gathering apparatus of the country.

However, there is a two-way interaction between budget deficits and inflation. Large budget deficits can lead to rapid inflation by causing governments to print money to finance the deficit. In turn, high inflation increases the measured deficit. There are two main mechanisms whereby inflation increases budget deficits.

The Tax-Collection System

As the inflation rate rises, the real revenue raised from taxation falls. The reason is that there are lags in both the calculation and payment of taxes. Suppose, to take an extreme example, that people pay taxes on April 30 on the income they earned the previous year. Consider someone who earned $50 000 last year, who has a tax bill of $10 000 due on April 30. If prices have in the meantime gone up by a factor of 10, as they might in a hyperinflation, the real value of the taxes is only one-tenth of what it should be. The budget deficit can rapidly get out of hand.

---

[15] John Maynard Keynes, A *Tract on Monetary Reform* (New York: Macmillan, 1923). This remains one of the most readable accounts of inflation. See also Thomas William Guttmann and Patricia Meehan, *The Great Inflation* (Gordon and Cremonsi, 1975); and Leland Yeager and associates, *Experiences with Stopping Inflation* (Washington, D.C.: American Enterprise Institute, 1981).

In principle the tax system can be indexed to adjust for the inflation, but that is difficult, especially for business taxation, and in any event even indexing lags behind. For example, if the monthly rate of inflation is 20 percent (equivalent to an annual rate of nearly 800 percent), then even if the amount that has to be paid is fixed according to the most recent price index, and if it takes a month to collect taxes, inflation causes the government to lose 20 percent of the value of its taxes.

Nominal Interest and the Budget Deficit

Nominal interest rates rise with the inflation rate and increase the measured budget deficit. To make this point we repeat equation (10):

$$\text{Total deficit} \equiv \text{primary deficit} + \text{interest payments} \qquad (10)$$

Suppose now that the government debt is at the relatively low level of just 20 percent of GDP. With an interest rate of, say, 10 percent, total interest payments are 2 percent of GDP (10 percent interest rate × 20 percent of GDP debt). Let the inflation rate rise by 90 percent, with the real interest rate remaining unchanged, so that the nominal interest rate goes up to 100 percent. Then total interest payments amount to 20 percent of GDP (100 percent interest rate × 20 percent of GDP debt), and the budget deficit measured as in (10) rises by no less than 18 percent of GDP. The data in this example are essentially those of Mexico in 1986, where the budget deficit during the inflation looked very large, despite the noninterest part of the budget being in surplus.

The problem here is that the conventional way of measuring the deficit includes *nominal* interest on the debt. This can give a distorted impression of the size of the deficit, because in fact the government is paying the high interest to offset the effect of inflation in reducing the value of its outstanding debt. We should recognize that at the same time as the government has to pay high interest, it also receives revenue from the decline in the value of its outstanding debt, owing to inflation. In the 1970s many economists began to calculate inflation-corrected budget deficits that took account of the government's gain from inflation because the value of its debt fell.

The inflation-corrected budget deficit calculates the budget deficit taking into account the effect of inflation in reducing the outstanding value of the government's debt.

We return to the previous example for an illustrative calculation. Suppose the real interest rate is 5 percent, and that the primary deficit is zero. Then, with a debt-GDP ratio of 20 percent, the budget deficit at a zero inflation rate is only 1 percent of GDP. When the inflation rate hits 95 percent, with a nominal interest rate of 100 percent, the calculated nominal deficit becomes 20 percent of GDP, but the inflation-corrected deficit is still only 1 percent of GDP, as long as the real interest rate remains at 5 percent.

Although the principle of the calculation of inflation-corrected deficits is clear, there is some controversy about whether they should be used. The question that should be asked is whether the private sector wants to maintain the value of the debt-to-GDP ratio. If so, it will willingly finance the apparently increased nominal deficit by purchases of bonds—people need to step up bond purchases precisely because the real value of their existing bonds is being reduced through inflation. If on the other hand the inflation rate is high as a result of unexpectedly high printing of money, then the inflation-corrected deficit does not give a good measure of the extent to which people are willing to continue financing the existing deficit at the existing real interest rate by purchasing bonds.

The Inflation Tax and Accelerating Hyperinflation

Rates of money growth are also very high during hyperinflations, of the same order of magnitude as the inflation rate.[16] The high rates of money growth originate in attempts to finance government spending.

However, as the inflations progress, and the tax collection system breaks down, the government reaches a point where it tries to raise more through money printing than the maximum amount IR^* that it can in Figure 17-9. It can succeed in raising more than IR^* *temporarily*, by printing money even faster than people expected. That increased money growth causes the inflation rate to increase and, as the government continues to try to spend more than IR^*, it continues driving up the inflation rate. The amount of real money balances that people hold becomes smaller and smaller, as they try to flee the inflation tax, and the government prints even more rapidly to try to finance its expenditure. In the end the process will break down.

Stopping Hyperinflations

All hyperinflations come to an end. The dislocation of the economy becomes too great for the public to bear, and the government finds a way of reforming its budget process. Often a new money is introduced, and the tax system is reformed. Typically, too, the exchange rate of the new money is pegged to that of a foreign currency, to provide an anchor for prices and expectations. Frequently there are unsuccessful attempts at stabilization before the final success.

The presence of so many destabilizing factors in inflation, particularly the collapse of the tax system as the inflation proceeds, together with an economy

---

[16] On average, though, the growth rate of money is below the inflation rate. That is because people are reducing their holdings of real balances during hyperinflation: if M/P is falling, then P has on average to be growing faster than M.

that is extremely dislocated by inflation, raises a fascinating possibility. A coordinated attack on inflation may stop the inflation with relatively little unemployment cost. This approach was used in Argentina and Israel in 1985, and Brazil in 1986, when the governments froze wages and prices. That stopped the inflation at a single blow. They also fixed their exchange rates, and there were significant changes in fiscal policy, to put the budget closer to long-run balances. In each case there was little increase in unemployment. Despite the early encouraging signs, the ultimate success of these stabilization programs remains to be established.

One more important feature of the stabilizations should be brought out. *Money growth rates following stabilization are very high.* Why? Because as people expect less inflation, nominal interest rates decline, and the demand for real balances rises. With the demand for real balances increasing, the government can create more money without creating inflation. Thus at the beginning of a successful stabilization there may be a bonus for the government: it can temporarily finance part of the deficit through the printing of money, without renewing inflation. But it certainly cannot do so for very long periods without reigniting inflation.

17-5 SUMMARY

1. A sustained monetary expansion typically expands output in the short run. In the long run higher money growth is translated fully into inflation. Real interest rates and output return to the full-employment level. Only under rational expectations and with full wage and price flexibility does a monetary expansion translate instantly into a more rapid rate of inflation with no impact on output.

2. A sustained change in money growth ultimately raises the nominal interest rate by the same amount. This positive association between inflation and nominal interest rates is called the Fisher effect.

3. In the short run increased money growth will lead to lower nominal interest rates if expectations adjust slowly. This is called the liquidity effect.

4. A sustained monetary expansion ultimately raises nominal interest rates and hence reduces the demand for real balances. That means that prices must on average rise faster than money in the transition to the new long-run equilibrium.

5. Inflation is a tax on real balances. To keep constant the purchasing power of holdings of money in the face of rising prices, a person has to add to nominal balances. In this fashion resources are transferred from money holders to money issuers, specifically the government.

6. A decision to finance a deficit through bond sales today may mean a higher inflation rate in the future if the government eventually has to finance the deficit through money printing. That is because the interest payments on the debt accumulate to increase future deficits, given a fixed primary deficit. This tradeoff exists when the interest rate exceeds the growth rate of output.

7. Hyperinflations have generally taken place in the aftermaths of wars. Large deficits are typical in hyperinflations. Governments can use the inflation tax to finance deficits to a limited extent, but if too large a deficit has to be financed, inflation explodes.

8. There is a two-way interaction between inflation and budget deficits. Higher inflation rates raise the deficit by reducing the real value of tax collection. Higher nominal interest rates raise the measured deficit by increasing the value of nominal interest payments in the budget. The inflation-corrected deficit adjusts for this latter effect.

9. Money growth rates are very high following a successful inflation stabilization, as people increase their holdings of real balances.

KEY TERMS

Fisher effect	Inflation tax
Liquidity effect	Seigniorage
Expectations effect	Inflation-corrected deficit
Hyperinflation	

PROBLEMS

1. (a) Show graphically the effects of a reduction in the growth rate of money on output and inflation.
    (b) Show also how the real interest rate adjusts over time. Be specific about the expectations assumption you are using.

2. In the above example show how the nominal interest rate adjusts to lower inflation.

3. We stated in the text that under rational expectations and with full price and wage flexibility, the inflation rate rises immediately to its new steady-state level when the growth rate of money increases. We also stated that real balance holdings decline when the expected inflation rate rises. How

can the level of real balances fall under rational expectations if the inflation rate is equal to the growth rate of money? (*Hint:* with prices fully flexible, they can change all at once when new information becomes available.)

4. (a) Explain the Fisher equation that describes the relationship between the nominal interest rate and expected inflation.
    (b) Use figure 17-8 to show that the real interest rate was very high in 1981.

5. Suppose the ratio of money base to GDP is 10 percent. The government is considering raising the inflation rate from the current 0 to 10 percent per annum and believes it will obtain an increase in government revenue of 1 percent of GDP by doing so. Explain why that calculation overestimates the inflation tax the government will receive at a 10 percent inflation rate.

6. During 1981–1986 the government of Canada added massively to the national debt. (a) Explain why you might worry that this is inflationary. (b) Explain whether you actually worry that the high deficits of the early eighties will lead to high inflation later.

7. At the height of the German hyperinflation, the government was covering only 1 percent of its spending with taxes. (a) What happened to the rest? (b) How could the German government possibly finance the remaining 99 percent of its spending? Refer to Figure 17-9.

8. (a) If the debt-GDP ratio is 30 percent, the nominal interest rate is 12 percent, the inflation rate is 7 percent, and the total budget deficit is 4 percent of GDP, calculate the inflation-adjusted deficit.
    (b) Suppose you were to discover in an inflationary economy that the inflation-corrected budget was in surplus. Explain why in that case the government might be able to sustain a low inflation rate if it could only find a way of getting the rate down to start with.

9. Explain how, following the end of hyperinflation, it was possible for the nominal money stock in Germany to increase by a factor of nearly 20 without restarting the inflation.

10. Why do budget deficits create such alarm? Distinguish the short from the long run in developing your answer.

CHAPTER 18

Current Issues in Macroeconomic Policy

The ideas of economists and political philosophers, both when they are right and when they are wrong, are more powerful than is commonly understood. Indeed, the world is ruled by little else.

John Maynard Keynes, 1936

As an advice-giving profession we are in way over our heads.

Robert E. Lucas, Jr., 1980[1]

In this chapter we describe the major currents of thought in macroeconomics since the 1960s, when the monetarist challenge to mainstream Keynesian discretionary policy first gathered strength. During the 1970s support for monetarism waned as it failed to deliver on its promise to deal with inflation. In the latter part of the decade, a more sophisticated critique of discretionary policy, developed by the *rational expectations* school, gained influence.

Any student may wonder about a field where opinions and policy prescriptions change so often, and you may worry too about the difference of views among macroeconomists at a given time. For instance, what should you conclude when one economist says that the budget deficit is the biggest problem facing the economy in the 1980s, and another says that it is better to maintain the current level of government spending and taxes by borrowing to finance the deficit?

There certainly are disagreements among economists, but it is also true that those disagreements, and the distinguishing features of different points of view, are systematically exaggerated by the media. Macroeconomic controversies are always in the newspapers because macroeconomics concerns some of the most important issues of daily life — whether jobs are hard or easy to find,

---

[1] The quotes are from J.M. Keynes, *The General Theory of Employment, Interest and Money* (London: Macmillan, 1936), p. 383; and Robert E. Lucas, "Rules Discretion, and the Role of the Economic Adviser," in his book *Studies in Business Cycle Theory* (Cambridge, Mass.: MIT Press, 1981).

whether prices are rising slowly or fast, whether living standards will rise fast or hardly at all. The disagreements are systematically exaggerated because disagreements are news.

Behind the rapidly changing macroeconomics fashions of the media is a more balanced macroeconomic analysis that addresses current economic problems while at the same time weighing carefully evidence that leads to changes —mostly small, but sometimes large—in macroeconomic theories.

18-1 MONETARISM

Milton Friedman and monetarism are almost synonymous. Monetarism appears, however, in many shades and covers quite a spectrum from a hard monetarism, beyond the Friedman variety, to eclectic Keynesianism. In that spectrum one would include Karl Brunner of the University of Rochester, Allan Meltzer of Carnegie-Mellon, Thomas Mayer of the University of California at Davis, Phillip Cagan of Columbia University, David Laidler and Michael Parkin of the University of Western Ontario, and William Poole of Brown University, to name only some of the most prominent. Monetarism is not confined to academic economists. Indeed, the Federal Reserve Bank of St. Louis has long been a haven for the monetarist perspective on macroeconomics. If monetarism admits of some diversity, it nevertheless comes down to the proposition that money is extremely important for macroeconomics, that money is more important than other things such as fiscal policy, and, in some variants, that money is virtually all that matters.

We define monetarism by describing Friedman's views, but we should warn you that in so doing we over emphasize Friedman's role in developing and sustaining monetarism. Friedman's views on macroeconomics have been laid out in a series of scholarly articles, books, and popular writing.[2] Outstanding among his publications is *A Monetary History of the United States, 1867–1960*, a book written jointly with Anna J. Schwartz of the National Bureau of Economic Research. Despite its length, the *Monetary History* is an absorbing book that skilfully relates the behaviour of the economy to the behaviour of the stock of money. The book generally attributes changes in the level of prices and in economic activity, including the Great Depression, to movements in the stock of money.

What are the main features of monetarism?

---

[2] Some of Friedman's major articles are reprinted in *The Optimum Quantity of Money* (Chicago: Aldine, 1969). See also his book *A Program for Monetary Stability* (New York: Fordham University Press, 1959), and Milton Friedman and Anna J. Schwartz, *A Monetary History of the United States, 1867–1960* (Princeton, N.J.: Princeton University Press, 1963).

Emphasis on the Stock of Money

Monetarism emphasizes the importance of the behaviour of the money stock in determining (1) the rate of inflation in the long run and (2) the behaviour of real GDP in the short run. Friedman has said:

> I regard the description of our position as "money is all that matters for changes in *nominal* income and for *short-run* changes in real income" as an exaggeration but one that gives the right flavor of our conclusions.[3]

The view that the behaviour of the money stock is crucial for determining the rate of inflation in the long run is consistent with the analysis of Chapter 17, as we noted there. The view that the behaviour of the money stock, by which Friedman usually means the *growth rate* of the money stock, is of primary importance in determining the behaviour of nominal and real GDP in the short run is not one we have accepted. Our treatment so far has given emphasis to *both* monetary and fiscal variables in determining the short-run behaviour of nominal and real GDP, but there is no doubt that monetary variables play an important role in determining nominal and real GDP in the short run.

An important part of monetarism is the insistence that changes in the growth rate of money—accelerations and decelerations—account for changes in real activity. Instability in monetary growth is mirrored in variability in economic activity. Thus Friedman argues:

> Why should we be concerned about these gyrations in monetary growth? Because they exert an important influence on the future course of the economy. Erratic monetary growth almost always produces erratic economic growth.[4]

Friedman's view of the primary importance of money is based in part on his careful historical studies, in which he was able to relate the booms and recessions of United States economic history to the behaviour of the money stock. In general, it appeared that increases of the growth rate of money produced booms and inflations, and decreases in the money stock produced recessions and sometimes deflations.

Long and Variable Lags

Monetarism has emphasized that although the growth rate of money is of prime importance in determining the behaviour of GDP, the effects of changes in the growth rate of money on the subsequent behaviour of GDP occur with long and

---

[3] "A Theoretical Framework for Monetary Analysis," *Journal of Political Economy*, March/April 1970, p. 217.

[4] "Irresponsible Monetary Policy," *Newsweek*, Jan. 10, 1972. Reprinted in Friedman's collection of public policy essays, *There's No Such Thing as a Free Lunch* (La Salle, Ill.: Open Court Publishing, 1975), p. 73.

variable lags. On average, it takes a long time for a change in the growth rate of money to affect GDP, so the lag is long. In addition, the time it takes for this change to affect GDP varies from one historical episode to another — the lags are variable. These arguments are based on empirical and not theoretical evidence. Friedman estimates the lags may be as short as six months and as long as two years.

The Monetary Rule

Combining the preceding arguments, Friedman argues against the use of active monetary policy. He suggests that because the behaviour of the money stock is of critical importance for the behaviour of real and nominal GDP, and because money operates with a long and variable lag, monetary policy should not attempt to "fine-tune" the economy. The active use of monetary policy might actually destabilize the economy, because an action taken in 1989, say, might affect the economy at any of various future dates, such as in 1990 or 1991. By 1991, the action taken in 1989 might be inappropriate for the stabilization of GDP. Besides, there is no certainty that the policy will take effect in 1991 rather than 1990. For example, suppose that the economy is currently in a recession, and that the money supply is increased rapidly today to increase the growth rate of real GDP. Today's increase in the growth rate of money might affect GDP within 6 months, and achieve its purpose. However, it might work only in 2 years, by which time GDP might well already have increased without the aid of the monetary policy action. If the expansionary monetary policy affects an economy by then close to full employment, inflation will result.

Thus monetarists argue that although monetary policy has powerful effects on GDP, it should not be actively used lest it destabilize the economy. Accordingly, their view is that the money supply should be kept growing at a constant rate, to minimize the potential damage that inappropriate policy can cause.[5]

The Unimportance of Interest Rates

In the *IS-LM* model changes in the money stock affect the economy primarily by affecting interest rates, which, in turn, affect aggregate demand and thus GDP. When interest rates are low, monetary policy seems to be expansionary, encouraging investment and thus producing a high level of aggregate demand. Similarly, high interest rates seem to indicate contractionary policy. Since the central bank can control the level of interest rates, and since interest rates provide a guide to the effects of monetary policy on the economy, it seems

---

[5] For a concise statement, see Milton Friedman, "The Case for a Monetary Rule," *Newsweek*, Feb. 7, 1972. Reprinted in Milton Friedman, *Bright Promises, Dismal Performance* (New York: Harcourt, Brace, Jovanovich, 1983), pp. 225–227. See too his article "The Role of Monetary Policy," *American Economic Review*, March 1968.

perfectly sensible for it to carry out monetary policy by controlling interest rates. Through the 1950s and most of the 1960s, central banks did carry out monetary policy by attempting to set the level of interest rates.

Friedman and monetarism brought two serious criticisms of the procedure of attempting to set interest rates as the basis for the conduct of monetary policy. The first is that the behaviour of nominal interest rates is not a good guide to the direction, whether expansionary or contractionary, of monetary policy. The *real* interest rate, the nominal interest rate minus the expected rate of inflation, is the rate relevant to determining the level of investment. A high nominal interest rate, together with a high expected rate of inflation, means a low real rate of interest. Thus monetary policy might be quite expansionary in its effects on investment spending even when nominal interest rates are high. Consequently, Friedman and other monetarists argued, the central bank should not concentrate on the behaviour of nominal interest rates in the conduct of monetary policy.

The second criticism is that attempts to control nominal interest rates might be destabilizing. Suppose that the central bank desired that monetary policy should be expansionary and that the interest rate should be lowered. To achieve these goals it buys bonds in the open market, increasing the money supply. The expansionary monetary policy itself tends to raise the inflation rate. It thus tends to raise the nominal interest rate as investors adjust their expectation of inflation in response to the behaviour of the actual inflation rate. However, then the central bank would have to engage in a further open market purchase in an attempt to keep the nominal interest rate low, and that would lead to further inflation, further increases in nominal interest rates, and further open market purchases. The end result is that an attempt to keep nominal interest rates low may lead to increasing inflation. Therefore, Friedman argues, the central bank should not pay attention to the behaviour of nominal interest rates in the conduct of monetary policy,[6] and should, rather, keep the money supply growing at a constant rate.

Each of these arguments on the dangers of conducting monetary policy by reference to nominal interest rates is important. It is indeed correct that real, and not nominal, interest rates provide the appropriate measure of the effects of monetary policy on aggregate demand. It is also true that the central bank could, by attempting to keep nominal interest rates low forever, destabilize the economy. However, once the latter danger has been pointed out, the probability that it will destabilize the economy by operating with reference to interest rates is reduced. The use of interest rates as a guide to the direction of monetary policy does not mean that the central bank has to attempt to keep the interest

---

[6] The details of the argument are spelled out in Friedman's "The Role of Monetary Policy," *American Economic Review*, March 1968.

rate fixed forever at some level. Instead, it may aim each month or quarter for an interest rate target that it regards as appropriate for the current and predicted economic situation.

The monetarist case for concentrating on the behaviour of the money stock in the conduct of monetary policy is a strong, but not conclusive, one. The major weakness in the argument is that the demand for real balances may change over time and indeed has done so. A simple numerical example should help make the point. Suppose that real income is constant, and that the nominal interest rate is constant. Suppose also that the demand for real balances is constant. Then if the money supply grows at, say, the rate of 5 percent, the price level, too, will grow at 5 percent, so that the stock of real balances remains constant. Now suppose, instead, that the demand for real balances is falling by 2 percent per year. Then if the nominal money supply increases at 5 percent per year, the price level has to increase at 7 percent per year to keep the supply of real balances equal to the demand. Thus, shifts in the demand for money affect the rate of inflation, given the growth rate of money. In this example, if the demand for real balances grew at 5 percent per year, 5 percent money growth would not be inflationary at all. These shifts in demand raise the possibility that concentration on the behaviour of the nominal stock may be seriously misleading and inappropriate for the conduct of monetary policy.

Because of shifts in the demand for money, the behaviour of the money stock is not a perfect guide to the conduct of monetary policy. Neither is the behaviour of nominal interest rates. However, the behaviour of the nominal money stock and the behaviour of nominal interest rates both provide some information about the direction in which monetary policy is pushing the economy, imperfect as each measure is. Accordingly, the central bank should pay attention to the behaviour of both interest rates and the supply of money in the conduct of its monetary policy.[7]

The Importance of Fiscal Policy

Friedman has frequently, if tongue in cheek, said that fiscal policy is very important. Although we noted earlier that he argues fiscal policy itself is not important for the behaviour of GDP, he does contend that it is of vital importance in setting the size of government and the role of government in the economy. Friedman is an opponent of big government. He has made the interesting argument that government spending increases to match the revenues available. The government will spend the full tax collection — and some more. Accordingly, he is in favour of tax cuts as a way of reducing government spending.

---

[7] The argument is worked out in Benjamin M. Friedman, "Targets, Instruments, and Indicators of Monetary Policy." *Journal of Monetary Economics*, October 1975.

Friedman stands out in arguing that fiscal policy does not have strong effects on the economy except to the extent that it affects the behaviour of money. Thus he has remarked:

> To have a significant impact on the economy, a tax increase must somehow affect monetary policy — the quantity of money and its rate of growth. . . .
>   The level of taxes is important — because it affects how much of our resources we use through the government and how much we use as individuals. It is not important as a sensitive and powerful device to control the short-run course of income and prices.[8]

The Inherent Stability of the Private Sector

The final aspect of monetarism we consider here is the monetarist view that the economy, left to itself, is more stable than when the government manages it with discretionary policy, and that the major cause of economic fluctuations lies in inappropriate government actions. This view is quite fundamental in that it underlies many other monetarist positions, and it may be the litmus test for distinguishing monetarists from other macroeconomists. It is because this point is so fundamental that a major stage in the acceptance of monetarism occurred when Friedman and Schwartz published their *Monetary History of the United States*. In it they provided evidence for the view that the Great Depression was the result of bad monetary policy rather than private sector instability, arising, say, from autonomous shifts in consumption or investment demand.

Summary: We Are All Monetarists

From the viewpoint of the conduct of economic policy, the major monetarist themes are (1) an emphasis on the growth rate of the money stock, (2) arguments against fine tuning in favour of a monetary rule, and (3) a greater weight that monetarists, as compared for example with Keynesians, place on the costs of inflation relative to those of unemployment.

Although we describe these as the major monetarist propositions relating to policy,[9] it is not true that macroeconomists can be neatly divided into two groups, some subscribing to the monetarist religion and others to a less fundamentalist faith called neo-Keynesianism. Most of the arguments advanced

---

[8] Milton Friedman, "Higher Taxes? No," *Newsweek*, Jan. 23, 1967. Reprinted in *There's No Such Thing as a Free Lunch, op. cit.,* p. 89.

[9] For a range of views on monetarism, see Franco Modigliani, "The Monetarist Controversy," *American Economic Review*, March 1977; Thomas Mayer, *The Structure of Monetarism* (New York: Norton, 1978); D. Batten and C. Stone, "Are Monetarists an Endangered Species?", Federal Reserve Bank of St. Louis, *Review*, May 1983; and J.H. McCulloch, *Money and Inflation* (New York: Academic Press, 1982).

by Friedman and his associates are technical and susceptible to economic analysis and the application of empirical evidence. Many of those propositions are now widely accepted and are no longer particularly associated with monetarism. As Franco Modigliani has remarked, "We are all monetarists now." He adds that we are monetarists in the sense that all (or most) macroeconomists believe in the importance of money.

Much of the analysis of this book would, in the past, have been considered monetarist. For example, we have assumed that the Phillips curve is vertical, a proposition that was originally associated with monetarism. We have laid considerable stress on the behaviour of the money stock and less stress on the behaviour of interest rates. We have emphasized that fiscal policy affects long-run inflation to the extent that it affects the long-run growth rate of money. Older readers will doubtless detect other places at which we appear monetarist to their eyes. That is all to the good. If economists, did not modify their analyses in the light of new theories and evidence, the field would be barren.

Friedman and his associates have indeed changed macroeconomics. The forceful and persuasive way in which he has emphasized the role of money has changed the views of most economists on the importance of monetary policy. It is always possible that those views would have changed anyway, in the light of the increasing inflation of the sixties. The fact remains, however, that it was Friedman, and not someone else, who hammered away at the importance of money.

18-2 MONETARISM AND THE BANK OF CANADA

As we saw in Chapter 12, in the early 1970s the Bank of Canada moved toward greater emphasis on the control of the money supply in implementing monetary policy. In 1975 it began the practice of announcing target ranges for the rate of growth of the money supply.

In his *Annual Report* for 1975, the governor stressed the importance of bringing down the rate of inflation and addressed the question of how this should be accomplished:

> One answer sometimes given to this question is that the Bank of Canada should do the job through a sharp and immediate reduction of the growth rate of the money supply to a rate approximately in line with the sustainable real growth of the economy. If that were to happen, it is asserted, inflation would readily come to an end.
>
> The trouble with this prescription is not with the medicine but with the dosage, which would be so great that the patient would suffer excessively while it was working. It would sharply curtail the growth of spending on goods and services in the face of continuing large increases in production costs already built into the economy, and this would almost certainly result in extremely weak markets, widespread bankruptcies and soaring unemployment. It must

be recognized that the annual rate of increase in average Canadian money incomes that is consistent with price stability is no higher than the trend rate of increase in national productivity, which is usually put at around 2 per cent per year, and we are a long way from that situation. All sorts of existing arrangements, including virtually all wage contracts, are based on the assumption of some continuing inflation. The attempt to force as rapid a transition to price and cost stability as this prescription involves would be too disruptive in economic and social terms to be sensible or tolerable.[10]

Thus the Bank of Canada clearly rejected a cold-turkey policy and opted for gradualism. This strategy was subsequently implemented by successive reductions in the target to the range of 4 to 8 percent established in February 1981. As can be seen in Figure 18-1, the Bank generally kept monetary growth within

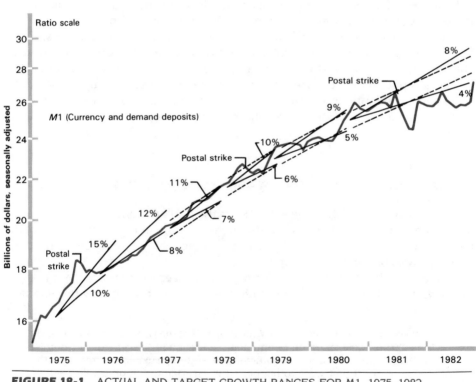

FIGURE 18-1   ACTUAL AND TARGET GROWTH RANGES FOR M1, 1975–1982

(*Source*: Adapted from Bank of Canada, *Annual Report*, 1982)

[10] Bank of Canada, *Annual Report*, 1975, p. 10.

the target range until the second half of 1981.[11] As discussed in the next section, the Bank abandoned gradualism at that time in response to a severe tightening of monetary policy in the U.S.

After the adoption by the Bank of Canada of a monetarist strategy, the governor annunciated the philosophy and principles underlying it on a number of occasions. In a statement before the House of Commons Standing Committee on Finance, Trade and Economic Affairs, the governor put forward three basic propositions. The first reaffirmed the overriding importance of bringing down the rate of inflation:

> For quite a few years now the nature of the major threat to the future economic welfare of the country has been unusually clear. That threat is inflation. The idea that some inflation is on balance helpful to the performance of an economy, that inflation is benign — an idea that was never more than superficially plausible but was nevertheless quite popular — is now thoroughly discredited. What has discredited it so effectively is not economic theory but economic experience. The experience of the world economy and the widely varying experience of its national members have shown beyond reasonable question that inflation is malignant. The matter is no longer seriously debated.

As to the role of monetary policy in fighting inflation, the governor stated:

> there is one proposition that must never be forgotten, and that is that in a free society no strategy for dealing with inflation will succeed unless it is well supported by firm and continuing control of the rate of monetary expansion in the society. That proposition is, I assure you, as reliable as any general proposition in the whole field of economics. Every central banker in the world knows it to be true, and I doubt that any serious and experienced student of financial affairs would question it. It is a very firm proposition indeed, and anyone who wants to participate responsibly in the debate on how to deal with inflation would be well advised to keep it uppermost in his mind.

In his third proposition, the governor put forward the distinction between real and nominal interest rates:

> The basic reason why interest rates are so high is because current and expected rates of inflation are so high. If you make allowance for the current rate of inflation, interest rates are not in fact unusually high. They are not so high as to provide savers with a large real return before taxes or in many cases with a real return at all after taxes. They are not so high as to discourage borrowers who expect continued high rates of inflation.[12]

---

[11] The exceptions have been periods in which the payments system was disrupted by postal strikes as indicated in the chart.

[12] Reprinted in the *Bank of Canada Review*, November 1980, pp. 13–19. The earliest statement was given in an address to the Canadian Chamber of Commerce in Saskatoon in September 1975. This speech has been dubbed the "Saskatoon monetary manifesto" by Thomas Courchene. See T. J. Courchene, *Monetarism and Controls: The Inflation Fighters* (C.D. Howe Research Institute, 1976).

Thus the Bank of Canada has made a clear commitment to an anti-inflation policy based on monetary gradualism. In doing so, it recognized the consequences not only for the levels of output and employment, but also for the behaviour of nominal interest rates. In his *Annual Report* for 1978, the governor stated:

> Whatever their object, however, central bank actions that have the effect of speeding up or slowing down the trend over time in the rate of growth of the money supply have longer run effects on the level of interest rates that can be quite the opposite of the effects produced in the short run. A stepped-up rate of monetary expansion that temporarily lowers interest rates will, if it is sustained, lead eventually to a higher rate of price increase than would otherwise have occurred. With money losing its value more rapidly, borrowers will be less reluctant to incur debt since they can repay in dollars of lesser value, while savers and lenders will for the same reason be more reluctant to provide loans. The consequence of rising inflation will thus be a growing excess demand for credit in relation to the supply which will put increasing upward pressure on interest rates. Thus the eventual result of letting the money supply grow too rapidly is not low interest rates but high interest rates.
>
> If a country wants to have and maintain low interest rates, there is no secret about how to achieve that. Monetary growth must be reduced until it is only just sufficient to finance the expansion in production that the economy is capable of achieving over the longer run without putting pressure on the over-all level of prices, and it must be kept there. The immediate effect of this policy will be to raise interest rates but the longer term effect will be to lower them. The low interest rate countries of the world are the ones that have had the greatest success over the years in resisting the temptation to allow inflationary pressures to be underwritten by excessive monetary expansion. The countries that have experienced less success in controlling the process of domestic monetary expansion have higher rates of inflation and higher interest rates.[13]

18-3 THE FIGHT AGAINST INFLATION

As discussed in the previous section, the Bank of Canada instituted a policy in late 1975 of gradually reducing the rate of growth of the money supply. At the same time, the government announced a program of wage and price controls to be administered by an Anti-Inflation Board (AIB). The board was given statutory power to control wages and profit margins of private firms with 500 or more employees. Provincial and municipal government wage setting was brought into the program through agreements with the provinces to apply the guidelines established by the federal board. The controls remained in effect until they were phased out beginning in April 1978. Let us examine the performance of the Canadian economy in response to these two policy initiatives.

---

[13] Bank of Canada, *Annual Report*, 1978, p. 14.

Wage Settlements and the AIB

The top panel of Figure 18-2 shows the average annual percentage increases in base rates of pay negotiated in wage contracts over the period 1974 to 1987. Prior to the formation of the AIB, wage settlements had risen to nearly 19 percent per year, but during 1976 and 1977 there was a substantial moderation in the rate of increase. However, as shown in the second panel of Figure 18-2, during the same period the seasonally adjusted unemployment rate rose from 6.8 percent to 8.4 percent. To measure the effect of the controls it is necessary to estimate on the basis of historical experience what wage increases would have occurred in the absence of controls given the actual economic conditions experienced.

In a study undertaken for the Economic Council of Canada, Cousineau and Lacroix estimated that the average annual wage increase in major collective agreements would have been 1.7 percentage points higher in the private sector and 4.3 percentage points higher in the public sector had the anti-inflation guidelines not been in force.[14] In another study, Auld, Christofides, Swidinsky and Wilton concluded that: "in the period of AIB wage controls, union wage settlements in the private and public sectors have been between 2½ and 3½ percentage points per annum lower than the pre-AIB wage structure would predict; by 1977 the cumulative wage affect of the AIB was on the order of 3.2 percent in the private and 4.6 percent in the public sectors."[15] Thus it would appear that controls had an impact particularly on public sector wages, but that they were responsible for a limited part of the moderation in negotiated wage increases that occurred.[16]

The Rate of Inflation

The third panel of Figure 18-2 shows the rate of inflation as measured by the percentage change in the Consumer Price Index over the same quarter of the preceding year. During 1976 the rate fell dramatically from the level above 10 percent recorded in 1975 to 5.9 percent. However, a closer look at the components of the CPI shows that very little of this decline in the rate of inflation can be attributed to the AIB controls. A major contributing factor was the sharp decline in the rate of increase of food prices which were not subject to controls.

---

[14] See Economic Council of Canada, Fourteenth Annual Review (1977), p. 20.

[15] D. Auld, L. Christofides, R. Swidinsky, and D. Wilton, "The Impact of the Anti-Inflation Board on Negotiated Wage Settlements," *Canadian Journal of Economics*, May 1979, p. 209.

[16] For a review of empirical studies on the effect of the AIB, see W.C. Riddell, "Dealing with Inflation and Unemployment in Canada," Royal Commission on the Economic Union, Vol. 25, University of Toronto Press (1986), pp. 78–84.

* Percent change over the same quarter of the preceding year.

FIGURE 18-2 INFLATION AND UNEMPLOYMENT, 1974-1987

(*Source: Adapted from Bank of Canada Review*)

Since food prices typically exhibit wide variations from year to year, it is common to use the CPI excluding food as a measure of the underlying trend in the rate of inflation. As can be seen in the bottom panel of Figure 18-2, this index shows a slow but steady decline from the fourth quarter of 1975 to the second quarter of 1978 when it fell to 6 percent. Unfortunately in the third quarter of 1978, the downward trend in the underlying rate of inflation was reversed, and by the third quarter of 1981, the CPI excluding food was increasing at a rate above 13 percent, in spite of the fact that the unemployment rate had remained above 7 percent since mid-1976.

In June 1982, the federal government introduced a limited program of wage controls known as the 6 and 5 program that limited wage increases to 6 percent in the first year and 5 percent in the second. The restrictions applied only to the federal public service and Crown corporations. Federal agencies which regulate prices such as telephone rates were asked to adhere to the guidelines and most provincial governments introduced similar restraint programs.

Concern about the rising rate of inflation also led to a severe tightening of monetary policy. During the first half of 1981, the Federal Reserve pushed up interest rates sharply in the U.S. and the Bank of Canada followed suit. By the middle of the year short-term interest rates in Canada had risen above 20 percent. As can be seen in Figure 18-2, the rate of inflation subsequently declined sharply, but this was achieved by exploiting the short-run Phillips curve tradeoff and allowing a drastic increase in the unemployment rate.

Was Monetarism a Failure?

The performance of the Canadian economy over the period 1975 to 1983 led to considerable controversy over the monetarist strategy of the Bank of Canada.[17] The success of the Bank's policy was hindered by the impact of supply shocks, problems with the implementation of gradualism, and difficulties in using money supply measures as targets of policy.

Supply Shocks and Inflation

One can accept the monetarist view that control of the money supply is an essential part of any anti-inflationary policy while at the same time recognizing that other factors influence short-run movements in the price level. In particular, the sharp increases in world prices of oil and other commodities that

---

[17] See for example the following two studies sponsored by the Canadian Institute for Economic Policy: A. W. Donner and D. D. Peters, *The Monetarist Counter-Revolution, A Critique of Canadian Monetary Policy 1975–1979*; and C. L. Barber and J. C. P. McCallum, *Unemployment and Inflation, the Canadian Experience*.

occurred in 1973–74 and 1978–79 led to increases in both the rate of inflation and the unemployment rate.

Gradualism

The Bank of Canada has argued on a number of occasions that the failure of its anti-inflation policy over the period 1975–1980 was in part caused by excessive gradualism. For example, in a statement before the House of Commons Standing Committee on Finance, Trade and Economic Affairs, Governor Bouey stated:

> The experience of the past few years appears to have led some observers to conclude that the Bank's approach to reducing inflation has failed. If they mean that progress in reducing inflation is less than the Bank hoped, I agree with them. But if they mean, as I think some of them do, that the Bank's approach was misconceived, then they have misread the history of the period. What they should conclude is that given the economic and financial developments over that period, many of which were unpredictable, it would have been better if the slowing of monetary growth had been less gradual so that it would have had more impact on inflation. That is the moral that should be drawn. In this connection I would point out that the rate of monetary expansion today is very much lower than it was five years ago and although we have arrived at this position through a very gradual process, the impact on total spending can be expected to be much firmer from now on than it was when we started on this path.[18]

This view was supported by the experience of the period 1981–1983 when the Bank of Canada abandoned gradualism. Following the lead of the Federal Reserve in the United States and Prime Minister Thatcher's government in Britain, the bank brought down the inflation rate by a severe tightening of monetary policy. Experience in all three countries showed that controlling monetary growth can indeed bring down the rate of inflation, but, because of the long lags, the process is very slow unless the economy is pushed into a very deep recession.

The Use of Monetary Targets

The Bank of Canada's Annual Reports for 1981 and 1982 both contained detailed discussions of the Bank's experience with the use of M1 as a target of monetary policy. It is argued that the usefulness of this measure of the money supply has been impaired by innovations in banking practice such as daily interest savings accounts and expanded cash management services for businesses. Initially the Bank attempted to adjust for these influences on the

---

[18] See *Bank of Canada Review*, November 1980, p. 1.

demand for money, but in November 1982 it announced that it would no longer establish M1 targets.

As we saw in Chapter 12, the use of money supply targets is appropriate when the demand for money is stable and the main source of disturbances is the goods market. The breakdown in the stability of the money demand thus forced the Bank to abandon money supply targets.

Recovery From the 1981–82 Recession

As we noted above the 1981–82 recession was brought on by a severe tightening of monetary policy that led to a reduction of the inflation rate at the expense of a sharp increase in unemployment. Figure 18-3 shows the pattern of recovery from 1983 to 1987. The unemployment rate remained above 10 percent through the end of 1985, but by the end of 1987 it was approaching 8

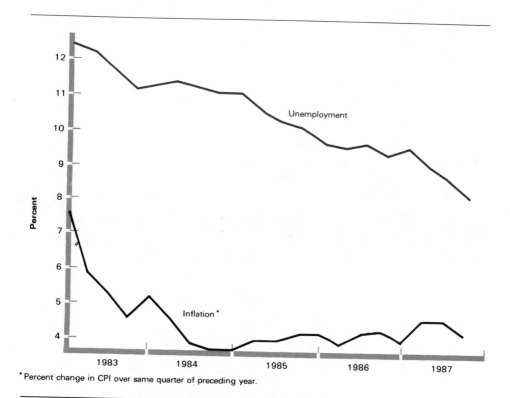

* Percent change in CPI over same quarter of preceding year.

FIGURE 18-3   RECOVERY FROM THE 1981–82 RECESSION

(Source: Bank of Canada Review)

percent. The inflation rate fell to 4 percent in 1984 but remained close to that level for the succeeding three years.

At the beginning of 1987, John Crow assumed the position of governor of the Bank of Canada. In a lecture given at the University of Alberta a year later, he reaffirmed the Bank's commitment to price stability as a major goal of monetary policy. In particular, he made the following case that the battle against inflation had not yet been won:

> It is sometimes argued that the necessary ingredient from the monetary side for good economic performance is not a stable general price level but just predictability in the general rate of inflation. In my view, the notion of a high, yet stable rate of inflation is simply unrealistic.
>
> The crux of the matter is that success in what is in effect an attempt to mimic price stability by achieving a stable inflation rate depends on strong public confidence that the authorities would not accept a further acceleration in the rate of inflation. However, if the authorities were unwilling to act to get the rate of inflation down from, for example, 4 percent, why should anyone believe they would be any more willing to get it back to 4 percent if for one reason or another upward pressures on prices led the inflation rate to rise to 5 percent? And so on. This is why a commitment to a steady inflation rate is ultimately not credible.[19]

18-4   THE RATIONAL EXPECTATIONS–EQUILIBRIUM APPROACH

The failure to reduce inflation in the 1970s and the apparent inability of macro policy to achieve its goals led to a reconsideration of the premises of modern macroeconomics. The reconsideration places great emphasis on expectations, on the credibility of policies, and on the limited scope for discretionary stabilization policies. These are among the hallmarks of what is called the *rational expectations approach* to macroeconomics. Among the leading members of the school are Robert Lucas of the University of Chicago, and Edward Prescott, Thomas Sargent, and Neil Wallace of the University of Minnesota.[20]

---

[19] See *Bank of Canada Review*, February, 1988, pp. 4–5.

[20] For an introduction see Thomas Sargent and Neil Wallace, "Rational Expectations and the Theory of Economic Policy," *Journal of Monetary Economics*, April 1976. See also Robert Lucas, "Understanding Business Cycles," in Robert E. Lucas (ed.), *Studies in Business Cycle Theory*, MIT Press, 1981; Bennett McCallum, "Macroeconomics after a Decade of Rational Expectations: Some Critical Issues," in Federal Reserve Bank of Richmond, *Economic Review*, November/December 1982; Arthur Okun, "Rational-Expectations-with-Misperceptions as a Theory of the Business Cycle," *Journal of Money, Credit and Banking*, November 1980, part 2. Two textbooks review the tools and propositions. These are Steven Shelfrin, *Rational Expectations* (London: Cambridge University Press, 1983), and David Begg, *The Rational Expectations Revolution in Macroeconomics* (Baltimore: Johns Hopkins University Press, 1983).

The rational expectations approach acquired that name because the assumption of rational expectations in the context of the expectations-augmented aggregate supply curve of Chapter 15 has such striking implications. Recall that in Chapter 15 we defined the rational expectations hypothesis as assuming *individuals form expectations using information efficiently and do not make systematic mistakes in expectations.*

We saw that rational expectations applied to the expectations-augmented aggregate supply curve implied that an expected reduction in the growth rate of money would reduce the inflation rate without causing a recession. We also noted in the same context that only unexpected changes in monetary policy would have real effects, and we discussed the important role of credibility of the intentions of policy makers.

The group known as the rational expectations school has a broader aim. The rational expectations–equilibrium approach aims to build all of macroeconomics on sound microeconomic foundations, in which individuals maximize utility, firms maximize profits, and markets are in equilibrium. The emphasis on markets being in equilibrium is far more fundamental than just the rational expectations assumption. It is for that reason that we add "equilibrium" in referring to the approach as the rational expectations–equilibrium approach.

In the remainder of this section we briefly take up the rational expectations part of the approach. In the next section we turn to the equilibrium approach.

Rational Expectations As a Theory of Expectations

The assumption that expectations are rational, based on the efficient use of information, and not systematically incorrect, is made on occasion by almost all macroeconomists. Its use does not automatically qualify the user as a member of the rational expectations–equilibrium school.

The question of whether individuals make systematic mistakes in expectations is an empirical one. Indeed, there is some evidence that individuals do make systematic mistakes.[21] At the level of individual firms forecasting sales, some firms seem to be perpetual optimists, others perpetual pessimists. It has to be recognized that firms or individuals may make mistakes in expectations for long periods. In normal times, they may use simple rules of thumb for forecasting. Nonetheless, the rational expectations approach suggests that if forecast errors are expensive to the forecaster, any systematic errors will eventually be corrected by the people making them.

Beyond that, rational expectations as a theory of expectations implies that policy cannot rely for its effectiveness on systematic misunderstandings by the

[21] See Michael C. Lovell, "Tests of the Rational Expectations Hypothesis," *American Economic Review*, March 1986. See, too, the challenging paper by Amos Tversky and Daniel Kahneman, "Judgment Under Uncertainty: Heuristics and Biases," *Science*, 185, pp. 1124–1131, 1984.

public. For instance, if at first the public does not understand that counter-cyclical tax changes are transitory, those changes will have powerful effects on the economy. However, as people begin to realize that tax changes are reversed as the economy reaches full employment, such a policy comes to have less powerful effects because the tax changes are understood to be transitory. The expectations part of rational expectations suggests that it is best, in formulating policy, to assume that the public will soon understand how a particular policy is working. It also implies that any policy which works for some time only because the public does not correctly anticipate its effects is doomed to eventual failure.

18-5   THE EQUILIBRIUM APPROACH

The equilibrium component of the rational expectations–equilibrium approach is also known as the *new classical macroeconomics*. The approach accepts as its basic challenge the need to explain the fluctuations in output and employment that take place in the business cycle.

Money and Business Cycles

The early work in this area was done by Robert Lucas. Lucas saw the Phillips curve, the tradeoff between inflation and unemployment, as the central empirical fact that had to be explained, and he aimed to explain it in a model in which prices can move to make supply equal to demand.[22]

Why is the Phillips curve a central problem for an equilibrium approach to macroeconomics? Recall that we showed in Chapter 7 that when prices are flexible, an increase in the money stock is fully neutral, raising prices but not output. If prices are not assumed to be sticky — and the equilibrium approach assumes prices are free to move to clear markets — it is necessary to explain why an increase in the money stock that raises prices apparently is accompanied also by higher output. Equivalently, it has to be explained why it appears impossible to reduce the inflation rate without creating a recession.

Lucas focussed on the tradeoff between output (rather than unemployment) and inflation. The explanation assumed that individuals have imperfect information about the current price level and thus mistake movements in *absolute* prices for *relative* price changes.

The model starts from the supply of a particular good, call it good i; quantity supplied increases with the *relative* price of that good. This is simple microeconomics. The aggregate price level (P_t) is not known at the time suppliers have to decide how much to produce and sell. Instead suppliers base their

[22] The most influential single article is Robert E. Lucas, "Some International Evidence on Output-Inflation Tradeoffs," *American Economic Review*, September 1973.

output decisions on the estimated or expected aggregate price level, P_t^e. *The price of the particular good i is P_{it}.* The supply curve of good i is

$$Y_{it} = f\left(\frac{P_{it}}{P_t^e}\right) \tag{1}$$

Y_{it} is the output of the ith good.

In a competitive market each supplier knows the price in his or her market, but because information is imperfect, all suppliers know only P_{it} in their individual market, not any other prices or the aggregate price level. On the basis of P_{it} and the price level they expected, P_t^e, they have to make a best estimate of the actual relative price of good i, that is, of P_{it}/P_t.

Individuals know that there are two types of shocks in the economy. Some shocks are *relative*, or specific to individual markets. These relative shocks sum to zero across the markets, some markets having higher than average demand, others having less than average. There are also *aggregate* shocks, which raise quantity demanded at a given price in every market. An unexpected increase in the money stock is one such shock.

Consider the supplier who has some expectation of the aggregate price level, P_t^e, and who now learns the relative price in the market. Suppose the relative price is high. The supplier has to decide whether that is because there has been an increase in demand in all markets, raising the aggregate price level, or just in his or her market, raising the relative price. If the high price in market i is a result of a shock to the money stock that affects all markets, the supplier will not want to raise output. If the shock is specific to market i, the supplier will want to raise output.

The key result that Lucas establishes is this: the rational calculation is to assume that when price in market i is high, that is partly because the aggregate price level is high and partly because there has been a relative shock in market i. The statistically best guess that individuals in the market can make, assigns responsibility for the high price between its two possible sources. That means that when seeing a price that, relative to the expected aggregate price level, seems high, a supplier will react to the higher price by producing more — though the reaction is less than if the supplier was certain the relative price in his or her market was high.

The next step is to look at all markets together. If there has been no shock to the money supply, the relative shocks will cancel out in their total effects on output. Output will be higher than average in some markets, lower than average in others. However, if there has been an unexpected increase in the money stock, output will on average be higher than normal—because everyone partly mistook the increase in aggregate demand as a shift in relative demand and produced more than average. Adding up output across markets, total production will be higher when the money stock has unexpectedly increased, and on average prices will be higher, because demand in each market was greater.

Lucas thus succeeded in producing a Phillips curve type of tradeoff in which a higher average price level would be accompanied by higher output. This is remarkable, but so is the accompanying implication, that *only unexpected changes in the money stock affect output.*[23] If the changes had been expected, suppliers in individual markets could have figured out the effects on the aggregate price level, taken them into account, and would not have increased production in response to a higher price level.

The Lucas demonstration of a possible Phillips curve based on incomplete information attracted much attention, particularly the demonstration that with regard to monetary policy, only unexpected changes in the stock of money affect the price level. Under these circumstances, there appears to be no role for monetary policy to systematically affect output or unemployment. Any systematic policy, such as increased monetary expansion in a recession (remember that recessions are possible as a result of surprises) would be predicted by market participants, and wages and prices would be set accordingly.[24] Unless the central bank had better information, or shorter reaction lags than the market, it could not, according to this theory, have a systematic *real* effect.

Empirical Testing

The proposition that only monetary *surprises* affect output has been the subject of intense empirical research. Early work by Robert Barro[25] appeared to support the proposition. Later research by, among others, Frederic Mishkin and Robert Gordon cast substantial doubt on the early findings.[26] The later results suggest that both expected and unexpected changes in the money stock affect output. By this stage, the evidence does not support the strong implication of the market clearing approach that only unanticipated changes in the money stock affect output. Accordingly, the evidence also does not support the view that systematic monetary policy does not affect the behaviour of output.

---

[23] We have already seen a result like this in Chapter 15, but we did not there use the microeconomic underpinnings that Lucas provides.

[24] You might wonder at this stage whether the equilibrium approach does not also imply that the economy should return immediately to equilibrium following a shock. We show below that is not necessarily the case.

[25] Robert J. Barro, "Unanticipated Money, Output, and the Price Level in the United States," *Journal of Political Economy*, August 1978.

[26] Frederic Mishkin, "Does Anticipated Monetary Policy Matter? An Econometric Investigation," *Journal of Political Economy*, February 1982 (this is difficult reading); and Robert Gordon, "Price Inertia and Policy Ineffectiveness in the United States, 1890–1980," *Journal of Political Economy*, December 1982.

Equilibrium Real Business Cycles

The weakness of the empirical evidence for the view that only unanticipated money affects real output led to two reactions. Some economists believed that better explanations would have to be found for the role of money in the business cycle. Others questioned the evidence linking money with the business cycle at all.

In particular, economists working on the equilibrium approach developed *equilibrium real business cycle* theory, the view that fluctuations in output and employment are the result of a variety of real shocks hitting the economy. They explained the apparent link between money and output as a result of the money stock accommodating movements in output. Thus money could be correlated with changes in output, but would not necessarily cause them.[27]

With monetary causes of the business cycle assumed out of the way, real business cycle theory is left with two tasks. The first is to explain the *shocks* or *disturbances* that hit the economy, causing fluctuations in the first place. The second is to explain the *propagation mechanisms.* A propagation mechanism is the means through which a disturbance is spread through the economy. In particular, the aim is to explain why shocks to the economy seem to have long-lived effects.

Propagation Mechanism

Many of the mechanisms that real business cycle theory relies on to explain why a shock to the economy affects output for several years have already been discussed. Among these are inventory adjustments and changes in investment caused by shifts in profitability. These are part of anyone's theory of the business cycle.

The one mechanism that is most associated with equilibrium business cycles though is *the intertemporal substitution of leisure.* Any theory of the business cycle has to explain why people work more at some times than at others; during booms employment is high and jobs are easy to find; during recessions people work less.

A simple equilibrium explanation would be that people work more in booms because wages are higher. That way they would voluntarily be supplying more labour in response to a higher wage. (Remember that the equilibrium approach requires people to be on their supply-and-demand curves at all times.) However,

---

[27] This view is developed in a technically very advanced paper by Robert King and Charles Plosser, "Money, Credit and Prices in a Real Business Cycle Model," *American Economic Review*, June 1984. A nontechnical review is in Carl Walsh, "New Views of the Business Cycle," Federal Reserve Bank of Philadelphia *Business Review*, January–February 1986.

the facts are not strongly in favour of that argument because the real wage changes very little over the business cycle. People are thus not obviously working more in response to higher wages.

The Keynesian or monetarist approaches explain these movements in output by saying that the demand for labour shifts as aggregate demand shifts, and that people may be unemployed in recessions because they cannot get work despite their willingness to work at the going wage.[28] However, the equilibrium approach constrains itself to assume markets are in equilibrium. The explanation for the large movements in output with small movements in wages is the following: there is a large elasticity of labour supply in response to temporary changes in the wage, or, as the argument is put, people are willing to substitute leisure intertemporally.

The argument is that people care very little about when in any given period of a year or two they work. Suppose that within a 2-year period they plan to work 4000 hours at the going wage (50 weeks each year for 40 hours a week). If wages are equal in the 2 years, they would work 2000 hours each year, but if wages were just 2 percent higher in one year than the other, they might prefer to work, say 2200 hours in one year, forgoing vacations, and working overtime, and 1800 hours in the other. That way they work the same total amount and earn more total income.

This intertemporal substitution of leisure is clearly capable of generating large movements in the amount of work done in response to small shifts in wages — and thus could account for large output effects in the cycle accompanied by small changes in wages. However, there has not been strong empirical support for this view either.

Similar intertemporal substitution arguments have been advanced to explain fluctuations in consumption over the course of the business cycle. In this case the real interest rate is assumed to move, with individuals reducing current levels of consumption when the interest rate is high in order to take advantage of the higher rate of return on saving.

Disturbances

The most important disturbances isolated by equilibrium business cycle theorists are shocks to *productivity*, or supply shocks, and shocks to *government spending*.

---

[28] In some versions of the Keynesian model, including that of Keynes in the *General Theory*, it is assumed that output is determined by the demand for labour curve (see the neoclassical labour demand curve in the appendix to Chapter 14). That implies the real wage would be higher in recessions than in booms — firms hire more labour in booms because it is profitable to do so. Since the real wage does not move much in the cycle, this explanation, too, cannot be correct. In the model developed in Chapters 14 and 15,

A productivity shock raises output as of a given level of input. Good weather and new methods of production are examples. Suppose there is a temporary favourable productivity shock this period. Then individuals will want to work harder to take advantage of the higher productivity. In working more this period they raise output. They will also invest more, thus spreading the productivity shock into future periods by raising the stock of capital. If the intertemporal substitution of leisure effect is strong, even a small productivity shock could have a relatively large effect on output.

Increased government spending is another type of shock. To provide the extra goods the government needs, individuals will work harder if the real wage rises, and save more if the real interest rate rises. Thus we should expect an increase in government spending to raise the real interest rate and the real wage.[29]

There is less certainty in the real business cycle approach about the effects of a cut in taxes than about the effects of an increase in government spending. As we discussed in Chapter 13, the Ricardian view is that individuals recognize that a cut in taxes today is just an increase in taxes tomorrow, and that they therefore should not increase consumption when taxes are cut.

Summary

The equilibrium real business cycle approach is still a subject of intense research. Its goal of building macroeconomics on sound microeconomic foundations is surely widely shared. There is no doubt too that some of the mechanisms, such as inventory accumulation and investment dynamics, that underlie its explanation of the dynamics of the business cycle, will form part of future business cycle models. However, there is room to doubt that the attempt to build business cycle models in which there is no role for monetary factors will be ultimately successful.

18-6 THE RATIONAL EXPECTATIONS–EQUILIBRIUM APPROACH TO POLICY

The rational expectations approach has led to a sophisticated view of policy making. The rational expectations approach emphasizes that economic agents do not react mechanically to every policy change. Rather, they try to figure out

---

the real wage is constant as a result of markup pricing, and employment changes with aggregate demand. Constancy of the real wage is a reasonable approximation to actual wage behaviour.

[29] Note that increased government spending raises the real interest rate in the *IS-LM* model, too, though there the crowding out is more of investment than consumption.

what the policy change means for the behaviour of the economy, and for future changes in policy, and they behave accordingly. For instance, as we noted in Chapter 8, economic agents adjust their consumption more in response to a permanent income tax cut than to a transitory tax cut of the same size.

Credibility

The approach leads naturally to the emphasis on the credibility of policy makers to which we have referred above. Individuals' reactions to policy decisions depend so much on their interpretations of what future policy decisions are implied that believability of policy becomes crucial.

Suppose the central bank announces a reduction in the growth rate of money. If people believe it, the rate of wage increase will slow and the central bank will be able to reduce the growth rate of money without any significant output cost. Suppose they do not believe the central bank. Then it is faced with the decision of whether to do what it said and create a recession, or not to do it, thereby avoiding the recession but losing credibility.

Indeed, it is even possible to see how under rational expectations individuals' beliefs can be self-justifying. Suppose the central bank announces that it will reduce money growth. Suppose people believe it and wage increases slow. Then the central bank will do it, and the expectations were right. Suppose they do not believe it and wages go on rising as before. Then if the central bank fears a recession, it will not cut the growth rate of money. The people were right again. This example illustrates the value of credibility.[30]

Institutional Reform

The approach leads also to an emphasis on institutional changes as ways of altering the behaviour of the economy. Members of the rational expectations school are less interested in what policy should be *now* than they are in ways of making it possible for policy to operate better in general. The quote from Lucas at the beginning of this chapter shows a general attitude toward attempts to predict the effects of a particular policy action. Members of the rational expectations school doubt that we know enough to predict how the public will respond in the short run to a particular policy change, because the response depends on how the policy measure affects expectations. However, in the long run the public will catch on to the effects of any policy change, and it thus

---

[30] The development of the rational expectations approach to policy has led to much game theoretical (the mathematical theory of games) research on policy, like the above example.

becomes possible to predict the long-run effects of long-run policy changes. A member of the rational expectations school might support a legal requirement to balance the budget, in part because such a law should have a very strong predictable effect on expectations.

Similarly, a rational expectations economist confronted with the inflationary experience of the seventies would argue that the best way to change the behaviour of the central bank is to change the institutional environment in which it works. Accordingly, such an economist is likely to support a monetary rule, for example, requiring the money supply to grow at 4 percent per year.[31]

The Rational Expectations–Equilibrium Approach, Monetarism, and the Mainstream

There is considerable overlap between the policy views of monetarists and those of members of the rational expectations school. The similarity extends to the usually conservative views of policy held by members of both groups, but there are important differences between the monetarist and rational expectations approaches to macroeconomics. Monetarists are willing to assume that expectations may be systematically wrong and that markets are very slow to clear, whereas a member of the rational expectations school would not make such assumptions. Monetarism can be viewed as operating within the same framework and model as Keynesianism, while disagreeing over the relative importance of monetary and fiscal policy. The rational expectations school believes that the standard framework is fundamentally flawed and thus has developed the market clearing approach, which argues that imperfect information is responsible for the business cycle. It is thus a more radical attack on standard macroeconomics than is monetarism.

Where will the rational expectations–equilibrium alternative to conventional macroeconomics lead? It has already had a substantial influence on the way macroeconomists think. First, rational expectations is widely used as a theory of expectations. Second, the sophisticated view of policy, in which responses to policy depend on the public's analysis of what policy measures will do to current and future behaviour of the economy, is widely adopted. The equilib-

---

[31] You might wonder why members of the rational expectations school should care at all about monetary policy if they believe that (1) only unexpected changes in money affect real output, and (2) the public's expectations eventually catch up with reality. The two assumptions (1) and (2) seem to suggest that whatever the central bank is doing, it will eventually have no effect on real output. However, the strong form of rational expectations does not argue that monetary policy is irrelevant to the behaviour of *prices*. Thus members of the rational expectations school concerned about keeping inflation low can logically be in favor of a monetary rule that will prevent the average rate of growth of money from becoming high.

rium approach, however, is more controversial than other components of the rational expectations view, and it seems to be inconsistent with the slow reaction of the economy to policy measures.[32]

18-7   SUPPLY-SIDE ECONOMICS

Supply-side economics was all the rage in the United States in 1981, the first year of the Reagan administration.[33] Supply-side economists lay heavy stress on the incentive effects of taxation in determining the behaviour of the economy. Beyond that broad agreement there are really two separate groups. The mainstream group includes economists such as Martin Feldstein, President of the National Bureau of Economic Research, and Michael Boskin of Stanford University. This group stresses the importance of tax incentives in promoting growth, by affecting saving and investment. Similarly it analyzes the effects of tax changes on labour supply, the effects of public pensions on saving and retirement decisions, and a host of other important issues.

The mainstream group has been presenting the results of its research in scholarly journals for many years and is influential and active within the economics profession. In Canada, supply-side economics, in the form of investment incentives such as investment tax credits, has long been a feature of fiscal policy.

However, there is a radical fringe of the supply-side group in the U.S. that has made exaggerated claims for the effects of tax cuts on savings, investment, and labour supply and for the effects of tax cuts on total government revenue from taxation.[34] Among the leaders of the radical fringe are Arthur Laffer, whose curve was described in Chapter 13, and George Gilder, whose radical supply-side book *Wealth and Poverty*[35] was on the best-seller list in 1981. The radical

---

[32] See the discussion in the special issue of the *Journal of Money, Credit and Banking,* November 1980.

[33] Paul Craig Roberts, *The Supply-Side Revolution* (Cambridge, Mass.: Harvard University Press, 1984), presents an insider's view of the supply-side impact on U.S. economic policy in the first Reagan administration. Various arguments of the supply-side case are brought together in the collection edited by Richard Fink, *Supply Side Economics* (University Publications of America 1982).

[34] The distinction between mainstream and radical groups is drawn by Harold McClure and Thomas Willett in "Understanding the Supply Siders," in W. C. Stubblebine and T. D. Willett (eds.), *Reaganomics A Midterm Report* (Institute of Contemporary Studies, 1983). See this paper and a paper by Richard Rahn in the same volume for more details on supply-side economics and for lists of the players in the two groups.

[35] New York: Basic Books, 1981.

fringe argued (1) that tax rate reductions would have such powerful effects on work effort that total tax revenues would rise, and (2) that the supply-side effects of the tax cuts would have a powerful effect in reducing inflation by increasing the growth rate of output.

Radical supply-side economics was thus an essential part of the rhetoric supporting President Reagan's policy of cutting taxes. However, the events of the two years following these tax cuts do not support the views of the radical supply-siders. Inflation was indeed reduced, but the reduction was a result of tight monetary policy and not of expansionary fiscal policy. Output did not increase but rather fell rapidly. Similarly, the rapid recovery that took place in the U.S. in 1983 and 1984 appears to have resulted from rapid growth of the money stock and large increases in the fiscal deficit.

18-8   RECENT APPROACHES

Under the challenge of the rational expectations–equilibrium approach, there has been substantial research since 1973 attempting to explain why wages and prices are sticky. We have already mentioned several of the new approaches, but draw them together here for review.

BOX 18-1   DISEQUILIBRIUM ECONOMICS AND POST-KEYNESIAN ECONOMICS

In the main text we have developed the history of ideas as running from Keynesian economics to monetarism and the rational expectations–equilibrium challenge, with supply-side economics as a flashy sideshow. However, two other strands of macroeconomics are sufficiently distinct and fruitful to deserve attention.

The Disequilibrium Approach

As early as the 1950s economists recognized the implications of disequilibrium in one market for supply or demand in other markets. If workers cannot sell all the labour they wish at the going wage, and cannot borrow, how will this affect their consumption decision? If they cannot buy all the goods they wish at the going prices, how does this affect their supply of labour or their demands for money and other assets? If firms cannot sell at the going price all the output they would like to produce, how does this affect their demand for labour?

The disequilibrium approach answers these questions by constructing a model of the economy that explicitly takes into account the *quantity constraints* on the decisions which households and firms face. Quantity constraints are present when households or firms cannot, at the going wages or prices, buy or sell all the quantities they wish. Central to the approach is the assumption that wages and prices do not move rapidly, leaving markets in disequilibrium, which gives rise to quantity adjustments. These quantity adjustments in different markets are interdependent through the quantity constraints under which households and firms make their optimal decisions.*

The most interesting contribution of the disequilibrium approach so far has been to influence empirical work. For example, studies of consumption pay close attention to the role of income and wealth, reflecting the possibility that individuals cannot borrow against future income so that *liquidity constraints* affect spending behaviour. In studies of the labour market the approach suggests the important distinction between "high-wage" or classical unemployment on one side and Keynesian or "lack of demand" unemployment on the other. (See Section 18-9.)

Post-Keynesian Economics

Post-Keynesians are a diverse group of economists who share the belief that modern macroeconomics leaves aside or explicitly assumes away many of the very central elements of Keynes' *General Theory*.†

Five elements of this approach stand out distinctly. First, adjustment, just as in the disequilibrium approach, takes place primarily through quantity adjustment, not price changes. Indeed, price changes where they occur are often seen as disequilibrating. Second, the distribution of income between profits and wages plays a central role in affecting consumption and investment decisions. Third, expectations (Keynes' animal spirits), together with profits, are the chief determinant of investment plans. Fourth, institutional features — credit constraints on households and self-finance by firms, as well as the financial structure involving credit creation in a pyramid — interact in shaping the business cycle and on occasion financial crises. Finally, unlike in classical macroeconomics, the focus of post-Keynesian economics is to explain why the economy does not work well.

---

*The early reference is D. Patinkin, *Money, Interest and Prices* (New York: Row, Peterson, 1956), Chapter 13. The complete working out of these ideas can be found in R. Barro and H. Grossman, *Money, Employment and Inflation* (London: Cambridge University Press, 1976); and E. Malinvaud, *The Theory of Unemployment Reconsidered* (Oxford: Basil Blackwell, 1977), and *Profitability and Unemployment* (Oxford: Basil Blackwell, 1981).

†For an introduction see A. Eichner (ed.), *A Guide to Post-Keynesian Economics* (White Plains, N.Y.: M. E. Sharpe, 1979), and the essays on post-Keynesian economics in the *American Economic Review*, May 1980.

Post-Keynesian economics remains an eclectic collection of ideas, not a systematic challenge, as, for example, the rational expectations hypothesis. It has influenced economists in their research program, but the deliberate downplaying, indeed rejection, of individual rationality and maximization as a basis of behaviour by firms and households has kept the approach at odds with the mainstream of the profession that has been attempting to bring macroeconomics into closer touch with microeconomics.

Relative Wages, Wage Contracts, and Rational Expectations

The strongest form of the rational expectations–equilibrium approach assumes markets clear every period and attributes the effects of monetary policy to imperfect information. That model has not been empirically successful. There are, however, models that use rational expectations as a theory of expectations but also recognize economic institutions such as long-term contracts and the importance of the relative wages of various groups in the labour market.[36] Relatively simple amendments have gone far in removing some of the least plausible implications of the strong market clearing form of rational expectations theory.

Suppose we have 2-year labour contracts and that half the contracts in the economy come up for renewal every year. Suppose further that we start from price stability and that an unanticipated decline in the money stock occurs. If all wages and prices were instantaneously flexible, they would immediately decline in proportion to the fall in money, and no real effects would arise. This does not occur, however, if we have long-term contracts that fix nominal wages. With a lowering in the money stock, there is potentially a decline in employment. Unemployed workers whose wages come up for renewal now have the choice of reducing their wages enough to become employed. If they do so, the price level will fall because the average wage has fallen, but when the price level falls, the real wage being paid to workers on existing contracts rises (the nominal wage they receive is fixed, and the price level has fallen), and some of them lose their jobs.

In addition, workers may be concerned that their *relative* wages not fall. If those whose contracts come up for renewal now accept cuts in wages large enough to keep them fully employed, their wages will have to fall relative to those whose wages were negotiated earlier. Workers may be willing to accept

---

[36] The discussion here follows a paper by John Taylor, "Staggered Wage Setting in a Macro-Model," *American Economic Review*, May 1979. For a careful, advanced introduction see D. Begg, *The Rational Expectations Revolution in Macroeconomics* (Baltimore: Johns Hopkins University Press, 1983).

some unemployment if they can keep their wages in line with those of others. If so, current wages will be set somewhere in between the full-employment level and the level of wages contracts still running. That means wages do *not* adjust immediately to money changes; that is, wages are less than fully flexible. It takes some time until the whole wage structure adjusts. The fact that we have long-term, nonsynchronized wage setting, and that relative wages matter, directly implies the possibility of extended periods of wage stickiness and unemployment.

The model is thus able to explain simultaneous wage inflation and unemployment. Suppose there is a contraction in demand, as we have just discussed, and that labour knows that policy will be expansionary in the future. Then those whose wages are currently up for renegotiation recognize that if they set too low a wage, they will be out of line with the wages that will be set next year by a group that will then be facing strong demand. Accordingly, even with the possibility of current unemployment, the prospect of expansionary aggregate demand policies in the future will make current economic slack less effective in dampening wage and price inflation. Rational expectations enter here in that the groups currently setting their wages look ahead and ask themselves what will be the macroeconomic environment in which other groups set their wages next period. If the policy setting next period is expected to be expansionary, this fact will already be anticipated in this year's wages.[37]

The relative wage model, combined with rational expectations, thus has two important features: first, wages are sticky downward in the face of unemployment; and second, wage inflation may persist in the face of unemployment. The extent of persistence is determined by, among other things, the degree to which the policy setting is accommodative or not.

Efficiency Wages

As we have noted, the basic question to answer is why wages and prices do not move quickly to clear markets when there is unemployment. *Efficiency wage theory argues that wages are not cut because doing so reduces a firm's profits.*[38]

There are several explanations for this assumption. The simplest occurs in very poor countries where individuals cannot feed themselves adequately

---

[37] Similar implications follow if workers are concerned about the real wages they will be receiving in future years, rather than relative wages.

[38] See Janet Yellen, "Efficiency Wage Models of Unemployment," in *American Economic Review*, May 1984. For a more extensive examination, see Lawrence Katz, "Efficiency Wage Theories: A Partial Evaluation," in *NBER Macroeconomics Annual* (Cambridge, Mass.: MIT Press, 1986). See, too, Assar Lindbeck and Dennis Snower, "Explanations of Unemployment," *Oxford Review of Economic Policy*, no. 2, 1985, and, by the same authors, "Wage Setting, Unemployment and Insider–Outsider Relations," *American Economic Review*, May 1986.

unless they receive a reasonable wage. Cutting wages in such a country would reduce the physical ability of the workers to perform their tasks. Even if there were substantial unemployment, it would not pay an employer to cut wages because doing so would reduce profits as the efficiency of workers fell owing to poor nutrition.

Physical efficiency is not the problem in developed countries. One efficiency wage explanation is that it is often difficult to observe the amount of effort put out by workers. To give the right incentive to work, there has to be a benefit to having this particular job. To create the benefit, so that the worker really wants to keep the job, the firm pays above-market wages. Then anyone who is found not be working hard pays the price by being fired and going back into the labour market to look for a lower-paid job.

This view suggests that there may be two types of jobs—high-paying desirable jobs that are difficult to find because the wage is above the market equilibrium wage and other jobs where firms can easily observe the workers' efforts and where jobs are easy to find, at a lower wage. That description brings to mind such jobs as driving a cab, in which there are almost always available positions, even when there is unemployment.[39]

Alternatively, there may simply be a social custom that wages are not cut. If workers whose wages are cut regard that as unfair and reduce their work effort in response, then wage cutting will not take place. This fairness argument is not fully satisfactory, because there is no explanation of how the custom developed, but it, too, is plausible.

Small Menu Costs

There is a puzzling aspect of business cycle theories based on the assumption that wages are slow to adjust. Unemployment is a very serious problem, creating large costs for the society. Changing a wage or price is a relatively simple and apparently cheap matter. The payroll has to be reprogrammed, or a new price tag has to be put on. The puzzle is why these apparently small costs stand in the way of adjusting prices so as to get rid of unemployment.

A very recent development is the so-called small menu cost approach, which argues that small costs of changing prices can have large effects.[40] The argument is technical, but asserts that when firms set prices optimally, they lose very little by meeting increases or decreases in demand by producing more or

---

[39] Sometimes the two types of jobs are described as primary and secondary, primary jobs being the better ones. This is the so-called *dual-labour market hypothesis.*

[40] The simplest such model is N. Gregory Mankiw, "Small Menu Costs and Large Business Cycles: A Macroeconomic Model of Monopoly," *Quarterly Journal of Economics,* May 1985. A more extensive model is developed in George Akerlof and Janet Yellen. "A Near-Rational Model of the Business Cycle, with Wage and Price Inertia," *Quarterly Journal of Economics,* supplement, 1985.

less without changing prices.[41] Then if there is some small cost for the firm of changing its prices or wages, a small shift in demand will not trigger a price or wage change. However, if firms do not change prices in response to shifts in demand, then the economy exhibits price (and/or wage) stickiness. Theoretical work in this area shows that extremely small costs of changing prices can generate enough wage and price stickiness to give changes in the money stock substantial real effects.

Profit Sharing

Another response to the macroeconomic difficulties of the seventies and the continuing problems of European economies, to which we turn below, has been the *profit-sharing* proposal of Professor Martin Wietzman of MIT.[42] The proposal is that workers take part of their pay as a share of profits rather than as a fixed wage.

By taking part of their pay as a share of profits, workers would cut the base wage firms would have to pay. This would tend to encourage employment. In effect, profit sharing makes the wage more flexible.[43] Weitzman argues that the Japanese have essentially a profit-sharing scheme. Japanese workers receive a substantial part of their income (often around one-third) in the form of a bonus. If their company has a good year, the bonus will be higher; if it has a bad year, the bonus can be cut. Of course the Japanese have by far the lowest unemployment rate of any of the major economies.

Weitzman suggests that similar benefits could flow from the adoption of profit sharing in other economies. He recommends that governments provide tax subsidies for profit sharing. The scheme will not get off the ground otherwise, he argues, because there is no benefit to one company of introducing profit sharing unless other firms do it too. The benefits come from both lower unemployment and greater macroeconomic stability that would occur if the scheme were implemented on a major scale.

The profit-sharing proposal has attracted considerable attention, especially in Europe. The British government in 1986 announced it would promote wage-sharing. Critics question whether workers would want to receive part of their income as an uncertain amount of profits rather than a known wage. In response Weitzman contends that employment would be more stable for most people

---

[41] An essential assumption is that the firm *sets* prices or wages; this means the firm cannot be perfectly competitive, taking the price or wage as given by the market.

[42] Martin Weitzman, *The Share Economy* (Cambridge, Mass.: Harvard University Press, 1984).

[43] Weitzman prefers to emphasize the effect of profit sharing on increasing employment because of a lower base wage, rather than the flexibility of the real wage that it creates.

than it is now — when the prospect of unemployment certainly creates uncertainty about income for those in serious danger of losing their job.

18-9   KEYNESIAN VERSUS CLASSICAL UNEMPLOYMENT

Table 18-1 presents an international comparison of unemployment experience over the past 25 years. A striking feature of these data is the rising unemployment rate in Europe and the U.K. In the sixties and early seventies their unemployment rates were well below those in North America. However, by the eighties unemployment in Europe and the U.K. had risen well above North American rates.

TABLE 18-1   COMPARATIVE UNEMPLOYMENT RATES, PERCENT

	Canada	U.S.	Japan	Germany	France	U.K.
1960–1966	5.4	5.1	1.3	0.7	1.2	1.4
1967–1973	5.2	4.5	1.2	1.0	2.4	2.4
1974–1980	7.2	6.8	1.9	3.5	4.8	4.7
1981–1984	10.4	8.5	2.5	7.8	8.3	11.7
1985	10.5	7.1	2.6	8.6	10.1	13.2

Sources: OECD *Historical Statistics,* 1960–1980, and OECD *Economic Outlook*, no. 39, May 1986.

The overall picture of an inexorable rise in European unemployment rates is remarkable. So are some of the details; for instance, the unemployment rate in France has risen every single year since 1973. The British unemployment rate in particular is remarkably high.

Such a prolonged increase in unemployment, to such high levels, calls for an explanation. The argument in Europe was over whether excessively high real wages or insufficient aggregate demand was the chief source of the problem. Figure 18-4 helps sort out the issues. The figure shows the labour demand schedule — the marginal product of labour (MPN) — with the real wage on the vertical axis and N as the full-employment labour supply. The full-employment real wage is $(w/P)_0$.

One interpretation of the unemployment problem of the early 1980s was that the economy was at a point such as A at a real wage $(w/P)'$. At point A firms hire only an amount of labour N' which falls short of full employment because the real wage is too high. The economy suffers from *classical*, or *real wage*, *unemployment*. The cure is either a reduction in the real wage to $(w/P)_0$ or else

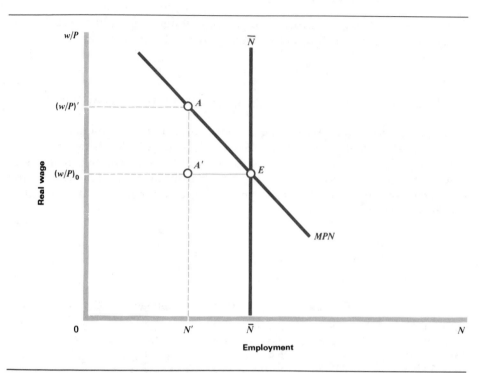

FIGURE 18-4   CLASSICAL OR KEYNESIAN UNEMPLOYMENT? The schedule *MPN* is the marginal product of labour or the demand curve for labour. The full-employment labour supply is $\overline{N}\overline{N}$. At a real wage $(w/P)'$ there is "high real wage" unemployment because firms only want to hire a labour force of N', which falls short of the supply $\overline{N}$, but it is also possible that even at the lower wage $(w/P)_0$ firms only want to hire N' of labour because they cannot sell the output that would be produced by a larger labour force. The question is to know whether the unemployment results from high real wages, as at point *A*, or from insufficient aggregate demand, as at point A'.

productivity growth or increased investment that shifts the *MPN* schedule out and to the right and thus reduces unemployment.

An alternative interpretation is that the economy was at a point such as A'. Again there is unemployment, but this time the real wage is not the problem. Firms are not willing to hire more workers than N' because they cannot sell the output. Aggregate demand is insufficient to absorb more output than is produced by an employment level N'. Therefore firms do not hire more workers, and accordingly, there is *Keynesian unemployment*. The cure, in this case, is not a cut in real wages but rather an expansion in aggregate demand through monetary or fiscal stimulus.

In both cases there is unemployment. In both cases it is unprofitable for firms to hire more labour than N'. In one case the problem is that labour is too expensive; in the other there is no market for the increased output, but it is essential to identify what kind of unemployment the economy faces before designing policy action. Because we do not know the equilibrium real wage, there is no direct way to decide whether unemployment is Keynesian or classical.

In all likelihood in the early eighties, there was some classical unemployment in Europe, because real wages had not adjusted enough in response to the increased price of oil and reduced productivity growth. In addition a dose of Keynesian unemployment was superimposed between 1980 and 1982, so that the economy was to the left of point A. In that case expansionary aggregate demand policies would go some way toward reducing unemployment, but there was also a need to cut labour costs relative to labour productivity.

There is also a question of why, if the real wage is too high, the existence of massive unemployment has not driven it down. The argument that has been advanced here distinguishes between insiders and outsiders in a firm. The wage is set between the firm and those working inside it. There is no easy way for the outsiders — the unemployed — to affect the wage. These theories do not explain, however, why other firms are not set up to hire the unemployed at low wages.

The European unemployment problem is becoming so severe and prolonged that the influence of that event will almost certainly substantially change theories of unemployment in the next few years. One possible change may be that the natural rate of unemployment will come to be seen as being heavily influenced by the recent behaviour of unemployment, with high unemployment driving the natural rate up.[44]

18-10 WHERE DOES IT ALL LEAD?

At the start of this chapter we asked why macroeconomics suffers from such rapidly changing opinions. The answer is that it does not. There has been an evolution from simple Keynesianism toward a more sophisticated approach, not a series of rapidly changing beliefs. Macroeconomics has evolved, and it now gives more weight to monetary factors and to aggregate supply, emphasizing the roles of both expectations and labour market institutions. The recent work reviewed in Section 18-8 does not lead to a significantly different overall view of the economy — rather it should be viewed as attempting to develop microeconomic foundations for existing macroeconomics.

The rational expectations–equilibrium approach does pose a more radical challenge to the standard way of viewing the economy, and it has already had a major impact on mainstream macroeconomics. As of now, it remains far from

---

[44] A theory of this type is developed in Olivier Blanchard and Lawrence Summers, "Hysteresis and the European Unemployment Problem," *NBER Macroeconomics Annual* (Cambridge, Mass.: MIT Press, 1986).

a major empirical success, though it has more theoretical appeal. Whether it will lead to the replacement of current mainstream macroeconomics with a new standard model remains to be seen—and time and evidence will determine that.

It is hoped that careful study will cumulate over the years to improved knowledge. Opinions, of course, change as new evidence accumulates, but genuine revolutions in thinking are rare. There was a Keynesian revolution in the thirties and a significant shift toward monetarism in the fifties and sixties—which was easily accommodated by expanding the Keynesian framework. There may be a rational expectations revolution in progress. Even if it succeeds, it will build in much of the existing structure of macroeconomics. And even if it does not radically reshape macroeconomics, it will, nonetheless, make for serious changes in understanding of the formation of expectations and the operation of economic policy. It has, in addition, spurred new work on the microfoundations of wage and price determination.

18-11 SUMMARY

1. Monetarism lays heavy stress on the money stock as determining the level of output in the short run and the inflation rate in the long run.

2. Monetarists generally view the money supply as having powerful, but not easily predictable, effects on the economy. Money works with long and variable lags, and for that reason monetarists favour a monetary rule. They argue that interest rates are a poor guide to the direction of monetary policy, and they also believe that the private sector of the economy is inherently stable.

3. Monetarism's influence on monetary policy in Canada was reflected in the adoption of money supply targets in 1975. This practice was abandoned in 1982 because of instability in the demand for money.

4. The rational expectations–equilibrium approach to macroeconomics has two components. The first is a theory of expectations, arguing that people form expectations using all available information and do not make systematic mistakes. The second is the equilibrium approach. This assumes that markets are in equilibrium each period and attributes deviations of output from normal levels to imperfect information.

5. The equilibrium approach implies that monetary policy can affect real output only by creating surprises. Early empirical evidence supported this view, but later evidence is less favourable.

6. Equilibrium real business cycle theory denies any causal role for money in the business cycle. Rather the cycle is seen as resulting from real shocks

hitting the economy, being then distributed through the economy and also into future periods by a variety of propagation mechanisms. The main real shocks are to productivity and government spending. The main propagation mechanism is intertemporal substitution of leisure and consumption. More standard mechanisms, such as inventory accumulation and investment in physical capital, also play a role.

7. The rational expectations approach to policy making emphasizes the credibility of policies as an important factor determining their success or failure. The approach views institutional reform as the main way to get better policy.

8. Supply-side economics focusses on the incentive effects of taxation. There are two groups — mainstream and radical. The radical group attracted much attention at the time the new Reagan fiscal policy was going into effect in the U.S. in 1981. They argued that incentive effects of taxes were powerful enough that tax cuts would not cause a major budget deficit and would have a powerful supply-side effect on inflation. Neither argument was supported by later events. Mainstream supply siders continue to be influential in both policy making and economics.

9. A synthesis combines rational expectations assumptions with institutional features of the economy, such as long-term labour contracts. This can explain the slow adjustment of the economy to changes in monetary policy.

10. Efficiency wage theories explain wage stickiness as a result of losses in productivity that would occur if firms cut wages. In combination with small menu costs, efficiency wage theory can produce sticky wages and prices.

11. Profit sharing has been suggested as a means of increasing the level and stability of employment. The proposal has received attention especially in Europe, where unemployment has continued rising over 15 years. Explanations for European unemployment focus on high real wages and on inadequate demand.

EY TERMS

Monetary rule	Intertemporal substitution of leisure
Rational expectations–equilibrium approach	Supply-side economics
Credibility	Efficiency wage
Imperfect information	Small menu costs
Real business cycles	Profit-sharing
Propagation mechanism	

PROBLEMS

1. (a) In what ways is monetarism closer to Keynesianism than to the rational expectations–equilibrium approach?
    (b) In what ways is monetarism closer to the rational expectations–equilibrium approach than to Keynesianism?

2. Distinguish and define the two components of the rational expectations–equilibrium approach to macroeconomics.

3. Suppose that people did not believe the Bank of Canada was serious about stopping inflation in 1980, and 1981. Can you then reconcile the 1981–1982 recession with the rational expectations approach? Explain.

4. (a) Explain why, in the aggregate supply and demand model of Chapter 15, more work is done in booms than recessions.
    (b) Contrast this with the real business cycle explanation.

5. Supply-side economics points, appropriately, to the importance of incentives in determining economic behaviour. Why then have mainstream macroeconomists generally been critical of radical supply-side economics?

6. (a) Why according to efficiency wage theory are employers reluctant to cut wages?
    (b) Suppose there were always some jobs available at a low enough wage. Could efficiency wages still help explain why high unemployment can continue for year after year?

7. (a) Explain the idea of profit sharing.
    (b) In what ways could profit sharing improve macroeconomic performance?

8. (a) Check a source such as the *Quarterly Economic Review* of the Dept. of Finance to find out whether the European unemployment picture has improved at all since 1985.
    (b) Why is high European unemployment a challenge for economics to explain?

9. Evaluate the quote of Keynes with which this chapter begins.

10. In the introduction we note contradictory views on the budget deficit. One group of economists believes that large deficits cause high real interest rates. Another group believes that the budget deficit has no real effects. Going back to Chapter 17, trace the key point that leads to this difference of opinion. What is your opinion of this issue in light of Chapter 17?

CHAPTER

Macroeconomic Policy and Inflation in an Open Economy

The analysis of income determination and the balance of payments in Chapters 5 and 6 was developed on the assumption that domestic prices were fixed and did not respond to changes in demand. In this chapter, we consider a more realistic model incorporating the aggregate demand and supply analysis of Chapters 7 and 14 to 16.

In the first section we consider the determination of income, prices and the trade balance under fixed exchange rates. The second section considers the flexible exchange rate case, and is followed by a review of Canadian experience under a flexible rate since 1970. The chapter concludes with further issues concerning the functioning of a flexible exchange rate system.

19-1 TRADE BALANCE AND PRICES UNDER FIXED EXCHANGE RATES

We begin by considering the adjustment of income, prices, and the trade balance under fixed exchange rates. In this section we ignore capital flows and treat the trade balance as the total balance of payments.

Aggregate Demand in an Open Economy

In the closed economy case, considered in Chapter 7, the process by which the price level affects aggregate demand is as follows. A higher level of prices implies lower real balances, higher interest rates, and lower spending. In an open economy, the relation is slightly more complicated because now an increase in our prices reduces demand for our goods for two reasons. The first is the familiar higher interest rate channel summarized above. The second is that an increase in our prices leads to a loss of competitiveness. For a given exchange rate, an increase in domestic prices decreases the relative price of imports and raises the relative price of exports in foreign markets. Thus demand shifts from domestic goods to foreign goods.

The relative price that affects the trade balance and the demand for domestic goods can be represented in terms of the three determining variables as follows:

$$\frac{eP_f}{P} \tag{1}$$

P denotes the domestic price level, P_f denotes the price of foreign goods in terms of foreign currency (pounds per unit), and e is the domestic currency price of foreign exchange (Canadian dollars per pound). Thus the numerator of expression (1) is the price of foreign goods in terms of domestic currency. This relative price is often referred to as the *terms of trade*.

In Figure 19-1, we show the downward-sloping demand curve for domestic goods, *AD*. It is drawn for a given level of the nominal money supply and given fiscal policy. In addition, the level of foreign prices (P_f) and the exchange rate (e) are given.

Internal and External Balance

The short-run aggregate supply curve, *AS*, and the full-employment level of output are also shown in Figure 19-1. The economy is shown in equilibrium at the point *E* where output is at full employment so that we have internal balance.

The external balance schedule *NX* is the set of combinations of income and the domestic price level, along which we have a zero balance of trade for given levels of the exchange rate and foreign prices. An increase in domestic income raises imports and worsens the trade balance. To restore external balance domestic prices must fall so as to improve domestic competitiveness. Thus we show the external balance schedule as downward sloping.[1] We assume that it is steeper than the aggregate demand schedule.

The Adjustment Process

At the equilibrium point *E* in Figure 19-1, the domestic price level is too high in relation to the foreign price level so that we have a trade deficit. To achieve

---

[1] We assume that a decline in prices improves the trade balance. This requires that exports and imports are sufficiently responsive to prices. It is possible that a reduction in our price level (which reduces the prices of our exports) lowers our revenue from exports because the increased sales are not sufficient to compensate for the lower prices. We shall assume that this possibility does not occur.

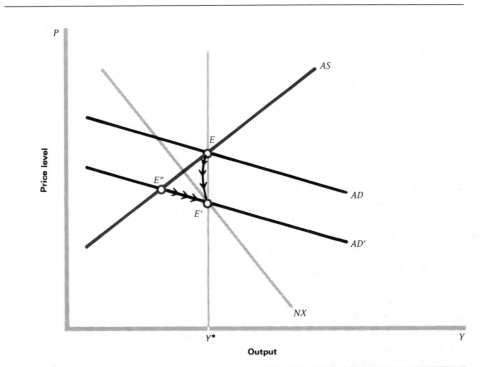

FIGURE 19-1   OPEN ECONOMY EQUILIBRIUM WITH PRICE ADJUSTMENT. At the point *E*, aggregate demand is equal to aggregate supply but the price level is too high so that we have a trade deficit. External balance can be achieved by contractionary policy that leads to a short-run equilibrium at *E"* and an adjustment path among *AD'* to *E'*. Alternatively, under a fixed exchange rate with no sterilization, the money supply will decline and the economy will move from *E* to *E'* along the path shown.

external balance, we have to use contractionary policies to shift the aggregate demand curve down to *AD'* so that it intersects the external balance schedule at *E'*. The short-run equilibrium will be at *E"* where we have unemployment. This puts downward pressure on wages and prices so that the aggregate supply curve shifts to the right and the economy moves along *AD'* to *E'*. Thus we are forced to push the economy into a recession to achieve external balance.

This process would occur automatically if the government did not pursue an active stabilization policy and peg the exchange rate without engaging in sterilization operations. As we saw in Section 5-5, in the absence of offsetting open market operations there will be a link between the balance of payments and the domestic money supply. Indeed, the central bank cannot offset a trade deficit indefinitely through sterilized exchange market intervention, since it will use up its stock of foreign exchange reserves.

Since there is a deficit at point E, pegging the exchange rate without sterilization will lead to a decline in the stock of high-powered money (and hence the money supply) as the central bank sells foreign currency in exchange for domestic currency. This will cause the aggregate demand curve to shift down, thereby creating excess supply. This will cause the aggregate supply curve to shift down as well so that the economy will follow the alternative adjustment path shown in Figure 19-1.

Price Level Versus Exchange Rate Adjustment

The adjustment process we have just described is called the *classical adjustment process*. It relies on price adjustments and an adjustment in the money supply based on the trade balance. This process "works" in the sense that it moves the economy to a long-run equilibrium with internal and external balance. However, the mechanism is far from attractive since it imposes a protracted recession simply to achieve a cut in prices.

An alternative solution is to recognize that external balance can be achieved in either of two ways. To restore competitiveness, domestic prices have to decline relative to foreign prices. As can be seen from the expression given in (1), this can occur either through a decline in domestic prices (P) as in the classical adjustment process, or by a devaluation of the currency (increase in e) with unchanged domestic prices. An appropriate devaluation will shift the NX schedule up so that it intersects the AS and AD schedules at the point E.

The devaluation strategy has the obvious advantage that it does not require a protracted recession to reduce domestic wages and prices. However, it is important to recall the analysis of a devaluation given in Section 5-3. In order to achieve internal and external balance it is necessary to combine the devaluation with contractionary policies that reduce aggregate demand. If this is not done, the aggregate demand curve will shift up and to the right as a result of the effect of the devaluation on demand for domestic goods. We will then have excess demand for domestic goods and a consequent increase in wages and prices. In the end, the improvement in competitiveness, achieved through the devaluation, will be offset by an increase in domestic wages and prices.

BOX 19-1   MEXICO: EXTERNAL DEBT, OIL, AND ADJUSTMENT PROBLEMS

In the short run, payments deficits can be financed by borrowing abroad. In the long run, they require adjustment. Politically, however, there is never a good time for adjustment — and that is often how extreme policy difficulties arise. Mexico is a case in point.

Mexico is an oil-exporting country. It discovered and began to exploit its large oil reserves in the 1970s, when oil prices skyrocketed. Mexico enjoyed a large increase in export revenues. Even so, its domestic spending increased so fast that Mexico ran big trade deficits. These deficits were financed by borrowing abroad. Foreign banks were willing to lend to Mexico because it was oil-rich and its prospects looked good for being able to pay interest on the debt and repay the amounts borrowed. By 1982 the Mexican external debt had reached $82 billion, about 50 percent of GNP.

Mexican external balance problems came to the fore in 1982. Real interest rates in the world market increased sharply in 1981. That meant Mexico had to pay more interest on every dollar of its debt. At the same time oil prices started to fall. Losses of export revenues and higher interest bills led to a loss of confidence in the Mexican currency, which resulted in massive capital outflows. The government financed these outflows by borrowing U.S. dollars abroad to defend the exchange rate from collapse.

By 1982 Mexico entered into deep debt difficulties. External borrowing became impossible. At the same time Mexico was not earning enough U.S. dollars to pay interest on the debt. In August 1982, Mexico had to enter a moratorium — telling its creditors that it could not pay the full amounts due and that debts would have to be serviced (interest paid and debt rolled over) on an adjusted basis. Since that time, extensive adjustment and sharply falling oil prices have put Mexico into even further economic difficulties. Table 1 shows the extent of adjustment.

TABLE 1   MEXICO'S EXTERNAL BALANCE ADJUSTMENT

	1980–1982	1983	1984	1985
External debt ($U.S. billion)	75	94	97	97
Trade balance ($U.S. billion)	−0.3	13.8	12.8	8.4
Oil price ($/barrel)	34	29	27	26
Real wage*	100	77	71	71

*Index 1980–1982.

Note that the trade balance after 1982 shows a large surplus. The surplus was achieved by cutting spending and by a depreciation of the peso, but even this large surplus was not enough to pay all the interest on the accumulated debt. The extent of adjustment shows in the sharp decline in real wages. Real wage reduction is the counterpart of a gain in competitiveness (a depreciation of the real exchange rate) which is the instrument for improving the external balance.

Even Table 1 understates the full extent of Mexico's difficulties, for at the end of 1985 the price of oil collapsed, falling below $15 per barrel. By the middle of 1986 it seemed that Mexico would have to undertake even further adjustment.

An Increase in the Foreign Price Level

We conclude this section with an analysis of the domestic policy options in the face of an increase in the foreign price level. As discussed in Section 19-3 below, this was the situation faced by Canada in the second half of the 1960s when the inflation rate was rising in the U.S.

Figure 19-2 illustrates an initial equilibrium at point E with both internal and external balance. An increase in the foreign price level shifts the NX curve up to NX'. What will be the increase in the domestic price level represented by the vertical shift in this curve? In order to restore trade balance at the same level of income, the domestic price level must increase *in proportion* to the foreign price level in order to restore the initial relative price of foreign and domestic goods.

The improvement in competitiveness also shifts the AD curve up to AD'. The short-run equilibrium is thus at E', where we have excess demand for domestic goods and a trade surplus.

Policy Options

One option to restore internal and external balance is to allow the automatic adjustment process to operate. Since there is a trade surplus at E', pegging the exchange rate will cause the money supply to rise and the aggregate demand curve to shift up. Since we also have excess demand for goods, the aggregate supply curve will also shift up and the economy will move along an adjustment path like the one shown in Figure 19-2.

The final equilibrium will be at the point E'' where internal and external balance are restored. The relative price of foreign and domestic goods will be unchanged from its initial value since the domestic price level will have risen in proportion to the foreign price level.

In this case, devaluation is again a more attractive option. If the domestic currency is devalued in proportion to the increase in the foreign price level, the relative price of foreign and domestic goods will remain unchanged and the economy will stay at point E. Thus a devaluation enables the domestic economy to maintain a stable price level and avoid importing foreign inflation.

The important implication of this analysis is that a country on a fixed exchange rate ties its price level to that of its trading partners and is forced to import foreign inflation.

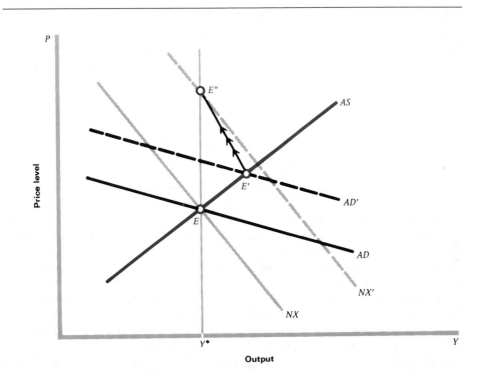

FIGURE 19-2 AN INCREASE IN THE FOREIGN PRICE LEVEL. An increase in foreign prices shifts both the *AD* and the *NX* curves upward and to the right. The short-run equilibrium is at *E′* where we have excess demand for goods and a trade surplus. In the absence of sterilization, the money supply will increase and the *AS* curve will shift up so that the economy moves along an adjustment path to *E″*. At this point internal and external balance are restored with an increase in the domestic price level proportional to that of the foreign price level. Alternatively, if the domestic currency is devalued in proportion to the foreign price increase, the economy will remain in equilibrium at the point *E*.

The Collapse of the Fixed Exchange Rate System

From 1946 to 1973 most countries had exchange rates that were fixed in terms of the U.S. dollar. This was the *Bretton Woods system* that at the end of World War II replaced the unstable exchange rates and restrictive trade policies of the 1930s. Under the Bretton Woods system, countries fixed exchange rates by specifying the rate at which the central bank would buy or sell U.S. dollars in the foreign exchange market.

As we have seen, a system of fixed exchange rates requires that countries pursue very similar policies so that prices of goods in different countries do not get out of line. This was not the case in the late 1960s when the inflation rate in the United States increased significantly without a similar increase in other countries. Other countries, particularly Germany, were forced to buy up huge amounts of U.S. dollars in an effort to hold down the value of their currencies. In May 1973, the fixed rate system was abandoned and the world economy moved to flexible exchange rates.[2]

19-2   MONEY AND PRICES UNDER FLEXIBLE EXCHANGE RATES

In this section we consider the effects of price level and exchange rate changes on income and the interest rate under flexible exchange rates. As in Chapter 6, we make the simplifying assumption of perfect capital mobility so that the domestic interest rate is always equal to the foreign rate. An incipient decline in interest rates because of, say, an increase in the money supply, leads to an *immediate* depreciation and income expansion that counteracts the tendency for the interest rate to fall.

For purposes of graphical illustration, we return to the *IS-LM* framework of Chapters 4–6. However, we relax the assumption of fixed prices maintained in those chapters and assume that prices rise when output is above full employment and fall when output is below full employment.

Figure 19-3 summarizes the adjustment process. At points to the right of full employment, prices are rising and at points to the left, prices are falling. The *BP* schedule is horizontal at the foreign interest rate, and at points above it the currency is appreciating while at points below it the currency is depreciating.

Short- and Long-run Effects of a Monetary Expansion

We saw in Chapter 6 that with fixed prices and flexible exchange rates, an increase in the money supply leads to a depreciation and an increase in income. We now ask how that result is modified once we take adjustments in prices into account. We will show that the output adjustment is now only transitory. In the long run a monetary expansion leads to a currency depreciation and to higher prices with no change in competitiveness.

In Figure 19-4 we start at an initial equilibrium with full employment, payments balance, monetary equilibrium, and equilibrium in the domestic goods market. All this occurs at point *E*. Now a monetary expansion takes place and shifts the *LM* schedule to *LM'*. The new goods and money market equilibrium at *E'* involves an interest rate below the world level, and therefore the currency

---

[2] As we noted in Chapter 6, Canada had already moved to a flexible exchange rate in 1970.

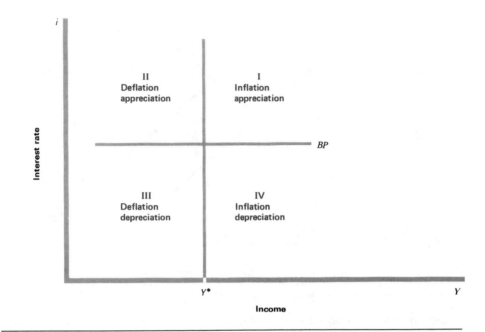

FIGURE 19-3 ADJUSTMENT OF EXCHANGE RATES AND PRICES. Prices move in response to the deviation of the economy from full employment. When output is above potential, prices are rising (regions I and IV), and they are falling at output levels below potential (regions II and III). With perfect capital mobility the balance of payments is highly sensitive to interest rates. If our interest rate falls below the foreign level, capital tends to flow out, and that leads to a deficit and depreciation of the currency (regions III and IV). Conversely, a rise in interest rates leads to capital inflows, a surplus, and appreciation (regions I and II).

immediately depreciates, raising home competitiveness and thus shifting the *IS* schedule to *IS'*. The economy moves rapidly from *E* via *E'* to *E"*. Output has risen, the currency has depreciated, and the economy has thereby gained in external competitiveness, but that is not the end of the story.

At *E"* outut is above the full-employment level. Prices are therefore rising, and that implies real balances are falling. As the real money stock *M/P* declines because of rising prices, the *LM* schedule starts shifting to the left. Interest rates tend to rise, capital tends to flow in, and the resulting appreciation leads now to a decline in competitiveness that also shifts the *IS* schedule back toward the initial equilibrium. Both the *IS* and *LM* schedules thus move back toward point *E*. The process continues until point *E* is reached again.

What adjustments have taken place once the economy is back to point *E*? At point *E* interest rates have returned to their initial level and so have relative

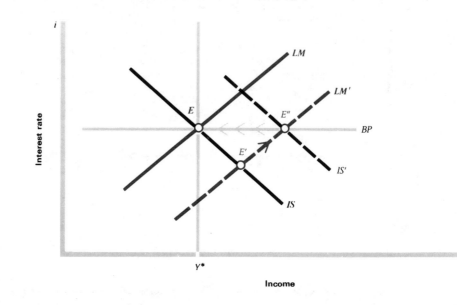

FIGURE 19-4   THE SHORT- AND LONG-RUN EFFECTS OF A MONETARY EXPANSION.
The economy is in initial equilibrium at E when a monetary expansion shifts the LM schedule to
LM'. The goods and money market equilibrium at E' involve an interest rate below the foreign
level. Capital outflows now lead to immediate depreciation, and therefore the IS schedule shifts
to IS'. The economy thus moves rapidly from E to E'', but at E'' there is overemployment, and
hence prices are rising. Rising prices reduce real balances and shift the LM schedule back toward
E. As real balances decline, interest rates tend to rise, drawing in capital and leading to
appreciation, which shifts the IS' schedule back toward E. In the long run, output returns to
normal, and money, prices, and the exchange rate all rise in the same proportion.

prices eP_f/P. In moving from E to E' the exchange rate depreciated immediately,
ahead of the rise in prices, but when prices increased and real balances fell,
some of that depreciation was reversed. Over the whole adjustment process,
prices and exchange rates rose in the same proportion, leaving relative prices
eP_f/P and therefore aggregate demand unchanged. In the long run money was
therefore *entirely neutral*. Table 19-1 summarizes these results. Neutrality of

TABLE 19-1   THE SHORT- AND LONG-RUN EFFECTS OF A MONETARY
EXPANSION

	M/P	e	P	eP_f/P	Y
Short run	+	+	0	+	+
Long run	0	+	+	0	0

money means, in terms of the second row of the table, that nominal money, prices, and the exchange rate all increase in the same proportion so that real money and relative prices are unchanged.

Purchasing Power Parity

The long-run neutrality of money discussed above illustrates the potential role of exchange rates in offsetting the effects of change in the price level at home and abroad on the terms of trade. In the preceding analysis, the exchange rate rose by precisely the right amount to offset the effects of domestic inflation on the terms of trade. That is, the exchange depreciation maintained the *purchasing power* of our goods in terms of foreign goods between the initial and the final equilibrium positions.

An important view of the determinants of the exchange rate is the theory that exchange rates move primarily as a result of differences in price level behaviour between the two countries in such a way as to maintain the terms of trade constant. This is the *purchasing power parity* (PPP) theory. The theory argues that exchange rate movements primarily reflect divergent rates of inflation. Examining the terms of trade, eP_f/P, the theory maintains the following: When P_f and/or P change, e changes in such a way as to maintain eP_f/P constant.

PPP is a plausible description of the trend behaviour of exchange rates, especially when inflation differentials between countries are large. In particular, we have seen that the PPP relationship does hold in the face of an increase in the money stock. If price level movements are caused by monetary changes — as they are likely to be if the inflation rate is high — then we should expect PPP relationships to hold in the long term.

Figure 19-5 shows the exchange rate (Canadian dollar price of one U.S. dollar) and the terms of trade in relation to the U.S. The terms of trade is calculated using the U.S. and Canadian GNP deflators to measure P_f and P.

From 1954 to 1967 similar inflation rates were experienced in the two countries so the two indexes moved together. The U.S. rate of inflation was above the Canadian rate during the period 1968 to 1971, and this is reflected in an improvement in the competitive position (or worsening of the terms of trade) in 1968 and 1969. Following the floating of the Canadian dollar in 1970, there was a sharp appreciation which dominated the movement of the terms of trade. From 1972 to 1976, the Canadian inflation rate was substantially above the U.S. rate, and the terms of trade improved until late 1976 when the Canadian dollar began to depreciate. By 1978 Canada's competitive position had been restored to the level of the early 1970s, and from 1979 to 1983 the terms of trade fluctuated within a narrow range.

Figure 19-5 suggests some tendency for the terms of trade to maintain a constant level in the long run, but there is considerable short-run variation. This reflects two important qualifications to the PPP theory. First, even a monetary disturbance affects the terms of trade in the short run. Exchange rates

FIGURE 19-5   EXCHANGE RATE AND TERMS OF TRADE RELATIVE TO THE U.S.

(*Source*: Department of Finance, *Economic Review*; U.S. Department of Commerce, *Survey of Current Business*)

tend to move quite rapidly relative to prices, and thus we observe substantial deviations from PPP.

The second important qualification concerns the role of nonmonetary disturbances in affecting exchange rates. For example, we saw in Chapter 6 that an increase in exports improves our terms of trade or leads to currency appreciation at unchanged domestic prices. If we look at an increase in potential output as another example, we will find that the equilibrium terms of trade worsen. To absorb the increased output, demand must rise, implying a decline in the relative price of our goods. Thus, it is apparent that, over time, adjustments to *real* disturbances will affect the *equilibrium* terms of trade. In the longer run, exchange rates and prices do *not* necessarily move together, as they do in a world where all disturbances are monetary. On the contrary, we may have important changes in relative prices. Such changes run counter to the purchasing power parity view of exchange rates.

Exchange Rate Expectations and Inflation

In Section 6-3 of Chapter 6, we modified our model, in the case of flexible exchange rates and perfect capital mobility, by introducing the interest parity condition. We replaced the condition that the domestic interest rate (i) is equal to the foreign rate (i^*) with

$$i = i^* + x \qquad (2)$$

where x is the expected rate of depreciation of the domestic currency.

As we indicated in our discussion in Chapter 6, exchange rate expectations can be a source of short-run instability. In the longer run, we would expect differences in inflation rates between countries to be the major factor in the trend movements in exchange rates. Thus, in long-run equilibrium, a country with a relatively high inflation rate would have a relatively high nominal interest rate (because of the Fisher equation discussed in Chapter 17), and a depreciating currency. The rate of depreciation would match the inflation differential in order to maintain the terms of trade at a constant equilibrium level.

Denoting the domestic and foreign inflation rates by gp and gp^* respectively, and substituting the differential for x in Equation (2), we obtain

$$i = i^* + gp - gp^*$$

or $\qquad\qquad\qquad\qquad\qquad\qquad\qquad\qquad\qquad\qquad (3)$

$$i - gp = i^* - gp^*$$

Thus, in long-run equilibrium, the interest parity condition states that *real* interest rates are equalized across countries. Nominal rates will differ according to the differences in inflation rates.

19-3 THE EXCHANGE RATE AND MONETARY POLICY IN CANADA SINCE 1970

In Chapter 6, we reviewed the Canadian experience under flexible exchange rates in the 1950s when inflation was not a serious problem for policy makers. In this section, we consider the operation of a flexible rate since 1970 when inflation became a major preoccupation.

The Build-up of Inflation in the 1970s

The inflation problem of the 1970s had its origins in the second half of the 1960s when the U.S. economy was experiencing boom conditions to a considerable extent as a result of expenditures related to the Vietnam War. Demand pressure in the United States spilled over into Canada in the form of demand for our exports, and this resulted in a large surplus on merchandise trade as shown in Figure 19-6. This process was intensified by the favourable competitive position that Canada enjoyed at the time. The longer term trends in the Canada-U.S. terms of trade shown in Figure 19-6 suggest that the choice of 92.5 U.S. cents when the Canadian dollar was pegged in 1962 involved a substantial undervaluation of our currency. This proposition is confirmed by the fact that maintenance of this rate required substantial intervention in the foreign exchange market. As can be seen in Figure 19-6, official reserves rose in every year of the fixed rate period, with the exception of 1966, as the Bank of Canada held down the exchange rate by supplying Canadian dollars to the market in exchange for foreign currency.

As pressure on the Canadian dollar built up, the Bank of Canada was unwilling or unable to sterilize the effects of exchange market intervention on the money supply. Thus the classical adjustment process discussed in Section 19-1 was brought into play and the rate of growth of the money supply increased (see Figure 19-6). In 1967, the rate of growth of $M1$ was nearly 10 percent as compared with an average of about 5 percent between 1960 and 1964. In 1968, the inflationary pressure was intensified by an acceleration of inflation in the United States. As pointed out in the previous section, the U.S. inflation rate was above the Canadian rate from 1968 to 1972.

The freeing of the Canadian dollar in 1970 provided the Bank of Canada with an opportunity to stem the inflationary pressures. The rate of growth of the money supply was sharply curtailed and the inflation rate eased thereafter. As would be expected, there was a substantial appreciation of the Canadian dollar. However, shortly after the Bank of Canada had freed itself from the restrictions imposed by a fixed exchange rate and made substantial progress in bringing inflation under control, it appears to have become reluctant to exploit the benefits of a flexible rate.

To begin with, the Bank of Canada attempted to resist the appreciation of the Canadian dollar in 1970 and 1971 by intervening heavily in the foreign exchange market. This is reflected in the large increase in official reserves shown in Figure 19-6. A substantial appreciation was required to restore the terms of trade to the equilibrium level, and intervention to prevent this from taking place intensified inflationary pressure in Canada.

The second error in policy was the sharp turnaround in monetary policy that occurred in 1971. Subsequent events indicated that the Bank of Canada overreacted to the slowdown in economic activity and rising unemployment experienced in 1970. As can be seen in Figure 19-6, the rate of growth of $M1$ shot up to a level close to 13 percent in 1971 and rose to 14 percent in 1972. In 1973, there was a sharp increase in the inflation rate, and by 1975 the consumer price index was rising at a rate in excess of 10 percent. There was an increase in the rate of inflation in the United States as well but the acceleration was more

FIGURE 19-6   MONETARY POLICY, INFLATION AND THE BALANCE OF PAYMENTS, 1965-1987

(*Source*: Adapted from *Bank of Canada Review*)

rapid in Canada. As shown in Figure 19-5, the exchange rate was held close to 100 U.S. cents over the period 1972 to 1976 while the difference in inflation rates lead to a substantial deterioration in our competitive position.

In retrospect, it appears that Canada missed an opportunity to avoid at least some of the inflation that plagued the world economy in the 1970s. Monetary policy was immobilized in the late sixties by a commitment to a fixed exchange rate at a time when inflation rates began to rise in other countries. In the early 1970s the full benefits of a flexible rate were not realized, since the Bank of Canada resisted the appreciation of the Canadian dollar. It appears to have been influenced by a misguided concern for the effect of an appreciation on the competitive position of Canada's export industries. This led the Bank to hold down the appreciation by direct intervention in 1970 and 1971, and to stabilize the rate near 100 U.S. cents in 1972 and 1973 by permitting a rapid rate of growth in the money supply. As indicated by the discussion of a money supply increase in the previous section, the short-run effect of an expansionary monetary policy is to hold down the exchange rate. However, the longer-run consequence is an increase in prices which restores the competitive position of domestic industries to the equilibrium level. In this case, the monetary expansion induced an overshooting of the price level and a temporary improvement in our competitive position that was reversed by the depreciation that began in late 1976.

A second reason for the mismanagement of monetary policy in the early 1970s was the delayed recognition of the importance of controlling the rate of growth of the money supply. As indicated in Chapter 12, it was not until 1973, when inflationary forces were already entrenched, that the Bank of Canada began to move towards greater emphasis on control of the money supply; explicit target rates of growth were not adopted until late 1975.

Monetary Policy and the 1981–82 Recession

As we saw in Chapter 18, the Bank of Canada's gradualist strategy of bringing down the rate of growth of the money supply in successive stages achieved limited success in bringing down the rate of inflation. The abandonment of gradualism came in the first half of 1981 when the Federal Reserve pushed up interest rates sharply in the U.S. and brought on a severe recession that finally produced a substantial easing of the inflation rate.

What options did the Bank of Canada have in the face of this sharp rise in interest rates in the U.S.? The effects of an increase in the foreign interest rate are illustrated in Figure 19-7. The initial equilibrium is at E and the increase in the foreign interest rate is represented by an upward shift in the BP schedule. In the absence of a parallel reduction of the money supply in Canada, the Canadian dollar undergoes an immediate depreciation, causing the IS curve to shift up and to the right so that the short-run equilibrium is at E'. At this point

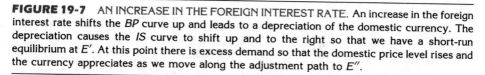

FIGURE 19-7 AN INCREASE IN THE FOREIGN INTEREST RATE. An increase in the foreign interest rate shifts the *BP* curve up and leads to a depreciation of the domestic currency. The depreciation causes the *IS* curve to shift up and to the right so that we have a short-run equilibrium at *E'*. At this point there is excess demand so that the domestic price level rises and the currency appreciates as we move along the adjustment path to *E"*.

there is excess demand so that the price level rises and the Canadian dollar appreciates as we move along the adjustment path to *E"*.

We thus conclude: If the Bank of Canada does not respond by reducing the growth rate of the Canadian money supply, a tightening of monetary policy in the U.S. will cause the Canadian dollar to depreciate and create inflationary pressure in Canada. For this reason, the Bank of Canada was reluctant to maintain an independent policy strategy and followed the American lead. The result was a sharp decline in the Canadian inflation rate, but as we have noted this was achieved by exploiting the short-run Phillips curve tradeoff and allowing a drastic increase in the unemployment rate.[3]

---

[3] For a further discussion of the policy response to a change in foreign interest rates, see G.R. Sparks, "The Theory and Practice of Monetary Policy in Canada: 1945–83", in J. Sargent (ed.), *Fiscal and Monetary Policy*, Royal Commission Research Studies, Vol. 21 (University of Toronto Press, 1986), pp. 141–143.

The spillover effects of U.S. tight money in this period created problems for other industrialized countries as well. Policy makers were forced to accept higher inflation caused by American policy or to change their own policy. Since most countries did not want to import inflation, they reacted by tightening money. This reduced the effects on exchange rates but it also meant that American tight money and recession became the world's tight money and a world recession.

19-4 EXCHANGE RATE CHANGES AND TRADE ADJUSTMENT: TWO EMPIRICAL ISSUES

In this section we take up two important empirical issues related to the possibilities for adjusting current account imbalances by changes in the exchange rate. In our theoretical model of Chapter 6, we assumed that prices here and abroad were fixed, so that exchange rate changes affected relative prices one for one. In this chapter, by contrast, we explore a world where prices (and wages) are flexible and full employment is maintained in the long run. In this section, we consider the alternative possibility, that wages and prices are flexible, but that they may respond to movements in the exchange rate in a way that makes it impossible or at least difficult to change relative prices through changes in the exchange rate. This issue is particularly important if formal wage indexation arrangements link wage behaviour to import prices and thus to the exchange rate.

The second issue we consider is whether changes in relative prices, assuming that they are possible, will affect the current account in the direction we have so far assumed. The assumption, so far, has been that a decline in the relative price of our goods improves the current account, but the possibility arises that at least in the short run there might be a perverse reaction. With import prices rising, for example, import demand may not decline sufficiently to compensate for higher prices, and thus total import spending (price times quantity) may actually increase. We turn now to these two issues.

Exchange Rates and Relative Price Adjustment

In studying the flexible wage-price model, we assumed that wages and prices adjust to achieve full employment. Now we consider as an alternative the possibility that prices are based on labour cost or wages and that wages are inflexible in real terms. Suppose that labour wants to maintain the purchasing power of wages or to keep real wages constant. In such a world, changes in the cost of living would lead to changes in money wages, in labour cost, and therefore in prices, which in turn feed back into wages. Two points emerge from this description. The first is that in such a world, we may not be able to get to full employment. Labour may set the real wage too high, and at least in the intermediate run, the full-employment level of output cannot be sustained. The second point is that a process in which changes in prices feed back into wages and from there into prices is one of a *wage-price spiral* that may produce considerable volatility in the price level. Small disturbances can set off quite large changes in the price level.

Suppose, first, that the real wage is fixed in terms of the consumer price index that includes both domestic goods and imports. Let us assume, second, that changes in the consumer price index are fully passed on into wages, and third, that changes in wages are fully passed on into increased domestic prices. Now assume that starting from an initial equilibrium, there is a currency depreciation brought about by some short-term, reversible disturbance. The depreciation raises import prices and thereby has a direct effect on consumer prices and wages. To maintain the purchasing power of their wages, workers increase money wages and firms pass on the wage increase into higher prices. Where are we after the process ends? Real wages are constant, which means wages and the price level (a weighted average of the prices of domestic and imported goods) have risen in the same proportion; wage increases have been fully passed on, which means that real wages *in terms of domestic output* are also unchanged. The two results imply that relative prices are unchanged, or that the exchange depreciation is fully matched by domestic inflation.

Of course, this is not really the end because we have to ask how the higher price level affects the macroeconomic equilibrium. To the extent that lower real balances lower aggregate demand, we would have a reduction in employment. To round out our story, we can imagine that the central bank steps in to prevent unemployment by raising the money stock. If nominal money rises in proportion to the price increase, then the full-employment equilibrium, at the same terms of trade, is reestablished but, of course, at a higher level of wages and prices. This is an economy where there is very little stability in the price level because the slightest change in exchange rate expectations leads to actual exchange rate movements that are fully *validated* by domestic wage, price, and monetary developments.

A second context in which the idea of *sticky real wages* is important is that of real disturbances. Suppose our export demand declines permanently because of, say, the introduction of superior technology abroad. To return to full employment, the relative price of our goods must fall so as to encourage foreign demand, but how can the relative price fall? In Chapter 6, we argued that the exchange rate will depreciate, thereby raising import prices relative to domestic prices and restoring our competitiveness. In the present context we have to recognize that important price increases would be immediately matched by wage increases and that these wage increases would be fully passed on into price increases. Relative prices cannot change. The consequence would, of course, be protracted unemployment. Unemployment would continue until the *real* wage declined.

The empirical question, then, is, How flexible are real wages? This is, to an important extent, a question of institutional arrangements. In small open economies with substantial cost-of-living indexation in wage agreements, it may indeed be very difficult to change real wages and relative prices through exchange rate changes. The governor of the Bank of Canada has argued that this problem is of some importance in Canada. For example, in a speech given in November, 1980, Governor Bouey stated:

> In certain circumstances, for example, a significant decline in the exchange value of the Canadian dollar brought about by unusual interest rate relationships between Canada and the United States would not only add almost immediately to the upward pressure on prices and spending but would also, before long, threaten to put increased upward pressure as well on negotiated wage settlements and thus on our on-going costs of production.[4]

Relative Prices and the Trade Balance: The J Curve

We come now to the second issue, the effect of changes in relative prices on the trade balance and the possibility that a depreciation *worsens* the trade balance. To make this point, we write out the trade balance, measured in terms of domestic goods, as

$$NX = X - \frac{eP_f}{P}Q \tag{4}$$

where X denotes the foreign demand for our goods or exports and Q denotes our own import quantity. The term $(eP_f/P)Q$ thus measures the *value* of our imports in terms of domestic goods.

Suppose that we now have a currency depreciation and that in the first instance, domestic and foreign prices, P and P_f, are unchanged. Then the relative price of imports, eP_f/P, rises. This leads to two effects. First, if the physical *volume* of imports does not change, their *value* measured in domestic currency unambiguously increases because of the higher price. With unchanged physical import volume, Q, higher prices mean increased import spending and thus a worsening of the trade balance. This is the source for the potentially perverse response of the trade balance to a depreciation. However, there is an adjustment that runs in the opposite direction. The increased relative price of imports makes us more competitive and shifts demand in volume terms toward domestic goods. This *volume effect* of substitution in response to changed relative prices shows up in equation (6) in the form of increased export volume, X, and reduced import volume, Q. The volume effects thus ambiguously improve the trade balance.

---

[4] See *Bank of Canada Review*, November, 1980, p. 10.

The question, then, is whether the volume effects on imports and exports are sufficiently strong to outweigh the price effect, that is, whether depreciation raises or lowers net exports. The empirical evidence on this question is quite strong and shows the following result: *The short-term volume effects, say, within a year, are quite small and thus do not outweigh the price effect.*[5] *The long-term volume effects, by contrast, are quite substantial, and certainly enough to make the trade balance respond in the normal fashion to a relative price change.*

Where does this asymmetry come from, and what does it imply about trade adjustment to relative prices? First, the low short-term and high longer-term volume effects result from the time consumers and producers take to adjust to changes in relative prices. Some of these adjustments may be instantaneous, but it is clear that tourism patterns, for example, may take six months to a year to adjust and that relocation of production internationally, in response to changes in relative costs and prices, may take years. A case in point is increased foreign direct investment in Canada, like, for instance, Volvo moving assembly operations from Sweden to Nova Scotia. In the long term, such direct investment leads to reduced Volvo imports by Canada, and thus to an improved trade balance, but such an adjustment takes years, not weeks or months.

The lag in the adjustment of trade flows to changes in relative prices is thus quite plausible. The next question is, What do these lags imply about the impact of relative price changes on the trade balance? Suppose that at a particular time, starting with a deficit, we have a depreciation that raises the relative price of imports. The short-term effects result primarily from increased import prices with very little offsetting volume effects. Therefore, the trade balance initially worsens. Over time, as trade volume adjusts to the changed relative prices, exports rise and import volume progressively declines. The volume effects come to dominate, and in the long run, the trade balance shows an improvement. This pattern of adjustment is referred to as the *J-curve effect*, because diagrammatically the response of the trade balance looks like a *J*.

The medium-term problem of sticky real wages and the J-curve effect are important qualifications to the macroeconomics of flexible rates as spelled out in Sections 19-1 and 19-2. They imply that flexible exchange rates do not provide for instant, costless flexibility of relative prices and trade flows. At the same time, these considerations provide important clues for the interpretation of macroeconomic experiences across countries, particularly in showing why depreciations typically do not lead to improvements in the current account in the short term.

---

[5] See Michael C. Deppler and Duncan M. Ripley, "The World Trade Model: Merchandise Trade," *IMF Staff Papers*, March 1978; Duncan M. Ripley, "The World Model of Merchandise Trade: Simulation Applications," *IMF Staff Papers*, June 1980; and "Issues in the Assessment of the Exchange Rates of Industrial Countries," *IMF Occasional Paper No. 29*, July 1984.

19-5 EXCHANGE RATE FLUCTUATIONS AND INTERDEPENDENCE

In the 1960s there was growing dissatisfaction with fixed exchange rates. The Bretton Woods system was called a crisis system because from time to time exchange rates would get out of line and expectations of exchange rate changes would mobilize massive capital flows that often precipitated the exchange rate changes that speculators expected. Is the flexible rate system of the 1970s and early 1980s better? Is it less crisis-prone, and does it provide a better framework for macroeconomic stability? Before providing an answer, we look briefly at how flexibly the system has, in fact, operated.

Dirty Floating and Intervention

Under *fully* flexible exchange rates the government takes no action in the foreign exchange market. Far from buying or selling foreign exchange at a fixed price, the government does not conduct *any* foreign exchange transactions. It stays out of the foreign exchange market, whatever happens to the exchange rate. Such a system is almost unheard of, although the United States did behave that way briefly in 1981–1982. More commonly, governments intervene in the foreign exchange market to a lesser or greater extent. Foreign exchange market *intervention* occurs when a government buys or sells foreign exchange in an attempt to influence the exchange rate. The extent to which governments intervene varies substantially. They may only try to offset short-term fluctuations and buy or sell foreign exchange to maintain "orderly markets," but they also may try to keep an overvalued exchange rate from depreciating or an undervalued exchange rate from appreciating. *Dirty floating* (as opposed to clean) is the practice of using substantial intervention to try to maintain an exchange rate against the pressure of market forces.

During the 1973–1986 period, exchange market intervention has been of the decidedly dirty variety. Governments have intervened on a very large scale. This leads naturally to the question of why a government should try to resist market forces to prevent an appreciation or a depreciation of the currency.

Why Governments Intervene

Central banks intervene to affect exchange rates for several reasons. Probably the main reason is the belief that many capital flows represent merely unstable expectations and that the induced movements in exchange rates move production in the economy in an unnecessarily erratic fashion. The second reason for the intervention is a central bank's attempt to move the terms of trade in order to affect trade flows. The third reason arises from the effects of the exchange rate on domestic inflation. Central banks sometimes intervene in the exchange market to prevent the exchange rate from depreciating, with the aim of preventing a depreciation-induced increase in the inflation rate.

Should central banks intervene in the exchange market? The basic argument for such intervention is that it is possible for intervention to smooth out fluctuations in exchange rates. At one extreme, the argument would assert that any movements in exchange rates produce unnecessary fluctuations in the domestic economy and that exchange rates therefore ought to be fixed. This is the basic argument for dirty floating. The only — and overwhelming — objection to the argument that the central bank should smooth out fluctuation is that there is no simple way of telling an erratic movement from a trend movement. How can we tell whether a current appreciation in the exchange rate is merely the result of a disturbance which will soon reverse itself, rather than the beginning of a trend movement in the exchange rate? There is no way of telling at the time a change occurs, although with the benefit of hindsight one can see which exchange rate movements were later reversed.

There is one circumstance under which central bank intervention might be desirable. It is clear from our earlier analysis that one of the key determinants of exchange rate behaviour consists of expectations of economic policy. It may sometimes be possible to make it clear that there has been a change in policy only by intervening in the foreign exchange market. This is a case of putting your money where your mouth is.

Should Governments Intervene?

There is disagreement on whether governments should intervene in the foreign exchange market. The United States, for example, in 1981–1982 strongly refused consideration of any kind of intervention. The reason was that policy makers in the United States, unlike those in Europe, felt the market knows better than policy makers what level the exchange rate should be. However, there is another and more interesting disagreement: it concerns the effectiveness of intervention. Does it make any difference to the exchange rate if the Bundesbank sells $1 billion from its reserves?

To judge the effectiveness of intervention we must make a distinction between *sterilized* and *nonsterilized intervention*. In the case of sterilized intervention a central bank, say, buys foreign exchange, and issues domestic money, but then the increase in home money is reversed by an open market sale of securities. In the sterilized intervention case, therefore, the home money supply is kept unchanged. By contrast in the case of nonsterilization, there is a change in the money stock equal to the amount of intervention.

Thus nonsterilized intervention results in a change in the money stock. It is widely agreed that nonsterilized intervention, because it changes the money supply, will affect exchange rates. There is widespread skepticism, however, about the effectiveness of sterilized intervention. In 1978–1979 the U.S. dollar was depreciating in currency markets even though there was intervention on a massive scale, but that intervention was carefully sterilized. Only in late 1979, when the dollar depreciation had come to alarm the Federal Reserve did a change in policy take place. Monetary policy was tightened, and immediately the dollar depreciation was stopped and soon massively reversed.

That episode strongly suggests the effectiveness of nonsterilized intervention and of intervention that is backed by credible policies. The earlier failure of sterilized intervention suggested that only unsterilized intervention could affect the exchange rate, but a more recent episode gives cause for rethinking that issue.

The very large appreciation of the U.S. dollar from 1980 to 1985 was a major concern to policy makers in the United States, Europe, and Japan.[6] Many policy makers thought that the markets had pushed the dollar too high, and that only speculative forces were keeping it up. In September 1985 the finance ministers of the Group of Five (the United States, Japan, Germany, France, and the United Kingdom) announced their view that the dollar was too high, and their central banks went into action to sell dollars to drive the rate down. The dollar responded quickly, suggesting that concerted action can affect the exchange rate even if there is no obvious change in monetary policy. Such action is certainly not guaranteed to work, but could work if there is widespread speculation in the markets about the future course of policy and if announcements and intervention suggest that future policy will try to move the exchange rate in a particular direction.

Interdependence

It used to be argued that under flexible exchange rates countries can pursue their own national economic policies—monetary and fiscal policy and the inflation rate—without having to worry about the balance of payments. That is certainly correct, but it is also misleading. There are important linkages between countries *whatever the exchange rate regime*.

These *spillover*, or *interdependence*, effects have been at the center of the discussion about flexible exchange rates. As we saw in Section 19-3 above, the effects of the tight U.S. monetary policy in 1980–1982 created problems for all industrialized countries. The reason is clear from our models: As the United

---

[6] See Federal Reserve Bank of Kansas City, "The U.S. Dollar — Recent Development, Outlook and Policy Options," 1985, which includes a discussion of many of the issues raised by the strong dollar, intervention, and coordination. See also Jeffrey Frankel, "Six Possible Meanings of Over-valuation: The 1981–85 Dollar," *Essays in International Finance* (Princeton, N.J.: Princeton, December 1985), and the Symposium in the Brookings Papers on Economic Activity, I, 1986.

States tightens monetary policy, U.S. interest rates rise, and this attracts capital flows. The U.S. dollar appreciates and other currencies depreciate. Table 19-2 shows the effects on other countries.

TABLE 19-2 MONETARY AND FISCAL POLICY EFFECTS WITH INTERDEPENDENCE

	U.S. MONETARY EXPANSION		U.S. FISCAL EXPANSION	
	U.S.	Rest of World	U.S.	Rest of World
Exchange rate	U.S. $ depreciates		U.S. $ appreciates	
Output	+	−	+	+
Inflation	+	−	−	+

The U.S. appreciation implies a loss in competitiveness. World demand shifts from U.S. goods to those produced by competitors. Therefore, American output and employment decline while output and employment expand in other countries.

There are also spillover effects through prices. When the U.S. dollar appreciates, import prices in the U.S. fall and the U.S. inflation rate declines. However, the opposite occurs in other countries. Their currencies depreciate and therefore prices increase. Inflation thus rises in other countries which may welcome an increase in employment as a side effect of U.S. monetary policy, but do not welcome the inflation.

In the same way, U.S. fiscal policies exert effects elsewhere. A U.S. fiscal expansion such as occurred during the 1980–1985 period will lead to appreciation of the U.S. dollar and a loss in competitiveness. The direct increase in American spending and the deterioration in U.S. competitiveness are the channels through which American expansion is shared with other countries that experience increased exports. At the same time the appreciation of the U.S. dollar will reduce inflation in the U.S. but increase inflation in other countries. Table 19-2 summarizes these interdependence effects.[7]

Policy makers in other countries therefore must decide whether to accept the higher employment–higher inflation effects of U.S. policies or whether they

---

[7] We showed before that in a country that takes foreign interest rates and income as given, a fiscal expansion leads to *full* crowding out. Table 19-2 shows that once interactions with the rest of the world are taken into account, there is a world expansion. We do not prove this result here. For a demonstration see Robert Mundell, *International Economics* (New York: Macmillan, 1968).

should change their own policies. If the rest of the world does not want *imported inflation*, then their response must be to tighten money. This response on the part of Canada and other countries led to a spreading of the 1981–1982 recession throughout the world.

Policy Synchronization

The large changes in exchange rates that arise when policies are not fully synchronized between countries pose a major threat to a world of free trade. When import prices fall by 20 to 30 percent because of a currency appreciation, large shifts in demand will occur. Domestic workers become unemployed, and they have no trouble seeing that it is foreigners who gain the jobs they just lost. Accordingly, there will be pressure for protection — tariffs or quotas — to keep out imports that are "artificially cheap" due to the currency appreciation. In the United States repeated calls for protection in the automobile industry, in steel, and in many other industries reflect in large part the side effects of a dollar that appreciated sharply in response to tight money.

On the question of independence or interdependence under flexible exchange rates, the experience of the last 14 years offers a quite unambiguous answer. Under flexible exchange rates there is as much or more interdependence as there is under fixed rates. Moreover, because exchange rates are so flexible and so ready to respond to policies (good or bad), macroeconomic management does not become easier. Further, to the extent that exchange rate overshooting causes sharp changes in competitiveness, it leads to protectionist sentiment.

On all counts then, flexible rates are far from being a perfect system. But there is no better system. Therefore we can ask only whether through international coordination of interests and policies, we can make the system work better than it has in the recent past. In 1985 and 1986 the leaders of the major industrial countries recognized their independence and agreed to work toward more coordinated policies. But there were as yet no major institutional changes that would provide a mechanism to ensure that coordination would take place.

19-6 SUMMARY

1. In an open economy, aggregate demand is reduced by an increase in the price level through a reduction in domestic competitiveness as well as through a reduction in real balances as in the closed economy case.

2. If there is a trade deficit at full employment, contractionary policy is required to reduce the price level so as to achieve external balance. This

adjustment occurs automatically via a decline in the money supply if the central bank pegs the exchange rate without sterilization. Devaluation can also be used to achieve external balance.

3. A country on a fixed exchange rate ties its price level to that of its trading partners. Canada was on a fixed rate in the second half of the 1960s and was forced to import U.S. inflation.

4. From 1946 to 1973, most countries had fixed exchange rates. This system collapsed because of divergent policies followed in the major industrial countries.

5. In the short run, an increase in the money supply leads to a depreciation and an increase in income. In the long run the initial levels of income and the terms of trade are restored by proportional increases in the price level and exchange rate. This neutrality result leads to the purchasing power parity theory of exchange rates. It does not always hold because the terms of trade varies in response to nonmonetary disturbances and is affected even by monetary factors in the short run.

6. In the long run, high inflation countries have high nominal interest rates and depreciating currencies. The interest parity condition implies that real interest rates are equalized across countries in the long run.

7. The floating of the Canadian dollar in 1970 did not stem inflationary pressure because the Bank of Canada failed to control the rate of growth of the money supply until it adopted money supply targets in 1975.

8. The 1981–1982 recession was brought on by tight monetary policy in the U.S. which forced other industrial countries to follow a similar policy to avoid an increase in inflation rates. This was an example of the interdependence among countries that exists even with flexible exchange rates.

9. A currency depreciation can, in the short run, lead to a worsening of the trade balance. This occurs when the effect of changes in relative prices on the volume of trade is small because adjustments take time. Over time, trade adjusts and the depreciation improves the trade balance. This is called the J-curve effect.

10. Because it raises import prices, depreciation of the exchange rate raises the cost of living and may spill over into increased wage demands. If such spillovers are substantial, then a flexible rate system will have large movements in nominal prices, and exchange rate movements may perform poorly in bringing about relative price changes.

11. Governments can intervene in exchange markets to limit the impact of exchange rate fluctuations, stemming from asset market disturbances, on output and prices. But intervention is very problematic when the

authorities cannot determine whether the exchange rate is moving on account of fundamentals or noise.

12. Even under flexible exchange rates economies are closely tied to one another. A monetary expansion at home will lead to unemployment and disinflation abroad. A fiscal expansion will cause an expansion abroad along with inflation. These interdependence effects make a case for coordinating policies.

KEY TERMS

Terms of trade   The J curve
Classical adjustment process   Intervention
Bretton Woods system   Dirty float
Purchasing power parity   Interdependence

PROBLEMS

1. Consider the model depicted in Figure 19-1. Illustrate the short-run equilibrium of an economy with unemployment and a zero balance of trade. Show the adjustment process assuming (a) sterilization, and (b) no sterilization.

2. Consider an economy with a fixed exchange rate and perfect capital mobility. Use LM, IS and BP curves to analyze the effects on domestic income and prices of a change in government spending. What are the short-run and long-term effects on the terms of trade? (You may need to review the analysis of Chapter 5 to do this question.)

3. Suppose in year 1 we have price levels $P = 100$ and $P_f = 100$. Suppose next that in year 2 the respective price levels are $P_2 = 180$ and $P_{2f} = 130$. Let the exchange rate initially be $2/£.
   (a) If there were no real disturbances between year 1 and year 2, what would be the equilibrium exchange rate in year 2?
   (b) If the real exchange rate, eP_f/P had deteriorated between years 1 and 2 by 50 percent, what would the exchange rate be in year 2?

4. Explain why an expansionary fiscal policy reduces foreign income less than direct intervention by the central bank in the foreign exchange markets to depreciate the exchange rate.

5. Assume that there is perfect mobility of capital. How does the imposition of a tariff affect the exchange rate, output, and the current account? (Hint: Given the exchange rate, the tariff reduces our demand for imports.)

6. How would the adjustment path in response to an increase in the money supply (see Figure 19-4) change if we take account of the interest parity condition discussed in Section 6-3 of Chapter 6?

7. Explain the purchasing power parity theory of the long-run behaviour of the exchange rate. Indicate circumstances under which you would not expect the theory to hold.

8. Discuss the extent to which the Bank of Canada can set interest rates in Canada independently of rates in the United States. Does the Bank have more control over nominal rates or real rates?

CHAPTER

Long-Term Growth and Productivity

In this chapter we turn our attention away from the short-run problems of the business cycle to look at where the economy has been and may be heading in the long term. From 1870 to 1987 real income in Canada grew at an average annual rate of 3.9 percent. This trend rate is shown in Figure 20-1 along with actual real income. In per capita terms, the average rate of growth was 2.1 percent. With this growth rate, per capita income doubles every 33 years.

Table 20-1 shows that growth in Canada in the period from 1973 to 1983 was below the historical average. During that decade per capita real income grew at only 1.6 percent. At that rate it would take 44 years to double.

To analyze the long-run behaviour of the economy we focus on *trend* or *potential output*. We pose the following major questions: What determines the *growth rate* of potential output? Why does output grow over time and how fast? Will growth in the future be as high as it has been in the past? Will the economy keep on a trend of rising output per capita, as it has been in the past century?

In discussing the growth of potential output we are also posing the question: What are future levels of output likely to be? Even small differences in the growth rate of potential output cumulate over time to large differences in the level of per capita income and hence in the standard of living. With a growth rate of 2 percent per year it takes 35 years for per capita income to double, but if the growth rate is only 1 percent, it takes 70 years to achieve a doubling of income per head. The growth rate of potential output is thus of central importance.

Table 20-2 shows an international comparison of income levels.[1] It is interesting to note that growth rates are lower in the U.S. and Canada than Japan

---

[1] For historical international comparisons see Angus Maddison, *Phases of Capitalist Development* (London: Oxford University Press, 1982). The difficulties with comparing incomes across countries and a methodology for these comparisons are presented in Irving Kravis et al., *World Product and Income* (Baltimore, Md.: Johns Hopkins University Press, 1982).

FIGURE 20-1   REAL INCOME, 1870-1987

(*Source*: M.C. Urquhart, "New Estimates of Gross National Product, Canada, 1870-1926," in S.L. Engerman and R.E. Gallman (eds.), *Long-term Factors in American Economic Growth*, NBER, 1986; Statistics Canada, 11-505, 13-201)

TABLE 20-1   AVERAGE ANNUAL GROWTH RATES, 1870–1987

	1870–1953	1953–1973	1973–1983	1983–1987
Real Income (%)	3.7	5.0	2.9	4.4
Per Capita Real Income (%)	2.0	2.9	1.6	3.4

Source: See Figure 20-1.

TABLE 20-2   COMPARATIVE PER CAPITA INCOME LEVELS ($U.S. in 1983)

	U.S.	Canada	Japan	Korea	Brazil	Mexico
Per capita income (1984 $)	15 390	13 280	10 630	2 110	1 720	2 040
Growth rate of per capita income 1965–1984 (% per year)	1.7	2.4	4.7	6.6	4.6	2.9

Source: World Bank, *World Development Report 1986.*

and the developing countries shown, but the level of per capita income is higher. However if Korea, for example, maintains a high growth rate long enough it will ultimately catch up with and even surpass North American income levels. Using the growth rates in Table 20-2, we can calculate that it would take 42 years to get to the U.S. income level. That may seem to be a long period, but it might be instructive to think of Japan in the post-World War II period. In the past 40 years U.S. real income per capita only doubled, but that of Japan increased by a factor of more than 10. In that perspective many of the newly industrialized countries in Asia and Latin America may well get within the reach of the old and established nations like the United Kingdom, Germany, or even the U.S. within the next 30 to 50 years.

Because future per capita income levels are so sensitive to the growth rate of potential output, it is worth worrying about changes of even $\frac{1}{10}$ of 1 percent in the long-run growth rate of output. To answer questions about the growth rate of potential output, we go back to fundamentals. With output at the full-employment level, and hence the available factor supplies fully utilized, there are only two possible sources of growth. *Factor supplies may grow, or the productivity of factors of production may increase*. This, in turn, raises the questions of what determines the growth of factor supplies and their productivity, and what the quantitative link is between growth in factor supplies and productivity, and output growth.

There are two complementary approaches to these questions. One is *growth theory*, which models the interactions among factor supplies, output growth, saving, and investment in the process of growth. The other is *growth accounting*, which attempts to quantify the contribution of different determinants of output growth. The two approaches draw on a common analytical framework which we now outline.

20-1 SOURCES OF GROWTH IN REAL INCOME

In this section we use the production function to identify the *sources of growth*. We show that growth in labour, growth in capital, and improved technical efficiency are the three sources of growth.

The Production Function

In earlier chapters we introduced the concept of a production function. The *production function* links the amount of output produced in an economy to the inputs of factors of production and to the state of technical knowledge. Equation (1) represents the production function in symbols:

$$Y = AF(K, N) \tag{1}$$

where K and N denote the inputs of capital and labour and A denotes the state of technology. The production function $AF(K, N)$ in (1) states that the output produced depends on factor inputs K and N and on the state of technology. Increases in factor inputs and improved technology lead to an increase in output supply.

The next step is to make these links more precise by looking at an expression for the growth rate of output. In equation (2) (which is derived in the appendix) we show the determinants of output growth.[2]

$$\Delta Y/Y = (1 - \theta) \times \Delta N/N + \theta \times \Delta K/K + \Delta A/A \qquad (2)$$

| Output growth | = | labour share | × | labour growth | + | capital share | × | capital growth | + | technical progress |

where $(1 - \theta)$ and θ are weights equal to the income share of labour and of capital in production.

Equation (2) summarizes the contributions of growth of inputs and of improved productivity to growth of output:

1. The contribution of the growth of factor inputs is seen in the first two terms. Labour and capital each contribute an amount equal to their individual growth rate *multiplied by the share of that input in income*.
2. The rate of improvement of technology, called *technical progress* or the *growth of total factor productivity*, is the third term in equation (2). The growth rate of total factor productivity is the amount by which output would be increasing as a result of improvements in methods of production, with all inputs unchanged. In other words, there is growth in total factor productivity when we get more output from the same factors of production.[3]

Example

Suppose the income share of capital is 0.3 and that of labour is 0.7. These values correspond approximately to the actual values for the Canadian economy. Furthermore, let labour force growth be 1.8 percent and growth of the capital stock be 4 percent, and suppose technical progress proceeds at the rate of 1.5 percent. What is the growth rate of full-employment output? Applying Equation (2) we obtain a growth rate of 4.0 percent ($= 0.7 \times 1.8$ percent $+ 0.3 \times 4$ percent $+ 1.5$ percent).

---

[2] Equation (2) applies when there are *constant returns to scale* in production; that is, increases in both inputs, in the same proportion, increase output in that proportion.

[3] There is a distinction between *labour productivity* and total factor productivity. Labour productivity is just the ratio of output to labour input, Y/N. Labour productivity certainly grows as a result of technical progress, but it also grows because of the accumulation of capital per worker.

An important point to note in Equation (2) is that the growth rates of capital and labour are weighted by the respective income shares. The reason for these weights is that the importance of a 1 percent change in capital or labour to production differs, and that difference in importance is measured by their relative income shares. Specifically, if labour has a larger share than capital, output rises more when labour increases by, say, 10 percent than if capital increases by 10 percent.

Returning to our example, if labour alone grows by 1 percent, output will grow by 0.7 percent, using the 0.7 income share for labour. If capital alone grows by 1 percent, output will only grow by 0.3 percent, reflecting the smaller importance of capital in production. But if each grows by 1 percent, so does output.

This point—that growth in inputs is weighted by factor shares—turns out to be quite critical when we ask how much extra growth we get by raising the rate of growth of the capital stock, say by supply-side policies. Suppose in the example above, with everything else the same, capital growth had been 7 percent instead of 4 percent. Doing the calculations with the help of Equation (2) we find that output growth would increase to 4.9 percent, rising by less than a percentage point even though capital growth rises by three percentage points.

Empirical Estimates of the Sources of Growth

The previous section prepares us for an analysis of empirical studies that deal with sources of growth. Equation (2) suggests that the growth in output can be explained by growth in factor inputs, weighted by their shares in income, and by technical progress. An early and famous study by Robert Solow of MIT dealt with the period 1909–1949 in the United States.[4] Solow's surprising conclusion was that over 80 percent of the growth in output per labour hour over that period was due to technical progress, that is, to factors other than growth in the input of capital per labour hour. Specifically, Solow estimated for the United States an equation similar to equation (2) that identifies capital and labour growth along with technical progress as the sources of output growth. Of the average annual growth of total output of 2.9 percent per year over that period, he concluded that 0.32 percent was attributable to capital accumulation, 1.09 percent per annum was due to the increases in the input of labour, and the remaining 1.49 percent was due to technical progress. Per capita output grew at 1.81 percent, with 1.49 percent of that increase resulting from technical progress.

The very large part of the growth contribution that is taken up by "technical progress" makes that term really a catchall for omitted factors and poor mea-

---

[4] "Technical Change and the Aggregate Production Function," *Review of Economics and Statistics*, August 1957.

surement of the capital and labour inputs. Further work therefore turned quite naturally to explore this residual, that is, growth not explained by capital accumulation or increased labour input.

Perhaps the most comprehensive of the subsequent studies is that by Edward Denison.[5] Using data for the period 1929–1982, Denison attributed 1.9 percent of the 2.9 percent annual rate of increase in real output to increased factor inputs. Output per labour hour grew at the rate of 1.58 percent, of which 1.02 percent was due to technical progress. Denison's findings thus support Solow's estimate that most of the growth in output per labour hour is due to technical progress.

The methods used by Denison have been applied to Canadian data for the period 1946 to 1967 in a study done for the Economic Council of Canada. Table 20-3 shows a breakdown of the contributions to growth of real output over this period. Out of an average rate of growth of 4.61 percent, 2.25 percent was estimated to be attributable to growth in factor productivity as a result of technical progress.

TABLE 20-3   SOURCES OF GROWTH OF REAL OUTPUT, 1946–67

Source of growth	Growth rate (percent per annum)
Total factor input	2.36
Labour:	1.24
Capital:	1.12
Output per unit of input	2.25
Total output	4.61

Source: Economic Council of Canada, *Seventh Annual Review*, 1970, p. 93.

Technical progress explains almost half the growth in output, with growth in total factor inputs accounting for the other half of growth. Consider now the breakdown between labour and capital. Here increases in the labour force get a very large credit for their contribution to growth. Why? Because labour grows very fast? The answer is provided by Equation (2), which suggests that labour's growth rate has a relatively large weight because labour's share of income is relatively large. The counterpart is obviously the relatively low share of capital. Thus, even if capital and labour grew at the same rate, the fact that they have

---

[5] *Accounting for United States Economic Growth 1929–1969* (Washington, D.C.: The Brookings Institution, 1974). See also E. Denison's *Accounting for Slower Economic Growth: The United States in the 1970s* (ibid., 1980), and *Trends in American Economic Growth, 1929–1982* (Washington, D.C.: The Brookings Institution, 1985).

different shares in income — labour having a share of about 70 percent and capital having a share of about 30 percent — implies that labour would be credited with a larger contribution toward growth.

The remaining significant part of technical progress is *economies of scale*. This is a bit troublesome because we assumed away economies of scale in deriving equation (2). In deriving that equation, we explicitly assumed constant returns to scale, but as the scale of operation of the economy expands, fewer inputs are required per unit output, presumably because we can avail ourselves of techniques that are economically inefficient at a small-scale level but yield factor savings at a larger scale of production.

The major significance of Denison's work, and the work in this area of others, including Nobel laureate Simon Kuznets (1901–1985) and J. W. Kendrick, is to point out that there is no single critical source of real income growth. The early finding by Solow that growth in the capital stock makes a minor, though not negligible, contribution to growth stands up well to the test of later research. Capital investment is certainly necessary — particularly because some technological improvements require the use of new types of machines — but it is clear that other sources of growth can make an important contribution. Furthermore, since for most purposes we are interested in output per head, we have to recognize that we are left with only technical progress and growth in capital to achieve increased output per head. Here we have to ask, What are the components of technical progress? *Advances in knowledge stand out as a major source and point to the roles of research, education, and training as important sources of growth.*[6]

20-2   POTENTIAL OUTPUT AND PRODUCTIVITY

When policy makers decide to use monetary or fiscal policy to bring the economy closer to full employment, they need to know where to aim. If the full-employment unemployment rate were 6 percent, it would not make much sense to use expansionary fiscal policies at a 5.5 percent unemployment rate. Thus we need measures of the full-employment unemployment rate and the corresponding level of *potential output* or *full-employment output*. The concept draws on the ideas of growth accounting to construct a GDP series that can serve as a benchmark for policy planning.

There are two steps in estimating potential output. The first is to estimate the production function, Equation (1), and the second is to estimate the full-employment levels of capital and labour and any other inputs that might be

[6] A collection of useful papers on the sources of growth is contained in Edmund Phelps (ed.), *The Goal of Economic Growth* (New York: Norton, 1969), and Dennis C. Mueller (ed.), *The Political Economy of Growth* (New Haven, Conn.: Yale University Press, 1983).

taken into account. For example, in the production function of the "MACE" model of the Canadian economy, constructed by John Helliwell at the University of British Columbia, three factors of production are taken into account. In order to estimate the impact of the energy crisis, the production function determines output of the energy-using sectors of the economy as a function of labour, capital and energy inputs. This approach makes it possible to estimate the impact of the sharp increase in the price of energy in the 1970s.

Productivity Growth

Table 20-4 shows a breakdown of the contributions to productivity growth in Canadian manufacturing as estimated by the Economic Council of Canada.

TABLE 20-4   CONTRIBUTIONS TO PRODUCTIVITY GROWTH IN MANUFACTURING, 1958–76

| Period | Growth rate of output per person-hour | Inputs per person-hour | | | Total factor productivity |
		Capital	Energy	Materials	
1958–76	3.43	0.30	0.07	2.33	0.74
1958–66	3.48	0.19	0.08	2.32	0.89
1967–73	4.26	0.35	0.07	2.91	0.94
1974–76	1.35	0.48	0.03	1.03	−0.18

Source: Economic Council of Canada, *A Climate of Uncertainty*, Seventeenth Annual Review, 1980, Table C-1.

The estimates for the subperiods reveal a striking decline in the contribution of factor productivity in the 1970s. This is confirmed in Figure 20-2, which shows a slowdown in the growth of real GDP per person employed after 1973.

   This marked decline in productivity growth has been the subject of considerable interest and investigation. In a study undertaken by the Department of Finance, two factors were identified as being significant.[7] About one-quarter of the decline in overall productivity growth was attributed to a fall in productivity in the oil and gas industry. Output per person in this sector declined on average by nearly 10 percent per year over the period 1962 to 1973. Over the remainder of the 1970s, employment, particularly in the areas of exploration and drilling, grew rapidly, while output of oil declined and output of natural gas remained close to the 1973 level.

[7] Department of Finance, *Recent Changes in Patterns of Productivity Growth in Canada*, April 1980.

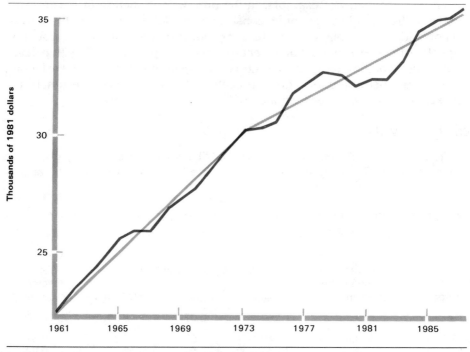

FIGURE 20-2   REAL OUTPUT PER PERSON EMPLOYED, 1961-1987

(*Source*: Department of Finance, *Quarterly Economic Review*, Annual Reference Tables)

Another 25 percent of the post-1973 decline in productivity growth was attributed to a decline in the growth of the capital-labour ratio. Four other factors were examined but were found not to have had a significant impact. These were: (1) changes in the demographic composition of the labour force, (2) shifts in the share of employment from goods producing to services-producing industries, (3) governmental pollution-abatement regulations, and (4) changes in average hours worked per employee.

Analysis of the productivity slowdown based on the MACE model referred to above provides a quite different perspective.[8] As indicated, this model focusses on the energy using sectors and Helliwell estimates that 30 percent of the decline in labour productivity between 1973 and 1982, relative to a steady growth case, is attributable to substitution of labour for energy. This represents, of course, a desirable response of producers to the sharp increase in the relative cost of energy.

---

[8] See J.F. Helliwell, "Stagflation and Productivity Decline in Canada, 1974–1982," *Canadian Journal of Economics*, May 1984, pp. 191–216.

According to Helliwell's analysis, the other major factor in the productivity slowdown was the low level of capacity utilization. This conclusion is particularly important for projecting into the future. It implies that if we are able to return to more normal utilization rates then we can expect the longer term trend growth of productivity to resume.

20-3   OUTPUT GROWTH AND SUPPLY-SIDE ECONOMICS

In the early 1980s, partly as a result of disappointment with slow growth and generally poor macroeconomic performance, *supply-side economics* (discussed in Chapter 18) attracted much attention. We now concentrate on the solid aspect, which argues that the level and/or the growth rate of output could be significantly increased through policies designed to promote greater efficiency, reduced regulation, greater willingness to work, and greater willingness to save and invest.[9]

In discussing full-employment output in earlier chapters we took the labour supply to be given and independent of the real wage, and similarly, we assumed a given stock of capital. However, the basic premise of supply-side economics is that capital and labour supplies are not given, independent of incentives to work, save, and invest. On the contrary, it is argued that the labour-leisure choice is strongly affected by the *after-tax* real wage and that the willingness to save and invest is likewise affected by the *after-tax* rates of return on assets. This perspective directs attention to fiscal policy as influencing factor supplies and hence the level and rate of increase of output.

Labour Supply

Households have to choose how much labour to supply. In practice that means choosing how many members of the family work and for how many hours per week or month. At first sight there appears to be little choice since the typical job comes with a given number of working hours per week, but that is not quite the case once we take into account the possibility that more than one family member might work or the possibilities of working overtime hours or holding part-time jobs. Households' labour supply can thus vary in response to incentives.

The main determinant of labour supply is the after-tax real wage. Suppose it rises. Then some family members who had preferred to stay home may now

---

[9] On supply-side economics see particularly Barry Bosworth, *Tax Incentives and Economic Growth* (Washington, D.C.: The Brookings Institution, 1984), Charles Hulten and Isabel Sawhill (eds.), *The Legacy of Reaganomics,* (The Urban Institute, 1984), Laurence Meyer (ed.), *The Supply Side Effects of Economic Policy* (Federal Reserve Bank of St. Louis, 1981), and Martin Feldstein, "Supply Side Economics: Old Truths and New Claims," *American Economic Review*, May 1986.

be tempted into the labour force. For those already working, the real wage increase has ambiguous effects on labour supply. The *income effect* of the wage increase tends to reduce labour supply because it is now possible to work less and earn more, but because every hour of leisure is now more costly, the *substitution effect* tends to increase labour supply. The outcome of conflicting income and substitution effects is thus a matter for empirical study. In addition, of course, higher participation in the labour force will tend to increase labour supply when the after-tax real wage rises.

Empirical Evidence

Jerry Hausman of MIT has shown in a number of studies that the household labour supply in the U.S. increases *significantly* in response to increased after-tax real wages.[10] This implies that changes in the tax structure that increase the after-tax real wage would increase labour supply and output. Hausman finds that the progressivity of income taxes reduces labour supply. The magnitude of the effect can be judged from the following experiment. Suppose the progressive income tax structure were eliminated and replaced by a flat 15 percent income tax which would lead to the same amount of revenue. What would happen to labour supply? Hausman estimates that total labour supply would rise by 5 percent. With an income share in the U.S. of 0.75, a 5 percent growth in labour supply would increase the level of full-employment output by 3.75 percent. This is certainly a nonnegligible gain, although the policy experiment —the move to a flat income tax—would be a major and controversial change in the structure of taxation.

Supply of Capital

The supply of capital represents the cumulation of past investment. The capital stock grows if additions to the stock more than offset the depreciation due to wear and tear and to obsolescence.

A supply-side point of view emphasizes the links between saving and investment. Recall that when the goods market clears and when net exports are zero, investment minus saving equals the budget surplus, or

$$I = S + (T - G) \tag{3}$$

Equation (3) shows that to raise investment, and thus growth of the capital stock, we require increased saving or reduced government budget deficits. Supply-side economics has focussed on the incentives to save and invest. Supply-side economists argue that regulation has reduced the productivity of

---

[10] See J. Hausman, "Labor Supply and the Natural Unemployment Rate," in L. Meyer, *The Supply Side Effects* op. cit., and Hank Aaron and Joe Pechman (eds.), *How Taxes Affect Economic Behavior* (Washington, D.C.: The Brookings Institution, 1981).

investment and that corporate and personal income taxes further reduce the rate of return eventually received by the savers who provide the funds needed to finance investment. If savers receive a lower rate of return as a result of taxation, say the supply-siders, they reduce saving, and therefore capital accumulation is reduced.

For instance, consider an investment that yields 12 percent per year in real terms. That is, someone who undertakes the investment, costing $100 in year 1, earns $12 per year in real terms forever after (net of labour and material costs). If the income tax rate is 40 percent, the saver can at most earn, after tax, 60 percent of 12 percent, or 7.2 percent. As a result of taxation, the return to saving is substantially reduced. Accordingly, claim supply-siders, the higher the tax rate, the less saving there will be.[11]

What supply-side policies increase the yield on saving? There are a variety of means of exempting the return on saving from taxation. For instance, the Canadian income tax exempts from taxable income contributions up to specified limits to a Registered Retirement Savings Plan. Some argue for the complete exemption of savings from tax by replacing the income tax with a *consumption tax*. A consumption tax levies taxes only on consumption spending, not on income. Since the difference between income and consumption is saving, a consumption tax effectively exempts any amount that is saved from being taxed in the year it is earned, and thereby encourages saving.

There is considerable disagreement on the issue of the response of saving to changes in its return. The contention that increased after-tax rates of return to saving will *strongly* raise saving does not have much support. Once again we have two opposing effects: With increased interest rates, less saving is needed to ensure a given future income, say, for retirement. This effect (actually an income effect) reduces saving. At the same time a dollar saved today yields increased future wealth and consumption and would therefore lead households to postpone consumption and increase saving (this is the substitution effect). The balance of effects is theoretically uncertain.

The empirical evidence does not settle the issue of whether changes in the after-tax rate of return affect the rate of saving.[12] Therefore policies that reduce taxes on saving as a means of generating more saving, capital formation, and growth have an uncertain effect on the economy.

---

[11] See M. Boskin, "Economic Growth and Productivity," in M. Boskin (ed.), *The Economy in the 1980s: A Program for Growth and Stability* (San Francisco: Institute for Contemporary Studies, 1980); the *Economic Report of the President,* 1982 and 1983; and especially, Michael K. Evans, *The Truth about Supply-Side Economics* (New York: Basic Books, 1983).

[12] Gerald A. Carlino, in "Interest Rate Effects and Intertemporal Consumption," *Journal of Monetary Economics*, March 1982, reviews and extends the (ambiguous) evidence. See, too, Larry Kotlikoff, "Taxation and Savings: A Neoclassical Perspective," *Journal of Economic Literature*, December 1984.

Another line of argument questions the quantitative importance of policies to promote saving. We have noted that growth in capital receives a very small weight in determining output growth. Even if policies led to a 10 percent rise in the capital-labour ratio, output per head would only increase by 3 percent.

Regulation

Government regulation involves a tradeoff. Government regulations serve some social purpose (the environment, safety, conservation), but they also involve costs to firms that have to abide by them. Regulation therefore reduces business profitability. Policy makers are keenly aware that the tradeoff exists and therefore, rightly, focus on inefficient regulation and particularly costly (nonmarket) regulation as requiring review. That process has been under way for some time, but it would be a mistake to expect major growth in output from reduced regulation.

Budget Deficits and Growth

In equation (3) we showed that private investment and capital formation will be higher when saving is higher and the government budget deficit is smaller.[13] Government budget deficits thus imply, other things equal, a reduction in full-employment output growth. Government budget deficits absorb private saving — households buy government securities rather than the stocks or bonds that firms issue to finance their investment. Therefore, funds are diverted from growth toward other purposes. It is clear that if the only objective is to promote growth, the government should balance the budget or even run a surplus to free resources for investment. However, there is a tradeoff between growth and the social objectives that may lie behind a budget deficit.

Evaluating Supply-Side Economics and Growth Incentives

The emphasis on increasing incentives to work, save, and invest is the valid core of supply-side economics. There are two questions here. 1. Will the proposed policies work, that is, increase future potential output? 2. If the policies do work, how far should we go in creating incentives to increase future potential output?

Policies to increase the labour supply by reducing taxes and policies to increase investment by reducing government budget deficits and through investment subsidies would be effective in increasing potential output today and in the future. Thus supply-side policies are available, but we can also go overboard on such policies. If we are reducing government budget deficits while

---

[13] To the extent that deficits are used to finance government investment, they, of course, do not reduce total investment.

reducing other taxes, we are also reducing government spending. We could reduce government spending by getting rid of the post office, but most people would think it better to have higher taxes and a post office than lower taxes and no post office. Similarly, the government provides many useful services through its welfare programs — services that most people prefer to have — rather than aiming purely to maximize the level of investment.

Further, given government spending, and at full employment, increases in saving imply reductions in consumption. Thus in supply-side economics we are trading off current consumption for future consumption. We are trading off the consumption of those now alive for the consumption of their children and children who come later yet. This process also can go too far. In the extreme, we (society) would not want to force the current generation to consume at a bare survival level just so their grandchildren can sit around their pools doing very little work while automated factories, made possible by a huge volume of past investment, produce a high level of output. Somewhere between not saving now and saving almost all of output, there is an optimal amount of saving to be done.

It is no easy task for society to decide what that optimal amount of saving is. Those who will be consuming in the future are not here to vote, because they have not yet been born. And those who are around now will have different views. Some may ask, as reportedly has Joan Robinson (1905–1984), the famous English economist, "What did posterity ever do for us?" Others may feel it is the duty of the parents to sacrifice for their children's sake. Ultimately the policy decisions that affect growth are settled politically.

20-4 GROWTH THEORY

We turn now from empirical issues and the historical record to the theory of economic growth. The theory of economic growth asks what factors determine the full-employment rate of output over time. Growth theory is important because it both helps explain growth rates and why per capita income levels differ among countries. One of the central results of growth theory, for example, is the proposition that between two countries with the same technology and saving rates, the one that has the higher rate of population growth will eventually have lower per capita income.

We have already examined the sources of growth in equation (2), where we showed that full-employment output growth depends on the growth in factor inputs and on technical progress. In this section we pursue the issue further to ask what determines the growth of factor supplies and what is the link to long-run per capita incomes or standards of living.

We take a rather simple formulation here by assuming a given and constant rate of labour force growth, $\Delta N/N \equiv n$, and also that there is no technical progress, $\Delta A/A$ = 0.[14] With these assumptions the only variable element left in equation (2) is the growth rate of capital.

Capital growth is determined by saving, which, in turn, depends on income. Income or output, in turn, depends on capital. We are thus set with an interdependent system in which capital growth depends, via saving and income, on the capital stock. We now study the short-run behaviour, the adjustment process, and the long-run equilibrium of that interdependent system.

Steady State

We start by discussing the steady state of the economy. Here we ask whether in an economy with population growth and saving, and therefore growth in the capital stock, we reach a point where output per head and capital per head become constant. In such a steady state, current saving and additions to the capital stock would be just enough to equip new entrants into the labour force with the same amount of capital as the average worker uses.

The idea of a steady state is this: If capital per head is unchanging, given technology, so is output per head; but for capital *per head* to remain unchanging even though population is growing, capital must grow at just the right rate, namely, at the same rate as population. More formally, if output per head is to remain constant, output and population must grow at the same rates, or $\Delta Y/Y = \Delta N/N = n$. Therefore, from equation (2), setting productivity growth equal to zero, we have $0 = \Delta K/K - n$, or

$$\frac{\Delta K}{K} = n \qquad (4)$$

Equation (4) states that in the steady state the growth rate of the capital stock is equal to the growth rate of population. Equivalently, in the steady state the amount of capital per head is constant.

We now show the steady state graphically in Figure 20-3. We put output per head on the vertical axis and capital per head on the horizontal axis. The production function, which is central to understanding growth, exhibits diminishing returns to capital. As capital per head increases, so that workers use increasing amounts of machinery, output per head increases, but at a diminishing rate. Thus an increase in the capital-labour ratio is productive, but there are diminishing returns. In steady state, the economy settles down to a fixed capital-labour ratio $(K/N)^*$. The production function shows the corresponding amount of output per head $(Y/N)^*$.

---

[14] For further simplicity we also assume that the entire population works, so that the labour force and the population are the same.

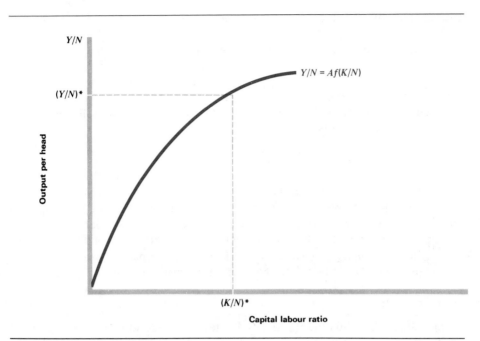

FIGURE 20-3 OUTPUT PER HEAD AND THE CAPITAL-LABOUR RATIO. The production function shows output per head as a function of the amount of capital per head, or the capital-labour ratio. The higher the capital-labour ratio is, the higher output per head is, but the increment to output from raising the capital-labour ratio grows progressively smaller as the capital-labour ratio rises.

Saving and Growth

We gain insight by examining the link between saving and the growth in capital. We are assuming there is no government. Accordingly, investment, or the gross increase in capital, is equal to saving. To obtain the increase in the capital stock, however, we have to deduct depreciation. Therefore the net addition to the capital stock is equal to saving less depreciation.

$$\Delta K = \text{saving} - \text{depreciation} \qquad (5)$$

Two assumptions take us from (4) and (5) to a complete description of the steady state. In (5) we need to specify saving behaviour and to make an assumption about depreciation. We assume first that saving is a constant fraction s of income Y. Second, depreciation is at a constant rate of d percent of the capital stock. Concretely, we might assume that people save $s = 15$ percent of their income and that depreciation is at a rate of 10 percent per year so that every year 10 percent of the capital stock needs to be replaced to offset wear and tear.

Substituting these assumptions in equation (5) yields

$$\Delta K = sY - dK \qquad (5a)$$

or placing the right-hand side in equation (4), we arrive at the following result that describes the steady state:[15]

$$sY = (n + d)K \qquad (4a)$$

Equation (4a) states that in the steady state, saving (sY) is just sufficient to provide for enough investment to offset depreciation (dK) *and* to equip new members of the labour force with capital (nK). If saving were larger than this amount, net investment would be sufficiently large to make capital per head grow, leading to rising income per head. Conversely, if not enough were saved, capital per head would be falling and with it income per head.

The Growth Process

We next study the adjustment process that leads the economy from some initial capital-labour ratio over time to the steady state. The critical element in this transition process is the rate of saving and investment compared with the rate of depreciation, and population growth.

Notation

The argument is made easier by a bit of new notation. We define the amount of output per head as $x = Y/N$ and the amount of capital per head, or the capital-labour ratio, as $k = K/N$. This is simply notation and in no way changes our model.

$$k \equiv \text{capital-labour ratio} = \frac{K}{N} \quad x \equiv \text{output per head} = \frac{Y}{N} \qquad (6)$$

Thus in terms of Figure 20-3 the vertical axis is labeled x and the horizontal axis k.

Capital Accumulation

We now turn to the transition to the steady state. Note from equation (2) that output per head will grow if capital per head grows and that capital per head

---

[15] Placing Eq. (5a) in Eq. (4) yields $(sY - dK)/K = n$. By multiplying both sides by K and collecting terms, we obtain $sY = (n + d)K$.

will grow if saving is *more than sufficient* to cover depreciation of the capital stock and also to equip new members of the population with capital. This can be formalized by writing the change in the capital-labour ratio as follows:[16]

$$\Delta k = sx - (n + d)k \tag{7}$$

The growth process can now be studied with the help of Equation (4a) and Figure 20-4. Here we reproduce the production function from Figure 20-3, writing output per capita as a function of the capital-labour ratio.

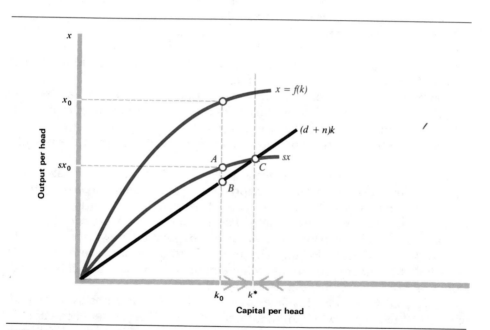

FIGURE 20-4 SAVING, INVESTMENT, AND CAPITAL ACCUMULATION. The saving function shows at each capital-labour ratio the part of income that is saved, sx. The straight line $(d + n)k$ shows the investment requirement. At low capital-labour ratios, saving exceeds the investment requirement, and hence output per head grows. Conversely at high capital-labour ratios, saving is less than the investment requirement, and capital per head is falling. The steady-state capital-labour ratio is k^*, where saving is just sufficient to maintain the capital-labour ratio constant.

---

[16] The percentage growth rate of the capital-labour ratio is equal to the difference between the growth rate of capital and the growth rate of labour, or $\Delta k/k = \Delta K/K - n$. Now using Eq. (5a) to replace ΔK, we have $\Delta k/k = sY/K - d - n = \dfrac{s(Y/N)}{K/N} - (d + n) = \dfrac{sx}{k} - (d + n)$. Multiplying both sides by k yields Eq. (7) in the text.

We have added the savings function, which, for each capital-labour ratio, is simply the fraction s of output. Thus, for any capital-labour ratio, say, k_0, the corresponding point on the saving schedule tells us the amount of saving per head, $sx(k_0)$, that will be forthcoming at that capital-labour ratio.

We know that all saving is invested, so that gross investment or gross additions to the capital stock, in per capita terms, are equal to sx, given a capital-labour ratio of k_0. We know, too, from Equation (7) that the increase in the capital-labour ratio falls short of that gross addition for two reasons:

- Depreciation reduces the capital-labour ratio, and part of gross investment must be devoted to offsetting depreciation. In particular, if the depreciation rate is d, an amount dk is required as a depreciation allowance. For example, if the depreciation rate is 10 percent and the capital-labour ratio is 10 machines per person, each year the equivalent of 1 machine would depreciate and would have to be replaced: that is, 10 percent times 10 machines equals 1 machine that has to be replaced.
- Growth in the labour force implies that with a given stock of capital, the capital-labour ratio would be declining. To maintain the amount of capital per head constant, we have to add enough machines to the stock of capital to make up for the growth in population; that is, we need to invest at the rate nk.

It follows that we can write the investment required to maintain constant the capital-labour ratio in the face of depreciation and labour force growth as $(n + d)k$. When saving and hence gross investment are larger than $(n + d)k$, the stock of capital per head is increasing. If saving and gross investment are less, then we are not making up for depreciation and population growth, and, accordingly, capital per head is falling. We can therefore think of the term $(n + d)k$ as the investment requirement that will maintain constant capital per head and therefore, from Figure 20-3 output per head.

In Figure 20-4 we show this investment requirement as a positively sloped schedule. It tells us how much investment we would require at each capital-labour ratio just in order to keep that ratio constant. It is positively sloped because the higher the capital-labour ratio, the larger the amount of investment that is required to maintain that capital-labour ratio. Thus, with the depreciation rate of 10 percent and a growth rate of population of 1 percent, we would require an investment of 1.1 machines per head per year at a capital-labour ratio of 10 machines per head to maintain the capital-labour ratio constant. If the capital-labour ratio were 100 machines per head, the required investment would be 11 machines (= 100 machines per head times 11 percent).

We have seen that the saving schedule tells us the amount of saving and gross investment associated with each capital-labour ratio. Thus, at a capital-labour ratio of k_0 in Figure 20-4, saving is sx_0 at point A. The investment requirement to maintain constant the capital-labour ratio at k_0 is equal to $(n + d)k_0$ at point

B. Clearly, saving exceeds the investment requirement. More is added to the capital stock than is required to maintain constant the capital-labour ratio. Accordingly, the capital-labour ratio grows. Not surprisingly, the increase in the capital-labour ratio is equal to actual saving or investment less the investment requirement and is thus given by the vertical distance *AB*.

In the next period, capital per head will be higher. Thus on the horizontal axis we draw an arrow showing *k* increasing. You recognize the line of argument we are taking. From Figure 20-4 it is clear that with a somewhat higher capital-labour ratio, the discrepancy between saving and the investment requirement becomes smaller. Therefore, the increase in the capital-labour ratio becomes smaller. However, the capital-labour ratio still increases, as indicated by the arrows.

The adjustment process comes to a halt at point *C*. Here we have reached a capital-labour ratio *k** for which saving and investment associated with that capital-labour ratio exactly match the investment requirement. Given the exact matching of actual and required investment, the capital-labour ratio neither rises nor falls. We have reached the steady state.

We can make the same argument by starting with an initial capital-labour ratio in excess of *k**. From Figure 20-4 we note that for high capital-labour ratios, the investment requirement is in excess of saving and investment. Accordingly, not enough is added to the capital stock to maintain the capital-labour ratio constant in the face of population growth and depreciation. Thus, the capital-labour ratio falls until we get to *k**, the steady-state capital-labour ratio.

To review our progress so far:

- To maintain the capital-labour ratio constant, saving and investment have to be sufficient to make up for the reduction in capital per head that arises from population growth and depreciation.
- With saving a constant fraction *s* of output, we established that the capital-labour ratio moves to a steady-state level *k** at which output and therefore saving (investment) are just sufficient to maintain constant the capital-labour ratio.
- The convergence to a steady-state capital-labour ratio *k** is ensured by the fact that at low levels of the capital-labour ratio, saving (investment) exceeds the investment required to maintain capital per head and therefore causes the capital-labour ratio to rise. Conversely, at high capital-labour ratios, saving (investment) falls short of the investment requirement, and thus the ratio declines.

Now we turn to a more detailed study of the steady-state equilibrium and the adjustment process. We note that the steady-state level of capital per head is constant, and thus the steady-state level of output per head is also constant.

The steady-state is reached when all variables, in per capita terms, are constant. This means that in the steady state, output, capital, and labour all grow at the same rate. They all grow at a rate equal to the rate of population growth. Note particularly that the steady-state growth rate is equal to the rate of population growth and therefore is *not* influenced by the saving rate. (Recall that we are assuming no technical progress.) To explore this property of the steady state in more detail, we investigate the effects of a change in the saving rate.

A Change in the Saving Rate

Why should the long-run growth be independent of the saving rate? If people save 10 percent of their income as opposed to 5 percent, should we not expect this to make a difference to the growth rate of output? Is it not true that an economy in which 10 percent of income is set aside for additions to the capital stock is one in which capital and therefore output grow faster than in an economy in which only 5 percent of income is saved?

We show here that an increase in the saving rate does the following: In the short run, it raises the growth rate of output. It does not affect the *long-run growth rate* of output, but it raises the long-run level of capital and output per head.

Consider Figure 20-5 with an initial steady-state equilibrium at point C, where saving precisely matches the investment requirement. At point C, exactly enough output is saved to maintain the stock of capital per head constant in the face of depreciation and labour force growth. Next consider an increase in the saving rate. For some reason, people want to save a larger fraction of income. The increased saving rate is reflected in an upward shift of the saving schedule. At each level of the capital-labour ratio, and hence at each level of output, saving is larger.

At point C, where we initially had a steady-state equilibrium, saving has now risen relative to the investment requirement, and as a consequence, more is saved than is required to maintain capital per head constant. Enough is saved to allow the capital stock per head to increase.

It is apparent from Figure 20-5 that the capital stock per head will keep rising until we reach point C'. At C', the higher amount of saving is just enough to maintain the higher stock of capital. At point C', both capital per head and output per head have risen. Saving has increased as has the investment requirement. We have seen, therefore, that an increase in the saving rate will in the long run raise only the level of output and capital per head, and not the growth rate of output per head.

The transition process, however, involves an effect of the saving rate on the growth rate of output and the growth rate of output per head. In the transition from k^* to k^{**}, the increase in the saving rate raises the growth rate of output. This follows simply from the fact that the capital-labour ratio rises from k^* at

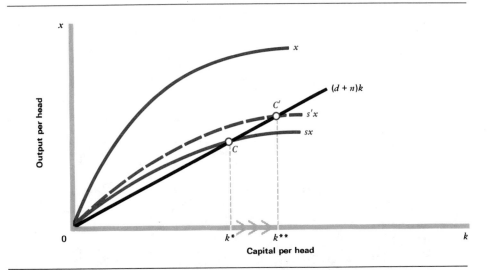

FIGURE 20-5 AN INCREASE IN THE SAVING RATE. An increase in the saving rate implies that at each capital-labour ratio a larger fraction of output is saved. The saving schedule shifts upward to $s'x$. At the initial steady state, saving now exceeds the investment requirement, and hence the capital-labour ratio rises until point C' is reached. An increase in the saving rate raises steady-state per capita income. The growth rate rises only in the transition from C to C'.

the initial steady state to k^{**} in the new steady state. The only way to achieve an increase in the capital-labour ratio is for the capital stock to grow faster than the labour force (and depreciation). This is precisely what happens in the transition process where increased saving per head, owing to the higher saving rate, raises investment and capital growth over and above the investment requirement and thus allows the capital-labour ratio to rise.

In summary, the long-run effect of an increase in the saving rate is to raise the level of output and capital per head but to leave the growth rate of output and capital unaffected. In the transition period, the rates of growth of output and capital increase relative to the steady state. In the short run, therefore, an increase in the saving rate means faster growth, as we would expect.

Figure 20-6 summarizes these two results. Figure 20-6a shows the level of per capita output. Starting from an initial long-run equilibrium at time t_0, the increase in the saving rate causes saving and investment to increase, the stock of capital per head grows, and so does output per head. The process will continue at a diminishing rate. In Figure 20-6b we focus on the growth rate of output and capital. The growth rate of output is equal to the growth rate of population in the initial steady state. The increase in the saving rate immediately raises the growth rate of output because it implies a faster growth in capital and therefore in output. As capital accumulates, the growth rate decreases, falling back toward the level of population growth.

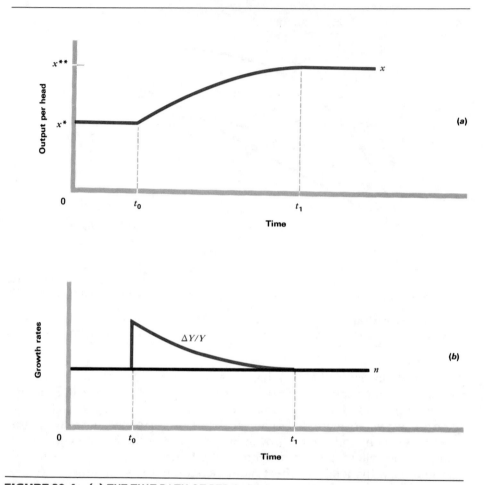

FIGURE 20-6 (**a**) THE TIME PATH OF PER CAPITA INCOME. A rise in the saving rate leads to a rising capital-labour ratio and therefore to increasing output per head until a new steady state is reached. (**b**) THE TIME PATH OF THE GROWTH RATE OF OUTPUT. An increase in the saving rate raises investment above the investment requirement and thus leads to capital accumulation. Output growth transitorily rises and then falls back to the growth rate of population.

BOX 20-1   THE LIMITS OF GROWTH

The record of growth since 1870 reviewed in Table 20-1 is impressive indeed. Per capita GDP in Canada has been doubling every 33 years over a period of more than a century. The question of the limits to growth is whether limited resources and the pressure of population on scarce land and food will ultimately bring the growth process to a dramatic halt. Are growing economies headed toward stagnation or even disaster?

The disaster scenario is a simple one. First, only so much oil, coal, copper, and other raw materials are in the earth. One day they will all be used up. Then what do we do? The "one day" seemed to come very close in the early seventies when many experts were predicting we would run out of oil by the year 2020. Second, there is the problem of an ever-growing population. The world, being of finite size, cannot accommodate an ever-growing population. Unless we can colonize other planets, population growth has to decline. In particular, there is the problem of food. Can we grow enough food to feed the nearly 6 billion people (compared with a current 4.5 billion) expected to be alive at the turn of the century? If not, will world population be forced down through starvation, as Malthus long ago predicted?*

The standard retort of the growth-oriented economist is to point out that all the concerns we have today about the limits to growth were equally valid a century ago. Indeed, in 1865 the famous English economist W. S. Jevons wrote a book about the impending exhaustion of Britain's coal resources — coal that is still being mined today.† The experience after the oil price shock in 1973 was that price changes can cause massive conservation of resources, and thus there is reason to hope that most *exhaustible* resources — resources present on earth in limited quantities — will be around for a long time, albeit with rising relative prices.

A more important challenge to the limits set by exhaustible resources is technical progress. Much technical progress takes the form of inventions and processes that save on scarce resources used up in production. The expectation or hope is that the same technical progress that has proved an important source of real growth in the last century will help overcome the effects of the reduced availability of raw materials.

Of course there is no assurance that the right technical progress will come along to bail us out when coal or oil run short in supply. Perhaps we should not bank on technical progress, innovation, and ingenuity to help us out. At the same time, it would surely be irresponsible to dismiss entirely the extraordinary record of technical progress that has contributed around one-half of the average growth in real income. Public policy directed at encouraging research and development could help ensure continued technical progress.

---

*Thomas Malthus, *The Principle of Population* (Homewood, Ill.: Richard D. Irwin, Inc., reprint).

†W. S. Jevons, *The Coal Question*, 1885 (New York: Augustus M. Kelly Publishers, 1965, reprint).

The idea of a convergence in per capita incomes among different countries has been suggested by William Baumol.‡ Studying the long-term behaviour of productivity growth, he finds that industrial countries, and even the newly industrializing countries, tend to converge over time in their levels of per capita income. This convergence occurs because growth rates of productivity slow down as differences in per capita incomes narrow. The countries that lag in terms of development tend to experience higher growth rates of productivity until they have caught up, and the countries that are ahead in terms of the level of productivity have lower growth in productivity.

The catching up hypothesis seems to be particularly applicable to Japan in the postwar period, but also to the *newly industrialized countries*, or *NICs*, like Korea or Brazil. These countries have shown particularly high growth rates in the 1960s and 1970s. However, the debt crisis of the 1980s, particularly affecting countries in Latin America, may well have imposed at least a temporary slowdown if not a stop to this rapid growth pattern.

---

‡William Baumol, "Productivity Growth, Convergence and Welfare: What the Long Run Data Show," C. V. Starr Center for Applied Economics, New York University, August 1985.

Population Growth

The preceding discussion of saving and the influence of the saving rate on steady-state capital and output makes it easy to discuss the effects of increased population growth. The question we ask is, What happens when the population growth rate increases from n to n' and remains at that higher level indefinitely? We will show that such an increase in the rate of population growth will *raise* the growth rate of output and *lower* the level of output per head.

The argument can be conveniently followed in Figure 20-7. Here we show the initial steady-state equilibrium at point C. The increase in the growth rate of population means that, at each level of the capital-labour ratio, it takes a larger amount of investment just to maintain the capital-labour ratio constant. Suppose we had 10 machines per head. Initially, the growth rate of population is 1 percent and depreciation is 10 percent, so that we require per year 11 percent times 10 machines, or 1.1 machine, just to offset population growth and depreciation and thus maintain capital per head constant. To maintain the capital-labour ratio constant in the face of higher growth rate of population, say, 2 percent, requires a higher level of investment, namely, 12 percent as opposed to 11 percent. This is reflected in Figure 20-7 by an upward rotation of the investment requirement schedule.

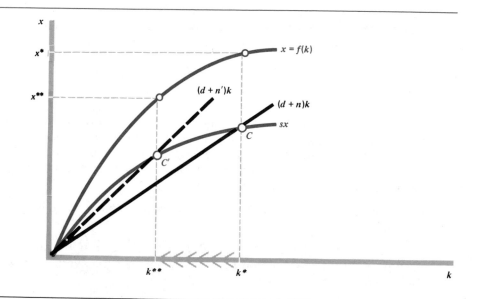

FIGURE 20-7   AN INCREASE IN THE POPULATION GROWTH RATE REDUCES PER CAPITA INCOME. Increased population growth raises the investment requirement, rotating the schedule upward to $(d + n')k$. At point C saving is insufficient to maintain capital per head constant in face of the more rapidly growing population. Capital and output per head decline until a new steady state at C' is reached.

It is clear from the preceding argument that we are no longer in steady-state equilibrium at point C. The investment that was initially just sufficient to keep the capital-labour ratio constant will no longer be sufficient in the face of higher population growth. At the initial equilibrium, the higher population growth with unchanged saving and investment means that capital does not grow fast enough to keep up with labour force growth and depreciation. Capital per head declines. In fact, capital per head will keep declining until we reach the new steady-state equilibrium at point C'. Here the capital-labour ratio has declined sufficiently for saving to match the investment requirement. It is true, too, that, corresponding to the lower capital-labour ratio, we have a decline in output per head. Output per head declines from x^* to x^{**}.

The decline in output per head as a consequence of increased population growth points to the problem faced by many developing countries. Fast growth in population, given the saving rate, means low levels of income per head. Indeed, in poor countries one can trace poverty, or low income per head, to the very high rate of population growth. With high population growth, saving will typically be too small to allow capital to rise relative to labour and thus to build up the capital-labour ratio to achieve a satisfactory level of income per head.

In those circumstances, and barring other considerations, a reduction in the rate of population growth appears to be a way of achieving higher levels of steady-state per capita income and thus an escape from poverty.

20-5   SUMMARY

1.   A production function links factor inputs and technology to the level of output. Growth of output, changes in technology aside, is a weighted average of input growth with the weights equal to income shares. The production function directs attention to factor inputs and technological change as sources of output growth.

2.   Growth theory studies the determinants of intermediate-run and long-run growth in output.

3.   In Canada over the 1946–1967 period, growth in factor inputs and technical progress each accounted for roughly one-half the average growth rate of 4.6 percent of output.

4.   Per capita output grows faster the more rapidly the capital stock increases and the faster is technical progress. In Canadian history since 1870, output per head has grown at an average rate of 2.2 percent.

5.   From 1953 to 1973, per capita real GDP grew at an average rate of 2.9 percent, but over the following ten years, the growth rate dropped to 1 percent.

6.   Supply-side economics argues that the level and rate of growth of potential output can be increased by creating improved incentives for work, saving and investment.

7.   The concept of steady-state equilibrium points (in the absence of technical change) to the conditions required for output per head to be constant. With a growing population, saving must be just sufficient to provide new members of the population with the economy-wide amount of capital per head.

8.   The steady-state level of income is determined by the saving rate and by population growth. In the absence of technical change, the steady-state growth rate of output is equal to the rate of population growth. An increase in the growth rate of population raises the steady-state growth rate of total output and lowers the level of steady-state output per head.

9.   An increase in the saving rate transitorily raises the growth rate of output. In the new steady state, the growth rate remains unchanged, but the level of output per head is increased.

10. With technical change, per capita output in the steady state grows at the rate of technical progress. Total output grows at the sum of the rates of technical progress and population growth.

11. Potential limits to growth pose a serious question about continued increases in real per capita income or even the maintenance of current consumption standards. The historical record is one of technological progress that offsets limitational factors and scarce resources. There is no certainty that this offset will continue, but so far it has done so. Public policy to encourage research and development can make a contribution in that direction.

KEY TERMS

Potential output

Production function

Growth accounting

Sources of growth

Labour productivity

Technical progress

Growth of total factor productivity

Supply-side economics

Steady state

Limits of growth

Catching-up hypothesis

PROBLEMS

1. Which of the following government activities have effects on the long-term growth rate? Explain how they can do so.
   (a) Monetary policy
   (b) Labour market policies
   (c) Educational and research programs
   (d) Fiscal policy
   (e) Population control programs

2. Discuss the role of government policy in raising (a) the supply of labour and (b) the supply of capital. How successful can such policies be?

3. Since 1973, the growth rate of productivity has sharply declined in most industrialized countries. List several of the factors that are responsible for this decline and discuss why the decline in productivity growth is an important issue.

4. Suppose the share of capital in income is 0.4 and the share of labour is 0.6. Capital grows by 6 percent, and labour supply declines by 2 percent. What happens to output?

5. An earthquake destroys one-quarter of the capital stock. Discuss in the context of the growth model the adjustment process of the economy, and show, using Figure 20-4, what happens to growth.

6. (a) In the absence of technical progress, what happens to output per head and total output over time? Why?
   (b) What is the long-run effect of the saving rate on the *level* of output per capita? On *growth* of output per capita?

7. Evaluate this statement: "The saving rate cannot affect the growth of output in the economy. That is determined by the growth of labour input and by technical progress."

*8. Suppose we assume a production function of the form

$$Y = AF(K,N,Z)$$

where Z is a measure of the natural resources going into production. Assume this production function obeys constant returns to scale and diminishing returns to each factor [like Equation (1)].
   (a) What will happen to output per head if capital and labour grow together but resources are fixed?
   (b) What if Z is fixed but there is technical progress?
   (c) Interpret these results in terms of the limits to growth.

*9. Use the model of long-run growth to incorporate the government. Assume that an income tax at the rate of t is levied and that, accordingly, saving per head is equal to $s(1 - t)x$. The government spends the tax revenue on public consumption.
   (a) Use Figure 20-4 to explore the impact of an increase in the tax rate on the steady-state output level and capital per head.
   (b) Draw a chart of the time path of capital per head, output per head, and the growth rate of output.
   (c) Discuss the statement: "To raise the growth rate of output, the public sector has to run a budget surplus to free resources for investment."

10. Use Figure 20-4 to explore the impact of a *once-and-for-all* improvement in technology.
   (a) How does technical progress affect the level of output per head as of a given capital-labour ratio?
   (b) Show the new steady-state equilibrium. Has saving changed? Is income per head higher? Has the capital stock per head increased?
   (c) Show the time path of the adjustment to the new steady state. Does technical progress transitorily raise the ratio of investment to capital?

11. Discuss the statement: "The lower the level of income, the higher the growth rate of output."

12. Explain the catching-up hypothesis that asserts that productivity growth is lower the higher the level of per capita income. What factors do you think are responsible for this observed pattern?

APPENDIX: PROPERTIES OF THE PRODUCTION FUNCTION

In this appendix we briefly show how the fundamental growth equation (2) is obtained. The material is presented for completeness; it is not essential to an understanding of the text.

We start with a production function that exhibits constant returns: increasing *all* inputs in the same proportion raises output in that same proportion. Thus if we double all inputs, output will double. With that property the change in output due to technical progress and to changes in inputs can be written as

$$\Delta Y = F(K, N)\,\Delta A + MPK\,\Delta K + MPN\,\Delta N \tag{A1}$$

where *MPK* and *MPN* are the marginal products of capital and labour, respectively. We remember that the marginal product of a factor tells us the contribution to output made by employing one extra unit of the factor. Dividing both sides of the equation by $Y = AF(K, N)$ yields the expression

$$\frac{\Delta Y}{Y} = \frac{\Delta A}{A} + \frac{MPK}{Y}\Delta K + \frac{MPN}{Y}\Delta N \tag{A2}$$

Equation (A2) further simplifies by multiplying and dividing the second term on the right-hand side by *K* and the third term by *N*.

$$\frac{\Delta Y}{Y} = \frac{\Delta A}{A} + \left(K\frac{MPK}{Y}\right)\frac{\Delta K}{K} + \left(N\frac{MPN}{Y}\right)\frac{\Delta N}{N} \tag{A3}$$

We now argue that the terms in parentheses are the income share of capital and labour. In a competitive market factors are paid their marginal product. Thus the term $N(MPN/Y) = wN/Y$, where w is the real wage. The right-hand side is recognized as the ratio of labour income to total income or the share of labour in income. Similarly, the term $K(MPK/Y)$ is the share of capital in income. With constant returns and competition, factor payments exhaust the total product. Therefore the shares of capital and labour sum to unity. Denoting the share of capital in income by θ and the labour share by $1 - \theta$, we arrive at equation (2) in the text.

We note a further property of the constant returns production function. When returns to scale are constant, we can write the production function as follows:

$$Y = AF(K, N) = NAf\left(\frac{K}{N}\right) \tag{A3}$$

or using the notation $x = Y/N$ and $k = K/N$,

$$x = Af(k) \tag{A5}$$

This is the form used in the growth theory section of the text, where output per head is a function of the capital-labour ratio.

cut here

STUDENT REPLY CARD

In order to improve future editions, we are seeking your comments on *Macroeconomics*, Third Canadian Edition, by Dornbusch, Fischer, and Sparks.

After you have read this text, please answer the following questions and return this form via Business Reply Mail. *Thanks in advance for your feedback!*

1. Name of your college or university: _____

2. Major program of study: _____

3. Are there any sections of this text which were not assigned as course reading? _____ _____ If so, please specify those chapters or portions:

4. How would you rate the overall accessibility of the content? Please feel free to comment on reading level, writing style, terminology, layout and design features, and such learning aids as chapter objectives, summaries, and appendices.

5. What did you like *best* about this book?

6. What did you like *least*?

If you would like to say more, we'd love to hear from you. Please write to us at the address shown on the reverse of this card.

cut here

cut here   *tape shut*

cut here

fold

BUSINESS
REPLY MAIL
No Postage Stamp
Necessary If Mailed
in Canada
Postage will be paid by

Canada Post / Postes Canada
7115

Attn: Sponsoring Editor, Business and Economics

The College Division
McGraw-Hill Ryerson Limited
330 Progress Avenue
Scarborough, Ontario
M1P 2Z5